Jane M. Murphy

Alec Leighton

PUBLIC AND PRIVATE FAMILIES

An Introduction

SECOND EDITION

PUBLIC AND PRIVATE FAMILIES

An Introduction

ANDREW J. CHERLIN
Johns Hopkins University

Consulting Editor

CRAIG CALHOUN
New York University

McGraw-Hill College

Boston   Burr Ridge, IL   Dubuque, IA   Madison, WI   New York   San Francisco   St. Louis
Bangkok   Bogotá   Caracas   Lisbon   London   Madrid
Mexico City   Milan   New Delhi   Seoul   Singapore   Sydney   Taipei   Toronto

McGraw-Hill College

A Division of The McGraw·Hill Companies

PUBLIC AND PRIVATE FAMILIES: An Introduction

This book is printed on acid-free paper.

3 4 5 6 7 8 9 0 VNH/VNH 9 3 2 1 0 9

ISBN 0-07-011987-2

Editorial director: *Phillip A. Butcher*
Senior sponsoring editor: *Sally Constable*
Senior developmental editor: *Rhona Robbin*
Marketing manager: *Leslie Kraham*
Project manager: *Amy Hill*
Production supervisor: *Debra R. Benson*
Design manager: *Kiera Cunningham*
Senior photo research coordinator: *Keri Johnson*
Photo research: *Inge King*
Supplement coordinator: *Carol Loreth*
Compositor: *Shepherd, Incorporated*
Typeface: *10/12 Garamond*
Printer: *Von Hoffmann Press, Inc.*

Library of Congress Cataloging-in-Publication Data

Cherlin, Andrew J., 1948–
    Public and private families: an introduction / Andrew J. Cherlin.
  — 2nd ed.
     p. cm.
    Includes index.
    ISBN 0-07-011987-2
    1. Family—United States. 2. Family. I. Title.
HQ536.C44   1998
306.85—dc21   95-18511

http://www.mhhe.com

ABOUT THE AUTHOR

 Andrew J. Cherlin is Benjamin H. Griswold III Professor of Public Policy in the Department of Sociology at Johns Hopkins University. He received a B.S. from Yale University in 1970 and a Ph.D. in sociology from the University of California at Los Angeles in 1976. His other books include *Marriage, Divorce, Remarriage* (revised and enlarged edition, 1992); *Divided Families: What Happens to Children When Parents Part* (with Frank F. Furstenberg, Jr., 1991); *The Changing American Family and Public Policy* (1988); and *The New American Grandparent: A Place in the Family, A Life Apart* (with Frank F. Furstenberg, Jr., 1986). In 1989–1990 he was chair of the Family Section, and in 1995–1996 he was chair of the Population Section of the American Sociological Association. In 1999 he will be president of the Population Association of America.

Professor Cherlin is a recipient of a MERIT (Method to Extend Research in Time) Award from the National Institutes of Health for his research on the effects of family structure on children. He was a member of both the Panel on Child Care Policy and the Committee on Child Development Research and Public Policy of the National Academy of Sciences. His recent articles include "Stepfamilies in the United States: A Reconsideration," in the *Annual Review of Sociology*; "Nostalgia as Family Policy," in *The Public Interest*; "Longitudinal Studies of the Effects of Divorce on Children," in *Science*; "Effects of Parental Divorce on Mental Health throughout the Life Course," in the *American Sociological Review*; and "By the Numbers," in *The New York Times Magazine*. He also has written many short articles for *The New York Times, The Washington Post, Newsweek,* and other periodicals. He has been interviewed on *ABC News Nightline,* the *Today Show,* network evening news programs, National Public Radio's *All Things Considered,* and other news programs and documentaries.

To Claire and Reid

CONTENTS IN BRIEF

CONTENTS

PART TWO · Race, Ethnicity, Class, and the State · 105

CHAPTER 4 · Social Class and Families · 107

PART SIX   Family and Society   493

CHAPTER 16   Social Change and Families   495

LIST OF BOXES

Families and Public Policy

Families in Other Cultures

How Do Sociologists Know What They Know?

PREFACE

The sociology of the family is deceptively hard to study. Unlike, say, physics, the topic is familiar (a word whose very root is Latin for "family") because virtually everyone grows up in families. Therefore, it can seem "easy" to study the family because students can bring to bear their personal knowledge of the subject. Some textbooks play to this familiarity by mainly providing students with an opportunity to better understand their private lives. The authors never stray too far from the individual experiences of their readers, focusing on personal choices such as whether to marry and whether to have children. To be sure, giving students insight into the social forces that shape their personal decisions about family life is a worthwhile objective. Nevertheless, the challenge of writing about the sociology of the family is to also help students understand that the significance of families extends beyond personal experience. Today, as in the past, the family is the site of not only private decisions but also activities that matter to our society as a whole.

These activities center on taking care of people who are unable to fully care for themselves, most notably children and the elderly. Anyone who follows social issues knows of the often-expressed concern about whether, given developments such as the increases in divorce and childbearing outside of marriage, we are raising the next generation adequately. Anyone anxious about the well-being of the rapidly growing elderly population (as well as the escalating cost of providing financial and medical assistance to the elderly) knows the concern about whether family members will continue to provide adequate assistance to them. Indeed, rarely does a month pass without these issues appearing on the covers of magazines and the front pages of newspapers.

In this textbook, consequently, I have written about the family in two senses: the *private family,* in which we live most of our personal lives, and the *public family,* in which adults perform tasks that are important to society. My goal is to give students a thorough grounding in both aspects. It is true that the two are related—taking care of children adequately, for instance, requires the love and affection that family members express privately toward each other. But the public side of the family deserves equal time with the private side.

ORGANIZATION

This book is divided into six parts and 16 chapters. Part One ("Introduction") introduces the concepts of the public and private families and examines how sociologists and other social scientists study them. It provides an overview of the history of the family and then examines the central concept of gender. Part Two ("Race, Ethnicity, Class, and the State") deals with the larger social structures in which family relations are embedded: social class hierarchies, and racial and ethnic divisions. A chapter is then devoted to the influences of the nation-state on family life. In Part Three ("Sexuality, Partnership, and Marriage"), the focus shifts to the private family—and specifically to the emergence of the modern concept of sexuality, to the formation of partnerships through dating, courtship, and cohabitation, and to the interpersonal relations between spouses and cohabiting partners.

Part Four ("Power, Conflict, and Disruption") deals with the consequences of conflict and of inequalities in power. First, the connections between the world of work and the balance of power and authority in the family are examined. Attention shifts to violence against wives, partners, and children. Then divorce, remarriage, and stepfamilies are discussed. Part Five ("Links across the Generations") explores how well the public family is meeting its caretaking responsibilities for children and the elderly. Finally, in Part Six ("Family and Society"), I discuss where the great social changes of the twentieth century have left the institution of the family.

SPECIAL FEATURES

This textbook differs from others in several ways. The first is the public versus private distinction, which underlies its structure. It is my hope that this organizing principle will lead to a more balanced portrait of contemporary family life. Furthermore, the focus on the public family leads to a much greater emphasis on government policy toward the family than in most other textbooks. In fact, every chapter except the first includes a short, boxed essay under the general title, "Families and Public Policy." Several of these essays are new in this edition, such as the roles of private charity and government in aiding poor families and the debates among feminists about anti-pornography laws. Given the attention currently paid to issues such as these, the essays should stimulate student interest and make the book relevant to current political debates.

Although the emphasis in the book is on the contemporary United States and other Western nations, no text should ignore the important historical and cross-cultural diversity of families. Consequently, in addition to relevant material in the body of the text, I have also included in every chapter except the first another boxed essay under the title, "Families in Other Cultures." The topics of these cross-cultural and historical essays include gender relations in China and Russia, parents' influence over the choice of marriage partners in Thailand, wife-beating in less-developed nations, and, new to this edition, "Love and Marriage in Japan." I hope that these essays will not only pique the readers' interest but also broaden the scope of their understanding. Moreover, both the policy essays and the cross-cultural essays should provide good starting points for class discussions.

The attention to the public family also led me to write several chapters that are rarely found in sociology of the family textbooks. These include Chapter 6, "The Family, the State, and Social Policy"; Chapter 14, "Children and Parents"; and Chapter 15, "The Elderly and Their Families." These chapters examine issues of great current interest, such as income assistance to poor families, the effects of out-of-home child-care, and the costs of the Social Security and Medicare programs. Throughout these and other chapters, variations by class, race, ethnicity, and gender are explored.

PEDAGOGY

Each chapter begins in a way that should engage the reader: the neither-men-nor-women *berdaches* of many Native American tribes; the nineteenth-century diary in which Maud Rittenhouse described her suitors; the plight of Lafayette and Pharoah

Rivers, two children growing up in a horribly violent Chicago neighborhood; the case of Danny Henrikson, taken from the stepfather who raised him and awarded by a judge to a father he did not know; and so forth. In fact, throughout the book, I have tried to write lively, succinct prose.

Each of the six parts of the book is preceded by a brief introduction that sets the stage. And each chapter contains an opening outline, key terms (highlighted in boldface where they are introduced and defined), and a chapter-ending summary and list of key terms. In addition, there is a comprehensive end-of-book glossary. Information is presented graphically in many charts and graphs. Numerous photographs illustrate important points in each chapter.

MAJOR CHANGES IN THE SECOND EDITION

Several instructors who used the first edition of this textbook suggested that I include more information about the research methods used by sociologists who study the family. Chapter 1 now includes a section titled, "How Do Family Sociologists Know What They Know?," which explains the ways that family sociologists go about their research. Then, in eight subsequent chapters I have included boxed essays under a similar title on subjects ranging from national surveys to feminist research methods to archival research. I hope this material gives students a better understanding of how sociological research is carried out and of the strengths and limitations of various methodological approaches.

In the few years that passed between finishing the first edition and beginning this revision, I found that the World Wide Web had changed from a pleasant diversion to an essential information-gathering tool. Almost every chapter in the second edition contains information that I gathered from the Web. For example, I often obtained the most up-to-date demographic statistics by downloading them from government statistical sites such as the Bureau of the Census web page. While using the Internet, I realized that it can be not only an indispensable research tool but also a powerful instructional tool. Consequently, at the end of each chapter I have added a section titled "Families on the Internet," in which I list web sites that students may find useful. I think that instructors will find many of these sites to be excellent sources of information for student papers and presentations.

In addition, I have included material on many topics, including Asian immigrant families (Chapter 2), the 1996 welfare reform legislation and its implications for families (Chapter 6), the changing nature of the AIDS/HIV problem (Chapter 7), the increased role of cohabitation in union formation (Chapter 8), a broadened conception of stepfamilies that includes nonmarital stepparents and stepchildren (Chapter 13), and the role of fathers in parenting (Chapter 14). I have, of course, updated all statistics and charts and have included a number of new summary charts and tables to assist students in learning and reviewing the material.

SUPPLEMENTS

The ancillary package that accompanies the second edition includes an instructor's manual with test item file prepared by Anne Smith Hastings of the University of North Carolina–Chapel Hill, a set of PowerPoint slides that feature the charts and graphs from the text, a selection of videos, and a computerized test bank in Windows and Macintosh formats. In addition, *Public and Private Families: A Reader,* edited by the author, can be used with the text. The readings are keyed to the 16 chapters in the text. (A special discount is available when the text and reader are ordered as a package.) Please contact your local McGraw-Hill representative for details concerning prices, policies, and availability of the ancillary materials, as some restrictions may apply.

ACKNOWLEDGMENTS

To write a book this comprehensive requires the help of many people. When writing the first edition, the initial drafts of eight chapters were assigned in Sociology of the Family classes at the University of North Carolina by Ronald R. Rindfuss and at the University of Pennsylvania by Frank F. Furstenberg, Jr. Their summaries of their students' experiences helped me to shape the revisions. Furstenberg also was kind enough to read drafts of some other chapters. Two other colleagues whose opinions I frequently rely upon, P. Lindsay Chase-Lansdale of the University of Chicago and Nancy E. Riley of Bowdoin College, provided excellent comments on several chapters. At McGraw-Hill, sponsoring editors Sylvia Shepard and then Jill Gordon provided me with editorial guidance, while senior developmental editor Rhona Robbin prepared detailed critiques that greatly improved every chapter. In producing the second edition, I again received valuable guidance from Rhona Robbin. In addition, the following individuals provided reviews of the first edition and suggestions for revision:

Vernon L. Bates, Pacific University

Mary Czarnezki, Marquette University

Teresa Cooney, University of Missouri at Columbia

Penny L. Deiner, University of Delaware

Robert W. Duff, University of Portland

Thomas P. Egan, Eastern Kentucky University

Lee K. Frank, Community College of Allegheny County

Rosalie Gilford, California State University at Fullerton

Lee Hamilton, New Mexico State University

Janet Hope, Saint John's University

Diane N. Lye, University of Washington

Stacy Rogers, University of Nebraska

Roger H. Rubin, University of Maryland at College Park

Jon A. Schlenker, University of Maine at Augusta

Martin Schultz, Eastern Carolina University

Elaine Wethington, Cornell University

Andrew J. Cherlin

Introduction

The family has two aspects. It is, first, the place where we experience much of our private lives. It is where we give and receive love, share our hopes and fears, work through our troubles, and relax and enjoy ourselves. Second, it is a setting in which adults perform tasks that are of importance to society, particularly raising children and assisting elderly parents. To be sure, people undertake these tasks not to perform a public service but rather to express love, affection, and gratitude. Nevertheless, family caretaking benefits us all by raising the next generation and by reducing our collective responsibility for the elderly. Indeed, one frequently expressed source of concern these days is whether changes in family life have reduced parents' abilities to raise their children well.

This book is about both the private and public aspects of families. It examines the contributions of family life not only to personal satisfaction but also to public welfare. The first three chapters provide an introduction to this perspective.

Chapter 1 explores the most useful ways to think about families. It reviews the debates about family life today; and it examines the approaches that sociologists and other social scientists use to study families.

Chapter 2 provides an overview of the history of the family. A knowledge of family life in the past can help us to understand families today. Over the past few decades, family historians have produced many studies that provide useful insights.

The experiences of women and men in families differ greatly. Consequently, gender—the social and cultural characteristics that distinguish women and men—will be discussed throughout the book. **Chapter 3** begins this discussion by examining the construction and maintenance of gender differences.

CHAPTER 1

Public and Private Families

INTRODUCTION

On December 17, 1990, three couples walked into the State of Hawaii marriage license bureau in Honolulu and requested licenses. In love and ready to commit to their partners, these women and men weren't much different from typical applicants, except in one crucial respect: All were in same-sex partnerships. The bureau refused to issue them marriage licenses. This did not come as a surprise to the two lesbian couples and the gay male couple; indeed, they had intentionally entered as a group in order to create the grounds for a lawsuit. Following the denial of their requests, they sued the State of Hawaii, charging that it is an unconstitutional violation of their rights to restrict marriage to heterosexual couples.

A lower court judge ruled against the couples and in favor of the State's interpretation of the marriage laws. But in 1993, after the couples appealed, the Hawaii Supreme Court disagreed with the lower court ruling (*Baehr* v. *Lewin,* 1993). It sent the case back to the lower court with orders to retry the case and to grant the marriage licenses unless the State could show that it "furthers a compelling state interest" to exclude same-sex couples. On September 10, 1996, testimony in the case, *Baehr* v. *Miike,* began before Judge Kevin S. C. Chang. News of the impending case had attracted great interest around the country. Opponents of same-sex marriage had even persuaded the U.S. Congress to pass the Defense of Marriage Act (Public Law 104-199) in 1996, which decreed that other states need not recognize a marriage license granted to a same-sex couple in Hawaii or elsewhere. Many states also enacted measures stating that they would not recognize such marriages.

Attorneys for the two sides—the couples and the State of Hawaii—presented a total of eight witnesses. Two were sociologists who study the family, one for each side: David Eggebeen of Pennsylvania State University testified in opposition to allowing same-sex marriages, and Pepper Schwartz of the University of Washington testified in favor of allowing them. Both testified as expert witnesses whose knowledge and experience qualified them to advise the court on the matter.[1]

The prominent role of sociologists in this landmark case demonstrates how much the field of the sociology of the family has become entwined with public debates about important social issues such as (alphabetically) abortion, caring for the frail elderly, children's well-being, the decline of marriage, divorce, gay and lesbian families, teenage childbearing, welfare, and women's equality. To be sure, the private relations between husbands and wives, intimate partners, and parents and children make up a large part of the field. In fact, the roots of twentieth-century sociology of the family lie in the study of marital interaction (see Chapter 9). But the field has also acquired a public dimension based on sociologists' studies of issues of concern.

Eggebeen and Schwartz's testimony reflects the way sociologists think about the family and the kinds of social scientific arguments they make. That they disagreed demonstrates that the kinds of evidence sociologists cite often lends itself to more than one interpretation. Often, the final interpretation—in this case the law about who may marry whom—must reflect moral or political beliefs that sociologists cannot prescribe.

David Eggebeen, testifying first, defined marriage in terms of **procreation:** having and raising children.

> EGGEBEEN: *Well, to me it's the . . . the conclusion is clear that marriage represents a gateway to becoming a parent. When people get married, by an extraordinary margin they intend to become parents.*
>
> ATTORNEY FOR THE STATE: *So in the minds of people, marriage would be synonymous with having children?*
>
> EGGEBEEN: *When 98 percent of the married individuals intend to become parents, I would say that's a very valid conclusion.*[2] (trial transcript, September 11, 1996, p. 42)

---

[1] In the spirit of full disclosure, let me state that I signed a friend-of-the-court brief in favor of extending marriage to same-sex couples.

[2] Eggebeen was referring to Jacobson and Heaton (1991), who reported that in a national survey 2.8 percent of men and 3.5 percent of women 39 or younger said that they did not have chilldren already and did not intend to have any.

Eggebeen then suggested reasons why gay marriages may not provide optimal settings for raising children. He cited research showing that children's well-being is, on average, lower in some respects in single-parent families and stepfamilies than in two-parent families. And gay couples with children are like stepfamilies, he argued, because often the children were conceived in heterosexual unions that the gay parent later left to live with a gay partner. In other words, he argued that gay marriages should be discouraged because they might not be as good for children as heterosexual marriages. Although some gay parents may do excellent jobs of raising their children, he acknowledged, on average they aren't as good.

Eggebeen's criteria emphasize one of the most public aspects of family life: the raising of the next generation, on which society depends. The belief that raising children is the central task of marriage is an old one, going back to the days when the survival of a family line couldn't be taken for granted. Procreation was seen as socially important work—not the sort of thing to risk by undertaking radical changes in marriage. Eggebeen admitted that there wasn't much research on whether or not same-sex couples are fit parents; but he drew the conservative conclusion that, in the absence of data, society should not take what he sees as a risk to children's development:

> EGGEBEEN: . . . my professional opinion is that if we do not have the studies done . . . that allow us to make generalizations, then my opinion is that we should not make any changes in how we view marriage or legal changes in marriages that would lead to [legalized gay marriage] (tr., September 11, p. 88).

In contrast, Pepper Schwartz, testifying on behalf of the couples, defined marriage more in terms of the private rewards it provides to adults than in terms of childrearing.

> ATTORNEY FOR THE COUPLES: Well, on the topic of what marriage means to people, Doctor Schwartz, why do people get married?
>
> SCHWARTZ: . . . What people think of when they want marriage is they want companionship, they want love, they want trust, they want someone who will be with them through thick and thin. Now, I wouldn't say this is what marriage means in all cultures but in our own it's an aspiration for—for intimacy and security. And that is the definition of marriage as people first and primarily think of it (tr., September 16, 1996, p. 59).

Children are an important part of marriage, she suggested, but they aren't as central as Eggebeen claimed:

> Yes, having children is a deep desire of the majority of young Americans . . . most of whom want kids when they get married. But it isn't, I think the reason that everyone gets married. They get married to have this partnership. It [having children] is a reason among many that people want to be married (tr., September 16, pp. 61–62).

As we will learn in Chapter 2, the view that private rewards such as intimacy and companionship are central to marriage wasn't widespread until the nineteenth and twentieth centuries. In a historical sense, it is a relatively new way to think about families. Schwartz's research, which has identified similarities and differences among married couples, heterosexual cohabiting couples, gay male couples, and lesbian couples, is focused mainly on the relationships among couples rather than on their childrearing (Blumstein & Schwartz, 1983; Schwartz, 1994).

But Schwartz and the attorneys for the couples realized that in order to win a favorable ruling from the judge, they had to address the question of whether allowing gay marriage is in the best interests of children. The attorneys for the couples knew that the other side would try to show that gay marriage was not in the best interests of children and that, therefore, prohibiting gay marriage furthered a "compelling state interest." So, under friendly questioning from the couples' attorneys, Schwartz argued that, according to social scientific research, gay parents could be as good as heterosexual parents:

> *ATTORNEY FOR THE COUPLES: Can a same-sex couple give a child the same love and attention that a different-sex couple can give?*
>
> *SCHWARTZ: Of course. I have no experience in my own research that there would be anything about same-sex couples that would give them less attention. And none of the research that I've read in reviewing for this case . . . indicates that there is any difference between the love and attention and parenting styles of heterosexual versus homosexual* (tr., September 16, p. 85).

Later, the same attorney asked Schwartz whether some lesbians and gay men enter into same-sex partnerships after having had biological children in previous, heterosexual relationships.

> *SCHWARTZ: Yes, yes, of course.*
>
> *ATTORNEY: And how effectively do those biological gay parents serve the needs of their children?*
>
> *SCHWARTZ: Well, I have every reason to believe from what I've read and what research I've done that they're good parents.*
>
> *ATTORNEY: And they are comparable to other biological parents?*
>
> *SCHWARTZ: That's my belief, yes.*
>
> *ATTORNEY: And what do you base that conclusion on?*
>
> *SCHWARTZ: Well, I base it primarily on, I don't know, what must there be near twenty studies comparing lesbian mothers with their own biological children compared to heterosexual mothers with their own biological children* (tr., September 16, p. 87).

Eggebeen, as we have seen, had a different reading of the evidence: On average, he believed children would not fare as well in same-sex partnerships as in marriages. (We will review the evidence in Chapter 14.) But under cross-examination, he acknowledged that gay and lesbian couples are capable of raising a healthy child and that there are some who do an excellent job. He also acknowledged that children who are being raised by gay couples would be helped if the couples could marry because many legal benefits (e.g., social security survivor's benefits for widows and widowers) are reserved for married couples.

Still, Eggebeen's (and the State's) position was that although children now being raised in same-sex partnerships would benefit if the partners could marry, same-sex marriages should be discouraged because, on average, children do better when raised by two biological parents. Therefore, they argued, the State has a compelling interest in prohibiting same-sex marriage. Schwartz (and the couples' attorneys) argued that the

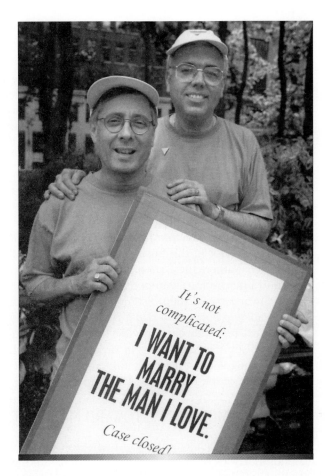

Whether to allow same-sex couples to marry became a controversial issue in the 1990s.

research base doesn't clearly show negative effects on children of being raised in gay partnerships and that making marriage available to them would increase the stability of their unions, give them important legal rights, and raise their status in the eyes of society. Thus, they concluded, the well-being of children might benefit, and is unlikely to suffer, if same-sex partners could marry.

Judge Chang listened to these arguments, studied the trial record and other materials, and on December 3, 1996, issued his ruling: The State of Hawaii had failed to prove that prohibiting same-sex marriage furthered a compelling interest.[3] He was not persuaded that enough negative evidence existed to plainly show that being raised by same-sex partners harms children, and he concluded that children being raised in same-sex partnerships would be helped if the partners were allowed to marry. He therefore declared the law unconstitutional and prohibited the State of Hawaii from denying a marriage license solely because the applicants are of the same sex. However, the State immediately appealed once again to the Hawaii Supreme Court, whose final ruling, either upholding or overturning Judge Chang's opinion, is expected to occur in 1998.

[3]Findings of Fact and Conclusions of Law of Judge Kevin S. C. Chang, filed December 3, 1996, First Circuit Court, State of Hawaii.

The same-sex marriage case reflects several themes of this introductory chapter and, indeed, of the rest of the book:

1 *Family life has both a public and a private dimension* Families can be thought of as places that do publicly valuable work by raising children and caring for the ill and the frail elderly; but, in addition, families provide private emotional rewards such as love, intimacy, and companionship. These two faces of the family are often connected; but they nevertheless represent different ways of viewing family life.

2 *The subject of this book, the sociology of the family, deals with important social issues* Far from dealing with topics of limited academic interest, sociological studies of the family engage some of the most hotly debated and difficult social issues of our time.

3 *Sociologists study the family by collecting data and interpreting it* Sociologists are not in the business of debating moral and political issues in the abstract. Rather, they attempt to contribute to public discussions by collecting and interpreting evidence obtained by studying families. Both Eggebeen and Schwartz based their testimony on existing studies.

4 *Sociological research can't, by itself, resolve moral and political issues* Sociological research can provide helpful information about social issues such as same-sex marriages. But in order to resolve these issues, citizens, legislators, and judges must also rely on values and principles that, strictly speaking, are outside of the domain of sociological research.

AMERICAN AMBIVALENCE TOWARD MARRIAGE AND THE FAMILY

The national uproar over the gay marriage case provided a puzzle: It was surprising to find, in a society in which sexual relations among unmarried adults are accepted, cohabiting unions are becoming the norm, and births outside of marriage are increasingly common, that so many people cared about the definition of marriage. Given the decreasing importance of marriage for sexual behavior and childbearing, why were so many people concerned? One obvious reason is widespread disapproval of homosexual activity. In a 1996 national survey, 66 percent of those questioned said that they thought sexual relations between two adults of the same sex was "always wrong" or "almost always wrong" (Davis & Smith, 1996).[4] But I think a more general reason is the profound ambivalence among many Americans toward marriage and the family. On the one hand, a family life centered on marriage remains the preference of most Americans. When young adults are asked their plans for the future, the overwhelming majority respond that they plan to marry and then have children.

On the other hand, Americans are much more tolerant than they used to be of those who aren't married. In 1957, at the height of the post–World War II baby boom, and again in 1976, national samples of Americans were asked what they would think about a person if all they knew was that he or she did not want to get married. In 1957, half responded that the person must be sick, selfish, immoral, or otherwise deficient. But in 1976, only a third responded negatively; most were neutral (Veroff, Douvan, & Kulka, 1981). To be unmarried in the 1950s was to be an outcast; in the 1970s—and even more so, I believe, in the 1990s—it is acceptable.

[4]See Chapter 7.

In fact, many of those who were so concerned about the outcome of the same-sex marriage case belong to a generation of women and men that has postponed marriage to an extent not seen since the beginning of the twentieth century. The postponement can be attributed to several factors, which are described more fully in subsequent chapters: The greater investment by young women in labor market skills and work experience, the decline in young men's earning power, the greater acceptance of premarital sex, the increase in cohabitation (unmarried couples living together), and the ability to avoid unwanted pregnancies and births through contraception and abortion. These developments have made women and men more independent of each other. Moreover, they have made possible the separation of three spheres of behavior that were closely linked earlier in this century: marriage, sex, and childrearing. It used to be that many, if not most, Americans had sexual relations only with the person they married; and it used to be that all but a small percentage of children were born to married parents.

The postponement of marriage also stems from a broader cultural shift. Over the past few decades, Americans, like the citizens of other Western nations, have come to place a higher value on emotional satisfaction and a personally fulfilling sense of self. The men and women in the 1957 and 1976 national samples were asked what gave them a sense of satisfaction and well-being in life. In 1957, respondents frequently mentioned the sense of satisfaction they derived from performing the social roles that were expected of them—being a good parent, a loyal spouse, or a reliable worker. They told of the satisfaction gained from meeting obligations and commitments to family, friends, and coworkers. By 1976, however, Americans spoke less about what they were doing for others and more about how they were feeling about themselves. They focused more on their personal relationships and less on their obligations and commitments. Increasingly, they judged their well-being by whether their relationships with others felt fulfilling, seemed emotionally satisfying, and provided opportunities for personal growth.

This broader cultural change has influenced what people value about families. For example, in a 1989 national survey, 1,200 individuals were read a list of 28 "value statements." For each statement, they were asked to give a number between one and four depending on how well the term "family values" described the statement. One, the lowest rating, meant "not at all well"; four, the highest rating, meant "very well." The survey researchers computed a mean (average) score for each statement and ranked them from highest score to lowest. The results, shown in Table 1.1, provide some evidence of what Americans currently think are the most important family values. Consistent with the trend observed from 1957 to 1976, the highest-rated statements in 1989 concerned emotional satisfaction (number 1), feelings (5), and personal relationships (2, 3, and 4). Although numbers 2 and 4 also imply responsibility to others, the general theme of these top-rated statements is that warm, personal relationships matter most.

How highly did the survey respondents rate the importance of performing the social roles once expected of adults? The statements pertaining to these social roles rank much further down the list. "Having children" is number 18, and "earning a good living" is number 21. What seems to matter most about marriage is not whether you are married per se but whether you are happy: "having a happy marriage" (6) ranks ahead of "being married to the same person for life" (12). Both are rated higher than "being married" itself, which, at number 16, ranks just below "being physically fit." Examples of the particular "family values" promoted by the social conservative movement of the 1980s and 1990s rank near the bottom of the

TABLE 1.1

In a national survey, 1,200 persons were read 28 "value statements" and were asked how well the term "family values" described each statement. For each statement, the respondent gave a number form 1, "not at all well," to 4, "very well." The mean rankings for each statement are displayed, in order from highest to lowest.

VALUE STATEMENT	MEAN
1. Being able to provide emotional support to your family	3.67
2. Respecting one's parents	3.66
3. Respecting other people for who they are	3.65
4. Being responsible for your actions	3.64
5. Being able to communicate your feelings to your family	3.61
6. Having a happy marriage	3.59
7. Respecting one's children	3.59
8. Respecting authority	3.52
9. Living up to my full potential	3.46
10. Having faith in God	3.45
11. Leaving the world to the next generation in better shape than we found it	3.40
12. Being married to the same person for life	3.39
13. Following a strict moral code	3.37
14. Having good relationships with your extended family, including aunts, uncles, and cousins	3.31
15. Being physically fit	3.30
16. Being married	3.28
17. Having a rewarding job	3.28
18. Having children	3.28
19. Being well-educated and cultured	3.27
20. Being independent	3.25
21. Earning a good living	3.23
22. Being financially secure	3.19
23. Having leisure time for recreational activities	3.14
24. Helping your community or neighborhood	3.14
25. Being in favor of prayer in school	2.92
26. Having nice things	2.75
27. Opposing abortion	2.72
28. Being free of obligations so I can do whatever I want to do	2.33

Source: Table 3 from Mark Mellman, Edward Lazarus, and Allan Rivlin, "Family Ties, Family Values," in David Blankenhorn, Steven Bayme, and Jean Bethke Elshtain, eds., *Rebuilding the Nest: A New Commitment to the American Family* (Milwaukee: Family Service America, 1990), 73–92.

list: "being in favor of prayer in school" is number 25, and "opposing abortion" is number 27. The rankings suggest, as Pepper Schwartz's testimony implied, that Americans value families for the personal fulfillment they can provide more than for the chance to play the role of spouse or parent.

Earlier in the twentieth century, in contrast to circumstances today, marriage was an economic necessity. Women and men needed to pool their resources in order to meet a minimum standard of living. Moreover, it was an expected, almost obligatory part of life. But our standard of living is far higher today. In addition, most married women are employed outside the home—a sharp change, as we will learn, from midcentury. Consequently, men and women are less dependent on each other economically than they were 50 or 100 years ago. Among the middle class, marriage must now compete with alternatives such as staying in school longer to obtain a higher degree, taking more time to develop a career, living with a partner without marrying, or childbearing outside marriage. Among middle-class young adults, this competition is increasingly judged by a single criterion: self-fulfillment. And by this criterion, marriage does not always come out the winner. Most Americans still want to marry but have less of a need to do so. Most want to have children, but they also value other uses of their time and money—such as investing in a career or building a vacation home. Many are ambivalent about marriage, at once drawn by its promise of intimacy and wary of its commitments and constraints.

The poor and near poor have not been immune to these cultural trends; but economics, of necessity, has played a greater role in their behavior. Since the early 1970s, the job prospects of young men without a college education have deteriorated. Their earnings have declined so severely that, among young men who had recently left school, the average high school graduate in the 1980s earned less than the average high school dropout in the 1970s (U.S. Bureau of Labor Statistics, 1993). Moreover, the income gap between the poorest and wealthiest families has widened.[5]

MARRIAGE AND THE FAMILY: CONTRASTING SOCIOLOGICAL VIEWPOINTS

Amid this ambivalence, social scientists also have been uncertain about the current and future role of marriage and the family in American society. From the end of World War II to the late 1970s, rates of marriage, divorce, and childbearing went up and down in a roller-coaster pattern that left experts scurrying to keep up. The pace of change slowed in the 1980s, allowing commentators to catch their breath and take stock of what had happened. Their assessments ranged from glee to gloom.

An Optimistic View   The optimists, most of whom are political liberals, claim that the family isn't in any great difficulty, it's just changing. Families, these observers remind us, have always been changing. What's more, so this argument goes, the family is good at adapting to change—it's a flexible, resilient institution. In this vein, the editors of a collection of essays write:

> *The American family is changing, but then it always seems to be changing. It is stable in its flexibility, its adaptation to changing social conditions. Instead of viewing with alarm the rapidity of change in family structures, we should step back a bit and be aware of the continuity of familial change* (Dornbusch & Strober, 1988).

No cause for alarm? What about the likelihood that about 40 percent of all children will witness the breakup of their parents' marriages and perhaps 10 percent will witness two divorces? Or that about 450,000 teenagers, many of them poor and unmarried, bear children every year? Or that one out of five children is living in a family with an income below the poverty line? The more forthright of the optimists face up to these facts but nevertheless argue that, as in the past, the family will adjust. They urge greater governmental effort in providing childcare for employed parents, helping teenage mothers finish school, ensuring that divorced fathers pay the child support they owe, and so forth. They note that wives

[5] See Chapter 4.

in dual-earner marriages still bear most of the burden of cooking, cleaning, and childcare and urge fathers to do more.

The less forthright of the optimists merely step gingerly around divorce, child-bearing outside of marriage, and childhood poverty and instead accentuate the positive. And there are positives. Americans value the increased independence that they have achieved in their private lives; although this achievement is easy to criticize, few critics would volunteer to be the first to give up their own autonomy. Moreover, the changes in women's work and family roles over the past few decades have given American women broader opportunities, the ability to leave abusive relationships, and much greater control of their own lives.

A Pessimistic View   The pessimists, who tend to be political conservatives, see the family in a very different light. Near the end of the introductory essay in his edited volume on marriage, Kingsley Davis, who was a leading sociological theorist, wrote:

> *The general direction of the changes in marriage that the present book documents during the last forty years is toward a weakening of marriage as an institution. If this goes far enough, and if no satisfactory substitute for marriage emerges, industrial societies will not survive. In fact they are not replacing themselves now, in either number or quality of the next generation. The nonindustrial two-thirds of the world, ill equipped to provide adequate education, is producing 92 percent of the world's next generation. There is thus no assurance that industrial societies, as we have known them, will survive* (Davis, 1985).

Whereas liberal defenders of family change focus on the emotionally enhanced relationships between adults and on the increased autonomy of women, conservatives such as Davis focus on instability and on children—and in Davis's case, on the lack of children in sufficient "number or quality." Without doubt, there are some valid issues about low birthrates that will be discussed in later chapters: How will a relatively smaller workforce pay for social security and health care benefits for a large elderly population? With fewer children and more women at work, will the elderly be able to rely on assistance from their families, as many do today? If low population growth means fewer new firms, will job opportunities be limited? Will the pace of technological innovation slow? Despite such questions and concerns, the end of industrial societies, as we have known them, is not in sight. Moreover, as will be noted later, birthrates of women over age 30 increased in the 1980s as many later-marriers sought to make up for lost time.

Conservative critics, I think, tend to minimize the family's ability to adapt to new developments, such as the increased employment of married women or the introduction of the birth control pill. Dire warnings of the family's failing health have been put forth for decades. Consider this false alarm, written by an expert on the family during the low-birthrate years of the Great Depression:

> *The family is not indefinitely adaptable to modern society. . . . Only two logical alternatives appear feasible for governments wishing to induce births. They can go back to a rural-stable regime, or they can invent a new system of reproductive institutions* (Davis, 1937; Modell, 1985).

This fear of a shrinking population proved groundless. It turned out later that the family had not yet reached the limit of its ability to adapt and that governments did not have to invent a new system for encouraging births. What the expert did not and could not foresee was the great increase in births that occurred after World War II. Who was this expert? None other than Kingsley Davis, writing in 1937 at the beginning of his career. This is not to say that we should expect another baby boom, nor that the family is as malleable as its liberal champions proclaim. The point is rather that the family has shown an ability to adjust to changing circumstances that is often underestimated by conservatives, albeit overestimated by liberals. The problems of the contemporary family are real and should not be minimized, but they do not suggest that the institution of the family is fatally wounded.

Steering a Middle Course   Consequently, the challenge for a social scientist writing about the family—and for a reader—is to avoid the two extremes of boundless optimism and prophesies of doom. Too many observers stake out a position at one pole and try to defend it against all challengers. We must accept, rather, that the changes in the family have had both benefits and costs. Take divorce, for instance: Adults are freer to end unhappy marriages, which is an advance; but they do so through a process that is often gut-wrenching and economically draining for parents and traumatic for children. Moreover, we must realize that family change is continuing and that the end point if there will be one is not clear. It is too soon to know, for example, to what extent living together will supplant marriage. Except among the poor, cohabitation outside marriage has been noticeable only since about 1970, and it is still increasing. Although one can argue that cohabitation has not yet challenged the primacy of marriage in the United States, it is unclear what its impact will be 10 or 20 years from now. The changes in the family since midcentury have been so sharp and so recent that an eminent French demographer titled his book *La Famille Incertaine*—the uncertain family. He concluded that for observers of the family:

> the attitude which makes the most sense is to accept that uncertainty is, for a time, our destiny, or rather the challenge we must confront. This should stimulate, not discourage, research. Without doubt, what research will reveal to us over the course of the coming years will not correspond to today's received wisdom[6] (Roussel, 1989, p. 279).

In writing this book, I have tried to steer a middle course that respects the complexity and uncertainty of social changes in the family. First, I have attempted to confront both the costs and the benefits of the kinds of family lives Americans now live. It is more difficult to hold the pluses and minuses in one's head than to argue the case that changes have been unequivocally for the better—or for the worse; but I think it is necessary to do so. Second, I have tried not to envision an end point for a process that is still playing out. The implications of the great changes we will examine in this book defy a simple, assured summary.

Still, there is plenty of room in the middle ground for reasoned disagreements about the state of the American family. A number of observers concede that the family is in no danger of fading away but nevertheless insist that it is in decline. David Popenoe notes that marriage has become much more unstable and that there are acceptable alternatives—lifelong singlehood, cohabitation—to getting married at all. He argues that people value the survival and strength of the family

---

[6]Louis Roussel, *La Famille Incertaine* (Paris: Editions Odile Jacob, 1989), quoted at 279. The translation is mine.

unit less and self-fulfillment more. And he charges that parents are doing a poorer job of bringing up children due to the increase in single-parent families (a theme in David Eggebeen's testimony), the higher percentage of mothers working outside the home, and what he claims is a thinner family culture in the home (e.g., fewer joint activities, fewer family-centered traditions) (Popenoe, 1988; Popenoe, 1991).

Others admit that change has brought some problems but argue that, on balance, the family is not in decline—just becoming different and more diverse. They argue that American society can adjust to the new family forms, such as two-earner couples and single-parent households, by changing the ways in which the workplace and the school are organized. They assert that there is little evidence to back up the claim that having a working mother hurts children. Moreover, they ask, "decline for whom?" and note that the authority and stability of the 1950s family was achieved, in part, by severely limiting the opportunities of women. It is an important debate—one that I will touch upon throughout the book and then evaluate in the final chapter.

Diversity　Both sides can agree on the growing diversity of American families. At midcentury, most families consisted of a married couple, neither of whom had been married to someone else previously, and their children. Beginning in the 1960s, however, family patterns were altered by great rises in divorce, childbearing

U.S. families are more diverse today than in earlier times because of the great changes that have occurred since midcentury. Single-parent families, extended families, and complex families formed by remarriages are among the kinds of families with which the two-parent, first-marriage family must share the spotlight.

outside of marriage, and, since about 1970, cohabitation. As a result, the first-marriage, two-parent family must now share its prominence with single-parent families and families formed by remarriages. The large numbers of immigrants from Latin America and Asia have brought their own cultural traditions, which often include a greater emphasis on ties to other kin beyond the parents-and-children household, such as grandparents, uncles, and aunts. Among African Americans, the percentage of two-parent households has declined greatly, while the importance of ties to other kin has increased. Across all racial and ethnic groups, married women have become much more likely to work outside the home. The causes of this growing diversity and its consequences for adults and children will be examined throughout this book.

PERSPECTIVES ON THE FAMILY

THE SOCIOLOGICAL PERSPECTIVE

In this book, the singular form "the family" rather than the plural form "families" will be used when discussing the family as a **social institution**. This term refers to a set of roles and rules that define a social unit of importance to society. The roles give us positions such as parent, child, spouse, ex-spouse, stepfather, partner, and so forth. The rules offer us guidance about how to act in these roles. But the use of the singular is not meant to imply that there is only one kind of family. On the contrary, there are many forms. Similarly, one might write about "the corporation" in a textbook on social organizations without implying that there is no difference between IBM and a chain of grocery stores. Or an author might discuss "the hospital" in a text on medical sociology while recognizing the difference between a giant teaching hospital in a central city and a community hospital out in the suburbs. In addition, referring to "the family" is not meant to imply that the interests of wives, husbands, and children are always identical—any more than that the interests of workers and managers in corporations are identical.

In all of these cases, the use of the singular would signal the study of the family as a social institution rather than just a set of interpersonal relationships. An institution can grow stronger or weaker over time; it can take on somewhat different forms at different times and places; and it can be difficult to define at its margins. But it is a visible structure that people can recognize and understand. It also does something important for society. The "family" fits this description. Its important functions include rearing children, caring for the elderly, and providing comfort and emotional support to its members.

If the family can be viewed as a social institution, then sociology can help us understand it better. Sociologists specialize in, among other topics, the study of institutions. They analyze the consequences for individuals of the roles that exist and the rules about how these roles should be played. For example, in my work analyzing remarriage after divorce, I have argued that some of the common problems occur because the rules of the institution of the family assume that individuals are in first marriages. There are no widely accepted norms for how harshly a stepparent can discipline his or her stepchild, nor for how much emotional and financial support a stepparent owes to a stepchild. This lack of norms can lead to confusion and conflict as remarried persons and their children attempt to build a successful stepfamily (Cherlin, 1978). (See Chapter 13.)

When sociologists study institutions, they also look outward. They search the social world for important external forces, such as the degree of opportunity provided by the labor market, the restrictions imposed by racial prejudice and discrimination, the domination of women by men, and the impact of new ideas and values. This book will discuss how forces such as these influence the family. In other words, sociologists argue that the family cannot be studied in a vacuum; rather, it must be studied in its social context. The sociological perspective on the family emphasizes the rules, roles, and relationships that are created and maintained by the larger society.

OTHER PERSPECTIVES

Nevertheless, the sociological perspective on the family does not provide a complete understanding. There is a vast amount of psychological literature on the family that focuses on the individuals involved. Whereas sociologists studying the family tend to look outward toward society, psychologists tend to look inward toward people's personalities and their interactions with other family members. They study how children come to understand the world around them and how they develop a sense of self. They observe how people's behavior is shaped by their family experiences. Several psychologists, for example, have observed in detail the effects on children of experiencing the breakup of their parents' marriages, as will be noted in Chapter 12. Moreover, as the next chapter will make clear, historians writing since about 1970 have greatly increased our understanding of how the contemporary family has emerged. Valuable work has also been done by economists who have applied their theories to family life. This book will draw upon these contributions from other social science disciplines, but it cannot provide a comprehensive account of them.

Nearly all sociologists believe that most of the differences in the roles men and ·women play and in the behaviors they show are social and cultural in origin. Yet some also think that the institution of the family has biological roots and, correspondingly, that the differences between women and men have both social and biological origins, and that it is likely that a person's sexual orientation (heterosexual or homosexual) has a substantial biological component. These statements may strike many readers as unexceptional or even obvious. In the academic debates about family, gender, and sexuality, however, they set proponents of these views, myself included, apart from a respected and influential camp that claims biological influences are minimal.

A number of studies build a plausible case that the greater aggressiveness that men, on average, show may be biologically based in part.[7] The evidence is suggestive but less solid that women, on average, may be more adept at enabling and maintaining relationships[8] (Rossi, 1984); and that men may be more inclined to pursue sex outside of lasting relationships.[9] As will be discussed in later chapters, the existence of these biological differences could account in part for the persistent differences in how women and men interact and in how they care for young children.

Why might biology underlie some of the differences in the ways that women and men go about finding partners and building family lives? Scholars from the emerging subdiscipline of **evolutionary psychology** claim that some of the differences are

[7]See Chapter 3.
[8]See also Chapter 3.
[9]See Chapter 7.

the result of the same evolutionary pressures that Charles Darwin recognized in plants and animals (Symons, 1979; Buss, 1994; Pinker, 1997). The basic argument is that animals, including humans, tend to behave in ways that maximize the chances that they will be able to reproduce themselves. These tendencies are rooted in the genes that the animals carry. Animals that are successful have offspring; whereas animals that are not die off. Over eons of time, therefore, genes that lead to behavior that increases the chance of bearing offspring spread through the species.

But why might men, on average, have genes that predispose them to different reproductive strategies than women? Here the evolutionary psychologists and like-minded sociologists note the different roles that men and women played in the hunter-gatherer bands in which most humans and their evolutionary predecessors lived until about 8,000 B.C. These differences will be noted in more detail in Chapter 2. In particular, women not only bore children but also cared for them while young and breast-fed them for several years. Under these conditions, the evolutionists hypothesize, women maximized their chances of having and raising children by finding men who would provide resources and protection exclusively to them for at least the first several years of pregnancy and childcare. Men, on the other hand, maximized their reproductive potential by impregnating many women; and they benefited from being aggressive enough to dominate other males and therefore control sexual access to many women. Thus, it is said, women, on average, came to value sex in the context of relationships and commitment more than men, whereas men were more likely to value sex outside of lasting relationships and to behave aggressively.

Although these evolutionary explanations are plausible, sociologists (and some psychologists) have produced alternative explanations that point to social structure and culture, rather than genes, as the causes of differences in women's and men's behavior. In particular, sociologists have uncovered evidence of the many ways in which boys and men receive different messages than girls and women about how they are supposed to behave; this literature will be reviewed in Chapter 3. Consequently, the behavior the sociologist sees is a composite of social and biological influences. Moreover, biological differences between men and women cannot explain changes in the family over the past few decades, or even over the past few centuries, because evolution occurs so slowly (Udry, 1994). For the same reason, the theory of evolution cannot explain the great changes in sexual behavior over the past few decades.[10] Nor can it explain the numerous differences in family behavior across nations and cultures today.

What is more, even if evolution and genes are important, they do not imply that any particular form of the family is biologically rooted. For example, there is little reason to believe that a family in which the wife stays home to raise the children and the husband works for pay outside the home is more biologically "natural" than one in which they both work outside the home. In fact, in the hunter-gatherer societies that existed for so much of our past, women tended to provide half or more of the food that was consumed. They did so through the gathering of edible plants—all the while caring for young children without much help from men. This picture of early human society, as some authors have noted, seems more similar to contemporary single-parent families than to nuclear families (Tanner & Zihlman, 1976).[11] Many people mistakenly assume that the "traditional" family fits

[10]See Chapter 7.
[11]See also Chapter 2.

the breadwinner-homemaker mold. To the contrary, as will be demonstrated in the next chapter, the breadwinner-homemaker family is historically unusual.

In recent years, a number of studies, to be discussed in Chapter 7, have suggested that there is a biological basis for a person's sexual orientation. Here again, the evidence is not definitive. Yet unlike the sociological explanations for gender differences, there is no convincing counterexplanation put forth by sociologists. In other words, whereas sociological studies leave no doubt that parents, peers, and the media often provide different messages to girls and boys, few studies demonstrate that they provide different messages to children who will grow up to have a homosexual orientation than to those who will have a heterosexual orientation. Even so, the historical and cross-cultural variations in the role of homosexuality suggest that society also has an important influence on sexual orientation.

These conclusions are not meant to imply that one kind of role for women or men in the family, or one kind of sexual orientation, is superior or more "natural" than others. Rather, they suggest that our biological makeup creates predispositions toward some behaviors and away from others. Whether we, in fact, exhibit these behaviors depends on the social circumstances of our lives: the upbringing we received from our parents; the cultural influences we absorbed from peers, neighbors, ministers, and the media; and the economic constraints or racial prejudices we may have faced. These social factors sometimes exaggerate biological differences between women and men, so that the differences we see can be greater than biology alone would create. Moreover, evolutionary perspectives can lead us to overlook the substantial similarities between men's and women's approaches to sexuality and family life (Schwartz & Rutter, 1998). Biological predispositions, then, do not determine a person's behavior. Rather, they create tendencies and leanings. On average, a group of people who share a predisposition (toward, say, aggressive behavior) are likely to show more of it than is a group who do not share it; but it is difficult to predict how any single member of the group is likely to behave.

WHAT IS A FAMILY?

How the family is defined has important social and economic consequences. On the level of morality, it is a statement of the kinds of personal relationships that we value highly. When President Jimmy Carter proposed a White House Conference on Families in the late 1970s, a bitter battle ensued between social conservatives who wanted the plural "families" replaced with "the family" in the title and liberals who wanted to preserve the original title. The social conservatives pressed the Carter administration to use the singular form because it symbolized their belief that there is only one proper kind of family: the "traditional" two-parent family in which the husband is employed outside the home and the wife cares for the children. Liberals fought off the conservative challenge, but it was a Pyrrhic victory; the conference was seriously weakened by the controversy.

The definition of the family is also important economically. Rules specifying who is a "family member" determine billions of dollars of government and corporate benefits. For example, I am eligible for health insurance coverage through my employer for my "family," which is defined as a spouse and children under 18. If I were unmarried but living with a woman who was the mother of my children, I could insure the children but not the mother. If I had been living for years with a man whom I considered my lifelong partner, I probably could not insure him. Moreover, how one defines a family plays an important role in the debate over whether the family has declined.

The definition of the family also varies from culture to culture. This book is primarily about families in the **Western nations,** the countries of Western Europe and the overseas English-speaking countries of the United States, Canada, Australia, and New Zealand. The main focus is on the family in the United States; but there are strong similarities between the American family and the family in other Western nations (Cherlin & Furstenberg, 1988). The primary unit in all these countries is the small, household-based family of parents and children. Young adults choose their spouses with modest input from their parents, and marriage is monogamous. (**Monogamy** is a marriage system in which persons cannot have more than one spouse.) Substantial proportions of married women work for pay outside the home (although that was not the case earlier in the twentieth century). Over the past few decades, nearly all the Western nations have undergone similar increases in cohabitation, childbearing outside of marriage, and divorce.

Nevertheless, we can draw important lessons by studying families elsewhere in the world. Therefore, this book will include numerous examples of family patterns in non-Western countries, including the developed nations of East Asia such as Japan and Taiwan, and developing countries through the world. In many of these countries, ties to parents and other kin play a larger part in the structure of the family. Often, parents provide substantial guidance to children in choosing spouses. In some countries, women rarely work outside the family home or compound. In many countries in Africa, Arabic Asia, and other areas, polygamous marriage is allowed. (**Polygamy** is a marriage system in which men or women [or both] are allowed to have more than one spouse at a time.) At the same time, significant changes have occurred in family patterns in much of the developing world over the past several decades; examining these changes can help us better understand the changes that have occurred closer to home. Similar insights can be drawn from studying the changes in family life in Western history. Each of the subsequent chapters of this book will include a separate, short essay on families in other cultures, with "other cultures" occasionally defined to include Western history.

For the United States and other Western nations, I would argue that there is no single definition of a family that is adequate for all purposes. Rather, how you define a family depends on what questions you want to answer. Two key questions are:

1 How well are family members taking care of children, the chronically ill, and the frail elderly?
2 How well are families providing the emotional satisfaction people value so highly—intimacy, love, personal fulfillment?

These questions address, respectively, the public responsibilities and the private pleasures the family is called upon to meet. For each of these questions, I submit, one of two definitions of the family will be helpful; I will call them the public family and the private family. These definitions provide two useful ways of looking at the same reality—and often the very same group of adults and children. Some observers may impose their own theological definitions of what constitutes a family from religious works such as the Bible or the Koran. But social science cannot determine the moral essence of the family, nor need it do so.

THE PUBLIC FAMILY

In examining the concept of the public family, it's useful to borrow a few terms from the field of economics. Economists who specialize in public welfare have introduced the notion of **externalities**, of which there are two types.[12] First, **negative externalities** occur when an individual or a business produces something that is beneficial to itself but imposes costs on other individuals or businesses. For example, factories that release sulfur dioxide through smokestacks impose a cost on everyone else by polluting the air. The factory gains by producing goods without having to install expensive smokestack scrubbers, but everyone else loses. Second, **positive externalities** occur when an individual or business produces something that benefits others but for which the producers are not fully compensated. For example, a corporation may start an expensive job training program in order to obtain qualified workers; but some of the workers may take jobs with rival firms after completing the training. The other firms obtain skilled workers without paying the cost of their training.

Some positive externalities involve the production of what are called **public goods**. These goods have a peculiar property: It is almost impossible to stop people who don't produce them from enjoying them. As a result, public goods are often produced in smaller quantities than is socially desirable. Suppose a town raises taxes to build a water filtration plant that cleans a polluted river. It cannot stop residents of other towns downstream from enjoying the cleaner water; yet these fortunate residents have paid nothing for the cleanup. In a situation like this, it is clearly in each town's interest to have some other town farther up the river produce the public good—the treatment plant. Yet if no town builds the plant, no one will enjoy cleaner water. One solution to this dilemma is for the county or state government to raise taxes in all the towns and then build the plant. Another is for the towns to reach an agreement whereby one will build the plant but all will contribute to the costs. Either solution compensates the producer of the public good for the benefits that others obtain.

Although it may seem like a long leap from factories to families, the concepts of externalities and public goods still apply. Families do produce valuable public goods—most notably, children (Folbre, 1994). For example, when I retire, I hope to receive a social security check from the government each month, just as retired people do today. The funds for those checks will come from payroll taxes paid by workers. After 2010, the many men and women born during the post–World War II baby boom will begin to reach retirement age; I hope to be one of them. Currently, there are about five persons of working age for each retired person; but by 2025 there may be only three persons of working age for every retired person.[13] This means that the burden of supporting the elderly will increase greatly. It's in my interest, then, for families to have and rear children today who will be productive workers when they grow up. But children are costly to raise, and I will receive the same social security check whether or not the workers were raised by me. Therefore, it's in my economic interest to remain childless and to have every other family except mine raise children. Yet if everyone followed this strategy there would be no next generation. Luckily, people have children for reasons other than economic self-interest. At the moment, however, they are barely having enough to replace the current generation of parents. Everyone benefits from the

---

[12]A standard treatment of these topics can be found in Stiglitz (1988).
[13]Considering 20 to 64 as working age and 65 or older as retirement age. See Palmer and Gould (1986).

Family members, such as this adult daughter combing her mother's hair, provide much of the care for the frail elderly.

child rearing that parents do.[14] A National Academy of Sciences panel estimated that if the government had to purchase all the childcare services parents and relatives now provide for free, the cost would be $126 billion per year (Hayes, Palmer, & Zaslow, 1990).

In addition, families provide other services that have the character of public goods. As will be noted in Chapter 15, adult children still provide the bulk of the care for the frail elderly. If I am old and ill, I will benefit if I have adult children who will care for me. But others will also benefit from the care that my family provides. Without them, I would need more assistance from the government-funded medical insurance programs for the elderly (Medicare) and for the poor (Medicaid). Consequently, the care my family provides will keep government spending, and hence taxes, lower for everyone. The same logic applies to care that family members provide for the chronically ill.

The first definition, then, concerns the view of the family you take when you are concerned about the family's contribution to the public welfare—the useful services family members provide by taking care of one another. It is a definition of what I will call the **public family**: *One adult, or two adults who are related by marriage, partnership, or shared parenthood, who is/are taking care of dependents, and the dependents themselves.* Dependents are defined as children, the frail elderly, and the chronically ill. The family members usually reside in the same household, but that is not essential. For example, an elderly person may live in her own apartment but still receive daily assistance from her daughter or son. Nor is it essential

[14]This example holds only, however, for developed countries such as the United States, where the birthrate is at or below the level needed to replace the population. In developing countries with very high birthrates, children can impose negative externalities. Given the high death rates in the poorest developing countries, it is in the interest of a peasant farmer to have many children to ensure that at least one or two will still be alive when the farmer is too old to work. But if every family follows that logic, the land may become overpopulated and the country's development may slow. See Cain (1983).

that the family members be married or of the opposite sex. The important fact is that they are taking care of dependents and, in doing so, producing public goods. This definition would include, of course, a married couple and their children or their elderly parents. But it would also include a divorced (or never-married) mother and her children, a cohabiting couple with children, a lesbian couple who are jointly raising a child that was born to one of them, or a gay man caring for a partner with AIDS. Note also who would be excluded by this definition: a childless married couple with no dependent or elderly relatives, or opposite-sex or same-sex cohabitors without children, the elderly, or ill dependents.

The boundaries of the public family are sometimes unclear. Suppose that after a divorce a father makes regular child support payments to his ex-wife and sees his children often. You might argue that he is still sharing parenthood and therefore part of the family under this definition. If the mother remarries, her new husband could also be considered part of the family. As will be discussed in later chapters, divorce, remarriage, and childbearing outside of marriage have made older notions of family boundaries unsatisfactory. Yet no social or legal consensus exists on what new boundaries should be accepted.

There is another kind of caretaking that goes on in many households with married or cohabiting couples, a kind that I have not included in the public family perspective. In most such households the wives (or women partners) do the majority of the housework: cooking, cleaning, shopping, washing, ironing. In doing so, they care for their husbands (or male partners), who do less than their share of the housework. Women's housework is socially valuable labor. Yet there is a difference between caring for husbands and caring for dependents such as children and the frail elderly: The latter are not capable of caring for themselves, whereas husbands are. When parents stop taking care of their children, the government is often obliged to step in and pay for the care. If wives stopped doing housework for their husbands, the government could tell husbands to care for themselves. That is why I have not listed childless couples under this definition.

The production of public goods invites public scrutiny, and public families are easily identifiable to outsiders by the presence of dependents. Because society has an interest in how well families manage the care of dependents, the law allows for some regulation of these families—despite strong sentiment in the United States against intervening in family matters. For example, we require families to send their children to school until age 16. And state social welfare agencies have the power to remove children from homes judged to be harmful. More recently, several states have required medical personnel to report suspected cases of physical abuse of children. The public family, then, is about caretaking and dependency. It points us toward the kinds of kinship ties that are important for nurturing the young and caring for the elderly and the ill. It is a useful perspective for answering questions such as: How adequately will our society raise the next generation? How will we care for the growing number of elderly persons?

THE PRIVATE FAMILY

At the same time, the family is much more than a public service institution. It also provides individuals with intimacy, emotional support, and love. Indeed, most people today think of the family and experience it in these private terms. Although some of the intimacy is expressed sexually, the family is also where we get hugs as children and back rubs as adults. It is where children form first attachments, teenagers take steps toward autonomy, and adults share their inner selves with someone else. The public family is not the most useful perspective in this regard because the central question is not how we will care for dependents but, rather, how we will obtain the intimacy and emotional support we desire.

An appropriate definition of the private family must, therefore, encompass intimate relationships whether or not they include dependents. Yet if we are to maintain our focus on the family as a social institution, the definition still must encompass some rules for defining what kinds of intimate relationships constitute a family. The rules were relatively easy to formulate in the case of the public family: A dependent and a caregiver had to be present. Twenty or 30 years ago, it would also have been easy to find rules for the private family, but now it is much more difficult. At the earlier time, one could simply have adopted the definition of a family that was then, and is still now, used by the U.S. Bureau of the Census: A family is two or more persons, living in the same household, and related by blood, marriage, or adoption. The term **relationship by blood** means sharing a common ancestor, including cross-generational kinship ties such as parent and child (whose common ancestors are the parents' parents) or same-generation ties such as brother and sister (whose common ancestors are their parents). The Census Bureau definition would include a married couple with or without children as well as an unmarried mother and her child (who are related by "blood"). It is no longer satisfactory for several reasons. For example, consider the great rise in cohabitation since about 1970. Nearly half of all adults live with a partner before they marry, as mentioned earlier. According to the Census Bureau definition, a couple who live together for three years and then marry would not become a family until their wedding day. Some people might still support this definition on moral grounds, but it is increasingly out of step with the way young adults are

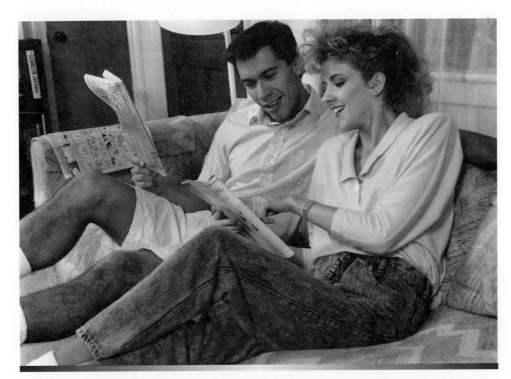

Cohabiting couples fit the definition of the private family.

leading their personal lives. Excluding cohabitation may still be valid as a state-ment of what family life should be, but it is deficient as a statement of what it is.

Moreover, Americans' increased tolerance of nonmarital relationships has led to a debate about whether to consider homosexual couples as families. The same-sex marriage trial was one manifestation of that debate. Advocates argue that most gay or lesbian couples who do not qualify as families under the Census Bureau definition because they are neither married nor related by blood have long-term intimate relationships that differ little in emotional content from heterosexual unions. Others, including some religious leaders, believe that heterosexual, marital unions are the only morally acceptable basis for family life. If one includes the care of dependents as part of the definition, as I have done above in defining the public family, the majority of gay and lesbian couples would be excluded. But if one's concern is with intimate relations, as mine is here in defining the private family, then gay and lesbian couples fit the definition descriptively.

Thus, it is difficult to define the family in terms of sentiment and intimacy be-cause of the decline of marriage and of kinship by blood as the sole markers of family-like relationships among adults. Some even see this decline as an indicator that the concept of the family is outmoded and should be discarded. In a recent book, four sociologists argued that the concept of the family is too restrictive and should be replaced altogether by the broader concept of close relationships, and in particular what they call a **sexually based primary relationship**, which they mer-cifully abbreviate as SBPR (Scanzoni, Polonko, Teachman, & Thompson, 1989). It is defined as an erotic, close relationship that is "one of strong, frequent, and di-verse interdependence that lasts over a considerable period of time." So defined, an SBPR could include a wide variety of relationships, from a couple married for many years to two people who live in different apartments and see each other a few times a week. There may be times when a concept this general is useful. But in rejecting the concept of families (not to mention "the family"), this approach de-nies an important reality that, I think, is still in people's heads. Most people still believe that there is something called the family, even if they have trouble defining its boundaries. There is still a public sense, which I share, that the institution is worth preserving. This sense is strongest when the rearing of children is at issue. And here the close-relationship approach is at its weakest, for the SBPR, as a sex-ual bond, excludes by definition the roles of parent and child.[15]

Yet, although the notion of an SBPR seems too broad to me, it is not evident where to draw the boundaries of the private family. Here uncertainty, as the French demographer said, is the challenge we must confront. Rapid change has undermined the consensus among Americans about the norms of family life—the social rules about what constitutes a family and how people should behave when they are in one. Let me offer, then, a definition of the **private family** not as an au-thoritative statement but rather as a starting point for analyzing this uncertainty: *two or more individuals who maintain an intimate relationship that they expect will last indefinitely—or, in the case of a parent and child, until the child reaches adulthood—and who live in the same household and pool their income and house-hold labor.* This definition allows for children to be part of the private family, al-though the character of the intimacy between parents and children is clearly differ-ent from that between adult partners. It does not require that the individuals be of

---

[15]The authors make an unconvincing attempt to bring children into their framework in Chapter 7 of Scanzoni, et al. (1989).

opposite sexes. In addition, the definition is more restrictive than an SBPR in two ways. First, the relationship must be one in which the commitment is long-term, in which the expectation is that the adult partners will stay together indefinitely. I do not require that they expect to stay together for life because it's not clear how many married couples even expect as much, given that about half of all marriages now end in divorce. Second, the definition includes the notion that the partnership usually is household-based and economic as well as intimate shared residence, common budgets. This reflects my sense that intimate relationships in families are not merely erotic and emotionally supportive but also involve sharing the day-to-day details of managing one's life.

To be sure, individuals also receive emotional support and material assistance from kin with whom they are not in an intimate relationship. The word "family" is sometimes used in the larger sense of relationships with sisters, uncles, grand-mothers, and so forth. These broader kinship ties are still an important part of the setting in which people embed their intimate relations to spouses, partners, and children. The usual definition of "kin" is the people who are related to you by descent (through your mother's or father's line) or marriage. Yet the concept of kinship is also becoming broader and harder to define, as this book will show. In settings as varied as sharing networks among low-income African Americans, friend-based support networks among lesbians and gay men, and middle-class networks of adults who are related only through the ties of broken marriages and remarriages, people are expanding the definition of kinship creating kin, as it were, out of relationships that don't fit the old mold. In fact, throughout the book I will distinguish between what I will call **created kinship**—kinship ties that people have to construct actively and **assigned kinship**—kinship ties that people more or less automatically acquire when they are born or when they marry. And I will return in the final chapter to the changing nature of kinship and its implications for family life.

TWO VIEWS, SAME FAMILY

Many, perhaps most, family units will appear before your eyes no matter which perspective—public or private—you choose. That is to say, both perspectives may apply to the same family unit. A married couple may be providing each other with love and intimacy and also raising children. Indeed, the public and private dimensions of the family often overlap. For example, it's difficult for families to provide good childcare without love and emotional support. Moreover, even the private family is influenced by the larger society. As will be discussed in Chapter 2, the development of the private family depended upon, among other things, the availability of wages high enough so that family members no longer needed to focus their attention on day-to-day subsistence. The two perspectives, then, can be thought of as complementary and sometimes overlapping ways of looking at the same reality: the institution of the family.

In sum, to examine the contributions of families to the public welfare is to look at relationships through the lens of the public family. To examine the family's provisions of intimacy, love, and fulfillment is to look through the lens of the private family. Both perspectives are embedded in each of the chapters that follow. Which is better? Neither. They are two takes on the same reality. Many textbooks emphasize the private family by focusing primarily on interpersonal relationships in courtship, cohabitation, and marriage. In doing so, they pay less attention to the socially valuable work that families do. Although this book, too, will have much to say about the private family, it will also emphasize the public family. In addition to the essays on families in other cultures, each subsequent chapter will include a short essay on families and public policy; and chapters such as "The Family, the State, and Social Policy," "Children and Parents," and "The Elderly and Their Families" will be directed primarily toward public issues.

HOW DO FAMILY SOCIOLOGISTS KNOW WHAT THEY KNOW?

Sociologists collect and analyze data consisting of observations of real families and the people in them. For the most part, they strive to analyze their data using objective, scientific methods. **Objectivity** means the ability to draw conclusions about a social situation that are unaffected by one's own beliefs. But it is much more difficult for a sociologist to be objective than it is for a natural or physical scientist. Sociologists not only study families, they live in them. They often have strong moral and political views of their own (indeed, strong views about social issues are what lead many people to become sociologists), and it is difficult to prevent those views from influencing one's research. Indeed, there are some sociologists who argue that objectivity is so difficult to achieve that sociologists shouldn't try. Rather, they argue, sociologists should try to do research that advances the social causes they believe in (Reinharz, 1992; see *How Do Sociologists Know What They Know?* Feminist Research Methods, in Chapter 3).

But most sociologists, although aware that their views can influence the way they interpret their data, model their research on the scientific method. For a detailed examination of the scientific method in sociology, consult any good introductory sociology textbook. For example, Schaefer and Lamm (1998, p. 37) define the **scientific method** as "a systematic, organized series of steps that ensures maximum objectivity and consistency in researching a problem." The essence of the scientific method is to formulate a hypothesis that can be tested by collecting and analyzing data. (A **hypothesis**, Schaefer and Lamm [1998] write, is "a speculative statement about the relationship between two or more factors" [p. 39].) It's easy to come up with a hypothesis (God is a woman), but the trick is to find one that can be shown to be true or false by examining data. Sociologists therefore tend to formulate very specific hypotheses about family life that can be confirmed or disconfirmed by observation. For example, sociologists have hypothesized that having a first child as a teenager lowers, on average, the amount of education a woman attains; and statistical data support this claim.

Even so, there are inherent limitations in how well social scientists can use the scientific method. The best way to confirm or disconfirm a relationship between two factors is to conduct an experiment in which all other factors are held constant. Scientists do this by randomly assigning subjects to one of two groups: an experimental group and a control group. For example, doctors will study whether a new drug speeds recovery from an illness by assembling a group of volunteers, all of whom have the illness, and then randomly giving half of them (the experimental group) the new drug. By randomizing, the doctors hope that all other confounding factors (such as past medical history) will be equalized between the two groups. Then they compare the average recovery times of the experimental group and the control group (those who did not receive the drug).

But it is rarely possible for sociologists to conduct randomized experiments on families. Without randomization, there is always the possibility that another, unobserved factor, lurking just beneath the surface, is causing the relationship we see. Consider again teenage childbearing. Women who have a first child as a teenager tend to come from families that have less education and less money, on average, than do other women. So the reason that teenage mothers attain less education may reflect their disadvantaged family backgrounds rather than having a child; in others words, they might have had less education even if they hadn't had children as teenagers. To truly settle this issue, a truth-seeking but cold-blooded sociologist would want to obtain a list of all families with teenage girls in the United States and then to assign *at random* some of the girls to have children and others to remain childless until their twenties. Because of the random assignment, teenage childbearing would be about as likely to occur in middle-class families as in poor families. In this way, the social scientist could eliminate family background as a cause of any differences that emerge between teenage mothers and nonmothers.

For very good ethical and legal reasons, of course, sociologists simply cannot conduct this type of study. Without random assignment, we can't be sure that having a child as a teenager *causes* a woman to have less education. (See *How Do Sociologists Know What They Know?* The Self-Selection Problem, in Chapter 8.) Still, the lack of randomized experiments does not mean that sociologists should abandon the scientific method. Astronomers, after all, can't do experiments either. But this limitation makes the task of deciding whether a sociological study confirms or disconfirms a hypothesis more difficult.

If not from experiments, where does the data that family sociologists use come from? Generally, from one of two research methods. The first is the **survey**, a study in which individuals or households are randomly selected from a larger population and asked a fixed set of questions. Sociologists prepare a questionnaire and give it to a professional survey research organization. The organization then selects a sample of households randomly from an area (a city, a state, or the entire nation) and sends interviewers to ask the questions of one or more family members in the households. The responses are coded numerically (e.g., a "yes" answer is coded 1 and a "no" is coded 0), and the coded responses for all individuals are made available to the sociologists as a computer file.

The random selection of households is done to ensure that the people who are asked the questions are representative of the population in the area. This kind of random selection of households shouldn't be confused with conducting a randomized experiment. A random-sample survey is not an experiment because the households that are selected are *not* divided into an experimental group and a control group. Nevertheless, data from surveys provides sociologists with the opportunity to examine associations among characteristics of a large number of individuals and families. (See *How Do Sociologists Know What They Know?* The National Surveys, in this chapter.)

The advantage of the survey method (assuming that the households are randomly selected) is that its results are representative not only of the sample that was interviewed but also of the larger population in the area. The main disadvantage is the limited amount of information that can be gathered on each person or family. Most people won't participate in an interview that takes more than an hour or two. Moreover, the same set of questions is asked of everyone, with little opportunity to tailor the interview to each participant. Another disadvantage is that it's difficult to determine whether the people in the sample are responding

How Do Sociologists Know What They Know?

The National Surveys

Sociologists who study the family in the United States draw many of their findings from a series of national surveys that have been conducted over the past few decades. These surveys interview randomly selected samples of the U.S. population. They are similar to the opinion-poll surveys you see in the newspapers (e.g., what percent of the public thinks the president is doing a good job?), but they differ in several important ways:

- *They are larger* The surveys in the newspapers typically interview 500 to 1,500 individuals. The social scientific surveys typically interview 5,000 to 10,000 individuals or more. Because of this larger size, the social scientific surveys can provide reliable information on subgroups of the population, such as couples who are living together outside of marriage, currently divorced individuals, and never-married adults.
- *They are carried out using in-person interviews* In contrast, most of the newspaper polls are conducted by randomly dialing

telephone numbers and speaking to people over the telephone. In-person interviews can be longer and more detailed (because people tire of telephone conversations more quickly than in-person conversations) and can be more flexible (e.g., the interviewer can give the subject a self-administered questionnaire for her husband or partner to fill out). But in-person interviews are also much more expensive to carry out. There is no master list of American households from which survey research centers can randomly select households. Rather the survey center must select neighborhoods at random around the country and then send its staff to make a list of all the households in them. Only then can the survey center randomly select households and send its interviewers out to knock on doors and do interviews.

- *They are longitudinal* Whereas the typical newspaper poll is a one-time activity, social scientists prefer a **longitudinal survey,** meaning a survey in which interviews are conducted several times at regular intervals. This design

allows social scientists to study social change. The surveys typically select families or individuals at random and then reinterview them annually or biennially about how their lives are changing.

- *They are intended to be public resources* Most newspaper polls are meant for **primary analysis,** meaning they are analyzed by the people who collected the information. The data from these polls are then forgotten. The social scientific studies are designed for **secondary analysis,** meaning analysis of the data by people other than the group that collected it. The questionnaires are intentionally broad so that the interviewers can collect a wide range of information that will be of interest to many researchers. The results are coded numerically onto computer tapes or CD-ROMs and made available to anyone who wants to analyze them.
- *They are conducted by academic research centers rather than by commercial polling firms* The academic centers, such as the National Opinion Research Center at the University of Chicago

honestly, especially if the questions touch upon sensitive issues. (See *How Do Sociologists Know What They Know?* Asking about Sensitive Behavior, in Chapter 7.)

The second widely used research method is the **observational study,** also known as *field research,* in which the researcher spends time directly observing each participant in the study—often much more time than an interviewer from a survey organization spends. The researcher may even join the group she or he is studying for a period of time. The individuals and families to be studied are not usually selected randomly; rather, the researcher tries to find families that have a particular set of characteristics he or she is interested in. For example, in a classic observational study of a low-income area of Boston, Herbert Gans (1982) moved into an Italian neighborhood for eight months and got to know many families well. He was able to argue that the stereotype of slum families as "disorganized" was not true. The strength of the observational method is that it can provide a and the Survey Research Center at the University of Michigan, typically take extra steps in designing and carrying out a survey so that the results are of better quality (e.g., the data conforms better to the statistical theory underlying random-sample surveys; a greater percentage of the selected subjects are reached and interviewed).

Because of the large sample size, longitudinal design, use of in-person rather than telephone interviews, and extra care in the fieldwork, the social scientific surveys are very expensive. Most are sponsored by U.S. government agencies such as the National Institutes of Health, the National Science Foundation, or the Bureau of Labor Statistics. The agencies support those large surveys to provide information on many research questions so that hundreds of researchers can analyze the data.

One such study is the National Survey of Families and Households. Interviews were first conducted during 1987 and 1988 with a randomly selected sample of 13,007 individuals, including oversamples of African Americans, Puerto Ricans, Mexican Americans, single-parent families, families with stepchildren, cohabiting couples, and recently married persons. A broad range of questions about personal background and family life were asked. From 1992 to 1994, reinterviews were conducted with 10,007 of these individuals.

Another study is the Panel Study of Income Dynamics. In 1968, researchers at the University of Michigan interviewed 5,000 American households selected at random. They have reinterviewed the members of these households every year since then. When children grew up and left home, or adults divorced and moved out, the study followed them and interviewed them in their new households. The Panel Study of Income Dynamics greatly increased our knowledge of the economic fortunes of family over time. For example, the results indicate that few families are poor every year, but over the course of a decade many families, perhaps one-fourth, experience at least a year in which they are poor (Duncan, 1984).

A third study is the National Longitudinal Survey of Youth. It began in 1979, with interviews with a random sample of 12,686 young women and men age 14 to 22. They have been interviewed every year or two since then. The survey has helped us understand how young people make the transition to adulthood. Moreover, beginning in 1986, the children born to survey members were given mental tests and their parents were asked about their behavior and their childcare arrangements. The resulting data have been used to study the effects of parental work and out-of-home childcare on young children (see Chapter 14).

Throughout the book, findings from these and other national surveys will be presented. Although not without limitations (See Chapter 7, *How Do Families Know What They Know? Asking about Sensitive Behavior*), they constitute a valuable resource to everyone interested in families, households, parents, and children. The "Families on the Internet" feature at the end of this chapter lists the World Wide Web addresses at which information about these surveys can be obtained.

much more detailed and nuanced picture of the individuals and families being studied than can the survey method. Sociologist-observers can view the full complexity of family behavior and can learn more about them. Observational studies are also valuable during the early stages of a research project, when the researchers are still learning about the phenomenon they wish to study and may not know what all of the most important questions are. Under these circumstances, sociologists may need the results of an observational study before they can write a good questionnaire to give to a survey organization.

The disadvantage of observational studies is that it is hard to know how representative the families being studied are of similar families. Because it takes a great deal of time to study a family in depth, observational studies typically are carried out with far fewer families than are surveys. Moreover, sociologists who do observational studies usually can't choose their families randomly by knocking on

TABLE 1.2	COMPARING SURVEY STUDIES AND OBSERVATIONAL STUDIES		
Who Is Studied	**How Are They Studied**	**Strengths**	**Limitations**
SURVEY STUDY			
Large, random sample of individuals or families	An interviewer asks questions from a predesigned questionnaire and records the answers	Results can be generalized to the population of interest	Only limited knowledge can be obtained; hard to judge honesty of responses
OBSERVATIONAL STUDY			
Small, purposefully chosen sample of individuals or families	A researcher observes them in depth over a long period of time, sometimes participating in their daily activities	Detailed knowledge is obtained	Findings may not be representative of other, similar individuals or families

doors or calling on the telephone because they must win a family's cooperation and trust before the family will agree to be studied in such detail. So although observational studies may yield a great deal of information about a small number of families, we may be unsure that we can generalize this knowledge to other similar families that weren't in the observational study.

Surveys and observational studies, consequently, have complementary strengths and limitations. They are summarized in Table 1.2. If the knowledge from sociological studies could be stored in a lake, a survey-based lake would be wide (because of the large number of people reached) but shallow (because of the limited time spent with each family), whereas an observationally based lake would be narrow but deep. Ideally, it would be best to employ both methods to study a problem, and some research projects attempt to do so. But to choose a large number of families randomly and then to send in sociologists to observe each family intensively over weeks and months is too expensive to be feasible. Moreover, the set of skills necessary to do survey research versus observational research is so distinct that sociologists tend to specialize in one or the other.

Sociologists sometimes use other research methods as well. For some topics, it is useful to examine historical sources. Chapter 9 describes a study in which magazine articles from 1900 to 1979 were used to study changing conceptions of marriage. Occasionally, it is even possible to do an experiment. In the 1960s and 1970s, the Federal government sponsored experiments to learn about the consequences of providing families with a guaranteed minimum income. In several communities, families were selected and randomly divided into experimental and control groups. Families in the experimental group received checks from the experimenters if their incomes fell below a threshold. The results indicated that a guaranteed income produced some reduction in work effort and possibly an increase in marital disruption (Robins, Spiegelman, Weiner, & Bell, 1980).

These are the major methods that sociologists use to study families. In several of the chapters of this book, we will examine the methodology of key studies so that you may better understand how family sociologists develop their research findings.

SOCIOLOGICAL THEORY AND THE FAMILY

Let me present a brief introduction to the theoretical perspectives that sociologists have developed for studying social institutions such as the family. These perspectives are best thought of as conceptual frameworks—road maps that show the important people and places, their characteristics, and how they relate to one another. I will draw upon these perspectives often in this book.

THE FUNCTIONALIST PERSPECTIVE

The dominant sociological perspective in the 1950s was **functionalist theory**. The functionalist theorists tried to determine the functions, or uses, of the main ways in which a society is organized. Functionalism had been developed earlier in the century by anthropologists who undertook field research among tribes and small societies in Africa, Asia, and Latin America. The anthropologists wanted to show that seemingly strange customs in other cultures had important uses and were valid, alternative ways of organizing a society—in other words, they wished to demonstrate that our culture was not superior to others. Their books documented the roles, relations, and practices of particular societies and then explained how these systems were able to maintain their societies' existences.

Beginning in the 1940s and continuing through the 1950s, numerous sociologists employed the functionalist approach to explain aspects of the ways social institutions were organized, including the institution of the family. The foremost practitioner of functionalism in sociology was Talcott Parsons, whose theoretical writings profoundly influenced other sociologists. Ironically, the effect of Parsons's writings about the American family was the opposite of the anthropologists' writings about exotic cultures. Whereas the anthropologists' message seemed to be that there were many valid ways of organizing family life, Parsons's message—whether intentional or not—seemed to be that the American family in the 1950s was the natural, superior form.

As will be described in Chapter 2, the middle-class ideal in the 1950s was the two-parent family in which the husband worked outside the home and the wife stayed home and did the housework and childcare. Robert Bales, a psychologist and colleague of Parsons on the Harvard faculty, had conducted a series of experiments with small groups, in which they were observed discussing how to go about some task. Bales claimed that in each group, one person emerged as the "instrumental" leader who led the group discussion about how to accomplish the task they had been assigned. A different person emerged as the "expressive" or "socioemotional" leader who kept up the group's spirit with warm, supportive remarks and jokes. This general tendency of small groups to divide the leadership tasks between two people, according to Bales, was functional in the sense that the coexistence of both kinds of leadership contributed to a better performance by the group.

Parsons and Bales then leaped to the assumption that since the family was a small group, it was functional for one adult member to specialize in instrumental leadership and for the other to specialize in expressive leadership. Lo and behold, that was how the middle-class 1950s family was organized. The husband, they wrote, was the instrumental leader because his labor provided the financial support for the family; and the stay-at-home wife was the expressive leader because she provided emotional support to her husband and children. Consequently, Parsons and Bales argued that the breadwinner-homemaker family was well organized to fulfill the tasks that society assigned to it providing the material goods necessary for a decent living, providing emotional support to adults, and raising children (Parsons & Bales, 1955). Although they never said it was superior to other ways of organizing families, by implication it was, for if wives worked outside the home there would no longer be a full-time expressive specialist.

But work outside the home they did. Although Parsons and Bales seemed to view the breadwinner-homemaker family of the 1950s as if it were timeless, it was, in fact, unusual in historical perspective. As married women poured into the workforce in the 1960s and 1970s, the breadwinner-homemaker family lost its dominant position (see Chapter 2). Much of the sociological writing about the family in the 1960s, 1970s, and 1980s was devoted to refuting Parsons's implicit conclusion that this change in the family was for the worse. This antifunctionalist viewpoint was congenial to the growing body of sociological research influenced by the resurgence of the feminist movement in the 1960s. Still, no single theoretical perspective has dominated the post-1950s literature. Rather, most writers have borrowed eclectically from several theoretical traditions, which are examined briefly.

THE CONFLICT PERSPECTIVE

One of these is **conflict theory**. Whereas functionalism focuses on stability and cooperation among members of a group, conflict theory focuses on inequality, power, and social change. Conflict theorists study how individuals, or groups of individuals, come to dominate others and the circumstances under which those who are dominated are able to reduce or eliminate the disadvantages they face. When analyzing the family, conflict theorists see men as more powerful and women as less powerful. For example, Randall Collins states that male dominance rests on two sources of coercion: physical force and control of economic resources. In societies in which men's use of physical force is curtailed by the state or by custom, men cannot be as dominant; nor can they be as dominant in societies in which women produce valuable goods and services outside the household (Collins, 1971). Conflict theorists have a much less favorable view of the 1950s family than did Parsons because of what they see as women's domination by men, due, in large part, to women's lack of economic resources.

Conflict theorists also see other groups as subject to domination. Marxist writers, for example, have emphasized the conflicting interests of capitalists—the people who own factories and businesses—and the workers in those enterprises. The owners obtain their incomes by paying workers less than the value of the goods the factory or business sells and keeping the difference. Some Marxist-influenced writers on the family claim that women's unpaid work in the home benefits employers in two ways. First, the housework women do allows employers to pay workers less than what would be required if workers had to pay for household services. Second, the emotional support wives provide to husbands eases the burdens of the often alienating and monotonous work that employers require them to do (Zaretsky, 1986).

THE EXCHANGE PERSPECTIVE

A third perspective is **exchange theory**. This sociological approach is similar to the model of human behavior that economists use. People are viewed as rational beings who decide whether to exchange goods or services by considering the benefits they will receive, the costs they will incur, and the benefits they might receive if they chose an alternative course of action. In the rational choice–based theory of the family that won Gary Becker the 1992 Nobel Memorial Prize in economics, women often choose rationally to exchange the performance of household and childcare services in return for receiving the benefits of a man's income. If men are more "efficient" at market production—meaning they can earn higher wages—and women are more "efficient" at home production—meaning they are better at raising small children—then both partners gain from this exchange, argues Becker (1991). Thus, Becker's model is consistent with the Parsonian analysis of the family.

But in the hands of others, exchange theory can shade into conflict theory and lead to very different conclusions. Many sociologists maintain that exchanges take on a different character if the two actors come to the exchange with unequal resources. Richard Emerson and his colleagues developed a version of exchange theory that is useful in studying families (Emerson, 1972; Cook, O'Brien, & Kollock, 1990). According to Emerson, if person A values goods or services person B has to offer, and if person A has few alternative sources of obtaining these goods or services, then person A is said to be dependent on person B. The degree of dependency is greater the more highly A values these goods or services and the fewer alternative sources A has. And the more A is dependent on B, the greater is B's power over A. When one person is more powerful than another, he or she may be able to shape the exchange so that he or she receives greater benefits and incurs fewer costs than does the other person. Husbands, many writers have suggested, are in a stronger bargaining position when they are the sole earners in their families because their wives have fewer alternative sources of income. According to exchange theory, when wives earn money on their own, their dependence decreases and therefore their husbands' power over them decreases (Scanzoni, 1972).

THE SYMBOLIC INTERACTIONIST PERSPECTIVE

Less common but still important is the distinctive perspective of **symbolic interaction theory**. The major figure in symbolic interaction theory was philosopher George Herbert Mead, who taught at the University of Chicago early in the twentieth century.[16] Among all animals, only human beings, the symbolic interactionists point out, do not merely react instinctively to what others of their species do but rather *interpret* what others do. We interpret symbols—gestures, words, appearances—whose meanings we have come to understand. This interpretation occurs in situations in which we interact with someone. It is this process of the interpretation of symbols during social interaction that the symbolic interactionists study. Some symbols are so clear and uniform that interpretation is straightforward; thus, we all know that the traffic officer's raised hand, palm facing the driver, means stop. But some symbols are harder to interpret. Symbols involving differences between women and men, it has been argued recently, are particularly problematic and in need of continual affirmation (see Chapter 3). For example, husbands who don't want to change their babies' diapers may make a grand display of fumbling at the changing table when called upon by their wives, thus exhibiting their male "inferiority" at the task. The interactionist perspective is also useful in analyzing situations where family relations seem less institutionalized, less set in concrete—such as in newly formed stepfamilies or dual-career marriages. It helps sensitize us to the ways in which people create shared understandings of how family members should act toward one another.

[16]For an account of Mead's viewpoint by his foremost interpreter in sociology, see Blumer (1962).

These shared understandings become the bases of the social roles people play in families—spouse, parent, breadwinner, homemaker, child, and so forth.

THE FEMINIST PERSPECTIVE

Feminist theory, which has arisen from the feminist movement over the past two decades, is a theoretical perspective that differs from the other perspectives in that it is focused on a problem, rather than on a mechanism such as an exchange based on costs and benefits, coercion based on the threat of force, or the use of symbols to create shared understandings. The problem is the domination of women by men. Nevertheless, feminist theory shares with conflict theory an orientation toward relationships of power and inequality. The central concept in feminist theory is **gender**, which is usually defined as the social and cultural characteristics that distinguish women and men in a society (see Chapter 3). Feminist theorists argue that nearly all the gender differences we see in the roles of women and men are of cultural origin and have been socially constructed. By socially constructed, they mean arising not from biological differences but rather from culturally accepted rules, from relationships of power and authority, and from differences in economic opportunities. For example, the culture might include a rule that women should not work outside the home (as was the case among the American middle class from the mid-nineteenth to the mid-twentieth centuries). Or the opportunities for women might be limited to jobs that tend to pay less than comparable jobs in which most workers are men.

Moreover, feminist theorists assert that these cultural differences are constructed in ways that maintain the power of men over women (Thorne, 1992). For instance, feminist theorists criticize the idea that the breadwinner-homemaker family provided an exchange that was equally beneficial to women and men. Rather, they note that women's direct access to money through paid employment was restricted in this type of family, which maintained women's dependence on men. The cultural belief that "women's place is in the home" and the lower wages paid to women employed outside the home compelled married women to give up the idea of paid employment. Under these constraints, their best strategy may indeed have been to trade household services for a male income; but it was a forced choice set up by a social system that favored men.

Sociologists have intensively studied gender roles, the patterns of behavior that typically occur among one gender but not the other. Many articles, for instance, document how parents, friends, and the media influence boys and girls to act in different ways. More recently, the study of gender roles has fallen out of favor among some feminist theorists (Ferree, 1990). Gender distinctions are such a ubiquitous part of our society, the theorists have claimed, that they can't be reduced to mere roles. Instead, the theorists have suggested that we analyze entire social institutions, such as the educational system or the labor market, to see how their organization maintains the inferior position of women.

Still, many sociologists think it is useful to examine social roles people play, such as mother, father, wife, or husband, and we will do so in this book. In addition, as stated earlier, a number of sociologists think there are some limited but potentially important biologically based differences in the ways women and men act in families. A minority of feminist social scientists are among those who believe it is important to explore biological differences and their implications for family life. "An ideology that does not confront this basic issue," writes one, "is an exercise in wishful thinking" (Rossi, 1984, p. 15).

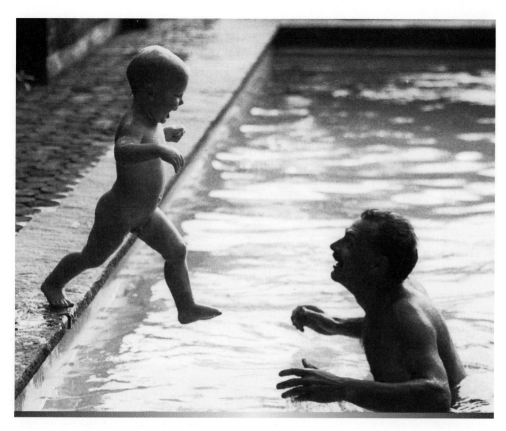

As Chapter 3 will describe, sociologists have studied how parents influence the gender roles of their children.

Some feminist theorists maintain that the family is itself an artificial creation that has been organized to maintain male dominance. They would deny that there are any deep-seated predispositions among people that would lead to the formation of the kinds of families that we see. In fact, some would argue that we shouldn't even try to study the family anymore because to do so accepts as "natural" the inequalities built into it. Rather, we should merely study households and the relations among people within them. Needless to say, these critics would reject the contention that there is any biological basis for the ways in which men and women act in families. At the extreme, some maintain that even sexual intercourse, pregnancy, and giving birth are best viewed as, in the words of two anthropologists, "cultural facts, whose form, consequences, and meanings are socially constructed in any society" (Yanagisako & Collier, 1987).

Whether or not you think it's useful to study the family (as I obviously do), there is an important insight to be gained from feminist theory. It makes us aware that the experience of living in a family is different for women than it is for men. Arrangements that make men happiest don't necessarily make women happiest. A husband might prefer that his wife stay home to care for their children and do household work full time. His wife might prefer to combine a paying job with housework and childcare, and she might wish that he would share more of the household tasks. In other words, women's interests in the family are not necessarily the same as men's interests. The breadwinner-homemaker bargain may have been great for men (except for those who wanted an active role in raising their children), and it may have been great for women who wished to raise children and do housework full time, but it frustrated other women by restricting the possibility of developing a satisfying career outside the home. Feminist theory urges us to view families through a prism that separates the experiences of men and women rather than just considering what's best for the family as a whole. It is a view that I will take repeatedly in this book.

Currently, most Americans seem to view the family primarily in emotional, personal terms—the terms of the private family—and to pay less attention to the commitments and obligations of the public family. This emphasis on sentiment and self-fulfillment might lead one to assume that the private family is the older, more-established perspective. But that isn't so. The emergence of the private family is a relatively new development in history. Its origins lie in the upper-class and merchant families of Western Europe in the 1600s and 1700s. It did not spread to the masses until the late 1800s and 1900s. Most people have used the public perspective in thinking about families throughout most of history. The historical development of the family is the subject of the next chapter.

SUMMARY

1. Many Americans seem to be ambivalent about marriage and the family. On the one hand, surveys show that most young adults plan to marry and to have children. On the other hand, young adults are postponing marriage. A number of factors, such as changes in women's participation in the paid labor force, increased cohabitation, greater acceptance of premarital sex, and improved contraception, underlie this postponement. Moreover, Americans increasingly value marriage for the personal fulfillment it can bring, rather than for the opportunity to play valued social roles such as spouse or parent.

2. Observers disagree on the current state of the family in the United States. The optimists claim that the family isn't in difficulty but rather is just changing. They note the emotionally enhanced relationships between adults and the increased autonomy of women. The pessimists contend that the family is in decline; they note the increases in divorce and childbearing outside of marriage, and they claim that the well-being of children has deteriorated.

3. Sociologists study the family as a social institution. They analyze the consequences for individuals of the roles that exist and the rules about how to play them. Sociologists also look at the influences of the external social world on the family. Overall, they would argue that the family must be studied in its social context. Psychologists tend to study how people's personalities and behaviors are shaped by their family experiences. Social scientists disagree about whether there are any biological influences on the family that are worth noting.

4. Sociologists collect and analyze data consisting of observations of real families and the people in them; and, for the most part, they try to analyze their data objectively using the scientific method. They formulate hypotheses that can be tested by collecting data that will confirm them or disconfirm them. There are limits, however, to how well sociologists can use the scientific method, notably the difficulty of doing randomized experiments. The two most common research methods are (1) the survey, a study in which individuals or families from an area are selected randomly and asked a fixed set of questions; and (2) the observational study, in which the researcher spends time directly observing each participant in the study. The two methods have complementary strengths and limitations.

5. The definition of the family depends on what questions one is concerned about. This book proposes two definitions. The public family perspective is useful if you are concerned about the contributions the family makes to the public welfare by taking care of dependents. It defines the family in terms of the presence of caregivers and dependents. The private family perspective is useful if you are concerned about the level of intimacy and love that the family provides to individuals. It defines the family in terms of an indefinite, intimate relationship between two or more individuals who live in the same household and share the fruits of their labor. These two perspectives constitute different views of the same reality; a given family unit might fit both of them.

6. Sociologists have developed several theoretical frameworks for studying social institutions such as

the family. These include functionalist theory, which emphasizes the functions, or uses, of the main ways that a society, or a social institution, is organized; conflict theory, which analyzes the consequences of power, domination, and resistance; exchange theory, which considers individuals as rational beings who exchange goods or services on the basis of costs and benefits; and symbolic interaction theory, which emphasizes the ways in which people create shared understandings through social interaction. In addition, feminist theory has arisen as a way of understanding inequalities between women and men.

KEY TERMS

procreation
social institution
evolutionary psychology
Western nations
monogamy
polygamy
externalities
negative externalities
positive externalities
public goods

public family
relationship by blood
sexually based primary relationship
private family
created kinship
assigned kinship
objectivity
scientific method
hypothesis
survey

longitudinal survey
primary analysis
secondary analysis
observational study
functionalist theory
conflict theory
exchange theory
symbolic interaction theory
feminist theory
gender

FAMILIES ON THE INTERNET

The Internet is a great source of information about family issues. Throughout this book, the "Families on the Internet" section will provide you with suggested World Wide Web sites. Keep in mind that web sites come and go on the Internet and that the contents of each web site change often. This flux means that you might occasionally not find a web site or specific piece of information within a site that is listed in this section. I will attempt, however, to suggest sites that are likely to be long-lived.

The first way to obtain information on the family is pure web surfing: Click the search button on your Internet browser and enter a phrase; the search engine will respond with corresponding links to web sites. As you know, the phrase can't be too broad: Entering "family" will cause the search engine to return a blizzard of links. But a more focused entry can be useful: Typing "gay marriage and Hawaii," for example, returns a number of useful links. It also, however, returns some not-so-useful links, and it can be difficult and time-consuming to distinguish the good sites from the bad, or simply irrelevant, sites.

Consequently, it helps to have some suggested links to broader web sites that provide issue-oriented information on a number of topics. For almost any public issue involving the family, two such "umbrella" sites are good places to start. The first is the Electronic Policy Network, **www.epn.org**, a site that provides links to many liberal organizations and publications. Entering "gay marriage," for example, at the epn.org site returns several interesting links. The second umbrella site is **www.townhall.com**, which has links to many conservative organizations and publications. By the time you read this chapter, the Hawaii Supreme Court may have ruled on the State of Hawaii's appeal of Judge Chang's decision in *Baehr* v. *Miike*. If so, both townhall.com and epn.org should have information and commentary.

One of the links at townhall.com is to the Family Research Council, **www.frc.org**, where a search on "homosexual marriage" will return several articles opposing same-sex marriage and favoring the "Defense of Marriage Act" that Congress passed in 1996. For information in favor of same-sex marriage, try **www.freedomtomarry.org**, which has links to several other like-minded sites.

The organizations that maintain the major national surveys have web sites. Information on the National Survey of Families and Households is available at **www.ssc.wisc.edu/nsfh/home.htm**. Information on the Panel Study of Income Dynamics is available at **www.isr.umich.edu/src/psid**. The U.S. Bureau of Labor Statistics maintains information about the National Longitudinal Survey of Youth at **www.bls.gov/nlsyouth.htm**.

CHAPTER 2

The History of the Family

INTRODUCTION

The serious study of the history of the family began in 1960, when the manager of a tropical fruit importing firm in France, a self-described "Sunday historian," published a book about the history of childhood (Ariès, 1960). Philippe Ariès, curious about family life in the Middle Ages, had examined works of art dating back 1,000 years. Any artist will tell you that children's heads are larger in proportion to

Marriage of Giovanni Arnolfini and Giovanna Cenami, *Jan van Eyck's famous painting of the wedding vows of a wealthy couple in 1434, shows a late medieval view of marriage. Wives were valued primarily for their childbearing and domestic roles: The bride is shown holding her long gown over her womb, as if she were pregnant. In back of her is a statuette of St. Margaret, the patron saint of childbearing women. A whisk broom symbolizes wives' domestic work. Arnolfini stands straight, his facial expression stern, as if ready to assume his role as head of the household. His wife's pose is more submissive: her head slightly bowed, her eyes slightly downcast. A dog symbolizes the faithfulness expected of the couple.*

the rest of their bodies than adults' heads. Yet many early medieval artists used adult proportions when painting children's heads and bodies, as if their subjects were, in fact, small adults. Moreover, the artists dressed children in the same clothes as adults. From such evidence Ariès concluded that the concept of childhood was a modern invention.

Of course, there always had been children, but until the 1700s, wrote Ariès, the long stage of life we call childhood wasn't recognized by most people. American historian John Demos put forth a similar argument about the Puritans in Plymouth Colony in the 1600s: "Childhood as such was barely recognized in the period spanned by Plymouth Colony. There was little sense that children might somehow be a special group, with their own needs and interests and capacities." (Demos, 1970). According to historians such as Ariès and Demos, parents withheld love and affection from infants and toddlers because so many of them died. The great French essayist Montaigne wrote in the late 1500s, "I have lost two or three children in their infancy, not without regret, but without great sorrow."[1] *Two or three*—Montaigne couldn't even remember how many. If children survived, wrote Ariès and Demos, they were treated as little adults. By age seven, boys and girls performed useful work—helping fathers in the fields or mothers at the hearth—and played the same games and attended the same festivals as adults. Ariès argued that it was only with the spread of schooling and the decline in child deaths—

[1]From vol. 2, no. 8, of Montaigne's ***Essais.*** Quoted on p. 39 of Ariès (1960).

neither of which occurred on a large scale until the 1800s outside the noble and middle classes—that the notion of a protected, extended stage of childhood emerged.

Ariès's influential book launched a new generation of historians who studied ordinary families rather than royal families. His contribution is still respected even though many historians now believe that he underestimated parents' appreciation of childhood as a stage of life. For every Montaigne, the revisionist historians have found a Martin Luther, who wrote in the 1500s after the death of his infant daughter, "I so lamented her death that I was exquisitely sick, my heart rendered soft and weak; never had I thought that a father's heart could be so broken for his children's sake."[2] When historian Linda Pollock located and read 68 diaries written by American and British parents in the 1600s and 1700s, she found that most of them were aware that children were different from adults and that they needed parental guidance and support. The diarists frequently referred to their children as "comforts" and showed pride in their accomplishments. "I doe not think one child of 100 of his age durst doe so much," wrote one proud father (Pollock, 1983). Nevertheless, parents of this period did seem less saddened by the death of an infant than of an older child.

The family history industry that Ariès spawned has produced hundreds of volumes and thousands of articles. During the same period, a related field, the history of women, has grown just as fast. Together, these fields provide an anchor for the study of the contemporary family. They describe the context in which the contemporary family has developed. Among other things, they tell us that the public family is as old as human civilization but that the private family blossomed only during the past few hundred years. For the sociologist studying the contemporary family, the historical literature is a wonderful source of insights. This chapter will provide a brief guided tour of that literature. Of necessity, it will be a highly selective tour; the topics that have been selected are those that provide the best foundation for the detailed study of the present in the remaining chapters of this book. But first we must go back even further in time than the historians have traveled.

WHAT DO FAMILIES DO?

THE ORIGINS OF FAMILY AND KINSHIP

We have all seen pictures of a new colt, minutes after birth, standing on its four legs. My local newspaper recently printed a photograph of a one-day-old dolphin swimming with its mother. In contrast, the average human baby cannot sit up until it is about six months old and cannot walk until it is about a year old. This difference in maturation time between humans and other animals is not an accident of nature; rather, it reflects the evolution of our species. Throughout most of their existence, human beings have been **hunter-gatherers**: They wandered through the forests in small bands, hunting animals and gathering edible plants. According to the theory of evolutionary biology, they evolved from four-legged primates to beings that could walk upright and hunt or gather with two arms. Because those with greater thinking power were more likely to survive, the size of their brains increased through natural selection.

---

[2]Quoted in Ozment (1983). For an overview of the revisionist scholarship, see Nicholas (1991).

These advances, however, came at a cost. The larger brain meant that babies' heads were larger at birth, but the shift to an upright posture limited the size of the pelvic opening through which the baby must pass. Consequently, humans are born smaller (relative to their adult size) than most other mammals and develop more after birth.[3] Infants need prolonged, intensive care in order to survive. In hunter-gatherer societies, as in nearly all other known societies, mothers provide most of the care during the first few years of children's lives. Anthropologists who have studied the few remaining hunter-gatherer societies report that mothers carry their young with them during the first year and continue to breast-feed them for several years (Howell, 1979). As a result, women specialize in finding plants and hunting small animals within a limited area, whereas men range farther afield in search of larger animals.

About 10,000 years ago, humans discovered the advantage of remaining in one place and planting crops. Settled agriculture revolutionized human organization because it allowed humans to accumulate surpluses of grain that could support larger kinship groups than was possible in hunter-gatherer societies. Indeed, human societies were often organized around large kinship groups. In societies where a tribe ruled a territory and there was no other strong government, people often traced descent through either the father's or the mother's line, but not both. What resulted were kinship groups called **lineages**: **patrilineages** if descent is traced through the father's line, **matrilineages** if through the mother's line. They seem odd, at first, to people in Western nations, who trace descent through both the father's and mother's line; but the structure serves a purpose. Among other virtues, lineages limit the number of people who are related to a person and with whom that person must share land, water, animals, and other resources. In a patrilineage, my sons will marry women from outside the lineage; then the couples will live near me (sometimes with me) and remain in my lineage. My grandsons will do the same. But my daughters and granddaughters will marry men from other lineages, move to their land, and leave my lineage. Consequently, I need to share my resources with, and to defend, only those persons related to me through my father, my brothers, and my sons. If a maternal uncle needs assistance, that's his lineage's problem; I am not my mother's brother's keeper.

Kinship, as one anthropologist has written, developed as "a weapon in the struggle for survival" (Fox, 1967). In tribal societies, family ties provide the structure that holds the society together: You are a member of the tribe not because you are a citizen (a concept that can't exist without a state) but rather because you are related to the other members. You obey rules set by the tribal elders, not laws set by a government. You tend farmland not because you purchased it but because the tribe lets you use it. Kinship groups ensure order, recruit members from outside the group (usually through marriage), defend against other outsiders, provide labor at harvesttime, and assist the less fortunate. Anthropologists who study social organization in tribal societies focus on family and kinship because, to a large extent, that *is* social organization.

In most societies, kinship groups are made up of smaller family units, consisting of a mother and children always, a husband usually, and other household members sometimes. In many of the Western nations the larger kinship groups have been weak, and the smaller husband-wife-children unit has dominated. This smaller unit of husband, wife, and children is referred to as the **conjugal family**; the word "conjugal" is from the Latin term for joining together in marriage. If any other

[3]For an overview, see Rossi (1977).

relatives are present in the household—such as a grandparent or uncle—the household is said to contain an **extended family**. Many Americans assume that most families in the past were like those in the television series *The Waltons,* with Grandma, Grandpa, Mom, Dad, and the kids sitting around the hearth, swapping stories, and enjoying one another's company. To be sure, there were substantial numbers of extended families in many European nations (Kertzer, 1991). But there were fewer families like that in the United States, England, or Northern France for two reasons. First, young people in these areas typically waited until they could start a new household before they married. This might mean waiting for the father to retire and turn over his land or moving to the city to work for a merchant. Second, Grandma and Grandpa often didn't live long enough to share a household with their grandchildren, although most elderly people continued to live with one child, often unmarried at first, who remained at home (Ruggles, 1994). That child might marry after being granted the right to farm his or her parents' land. This arrangement, in which one, and only one, child remained in his or her parents' household even after marriage, is called a **stem family**. Life expectancy was so short, however, that the stem family was unlikely to last long.

In other parts of the world, larger family units have been more common. The traditional Chinese family was patrilineal, and the cultural ideal was for five male generations (and their wives and children) to live under one roof, ruled by the oldest male. Here, too, few families reached this ideal because the oldest generations rarely lived long enough and because a family had to be affluent to support such a large dwelling. Nevertheless, households containing extended families were more common in China than in the Western nations. In many African societies, men were allowed (and in some countries still are allowed) to have more than one wife, a practice known as **polygyny** (literally, in Greek, "many women"). A wealthy man might take a second or third wife and establish each of them in separate dwellings in the same compound. All the wives and children might cook and eat together,

The cultural ideal for the traditional Chinese family was for several male generations (and their wives and children) to live under one roof, ruled by the oldest male.

Most Native Americans lived in tribal societies based on lineages.

under the direction of the senior wife. In a much smaller number of societies, women were allowed to practice **polyandry**, having more than one husband.

NATIVE AMERICAN FAMILIES

An exception to the rule that small kinship groups prevailed on the North American continent is provided by Native Americans. Although there is little direct evidence about Native American societies before the 1800s, scholars think that most Native Americans lived in tribal societies based on lineages. We do know that the Native American population was devastated by diseases brought by Europeans, such as smallpox—diseases to which the native population had developed no immunities. Moreover, we know that large numbers of American Indians were killed in wars and massacres (Shoemaker, 1991). How these catastrophic events modified family and kinship is unclear. In the absence of direct evidence, scholars have assumed that the numerous accounts of American Indian societies in the 1800s and early 1900s can be generalized back in time. (The term **Native American** refers to the original, indigenous people who had settled in North America thousands of years before Columbus. The term **American Indian** is often used for a subset of all Native Americans, namely those who had settled in the territory that later became the 48 contiguous United States [Snipp, 1989]. Indeed, it was because Columbus mistakenly believed that he had reached India that he gave this aboriginal population the misnomer "Indian.") Although the assumption that present arrangements accurately reflect the past ignores the historical changes that occurred to Native American societies after the arrival of the Europeans, the outlines of Native American family and kinship seem clear.

Both patrilineal and matrilineal tribes existed. Related lineages were often organized into larger clans that provided the basis for social organization and governing. In matrilineal tribes such as the Hopi, for example, a person traced his or her relatives through his or her mother's line.[4] If you were a child, your father was a guest in

---

[4]This account of Hopi kinship draws from Queen, Habenstein, and Quadagno (1985).

your mother's home. Although strong bonds existed between wives and husbands, a woman's ties to her maternal kin—her mother, her mother's brothers, her maternal cousins—were generally stronger. Consequently, your maternal uncles played an important role in your upbringing. They, not your father, had to approve your choice of spouse. Still, if you were a boy, you did learn many of the skills of an adult male— growing crops, herding animals—from your father. It was as if you had two kinds of fathers: a biological father who taught you skills and an uncle-father who held greater authority over you. If you were a girl, you spent less time with your father.

When Hopi boys reached puberty, they moved out of the household, sleeping in the men's ceremonial house and eventually marrying into another clan. Girls, on the other hand, remained in or near their mothers' homes throughout their lives, bringing husbands from other clans into their dwellings. In all tribal societies, the common requirement that individuals marry someone outside their clan forged alliances across clans. If clan A and clan B frequently exchanged young adults as marriage partners, the two clans would likely consider themselves as allies in any disputes with other clans in the tribe. Thus, the lineage and clan organization of Native American societies served to strengthen the social order and to protect individuals against unfriendly outsiders.

In sum, family and kinship systems were developed to provide for people's fundamental needs, such as producing sufficient food and defending against outsiders. Although kin often shared strong emotional bonds, families did not develop primarily out of people's desire for love and intimacy; rather, they developed out of their will to survive, prosper, and raise children. The origins of family and kinship are best analyzed from the perspective of the public family introduced in Chapter 1: the view of families as settings in which people take care of one another and depend on one another. In contrast, the perspective of the private family, which emphasizes intimacy and personal fulfillment, is less useful; its utility is greater for analyzing contemporary families, as will be noted later.

MODES OF PRODUCTION

Until the past 250 years or so, most Western families performed three basic activities:

1 *Production*   They produced much of the food, clothes, and other goods and services they used.
2 *Reproduction*   They bore and raised children.
3 *Consumption*   They consumed food, firewood, and other essentials as a unit.

Today, in the United States and other Western countries, families still reproduce and consume. But few families produce many of the goods and services that they use. Instead, they exchange their labor for money, which they use to buy goods and services. Even farmers are no longer self-sufficient producers; rather, they grow one or two crops, sell them on the market, and buy most of the food they eat. The shift from producing most of what the family consumes to buying most of what the family consumes is the most fundamental change in the Western family over the past few centuries. A typical family under the old system, referred to as the **familial mode of production**,[5] would be a largely self-sufficient, farming family

---

[5]There are several terms in the literature for modes of production. Some authors refer to the familial mode of production as the "domestic mode of production" or the "family economy" and to the labor market mode of production as the "capitalist mode of production" or the "family wage economy." I follow the usage in Caldwell (1982).

whose members grow grain, tend a vegetable garden, keep animals for milk or meat or eggs, make most of the clothes they wear, and with the help of other kin build their own dwellings.

Most white families in the American colonies prior to the Revolutionary War fit this description reasonably well, although, in reality, almost no colonial family was completely self-sufficient. For example, craftsmen such as blacksmiths sold their wares; and merchants bought and sold grain, tobacco, or spices. Actually, as far back as the 1200s, British rural families sold some of what they produced and employed hired laborers (Macfarlane, 1978). Nevertheless, most white colonial American families and Western European families were production units as well as consumption units. For American slave families, of course, the description is not relevant. As for Native American families, their great diversity, and the lack of research on them, makes generalizations perilous. For some migratory tribes, the concept of a self-sufficient, landowning farm family makes little sense. Even when Native American populations did not move, larger family units, encompassing more than one dwelling, may have been the central production units (Shoemaker, 1991).

The familial mode of production began to decline in the mid-1700s in the American colonies and England, and in the early 1800s elsewhere in the Western nations. A new system took hold in which most men, and many unmarried women, worked for wages. Families purchased more clothing and made less of it at home. In the expanding cities, families could not easily grow their own food; rather, they had to buy it. Consequently, they produced less at home and bought and sold more on the market. The advent of the new system of production for exchange (working for wages which then are exchanged for goods) rather than for use (working to grow food and eat it) accelerated in the 1800s, as more and more men began to work for wages. This system, referred to as the **labor market mode of production**, solidified by the late 1800s, when working for wages in factories became a widespread way for men to make a living—and also for many immigrant and working-class women and even their children. The transition from the familial to the labor market mode of production had two important consequences for family life. First, it separated the workplace from the home. Before, it had been common for husbands, wives, and children to work together in a common family enterprise. Then in the 1800s, as more and more husbands began to work in factories or offices, a gap opened between the world of work and the world of the family. Second, the transition eroded the authority of fathers over their children because fathers no longer controlled a key resource—land—that sons needed in order to attract a wife. Let us trace these themes in the history of the American family.

THE AMERICAN FAMILY BEFORE 1776

THE PRIMACY OF THE PUBLIC FAMILY

In the previous chapter, the public family was defined in terms of taking care of dependents—children and the frail elderly. Those are the only public goods that most contemporary American families produce. In contrast, the colonial American family performed public services of many kinds. Consider education. In Plymouth Colony, children received their basic education from their parents and, if they were working as servants, in another family's home. Demos found that in Plymouth Colony parents and masters were required by law to teach reading to their children

In the 1600s and early 1700s, most children in the American colonies received their education from parents.

and young servants so that they could at least "be able to duely read the scriptures" (Demos, 1970). Why weren't these children learning to read in school? Because there was no school—or, rather, because the family *was* school. In addition to providing schooling, wrote Demos, all Plymouth Colony families were expected to provide vocational training. Through apprenticeship and service, working next to an adult, children and youths learned the skills they needed to farm, trade, garden, cook, and make clothes. All families were also expected to supplement church services by engaging in "family worship," praying and meditating daily.

Selected Plymouth Colony families also functioned as

- *Hospitals* Some adults who supposedly had specialized knowledge took sick persons into their homes for treatment.
- *Houses of correction* Judges ordered some idle or criminal persons to live in the homes of upstanding families to learn how to change their ways.
- *Orphanages* Children whose parents died—a far more common occurrence than today—were taken in by the household of a relative or family friend.
- *Nursing homes* Frail elderly parents were cared for in their homes by their children.
- *Poorhouses* Families sometimes took in poor relatives who needed food and shelter (Demos, 1970).

Today, all these activities, with the exception of caring for the elderly, are carried out primarily outside the home, mostly by publicly supported institutions. In Plymouth Colony, then, the family's public role was much broader than it is now.

In contrast, the family's private role was much smaller. The kind of privacy that Westerners today take for granted hardly existed a few hundred years ago. This is apparent to anyone who visits the Puritan houses that still stand in Massachusetts. The downstairs area of a typical house contained one or two rooms. The larger of them was an all-purpose room called the "hall," in which the members of the household spent most of their indoor waking hours. It was dominated by a huge fireplace used for heating and cooking. In smaller houses, the second downstairs room would contain little except bedding. Most houses also had one or two second-story lofts with beds. Often, only the hall contained furniture for any activity other than sleeping. It was there, in this one room, that fathers, mothers, children (Plymouth families had an average of seven or eight children), servants or apprentices, and perhaps a grandparent ate, cooked, talked, prayed, sewed clothing, relaxed, and received visitors. Individuals simply could not find a place to get away from other household members.

Larger houses also lacked privacy because a key feature of home architecture had not yet been invented: the corridor. In England and in the colonies before the late 1600s, even the houses of the wealthy were built without corridors, so that the only way to get from room A to room B was to walk through all the rooms in between. Consequently, it was impossible to maintain your own room as a private space. In the 1700s, wealthier families began to include a central corridor in the floor plans of new houses. But most of the homes of common people still lacked them (Stone, 1977; Demos, 1970).

Not only was it difficult for individuals to maintain privacy, it was also difficult for the conjugal family to maintain privacy from other households. The colonists did not regard the conjugal family as separate from society but rather as an integral part of it. To a great extent, a family's affairs were considered public business. For example, Puritan laws required that married couples maintain harmonious relations and that parents raise their children properly—and imposed fines on those who didn't. It was accepted and common for friends and neighbors to call at one another's houses without advance notice. Given all the ways in which privacy was prevented, the idea of a private, conjugal family with its own separate space—and of individual privacy within the family—may not have been in the mind-set of most people. At best, privacy was dismissed as unattainable.

THE ROLE OF THE FATHER

The Puritans considered the father to be the rightful head of the conjugal family, the proper person to transmit God's will to spouses and children. Fathers dominated family life much more than they would after the Revolution. In town meetings, each family was given one vote, and the father normally cast it. The right of married women to own property or enter into legal contracts was limited. Yet even the restricted rights of married women in the colonies probably exceeded the rights of women in England (Demos, 1970). In the New World, where their labor was essential to the survival of the household (as exemplified by the quick remarriages of men whose wives died), women may have attained a stronger bargaining position. Nevertheless, they submitted more fully to male authority than was the case in the nineteenth and twentieth centuries.

Fathers also were the unchallenged rulers of children. Puritan theology taught that children were born tainted with sin, the source of which was the original sin of Adam and Eve that made God banish them from the Garden of Eden. Children, it was said, expressed their diabolical nature through stubbornness, willfulness, and disobedience. Consequently, it was the moral duty of good parents to defeat these expressions of sin. When two- and three-year-olds first began to act contrary, the task of the father was to "break the child's will" and instill obedience through stern discipline. In fact, childrearing advice in colonial times was addressed to the father, not the mother, for he was seen as the more important influence on his children's upbringing.

Unlike current practice, colonial fathers kept custody of the children in the small number of separations and divorces that occurred. They did so because children were seen primarily as economic assets, future sources of farm labor or home work in whom the father had invested much time and effort. Since fathers legally were the owners of most marital property, it followed that children also belonged to them. This does not imply that fathers didn't love their children; rather, it implies a worldview in which love and affection were less important than the daily struggle against hunger, cold, and disease. Nearly half the Pilgrims who sailed on the *Mayflower* died within six months of landing at Plymouth, weakened by the voyage and victimized by a harsh winter and inadequate shelter. Learning to obey your father and to do your job well is probably more important in a setting where the family's survival depends on the daily contributions of all its members than it is in most contemporary American families.

The father was less dominant in other parts of the American colonies, most notably in the Maryland and Virginia colonies surrounding the Chesapeake Bay. In the 1600s, a heavy in-migration of men created a shortage of women, which gave women greater bargaining power in choosing a husband (Smith, 1980). Moreover, a higher death rate also contributed. It turned out that the warmer climate of the South was more hospitable to disease than the colder New England climate. It was common for fathers to die before all of their children were grown, leaving them under the control of widowed mothers. By the mid-1700s, just as New England fathers were losing some of their dominance (see below), declining white, male immigration (which eliminated the shortage of women) and improving health conditions allowed Chesapeake fathers to become more dominant (Norton, 1984).

THE EMERGENCE OF THE "MODERN" AMERICAN FAMILY: 1776–1900

It is always difficult to pinpoint the beginnings of social change; rarely can we discern a great divide between an older way of life and an emerging one. Nevertheless, the decades surrounding the American Revolution seem to have been a watershed in the history of the American family. In an overview of the history of women and the family in the United States, Carl Degler (1980) claims that between 1776 and 1830, the outlines emerged of a kind of family that would remain prominent well into the twentieth century. It emerged most clearly among the white middle class, and, according to Degler, it had four new characteristics:

- Marriage was increasingly based on affection and mutual respect rather than on male authority and custom. As a consequence, women experienced increasing autonomy in the family. (But, I would add, they were increasingly restricted to the home.)
- The primary role of the wife became the care of children and the maintenance of the home. Women came to be seen as morally superior to men, and the home came to be seen as "women's sphere."

Under the ideology of "separate spheres" that developed in the 1800s, caring for children was seen as a central part of women's lives.

- The attention and energy of the husband and wife were increasingly centered on their children. Children came to be seen as needing not only discipline and economic support but also attention, affection, and loving care.
- The number of children per family declined, in part as a consequence of the greater investment of emotion and time that they now were seen as needing.

In the dusty records stored in county courthouses and town halls in New England, historians have found evidence of these changes. The records of Andover, Massachusetts, studied by Philip Greven, show, for example, that in the 1600s and early 1700s, fathers strongly influenced the timing of their sons' marriages. In order to attract a good wife, a young man needed the means to support her. In Andover, this meant access to land, which fathers owned. Only when fathers turned over control of the land could sons marry. Consequently, sons of first-generation colonists in Andover married at later ages than their fathers. By the late 1700s, this difference in marriage timing was smaller, suggesting that fathers were less inclined or able to use land ownership as a source of influence (Greven, 1970).

Daniel Scott Smith, using the records of Hingham, Massachusetts, uncovered evidence that parents' influence over their daughters' marriages declined during the 1700s (Smith, 1973). If parents played a major role in determining when and whom their daughters married, one might expect that they would have married off their oldest daughter first, then their second oldest, and so on. If, however, parental influence declined, then the records might show more daughters marrying out of order—that is, younger sisters marrying before older sisters married. In fact,

Smith found that the percentage of daughters marrying out of order did increase during the early 1700s and then again after about 1750.

THE DECLINE IN BIRTHS

Moreover, throughout the new nation, the birthrate began to fall sharply in the early 1800s. Demographers, the social scientists who study the growth, decline, marriage patterns, and movement of populations, often express the level of births through the **total fertility rate (TFR)**. The TFR is the average number of children that women would bear over their lifetime if birthrates were to remain the same. At the birthrates prevalent among women at different ages in 1800, the average white woman would have had seven children. This TFR of seven was higher than the TFR of any western European country at the time (Coale & Zelnik, 1963). Births were higher because marriage tended to occur at earlier ages, and was more universal, than in western Europe. Observers such as Benjamin Franklin linked earlier marriage in the colonies to the greater availability of land in the New World, which allowed young couples to start their own families sooner (Haines, 1996).

By 1850, however, the TFR for white women had fallen to about five children. This fall in births occurred before there was much industrialization in the United States, so the growth of nonfarm work cannot have been a major factor. Rather, historical demographers have argued that decreasing land availability played an important role. In the eastern areas that had been settled the earliest, the amount of available farm land fell as population grew. Demographers think that the land shortage forced young adults to reduce their family size, in large part by delaying marriages until they could obtain land (Yasuba, 1962). In the more sparsely settled areas to the west of the original colonies, where land was more plentiful, birthrates remained high for a longer period.

THE RISE OF INDIVIDUALISM

Land availability, however, wasn't the only factor that altered marriage and child-bearing. Many historians believe that the idea of individualism gained greater currency during the 1700s. To be sure, it was not a new idea, especially among the English.[6] But Lawrence Stone's influential account of British family history claims that individualism gained ground among the British middle and upper classes in the 1700s. Individualism, Stone wrote, had two meanings where the family was concerned. The first was a greater consideration of one's own self and, in particular, one's own sense of self-satisfaction. This led, in turn, to an increased emphasis on personal gratification in family relationships. The second meaning was of autonomy—individual freedom from constraints imposed by others. Consequently, Stone called this phenomenon the rise of **affective individualism**, meaning an outlook on personal relationships that emphasizes the emotional rewards to, and autonomy of, each individual more than that individual's obligations to care for and support others (Stone, 1977). Other historians dispute Stone, arguing that as far back as they can push their investigations of British family life—even as far back as the 1200s—the British had always been individualistic (Pollock, 1983; Macfarlane, 1978).

In any event, the changes in American family life in the 1700s and early 1800s were consistent with the growing individualism. It was probably not a coincidence

[6]On its increasingly long history in England, see Macfarlane (1978).

that in 1776 the Americans had begun a war of independence dedicated, as every schoolchild knows, to the values of "life, liberty, and the pursuit of happiness." Young adults successfully freed themselves from the control of their elders, and relations between husbands and wives and between parents and children became more affectionate.

Religion played a role in shaping these changes. The Puritan theology had strongly supported the authority of the father prior to the Revolution, but a wave of religious revivals that swept through many states in the early 1800s carried other values. If the Puritans saw children as depraved beings whose will needed to be broken, the revivalists viewed them as innocent beings who needed continual guidance and affection. And mothers, not fathers, were thought to be the parents who were better at this kind of childrearing (Ryan, 1981).

Consequently, this new view of how to care for children elevated the position of women in the family because they were to be entrusted with the major responsibility for childrearing. Married women's wishes and needs as individuals rose in importance (Degler, 1980). Women also had an interest in having fewer children because the large families of the 1700s made it difficult to provide each child with enough attention. In this way, the religious movements of the early 1800s promoted the growth of individualism in the family and the fall in the birthrate.

FROM COOPERATION TO SEPARATION: WOMEN'S AND MEN'S SPHERES

Another spur to family change was the transition from the familial mode of production to the labor market mode of production. It began sometime in the 1700s and early 1800s with the growth of commercial capitalism—an economic system in which the buying and selling of goods such as grain, tobacco, or cotton are important. Commercial capitalism created jobs for merchants, clerks, shippers, dockworkers, wagon builders, and others like them who were paid money for their labor. The opportunity to earn money outside the home undermined the authority of fathers. Because sons had alternatives to farming, fathers no longer had a near monopoly on the resources needed to make a living. The greater economic independence of adult children facilitated the growth of individualism. This transition accelerated in the mid-1800s with the spread of industrial capitalism, which created factory work for the great masses of immigrants and their descendants.

The heart of the change was the aforementioned movement of men's work out of the home. Instead of working together in a common household enterprise, husbands and wives worked on separate enterprises—he exchanging his labor for wages, she maintaining the home and raising the children. Instead of working in close proximity, they were physically separated during the workday. Moreover, wage work held no intrinsic value for most workers, and in nineteenth-century factories it was frequently exhausting and dangerous.

The sharp split between a rewarding home life and an often alienating work life led to the emergence of the idea of "separate spheres": men's sphere being the world of work and, more generally, the world outside the home; and women's sphere being the home, relatives, and children. Whereas men's sphere was seen as governed by the rough ethic of the business world, women's sphere came to be seen as morally pure, a place where wives could renew their husbands' spirituality and character. And whereas men's sphere was seen as providing no rewards other than a paycheck, women's sphere was the center of affection and nurturing, providing the emotional core for husbands and children.

Thus developed a nineteenth-century ideology, a set of beliefs, which historian Barbara Welter named "the cult of True Womanhood" (Welter, 1966). The True Woman was, first of all, the pious upholder of spiritual values. She was also pure: She was to have no sexual contact before marriage—although men might try to tempt her—and none afterward except with her husband. Moreover, the True Woman was submissive to men and particularly to her husband. And finally she was domestic: Her proper place was in the home, comforting her husband, lovingly raising her children.

Woman's sphere at once limited women's opportunities and glorified the domestic role they were left with. It was a more restricted role than wives in the colonial era experienced. To be sure, the Puritan wife was also home most of the day, but she was collaborating with her husband in the common family economy; without her contribution, her husband might not be able to feed and clothe their children. Then the movement to wage labor separated women from paid work. Men went out every morning into the wider social world, but their wives could not follow. In a culture that had begun to celebrate individualism, women were supposed to give up much of their individualism and care for their husbands and children. Seen from this vantage point, one might argue that women's lives were worse than they had been before the Revolution—more restricted in opportunity, less productive, more dependent on their husbands, more isolated from society. Indeed, many historians have argued as much.

But other historians, while acknowledging the restrictions and dependency inherent in the domestic sphere, argue that it nevertheless offered some benefits. By appointing women the guardians of moral values and giving them the major role in rearing children, it provided them with an area in which their influence was substantial. However circumscribed that area, it may have allowed wives to counter the authority of husbands that had been so pervasive in the colonial period. Moreover, by fencing in an aspect of life and assigning women to live in it, the ideology of women's sphere may have created a self-consciousness of, and an identification with, women as a group. Women established and maintained deep friendships with other women, reinforced by the segregation of their lives and by female rituals surrounding childbirth, weddings, illnesses, and funerals (Smith-Rosenberg, 1975). Some joined together in public associations to promote values consistent with domesticity, such as greater devotion to religion, assistance for the poor, or enlightened childrearing methods. These friendships and associations may have been a prerequisite for the development of feminist organizations in the nineteenth and twentieth centuries. Historian Nancy Cott captured the dual nature of women's sphere in the title of her book, *The Bonds of Womanhood* (Cott, 1977), for the bonds that tied women to the domestic sphere also bound them together in a subculture of sisterhood that prefigured their social and political movements decades later.

WORKING-CLASS FAMILIES

This was the picture for the white middle class. But life was different for the working class, especially for the tens of millions of immigrants who poured into American cities. The scale of immigration was simply massive between 1850 and World War I. Even in 1850, 10 percent of the population had been born in another country. Then began a sustained increase in immigration that peaked in the early 1900s. By 1880, 13 percent of the population was foreign born; by 1910 it was 15 percent (U.S. Bureau of the Census, 1975). In contrast, the comparable figure today is only about 6 percent, despite some grumbling among political leaders that the United States has too many immigrants (U.S. Bureau of the Census, 1991e). The migrants to the country's growing cities from overseas or from rural America worked long hours for low wages and lived in crowded, often unsanitary conditions. In Homestead, Pennsylvania, in the 1890s, workers labored at one of Andrew Carnegie's steel mills from 7:00 A.M. to 5:30 P.M., six days a week, for less than $15 a week. Some worked longer night shifts or all seven days. According to one report, half of the African-American and Slavic workers in the town lived in one- or two-room shanties without indoor plumbing or toilets (Mintz & Kellogg, 1988).

Living between Modes   Working-class families may or may not have aspired to the breadwinner-homemaker model, but in either case, it was a style of life they could not afford. Instead, they needed to pool the economic contributions of more than one family member in order to subsist. Before stricter child labor laws were passed, children as young as 10 or 11 might work alongside their fathers and older siblings at a factory. Unmarried sons and daughters contributed their wages to the family fund. To be sure, few wives worked for wages outside the home—just 2.5 percent of white married women (of all classes combined) did so in 1890 (Goldin, 1977). For a wife to work outside the home was such a sign of economic failure that white families avoided it unless there was no alternative except extreme hardship (Robinson, 1993). Instead, working-class wives made important economic contributions at home. Some earned money by doing laundry; others did piecework—literally work for which they were paid by the piece—such as stitching

In working-class families around the turn of the twentieth century, women and children earned money by doing piecework—such as making dried flower bouquets—at home.

shoes. Often they took into their households a kind of resident that has now almost disappeared—the boarder or lodger.

A boarder is someone who pays to live in a room and to eat meals in someone's household; a lodger is someone who pays for a room but does not eat in the household. Let me use the term "boarder" for both. In the nineteenth and early twentieth centuries, boarding was the most common living arrangement for unmarried adults who were not living with their parents. Very few people lived alone; as recently as 1900, only 5 percent of all households contained one person (Kobrin, 1976). Rather than live alone, unmarried people boarded for several reasons. First, few could afford to live alone because wages were too low. Second, the surge of immigrants created a housing shortage, which drove rents up further. Third, preparing meals required much more time and effort than is the case today. Since there were no refrigerators or freezers, people had to shop for food almost daily. There were no microwave meals, no TV dinners, no inexpensive fast-food restaurants. Fourth, having grown up in households larger than ours today, people may have preferred to live in the company of others. By one estimate, 15 to 20 percent of all urban households contained boarders at any given time (Modell & Hareven, 1973). The proportion of households that ever took in boarders was certainly much higher. In a sense, boarders were a replacement for grown children in the household's economy. When an older child who had contributed part of his or her earnings left home, a bed was freed and a hole was left in the family's budget. Families typically would take in a boarder in response.

These working-class families do not correspond neatly to either the familial or the labor market mode of production. Like families operating in the familial mode, they pooled the efforts of several members into a common family enterprise: The husband and his teenage son might work for wages, the wife might take in boarders and do piecework; an unmarried older sister might contribute her wages so that her brother could go to college. But unlike families in the familial mode, most members exchanged their labor for wages. It seems more accurate to say that working-class families from the mid-1800s to the early 1900s were living between modes, a phrase that has been used to describe most of the families that exist today in poor, less-developed countries (Caldwell, 1982). These families were organized the old way, as if they were still producing for their own use, even though some members worked for wages some of the time. Parents and children still contributed the fruits of their labor, be it cash or crops, to a common family fund. Individuals subordinated their own desires for the good of the family. And what was good for the family was decided by the parents, particularly the father.

Although living between modes was an admirable way for families to manage their lives with limited resources, it was an unstable system. Once older children decided that they needn't turn over most of their earnings to their parents, the authority of the father eroded. Once the husband's wages increased enough that his wife could cut back on piecework and boarding, the family became heavily dependent on his wages. In such families parents got smaller economic returns from children and were forced to expend more time and energy educating and rearing them. Families such as these were likely to decide that having fewer children and investing more in each was preferable to having many children. The result was a smaller, more isolated conjugal family—the kind we today recognize as familiar.

The Kinship Connection   Kinship ties to relatives outside the household were also beneficial to working-class families. It used to be conventional wisdom that industrialization caused the breakdown of the large, extended family. But this generalization has been battered. The first assault came from historical studies of western Europe, which showed that in some countries extended families had never been as common as had been assumed, for reasons discussed earlier in the chapter: higher death rates among adults and the expectation that young couples would start new households. The second assault has come from studies of early industrialization in England and the United States. In the early years of industrialization, the proportion of extended families actually increased; it then declined in the twentieth century (Ruggles, 1987).

One explanation for the temporary rise is that ties with kin were an important means of finding a factory job or a place to live in a newly industrializing city. Historian Tamara Hareven studied French Canadians who immigrated to Manchester, New Hampshire, in the first two decades of the twentieth century to work in what was then the world's largest textile mill. The developments she studied were similar to what had been occurring in other industrializing cities in the late nineteenth century. Hareven found that workers were recruited through networks of kin. For example, the eldest son in one Canadian family with seven children migrated to Manchester in 1908, after his mother's death, and became a weaver in the mill:

> He then brought his father and all his younger brothers and sisters. The father entered the same weaving room in which the son was working; subsequently, each child entered the mills upon reaching age 14 except for the youngest son, who became a barber and worked in the shop that his father set up after he left the mill (Hareven, 1982).

The plant often hired relatives recommended by their workers; Hareven estimates that 76 percent of the French-Canadian workers had relatives working in the mill at some point, often in the same room. In Manchester and elsewhere, when factory work proved unstable, workers used family networks as sources of information and temporary shelter as they moved from job to job. In sum, family ties remained vitally important to working-class Americans during industrialization, and supposedly old-fashioned forms of kinship gained new purposes.

AFRICAN-AMERICAN, MEXICAN-AMERICAN, AND ASIAN IMMIGRANT FAMILIES

Europeans, of course, were not the only immigrants to the United States. Three other groups were present early in the nation's history. Africans had been forced to immigrate—captured or bought in West Africa, transported across the ocean under horrible conditions that killed many, and sold as slaves upon arrival. Mexicans, in search of grazing land, had pushed north into the area that is now the Southwest. Asian immigrants first arrived in large number in the mid-nineteenth century, when they were used as laborers by the railroads and other enterprises. The family lives of all three groups differed from those of the Europeans.

AFRICAN-AMERICAN FAMILIES

None of the categories used in this chapter to describe various types of families applies to African-American families before the Civil War because of the institution of slavery. Until the appearance of new scholarship in the 1970s, most historians thought that the oppression and harsh conditions of slavery had destroyed most of the culture African slaves brought with them and left little in its place. The writings of both white and black scholars emphasized the losses imposed by slavery: the uprooting from Africa, the disruption of slave families through sales of slaves to new owners, the inability of slave fathers to protect their families from the sexual advances and other indignities imposed by masters. In an influential 1939 book, E. Franklin Frazier, a sociologist and an African American, argued that the white masters destroyed all social organization among the slaves. As a result, he argued, slave family life itself was disorganized. In particular, the only stable bond was between mothers and their children:

"Consequently, under all conditions of slavery, the Negro mother remained the most dependable and important figure in the family" (Frazier, 1939).

From Frazier and others, then, came the idea that most African-American families during and after slavery were headed by women and that African-American men were relatively powerless inside and outside the home. Then, in 1976, historian Herbert Gutman published a comprehensive study of plantation, local government, and Census records that suggested a much different picture (Gutman, 1976). Gutman found substantial evidence that slaves married and lived together for life, whenever possible, and that slaves knew and kept track of uncles, aunts, cousins, and other kin. He cited letters such as one that the field hand Cash sent to relatives on a Georgia plantation after he, his wife, Phoebe, and some of their children were sold away:

Clairissa your affectionate Mother and Father sends a heap of love to you and your Husband and my Grand Children. Mag. & Cloe. John. Judy. My aunt sinena . . . Give our Love to Cashes brother Porter and his Wife Patience. Victoria sends her Love to her Cousin Beck and Miley (Gutman, 1976).

African slaves maintained strong family ties despite the oppression of the slave owners, as this wedding in the slave quarters of a plantation shows.

Families in Other Cultures

The Process of Marriage in Sub-Saharan Africa

Historically in the United States and other Western countries (and, indeed in many less-developed countries), a marriage started on the day when a civil or religious wedding ceremony took place. Before that day, the couple was not married; after that day, they were. Yet in much of sub-Saharan Africa becoming married has traditionally been a process that could take months or even years. Moreover, it has been a process so ambiguous that it could be hard for outsiders to tell whether a couple had become married or not. Even the prospective husband and wife could redefine their marital status if their situations changed before the process was completed.

Among the Kpelle of Liberia, the process began with an initiation ritual for young women and men at roughly the time of puberty, which eventually was followed by a betrothal to a future spouse, living together, a ceremony in which the woman is "turned over" symbolically to the man, a payment from the family of the man to the family of the woman, and the bearing of a child or two (Bledsoe, 1980). The entire process could occur rapidly or slowly, and the steps could occur out of order. For example, a prepubescent girl could be betrothed to a man before her initiation ceremony. Or a man's family might not make a payment to a woman's family until after a woman had borne a child.

The central reason for these customs was the very high value most African societies placed on bearing children. In many societies, land was held in common by the tribal elders or the chiefs. They allocated land to adult men according, in part, to how many children they had (which also depended in part on how many wives they had in the many areas where polygyny was practiced). Thus, it was very important to a husband that his wife be capable of bearing children. Under these circumstances, some young men (and their parents) wished to wait until their partners gave birth to children before deciding that the marriage was final. Consequently, the final ceremonies of the marriage might not occur until the couple had

Moreover, Gutman argued, before and after slavery, in both the North and the South, most African-American families were headed by two parents. These family ties were forged by the slaves despite the frequent sales of husbands, wives, and children to other masters, the sexual abuse of slave women by slave owners, and the high rates of disease and death.

Still, there were some differences, both before and after the Civil War, between black and white families. It was common, for example, for a young slave woman to have a first child before marrying; if so, she was usually married within a few years, although not necessarily to the father (Jones, 1985). This pattern may have occurred in part because slave owners valued women who had many children, thus increasing the owner's wealth. Yet it is also consistent with customs in West Africa, where most of the slaves came from. In much of Africa, becoming married was a long process with many events, rather than a ceremony that occurred on a single day (Bledsoe, 1980). Parents and other kin watched over the process. Because fertility was also highly valued in Africa, it was not unusual for a young woman to become pregnant by a man who wished to marry her; afterward, her parents and his parents would negotiate the final terms of a marriage agreement. (See *Families in Other Cultures:* The Process of Marriage in Sub-Saharan Africa.)

Another difference between black and white families was that wives in rural black families after the Civil War worked seasonally in the fields, whereas white rural women didn't. According to 1870 Census figures for the Cotton Belt states, about 4 in 10 African-American wives told the Census taker that they had jobs, almost all as field workers. In contrast, 98 percent of white wives said they were cohabited and had a child. Alternatively, a man might begin to have sexual relations with his partner but not cohabit with her until she had borne a child (Little, 1973).

Moreover, families used the marriages of their children to establish alliances that could benefit them or to obtain goods and services. For instance, a family might betroth their daughter even before puberty to a powerful man who could provide access to land or other resources. Among the Kpelle, even when young people chose their own spouses, it was necessary that the parents agree to the match. Commonly, the groom's family might make a gift of money or cattle to the bride's family, a custom known as **bridewealth;** or he might

agree to work for a time for the bride's family, a variant known as **brideservice.** Until the gifts were transferred, or until the agreed-upon labor was completed, the bride's family might not consider the marriage to be final. A dispute over the status of the marriage could occur should the terms of the agreement not be fulfilled to both sides' satisfaction.

These customs have been changing over the past few decades. Anthropologists report that young adults are choosing their own marriage partners for love and companionship more than in the past, especially among the better educated (Harrell-Bond, 1975). Moreover, as women become better educated, they are less likely to wed men who already have wives. In Nige-

ria in 1990, 38 percent of young wives with no formal education were in polygynous unions, compared with 16 percent of young wives with secondary education or higher (Bledsoe & Cohen, 1993). As young adults have gained access to wage work, they have become more independent of their parents and in-laws. A young man with money has alternatives to relying on his parents for bridewealth or performing brideservice. Anthropologist Caroline Bledsoe reports that one Kpelle man told her that by giving your in-laws a lot of money, you don't have to work for them and you can keep them at bay (Bledsoe, 1980). Still, compared with Western nations, marriage in sub-Saharan Africa is less of an event and more of a process.

"keeping house" and had no jobs (Jones, 1985). Here again, the differences reflect a mixture of economic pressure and culture. The plots of land farmed by African-American sharecroppers in the late nineteenth century provided such a marginal standard of living that men and women (and often children) were needed in the fields, at least at harvesttime. Historian Jacqueline Jones also notes that "the outlines of African work patterns endured among the slaves," (Jones, 1985) in that West African women often had the major responsibility for cultivating food.

Moreover, black mothers with children were more likely to be living without a male partner than white mothers, although most black families still had two parents. This racial difference stemmed partly from the high mortality rates of black men; by one estimate, 42 percent of black wives were widowed by ages 45 to 50 around 1900 (Preston, 1992). But a difference still remains after mortality is taken into account (Morgan, McDaniel, Miller, & Preston, 1993). A much larger racial difference in household structure emerged after about 1960 (see Chapter 5).

When black families migrated to Northern cities in the twentieth century, black women continued to work outside the home in larger numbers than white women. About one-third of married nonwhite women worked outside the home in the 1920s and 1930s, compared with less than one-tenth of married white women (Goldin, 1977). Because of discrimination, black men were offered low-paying, physically challenging jobs that couldn't support a family. If a black man worked in a steel factory, for example, he might be stoking a blast furnace all day long. Staying home simply was not an option for most black wives, who also faced discrimination but found work as domestic servants. It wasn't until the 1960s that black women were able to break out of domestic service into occupations that had previously been reserved for white women. Women of both races still lag behind men in earnings, and black men's employment situation, although improved, remains difficult.

MEXICAN-AMERICAN FAMILIES

Like African Americans, Mexican Americans established a presence early in the history of what is now the United States—although, unlike African Americans, the descendants of the early residents are vastly outnumbered by more recent immigrants. In the early nineteenth century, well before migrants from the eastern United States arrived, frontier settlements of Mexicans were present throughout what was then northern Mexico (Moore & Cuèllar, 1970). These Mexican pioneers crossed deserts and fought with American Indians to reach as far west as California and as far north as Colorado. The early settlements generally included a landowning elite and poorer, farmer-laborer settlers. The landowning elite tended to be (or claimed to be) of nearly pure Spanish descent. Some owned vast tracts of land on which they grazed cattle or sheep. They arranged the marriages of their children with care and celebrated elaborate weddings and feasts, so as to preserve or merge their holdings with other wealthy families or with wealthy Anglo (non-Mexican) immigrants (Griswold del Castillo, 1979).

More numerous were the laborers who worked the great estates or who farmed or grazed animals on their own smaller holdings. They tended to be *mestizos,* people whose ancestors included both Spanish settlers and Native Americans in Mexico. There is some evidence that informal marriages—those in which the couple never underwent a formal ceremony—were more common among this group (Griswold del Castillo, 1979). Informal marriages allowed couples to evade the control of their parents and other kin; with fewer resources to protect than among the elite, the *mestizo* classes had less reason to control who married whom. The small landholders and laborers attempted to enlist the sponsorship and support of the well-to-do through the tradition of *compadrazgo:* a godparent relationship in which a wealthy or influential person outside the kinship group is asked to become the *compadre,* or godparent, of a newborn child, particularly at its baptism. The godfather and godchild were expected to retain a special relationship, and the godparent was supposed to assist his godchild, for example, by providing or finding a job (Camarillo, 1979).

This social structure was disrupted by a series of wars, revolts, and land grabs by U.S. troops and immigrants during the 1830s and 1840s. When it was over, the United States had acquired, by conquest, the current Southwest. Soon thereafter, most of the Spanish elite lost their land due to taxes, drought, and Anglo squatters. Instead of ranchers and farmers, Mexicans became more of a working-class community, employed by the growing numbers of Anglos (Camarillo, 1979). Census statistics for the Los Angeles district in the last half of the nineteenth century show a rising number of households headed by women without husbands present (Griswold del Castillo, 1979). Some of these women were probably married to men who migrated from harvest to harvest, picking crops; others were in informal marriages. Many were probably unmarried, their numbers reflecting the economic changes of the time. Mexican-American women, like African-American women, could find low-paying but steady work as domestics and launderers for wealthier Anglos, whereas Mexican-American men were losing their established positions as small ranchers and farmers.

As the number of Anglo immigrants rose, Mexican Americans were forced into *barrios,* segregated urban Mexican-American neighborhoods. Residents of the *barrios* faced high unemployment and low income as they provided low-wage labor to Anglo employers. Waves of new Mexican immigrants were drawn into the country during economic expansions, further depressing the wages of resident Mexican Americans (Camarillo, 1979). The Mexican immigrant families often were highly male dominant: Husbands were supposed to be powerful, respected, and in charge; wives were supposed to submit to their authority (Queen et al., 1985). But male dominance eroded under the low wages of urban employment or the separations of migrant workers from their families. Mexican-American families in the barrios today still show the effects of poverty and unemployment. Yet they remain distinctive in some respects, such as their high birthrates, as will be discussed in Chapter 5.

ASIAN IMMIGRANT FAMILIES

Before the middle of the twentieth century, most Asian-American families in the United States consisted of immigrants from China and Japan. Chinese immigrants began to arrive during the California gold rush in the 1850s. After the Civil War, Chinese immigrants were hired to build the railroads of the Southwest. Because the vast majority of these immigrant laborers were men, relatively few new families were formed. Some of the immigrants had left their wives in China, and many of these men sent **remittances**, cash payments sent to family members such as spouses or elderly parents in their country of origin. Laws in California and most other western states prohibited Chinese (and later Japanese) immigrants from marrying white Americans or becoming citizens. In fact, American sentiment against Chinese immigrants was so strong that Congress passed the Chinese Exclusion Act of 1882, which virtually ended Chinese immigration until after World War II (Olson, 1979).

Significant numbers of Japanese immigrants began to arrive in Hawaii (which the United States would soon annex) and the mainland United States in the 1880s. The ratio of women to men was more balanced than among the Chinese immigrants, so more families were formed. Both the Chinese and Japanese families were patrilineal. The authority of the father was strong, and ties to extended family members were important. Traditionally, parents or other relatives arranged the marriages of their children (Wong, 1988). Since the immigrants usually left their extended families behind, they developed other ways of building family-like ties in the United States. For example, people from the same region of China or Japan formed mutual aid societies. Wealthy merchants sometimes played the supervisory roles that village elders had in Asia (Olson, 1979).

Like the Chinese, Japanese immigrants faced discrimination. After the war with Japan began in 1941, some Americans warned that Japanese immigrants might be disloyal, even though many had been in the United States for decades. Bowing to these fears, the government rounded up Japanese immigrants, most of whom were in California, and sent them to internment camps in the interior. Aside from the imprisonment, humiliation, and economic losses suffered by the Japanese, the internment camps eroded the traditional authority of parents (Kitano, 1988). They had little to offer their children, who were exposed to American activities such as dancing to the music of the latest bands. Young men could even volunteer to join a much-decorated U.S. Army unit that fought in Europe. The children's autonomy contributed to sharp changes after the war in Japanese-American marriage patterns. Whereas the older generation's marriages were usually arranged by relatives and stressed obligations to kin and emotional restraint, the younger generation much more often chose their own spouses and valued romantic love and companionship (Yanagisako, 1985).

Overall, Asian immigration was modest in the twentieth century until Congress passed the **1965 Immigration Act**. It ended restrictions that had blocked most Asian immigration and substituted an annual quota of 170,000. Since then, the Asian population of the United States has expanded rapidly. The 1990 Census counted 6.9 million Americans of Asian origin, double the number in 1980. The two largest groups were Chinese (24 percent) and Filipinos (20.4 percent).[7]

Filipino immigration began as a small stream, mostly of students, after the United States captured the Philippines in the Spanish-American War of 1898. Many of the Filipino immigrants in the post-1965 surge were professionals, most notable nurses. Unlike China and Japan, families in the Philippines trace descent through both the father's and the mother's line, a system called **bilateral kinship**. (This is also the system followed in the United States.) This system usually provides women more independence than patrilineal kinship, and Filipino-American women have been more likely to work outside the home than women in Chinese or Japanese families (Kitano & Daniels, 1988).

THE RISE OF THE PRIVATE FAMILY: 1900–PRESENT

THE EARLY DECADES

An increase in premarital sex. A drop in the birthrate. A new youth culture rebelling against propriety, dressing outrageously, and indulging in indecent dance steps. And a rapidly rising divorce rate. Sound familiar? No, this is not a description of the present or even of the 1960s and 1970s. Rather, these were the concerns of American moralists, politicians, and social scientists during the first few decades of the twentieth century. Premarital sex had become more common, although much of the increase occurred among couples who were already engaged (see Chapter 7). As for the flourishing new youth culture, it was exemplified in the 1920s by the "flapper" girls. Independent, often employed outside the home, and brazen enough to bob their hair and wear lipstick and eyeliner in public, they patronized dance halls and movie theaters with their male companions. The divorce rate, perhaps the greatest source of concern, had risen to the point where a marriage begun in 1910 had about a 1-in-7 chance of ending in divorce. This may seem like a small risk today, but it represented a substantial increase over the 1-in-12 chance in 1880 or the 1-in-20 chance at the end of the Civil War (Cherlin, 1992b).

Yet the period from the 1890s through the 1920s was generally one of increasing prosperity, which raises the question of why such an increase in divorce would occur. In part, it was made possible by the growing economic independence of women, who were better educated, had fewer children, had likely worked outside the home before marrying, and therefore had greater potential to find work outside the home if their marriages ended (O'Neill, 1967). But this is not the whole story, for, as historian Elaine Tyler May notes, the marriage rate kept rising right

---

[7]Four other groups each constituted between 9 and 12 percent of the Asian population: Japanese, Asian Indian, Korean, and Vietnamese (U.S. Bureau of the Census, 1993h).

along with the divorce rate. What occurred in addition, she asserts, is that both women and men came to expect a greater amount of emotional satisfaction from marriage (May, 1988). They sought happiness, companionship, and romantic love in marriage more than ever before. If they found that their marriages fell short of their expectations, they became dissatisfied and asked for a divorce. (See *Families and Public Policy:* Divorce Reform: Have We Been Here Before?, on page 64.)

And so women and men came to see marriage and family as central to their quest for an emotionally satisfying private life. Before the twentieth century, emotional satisfaction had been less important to both husbands and wives. This was not because they were ignorant of the concept of emotional satisfaction—no Ariès-like claim is made here that the twentieth century discovered happiness. Rather, before this century the standard of living was so low that most people needed to concentrate on managing the day-to-day family tasks that kept them clothed, housed, and fed. Before 1900, pursuing personal pleasure was a luxury few people could indulge in. Most family members were too busy just trying to get by.

Even after 1900, large segments of the American population—immigrants and racial and ethnic minorities—had little time to invest in private life. My grandparents immigrated from Eastern Europe just after the turn of the century, started a grocery store, and raised 10 children. Had I been around to ask them whether their marriage was satisfying, they would have said of course—they were raising a big family. They would not have answered in terms of companionship, romance, sexual pleasure, excitement, or personal growth. Yet these were the ways in which more and more Americans came to define a successful marriage in the twentieth century.

Americans (and the citizens of other Western nations) were enlarging the scope of the *private family*. They were defining marital success in emotional terms, not material terms; they were beginning to derive their greatest satisfaction not from the roles they played (breadwinner, homemaker, father, mother) but from the quality of the relationships they had with their spouses and children. This process had certainly begun long ago among the more prosperous classes, and it continued throughout the twentieth century. But in some eras its ascendancy was more noticeable, and the first few decades of the twentieth century was such an era.

These developments were occurring as the family was becoming less of a dominant force in people's lives. The many public goods that the colonial family had provided gradually diminished. Compulsory schooling replaced education at home; hospitals replaced sickbeds; department stores replaced home crafts; and so forth. As marriage became less necessary economically and materially, it was redefined as a means of gaining emotional satisfaction. A well-known text on the family described this transformation in marriage as a shift "from institution to companionship" (Burgess & Locke, 1945). (See Chapter 9.) In this process, marriage became more fragile. The bonds of sentiment were weaker than the ties forged by working together on a family farm or than the unchallenged authority of the patriarch. In addition, an institution which had been designed to enhance survival and security creaked under the weight of expectations that it provide so much emotional satisfaction. One result was a more or less continuous increase in the divorce rate until a high plateau was reached about 1980.

Privacy also increased after 1900. Two demographic trends contributed to this increase. First, the birthrate declined, which meant, among other things, fewer persons per room. Second, adult life expectancy increased due to advances in medicine and a rising standard of living. As a result of these trends, parents were younger when they finished the stage of life in which they were raising children,

Divorce Reform: Have We Been Here Before?

At current rates, about one out of two marriages begun in the United States today will end in divorce. As noted, the divorce rate has been increasing since at least the Civil War. The most recent burst occurred between the early 1960s and the mid-1970s, during which time the probability that a marriage would end in divorce doubled. Since then, the rate has declined slightly (Cherlin, 1992). The rise in divorce has alarmed some commentators, who fear that it is undermining the institution of the family. (The effects of divorce will be discussed in detail in Chapter 12.)

Some writers have called for a toughening of divorce laws, which were relaxed in the 1970s and 1980s, when all states enacted "no fault" divorce legislation. One suggestion, for instance, is to require a longer waiting period before a person can obtain a divorce if children are involved (Galston, 1990/1991). Currently, a person who wishes to obtain a divorce against the wishes of his or her spouse needs to wait just a year or less after separating in most American states

(Glendon, 1987). In 1997, Louisiana passed a law allowing couples that were marrying to choose "covenant marriage." In the event of a serious dispute they were required to undergo counseling and to remain married for at least two years should one spouse oppose a divorce (Jeter, 1997).

Yet this is not the first time a debate has emerged about the consequences of divorce and restrictive legislation has been proposed. In fact, the divorce debates of the Progressive Era (1890–1930) bear an uncanny resemblance to the current discourse. As in the 1960s and 1970s, a rise in the divorce rate caused concern. So did a fall in the birthrate among native-born whites. John Watson, a leading psychologist, reflected the fears of many when he predicted that "in fifty years there will be no such thing as marriage" (Mintz & Kellogg, 1988). Arthur Calhoun, the leading historian of the family, acknowledged the sweeping changes but wrote approvingly that "we are in the midst of a social revolution" which would make a new, more democratic family "inevitable" (Calhoun, 1919).

Prior to the mid-1800s, in most states a person could obtain a divorce only by an act of the legislature. This requirement put divorce beyond the reach of everyone except the politically connected and the well-to-do. In midcentury, however, many legislatures delegated to the state courts the authority to grant divorces. Persons of more-modest means could now obtain divorces from judges, who were more liberal in granting them than legislatures had been. Then, in the 1890s and 1900s, the rising divorce rate led many legislatures, especially in the eastern states, to tighten divorce laws. According to historian Elaine Tyler May, between 1889 and 1906 state legislatures enacted more than 100 pieces of restrictive marriage and divorce legislation. For instance, 15 states forbade remarriage until one or two years after a final divorce decree, and 6 eliminated certain grounds for divorce. New York permitted divorce only in the event of adultery, and South Carolina prohibited it altogether (May, 1980).

The Progressive Era was a time of great and varied action by groups

and they lived longer after their last child left home. Consequently, a new stage of family life, the "empty nest" phase after the departure of all children, became common. Before the twentieth century, far fewer married couples ever reached it (Cherlin & Furstenberg, 1992).

Greater prosperity also meant that more apartments were built and more people could afford to live on their own, and the rise in individualism probably made more unmarried people *wish* to live on their own. Consequently, boarding and lodging went from commonplace to rarity during the first half of the century (Laslett, 1973). By 1950, 9 percent of all households contained one person; by 1970 the figure was 17 percent; and by 1990 it was 25 percent (Kobrin, 1976; U.S. Bureau of the Census, 1993c).[8] Yet during the first few decades of the century, it was still true that about two-thirds of young women, and perhaps 40 percent of

[8]The 1992 figure was also 25 percent.

seeking reform in order to increase democracy, efficiency, and the quality of life. What some historians have called the "social progressives" sought improvements in industrial working conditions and in the lives of parents and children (Skocpol, 1992). Many of the social progressives, including those interested in the family, sought reform through the passage of new laws. For example, an Inter-Church Conference led by Episcopal Bishop William Doane convinced Theodore Roosevelt to order the Bureau of the Census to carry out a new study on marriage and divorce. In Roosevelt's message to Congress in 1905, he wrote:

> There is widespread conviction that the divorce laws are dangerously lax and indifferently administered in some of the states, resulting in a diminished regard for the sanctity of the marriage relation.[1]

Roosevelt called for uniform divorce legislation in all states to eliminate overly liberal state laws.

Yet despite all this activity, despite numerous conferences on uniform divorce laws, and despite attempts in Congress to tighten state provisions, little was accomplished, and the divorce rate continued to rise. Why did the divorce reformers have so little success? Historians who have studied these events argue that the reformers were fighting against powerful cultural changes in the nature of marriage. Marriage was becoming more of a companionship, more of a relationship among equals. Increasingly, people sought personal satisfaction through marriage.[2] I would add that the rising standard of living in the early decades of the twentieth century allowed people to focus less on food and shelter and more on emotional satisfaction. Because of this emphasis, people who found their marriages lacking in satisfaction were more likely to consider divorce (see Chapter 9). Moreover, the increasing labor market participation of women decreased their economic dependence on men, making marriage less necessary.

Given the strength of these cultural and economic forces, the social progressives were unable to enact their program of divorce reform. Advances in one state would be stymied by setbacks in others. Resistance to more restricted divorce remained firm. The failures of the reformers may hold lessons for those who today urge public action to reduce the divorce rate. The same cultural and economic forces have continued to influence marriage and divorce throughout the twentieth century. Indeed, one could argue that they are more powerful now: The quest for personal fulfillment has led to widespread cohabitation outside of marriage; the loosening of cultural constraints has led to a toleration of childbearing outside of marriage; the economic independence of women has grown as a majority of wives now work outside the home. A look backward at the entire century, and particularly at the Progressive Era, suggests that today's divorce reformers have few promising strategies to push. Lowering the divorce rate through political action and moral suasion is a very difficult task.

[1] Quoted in O'Neill (1967).
[2] Mintz and Kellogg, May, and O'Neill all present arguments along these lines.

young men, didn't leave home until they married. If they did leave home before marrying, it often was because their parents lived in rural areas where the young adults couldn't find jobs. Later, in the 1940s and 1950s, the age at which young adults left home fell sharply because of earlier marriage and because so many young men left home to join the military during World War II and the Korean War (Goldscheider & Goldscheider, 1994).

The first few decades of the twentieth century, then, were an important time of change in the American family. The basis of marriage moved away from an economic partnership and toward emotional satisfaction and companionship. Men and women began to be more economically independent of each other. As a result of these developments, the bonds of marriage became weaker and divorce became more common. In addition, prosperity, lower birthrates, and longer life expectancy accelerated a trend toward more privacy, as exemplified by child-free older couples and people living alone.

THE DEPRESSION GENERATION

The prosperity of the early decades of the century was interrupted by the Great Depression, which began in 1929 and continued until the late 1930s. In addition to its effects on family finances, the Depression also undermined the authority and prestige of the father. If he lost his job, his family might view him as having failed in his role as the breadwinner. If his wife or his children were forced to find jobs, as many were, their labor was a constant reminder of his inability to fulfill their expectations. You might expect that the divorce rate would have risen as a result of these difficulties, but instead it fell temporarily. Couples stayed together not because they were happier—many were less happy—but because they couldn't afford to get a divorce and live in two households. Years later, after the worst of the Depression was over, there was a surge of divorce among couples who had married at the start of the Depression, had developed serious problems during it, but hadn't been able to divorce until it was over (Cherlin, 1992b).

The economic hardships forced many young adults to postpone marrying and to defer having children. The Depression was so long and so severe that some never had the opportunity to have children. As a result, levels of lifetime childlessness were higher for women who reached their peak childbearing years in the 1930s than for any other generation of women in the twentieth century: About one in five never had a child (Rindfuss, Morgan, & Swicegood, 1988). In contrast, only about 1 in 10 of the women who reached their peak reproductive years during the 1950s baby boom (see below) never had a child.

The hardships of the Great Depression strained many families in the 1930s. The family of farm laborer William Jones was photographed at "home"—blankets thrown over fence posts and containers—along a rural Missouri highway.

As fathers and mothers struggled to make a living, their children helped out. Teenage boys took whatever jobs they could find; teenage girls took over more of the household work if their mothers were forced to work outside the home. The result was what Glen Elder, Jr., called "the downward extension of adultlike experience": Girls took on the role of homemaker; boys took on the role of breadwinner. Elder was able to examine the records of a group of children who were observed at age 11 in 1932 and then followed through adulthood. He found that, when they reached adulthood, the men and women in the group who came from economically deprived families valued marriage and family life more highly than those whose families hadn't experienced hardship. Women from deprived families married at younger ages than other women. Perhaps the difficulties their families had faced when they were adolescents made the deprived group eager for secure marriage; or perhaps they viewed families as an important resource in case hard times returned. In any event, when they reached adulthood, they turned inward toward building their own family lives.

THE 1950s

In fact, when the young adults of the Depression generation began to marry and have children after World War II, they created the most unusual and distinctive family patterns of the century. They married at the youngest ages and had more children than any other twentieth-century generation. Figure 2.1 shows the percentage of 20- to 24-year-old men and women who had never married, from 1890 to 1995. This is the age group that is most sensitive to variations in age at marriage. The percentage is highest at the beginning and end of this chart, indicating that young men and women were most likely to be single (and therefore to marry at older ages) in the late 1800s and late 1900s. The percentage never married declined slowly during the first half of the twentieth century and then plunged to its lowest

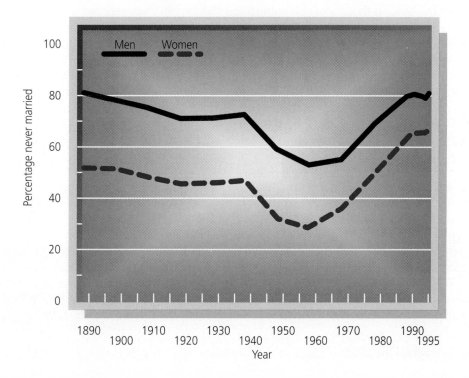

FIGURE 2.1 Percentage never married for men and women aged 20 to 24, 1890 to 1995. (*Sources:* for 1890–1960, U.S. Bureau of the Census, *Historical Statistics of the United States, Colonial Times to 1970,* pp. 20–21; for 1970–1995, U.S. Bureau of the Census, *Current Population Reports,* Series P20,"Marital Status and Living Arrangements," various issues.)

point during the 1950s. After 1960, it rose sharply again, especially for women, who by the mid-1990s were marrying later than at any time in the previous 100 years.

The years after World War II were also the time of the great **baby boom**. Couples not only married at younger ages, but they had children faster—and had more of them—than their parents' generation and, it would later turn out, their children's generation. Indeed, the late 1940s through the 1950s was the only period in the past 150 years during which the American birthrate rose substantially. It spiked dramatically just after the war, as couples had babies they had postponed having during the war. The spike ended after a few years; but then the birthrate began to climb again and peaked in 1957. Women who married during the 1950s had an average of slightly more than three children, the highest of the century (Evans, 1986).

Although the causes of the baby boom aren't fully clear, a strong post–World War II economy and a renewed cultural emphasis on marriage and children are viewed as important contributing factors. In addition, one explanation focuses on the unique circumstances of the young adults who married during the 1950s. Since most of them were born during the Depression, when birthrates were low, they constituted a relatively small **birth cohort**, as demographers call all people born during a given year or period of years. After the bad luck of growing up during the Depression and the war, they had the good fortune to reach adulthood just as the economy was growing rapidly. The Allied victory in World War II left the United States with the strongest economy in the world. Employers needed more workers, but the small size of the cohort meant that there were fewer workers to hire (at least given the widespread preference during the 1950s that married women not work outside the home). Therefore, wages rose for young men, making it easier for them to support larger families.[9]

This explanation, however, is incomplete. Birthrates rose not only among newlyweds in their early twenties but also among women in their thirties who had been married for years (Rindfuss et al., 1988). These older women belonged to larger cohorts, so that the small-cohort-size theory can't account for their behavior. Rather, the pervasiveness of the rise in births suggests that people's preferences about family size also shifted during the baby boom. It seems likely that there was a greater cultural emphasis on getting married and having children than was the case before or since—perhaps as a result of the trauma of the Depression and the war. It was an emphasis that had a broad effect on women and men in their twenties, thirties, and even early forties.

The strong economy and the marriage-and-childbearing orientation produced the high point of the breadwinner-homemaker family. In addition, the federal government helped by financing low-interest mortgages for armed forces veterans, which allowed millions of families to purchase single-family homes in the growing suburbs. For the first time, the "American dream" of marriage, children, and a single-family home was within the reach of not only the middle class but also many in the working class (Laslett, 1973). Figure 2.2, compiled from Census data by Donald Hernandez, shows the rise—and decline—of the breadwinner-homemaker family from 1790 to 1989, from the perspective of children aged 0–17. As this graph makes clear, the breadwinner-homemaker family is not the "traditional" American family.

The figure divides all children into four groups. The first is the percentage who were living with neither parent, a small number at all times. The second is the percentage who were living in two-parent farm families. As noted earlier, farm families

[9]The relative-cohort-size theory was expounded by Easterlin (1980).

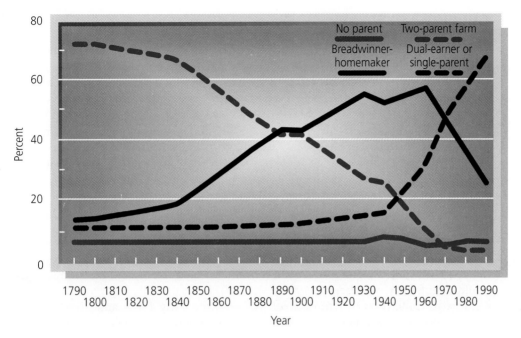

FIGURE 2.2
Percentage of children aged 0–17 living in each of four types of families, 1790–1989. (*Source:* Donald J. Hernandez, *America's Children: Resources from Family, Government, and the Economy,* New York: Russell Sage Foundation, 1993.)

do not fit the breadwinner-homemaker model because wives typically are involved in producing essential goods and services by tending livestock, growing vegetables, making clothing, helping with the harvest, and so forth. Note that living on a farm was the experience of a majority of children until the mid-1800s. The third group is the percentage living in breadwinner-homemaker families, defined here as two-parent, single-earner families not living on farms. This percentage was small early in the nation's history; it began to rise sharply in the mid-1800s, reached a temporary peak in 1930, fell briefly during the Depression, and then peaked again in 1960. The data show that this form was dominant only in the first half of the twentieth century and reached its zenith during the 1950s. After 1960, as the chart shows, its dominance ended.

The fourth group is nonfarm families that don't fit the breadwinner-homemaker mold, either because both parents work or because only one parent is present in the home. Only about 10 percent of children lived in these kinds of families before 1900, but after 1940, the percentage rose dramatically. By 1989, the last year in the chart, these families were by far the largest group, greatly exceeding the declining breadwinner-homemaker group. The reasons for the rise in single-parent and dual-earner families, and the consequences of this rise, will be discussed extensively in later chapters. Still, the breadwinner-homemaker family has not disappeared; in 1989, about one-fourth of all children lived in such a family.

Moreover, overlooked during the 1950s because of all the attention to the baby boom was a countercurrent that would loom large later in the century. An increasing number of married women went back to work outside the home after their children were of school age. They took jobs that had been typed as women's work, jobs that were relatively low paying but still required some education—secretary, nurse, salesclerk. As the service sector of the economy expanded, the demand for these pink-collar workers increased, and married women responded to the opportunities.

THE 1960s AND BEYOND

Just as social commentators confidently announced a return to large families, the roller-coaster car reached the top of its track and hurtled downward. The birthrate plunged from the heights of the baby boom to an all-time low in the 1970s and has risen only slightly since then. Women who were in their childbearing years in the 1970s and 1980s were likely to have an average of about 2.0 children.[10] The baby boom had begotten the baby bust. In addition, young women and men married at later and later ages; the age at which half of all first marriages occur increased by about four years for both women and men between the mid-1950s and the early 1990s (U.S. Bureau of the Census, 1992b). So the percentage of young adults who have never married, as Figure 2.1 shows, surpassed the levels of the early twentieth century. One might expect that, because they were marrying later, young adults also would have left home later. Yet the average age of leaving home did not increase much in the 1970s and 1980s. The reason is that more and more young adults were leaving home not to marry or even attend college but rather to live independently—to get a job, find an apartment, and be on their own (Goldscheider & Goldscheider, 1994).

Moreover, the divorce rate doubled between the early 1960s and the late 1970s and has declined just slightly since then. At current rates, about one in two marriages would end in divorce (Cherlin, 1992b). As at the beginning of the century, there is a great concern about the consequences of the high divorce rate. At the beginning of the century, optimists could at least argue that the marriage rate was increasing right along with the divorce rate; but that wasn't the case during the 1960s and 1970s. Young adults were postponing marrying, and divorced adults were postponing remarrying, although increases in **cohabitation**—the sharing of a household by unmarried persons who have a sexual relationship—accounted for some of this postponement (Bumpass, Sweet, & Cherlin, 1991).

There was one important continuity with the 1950s: Married women continued to work outside the home in ever larger numbers. Even women with preschool-aged children joined the workforce in large numbers. By the early 1990s, about two-thirds of all married women with school-aged children, and about 6 in 10 married women with preschool-aged children, were working outside the home. Whereas married women in the 1950s tended to drop out of the paid workforce when they were raising small children, married women today are much more likely to remain at their jobs throughout the childrearing years. This change in women's work lives has had a powerful effect on the family.

The most recent period in the history of the family—from about 1960 to the present—will be the main subject matter of this book. Future chapters will examine in detail the recent history of marriage, childbearing, divorce, cohabitation, and women's labor force participation in the United States and elsewhere in the Western nations as a prelude to understanding the present. In addition, these discussions will be informed by studies of non-Western countries, which can deepen our understanding of the nature of contemporary family patterns.

---

[10]Evans (1986). The figure cited is an estimate for women born in 1956, who have not yet completed their childbearing years.

SUMMARY

1. Family and kinship emerged as ways of ensuring the survival of human groups, which were organized as bands of hunter-gatherers until about 10,000 years ago. In societies where a tribe rules an area and there is no other government, family ties provide the structure that holds the society together, often through relationships among lineages. In the Western nations, the larger kinship groups have been weaker, and the smaller conjugal family has dominated.

2. Until the past 250 years or so, most Western families performed three basic activities: production, reproduction, and consumption. These kinds of families can be said to follow the familial mode of production. More recently, families have substituted working for wages and purchasing goods instead of directly producing what they need—a system that is called the labor market mode of production.

3. The colonial American family performed many activities that are now done mainly outside the family: educating children, providing vocational training, treating the seriously ill, and so forth. In contrast, the kind of privacy people today take for granted hardly existed. The family's affairs were, to a larger extent than today, viewed as public business. In the northern colonies, fathers dominated family life more than they would after the Revolution. Fathers, not mothers, were viewed as having the more important influence on children's upbringing.

4. Around the time of the Revolution, American family life began to change markedly. Between the Revolution and about 1830, a new kind of family emerged among the white middle class, one in which marriage was based on affection rather than authority and custom; the primary role of women became the care of children and the maintenance of the home; marriage was increasingly centered on children; and the number of children declined. Children came to be seen as needing continual affection and guidance, and mothers were thought better at providing it than fathers. Parents' influence over their children's marriage decisions and family lives seems to have declined. Commercial capitalism created opportunities for children to earn wages, thereby eroding the control parents had over their children's occupations. An increase in individualism, related to

the economic changes and to religious-based shifts in values, also seems to have occurred. The doctrine of separate spheres for women and men also emerged. One key to these changes was the movement of paid work to outside the home.

5. In the late 1800s, working-class families were more likely to combine elements of the older familial mode of production with newer, wage-oriented elements. Family members contributed to the common fund in several ways, such as wage earning by the husband and unmarried children, and taking in boarders or washing by the wife. Extended kinship ties became useful in finding jobs in newly industrialized cities.

6. As for African Americans, before the Civil War, slaves married and lived together for life, wherever possible, and knew and kept track of other kin. After the Civil War, there were some differences between African-American and white families: Rural black wives worked in the fields, and urban black wives worked for wages outside the home, more than white wives. Moreover, black mothers with children were more likely to be living without a male partner, although until recently the majority of black families with children consisted of two parents.

7. Early Mexican settlements in what later became the U.S. Southwest generally included a landowning elite and poorer, farmer-laborer settlers. Laborers sought the patronage of wealthier individuals for their children through the tradition of *compadrazgo*. After U.S. troops and immigrants seized the land, Mexicans became more of a working-class community and increasingly lived in *barrios*. A rising number of women headed households, in part because their husbands often worked as migratory farm workers. The descendants of the early settlers are far outnumbered by more recent immigrants. The strong male dominance in many Mexican-American immigrant families was eroded by unemployment, low wages, and the separations of migrant workers from their families.

8. Chinese and Japanese immigrants began to enter the United States in the 1800s. Initially, most Chinese immigrants were men, and few new families formed. Both Chinese and Japanese immigrants faced discrimination and prejudice; laws prevented them from marrying whites. The Chinese and Japanese families traditionally were patrilineal

and emphasized the authority of the father. Japanese families were interned in camps during World War II, an event that contributed to a loss of authority of parents over children. The 1965 Immigration Act eased restrictions on Asian immigration and has led to a great growth in the Asian population in the United States. The second largest Asian immigrant group today is Filipinos, nearly all of whom are descended from people who migrated to the United States in the twentieth century. Filipinos have a bilateral kinship structure that is more similar to the kinship system of Americans of European descent.

9. During the early decades of the twentieth century, the private family emerged. Rising standards of living allowed for greater attention to an emotionally satisfying private life, and the search for emotional satisfaction through family life became an even more important goal. The success of marriage came to be defined more in emotional terms than in material terms. There was much social concern about changes in family life, particularly the rise in divorce. Efforts to reduce the divorce rate through laws and regulations failed, demonstrating how difficult it is to decrease divorce through public policy. Demographic trends and greater prosperity produced the "empty nest" phase of family life as well as the beginning of a century-long increase in the number of people living alone. During the Depression years, economic hardships forced many adults to postpone marriage and defer having children.

10. In the 1950s, young adults married at earlier ages and the birthrate rose to a twentieth-century high. The baby boom was caused in part by the small cohort size and good economic fortune of the cohort that reached adulthood in the 1950s. In addition, a greater cultural emphasis on marriage and childbearing seems to have been present. The 1950s was the high point of the breadwinner-homemaker family, which was dominant only during the first half of the twentieth century. During the 1960s, the trends in marriages, divorces, and births all reversed: Age at marriage increased sharply, the divorce rate doubled, and the birthrate reached its lowest level. Moreover, married women were increasingly likely to work outside the home even when their children were young.

KEY TERMS

hunter-gatherers	Native American	*compadrazgo*
lineage	American Indian	*barrio*
patrilineage	familial mode of production	remittances
matrilineage	labor market mode of production	1965 Immigration Act
conjugal family	total fertility rate (TFR)	bilateral kinship
extended family	affective individualism	baby boom
stem family	bridewealth	birth cohort
polygyny	brideservice	cohabitation
polyandry	*mestizo*	

FAMILIES ON THE INTERNET

Although it's the most modern of media, the Internet is also a resource for historians. For instance, the Library of Congress maintains a site entitled "American Life Histories: Manuscripts from the Federal Writers' Project, 1936–1940." During the Great Depression, the government employed over 300 writers to gather life histories from 2,900 people in 24 states. You can view these documents and search them by keywords such as marriage, divorce, and children (**Lcweb2.loc.gov/wpaintro/wpahome.html**). The University of Rochester has placed on-line several monthly issues of *Godey's Lady's Book* from 1850, one of the most popular magazines of the nineteenth century. You can view articles, poems, and engravings (**www.history.rochester.edu/godeys/**). The Women's Studies Section of the Association of College and Research Libraries maintains a list of women's history sites (**www.utep.edu/library/acrlwss/history.html**).

CHAPTER 3

Gender and Families

THE *BERDACHE*

In 1841, the American traveler and artist George Catlin published his monumental *Manners, Customs, and Conditions of the North American Indians.* The result of his eight years of traveling among Native Americans in the West, it included about 300 engravings. One of them, entitled "Dance to the Berdache," is shown in Figure 3.1. It depicts warriors of the Sauk and Fox Indians dancing around a man wearing women's clothing. "For the extraordinary privileges he is known to possess," wrote Catlin of the man, "he is . . . looked upon as medicine and sacred, and a feast is given to him annually." Men like him, who dressed like women, performed women's occupations, and behaved like women, were called **berdaches** by French colonists. They existed in more than 100 Native American

FIGURE 3.1 George Catlin's "Dance to the Berdache," from Catlin's *Manners, Customs, and Conditions of the North American Indians,* 1841. Original sketch at the National Museum of American Art, Smithsonian Institution, Washington, D.C.

cultures (Callendar & Kochems, 1983).[1] In a smaller number of these cultures, female *berdaches,* who dressed and worked like men, were also found.

Most individuals became *berdaches* in one of two ways. First, some children displayed what their parents thought were *berdache*-like characteristics. Parents in some of the Native American cultures might develop a male child as a *berdache* if he showed "a gentle, androgynous [having characteristics of both sexes] nature" and showed great interest in the work of the other sex (Williams, 1986). Second, some men and women experienced spiritual visions at adolescence, or even later, that they took as signs to become *berdaches.* These visions usually involved some supernatural intervention, such as instructions from the female moon deity. *Berdaches* were generally accepted members of adult society; anthropologists report that attitudes toward them "varied from awe and reverence through indifference to scorn and contempt" (Callendar & Kochems, 1983). In many cultures they were credited with supernatural powers and exceptional skill at carrying out the other sex's work. The dance at the annual feast that Catlin sketched indicated that the Sauk and Fox respected the powers of the *berdache.* As neither ordinary men nor ordinary women, *berdaches* were able to undertake special tasks that women and men could not perform as easily, such as negotiating a marriage bargain between a woman's family and a man's family or settling a dispute between a man and a woman.

In many cultures, a *berdache* could marry a person of the same sex who was not a *berdache.* It appears that male *berdaches* typically engaged in homosexual intercourse and that the sexual relations of married female *berdaches* were lesbian. But many *berdaches* also had heterosexual relations; the Navaho, for example, permitted male *berdaches* any form of sexual intercourse with either sex (Callendar & Kochems, 1983). Moreover, a male *berdache* could renounce his role and return to being an ordinary

[1]According to a commentary by Sue-Ellen Jacobs appended to this article, the word *berdache* came from the Arabic *bardaj,* which in turn came from the Persian *bardah,* meaning "kept boy" or "male prostitute." This term represented the colonists' preconceptions and was inappropriate; nevertheless, it became common usage.

male. By some accounts, non-*berdache* males could have sex with a *berdache* without being considered primarily homosexual.[2]

Female *berdaches,* who were less common, were found in Native American cultures that had relatively egalitarian relationships between men and women and in which women owned and distributed the goods they produced. But in cultures with strong lineages, they were very rare. For instance, in matrilineal cultures, the children of a man's sister remained in his lineage under his control. Under these circumstances, females of reproductive age were too valuable to the men of the lineage to be allowed to take on the *berdache* role. But in less hierarchical cultures, some women could take on a male role without threatening the male social order (Blackwood, 1984). Put simply, female *berdaches* were more likely to be found in societies where men had less control over women.

As the influence of European culture on Native Americans grew during the nineteenth century, the number of *berdaches* declined rapidly; there were very few by the end of the century. Nevertheless, the story of the *berdaches* can help us begin to answer some important questions that will be addressed in this chapter.

1 *What is the difference between sex and gender?*   The social situation of the berdaches illustrates the distinction sociologists make between sex and gender. In most sociological writing, **sex** refers to the biological characteristics that distinguish women and men: sex chromosomes, reproductive organs, sex-specific hormones, and physical characteristics (Richardson, 1977). It is true that a very small number of people are born with ambiguous sex characteristics, but for the vast majority there is a clear sexual identification as either woman or man. **Gender,** in most sociological writing, refers to the social and cultural characteristics that distinguish women and men (Richardson, 1977). In our society, such characteristics include the different clothing that men and women wear or the expectation that boys shouldn't cry when they are hurt. Gender is said to be a social creation; sex is said to be a biological creation.

The distinction between sex and gender will be useful in examining many of the topics in this book. Nevertheless, it is occasionally more difficult to draw a line separating them than this definition at first suggests. For example, the literature on the *berdaches* indicates that parents sometimes perceived qualities in their young sons that were more typical of daughters and then raised them as *berdaches.* If sexual orientation is partly biologically determined, as evidence suggests (see Chapter 7), these parents may have recognized predispositions in their sons toward a homosexual orientation. Indeed, some students of the *berdaches* phenomenon have advanced this interpretation. Walter Williams wrote:

> Indian societies constructed an alternative gender and put their emphasis on the berdache's *character and social role rather than on only sexual behavior. This is certainly a social construction. . . . Yet, the* berdache *does have an identity, which seems much more a reflection of the individual's innate character* (Williams, 1986).

If correct, this view implies that the gender parents chose for their sons—*berdaches*—was socially assigned on the basis, in part, of innate, biological characteristics. In other words, a *berdache*'s gender was influenced by both culture and biology. In some real-world situations, it may not be possible to separate sex and gender as neatly as sociologists maintain.

[2]See the interpretation in Williams (1986).

2 *How many genders are there?*   The story of the *berdaches* shows us that gender need not be neatly mapped onto two sexes. Just what gender were the *berdaches?* Did a male *berdache* who dressed, acted, and married like a woman take on the female gender? Not quite, for he could not give birth, often had greater physical strength, was sometimes taken along on hunts, and differed in other ways (Williams, 1986). Rather, it appears that the *berdaches* occupied an intermediate position between male and female—a third gender of sorts. He was called not a "man" or a "woman" but rather a "halfman-halfwoman" or a "man-woman" or a "would-be-woman." Reflecting this mixture, the Zuni buried male *berdaches* in women's dress but men's trousers on the men's side of the graveyard (Callendar & Kochems, 1983).

In its blurring of the difference between male and female, its status as an in-between gender, the *berdache* demonstrates how gender categories are created by society and culture. Yet it is also clear that the existence of a third, *berdache*-like gender category is unusual; there are only a few non-Western examples[3] and in the Western nations, there seems to be no status like it. Recently, however, a number of adults who were born with ambiguous sexual organs have formed an organization in the United States, calling themselves **intersexuals** (Cowley, 1997). Most had surgery as children and long-term treatments with sex hormones to make their genitals and secondary sex characteristics more like those of males or females (see below). Their platform is to convince doctors and parents not to do so-called sex reassignment until the individuals are old enough to make informed choices.

Still, even though the *berdaches* story and the emergence of intersexual activists shows that female versus male is not the only way to make gender distinctions, the overwhelming predominance of the two-gender model suggests that it is the typical manner in which people have made sense out of sex. Consequently, the assumption throughout most of this chapter will be that there are two genders.

3 *Can a person's gender identity be modified?*   Native American men in some tribes were allowed to become *berdaches* in adolescence or even later if a supernatural event guided them to do so. And they were subsequently allowed to leave the status and return to the male gender. So it is clear that under some cultural circumstances, gender identity can be established after middle childhood and can be modified in adulthood. Yet even in this extraordinary case, the modification is not from male to female but rather from male to an in-between third gender. Research shows that most children develop a gender identity during their preschool years, that this identity is reinforced during middle childhood and adolescence, that it becomes a central part of their self-definition, and that it is altered in only a handful of exceptional cases.

A recent report illustrates how difficult it can be to completely override biological predispositions toward being a woman or man. While an infant, a boy had his penis accidently cut off during surgery. His parents accepted the recommendation of the doctors that he undergo further surgery to feminize his genitals and that he be raised as a girl. Early medical reports indicated that the child was behaving in appropriately feminine ways, and the case was widely cited as showing that gender identity can be socially assigned (Money & Tucker, 1975). However, a thirty-year follow up revealed a different story (Diamond & Sigmundson, 1997). The individual rebelled continually as a child against the clothing and play styles that were suggested to him and, as an

[3]See Nanda (1990).

adolescent, refused to be a girl. After being informed of his history, he elected to have further surgery and hormone treatments in order to masculinize himself physically. He subsequently lived as a man and has since married. In an editorial accompanying the medical journal report on the case, a physician writes, "the organ that appears to be critical to psychosexual development and adaptation is not the external genitalia, but the brain" (Reiner, 1997, p. 225). And it appears that the brain forms a gender identity in response to both biological and social cues.

4 *How much do gender differences reflect men's attempts to retain power over women?* We have learned that male *berdaches* were allowed in many Native American cultures throughout Western North America, but female *berdaches* were more restricted. Women had the freedom to modify their gender only in cultures where they had substantial resources relative to men and in cultures where the power of male-dominated lineages was weaker. In cultures where men had greater control over women, they blocked women's moves toward male roles. Are similar forces still operating today? As a social creation, notions of gender are likely to reflect the existing power relationships in a society. In fact, some scholars would restrict the definition of gender to sex-linked characteristics that reflect male power over women or would even argue more broadly that all gender differences reflect male power (Scott, 1986). Others would argue for a looser connection between gender and power. The connection between gender differences and male domination will be examined later in this chapter.

Overall, the story of the *berdaches* shows a flexibility and variability of gender that is unusual. Yet even in this unusual instance, as well as in the current controversy about sex reassignment, we can see evidence that both cultural norms and biological predispositions may influence a person's gender identity; that a shift in gender identity from male to female or vice versa rarely occurs; and that gender differences can be influenced by the degree of power men have over women in a society. Although the *berdaches* and the intersexuals show that alternative ways of organizing the culture and biology of sex and gender are possible, their rarity underscores how widespread is the familiar two-sex, two-gender model that we take for granted. Nevertheless, it can lead us to pose questions about the relationships among gender and family life in contemporary societies today.

The distinction between women and men, female and male, is basic to the study of the family because of the sharp differentiation, in nearly all societies, between what women and men do in families. Exactly what they do differs from society to society, but, almost universally, they tend to do different things. To understand families, you must understand gender. To understand gender, you must begin in childhood, for it is then that the paths of male and female begin to diverge. The origins and consequences of gender differences in childhood, and their maintenance in adulthood through social interaction and male domination, constitute the subject of this chapter. (A more general examination of how parents raise their children will be the subject of Chapter 14.)

THE CHILDHOOD CONSTRUCTION OF GENDER

Sociologists have borrowed the concept of roles from the theater, and they often write about the social roles people play. A **social role** is a pattern of behaviors associated with a position in society (e.g., parent, teacher, supervisor, elected official).

The term **gender roles** can be defined as the different sets of behaviors that are commonly exhibited by women and men. Gender roles usually occur in pairs, one for each gender. For example, in many marriages during the first half of the twentieth century, men tended to play the gender role of "breadwinner," the person who earns all the income for his family, whereas women tended to play the role of "homemaker," the person who specializes in caring for her children and housekeeping. Many sociologists define gender roles as entirely socially created, although a minority allow for biological influences, as will be discussed later. For example, in a book on gender roles, Jean Lipman-Blumen summarizes her view:

> *The family, and even gender roles, are social inventions, according to this perspective. More specifically, society magnifies biological sexual differences into artificially dichotomous gender roles. . . . These differences lead to the sexual division of labor, whose strict enforcement fosters the mutual, if unequal, dependence of men and women* (Lipman-Blumen, 1984).

Moreover, the division of labor reflects men's interests more than women's:

> *Some observers have noted that the current structure of the sex-gender system represents a centuries-old power relationship—often a power struggle—that persists despite the erosion of its original social bases* (Lipman-Blumen, 1984).

This power relationship will be discussed later in the chapter.

PARENTAL SOCIALIZATION

Researchers in the mainstream sociological tradition exemplified by Lipman-Blumen have argued that people first acquire gender roles through socialization in childhood. **Socialization**, according to the definition in one widely cited book, is "the process by which we learn the ways of a given society or social group so that we can function within it" (Elkin & Handel, 1984). It is how individuals learn to take on attitudes and behaviors that are considered culturally appropriate for them. The emphasis in the **socialization approach** to gender differences is on conscious, social learning: Children are rewarded for behavior adults think is appropriate for their gender and admonished or punished for behavior that parents don't think appropriate. By watching parents, teachers, television actors, and others, children learn the behavior of both genders, but they soon learn that they will be rewarded for one set of behaviors and not for the other (Mischel, 1966). For example, although at first little boys cry as much as little girls, they are admonished not to, and men cry less often than women. Lipman-Blumen reminds us that in 1972, Senator Edmund Muskie of Maine, running for the Democratic nomination for president in the New Hampshire primary election, was widely perceived to have suffered a major blow when his eyes teared while denouncing a newspaper's criticism of his wife (Lipman-Blumen, 1984). (Muskie did worse than expected in the primary and did not win the nomination.) More generally, men are expected to be aggressive, competitive, and independent, whereas women are expected to be less aggressive, more nurturing to children and adults, and better at enabling and maintaining personal relationships.

Parents, it has been argued in a large number of studies, act differently toward boys than toward girls from birth onward. In the first 24 hours after birth, according to one study, parents described boys as more alert, stronger, and firmer and girls as less attentive, weaker, and more fragile—even though there were no differences

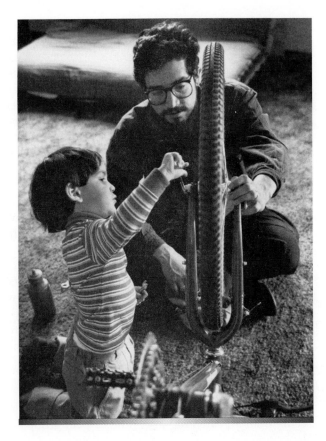

Children learn gendered behavior, such as how to use tools to fix a bicycle, in part from their parents.

between them according to tests and observations (Rubin, Provenzano, & Luria, 1974). Other studies show that parents react more to boys; they give both more positive feedback and more negative feedback. Parents, it is said, also hold boys more and give them more freedom to explore. They offer boys toys such as blocks and tools, which allow for invention and manipulation, whereas girls are offered toys such as dolls, which encourage imitation. When fathers play with their sons, they often engage in a rough-and-tumble style of play, but when they play with their daughters, they often do stereotypically female activities such as play with a tea set (Jacklin, 1984). Often with little conscious awareness, it is argued, parents teach girls different ways of behaving than they teach boys. At an early age, children, for their part, develop stereotypical conceptions of both genders, and they use these conceptions to organize their knowledge and behavior (Bem, 1981).

THE MEDIA

Nor is gender socialization confined to parents; children learn lessons from books and television, among other sources. As recently as the 1960s, schools made little effort to balance the gender content of the books children were assigned. Publishers produced stories and histories that mainly focused on boys and men. Then, spurred by the feminist movement, school systems began to demand more-balanced literature. Today, in most children's books, girls and boys receive much more equal treatment. For instance, a 1972 study of books for elementary school reading classes found that boy-centered stories outnumbered girl-centered stories by a ratio of 5 to 2 and adult male characters outnumbered adult female characters by 3 to 1. A similar study conducted in 1989 showed "much more egalitarianism" (Purcell & Stewart, 1990). Girls appeared just as often as boys and were portrayed in a wider range of activities than in 1972. Women appeared more often than in 1972, but still not as often as men. Two-thirds of the photographs still featured male characters. Studies such as these suggest that substantial progress has been made in presenting gender-balanced portrayals in children's books, although differences remain.

Over the past few decades, however, books have lost ground relative to television (and to educational computer software) as a source of information for children about the world around them. A study conducted in 1986 and 1987 found that children aged 2 to 5 watched an average of nearly $3^1/_2$ hours per day of television and 6- to 11-year-olds watched an average of 3 hours per day (Elkin and Handel, 1989). At least through the early 1980s, studies have shown that more of the characters in children's programming are male than female and that the characters by and large undertake gender-stereotyped activities (Barcus, 1983). Moreover, the newer cable channels watched by children and adolescents also show gender imbalances. A 1990 study of randomly selected music videos on Music Television (MTV) found that men appeared twice as often as women and engaged in significantly more aggressive and dominant behavior. Women were shown engaging in more implicitly sexual and subservient behavior and more often were objects of sexual advances (Sommers-Flanagan, Sommers-Flanagan, & Davis, 1993).

EARLY PEER GROUPS

Other researchers argue that much of the development of gender-specific behavior occurs from an early age in children's **peer groups**—similar-age children who play or perform other activities together. Between the ages of two and three, children begin to sort themselves into same-sex peer groups. Psychologist Eleanor Maccoby argues that these same-sex peer groups strongly influence the distinctive behavior patterns of boys and girls (Maccoby, 1998). Upon observing pairs of children who were, on average, 33 months old, Maccoby and her colleagues found that they were far more likely to show social behavior—offering or grabbing a toy, hugging or pushing, vocally greeting or protesting, and so forth—to children of the same sex than to children of the opposite sex. When girls were paired with other girls, they were just as active as were boys paired with boys; but when girls were paired with boys, they frequently stood back and let the boys monopolize the toys. The observers suggest that the rough-and-tumble play style and focus on competition and dominance among boys are unattractive to girls. Moreover, they argue, girls find it difficult to influence boys—between ages three and five, girls increasingly attempt to influence other children by making polite suggestions, whereas boys increasingly make direct demands (Serbin, Sprafkin, & Doyle, 1984).

In another study, five- and six-year-olds were observed playing in groups of four. An adult woman sat at one end of the playroom, then shifted to the other end of the room halfway through the session. When the groups were composed of all boys or all girls, they changed positions to remain equally distant from the adult before and after she shifted seats. In fact, all-girl groups moved farther away from the adult than all-boy groups. But in mixed-sex groups the girls tended to stay close to the adult and to move with her, whereas the boys did not—as if the girls thought the adult might moderate the rough, assertive play style of the boys (Greeno, 1989).

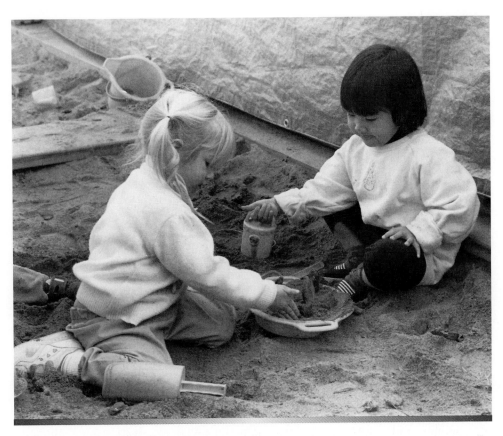

Young children, such as these three-year-olds at a childcare center, play together in peer groups, where they may learn gender-specific behavior.

Maccoby suggests that boys' peer groups reinforce a competitive, dominance-oriented interaction style that carries over into such adult male communication tactics as interrupting, boasting, contradicting, and threatening tactics that restrict conversation. Girls' groups, she suggests, reinforce a different style that carries over into adult female communication. Through expressing agreement or support, asking questions rather than making statements, and acknowledging other persons' comments, this style enables interactions to continue rather than restricting them. These styles, Maccoby asserts, may influence adult, mixed-sex interactions in school, at the office, and in families. Maccoby suggests that the ubiquitous same-sex peer groups emerge so early that both parental influence and biological predispositions may shape them (Maccoby, 1990).

CHILDREN'S PREFERENCES

The picture that emerges from this literature is of a barrage of messages, first from parents and then from peers, the media, and schools, that teach boys and girls different gender roles (Block, 1984).[4] Yet several studies suggest that these influences, although centrally important, are not the whole story of early differences between girls and boys. Consider children's preferences for toys. Before their second birthday,

---

[4]The major exception in this literature is an overview by Eleanor Maccoby and Carol Jacklin (1974) which concluded that the extent of the differences in the way parents treat girls and boys had been exaggerated, as had the differences in girls' and boys' behavior.

boys and girls begin to choose different kinds of toys. In one British study, two groups of children, 12 to 15 months old and 19 to 24 months old, respectively, were observed playing at home (Smith & Daglish, 1977). In both groups, boys played much more with cars and trucks, whereas girls played much more with soft toys and dolls. Boys also engaged in more active play and more forbidden play, such as climbing on furniture or attempting to touch wall plugs.

Many sociologists would say that even by this young age, children's activities are influenced by their parents' beliefs about what kinds of play boys and girls should be engaged in. Indeed, Lenore Weitzman writes:

> *From the minute a newborn baby girl is wrapped in a pink blanket and her brother in a blue one, the two children are treated differently. The difference starts with the subtle tones of voice adults use in cooing over the two cradles, and it continues with the father's mock wrestling with his baby boy and gentler play with his "fragile" daughter* (Weitzman, 1979, p. 1).

The authors of the British study did ask the parents what kinds of play they thought appropriate for girls and boys. They found, not surprisingly, that some parents held strongly stereotypical views—boys should play with trucks, girls with dolls, and so forth. But the views of the parents had no effect on the activities of their children. That is, sons of parents who didn't feel strongly that boys should play with trucks were just as likely to play with trucks as were the sons of parents who did feel strongly that boys should play with trucks. Daughters of parents who didn't hold strong stereotypes were just as likely to play with dolls as were daughters of parents who held strong stereotypes. The young children's preferences seemed to evolve independently of their parents' preferences.

In another study, children aged 21 to 40 months were observed playing and were also given a test to see if they could discriminate between genders: They were shown pictures of children and adults in stereotypically male or female activities and were asked whether the person in the picture was a boy or girl (or man or woman) (Fagot, Leinbach, & Hagan, 1986).[5] Overall, boys engaged in more aggressive behavior (hitting, pushing, shoving, taking objects, yelling, calling names) and were more likely to play with blocks, tools, cars, and trucks. Girls were less aggressive and somewhat more likely to play with dolls, dance, or dress up. Were these children already doing what they thought was appropriate for their own gender? Not so for the boys: Those who couldn't tell the genders of the people in the pictures were just as aggressive and just as likely to play with stereotypically male toys as were those who "passed" the gender test. The way they behaved seemed unaffected by their knowledge of what activities boys and girls are "supposed" to do. This finding suggests that the boys' greater aggressive behavior may have a biological basis, although it's also possible that they already had been socialized to be aggressive. For girls, however, the gender recognition test made a difference. Even girls who "failed" the test were less aggressive than boys and played with stereotypically female toys more than boys. Yet girls who "passed" the test showed a further drop in aggression—in fact, they showed virtually no aggressive behavior. Girls' responses suggest the possibility of both a biological predisposition toward less aggressive behavior and a conformity to social expectations about how they are supposed to behave.

---

[5]On toy preferences preceding gender recognition, see also Weinraub, Clemens, Sockloff, Ethridge, Gracely, and Myers (1984).

HORMONAL INFLUENCES

Some studies also suggest that the hormone levels that children were exposed to prior to birth can affect gender-typed behavior, although the authors tend to agree that socialization is also a powerful predictor of these behaviors. During the second trimester of pregnancy, male fetuses begin to produce male sex hormones, which cause the genitals to take on the male form and influence brain organization. Studies of girls who had been exposed to abnormally high levels of male sex hormones while in their mother's wombs have found that these girls showed higher levels of interest in strenuous physical activity—climbing trees, biking, playing football—and lower levels of doll play and infant care than did girls with normal hormonal histories. Similarly, boys who had been exposed to abnormally high levels of female sex hormones showed lower levels of physical activity and more doll play and infant care than boys with normal hormonal histories. These findings suggest that prenatal (before birth) hormone levels may influence behavior in ways consistent with gender stereotypes (Ehrhardt, 1985).

Further support for this thesis comes from a recently completed 30-year study of mothers who gave birth between 1960 and 1963 and their daughters, in California. Blood samples were taken from the mothers-to-be during each trimester of pregnancy and stored. In 1990, these blood samples were tested for levels of male and female sex hormones, both of which are normally present in women's blood. In addition, the daughters, who were by then aged 27 to 30, were interviewed. Their sex-hormone levels were measured, and they were asked a detailed series of questions about gender-typed behaviors and values, such as the importance of a career and of marriage; the number of gender-typed activities they engaged in; whether they liked caring for babies; and the number of births they had had. The responses to all these indicators were combined into a single measure of "gendered behavior." The authors found that the higher the level of male sex hormones in the mothers' blood in the second trimester, the more masculine was the gendered behavior of their daughters 27 to 30 years later, even after adjusting for the level of male sex hormones in the daughters' own blood. Still, no claim was made that hormone levels fully determined the daughters' behaviors; on the contrary, the authors note that the hormone levels of the mothers and daughters accounted for about one-fourth of the variation in gendered behavior. Social and cultural influences could have accounted for most of the other three-fourths of the variation (Udry, Morris, & Kovenock, 1995).

In addition, the authors asked the daughters whether, when they were children, their mothers had encouraged them to behave in stereotypically feminine ways (such as wearing dresses or taking an interest in sewing) and masculine ways (such as defending oneself physically or repairing things around the house). The standard parental socialization model would predict that daughters whose mothers had encouraged feminine behavior would act in more feminine ways as adults. In general, that is what the authors found; however, they also found that the higher the level of male sex hormones in the mothers' blood, the weaker was the effect of mothers' encouragement on their daughters' behavior (Udry, 1997). In other words, the study suggests that daughters who are exposed to higher levels of male sex hormones before birth are less receptive to suggestions that they behave in feminine ways and that daughters exposed to lower levels are more receptive. It may be that people's biologically derived predispositions and their social experiences work in combination to produce gendered behavior.

CULTURE AND BIOLOGY

In sum, studies of young children's preferences and activities suggest numerous influences on the different behaviors of girls and boys. Society's expectations about how to behave are transmitted to children through channels such as parents, books, television, and peer groups. In these ways, cultural differences between women and men are reproduced in the next generation. These differences are visible only on average; that is to say, a group of women will appear different from a group of men, even though some women will be more aggressive, say, than some men. Sociologists have clearly documented this cultural transmission of gender differences. Yet the evidence also suggests that children may have innate predispositions that affect gender differences in behavior. These predispositions appear to be stronger for boys than for girls. Boys seem to prefer blocks, trucks, and rough play regardless of how much their parents think that boys should play this way. Boys' toy preferences appear earlier than, and are more pronounced than, girls' preferences. The influences of same-sex peer groups may reflect both socialization and biological predispositions.

If biologically based gender differences exist, how might they have emerged? Sociologists who advocate what has been called the **biosocial approach** to human behavior (Rossi, 1977, 1984)—which views behavior as a composite of biological and cultural influences—apply the Darwinian evolutionary model discussed in Chapter 1. That is, like the evolutionary psychologists, they believe that women and men may have evolved different strategies for reproductive success. They note that the vast majority of the evolutionary past of humans was spent in hunter-gatherer societies (see Chapter 2). These societies evolved a system in which infants were born relatively immature and needed prolonged care to develop. In hunter-gatherer societies, women provided this care and gathered food, and men hunted and defended the group's territory. Evolutionary biology suggests that women may have evolved a greater capacity for the care of young children and men may have evolved a greater capacity for aggressive territorial behavior.

It is, however, a leap from forest dwellers to city dwellers, from mothers carrying children while gathering edible plants to parents placing children in day care centers while gathering spendable wages. To what extent evolutionary biology still is relevant is not clear. Many sociologists are reluctant to concede it any role, in part because social norms and behaviors are what they are trained to study. Some are also reluctant because biological explanations have been used in the past to deny equal opportunities to women. For instance, some doctors in the 1800s opposed higher education for women on the grounds that too much intellectual stimulation would diminish their ability to have babies (Freedman, 1990). Social scientists who advocate greater equality for women fear that biological explanations will again be used against their cause. Yet most social scientists who do believe that biology plays a role in shaping gender differences in behavior also believe that culture plays a crucially important role. Historian Carl Degler (1990) wrote:

> *What social scientists who are interested in the biological roots of our actions are asserting is that our evolutionary past, like our cultural past, continues to influence us. Yet neither past is so controlling that we cannot seek ways to alter or modify its influences* (p. 43).

Moreover, even if there are biological influences, these would not prevent boys and girls from acting in nonstereotyped ways. Biological models, like cultural models, predict that although men's and women's behavior will differ on average, both genders will show a wide range of behavior, with much overlap (Udry, 1994). Biological predispositions would operate to raise or lower thresholds that make a behavior more or less likely. As noted, male fetuses are exposed to a higher level of male sex hormones (androgens) and female fetuses are exposed to a higher level of female sex hormones (estrogens). Two authors who believe that this hormonal difference affects behavior wrote:

> *More androgen prenatally means that it takes* less *stimulus to evoke your response as far as strenuous physical activity or challenging your peers is concerned, and* more *stimulus to evoke your response to the helpless young, than would otherwise be the case.* How *you respond once you're over the threshold depends on many things—your age, health, strength, physical development, cultural heritage, gender schemas, environment, training, and experience—but not simply on your prenatal sex hormone exposure. . . . What the prenatal sex hormone mix did not do was to preordain sexual differences in you in an immutable formula that would either equip you or bar you from strenuous physical activity, dominance behavior, or parental behavior* (Money & Tucker, 1975, pp. 78 and 81).

THE PSYCHOANALYTIC PERSPECTIVE

There is another perspective on the reproduction of gender differences that has been developed by social scientists who, on the one hand, don't think biology has much effect, yet, on the other hand, are puzzled by the tenacity of the worldviews acquired in childhood and surprised by how hard it is to change them. For instance, Lillian Rubin writes:

> *Until recently I believed that we needed only to understand . . . socialization to explain stereotypic gender behavior. But more than a decade of watching women and men struggle to change—often with only limited success—has convinced me that there are differences between us that are not* simply *a product of role learning and socialization practices. . . . "Why?" I kept asking myself. "There must be something else necessary to explain the dogged persistence with which these ways of being resist our best efforts to change."*

Otherwise, Rubin reasoned, it wouldn't be so difficult to unlearn old ways of behaving even when we are intent on doing so.

> *The answer, I now believe, lies in some deep-seated psychological differences between women and men—differences, I hasten to add, that are not born in nature but are themselves a product of the social organization of the family* (Rubin, 1983, p. 40).

The answer that Rubin favors is derived from psychoanalytic theory. Its foremost proponent in sociology is Nancy Chodorow, who draws upon it to explain why women do the mothering in nearly all societies (Chodorow, 1978).

The **psychoanalytic approach** to gender differences is based on the psychoanalytic theory of children's development that was first put forth by Austrian psychiatrist Sigmund Freud at the turn of the twentieth century. Freud argued that children become like their same-sex parent by internalizing—unconsciously incorporating—a representation of that parent into their own personalities. So Freud's theory is about unconscious mental processes, whereas the socialization approach is about conscious processes. And whereas the central mechanism of the socialization approach is learning, the corresponding mechanism in psycho-analytic theory is internalization. We become like a parent through a process that is beyond our conscious control and not evident to us at the time.

The version of psychoanalytic theory borrowed by Chodorow asserts that the first several years of life are crucial to a person's development of a gender identity and a sense of self (Chodorow, 1978). After birth, it is said, the infant unconsciously experiences itself as merged and continuous with its first caretaker—who is almost always a woman. The young child, whether girl or boy, becomes deeply attached to the all-encompassing, comforting female figure and internalizes her image. There soon comes a time in boys' lives, however, when they realize they must establish their gender identities as males. To do so, they must transfer their attachment and identity from their mothers to their fathers (or to other males, if the father is not present). This is said to be a traumatic break for boys, who must do the difficult work of distancing themselves from their mothers. Consequently, the theorists argue, boys build psychological barriers between themselves and their mothers; they put fences around their gender identities—or, in the psychoanalytic language, they create rigid ego boundaries as a way of protecting their emerging identities. Girls, on the other hand, need not distance themselves from their mothers in order to establish their gender identities. They remain connected to their first attachment in life, and they have a longer, more continuous period of attachment as they come to identify themselves as female.

As a result, Chodorow writes, "The basic feminine sense of self is connected to the world, the basic masculine sense of self is separate" (Chodorow, 1978, p. 169). Boys and men, she asserts, establish more rigid emotional boundaries between themselves and others; women, on the other hand, have more permeable boundaries. Therefore, Chodorow and others argue, women have more empathy, which my dictionary defines as "identification with and understanding of another's situation, feelings, and motives" (Copyright 1997 © by Houghton Mifflin Company. Reproduced by permission from *The American Heritage College Dictionary, Third Edition*.). Put differently, they are said to have a greater capacity for relating to others and an easier time establishing close relationships. And because they value so highly the connectedness they experienced with their mothers, according to Chodorow, women *want* to have children and mother them so that they can re-create that fundamental attachment. They are also better at relating to infants, on average, than men because of their greater ability to respond to a small being who cannot verbally express its needs.

And so, argues Chodorow, women mother because they were mothered by women themselves and in the process developed a sense of self that makes them want to be mothers and also makes them better at it. If we wish to change this situation, she concludes, then we must make a concerted effort to involve men in the parenting of young children on an equal basis with women; anything less will not work. This psychoanalytic model implies that girls grow up to become mothers not so much because of the kinds of toys they are given, as the socialization perspective would have it, but because of *who* gives them the toys—their primary caretakers, their mothers.

The psychoanalytic approach has been criticized for its reliance on clinical case histories.[6] Individuals who seek psychotherapy are likely to be more troubled, on average, than other people. Psychoanalytic theorists claim, nevertheless, that the difficulties of their patients reflect differences in the population, albeit in exaggerated form. They argue that the deep insight that can be obtained from case histories far

---

[6]This section draws from a review symposium in the journal *Signs* on Chodorow's book (Lorber et al., 1981).

exceeds that which can be obtained from mere observation or large-scale sample surveys. Other critics also have charged that Chodorow overestimates how much change is possible in parenting roles if her model is true. Judith Lorber asks about Chodorow's proposed solution that men and women share primary parenting:

> If most men have developed nonaffective [low on emotion] personalities and strong ego boundaries, where are you going to find enough men with psychological capabilities to parent well and thus break the general pattern of the emotional primacy of the mother? (Lorber et al., 1981, p. 485)

Her critics, then, believe that Chodorow's system may be more resistant to change than she thinks.

THE CONTINUAL CONSTRUCTION OF GENDER

Recently, much sociological research and writing on the construction of gender differences has focused not on socialization or predispositions in early childhood but rather on the continual construction and maintenance of gender differences throughout childhood and adulthood. Criticizing the use of standard role theory, some scholars have argued that the concept of gender as a role should be dropped (Ferree, 1990). The rejection of the language of roles is in part a reaction to the 1950s structural-functionalist position that there are two natural roles which provide the best basis for a family: breadwinner (instrumental leader) and home-maker (expressive leader). Critics charge that the functionalists created the false impression that the breadwinner-homemaker division of labor was inevitable; that they also erred in implying that the two roles shared power equally; and that they ignored historical variation (Thorne, 1992).[7] The critics of role theory also argued that gender is a master identity, far too broad to be considered just one of life's roles (West & Zimmerman, 1987). A person's gender identity is so fundamental that others are intensely uncomfortable unless they can determine what it is. In addition, I think the attack on the use of role theory arose in the 1980s because research on early socialization for gender roles offered a distressing view for those who wished to change gender roles. As was just discussed, this body of research suggested that gender roles emerge at an early age through an elaborate system that may include differential rewards and opportunities, differing biological predispositions, and unconscious psychoanalytic processes. Such a powerful mixture might make later modification difficult. A theoretical framework that viewed gender identities as more fragile, more fluid, less determined in childhood, and more in need of continual support would be more congenial to change.

DOING GENDER

To develop such a framework, which is known as the **interactionist approach,** a group of sociologists hearkened back to symbolic interaction theory, which was described briefly in Chapter 1 (Blumer, 1962). How, we might ask, do a wife and husband come to understand that she should do most of the housework? From the socialization research in the previous section, we might conclude that doing the

---

[7]Yet by the 1980s, the functionalism of the 1950s was in full retreat and few writers used the term "role" in the strict functionalist sense; see Komarovsky (1992).

housework is part of the gender role that women learn beginning with the dolls and teacups they are given in childhood and the praise they get for helping their mothers wash the dishes.

The symbolic interactionists, while not denying that socialization occurs, emphasize that gender distinctions, such as who does the housework, get reproduced again and again in daily life. For example, a woman who was asked "What household work does your husband do?" in a study conducted by Sarah Fenstermaker Berk (1985) replied:

> *He tries to be helpful. He tries. He's a brilliant and successful lawyer. It's incredible how he smiles after he sponges off the table and there are still crumbs all over* (p. 206).

Here the husband's smile—the symbol—indicates to his wife that he is incapable of sponging all the crumbs off the table, despite having enough brains to be a brilliant and successful lawyer. It is a way for the husband to express a feigned helplessness, which he and his wife both interpret as meaning that she's the only one who can do a good job of cleaning up after dinner. Daily scenes such as these, Berk and others argue, not only produce clean tables, they also produce—and reproduce—gender distinctions as well. The interactionist approach focuses on people's actions in concrete situations such as this one in order to see how social meanings—in this case the shared understanding of who should do housework—are produced.

Implicit in this interactionist view is the premise that gender distinctions are fragile enough that they need to be reinforced and reproduced day after day; otherwise, there would be no need to keep reproducing them. Is this premise true? Socialization theorists and evolutionary psychologists would say no. However, adherents to the school of symbolic interaction known as ethnomethodology, and the gender theorists influenced by them, would say yes.[8] Ethnomethodologists claim that the social order we take for granted in everyday life is much more precarious, much more house-of-cards–like, than we think. People must spend a lot of time, they assert, creating and re-creating a shared sense of social order in their everyday lives. The ethnomethodologists study how we create that shared sense. According to this line of reasoning, we must continually "do" gender—do the work of creating a shared sense of what the relations between men and women are like (West & Zimmerman, 1987). Gender becomes a verb, usually in the passive voice: Housework is gendered, work for wages is gendered, childcare is gendered, over and over in hundreds of situations. The household, in Berk's phrase, becomes a gender factory that produces the shared reality of gender relations right along with crumb-free tables (Berk, 1985).

However, the interactionist approach, which emphasizes the continual construction of meaning, and the socialization approach, which tends to stress lessons learned early in life, are not necessarily contradictory. Consider the same-sex peer groups that are formed in school settings by children somewhat older than the ones we have been considering. Children are socialized, in part, through playing games and sports in same-sex, school-age peer groups. In these groups, children learn the behaviors expected of them, try out these behaviors with their peers, get feedback on how well they are performing, and try again. Sociologists have studied

---

[8]I am aware that many ethnomethodologists consider their perspective to be distinct from symbolic interaction; but I agree with Jonathan H. Turner (1986) that they are related.

how this interactive process produces and reinforces different behavior patterns in boys and girls. In a study of Little League baseball teams, Gary Alan Fine observed that boys were concerned with impression management—behaving in a way that met with approval by the other boys—as well as with winning or losing. They learned to control their emotions and not to cry; otherwise they would risk ridicule from their peers. They learned to value competition. Once, when an opposing team showed up with too few players, a coach offered his first-place team the options of winning by forfeit or playing the game anyway and taking the small risk that they would lose. All the best players argued for taking the forfeit; only two players argued in favor of going ahead with the game because they were supposed to be playing for fun. When the team voted overwhelmingly to take the forfeit, the boys learned a lesson about valuing competition over cooperative play—a lesson consistent with the expected behavior of men (Fine, 1987).

At least until the recent expansion of athletic programs for girls, elementary school boys tended to play organized games more than elementary school girls (Lever, 1976; Thorne, 1993). Boys more often played competitive games with a set of rules and a goal; their play involved larger groups with more mixing of different ages; it occurred more often outdoors; and their games lasted longer. In contrast, girls' play reinforced the relational and emotional skills women are expected to have. Girls tended to play indoors more; they played noncompetitive activities without a goal more often; and their play groups tended to be smaller. In these small groups, girls showed more affection than boys and learned to pick up non-verbal cues about their friends' moods. The traits that were reinforced by girls' play were consistent with an adult life that emphasizes home, family, emotional closeness, and cooperation.

Nevertheless, not all girls and boys follow these scripts. When Barrie Thorne (1993) observed children in elementary schools, she found that most play groups comprised either all girls or all boys. But a modest number of girls and boys played in groups with the other gender, and there was much crossing of the gender border as, for example, when boys and girls chased one another or invaded the other gender's space. The degree of separation between girls' and boys' worlds, Thorne concluded, was overstated. Thorne's approach to her study reflects many of the principles of feminist research methods (see *How Do Sociologists Know What They Know?* Feminist Research Methods).

The symbolic interactionists say that children develop a sense of self through activities such as peer group play—a "gendered" sense of self in this instance. As a girl (or a boy) formulates what she will say or do in the group, she imagines how the others are likely to respond. This process of imagining how others will respond to you is what George Herbert Mead called "taking the role of the other" (Blumer, 1962). It is, interactionists say, how children develop an internalized sense of what is appropriate behavior for them to engage in.

GENDER AND MALE DOMINATION

Another body of writing about the construction and maintenance of gender differences focuses not on social interaction or on socialization but rather on the very structure of society: its hierarchies of dominance and power and its economic system. According to this line of reasoning, gender differences are social creations deeply imbedded in the way society is organized. More specifically, the United

How Do Sociologists Know What They Know?

Feminist Research Methods

Sociologist Barrie Thorne (1993) begins her book about children's play groups, *Gender Play: Girls and Boys in School,* by writing not about her subject but rather about herself. She recalls that the segregation of girls and boys on the playgrounds of the elementary school she attended was considered "natural." She tells the reader that her views on gender were transformed by the women's movement of the 1970s and 1980s, which argued that the differences between the genders is not natural but rather a social construction. She describes her commitment to raise her own children in a nonsexist way.

Thorne then discusses how, in her own research, she took pains to learn the terminology that the subjects themselves used: "kids" rather than "children." She explained, "I found that when I shifted to 'kids' in my writing, my stance toward the people in question felt more side-by-side than top-down" (p. 9). Using "kids" helped her to adopt the viewpoint of her subjects as opposed to the viewpoint of an adult feminist scholar.

In fact, the entire first chapter consists of preliminary material about herself and her relationship with her subjects. The chapter illustrates a practice known as **reflexivity**: a researcher's examination of the nature of the research process that she or he is undertaking (Fonow & Cook, 1991). The researcher *reflects* upon the beliefs (e.g., feminism) and statuses (e.g., college professor, woman) she brings to the project—and, in particular, how those beliefs and statuses might affect the research project.

Reflexivity is part of a larger orientation toward research in sociology that is called *feminist research methods.*[1] It emerged from the feminist movement of the 1970s and 1980s and is linked to feminist theory, the set of principles about gender that was summarized in Chapter 1. A central tenet of feminist research methods is that scholars should conduct action-oriented research, meaning research that has the objective of advancing the liberation of women from oppression by men—and also ending the gender constraints placed on men (Fonow & Cook, 1991). Feminist researchers explicitly acknowledge this political agenda. More important, they argue that *all* social scientific research reflects the social and political beliefs of the researchers but that most social scientists hide their beliefs—sometimes even from themselves.

In contrast, most sociologists try to follow the *scientific method,* reviewed in Chapter 1. A key assumption of the scientific method as it is often practiced is that researchers are neutral figures who stand outside of the phenomena they study. The researcher's point of view, it is said, should not influence the methods she or he uses or the conclusions she or he makes. In this way, the social scientist strives for objectivity—a way of viewing the social world that is independent of personal beliefs (see Chapter 1).

But feminist researchers argue that objectivity is nearly impossible to achieve (Neilson, 1990). They argue that much supposedly "objective" social scientific research actually reflects male bias. They are often critical of large-scale surveys and other forms of statistical research. For example, they note that until a decade or so ago, the U.S. Bureau of the Census, in its surveys, defined the husband as the "head of household" in a married-couple family, no matter what the family's definition was. Similarly, violence by husbands and partners against women was greatly underre-

States and most other nations are said to build inequalities between women and men into their social systems through **patriarchy**. The most general definition of patriarchy is a social order based on the domination of women by men. Following some scholars, I prefer to reserve the term for conditions that are more common in agricultural societies, in which older men control their families and in which family groups are the main economic units. In industrialized societies, in which the family or lineage is no longer the main economic group, I prefer the simpler term "male domination" (Thorne, 1992; Orloff, 1993). But no matter which term one uses, the main point of this scholarship is that men have power over women in ways that are similar to how the wealthy have power over the poor and how whites have power over blacks. Like class (see Chapter 4) and race (see Chapter 5), gender is ported in crime statistics until feminists focused attention on the problem (Reinharz, 1992).

Scholars who use feminist research methods try to make connections to their subjects and to understand and take their subjects' points of view. That is why Thorne sought to use language and methods that made her more of a "side-by-side" observer than a "top-down" (i.e., detached and objective) observer. Only by understanding the meanings that research subjects themselves give to their actions can the researcher, according to feminist research methods, provide a full account of an issue.

In addition, proponents of feminist research methods frequently try to show that there is substantial variation from person to person in the ways that women and men act. They do so because they oppose generalizations about women that might be used to restrict their independence and equality (for example, the belief, prevalent at midcentury, that it is better for the husband to earn the money and for the wife to stay home and care for the children). They sometimes carry out research with the intent of demonstrating that generalizations about women are wrong. For

instance, Thorne warns, "One should be wary of what has been called 'the tyranny of averages,' a misleading practice of referring to average differences as if they are absolute" (pp. 57–58).

So Thorne ventured out to the elementary school playground to disprove the idea that boys and girls are inherently different in their play styles—boys more aggressive, more concerned with dominance in groups; girls more concerned with relationships with a small number of friends. On the playground, girls and boys did separate, for the most part, in the ways that the generalizations predicted. They were not, however, completely separate. Thorne provided an insightful analysis of contact between girls and boys during the "border work" that maintained this separation, such as invading the other gender's spaces and chasing one another. Thorne also found that there were a few children who defied the stereotype, such as a boy who played jump rope and an athletic girl who played sports with the boys. And she documented occasional mixed games of dodgeball and the like.

From evidence such as this, Thorne concluded that gender "has a

fluid quality" (p. 159) and that the claim that boys and girls have separate cultures "has outlived its usefulness" (p. 108). However, as a reviewer noted, the number of times that boys and girls cross the gender boundaries "are a tiny minority of her observations" (England, 1994, p. 283). Consequently, it may be an overstatement to claim that the average differences between boys and girls aren't important because some individuals cross the boundaries.

Nevertheless, even if one is not always convinced by the conclusions of Thorne or other researchers like her, one can find useful lessons in feminist research methods. Perhaps the main lesson is that researchers should pay more attention to where they are coming from: the reasons they choose to study a particular topic, the assumptions they have going into the research project, and the beliefs they have that might influence their conclusions. Feminist researchers have made a convincing case that, in the study of family and gender, objectivity has its limits.

[1]However, the use of reflexivity pre-dates feminist research methods in sociology. Researchers working in the tradition of symbolic interactionism (see Chapter 1) incorporated it into their methods.

said to be one of the basic ways in which society is stratified into more powerful groups—men, in the case of gender—and less powerful groups.

THE SEX-GENDER SYSTEM

Put another way, societies often take the biological sex differences between women and men and use them as the basis for a comprehensive social order in which men have advantages over women. Specific, limited sex differences become the basis for pervasive gender differences. Gender theorists refer to this transformation of biological differences into a social order that supports male domination as a **sex-gender system** (Rubin, 1975). Consider the economy, for example. In

Families and Public Policy

The Earnings Gap

In the early 1990s, women who worked full-time as financial managers earned 61 percent of what men who worked full-time as financial managers earned each week. Women bus drivers earned 73 percent of what men who worked as bus drivers made each week. Women computer programmers earned 85 percent of what men made (Reskin & Padavic, 1994). Why is it the case that in nearly all occupations women earn less than men? And why are women workers concentrated in lower-paying jobs? Do employers discriminate against women workers? Or are other factors responsible for the earnings gap?

In the 1960s and 1970s, some labor economists argued that the gap essentially reflected the different social roles that women choose. That is to say, they assumed that women preferred to devote a larger share of their lives to raising children than did men. Consequently, economists such as Solomon Polachek argued, women chose the kinds of jobs in which it was easier to drop out for a period of time and then reenter, and they left voluntarily when they had young children (Polachek, 1979). They earned less than men, according to this argument, because they had less work experience, on average, and invested less in their careers (by, for example, taking fewer job training courses). Moreover, economists such as Gary

Becker argued that discrimination against women workers (or any other group) was likely to fade away because it cost employers money (Becker, 1957). The logic was that if women had difficulty finding jobs because of discrimination, some employer would seek an advantage by hiring women at lower wages than men were paid and such an employer would make products more cheaply, increase sales, and gain greater profits. The discriminators, seeing their sales and profits falling, would finally hire more women, thus bidding up women's wages. In sum, women's personal choices were said to underlie wage differentials and market forces were said to reduce discrimination.

The evidence, however, has not supported this model—at least not as the sole explanation for the gap. Numerous studies have examined wage differences between women and men controlling for education, work experience, and other factors and have found that a substantial portion of the gap remains. Robert Michael, a labor economist and the chair of a National Academy of Sciences panel on Pay Equity Research, wrote in 1989:

> there exist sizeable and systematic wage differences between women and men that cannot be explained by measured differences in skill, experience, effort, job commitment, or most any other attribute of workers that has been studied. Some argue that

the unexplained differences constitute a serious inequity that should be addressed by public and private policy (Michael, Hartmann, & O'Farrell, 1989, p. vii).

If a gap still exists, why haven't market forces worked as they were supposed to by penalizing firms that pay women low wages? Paula England and George Farkas argue that feedback effects involving households and the labor market can prolong discrimination (England & Farkas, 1986). Suppose, as is often the case, that parents socialize girls to care for children and to be less concerned than boys about occupational careers. Then, when the girls grow up, suppose that employers pay them less, in part because of their lesser investment in their careers and in part because of discrimination. The lower pay, England and Farkas maintain, will feed back into their households: Perceiving that they are paid less, these women (and their husbands) will give their own daughters less encouragement to be career-oriented than they will give to their sons.

Meanwhile, employers may have become less inclined to discriminate, as economic theory predicts. Yet they note, accurately, that women have slightly higher rates of leaving jobs than men. Consequently, they hesitate to hire women for jobs that require expensive training and therefore tend to pay well. In other words, employers

Western nations, people must purchase the goods they need with money (as opposed to making their own clothes and building their own houses). Western societies are organized so that men have access to more money than do women: Men are more likely to work for pay, and when they do, they earn considerably higher wages and salaries than women (see Chapter 10). To be sure, men tend to have more education and work experience than women, in part because many women withdraw from the paid workforce to bear and rear children. Gender theorists

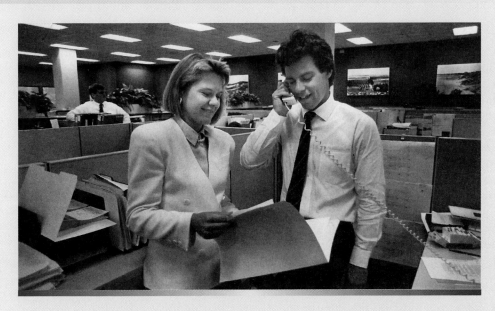

A gap still exists between the average pay of women and men.

engage in "statistical discrimination": When they interview a woman, they are wary of hiring her because they know that, as a group, women have higher turnover rates—even though the specific woman they are interviewing might never quit (England & Farkas, 1986). Their statistical discrimination, in turn, can affect how parents socialize the next generation, and so on. Consequently, discrimination tends to linger, even though employers' attitudes toward having women in the workplace have become more positive.

A subtler issue is **comparable-worth discrimination:** a situation in which women and men do different jobs of equivalent value in the same company but the women are paid less. A remedy for this problem is to have an expert body classify jobs according to their "worth," as defined by attributes such as skill, effort, responsibility, and working conditions. Then wages or wage guidelines would be set according to the ranking of jobs, usually by a government body. To be sure, it is difficult to decide how much value a given job produces relative to another. Yet in Australia and Great Britain, where government influence over wage levels is greater than in the United States, similar actions have been taken and have reduced the earnings gap (Gregory et al., 1989).

Modest progress has been made in closing the earnings gap over the past decade or two. In 1980, median weekly earnings of women who worked full-time were about 60 percent of men's earnings; in 1997 the figure had increased to 75 percent (Reskin & Padavic, 1994; U.S. Bureau of Labor Statistics, 1997). Still, women's earnings lag behind men's in nearly every occupation. And some of the progress in narrowing the gap has occurred because the wages of men without college educations have gone down, rather than because the wages of women have risen (Bernhardt, Morris, & Handcock, 1995).

argue, however, that the wage gap is far wider than differences in education and work experience would predict—and recent economic studies suggest that their argument is correct. (See *Families and Public Policy:* The Earnings Gap.) They argue that in a number of ways—such as when parents encourage sons to have careers more than they encourage daughters to do so, when employers discriminate against women in hiring or pay, and when long-established rules provide men with higher pay than women for comparable work—society creates and reinforces men's economic domination. Therefore, most women must depend on men if they wish to live in a household with a substantial income.

Just how men have come to have a dominant position in society is a subject of some debate. Many writers of this genre link male domination and capitalism—the economic system of the United States and most other nations (Shelton & Agger, 1993). **Capitalism**, which (along with socialism) will be discussed in more detail in Chapter 6, is an economic system in which goods and services are privately produced and sold on a market for profit. Gender theorists have maintained that economic inequalities between women and men benefit capitalists, the owners of businesses, in at least three ways. First, employers are able to save money by hiring women at lower wages than they would have to pay men. During the twentieth century, the sector of the economy that produces services, such as medical care, communications, insurance, restaurant meals, and the like, expanded faster than the factory sector. As this expansion occurred, women—especially unmarried women—were hired as nurses (but less often as doctors), secretaries (but not managers), and telephone operators (but not supervisors), and for other service jobs (Oppenheimer, 1970). Their wages tended to be substantially lower than the wages of men with comparable responsibility, thus providing employers with considerable savings. Second, the lower wages of women are said to create divisions between male and female workers that prevent them from organizing to protect their interests against the interests of capitalists.

Third, the unpaid work of housewives, gender theorists have argued, allows families to subsist on the often modest wages that men earn. Employers count on their male workers being married to women who will wash their clothes, cook their meals, and raise their children at no cost. Therefore, employers gain greater profits by paying their workers less than the full cost of raising a family. Indeed, in the first half of the twentieth century, this division of labor was enshrined as the "family wage system," in which husbands were supposed to earn enough so that their wives did not need to work for pay (see Chapter 6). Wives' unpaid work was, and still is, invisible economically: Government statisticians do not count housework and childrearing as part of the gross national product—the annual accounting of the total amount of goods and services produced in the country. Yet wives' unpaid work is economically valuable. In recent decades, as more married women have taken jobs outside the home, millions of families have discovered how expensive it is to pay someone else to care for their children while they work.

Still, the nature of the connection between male domination and capitalism is unclear. Most feminist theorists have maintained that the two fit well together but are at least partially distinct. For example, some have described the social and economic organization of the United States as "patriarchal capitalism," arguing that male domination of women and capitalists' domination of workers are intertwined, with each reinforcing the other (Hartmann, 1976). Male domination is said to have emerged before capitalism but to have broadened and strengthened once capitalism was established. An implication of this line of thought is that male domination would be reduced if capitalism were replaced by another economic system, such as socialism.

This implication, however, is undercut by cross-national research. Several scholars have studied the position of women in countries with a socialist economic system. Under **socialism**, the number and type of goods produced, and whom they are distributed to, are decided by the government rather than by the actions of a market. Theoretically, a socialist system should eliminate the economic disparities between women and men because there are no business owners who could profit from paying women lower wages or from having housewives subsidize the wages employers pay men. In fact, in socialist countries such as the former Soviet Union and its Eastern European satellites, nearly all urban women worked outside the home. Yet most positions of power and advantage in socialist nations are held by men. Feminist scholars who have studied China, for instance, have been particularly disappointed by the continuing gender inequalities there, especially given the feminist rhetoric of the leader of the Communist revolution, Mao Zedong. (See the box in Chapter 6, *Families in Other Cultures:* Women Hold Up Half the Sky.) Judith Stacey concluded from the Chinese experience that sex-gender systems are "relatively autonomous" from economic systems, be they capitalist or socialist (Stacey, 1983). Men's domination of women, in other words, is not just a function of the economic system of a nation; it may even be largely independent of the economic system. Although there are differences between the status of women in capitalist and socialist societies, male domination seems to be built into the social structures of most nations in ways that are compatible with either capitalism or socialism.

GENDER, CLASS, AND RACE

Rather than being reducible to class differences, then, many scholars argue that gender is a separate, distinctive way in which societies are stratified by power and advantage. It is now a basic tenet of gender theorists that gender should be thought of in the same way scholars think of class and race—namely, as a primary basis of social stratification. This is a viewpoint that is especially useful when one is studying differences in occupations or earnings, as the above discussion suggested. It is also a relevant viewpoint for the study of families. For instance, women's and men's choices about whether and whom to marry can be influenced by how much they could earn if they were single and how much they can expect a spouse to earn. These earnings levels, in turn, are influenced by the sex-gender system of the society in which they live.

Still, let me suggest that, in studies of the family, there is an important sense in which gender is not fully similar to either class or race. The sex differences in childbearing—the fact that women become pregnant, bear children, and can breast-feed them—may be relevant to the different family roles of women and men. I don't mean to suggest that the roles of women and men in families are predestined by these sex differences; but I would argue that the sex differences can't be ignored in studying the different behaviors of men and women. In her presidential address to the American Sociological Association, Alice Rossi said:

> *Gender differentiation is not simply a function of socialization, capitalist production, or patriarchy. It is grounded in a sex dimorphism [the occurrence of two distinct sexes] that serves the fundamental purpose of reproducing the species.*

Rossi argued that, to some extent, the parenting styles of women and men build upon biological differences. If so, she stated, "This is where the sociological analogy so often drawn between race and sex breaks down" (Rossi, 1984, pp. 1 and 10).

The analogy breaks down, she argued, because we could easily imagine a human society in which, as a result of intermarriage, there are no racial differences. We could even imagine (as Marx did) a society in which there are no class differences. Yet we cannot imagine a society in which there are no sex differences.

That is because women and men have different biological roles in reproduction. It is possible, then, that gender differences may not be *wholly* socially constructed and that they may not always reflect male domination and power. Although male domination shapes gender roles, it may not be the only force that does so. This is the sense in which the gender stratification perspective, although an important source of insight that I will draw upon throughout this book, needs to be supplemented by other views.

THE CONTRIBUTIONS OF GENDER STUDIES

We have reviewed several approaches to the study of gender differences (See Table 3.1). The socialization approach emphasizes conscious learning and interpretation by children from the world around them—their parents, peers, television, and so forth. The lessons very young children learn allow them to construct a sense of what society expects a girl or a boy to be like. The sex-gender system approach emphasizes the dominance men maintain over women through political and economic systems and through customs and traditions. (See *Families in Other Cultures:* China's Missing Girls.) Are these perspectives enough? Clearly, the tallest stack of direct evidence is in the hands of the socialization theorists; numerous studies show that boys and girls learn appropriate gender-role behavior from other children and from adults. No one disputes the importance of socialization in the

TABLE 3.1   APPROACHES TO THE STUDY OF GENDER DIFFERENCES

APPROACH	HOW GENDER IS CONSTRUCTED	EXAMPLES
Socialization	Through learning from adults, the media, peers, and the like, what kinds of behavior are expected of women and men.	Boys are given trucks and tools for birthday presents; girls are given dolls and stuffed animals. Boys are admonished not to cry; girls are allowed to cry.
Sex-gender system	Through the constraints of an economic and social system that restricts women's behavior in ways that favor men.	Women are paid less than men for working at the same job. Women who work outside the home are still expected to be the primary caregivers to children, even if they are married.
Biosocial	Through biologically based (e.g., genetic, hormonal) differences that have evolved over the history of the human existence.	Boys will sometimes insist on playing with trucks and tools even if they are given dolls and stuffed animals.
Psychoanalytic	Through relations with women caregivers early in life, which cause women to internalize a sense of connectedness to others and men to internalize a sense of separateness.	Women, on average, may find it easier to form close relationships with others; men may find it easier to be separate from others.
Symbolic interactionist	Through continual reinforcement of gender differences because of the everyday behaviors of women and men.	Husbands who are very competent outside the home will claim they're not good at washing dishes or changing diapers, and their wives will agree with them and do these tasks.

creation of gender roles. Moreover, few would dispute the notion that the structure of most societies reinforces male domination in many ways. To many sociologists, these perspectives are indeed enough. But a growing number of other observers are not satisfied.

Some of these observers find gender differences too tenacious, too difficult to change, to be supported by childhood socialization alone. Others question whether all the differences can be accounted for by men's greater political and economic power. Their views lead to two approaches to the study of gender differences that are less widely agreed upon: the biosocial and the psychoanalytic. Girls and boys, these approaches suggest, may have innate predispositions toward certain types of behaviors. These predispositions are reinforced or discouraged by the gender-specific socialization they receive. In her presidential address, Rossi (1984) said:

> It makes no sense to view biology and social experience as separate domains contesting for election as "primary causes." Biological processes unfold in a cultural context, and are themselves malleable, not stable and inevitable. So, too, cultural processes take place within and through the biological organism; they do not take place in a sociological vacuum (p. 10).

Finally, symbolic interactionists argue that gender is too problematic to be created merely through childhood socialization; rather, it must be created and recreated in the everyday lives of adults. Their views lead to another perspective, the interactionist approach, which emphasizes the need for continual reinforcement of gender differences. Throughout life, it is argued, people construct and maintain gender differences through their everyday interactions with others.

Despite their different perspectives—or perhaps because of them—sociologists who have studied gender (along with their colleagues in anthropology, history, and psychology) have made several important contributions to our understanding of the family. First, they have demonstrated that the roles men and women play in families are, in large part, socially and culturally constructed. Indeed, many sociologists would argue that the differences are almost entirely constructed by conscious social forces. But even those who believe that there is a psychoanalytic or biological component to gender-role distinctions would agree that our society greatly exaggerates these distinctions. That is to say, even if one believes that, on average, women are predisposed to relate somewhat better to infants and small children, that does not explain why so few husbands share the care of older children or of the housework. Biology cannot explain why a brilliant lawyer is unable to clean a table. Psychoanalytic theory cannot explain why the great 1950s liberal Adlai Stevenson told the 1955 graduating class of Smith College (a private liberal arts college for women) that their place in politics was to "influence man and boy" through the "humble role of housewife" (Chafe, 1972). Moreover, biology can't explain the social changes in gender roles and family life over the past few decades, or even the past few centuries, because evolutionary change is so slow. Consequently, the biological and psychoanalytic approaches may not be very useful to a sociologist who is trying to explain social change—although these approaches might be helpful in determining the difficulty of bringing about social change. The social and cultural construction of gender will be relevant to discussions in later chapters on changing conceptions of sexuality (Chapter 7), patterns of courtship, dating, and spouse choice (Chapter 8), and the relationships between married or cohabiting couples (Chapter 9).

Families in Other Cultures

China's Missing Girls

American fathers may have a slight preference for sons over daughters—studies show that married couples are somewhat less likely to divorce if they have boys than if they have all girls (Morgan, 1988). But most expectant couples are very happy if the woman gives birth to a healthy child of either gender. This is not as true in some other cultures. Consider China: Its families traditionally were patrilineal, defined in Chapter 2 as a kinship system in which descent is traced through the father. In such a system, a father transmitted his family line through his sons. His daughters, upon marrying, became part of their husbands' family lines. Moreover, China also has been **patrilocal**, meaning that a young wife goes to live in her husband's parents' home. As a result, from their parents' perspective, daughters neither continue the family line nor contribute to the family's well-being as adults. Sons on the other hand, continue the family line and are expected to remain at home to care for their elderly parents. Especially in rural areas where help with farm labor is highly valued, this patriarchal system created a distinct preference for sons over daughters. If a newly married man's wife gave birth to a girl, his relatives would console him with the saying that having a daughter brings in a son.

Many other cultures also have strong son preferences (see Das Gupta & Bhat, 1997, on India). But when the continuing preference for sons in China collided with the government's desire to reduce its rate of population growth, the consequences for girls—and for gender relations in general—were dramatic. China is the most populous nation on earth, making up one-fifth of humankind. In 1979, it instituted a "one-child policy," which limited urban families to one child and allowed most rural families only two. Because the state controlled people's access to jobs, housing, land, and consumer goods, it could—and did—penalize families that exceeded the limit.[1]

Under this rule, having a girl, rather than bringing in a son, often precluded one. Consequently, the strict policy evoked resistance. In a normal population, women give birth to about 106 boys for every 100 girls. (Because males have higher death rates, these numbers even out as the boys and girls age.) In China the sex ratio was very close to 106 in the 1960s and 1970s, before the one-child policy (Zeng et al., 1993). The ratio in China in 1989, the latest year for which good information is available, was 114 boys for every 100 girls; among women who had already borne one child, the ratio for their second child was 121 boys for every 100 girls (Zeng et al., 1993). Clearly, many fewer girl babies are being reported than would ordinarily have been born; they have become known as the millions of "missing girls" (Riley, 1996).

No one knows for sure what is responsible for this discrepancy. One factor is underreporting of girl babies who are hidden, sent to live with friends or relatives elsewhere, or given for adoption (Zeng et al., 1993). Because these girls are unreported, they will have more difficulty obtaining state-controlled medical care, education and, later in life, housing and employment. In some cases, families abandon newborn girls, often in places where they can be found and placed in overburdened orphanages, brimming with girls but bare of boys. Recent reports also suggest the importance of sex-selective abortions. The number of sophisticated ultrasound examination machines, which can determine the sex of a fetus, increased greatly in China in the 1980s and early 1990s. Some parents are learning the sex of fetuses through ultrasound and then selectively aborting females (Riley & Gardner, 1997). And finally, a small number may be allowing their infant daughters to die of neglect—not breastfeeding them as long as boys, for example—or even killing them.

The socialist revolution in China was supposed to end male dominance, but it has not done so. (See *Families in Other Cultures:* Women Hold Up Half the Sky, in Chapter 6.) It has certainly placed the goal of sharply reducing its population over the well-being of newborn, or would-

Second, sociologists of gender have taught us that gender distinctions sometimes (some would say *always*) reflect differences in power between men and women. Stevenson's speech was meant to convey to the Smith graduates how important their restricted political role was. But women whose only political influence is through their husbands are not equal in political power to men. After the rise of the feminist movement in the 1960s and 1970s and the increases in the

Chinese orphanages, such as this one in Shanghai, are populated almost exclusively with girls.

be-born, girls. The Chinese government argues that the sharp drop in birthrates will benefit women as well as men because women suffered more than men in previous economic crises (Riley, 1997). However, critics charge that the current policy reflects the lower value placed on women than on men. It places great pressure on Chinese women to bear sons at any cost. More generally, in the words of anthropologists Susan Greenhalgh and sociologist Jiali Li (1995), the one-child policy:

> . . . has shrunk the basic unit of social life, allowed the state to penetrate one of the few private spaces left by Chinese collectivism; pitted husband against wife, neighbor against neighbor, city against countryside; and raised terribly painful ethical dilemmas that can be dimly perceived through the haze of silence and shame that surrounds the issue of the missing girls in China's villages. (p. 636)

Moral questions aside, the one-child policy has helped China's economic development by reducing population growth. In the long run, however, it may cause some problems: When today's children reach adulthood, young men will find a shortage of young women to marry because of the sex-ratio imbalance. The elderly, who traditionally in China have relied on their children—especially their sons—for support, will have fewer children, and often no sons, to care for them. The Chinese government will have to increase its support of the elderly greatly as a result.

[1]Market-oriented economic reforms in China have reduced the power of the government to enforce the one-child family policy because more people now obtain jobs themselves through the labor market.

number of women elected to political offices, no male politician would make Stevenson's statement today. Feminist scholars argue, moreover, that power differences do not stop at the family's front door; rather, they argue that the roles women play within marriages often reflect their husbands' greater power—in particular, his greater economic power. Said differently, the lesson is that families are not islands isolated from the rest of society; rather, the relations of power and inequality that hold outside the home can also extend within it. Differences in power and the allocation of work within the household will be examined in Chapter 10. Other chapters will include discussions of the effects of male domination on family law and policy (Chapter 6), domestic violence against women (Chapter 11), and the economic circumstances of divorced women (Chapter 12).

Finally, sociologists have demonstrated that it is possible to accept the idea that women's and men's personalities may be fundamentally different, on average, in *some* respects without accepting the view that they are fundamentally different in *all* respects. Although this may seem like an obvious point, it signifies, in my view, a significant evolution in the debates about women's and men's roles. The terms of this debate had been set by leading structural-functionalist sociologists in the 1950s who, writing during a decade of prosperity and high birthrates, implied that the exaggerated division of labor in the breadwinner-homemaker family was timeless, natural, and for the best in this best of all possible worlds. The initial surge of feminist sociological scholarship in the late 1960s and 1970s was conducted in reaction to this view and took the form of demonstrating that gender differences were socially constructed by a male-dominated society.

During the debate, many feminist scholars were reluctant to admit that there were any deep-seated gender differences. Still, some authors began to write of a limited set of persistent differences: more separateness and aggressiveness in men and a greater sense of relating to others and caring for them in women. Chodorow's explanation for these persistent differences gained many adherents not because sociologists are enamored of psychoanalytic theory—they are not— but rather, I think, because it allowed sociologists to accept the idea of deep-seated gender differences without having to talk about biology. Thus, Rubin can solve her riddle of the "dogged persistence with which these ways of being resist our best efforts to change" by embracing an explanation that allows her to say "I hasten to add, that [these differences] are not born in nature."

An explicit consideration of biology is more than many sociologists can accept, but it is the logical step for those who suspect fundamental differences and find psychoanalytic theory an incomplete explanation. Indeed, sociologists with a biosocial perspective have produced evidence that there may be some fundamental differences in the range of behaviors of women and men. Raising the issue of biological influences can easily provoke a spirited debate, but in some ways there is less to this debate than meets the eye. For example, even if women were inherently better, on average, at caring for infants and toddlers, there still would be a range of capabilities within each gender. That is to say, there still would be some men who would be particularly good at caring for small children and there would be some women who would not be good; the distributions of caregiving ability would overlap. Moreover, it would be possible to reduce the difference somewhat, if society so chose, by providing training: If we want more men to care for infants well, says Rossi, give them childrearing classes, much as we give high school dropouts job training classes now (Rossi, 1984). And if the care of small children interferes with work careers, it should be possible to alter job conditions to make it easier for parents who are employed to do childcare—such as through generous work leaves for infant care, reduced or flexible work hours for parents, and so forth (see Chapter 10). Any differences in caregiving ability or in forgone career opportunities that remain after encouraging and instructing men and making the workplace more family-friendly should be substantially less significant than the exaggerated gender differences we see today.

SUMMARY

1. Sociologists distinguish between sex and gender, using sex to refer to differences between women and men that are biological and gender to refer to differences that are social and cultural—and therefore constructed by society. Gender differences often reflect male domination over women. Nevertheless, in some instances it is difficult to disentangle social and biological influences on gender differences. Other cultures have organized gender in different ways than the tradition of the Western nations, as the example of the *berdaches* illustrates. Individuals develop gender identities in early childhood; it is difficult to change these identities thereafter.

2. Several approaches attempt to explain differences in gender roles between men and women. According to the socialization approach, young children are taught lessons about stereotypical gender roles by parents, peers, teachers, and the media. The emphasis in this approach is on conscious, social learning. In general, children are taught to think that boys and men are aggressive, competitive, and independent, whereas girls and women are less aggressive, more nurturing, and better at enabling and maintaining personal relationships. Numerous studies have shown in detail how gender-specific messages are received by young children, who then construct the concept of gender in their minds. In fact, some scholars argue that gender is such a broad and central identity that it shouldn't be considered just another social role.

3. Some evidence indicates that typical gender roles are not totally the result of social learning. Especially among boys, toy preferences and an active play style emerge very early and appear to exist independently of their parents' beliefs about how boys and girls should play. Some studies suggest that variations in prenatal hormone levels can affect gender-typed behavior. Early same-sex peer groups also influence children's behavior, perhaps due to both parental influence and biological predispositions. Two approaches to gender roles attempt to account for these findings. First, the biosocial asserts that evolution has created predispositions among men and women that differ, on average, for a limited set of behaviors,

such as aggression. Second, the psychoanalytic approach suggests that gender differences emerge because women almost always do the mothering. Consequently, boys, who must separate from their mothers, develop a more separate sense of self; in contrast, girls, who need not separate, develop a sense of connectedness with the world around them.

4. The interactionist approach has been adopted by sociologists who believe that gender roles need continual reinforcement throughout life. They argue that everyday social situations, such as cleaning up the kitchen after dinner, re-create and reinforce gender distinctions. Starting in childhood, people create their own meanings through interactions with others. In constructing their own meaning, people "take the role of the other," that is, they consider how others would react if they were to behave in a certain way.

5. Many gender theorists argue that gender differences are built into the structure of nearly all societies. They identify a system of patriarchy, a social order based on the domination of men over women. Society, it is argued, uses limited sex differences to construct pervasive gender differences through a sex-gender system. Some writers maintain that male domination and capitalism, although somewhat distinct, are interrelated, with one reinforcing the other. Research on socialist societies, however, suggests that systems of male domination are compatible with either capitalism or socialism. Gender theorists argue that gender should be seen as a source of social stratification as basic as race and class.

6. Sociologists who study gender have made several contributions to our understanding of the family. First, they have demonstrated that the roles men and women play in families are, in large part, culturally constructed. Second, they have taught us that gender-role distinctions often reflect differences in power between women and men. Third, they have demonstrated that it is possible to accept the idea that women's and men's personalities may be fundamentally different, on average, in some respects without necessarily accepting the idea that they are fundamentally different in all respects.

KEY TERMS

berdache
sex
gender
intersexuals
social role
gender roles
socialization
socialization approach (to gender
    differences)

peer group
biosocial approach (to gender
    differences)
psychoanalytic approach (to
    gender differences)
interactionist approach (to gender
    differences)
reflexivity
patriarchy

sex-gender system
comparable-worth discrimination
capitalism
socialism
patrilocal

FAMILIES ON THE INTERNET

Information on gender and on women's issues abounds on the Internet. On the liberal side, the Institute for Global Communications maintains WomensNet (**www.igc.org/igc/womensnet**), which provides many links to sources of information elsewhere. The National Organization for Women, the leading feminist political organization, can be found at **www.now.org**. A conservative perspective is available from Concerned Women for America at **www.cwfa.org**. For an abundance of factual information on labor force issues such as earnings differences between women and men, go to the home page of the Women's Bureau at the U.S. Department of Labor, **www.dol.gov/dol/wb/welcome.html**.

PART TWO

Race, Ethnicity, Class, and the State

Families are affected by the larger social structures in which they are embedded. Differences between the social roles of women and men are so fundamental to families that they were discussed in Part One. There are other important divisions in society as well. Social class differences—the ordering of individuals in a society according to power, prestige, and privilege—influence the ways that family life is organized. Racial and ethnic groups also differ in their family lives. In addition, the government has a substantial influence on families through its policies and programs.

Chapter 4 explores the differences in family life among social classes. It includes an examination of how trends in the economy have affected families. The kin networks of the poor, the changing attitudes toward gender roles among the working class, and the importance of the conjugal family among the middle class are also discussed.

Chapter 5 considers the consequences for families of the divisions in society along racial-ethnic lines. The distinctive family patterns of African Americans are discussed. The chapter also examines commonly used categories such as "Hispanic" and "Asian," which include groups that vary greatly in their family patterns. For example, the differences among Mexican-American, Puerto Rican, and Cuban families are described.

In modern nation-states such as the United States, the state itself exerts a strong influence on family life. It does so through the many programs that can influence individuals' decisions about whether to marry, to work outside the home, to buy a house in the suburbs, and so forth. **Chapter 6** explores the influence of the state; in particular, it focuses on the political conflicts over measures that affect women's autonomy and that provide income assistance to poor families.

CHAPTER 4

Social Class and Families

Kenny and Bonita Merten and their two sons, of Des Moines, Iowa, are a rather typical working-class family. They were profiled in the *New Yorker* magazine in 1995.[1] Kenny earned $7.00 an hour at his first job after marrying Bonita in 1972. His wage peaked at $11.80 an hour on a factory assembly line in 1993. But he was fired; his supervisors said he worked too slowly and his work was of low quality. Kenny said that factories can be choosy and prefer to hire young men. In 1995, working for a company that puts up barriers, sandbags, and signs on highways, he made $7.30 an hour.

In the time since Kenny and Bonita married, the cost of consumer goods more than tripled because of inflation. Consequently, Kenny would have to be earning over $24 an hour to match the buying power he had in 1972. Instead, by 1995 his

---

[1]See Sheehan (1995). The entire article is reprinted in Andrew J. Cherlin, *Public and Private Families: A Reader.*

buying power had declined by 70 percent. "I know I'll never be able to earn $11.80 again," he said. "The most I can hope for is a seven-dollar-an-hour job that doesn't involve swinging sandbags. Maybe if I come home less tired at the end of the day, I can handle an evening job."

Bonita works the evening shift at a local nursing home. A recent raise boosted her pay to $7.40 per hour. Even with two incomes, the Mertens are often unable to pay all of their bills. "1995 has been a pretty hard year in a pretty hard life," she said. "We had our water shut off in July *and* August, and we ain't never had it turned off even once before."

Kenny and Bonita married at the end of a period of great prosperity in the United States. In the 1950s and 1960s, the American economy was strong and wages were rising. In fact, the average income of full-time workers, adjusted for inflation, doubled. Many workers without college educations found jobs in the expanding factories of the nation. But the 1973 decision by oil-producing countries to sharply raise the price of oil sent the U.S. economy into a tailspin, and wages have been stagnant ever since for workers without college degrees. Even after the United States adjusted to the oil price shock, it became clear that our employment base in manufacturing was not growing the way it had in the past. Corporations moved production overseas in order to take advantage of the lower wages paid to workers in the developing world. Computers and other technologies allowed employers to replace some workers with machines, such as the robots on automobile assembly lines. How recent changes in the economy may have affected families—and, more generally, how social class position, income, and poverty affect families—are the topics that will be addressed in this chapter. Let's discuss first, however, what sociologists mean by social class.

DEFINING SOCIAL CLASS

Class is a concept that is hard to define precisely but difficult to avoid using. It is used in two senses by sociologists. In the first sense, which derives from the writings of Karl Marx, a person's class position in a capitalist society, such as the United States, is determined by his or her relationship to "the means of production" (Marx, 1977). The latter term refers to the things necessary to produce goods and services, such as buildings, machines, and capital (money that can be used to buy equipment, place advertisements, hire workers, and so forth). Marx called those who owned the means of production the capitalist class. Those who traded their labor for wages paid by the capitalists he called the working class. Marx's basic, two-class model, however, is inadequate as a complete description of class in contemporary societies. It does not take into account, for instance, managers who are hired by business owners to supervise the work of others; independent professionals such as doctors in private practice; and owners of small businesses such as mom-and-pop grocery stores. As a result, many sociologists, some of them still working in the Marxian tradition, have developed multiclass models.[2]

Class in the second sense, for which the term **social class** is used, refers to an ordering of all persons in a society according to their degrees of power, prestige, and privilege. Whereas Marx's model focuses on economic factors, this definition is broader in scope. To be sure, wealthy people often have substantial power, prestige, and privilege, whereas poor people rarely do. Still, these three kinds of

---

[2]See, for example, Wright (1976).

rewards are not tied solely to how much money a person has or to whether he or she owns a business. **Power** is the ability to force a person to do something even against his or her will. Most powerful people, however, are able to exercise their power most of the time without resorting to force or coercion. The president of the United States—who in the mid-1990s was a man without great wealth who did not even own a home—has perhaps more power than any other person in the world. He is the Commander in Chief of the world's most powerful military, and he has great political power as Chief Executive. **Prestige** refers to honor and status in a society. Supreme Court justices have prestige far greater than their incomes alone would predict. A cardinal of the Catholic Church has great prestige and substantial power (by, for example, threatening excommunication) but little income. **Privilege** is a special advantage or benefit enjoyed by some individuals. It is more closely tied to income and wealth, for people with enough money can usually buy a privileged style of life, from beautiful homes to fine vacations to private schooling for their children.

In practice, a person's power, prestige, and privilege are heavily determined by her or his income, occupation, and education. Instead of a few distinct classes, this ordering might produce numerous layers, or "strata," in a society; consequently, some sociologists argue that, strictly speaking, one should not use the term "social class" in this second sense but rather speak of "social stratification."[3] However, the former term, which is more common, will be used in this book. This chapter will distinguish among families in four broad classes according to power, prestige, and privilege. In real life, there is considerable overlap among these four social classes, and not all families fit neatly into one category. Therefore they are meant as ideal types. Introduced by Max Weber, the term **ideal type** refers to a hypothetical model that consists of the most significant characteristics, in extreme form, of a social phenomenon. It is useful for understanding social life, even though any real example of the phenomenon may not have all the characteristics of the ideal type.

FOUR SOCIAL CLASSES

The four social classes are upper class, middle class, working class, and lower class. When American adults are asked which of these four classes they belong to without any instruction about what these categories mean—they overwhelmingly choose either middle class or working class. For instance, in the 1996 General Social Survey (GSS), an annual national survey of about 3,000 adults, 4 percent said they were upper class, 45 percent said middle class, 45 percent said working class, and 6 percent said lower class (Davis & Smith, 1996). Both extremes apparently sound unpleasant to people, probably because of the stigma of being a "lower-class" person or the embarrassment of admitting to be "upper class." By most reasonable criteria, the lower class is larger than 5 percent. For instance, 11 percent of American adults had incomes below the poverty level in 1996 (U.S. Bureau of the Census, 1997g).

There is little consensus on the size of the upper class or on just how to define it. In general, **upper-class families** are those that have amassed wealth and privilege and that often have substantial prestige as well. They tend to own large, spacious homes, to possess expensive clothes and furnishings, to have substantial investment holdings, and to be recognized as part of the social and cultural elite of their communities. Upper-class husbands tend to be owners or senior managers of large corporations, banks, or law firms. Their wives are less likely to work for pay

---

[3]A good discussion of how to define social class and social stratification can be found in Kohn and Slomczynski (1990).

outside the home than women in other social classes. Some engage in extensive volunteer work, whereas others devote considerable time to entertaining and socializing with other couples to help advance their husbands' careers. There is little good research on the upper class, and this chapter will focus mainly on the other three social classes.

Middle-class families are those whose connection to the economy provides them with a secure, comfortable income and allows them to live well above a subsistence level. Middle-class families can usually afford privileges such as a nice house, a new car, a college education for the children, fashionable clothes, a vacation at the seashore, and so forth. The jobs that middle-class men and women hold usually require some college education and are performed mainly in offices and businesses. Middle-class men tend to hold higher-paying jobs such as lawyer, pharmacist, engineer, sales representative, or midlevel manager at a corporation. Jobs such as these usually have some prestige and include fringe benefits such as health insurance, paid vacations, paid sick leave, and retirement pensions. Women in general are underrepresented in the higher-paying professional and managerial occupations, although their numbers are growing. Women professionals still tend to be found in occupations that require a college education, such as nursing and teaching, but that don't pay as much as male-dominated professions. Relatively few women work at blue-collar jobs such as plumber or bricklayer, although again their numbers are growing in jobs such as assembler and bus driver. In contrast, a large number have lower-paying jobs in offices and businesses, such as secretary, department store clerk, and telephone operator. These clerical jobs came to be seen as "women's jobs" early in the twentieth century, and until recently nearly all the workers in such positions were women (Oppenheimer, 1970).

Working-class families are those whose incomes can provide reliably for the minimum needs of what people see as a decent life: a modest house or an apartment, a car, enough money to enroll children at a state or community college, and so forth. Working-class men tend to hold manual jobs in factories, automobile repair shops, construction sites, and so forth. Layoffs are more common in manual occupations than in the office and business jobs middle-class men tend to have, so working-class men are more vulnerable to periods of unemployment. Moreover, working-class men and women are more likely to be contingent workers, who may not work a full week and who may have few fringe benefits. Clerical jobs, such as secretary, or service jobs, such as cafeteria cashier or hospital orderly, are common among working-class women; a minority work in factories.

Lower-class families are those whose connection to the economy is so tenuous that they cannot provide reliably for a decent life, either because they work steadily at low-paying jobs (the so-called "working poor") or because they are frequently unemployed. They may live in deteriorated housing in neighborhoods with high crime rates. They may not be able to afford adequate clothing for winter, and they may need government-issued food stamps to purchase enough food. Lower-class men, who have little education and few occupational skills, can find jobs that pay only at or slightly above the minimum wage and that have few, if any, fringe benefits and little security. Lower-class women may work at low-paying service jobs; some are dependent on cash assistance from the federal and state governments to low-income families—commonly known as "welfare." A small minority of lower-class families are homeless. As their numbers grew in the 1980s and early 1990s, "homelessness" became a much discussed social problem. (See *Families and Public Policy:* Homeless Families: The Tip of the Iceberg, on pages 112–113.)

CHANGING CONCEPTIONS OF SOCIAL CLASS

These categories, although useful, cannot capture the full complexity of the social stratification of families. They date from the social scientific literature of the mid-twentieth century, when most families had two adults present and when relatively few married women worked outside the home. Most women at that time attained their class position through their husbands' occupations. Consequently, the categories work best in describing the position of two-parent, single-earner families. In contrast, when both spouses work for pay, the line between a middle-class family and a working-class family, or between a working-class and a lower-class family, becomes less clear. Suppose, for example, that the wife and the husband are both high school–educated factory workers, with a joint income that provides a comfortable standard of living. Is this family working class because of the occupations of both spouses and their lack of college education, or is it middle class because of their comfortable joint income? There is no clear answer to this question. Still, when married women are asked what class they belong to, they rely heavily on their husbands' jobs; but their own education and income also figure into their answers (Baxter, 1994; Davis & Robinson, 1988).

Moreover, in the growing percentage of families in which a father is not present, the mothers' class position is not well defined. In these cases, the mothers' occupation, education, and sources of income (including child support payments, if any) must obviously be the criteria. A woman who works as a secretary might be comfortably middle class only as long as she is married to a man who earns substantially more than she does. If the marriage ends, her standard of living is likely to drop. Whether she necessarily becomes "working class" is unclear—she has less income, but she retains the same level of education and many of the same friends and interests. (More will be said about the economic situation of single-parent families below and in subsequent chapters.)

FAMILIES AND THE ECONOMY

To return to the story of families and the changing U.S. economy, every old city has seen the closing of factories that had formerly provided full-time jobs at good wages to workers without college educations. For example, the Singer Sewing Machine Company dominated Elizabeth, New Jersey, from its founding in 1873 until it closed in 1982—its market reduced by ready-to-wear clothes and its competitive edge lost to plants in developing countries that paid workers far lower wages. One longtime worker told anthropologist Katherine Newman:

> I worked there forty-seven years and one month. I was one of many people in my family. My niece worked there. My two brothers, my father. You see, Singer's in the old days, it was a company that went from one generation to the other (Newman, 1988).

THE IMPACT OF ECONOMIC RESTRUCTURING

Young workers without a college education have been particularly hard hit by the changes in the U.S. economy. The growth of semiskilled and skilled manufacturing jobs has slowed because of two factors. The first is technological change, such as growing use of computers in offices and factories; the new technologies allow firms

Families and Public Policy

Homeless Families: The Tip of the Iceberg

It is one of the paradoxes of public debates about the family that the phenomenon of homeless families, which emerged in the 1980s, has received so much attention compared with the more general problems of poor families. To be sure, homelessness is worthy of public concern. Although few homeless families were visible in 1980, by 1987 about 35,000 families a night stayed in shelters for the homeless (Burt & Cohen, 1989). Over the course of a year, a larger number—perhaps as many as 100,000 families—spent at least one night in a shelter (Rossi, 1994). (Reliable figures for the 1990s are not available.)

But these families are just a small share of the number with incomes so low that they face the same kinds of risks the homeless face. Several studies have examined why some families become homeless and others don't, and why the number of homeless families has increased.

To become homeless, a family must have both a low income and weak ties to other kin. That is to say, it must have too little money to pay rent and too few relatives it can call upon for shelter. Single-parent families are vulnerable on both counts; their incomes tend to be low, and they cannot rely on the resources of a second parent and his or her kin. That is why the vast majority of homeless families are single-parent families (Jencks, 1994). Yet most poor single-parent families are not homeless. Peter Rossi (1994) estimated that in the mid-1980s more than two million single-parent families had incomes that were less than half the poverty level. At

most, about 5 percent of these families spent a night in a shelter during a given year.[1] The other 95 percent constitute what Rossi calls the "precariously housed," those who are especially vulnerable to homelessness through deep poverty and the lack of a second parent but who manage to avoid it.

Why have a small but growing percentage of the poor appeared at the door of public shelters for the homeless since 1980? Several factors contribute. Rossi emphasizes the consequences of the restructuring of the economy, especially the worsening job opportunities for young adults without a college education. In an analysis consistent with this chapter, Rossi argues that the decline in manufacturing jobs has undercut the ability of many young adults to earn enough to marry. It may also have reduced the ability of other relatives to provide assistance. Moreover, marriage may have decreased among the poor and nonpoor alike for other reasons having to do with women's greater economic independence or with cultural changes such as increased individualism. In any event, the growth of poor single-parent families was a key factor. According to Rossi's estimates, in the 1970s there were 1 million single-parent families with incomes less than half the poverty level but by 1991 there were 2.5 million.

Rossi and Christopher Jencks also note that the average value of welfare payments has dropped substantially since the mid-1970s because Congress and state legislatures did not adjust them for increases in the cost of living. So families with no other sources of income have been less able to afford housing. (The time limits on welfare

passed by Congress in 1996 may therefore cause an increase in family homelessness; see Chapter 6.) Moreover, the supply of low-cost rental housing has declined since the 1980s, either through demolition, remodeling into high rent properties, or neglect and abandonment by slum landlords (Koegl, Burnam, & Baumohl, 1996).

Although rates of mental illness and substance abuse are higher among homeless families than among Americans in general, homeless families show *less* mental illness and substance abuse than do homeless adults. Compared with homeless adults, then, it seems that the problems that lead families to become homeless have more to do with poverty, housing, and the increase in single-parenthood among the poor than with mental illness or drugs (Shinn & Weitzman, 1996). In general, family homelessness is more common among minority groups than among non-Hispanic whites; but studies suggest that poor Hispanic families have a substantially lower rate of homelessness than do poor African-American families (González Baker, 1996). Part of the difference may reflect the greater tendency of Hispanic families to live in overcrowded housing.

Moreover, in a peculiar way, the growing number of shelters may have helped "cause" the increase in homeless families. Nearly all homeless families live in public shelters. Parents go to great lengths to spare their children the harsh difficulties of living in public spaces, and their relatives may accept great inconveniences to share apartments with them. Moreover, state agencies will often remove children from parents who are living in automobiles, at train stations, or on

Homeless families, such as this family living in a shelter, became a cause for public concern in the 1980s and 1990s.

streets (Jencks, 1994). When a new shelter is opened, parents in the worst housing situations—those doubling or tripling up in crowded apartments, living with abusive partners, or exhibiting behavior that makes their relatives want them to leave—take advantage of it. Since the early 1980s, the number of shelters for families has expanded rapidly; a 1988 government survey found that 41 percent of family shelters had been started in the previous four years (Rossi, 1994). The more shelters available, the more "precariously housed" families show up at their doors and are officially counted as homeless.

This is not to diminish the seriousness of the problems faced by very poor families who cannot maintain their own living quarters. Many of the shelters were started by organizations that responded to what they perceived as an increase in the number of families with difficulties so severe that they could not find and keep adequate places to live. The increases in very poor single-parent families in the 1980s and 1990s were real. It must be noted, though, that the increase in serious poverty affected many more "homed" families than homeless families, and yet public attention focused on the latter. Americans seemed far more sympathetic to families living in shelters than to the larger and growing number of poor families sharing cramped quarters with relatives or barely avoiding eviction from their own apartments.

The public reaction suggested that most Americans think every family ought to have a home, whether or not their poverty is in any sense their own making. Homelessness grabbed the guts of many Americans whose hearts were hardened against stories of hardships among the poor. But family homelessness is just the tip of the iceberg of serious poverty among families—an iceberg that grew ominously in the 1980s. Passengers aboard the Titanic learned the hard way that it's dangerous to ignore the rest of an iceberg. We would be wise to heed their lesson.

[1] I derived this figure by dividing 100,000 by 2 million and converting the result to a percentage.

to replace workers with machines. The second factor is the movement of factory production to developing nations such as Taiwan and Mexico, where wages are much lower. Due to these changes, there is a growing shortage of full-time jobs, with fringe benefits, that pay substantially above the minimum wage and yet are available to persons without a college degree. These were the kinds of jobs that used to allow high school–educated young adults in this country to support a family.

More and more, what's available to young workers without a college education is low-paying service and unskilled manual-labor jobs, often on a contingency basis. **Contingent workers** are those who are hired temporarily or on a part-time basis and who typically do not receive fringe benefits such as health insurance, retirement pensions, and paid vacations. Many corporations have dismissed some of their full-time employees and then adjusted to ups and downs in business by hiring and firing lower-paid contingent workers. The majority of new jobs created by companies in recent years have been part-time; by the early 1990s, about one-third of the labor force was made up of contingent workers (*Time,* 1993). Writes economist Frank Levy, "A declining proportion of jobs pay enough to support the middle-class standard of living" (Levy, 1987). Even middle-class jobs are not immune to these problems: As corporations "downsize" their managerial workforce to save money, middle-aged white-collar workers can find themselves out of work. Still, the problems of the job market are substantially worse for people without a college education.

In contrast, the 1950s and 1960s were prosperous times for American families. Between 1945 and 1973, the average income of full-time workers, adjusted for inflation, doubled (Levy & Michel, 1991). Young men and women growing up in the 1950s and 1960s expected that they would eventually earn more than their parents, just as their parents were earning more than their grandparents. In 1973, however, the Organization of Petroleum Exporting Countries raised the price of oil fourfold and the economies of the Western nations plunged into recession. Income growth stopped, and, more than 25 years later, wages are still stagnant. Particularly hard hit were the kinds of entry-level jobs for which young parents tend to be qualified. The impact of the economic slump was so great that the wages of the average male worker in his twenties and early thirties were lower in the mid-1980s than in 1970, after adjusting for inflation (Levy, 1987). Indeed, among young men who had recently entered the job market, high school *graduates* in the 1980s were earning less, on average, than high school *dropouts* in the 1970s (U.S. Bureau of Labor Statistics, 1993). Consequently, the gap between the wages of more-educated and less-educated male workers has widened considerably since the 1970s. To make matters worse, housing prices have risen substantially.

UNEQUAL DISTRIBUTION OF INCOME

Not only have wages failed to grow, but earnings have become more unequal. While the earnings of workers without a college education have been decreasing, the earnings of college graduates have been stable or increasing (Juhn, Murphy & Pierce, 1993). More generally, the distribution of family income has become more unequal. Suppose that every family in the nation tossed its annual income into one huge pot and then they all lined up, one family in back of the other. If we wanted the **distribution of family income**—the proportion of the total income of all families in the nation that each family receives—to be equal, we would simply give each family in line the same amount of money from the pot. If we wanted the distribution to be unequal, we might give, say, 35 percent of all the money in the pot to

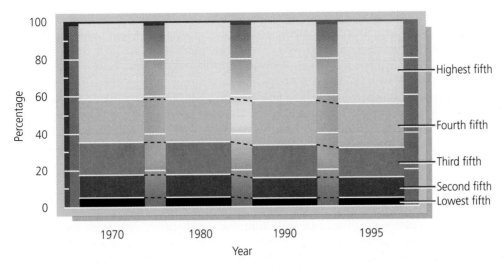

FIGURE 4.1 Share of income received by each fifth of families, 1970–1995. (*Source:* U.S. Bureau of the Census, 1997f. Historical Income Tables, Table F-2, "Share of Aggregate Income Received by Each Fifth and Top 5 Percent of Families, by Race and Hispanic Origin of Households." [On-line]. Available: www.census.gov. Accessed: December 24, 1997.)

the first one-fifth of families in the line, 30 percent to the next one-fifth, 20 percent to the next one-fifth, 10 percent to the next one-fifth, and just 5 percent to the last one-fifth. In fact, the actual distribution of family income in the United States is even more unequal than this hypothetical experiment would create. Moreover, inequality has increased since the early 1970s. Figure 4.1 shows the income shares of each fifth of families from 1970 to 1995. During this period, the share of income that went to the bottom fifth declined from 5.4 to 4.4 percent. Although this does not look like a substantial change, it means that the bottom fifth's income share dropped by about 20 percent. The second- and third-lowest fifths also saw their shares shrink. Even the next-to-highest fifth had a modest decrease. Only the top fifth of all families increased its income share substantially; it rose from 40.9 to 46.5 percent. During this period, then, the wealthy were getting wealthier while the poor were getting poorer and those in the middle were struggling to keep up.

Income inequality among families has increased for three reasons:

- The growing inequality in the earnings of men.
- The growth of single-parent families.
- The movement of middle-class wives into the workforce.

We might call the first reason the Kenny Merten effect: Men with less education and few skills have seen their incomes drop, on average, whereas men with more education have seen their incomes rise.[4] Consequently, the gap has widened between families with blue-collar husbands and families with white-collar husbands. The second reason is important because families with only one parent must rely on the earnings of one wage earner. And women's earnings are, on average, lower than men's (see *Families and Public Policy:* The Earnings Gap, in Chapter 3; and also Chapter 10). So the growth of single-parent families has widened inequality by creating a larger number of low- and moderate-income families.

[4]There is disagreement, however, among economists about the role of men's earnings in the rise of income inequality. Some economists argue that declines in the number of men who work full-time or who work at all are more important than differences in the earnings of employed men (Haveman, 1996).

The third reason is perhaps more subtle. A few decades ago, most of the married women who worked for pay came from poor and working-class families. In contrast, most middle-class married women did not work for pay. As a result, the net effect of wives' employment was to boost the incomes of poor and working-class families more than the incomes of middle-class families; and this effect reduced family income inequality. Over the last few decades, however, many middle-class wives have taken jobs outside the home. Their employment raised the incomes of families in which the husband already was earning a good income. Therefore, the rise in married women's employment since about 1970 has actually increased family income inequality (Burtless & Karoly, 1995).

Trends in Poverty   Poverty decreased in the United States during the prosperous 1950s and 1960s, but since then it has actually increased. Each year the U.S. government calculates an official **poverty line** and publishes statistics on the number of families with incomes below the line. The poverty line is a strange concoction that no one likes but no analyst can do without. It was established in the mid-1960s, when federal officials figured out how much it would cost to buy enough food to meet the Agriculture Department's standard for an "economy" diet—and then, on the assumption that families spend one-third of their income on food, simply multiplied by three (Katz, 1989). To account for inflation, this standard (which is adjusted for the number of people in the family) is multiplied every year by the increase in the cost of living. Advocates for the poor claim it is too low and therefore underestimates the low-income population; many conservatives claim it is too high. Its main virtue is that it can be used to examine changes over time in the percentage of families that fall above or below it. In 1996, the line stood at $15,991 for a family of two adults and two children under 18 and at $12,641 for a family of one adult and two children (U.S. Bureau of the Census, 1997g).

Figure 4.2 shows the percentage of families with children under 18 that fell below the poverty line each year from 1959 to 1996. Information on African-American families is available only from 1967 onward, and for Hispanic families

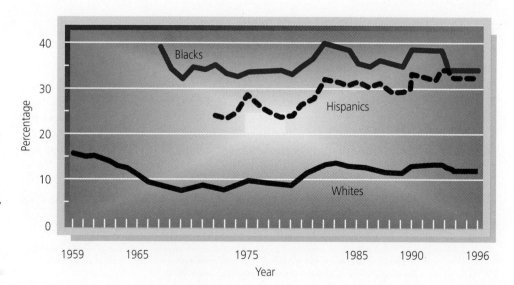

FIGURE 4.2 Percent of families with children under 18 that had incomes below the poverty line, for whites, blacks, and Hispanics, 1959–1996. (*Source:* U.S. Bureau of the Census. 1997g.)

(which may be of any race) from 1972 onward. As can be seen, the percentage of families below the line dropped for white families from 1959 through the early 1970s, and for African-American families from 1967 through the early 1970s. (Other statistics in the same government report suggest that African-American poverty had been declining sharply throughout the 1960s.) When the economy began to decline in the mid-1970s, however, the percentage of families in poverty began to rise for African Americans and whites and, by 1993, had attained levels not seen since the 1960s. Since 1993, poverty rates for African-American and white families have declined somewhat. Hispanic families showed a sharp rise in poverty between 1972 and 1982 and little change subsequently. In 1996, about one in eight white families with children under 18, and about one in three Hispanic and African-American families with children under 18 were living in poverty, according to the official definition, as were 21 percent of all U.S. children.

Not only did poverty increase during this period, it also became increasingly concentrated in the growing numbers of households headed by divorced, separated, never-married, or widowed mothers. Whereas about one-fourth of all poor families were headed by single mothers in 1960, more than one-half were headed by single mothers in 1996 (U.S. Bureau of the Census, 1997g). These single-parent families tend to remain poor longer than low-income two-parent families, according to a national study, the Panel Study of Income Dynamics (PSID), which is based on multiple interviews of the same families since the late 1960s. Economist Greg Duncan examined families in the PSID that were poor at any time between 1969 and 1978 and isolated two groups of low-income families: the "temporarily poor," who fell below the poverty line only 1 or 2 years during the 10-year period, and the "persistently poor," who fell below the line at least 8 of the 10 years. Most temporarily poor families, he found, had an adult male in the household, but 61 percent of the persistently poor families were headed by a single woman. In addition to family structure, race also affected the likelihood of being persistently poor. Regardless of family structure, most of the temporarily poor were white, but 62 percent of the persistently poor were black. Families in which the head was both black and a single woman made up 31 percent of the persistently poor (Duncan, 1984). (The connections among race, family structure, and poverty are explored in the next chapter.)

Prospects for Dual-Earner Couples   During the 1970s and 1980s, many families in the middle of the income distribution kept up with the cost of living only because wives took jobs outside the home. Figure 4.3 shows the trends since 1973 in the median incomes of three kinds of families. (The median is the midpoint in the distribution, the point at which as many families have higher incomes as have lower incomes. All dollar figures are expressed in 1992 dollars, adjusted for increases over time in the cost of living.) The bottom line shows that there was little change in the median incomes of families that were headed by women without husbands present. The middle line shows how married-couple families without wives in the paid labor force fared. The median income for this group declined by about 10 percent—a sharp break from the increases of the 1950s and 1960s. The only increase in income came for married-couple families in which the wife worked for pay, as shown by the top line. The gap between the median incomes of single-earner married couples and dual-earner married couples rose from about $11,000 in 1973 to about $23,000 in 1996 (U.S. Bureau of the Census, 1997f). With housing prices rising and young men's wages declining, families

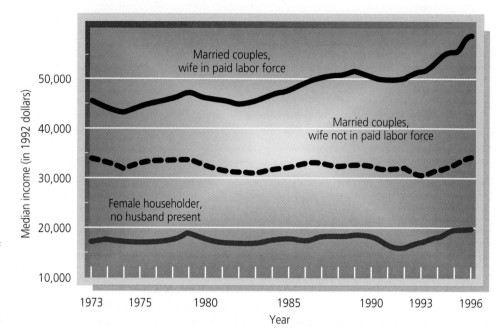

FIGURE 4.3 Median income of three types of families, 1973–1996. (*Source:* U.S. Bureau of the Census, 1993e, 1997f.)

needed a second income to live the kind of lives they aspired to. An increasing number of them chose to have wives enter the paid labor force.

These income trends led economist Frank Levy, in his study of U.S. income distribution since the 1940s, to write, "The most striking development is in families' connection to the economy" (Levy, 1987). In the 1940s, Levy notes, most families had two parents and one earner, whether they were rich or poor. There wasn't much variation in family structure. Yet by the 1980s, more than half of the wealthier families had two earners, while nearly half of the poorer families had no earners.[5] In the 1940s, the key economic difference between families was how much the husband earned. Today, the key difference increasingly is whether or not there is a husband in the household at all. As the link between family structure and poverty grows stronger, persistent poverty is becoming the property of single mothers and their children and prosperity is becoming the property of dual-earner, two-parent families.

CLASS DIFFERENCES IN FAMILY LIFE

In part because of the different ways they are connected to the economy, the family lives of parents and children vary from social class to social class. Families vary in how many parents are present, in how many steady earners are present, in the ways women and men interact, in the kind of assistance they receive from relatives living in the household and elsewhere, in their attitudes toward childrearing, and in many other ways. They are not completely different, of course; there are similarities that run across classes—similarities that would be apparent to someone visiting from a non-Western culture where, for instance, parents are heavily

[5]Specifically, in 1984, among the wealthiest 40 percent of all families, 60 percent had two earners, whereas among the poorest 20 percent of all families, 44 percent had no earner. See Levy (1987).

involved in helping their children choose spouses, newly married couples move in with the husband's family, and adult children care for their aged parents in their homes. And there is much variation within each social class. Nevertheless, there are some distinctive characteristics that are worth studying.

LOWER-CLASS FAMILIES

A large literature dating back to the Great Depression shows that a husband's place in the family is heavily dependent on whether he has a job.[6] In the cultures of all industrialized nations, men have been viewed as the main earners; providing a steady income has been seen as their responsibility. Rightly or wrongly, women's economic contribution has been viewed as secondary, although this perception may be changing as they increasingly work outside the home. When wives choose not to work for pay, or when they lose their jobs, they are not looked down upon. But when husbands lose their jobs, as happens frequently to husbands in lower-class families, their authority in their homes decreases, their self-respect declines, and other family members treat them with less respect as well. Chapter 10 examines in more detail how a husband's unemployment affects a married couple and their children.

Chronic Poverty and Kin Networks   When a man's unemployment problems are chronic—when he is unable or unwilling to find steady employment over many years—he may be viewed, and may view himself, as having failed to fulfill a central role in his life. In a community with many chronically unemployed men, young mothers rely less on marriage and more on other kinship ties for support. Commonly, in poverty areas, young mothers, many of them unmarried, receive help from their own mothers in raising their children. They may also get money or assistance from sisters and brothers, friends, and, sometimes, the fathers of their children. The result is **women-centered kinship**, a kinship structure in which the strongest bonds of support and caregiving occur among a network of women, most of them relatives, who may live in more than one household. Mothers, grandmothers, sisters, and other female kin hold most of the authority over children and provide most of the supervision.

One such community is Potter Addition, David Harvey's pseudonym for a poverty-ridden neighborhood on the rural-urban fringe of a city in the midwestern corn belt (Harvey, 1993). When studied by Harvey in the early 1970s, its residents, all white, had been driven off the land by the growth of large corporate farms that had replaced farm labor with more-efficient farm machinery. Having little education and few marketable skills, the members of this displaced rural population— and its young men, in particular—could find few steady jobs that paid well enough to provide adequately for a family. Instead, the men typically held a series of low-paying, unskilled jobs and experienced bouts of unemployment in between. Harvey writes:

> *I discovered jumbled job histories in which a man might begin his occupational life as a gas station attendant, graduate to being a roofer, take a job as a janitor, and then five or ten years later return to being a gas station attendant* (Harvey, 1993).

---

[6]See, for example, Robert Cooley Angell, *The Family Encounters the Depression* (New York: Charles Scribner's Sons, 1936); Ruth Shonle Cavan and Katherine Howland Ranck, *The Family and the Depression: A Study of 100 Chicago Families* (Chicago: University of Chicago Press, 1938); and Mirra Komarovsky, *The Unemployed Man and His Family* (New York: Octagon Books, 1971). This literature will be discussed in Chapter 10.

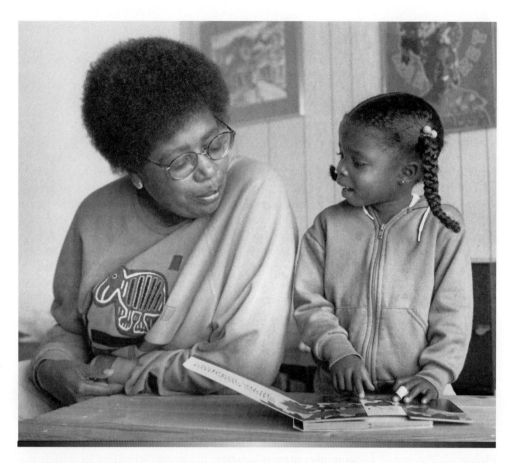

In the female-centered kinship networks often found among low-income families, grandmothers do much of the childcare.

Teenage pregnancy was common, and abortions were frowned upon. When a teenage girl became pregnant, parents and other kin pressured the father into marrying. But given the bleak employment prospects of the young man, his wife depended heavily on her mother and other kin for support. Although the man had become a father, his economic failure (or the expectation that he would likely fail) prevented him from playing the conventional role of husband. Without the respect due to a breadwinner, his ability to supervise and discipline his children was limited; rather, his wife often took charge of the discipline as well as the care. The husband's role within the household minimized, he spent most of his time in stereotypical male pursuits outside the household, such as working on cars or drinking with friends.

When the children of Potter Addition reached adolescence and themselves had children as teenagers, the result was a compression of the generations: Women often became mothers as teenagers and grandmothers in their thirties. Children were raised primarily by their grandmothers because their teenage mothers were too young to assume the main responsibility for raising them. This alternating-generation pattern of childrearing also occurred in a low-income African-American neighborhood studied by Linda Burton (1990). In both communities, a woman's first experience as the primary caretaker for a new baby often did not occur until she became a grandmother. The two central roles in the women-centered kin networks, Harvey argued, were, first, the grandmother who is also a "mother" to her grandchildren and, second, the young mother who, still in the care of her own mother, is something of a sister to her own children. Marriage, wrote Harvey, was usually a "secondary alliance" compared with the grandmother-mother-child axis.[7]

The extended kinship ties of the women-centered network help its members survive the hardships of poverty. If the members of a household have little to eat or are evicted from their homes, relatives and friends in their network will provide whatever assistance they can. Sisters or aunts who are themselves poor will nevertheless give food or money because they know that in the future they may need emergency help. In this way, the kinship networks of the poor spread the burdens of poverty, cushioning its impact on any one household and allowing its members to get by from day to day. In a widely cited study of The Flats, a low-income African-American neighborhood in the Midwest, anthropologist Carol Stack found that individuals could draw upon complex network of relatives and friends that extended over many households (Stack, 1974).

In fact, individuals actively cultivate these networks so that they will have assistance when they need it. For example, Stack writes of Lydia, a woman in The Flats who did not need assistance from kin as long as she was married and therefore did not want to be obligated to them. Instead of sharing with kin, Lydia used the money she and her husband were earning to buy a house and furniture. She generally refused to trade clothes or lend money, and on the few occasions when she and her husband gave something to a relative, they never asked for anything in return. Then, however, Lydia's marriage broke up. During the five-month period when the marriage was ending, Lydia suddenly began to give things to relatives. She gave some of her nice clothes to her sisters and nieces, a couch to her brother, and a television set to her niece (Stack, 1974).

By giving away these things, Lydia was attempting to create a kinship network that she could rely on when she was no longer married. Her actions are typical of how poor people actively construct extended kin networks by exchanging goods and services with others who are in need. Poor people cannot afford to rely solely on *assigned kinship*—the more restricted set of kinship ties that middle-class people acquire automatically at birth and when they marry: father, mother, grandparents, husband, wife, children. Rather, they make use of *created kinship* to recruit assistance wherever it can be found.

The Costs of Kin Networks   Yet membership in such a kinship network is not without cost—which is why Lydia was reluctant to exchange resources with kin as long as she was married. Because an individual's meager income must be shared with many others, it is difficult for her or him to rise out of poverty. Stack described what happened when an older couple unexpectedly inherited $1,500. At first, they wished to use the money for a down payment on a house. Then other members of their network, upon learning of the windfall, asked for help. Several relatives needed train fare to attend a funeral in another state; another needed $25 so her telephone wouldn't be turned off; a sister was about to be evicted because of overdue rent. Moreover, the public assistance office cut their children off welfare temporarily. Within six weeks, the inheritance was gone. The couple acquiesced to these requests because they knew they might need assistance in the future. Even someone who finds a good job may not withdraw from a network unless she is confident that the job will last a long time.

[7]Harvey (1993), quoted at 199. Instead of "women-centered," Harvey uses the term "uxoricentric," drawn from anthropological terminology.

Thus, these kinship-based sharing networks, admirable and necessary as a bulwark against destitution, can nevertheless serve to perpetuate poverty across generations. When another young woman in Stack's study decided to marry, the relatives and friends in her network tried to talk her out of it. Her contributions were valuable, and they did not want to lose her. Recognizing that she and her husband couldn't accumulate enough money to rise above poverty unless she left the network, the young woman married and then left the state that same night (Stack, 1974). In Potter Addition, a woman described how she and her husband moved to a farm outside town, only to see a stream of hard-luck relatives move in and out, eating their food. Of one relative who hoarded his food while eating hers, she said, "To this day, I can't figure out why I didn't throw him out." But then she recalled to the interviewer the many earlier times when she and her husband had received assistance from her guest (Harvey, 1993). Turning aside the demands of kin is a step poor people are reluctant to take unless they are sure they won't need help in the future. The problem is that unless a person denies some requests, it is difficult to accumulate any savings, and without savings it is difficult to leave the network.

WORKING-CLASS FAMILIES

How do sociologists view working-class families, perched above poverty although typically not by much? The predominant picture of working-class families still comes from several widely cited studies conducted in the 1950s, 1960s, and early 1970s. For example, after living in a working-class Italian-American neighborhood in Boston for eight months in 1957 and 1958, Herbert Gans reported that daily life centered around the family circle, a group of relatives and friends who lived near one another and who socialized largely with one another (Gans, 1982). Most households contained the conjugal family of husband, wife, and children, but conjugal families were embedded in the larger extended family and in many ways were secondary to it. Married couples tended to live near the wife's mother, who provided frequent assistance and emotional support. A study of working-class families in London in 1955 by Michael Young and Peter Willmott also found a strong bond between the wife and her "Mum," who tended to live nearby (Young & Willmott, 1986). When members of the family circle in Gans's neighborhood socialized, the women sat in one room and the men sat in another.

Gender-Role Segregation   In fact, women and men's worlds were highly segregated.[8] In the economic realm, it was seen as men's place to earn money and women's place to care for the children and the home. Even though low incomes often led wives to work at least part time outside the home, the ideal remained the breadwinner-homemaker family. Being the sole earner was a source of pride for men, an ideal to strive for. As one husband is quoted as saying in Lillian Rubin's study of working-class families in 1972:

> *She doesn't have to work. We can get by. Maybe we'll have to take it easy on spending, but that's okay with me. It's worth it to have her home where she belongs* (Rubin, 1992).

But this picture of working-class families is now out of date. Gans, Young and Willmott, and Rubin have reissued their books with new introductions and

[8]See also Elizabeth Bott, *Family and Social Network* (London: Tavistock, 1957).

postscripts. All of them report that the distinctiveness of the working-class family has faded somewhat. The family circle is not as central to the sons and daughters of the Italian Americans Gans studied, he concluded in 1982, because greater affluence has reduced the need for mutual assistance, because migration to the suburbs has spread relatives apart, and because resistance has grown to the conformity that the family circle demands (Gans, 1982). In other words, the more-prosperous (compared with the 1950s) next generation did not need as often to borrow money, clothes, or food from their parents and siblings. Moreover, it is harder for the sons and daughters to socialize because they don't live as close to one another as family members of their parents' generation did. And the cultural drift toward individual fulfillment clashes with the pressure to maintain the same lifestyle as other members of the circle. According to Young and Willmott, writing in 1986, migration out of the working-class neighborhood of London they studied has loosened the bond between the daughter and her mum.

Gans and Rubin both also observe that the strict division of roles between wife and husband has weakened, although most men still do substantially less of the childcare and housework. Rubin notes that even when the women in her original study were working outside the home, they defined themselves primarily as wives and mothers. Paid work was something they did to help their families, but it was not an important part of their identity. Many shared their husbands' views that, ideally, they ought to stay home. By 1992, wrote Rubin in a new introduction to her book, these attitudes had changed: Women viewed employment as a proper activity, necessary to maintain their families' lifestyles and also a source of satisfaction and self-esteem (Rubin, 1992).

Changing Attitudes toward Gender Roles   The General Social Survey (GSS) provides further evidence of the changes among working-class families in attitudes about married women working outside the home. In most years since 1972, the GSS has included the question "Do you approve of a married woman earning money in business or industry if she has a husband capable of supporting her?" For each year in which the question was asked, Figure 4.4 shows the percentage who approved among married men under age 50, divided into two groups. The

FIGURE 4.4 Percent approving of a married woman earning money in business or industry if she has a husband capable of supporting her, for married men under 50, by occupation, 1972–1996. (*Source:* Davis & Smith, 1996a.)

first group (top line) includes men with white-collar occupations: professionals, managers, sales, and clerical workers. These are the kinds of occupations that men in middle-class families are more likely to have. The second group (bottom line) includes those with blue-collar occupations, the kinds that men in working-class families are more likely to have: factory workers, people who operate machinery, and skilled and unskilled laborers. As you can see, in 1972, blue-collar husbands were substantially less likely than middle-class men to approve of a married woman earning money. Yet by the mid-1990s the gap between the two groups had narrowed greatly. Although both occupational groups grew more likely to approve of a married woman working for pay, blue-collar husbands had changed their opinions more. Thus, the figure supports the claim that working-class men have become more accepting of wives' employment probably because of the increasing economic importance of wives' earnings to working-class families.

At all times during the two decades covered by the GSS, most women said they approved of married women earning money in business or industry even if they had a husband capable of supporting them. In 1977, the GSS asked whether respondents agreed with the statement "It is much better for everyone involved if the man is the achiever outside the home and the woman takes care of the home and family." Among married women under 50, a majority of those who had worked last at clerical or blue-collar jobs said that they agreed—they thought it was better if the man were the achiever. Only among women professionals and managers did a majority disagree. These responses suggest that many married women in 1977 did indeed believe women, ideally, shouldn't work outside the home and that this belief was strongest among those who might be termed working class. By the early 1990s, however, clerical and blue-collar women were much more likely to disagree with the statement than they had been one and a half decades earlier: Only about one-third agreed. This change in attitude fits Rubin's report that women in working-class families have incorporated paid employment into their image of a wife's proper role.

MIDDLE-CLASS FAMILIES

The Primacy of the Conjugal Family   The core of middle-class kinship in the United States has been the conjugal family of wife, husband, and children (Schneider & Smith, 1973). Typically, the middle-class conjugal family is more independent of kin than the working-class version. The married couple is expected to spend their income on their children and themselves rather than to provide financial assistance to siblings or other relatives. Any assets or savings are passed from parents to children, rather than being spread throughout a kin network. Income sharing is not as necessary, to be sure, because the standards of living of kin tend to be higher than among the working class or lower class. Yet standards of living are higher in part *because* it is expected that the conjugal family will spend its savings on a down payment for a house rather than doling it out to relatives who need train fare to attend funerals or to pay bills and *because* it is expected that the family will move away from kin, if necessary, to pursue better job opportunities.

A clever survey of adults in the Boston area in 1984 and 1985 demonstrated people's beliefs about the restricted kinship obligations of the conjugal family (Rossi & Rossi, 1990).[9] Alice and Peter Rossi presented 1,393 people with a set of

[9]Of the respondents, 94 percent were white, only 2 percent were unemployed, and over half were Catholic. The vignettes described here are a subset of a larger set of vignettes that the authors used.

"vignettes": brief, hypothetical descriptions of relatives and friends who were experiencing crises that might require "some financial help" or "comfort and emotional support." For example: "Your unmarried sister has undergone major surgery and will be bedridden for a few weeks. This problem is straining her financial resources." From a list of relatives and friends (e.g., child, father-in-law, cousin, neighbor), eight crises (e.g., "run out of unemployment benefits and no job in sight"), and two obligations ("to offer some financial help," "to offer comfort and emotional support"), a computer program selected one relative or friend, one crisis, and one obligation at random and printed a vignette. The process was repeated until 26 crisis vignettes had been generated randomly to present to each of the survey respondents. We will focus on the vignettes for which the respondent was asked to rate "How much of an obligation would you feel to offer some financial help?" on a scale from 0 to 10, where 0 meant no obligation at all and 10 meant a very strong obligation.

The mean obligation scores for offering financial help, for 15 common relatives and friends, averaged across the various vignettes, was plotted by Rossi and Rossi on a "wheel of obligation," which is reproduced as Figure 4.5. The closer to the center of the wheel, the stronger the sense of obligation people felt: A mean score

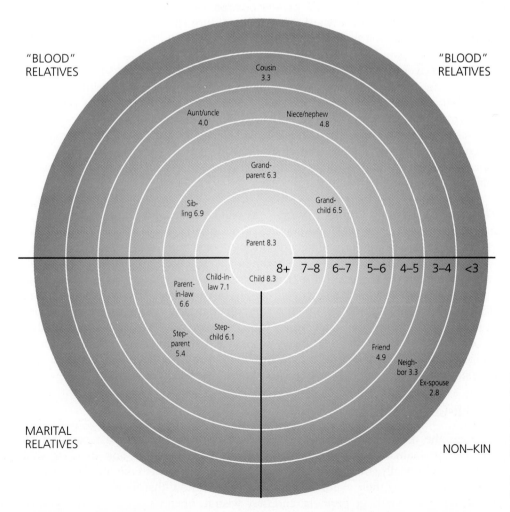

FIGURE 4.5 "Wheel of obligation": degree of obligation felt by survey respondents to various relatives and friends, for Boston-area adults, 1984–1985. (*Source:* Rossi & Rossi, 1990.)

of 10 would be plotted at the hub of the wheel, whereas a mean score lower than 3 would be plotted in the outer circle. Note first that most of the mean scores are close to the hub, indicating that people felt a moderate to high level of obligation to most kin. Only neighbors and ex-spouses had mean scores lower than four. (Of course, these are hypothetical obligations; we don't know whether people actually would provide financial assistance this freely.) Since it did not make sense to ask these kinds of questions about a person's current husband or wife, there is no score for spouses. Other studies suggest that strong bonds of obligation exist between spouses (Schneider, 1980).

Note also that the highest levels of obligation were expressed toward a person's parents and children. Indeed, all the relatives in the two circles surrounding the hub are related to a person through a child, a parent, or a spouse. This pattern suggests that adults felt the most obligation to the members of the conjugal or single-parent families in which they grew up and to the conjugal or single-parent families in which they have had children. These vertical kinship ties—up and down the chain of generations from parents to children to grandchildren—engender the strongest feelings of obligation. They are created by direct descent and by marriage. Contrast the degree of obligation adults felt toward more distant relatives such as aunts, uncles, nieces, nephews, and cousins: None has an average score of five or above. Kinship ties from a person's marriage—even a second marriage—are stronger than kinship ties toward these more distant blood relatives. For instance, note that the adults felt more obligation toward a stepchild than toward a cousin or a nephew. Obligations to the conjugal family, and to one's parents, seem to take precedence over those to other relatives.

The image of kinship suggested by these findings is of a tall, solid tree trunk with skinny branches: The vertical axis is strong as one moves from parents to children to grandchildren, but the horizontal links are weaker as one moves from parents to uncles, or from children to nieces. Resources are passed from a person's parents to his or her spouse and children, and then to the grandchildren. Assistance to elderly parents is likely to be much more substantial and more common than assistance to elderly aunts and uncles.

The Role of Women in "Doing" Kinship   As will be discussed further in Chapter 15, it is women who do most of the helping of other kin. This is true even in middle-class families, which are more likely than lower- or working-class families to have a husband living at home. On average, women spend more time than men doing the work of kinship (di Leonardo, 1987). They are more likely to send cards and flowers on birthdays and holidays, to plan family get-togethers, and to help a frail elderly parent. Many men rely on their wives to keep these contacts alive and to provide assistance. "On topic after topic," wrote Rossi and Rossi at the end of their book, "we have found that ties among women were stronger, more frequent, more reciprocal [i.e., both giving and receiving], and less contingent on circumstances [i.e., not just given in a crisis] than those of men" (Rossi & Rossi, 1990).

UPPER-CLASS FAMILIES

Whereas the main economic task for families from other classes is to accumulate wealth, the main task for upper-class families is to preserve and increase their wealth. Traditionally, this has meant that upper-class parents take an active role in determining whom their children will marry. They know that their children will be highly desirable marriage partners, and they wish to obtain a good match: someone from a family that also has wealth or, at least, someone who is likely to help the children manage their wealth wisely. In England in the 1500s, rich families usually chose their child's spouse, creating what is termed an **arranged marriage**. When two wealthy families were involved, arranged marriages often seemed more like economic alliances than romantic partnerships. Indeed, historians suggest that there was little romance in many aristocratic marriages (Stone, 1977).

However, by the 1600s, the ideals of companionship and intimacy in marriage spread and arranged marriages became less common. (They always had been uncommon among the poorer classes, who had less to gain by an arranged marriage.) Still, many parents strongly influenced their child's choice. Recall that records from Hingham, Massachusetts, show that prior to 1700 families tended to marry their oldest daughters first, then their next oldest, and so on, suggesting substantial parent involvement (Smith, 1973). Records from Andover, Massachusetts, indicated that in the 1600s and early 1700s, sons tended to marry only when their fathers were ready to turn over control of their land (Greven, 1970).

By the nineteenth century, parental influence over the timing of marriage and the choice of a partner had diminished substantially in the more prosperous classes. Even among the elite, it is likely that most children chose their spouse. Yet upper-class parents retained an indirect influence on their children's marriage partners through strategies that persist to this day. First and foremost was separate schooling. Wealthy children were much more likely to attend the nation's private boarding schools, where they met children from other wealthy families. John D. Rockefeller, Jr., heir to the most famous nineteenth-century fortune in the United States, met his future wife, Abby Aldrich, while attending Brown. Rockefeller certainly chose his wife; but he did so at an elite Ivy League university where, not coincidentally, the woman he chose came from a powerful Rhode Island family (Keller, 1991).

This pattern of separate education continued into the twentieth century. A study of marriage announcements in the Sunday *New York Times* from 1962 to 1972 found that 70 percent of the men and 84 percent of the women reported attending private schools, such as St. Paul's, Exeter, Andover, and Miss Porter's (Blumberg & Paul, 1975). Upper-class children were also more likely to attend elite universities: 52 percent of the men in the *Times* wedding announcements had attended an Ivy League college, and 29 percent of the women had attended one of the Seven Sisters colleges.

Until recently, at least, the vast majority of upper-class wives did not work outside the home. Still, wives of corporate executives and managers have had important roles to play in furthering their husbands' careers. The executive's wife was expected to host dinner parties, to attend charity events, to establish friendly relations with the wives of other executives, and to be ready to move to another city, should the executive be transferred. Not only her husband but also her husband's company expected that she would devote her efforts to his advancement. Hanna Papanek (1973) aptly labeled this phenomenon the "two-person career." Upper-class women are instrumental in maintaining ties among wealthy kin, as a study of a Mexican elite family demonstrated. (See *Families in Other Cultures:* Kinship Networks among the Mexican Upper Class.)

In sum, the upper class have historically sought to conserve their wealth and transmit it to their children first by arranging marriages, then by controlling access to land, and most recently by controlling whom their children meet. And in this century, they evolved a style of marriage in which wives' rewards came through supporting their husbands' careers. Let me caution, however, that we don't know

Families in Other Cultures

Kinship Networks among the Mexican Upper Class

It is well established that lower-class family members frequently belong to extended kin networks that share resources and provide support to one another. These networks enable individuals to survive the economic crises of poverty by turning to their relatives for aid. Among the middle class, extended kinship ties are less important. Yet among the upper class, the importance of kinship often rises once again (Goode, 1982). Anthropologist Larissa Adler Lomnitz has demonstrated the importance of kin in two studies of the extremes of poverty and wealth in Mexico City. First, she studied poor people living in shantytowns in the city—sprawling settlements made up of one-room shacks or brick cabins without running water. The residents of these neighborhoods survived by pooling their resources among a kinship network, much as the residents of Potter Addition or The Flats did (Lomnitz, 1977).

Lomnitz next studied kinship ties at the other end of the social spectrum, the Gómez family, which traces its roots back to Don Carlos Gómez, a nineteenth-century farmer and village trader (Lomnitz, 1987). In 1978, the Gómez family was a large, mostly wealthy network of business owners and their wives and children, compris-

ing 360 people in five main branches. The businesses were privately held and family controlled, rather than being publicly held corporations. Prominent family members hired cousins, nephews, and brothers-in-law from their own branch, and sometimes from others, to work in their firms. It was expected that sons, who started to work for their fathers at an early age, would eventually take over the businesses. But as long as the father was alive, he retained control.

These economic arrangements, Lomnitz found, were supported by—or perhaps better said, made possible by—the structure of family and kinship. The basic unit was the grandfamily, a three-generation family composed of a father and mother, sons and daughters and their spouses, and grandchildren. Although married couples lived in their own households, the grandfamily members lived near one another and met often. For instance, once a week they went to their father and mother's home for a family dinner. The women of the grandfamily saw one another almost every day; moreover, the women kept in contact with women in other grandfamilies, maintaining the links of kinship. In each generation of each branch, at least one woman seemed to specialize in maintaining the links of kinship; Lomnitz

called these **centralizing women.** Their conversations included not only personal news but also news about family businesses in their own branch and others. Frequent ritual events, such as christenings, first communions, marriages, and funerals, provided occasions for contact among members of different branches.

These extensive ties were useful for two reasons. First, wealthier family members were a source of employment and of money to invest in new business ventures. With so much wealth controlled by the family, individuals looked to their kin for economic opportunities. Second, kinship ties provided some protection against the risks of doing business. An individual could have trust, *confianza*, that a relative would abide by the terms of an agreement to produce, deliver, or sell goods. If a person broke a business agreement or was consistently unable to meet the terms of agreements, he would be subject to the ridicule and scorn of the other members of the family. Family ties thus enforced honesty and hard work.

Lack of trust in one's associates is an example of what economists and sociologists call **transaction costs:** the costs of organizing and carrying out exchanges (Williamson, 1981; Treas, 1993). In most developed countries, business exchanges are governed by

the extent to which these patterns still hold as the twentieth century ends. Beginning in the 1960s, the elite universities began to enroll more public school students and most of them became coeducational; consequently, the educational experiences of the children of the upper class may not be as distinctive as they were. Given the massive increases in the number of married women in the paid labor force—including increases in managers and professionals—it is not clear how many wives still devote themselves to the advancement of their husbands' careers. There is little current research on the upper class, in large part because sociologists are more interested in studying disadvantaged groups.

For many Mexicans, the basic family unit is a three-generational grandfamily composed of a father and mother, sons and daughters and their spouses, and grandchildren.

laws about contracts and agreements, and markets for materials and capital (e.g., stocks and bonds) are closely regulated. Persons who violate the regulations can be sent to jail (junk-bond financier Michael Milken is an example). These laws and regulations reduce the risk to an investor or producer that his or her partners will not carry out the terms of agreements. As Lomnitz notes, however, the Gómez family began its rise during a time when the Mexican state was weak and politically unstable. Consequently, there was little state regulation and enforcement of economic exchanges. Instead of relying on the power of the state, Gómez family members relied on trust in kin. Their extreme reliance on this strategy may now be outdated. Lomnitz reports that the refusal of the family to incorporate its businesses and to centralize management has placed it at a disadvantage compared with the large multinational corporations that are increasingly dominant in the Mexican economy. In any case, the stories of the Gómez family and the shantytown dwellers illustrate why extended kinship ties seem to be more important at the two ends of the social class hierarchy than in the middle.

SOCIAL CLASS AND THE FAMILY

Across all social classes, the changing economic roles of women and men over the past few decades have altered family lives. In the 1960s and 1970s, social commentators debated whether it was "necessary" for married women to work. After all, standards of living had been far lower in the first half of the twentieth century, and yet few married women had worked outside the home. However, the continuing economic slide since 1973 has more or less ended that debate. Among the working class, objections to married women working outside the home have faded as decent-paying entry-level blue-collar jobs—the kind of jobs young husbands used to take—have dwindled. Whereas in the 1970s wives' employment was seen by many working-class couples as a sign of a husband's failure to provide adequately for his family, now it is seen as a necessary and acceptable contribution.

Among middle-class couples with college educations, the employment situation has been better; still, as noted earlier, men's wages have stagnated. Only two-earner couples have been beating inflation. Moreover, the price of housing has risen far faster than wages, placing the American dream of homeownership out of reach of more and more single-earner couples. In the 1950s and 1960s, payments on a median-priced home required just 15 to 18 percent of the average 30-year-old man's income. That figure rose to 20 percent in 1973 and then doubled to 40 percent in 1987 (Levy & Michel, 1991). Consequently, for middle-class couples, too, wives' employment is seen as necessary and acceptable.

To be sure, there are other reasons for the increase in wives' employment over the past few decades. As birthrates declined after the baby boom, the number of years in which women have intensive childrearing responsibilities also decreased. Raising one or two children is simply not a full-time, lifelong job. Knowing this, many young women keep closer ties to the labor market before and even during the years in which they have small children. Having work experience is also prudent protection against the growing risk of a divorce and single motherhood.

Not all the forces for change have been economic. The rise in divorce, for example, has both economic and cultural roots (see Chapter 12). People's expectations about what constitutes a good life have also changed. Young middle-class couples could, in theory, aspire only to the standard of living of the late 1940s and early 1950s, which for many consisted of an apartment or a small, one-story home, one car, a clothesline in the backyard for drying the laundry, one telephone, no stereo system, few restaurant meals, no airplane travel, and of course no VCRs or computers, and still keep one parent home all day. This is not an appealing prospect in a country where people have gotten used to a higher standard that is promoted by advertising and reinforced by the media.

It is hard to foresee, therefore, any scenario under which fewer married women would work outside the home. To the contrary, further increases are likely. Moreover, the rise is likely to widen the income gap between middle-class families, on the one hand, and working-class or lower-class families. Inequality will increase because better-off families have recently sent, and are now sending, large numbers of women into the workforce. In contrast, wives from lower-income families were the first to enter the workforce in large numbers beginning at midcentury, a trend that actually reduced family income equality (Levy & Michel, 1991). Future growth in married women's labor force participation, however, will come increasingly from the middle class.

With regard to kinship, perhaps the most important difference among the lower-class, working-class, and middle-class families studied in this chapter is the relative autonomy of the parent-child unit from other kin. In lower-class families, ties between mothers and an extended network of kin are often a more important source of support to the mother than ties to the father of her children—even if the mother is still married to the father. In Potter Addition, a young mother's tie to her mother was usually stronger than her tie to her husband. In The Flats, mothers' ties to the fathers of their children commonly were weak, even nonexistent. Two-parent households are more often present in working-class families, yet ties to other relatives, particularly to the wife's mother, remain important sources of support. In contrast, the two-parent household of the middle-class family is typically independent of day-to-day support from other kin, in large part because family members and their kin have less need for economic assistance. Nevertheless, family members seem to retain strong obligations to assist relatives from whom they have descended—parents and grandparents—and relatives who descend from them.

Still, it is becoming increasingly difficult to speak of "the" social class position of a family anymore. The old way of measuring a family's social class, namely by considering only the husband's occupation and income, is inadequate, given the greater number of dual-earner and single-parent families. In addition, it may be that husbands have a firmer grip on their class position than their wives. As will be discussed in the chapter on divorce, women who gain a high-social-class position by marrying men with high-paying jobs can lose that position if their marriages break up. After a divorce many middle-class women experience downward mobility as they reenter the job market after a long absence, receive modest child support payments, and perhaps sell their family home and move to a less-expensive neighborhood.

Social class is not the only way American society classifies families. Rather, racial and ethnic distinctions are also frequently made. It is to racial and ethnic differences in family patterns that we now turn.

SUMMARY

1. Families can be thought of as occupying a social class position according to their degree of power, privilege, and prestige. Four broad social classes were defined: upper-class families, middle-class families, working-class families, and lower-class families. These categories are ideal types; in real life it is sometimes difficult to place a family unambiguously into one of these categories. These difficulties are greater among two-earner and single-parent families because the categories date from an era when most families had two parents but only the father worked outside the home.

2. The restructuring of the U.S. economy has caused a shortage of semiskilled and skilled jobs that do not require a college education but still pay substantially more than the minimum wage. These are the kinds of jobs that less-educated young men used to rely on to provide support for their wives and children. Now many of these jobs have moved to other countries where the wage rate is much lower. Since 1973, the year of the oil price rise, family incomes have increased only for the growing number of families in which both the husband and the wife work for pay outside the home. Persistent poverty that lasts for several years has become more concentrated among single-parent families.

3. Lower-class family members are often embedded in women-centered kinship networks, in large part because men cannot consistently earn enough to support their children. In these networks, poor people share what little they have with relatives and friends in order to cushion the hardships of poverty. Membership in a sharing network can also make it difficult for an individual to rise above poverty because it is hard to accumulate savings while providing financial help to many others.

4. Working-class kinship patterns are more likely to involve two-parent households than are lower-class kinship patterns, but even so, the household is often embedded in a larger extended family. Studies dating back a few decades suggested that wives remained very close to their mothers, with whom they exchanged support. The same studies also reported that the worlds of men and women were highly segregated, with both women and men believing strongly that it was a woman's place to stay home, if possible, to raise the family while the man earned the income. However, these distinctive qualities of the working-class family—its close ties to a family circle and its rigid division of labor and responsibility—appear to have lessened substantially over the past decade or two.

5. Middle-class kinship patterns are distinguished by a greater emphasis on the parent-child unit compared with ties to other kin. The strongest obligations are felt toward one's spouse, parents, and children. Ties created by marriage, even to stepchildren and to stepparents, are stronger than ties to blood relatives such as uncles, aunts, and cousins. The result is a kinship structure with a strong vertical axis of support from parents to children to grandchildren, and weaker horizontal support to other blood relatives. Women do most of the work of maintaining these kinship networks, keeping in contact with relatives and providing most of the support.

6. Upper-class kinship patterns are distinguished by parents' greater influence over their children's choice of spouse. Parents exert more influence because they wish to pass the wealth they have accumulated to their children's generation. In the twentieth century, the parents' major influence has come from educating their children separately from the other social classes. Upper-class wives of executives and professionals often worked hard behind the scenes to advance their husbands' careers. It is not known how much of the distinctiveness of upper-class kinship patterns exists today.

KEY TERMS

social class
power
prestige
privilege
ideal type
upper-class families

middle-class families
working-class families
lower-class families
contingent workers
distribution of family income
poverty line

women-centered kinship
arranged marriage
centralizing women
transaction costs

FAMILIES ON THE INTERNET

It used to be that you had to go to the library and sort through government publications to find statistics on income and poverty. Now most of the key statistics are available on-line, and you can download and print many reports. For statistics on poverty, the place to go is the U.S. Bureau of the Census home page, **www.census.gov**. Click on *Subjects A–Z,* then *P,* then *Poverty.* The Bureau's annual statistical reports on poverty, from which Figure 4.2 was tabulated, are in Portable Document Format (PDF) and can be downloaded using Adobe Acrobat

software (which itself can usually be downloaded free from the Adobe web site, www.adobe.com). Historical tables are available as well.

For basic information about measuring poverty, you can turn to the Institute for Research on Poverty at the University of Wisconsin, **www.ssc.wisc.edu/irp**. Its home page contains answers to frequently asked questions such as, "How is poverty measured?", "What is the poverty line?", and "What is the Consumer Price Index and how is it used?" The site also contains links to many other poverty-related sites.

CHAPTER 5

Race, Ethnicity, and Families

Perhaps more than any other nation, the United States is continually reinventing itself. It began as a society dominated by British settlers. They took land from an indigenous people whom the early European explorers, thinking they had reached Asia, called Indians. As the Southern plantation economy developed, the planters imported African slaves to work the land. In the nineteenth century, a war with Mexico and a purchase of land from France added vast territories that included Spanish-speaking and French-speaking people. In addition, immigrants from China were recruited to build the transcontinental railroad. From the mid–nineteenth century through the early twentieth century, a high tide of immigrants flowed in from Europe, first from Ireland, Germany, and other Northern countries and then from Italy, Poland, Greece, Russia, and other countries to the south and east.

   The great European immigration maintained the dominance of Western culture in the United States. So did laws that restricted the number of immigrants from Asia and Latin America, such as the Chinese Exclusion Act of 1882. As a result, the United States remained a society with a white majority of European descent, a substantial African-American minority, and smaller numbers of Asians, Latin Americans, and Native Americans. As recently as 1950, African Americans constituted about three-fourths of the non-European population (O'Hare, 1992).

Yet since midcentury, immigration has once again been reinventing the United States. A revision of immigration laws in 1965 allowed larger numbers of non-Europeans to enter the country. Economic opportunities and political change drew Latin American and Asian immigrants:

- Puerto Ricans (who are U.S. citizens at birth) moving from their Caribbean island to New York.
- Cubans fleeing the Communist revolution for Miami.
- Mexicans crossing their northern border both legally and illegally.
- Vietnamese allies evacuated by helicopter as Saigon fell.
- Chinese, Koreans, and other Asians flying across the Pacific.

Between 1980 and 1995, the Asian population more than doubled from 3.6 million to 8.7 million; and the Hispanic population nearly doubled from 14.6 million to 27.0 million. In contrast, the African-American population, without a large immigration stream to feed it, grew by a slower 21 percent from 26.1 million to 31.6 million (U.S. Bureau of the Census,1996e). As a result, for the first time in American history, African Americans now make up a minority (46 percent in 1995) of the non-European population of the United States.

Moreover, population projections indicate that, at current rates of immigration and births, Hispanics would surpass African Americans as the largest non-European group by 2010 (O'Hare, 1992). And if current rates were to continue until 2050, the demographic domination of white Europeans might come to an end—they would make up just 53 percent of the population (U.S. Bureau of the Census,1996e). (The white European population has been increasing far more slowly than other groups.) Of course, it is unlikely that current rates will continue unchanged; a similar projection 50 years ago would have missed the surge of Hispanic and Asian immigrants. Still, it is clear that the composition of the U.S. population is changing dramatically. Already, one in four adults and one in three children belong to a non-European racial or ethnic group (O'Hare, 1992).

RACIAL-ETHNIC GROUPS

All this, however, begs the question of what constitutes a racial or ethnic group. We generally think of racial groups as people with a common set of physical features that distinguish them from other groups. The boundaries of racial groups, however, vary from country to country and from the past to the present. For instance, in other New World countries such as Brazil, there is no sharp division between black and white but rather a continuum of skin color distinctions. As recently as 1910, the U.S. Census included a mixed black and white ancestry category labeled "mulatto." Yet during the twentieth century, the image of two distinct groups, black and white, became fixed in American culture, despite the mixed racial ancestry of many Americans.

Other racial categories remain more flexible, in part because none carries the long history of slavery and racial discrimination faced by African Americans. Consider the category **Native American**, which will be used, as in Chapter 2, to indicate individuals in the United States who are descended from the original, indigenous peoples of North America. These peoples include **American Indians**, the name still often used for Native Americans in the contiguous 48 states, and **Alaska natives**, such as the Eskimo and Aleut. The 1990 Census questionnaire presented "American Indian" as one of fifteen "race" categories.[1] Between 1970 and 1980 the number of people choosing "American Indian" rose by 72 percent, a far higher rate than counts of births and deaths during the 1970s would suggest. It appears that about 60 percent of the increase in the American Indian population occurred because more people chose to report themselves as American Indians in 1980 than in 1970 (Snipp, 1989). The increases in reporting were greater in California and the East than in traditional American Indian population centers. This pattern suggests that individuals residing in metropolitan areas far from tribal lands and having some Native American ancestry became more likely during the 1970s to think of themselves as American Indians (Eschbach, 1993). Perhaps as a result of the civil rights movement of the 1960s, more persons of at least partial Native American descent viewed their heritage positively enough to claim it as an identity. A similar, although smaller, increase in self-identification also seems to have occurred between 1980 and 1990 (O'Hare, 1992).

It is even more difficult to define an ethnic group than it is a racial group. Most generally, an ethnic group consists of people who think of themselves as distinct from others by virtue of common ancestry and shared culture—but not necessarily physical characteristics. For example, the skin color and physical features of Mexican Americans range from distinctly European to distinctly Native American, with most people displaying a mixture of the two. Given the ambiguities and overlap between race and ethnicity, let me combine them and define a **racial-ethnic group** as people who share a common identity and whose members think of themselves as distinct from others by virtue of ancestry, culture, and sometimes physical characteristics. Often racial-ethnic group members' shared identity is reinforced by the way they are treated by outsiders. For instance, racial prejudice and, until the 1960s, racially discriminatory legislation have contributed to the sharp distinction between blacks and whites.

Thus, racial-ethnic groups are largely social creations, reflecting cultural norms, social inequality, and political power. Consequently, people can redefine these groups or create new ones as circumstances dictate. The clearest recent example of the redefinition of a racial-ethnic group in the United States is the rise of Hispanic ethnicity. In this chapter, the term **Hispanic** refers to persons in the United States who trace their ancestry to Latin America.[2] A few decades ago, the term hardly was used; rather, one referred to specific groups such as Puerto Ricans, Mexican Americans, or Cuban Americans. There was no Hispanic category, for example, in the full 1970 Census. During the 1970s and 1980s, however, political leaders of Latin American ancestry formed alliances based on their shared interest in improving the lives of their disadvantaged constituents. A Hispanic caucus was

[1]Individuals were asked to choose one of the following categories: White, Black or Negro, American Indian, Eskimo, Aleut, Chinese, Filipino, Hawaiian, Korean, Vietnamese, Japanese, Asian Indian, Samoan, Guamanian, and "Other Asian or Pacific Islander." If none of these fit, an individual could choose a residual category, "Other race," which was included at the end of the list.
[2]Strictly speaking, "Hispanic" also includes people who trace their ancestry directly to Spain.

formed in Congress; the category "Hispanic" was added to the Census; and Hispanics came to be seen as a coherent racial-ethnic group. In the 1980 Census, after the individual responding for the household checked boxes indicating which of the so-called races each person in the household belonged to, she or he was asked "Is this person of Spanish/Hispanic origin or descent?" The categories were: (1) No; (2) Yes, Mexican, Mexican-American, or Chicano; (3) Yes, Puerto Rican; (4) Yes, Cuban; and (5) Yes, Other Spanish/Hispanic.

A similar scheme was used in the 1990 Census, in which about 9 percent of the U.S. population chose one of the Hispanic categories. This question was asked separately from the racial question because Hispanics can be of any race. In 1990, 43 percent of people who listed themselves and their household members as Hispanic checked none of the 15 specific racial categories but rather the catchall racial category "Other" (O'Hare, 1992). That 43 percent of Hispanics consider themselves to be neither white nor black may reflect both the Latin American tradition of intermediate racial categories and also the sentiment that Hispanics are a separate group from European whites and African blacks.

Similarly, the category **Asian American** has become an umbrella for an extremely diverse group of people who hail from nations as far apart as Japan and Pakistan—people who differ in language, religion, alphabet, and race. For instance, South Asians, such as Indians, Pakistanis, and Bengalis, are classified as Caucasian by physical anthropologists; they are mostly Hindus or Muslims; and they speak languages belonging to the same Indo-European family from which English evolved. Asian Indians alone numbered 815,000 in the 1990 Census, double their population in 1980 (U.S. Bureau of the Census, 1992a). East Asians (e.g., Chinese, Japanese) and Southeast Asians (e.g., Indonesians, Thais, Filipinos), in contrast, are classified as Mongoloid by anthropologists, are heavily Buddhist or Confucian, and speak languages of Asian and Pacific origin. They numbered over five million in 1990. Unlike the category "Hispanic," there was no overall "Asian" category in the 1990 Census but rather a list of many Asian nationalities (e.g., "Chinese," "Asian Indian") in the "race" question. Census tabulations of Asian Americans sometimes include U.S. residents who are Pacific Islanders—people indigenous to Hawaii and to the Pacific islands that are territories of the United States.

For studying the family, unfortunately, the category "Hispanic" is not very useful, and "Asian American" is not much better. As will be discussed, there is nearly as much variation in family patterns among the various subgroups of the Hispanic population as there is between Hispanic families and non-Hispanic families. Indeed, there is substantial variation in family patterns within each of the major racial-ethnic groups, and among European whites as well. Nevertheless, the political discourse on racial-ethnic groups in the United States is increasingly structured around four racial-ethnic groups: African Americans, Hispanics, Asian Americans, and Native Americans. The majority, residual category we can call **non-Hispanic whites**, meaning people who identify their race as white but do not think of themselves as Hispanic. These categories are still a subject of debate and controversy. (See *Families and Public Policy:* How Should Multiracial Families Be Counted?, on pages 140 and 141.)

Figure 5.1 shows the great differences in family structure among the four racial-ethnic groups and non-Hispanic whites. The 1990 Census defined a "family household" as a household that contained two or more persons related by blood, marriage, or adoption. Figure 5.1 shows all family households with children present in 1990. As the blue columns show, more than 80 percent of Asian-American family households were headed by a married couple, the highest percentage of any of

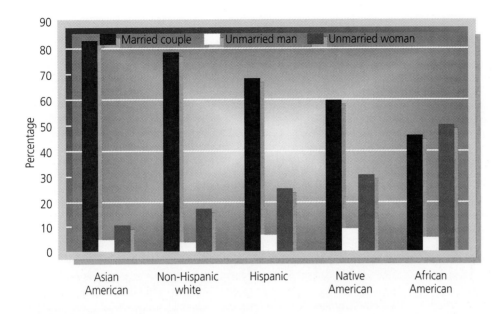

FIGURE 5.1 Percentage of family households with children that were headed by a married couple, an unmarried man, and an unmarried woman, by racial-ethnic group, 1990. (*Source:* O'Hare, 1992, Table 5.)

the five groups. In contrast, just 44 percent of African-American family households were headed by married couples—the lowest percentage of any of the groups. Non-Hispanic whites, Hispanics, and Native Americans were in between. Correspondingly, African Americans had the highest percentage of family households headed by an unmarried woman and Asian Americans had the lowest. Few households in any group were headed by an unmarried male, as the middle columns show.[3] Clearly, the racial-ethnic groups are dissimilar enough to be worthy of separate study. Sociologists study racial-ethnic variations in family patterns because different kinds of families can have different effects on individuals. The previous chapter, for instance, examined the benefits and costs of female-centered kinship among the poor, with its emphasis on sharing networks of extended kin.

AFRICAN-AMERICAN FAMILIES

When African Americans discuss the labor market, they often say they are last-hired and first-fired. The 1990–1991 economic recession (a recession is a downturn in the economy that is less severe than a depression) was a case in point. According to *The Wall Street Journal,* African Americans were the only large racial-ethnic group that suffered a net loss of jobs during the recession (Sharp, 1993). In contrast, whites, Hispanics, and Asians each gained thousands of jobs. (No figures were reported for Native Americans.) When large companies trimmed their workforces because of the downturn, African Americans were disproportionately laid off. At the Coca-Cola Company, where 18 percent of the workers were black in 1990, 42 percent of the workers who lost their jobs during the recession were black. The company reduced its blue-collar labor force of drivers and warehouse workers—which had been where black employees were concentrated—as sales of Coke fell. Other big employers such as Sears, Roebuck cut costs by

[3](O'Hare, 1992). The data were taken from 1990 Census Summary Tape File 1C. By "unmarried," I mean never married, divorced, separated, or widowed.

Families and Public Policy

How Should Multiracial Families Be Counted?

How can a child whose parents have different races have only one? Logically impossible, you might think; but until 1997, federal government statistical policy required that individuals check just one race for themselves or their children on official forms such as the Census of Population. And before 1997, the government recognized four races: (1) white, (2) black, (3) Asian and Pacific Islander, and (4) American Indian and Alaska Native. It also required its agencies, in a separate question, to ask about membership in one ethnic group: Spanish or Hispanic origin.

The federal policy on race dates from a time when there were few interracial marriages. (Not until the 1960s were the last state laws prohibiting interracial marriages struck down by the courts.) But over the past few decades, interracial marriages have been on the rise. Between the 1960 and 1990 Census, the number increased tenfold from about 150,000 to about 1.5 million (U.S. Bureau of the Census, 1996a). Figures for the 1990s suggest that the increase has continued.[1] And when interracial marriages increase, so do interracial children. According to one study of federal government data, the number of interracial births more than doubled between 1978 and 1992, reaching almost 133,200 in the latter year (Kalish, 1995). An estimated two million children lived in multiracial families in 1990 (Bennett, 1995).

African Americans still have the lowest intermarriage rates of any of the officially defined races. Among married blacks in their twenties in 1990, 92 percent of men and 97 percent of women had black spouses. Intermarriage is much more common among other minority groups. For example, the great majority of Asian Americans now marry non-Asians. Among married Asian Americans in their twenties in 1990, just 39 percent of men and 34 percent of women had Asian spouses. Hispanics marry outside their ethnic group more than blacks but less than Asians: 64 percent of Hispanic men and 63 percent of Hispanic women in their twenties in 1990 had Hispanic spouses (Qian, 1997).

To be sure, interracial couples and their children still represent a small share of all families. Only about 3 percent of married couples were interracial in 1995. Their numbers are large enough, however, that they have become a visible presence and a reminder that the old categories may not fit much longer. In 1993, Representative Thomas Sawyer of Ohio, chair of the subcommittee of the House of Representatives that oversees the census and statistical policy, listened to the testimony of Susan Graham, an advocate for multiracial children and a mother of two of them. She told Representative Sawyer:

When I received my 1990 census form, I realized there was no race category for my children. I called the Census Bureau. After checking with supervisors, the Bureau finally gave me their answer, the children should take the race of the mother. When I objected and asked why my children should be classified as their mother's race only, the Census Bureau representative said to me, in a very hushed voice, "Because in cases like these, we always know who the mother is and not the father" (U.S. House of Representatives, Committee on Post Office and Civil Service, Hearings, 1994).

Ms. Graham said her son had been classified as white by the census but black by the school he attended. Her solution: Add a new category, "Multiracial," to the official government list and to the 2000 Census. Yet this seemingly logical step was opposed by many of the political leaders of the minority groups that would be most affected. They opposed a multiracial category because the statistics that agencies collect are used not just to describe the population but also to determine whether federal laws have been carried out. Congress and the courts use the information on race and ethnicity from the census to determine whether congressional districts are providing fair representation to blacks and Hispanics. Agencies that oversee banks use the information to determine whether banks are willing to loan money to members of racial-ethnic groups. Other agencies use the information from employers to determine whether employers are discriminating on the basis of race or ethnicity. Consequently, the political leaders opposed a multiracial category because they feared it would lower the number of blacks, Hispanics, or Asians counted

A modest but growing number of families are interracial; their children do not fit within any of the official government racial categories.

in the census and would therefore dilute the political power that comes with greater numbers (Wright, 1994).

Faced with this dilemma, the government considered what, if anything, to do about Susan Graham's children and the many others like them when it fields the 2000 Census of Population. The Bureau of the Census conducted test surveys of minority populations to see how much the addition of a multiracial category would alter the statistics it reports. They found that only about 3 percent of people who now report themselves as black would choose a multiracial category or check more than one race box if allowed. An estimated 2 to 5 per-

cent of Hispanics and 4 to 12 percent of Asian and Pacific Islanders would report more than one race (U.S. Bureau of the Census, 1997h).

Finally, in 1997, a government statistical committee decided that the 2000 Census (and all other government surveys) will allow individuals to choose more than one race; but it rejected a separate "multiracial" category. It also decided to place the question about Hispanic ethnicity before the question on race (rather than after it, which is the current policy), a change that should increase the number of people who say they are "Hispanic" (U.S. Office of Management and Budget, 1997). So when

you fill out the 2000 Census, you will see five races (because native Hawaiians and Pacific Islanders wanted to separate themselves from the broad "Asian" category), whose new official names will be: (1) white, (2) black or African American, (3) Hispanic or Latino, (4) Asian, and (5) native Hawaiian or other Pacific Islander. And for the first time, you will be allowed to check all that apply to you.

[1]The available figures for the 1990s are from the Census Bureau's monthly Current Population Survey (CPS), which reports somewhat different totals from the Decennial Census; still, the CPS figures show an increase of 44 percent in the number of interracial married couples between 1990 and 1995 (U.S. Bureau of the Census, 1996a).

closing expensive inner-city distribution centers and relocating their operations to cheaper suburban locations. In fact, of all the blue-collar jobs lost at large corporations in the nation, African Americans lost one-third.

Even when the economy recovered later in the decade, blacks did not benefit as much as whites. Between 1992 and 1997, the black unemployment rate declined by 29 percent, while the white unemployment rate declined by 39 percent. Employers were slower to rehire workers for the kinds of jobs that black workers used to obtain.[4]

The fate of black workers during the ups and downs of the economy in the 1990s is a reminder of how hard the blue-collar workforce has been hit by the economic difficulties of the last decade or two—and how heavily this blow has fallen on African Americans. Many black workers have a precarious hold on working-class status; their low seniority makes them particularly vulnerable to economic downturns. The troubles of the U.S. economy, reviewed in the previous chapter on social class, have cost many African Americans the opportunity to hold jobs that pay substantially above the minimum wage. This economic reality has had a significant impact on lower-class and working-class black families. Without jobs such as these, some black men are reluctant to marry for fear they will fail to provide for their families, and some black women are reluctant to marry them. In fact, William Wilson argued in two influential books that the drop in semiskilled and skilled blue-collar jobs—their flight to the suburbs or to low-wage nations such as Mexico or Taiwan—is the major reason for the sharp decline in marriage among African Americans (Wilson, 1987, 1996).

THE DECLINE OF MARRIAGE

That there has been a sharp decline in the place of marriage in black family life is not in doubt. To be sure, the decline of marriage has also occurred among whites, but it has not been as great. Table 5.1 presents three indicators of the decline of marriage among African Americans and whites. The first row shows that the proportion of young adults who will ever marry has fallen more for African Americans than for whites since the 1950s. At current rates, only 70 to 75 percent of African-American young adults will ever marry. As will be discussed in Chapter 12, black women are less likely to marry, more likely to separate from their husbands if they do marry, and less likely to remarry than white women. The second row shows that for both groups, the percentage of children born to unmarried mothers increased sharply between 1970 and 1994. By 1994, 70 percent of all African-American births were to unmarried women. And the third row shows that the percentage of family households (meaning households containing parents and children under 18) that were headed by one parent rose for both groups between 1970 and 1996. A majority of African-American family households are now headed by one parent.

When we include cohabitation in the picture, the differences between blacks and whites are smaller but still substantial. Let me define **union formation** as the process of beginning to live with a partner either through cohabitation or marriage. The first unions formed by blacks are almost twice as likely to be cohabitations (rather than marriages) than is the case for whites. Therefore, studies that

---

[4]The figures compare June 1992 and June 1997 seasonally adjusted unemployment rates for blacks and whites age 16 and over in the civilian labor force (U.S. Bureau of Labor Statistics, 1997).

TABLE 5.1   INDICATORS OF THE DECLINE OF MARRIAGE AMONG AFRICAN AMERICANS AND WHITES

INDICATORS OF THE DECLINE OF MARRIAGE	AFRICAN AMERICANS	WHITES
The percentage of young adults who will ever marry has fallen more for African Americans than for whites[a]	88% in 1950s → 70 to 75% in 1980s	95% in 1950s → 90% in 1980s
The percentage of children born to unmarried mothers has risen for both African Americans and whites[b]	38% in 1970 → 70% in 1994	6% in 1970 → 25% in 1994
The percentage of family households headed by one parent has risen for both African Americans and whites[c]	33% in 1970 → 59% in 1996	9% in 1970 → 22% in 1996

[a]Bennet, Bloom, & Craig, 1989; Rodgers & Thornton, 1985

[b]U.S. Bureau of the Census, 1991e; U.S. National Center for Health Statistics, 1996.

[c]U.S. Bureau of the Census, 1997 [FM-2. All parent/child situation, by type, race, and Hispanic origin if householder or reference person: 1970 to present. On-line. Available: www.census.gov. Accessed: December 24, 1997.]

only examine the timing of first marriages produce greater differences between blacks and whites than do studies that examine the timing of first unions, either marital or cohabiting. In fact, racial differences in the timing of first unions are only about half the magnitude of racial differences in the timing of first marriages (Raley, 1996).[5]

THE SHORTAGE OF EMPLOYED BLACK MEN

African-American women and men seem to weigh economic considerations more heavily than white women and men in deciding when to marry—as might be expected, given their more precarious economic situation. For instance, in the 1987–1988 National Survey of Families and Households, never-married African Americans were more likely than comparable whites to rate such factors as "having one's spouse established in a job" as important in making the decision to marry (Bulcroft & Bulcroft, 1993). As noted earlier, recent job losses have hit African Americans especially hard. Fewer young black men work at all now than in the past: The proportion of 25- to 34-year-old high school dropouts who had earned any money in the previous year dropped from 93 percent in 1969 to 77 percent in 1984 (Duncan & Hoffman, 1991). According to a recent study, for every three black unmarried women in their twenties, there is roughly one unmarried black man with earnings above the poverty line (Lichter et al., 1992). Greater benefits available to mothers through public assistance may also have increased women's independence and reduced the pressure to marry. Studies suggest that the effect of welfare on marriage behavior is modest but may have increased during the 1980s (Moffitt, 1990).

In addition to job losses—or perhaps as a result of them—there are other reasons why young black women may face a difficult time finding a suitable spouse. Consider the terrible toll that violence and drugs are taking on young black men.

[5]Still, black cohabiting unions are less likely to lead to marriage (and more likely to lead to a breakup) than are white cohabiting unions (Manning & Smock, 1995).

Homicide rates for young African Americans have risen to appalling levels over the past decade. If the rates in 1993 were to continue, about 2 of every 100 black 15-year-old boys would die violently before reaching age 25; of the survivors, another 2 of every 100 would die violently before age 35.[6] The rates of imprisonment and institutionalization of young black males are also strikingly high. The prison population grew rapidly during the 1980s and 1990s, and about half of all inmates are black. On any given day, about 3 of every 100 black men in their twenties are behind bars. Moreover, about 1 of every 100 black men aged 18 to 44 is admitted to state and county mental hospitals each year, and others are incapacitated by drug addiction or alcoholism (Cherlin, 1992b).

Is the decline in marriage, then, due to the shortage of men who are "marriageable," as Wilson calls them, by virtue of steady employment? Recent studies suggest two conclusions: (1) the employment problems of black men are indeed an important factor in the decline in marriage, but (2) the racial difference remains substantial even after employment problems are taken into account. Several demographic studies have measured the relative numbers of employed black men in the local areas or states where black women live. The authors find that black women are more likely to marry if they live in areas with greater relative numbers of employed black men—thus supporting Wilson's hypothesis. Yet they also find that the drop in the availability of employed men cannot account for all—or even most—of the widening racial gap in marriage rates. Robert Mare and Christopher Winship, using Census data from 1940 through the mid-1980s, reported that although men who were employed were more likely to marry, the "recent declines in employment rates among young blacks are simply not large enough to account for a substantial part of the trend in their marriage rates" (Mare & Winship, 1991). Another team of sociologists, using data from a national survey that followed young adults for several years, found that lower numbers of employed black males were "a significant factor contributing to delayed marriage—and perhaps nonmarriage—among black women." Yet even after marriage market opportunities were taken into account, the rate of marriage among the young black women in the survey was still just 50 to 60 percent of the rate for comparable young white women (Lichter et al., 1992).[7] Reviewing the evidence in his most recent book, Wilson (1996, p. 97) acknowledges that "even though the joblessness among black men is a significant factor in their delayed entry into marriage . . . it can account for only a proportion of the decline in marriages in the inner city, including postpartum marriages."

A similar pattern can be seen in a comparison of Census data on the percentage of black and white family households that are headed by a married couple (as opposed to an unmarried woman or man). Figure 5.2, taken from 1980 Census tabulations by Reynolds Farley and Walter Allen, shows this comparison for family households at different income levels (Farley & Allen, 1987). As the reader can see, for both African Americans and whites, the higher the family's income, the greater is the percentage that are headed by a married couple. Clearly, among both African Americans and whites, married couples are less commonly found in low-income households. Note also, however, that at each income level, white family households are more likely to be headed by a married couple than black family households. Even when there are no income differences between the families

---

[6]Author's calculation from homicide rates for black males 15–24 and 25–34 in U.S. Bureau of the Census (1996e).
[7]Other similar studies are summarized in Cherlin (1992b).

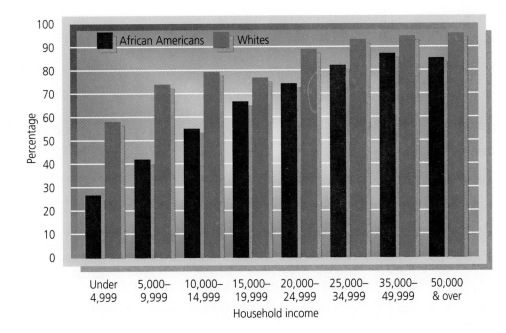

FIGURE 5.2 Percentage of family households that were headed by a married couple, by household income, for African Americans and whites, 1980. (*Source:* Farley & Allen, 1987, Table 6.1.)

being compared, a racial gap still exists, and the gap is particularly pronounced among the poor and near poor. Economics, it seems, is part of the story of racial differences in family structure; but it is not the whole story.[8]

AFRICAN-AMERICAN CULTURE

To more fully understand the differences in the family patterns of African Americans and whites, we must turn from economics to culture. There has been a resistance among liberal social scientists and activists to acknowledging the role of culture in shaping African-American family patterns. In part, this concern arises from the entirely negative way in which black families are often portrayed: problem-ridden, weak, overwhelmed. The strengths of black families are often overlooked. Figure 5.3, based on another comparison by Farley and Allen, helps to show where these strengths may lie. Graphed in Figure 5.3, across income levels from low to high, are the percentage of family households that are "extended"; that is, the percentage that contain relatives other than parents (or stepparents) and their children (Farley & Allen, 1987). Often the additional relatives are grandparents. Note that at all income levels—even among those earning more than $50,000 in 1980—black family households are more than twice as likely as white households to include a grandparent or other relative.

In fact, grandparents play a stronger role in African-American families, on average, than they do among white families. In 1982, just before Frank Furstenberg and I carried out a national survey of grandparents, we visited a group of black grandmothers at a senior citizens' center in Baltimore. The grandmothers told us how involved they were with their grandchildren's upbringing. Most of them had

---

[8]Farley and Allen state that additional analyses convinced them that the factors responsible for the remaining differences "are not simply other aspects of socioeconomic status."

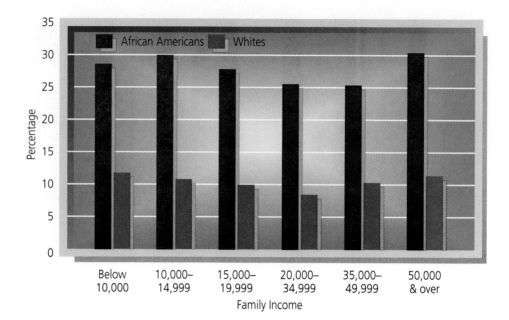

FIGURE 5.3 Percentage of family households that are extended (contain relatives other than parents and their children), by family income, for African Americans and whites, 1980. (*Source:* Farley & Allen, 1987, Table 6.4.)

lived at least temporarily with their grandchildren. One woman, for example, said about her grandchildren:

> *I was always named "sergeant"—"Here comes the sergeant." I loved them. I did for them, and gave to them, so that they had an education, so that they had a trade. I went to school regularly to check on them; they didn't know I was coming* (Cherlin & Furstenberg, 1992).

Very few white grandparents had this kind of hands-on involvement and authority. Our national survey confirmed that black grandparents, on average, were more involved in parentlike activities with their grandchildren than were white grandparents. Moreover, this racial difference still remained when we compared black and white grandparents of similar incomes. Even among working-class and middle-class families, black grandparents seem to play a stronger role than white grandparents.

More generally, in African-American families, ties to a network of kin are more important, compared with marital ties, than is the case in white families. When Alice and Peter Rossi measured the strength of people's feelings of obligations toward kin (see Chapter 4), they found that African Americans felt much stronger obligations to aunts, uncles, nieces, nephews, and cousins than did whites (Rossi & Rossi, 1990).[9] It follows, then, that when African Americans face adversity, they are probably more likely to seek help from kin than are whites. Moreover, Chapter 2 noted the possible influences of African cultural patterns: In West Africa marriage is more of a process than an event, with childbearing sometimes occurring before the process is completed. In addition, we saw in Chapter 4 that poor white families, such as those in Potter Addition, also show a pattern of relying less on spouses and more on parents and other kin (Harvey, 1993).

Recall that, in Potter Addition, the husbands were formally present in many households, even though they often had limited authority. In poor black families,

---

[9]The comparisons controlled for the respondent's age, gender, and education.

husbands are less often present.[10] In fact, mothers' partners are often incorporated into the kin networks on the basis not of whether they are the biological fathers of the mothers' children but rather whether they provide support to the children. Frank Furstenberg interviewed a group of low-income African Americans in an Eastern city who distinguished between "fathers" and "daddies." The former were biological fathers, whereas the latter were men who were providing support. A woman's current partner, for example, might become a daddy by helping with the care of a child from a previous relationship whose father provided little support. It was the daddies—the men who were providing assistance—not the fathers, who became members of the sharing networks (Furstenberg, Sherwood, & Sullivan, 1992).

The chapter on class also discussed the strengths and weaknesses of relying on kin for support. Briefly, membership in a network of kin helps people subsist because it allows them to spread the burdens of poverty by borrowing when they are in need and lending when they are able. It also, however, makes escaping from poverty more difficult because it is difficult and risky for poor people to withdraw from the network. Moreover, not all poor black single-parent households necessarily belong to strong networks. In a 1984 national survey, 68 percent of black single mothers, aged 19 to 26, lived in an extended-family household, received half or more of their income from someone other than their husband, or received unpaid childcare assistance. The comparable figure for white single mothers was 54 percent (Hogan, Hao, & Parish, 1990). Still, 32 percent of the black single mothers in this study did not receive any of the three kinds of assistance.

The greater amount of help received by black single mothers than white single mothers is consistent with Stack's (1974) influential account of African-American kinship networks in "the flats" (see Chapter 4). Yet statistical studies have found that black households, on average, don't receive more help from their social networks than do white households (Hofferth, 1984; Silverstein & Waite, 1993; Raley, 1995; Roschelle, 1997). In the 1987–88 National Survey of Families and Households, for example, black respondents did not report exchanging more childcare and household help with kin living elsewhere than did non-Hispanic whites; in fact, on some measures non-Hispanic whites were more likely to exchange services (Roschelle, 1997). Another study of the same survey found that young black never-married adults were more likely to live with kin, see their mothers and siblings, and socialize with relatives than were comparable whites; but they were not more likely to receive assistance from kin (Raley, 1995).

Ever since Stack's work and subsequent ethnographic accounts (e.g., Martin & Martin, 1978) appeared, most sociologists have accepted the premise that low-income black households give and receive more support from an extended network of kin than do white low-income households. Perhaps they do but statistical analyses of survey data just aren't rich enough in detail to substantiate the difference. There are, however, two other possibilities. The first is that the ethnographic studies, which were based on small samples and which usually lacked a comparison group of whites, overstated the differences between black and white families (Roschelle, 1997). The second is that poor people have fewer resources to share now than in the 1970s. We know, for instance, that the share of income going to the bottom fifth of the population has been declining. It may be that the poor are poorer than they were a generation ago, when widely cited studies of

---

[10]Harvey did his fieldwork in Potter Addition in the early 1970s. In 1980, he reported, 56 percent of the poor families in the county were headed by a husband and wife, down from 71 percent in 1970. Still, the 56 percent figure is higher than that for poor black families nationwide in 1980, as Figure 5.2 shows.

supportive kin networks were published. Some kin networks, therefore, may be overwhelmed by their members' needs.

In addition, studies of kin networks also show that support from kin tends to decline over time. In the 1984 national survey mentioned above, about two-thirds of the black single mothers were living with their own mothers at age 19, compared with about half of 21-year-olds and about one-third of 25-year-olds (Hogan, Hao, & Parish, 1990). This decline suggests that many single mothers move out of their mothers' homes as their children become older. Moreover, many of the grandmothers are themselves working outside the home and, therefore, are less available to their daughters. As the children enter adolescence, then, the support that kin provide to mothers may be substantially less than the support that was provided when the children were small. Several studies suggest that single mothers living without relatives provide less supervision and monitoring of their children's schoolwork and behavior than do mothers who live with a husband or other adult (Astone & McLanahan, 1991; Dornbusch et al., 1985). Despite their best efforts, many poor single mothers may have difficulty providing adequate parenting to their school-age children.

EXPLAINING THE CHANGES

How, then, can we explain the great decline of marriage among African Americans and the sharp increase in the proportion of children born to unmarried mothers? Although African Americans have had a higher proportion of single-parent households than whites since at least the beginning of the twentieth century (see Chapter 2), the difference has become more pronounced over the last few decades. There is no consensus as to why. Without doubt, changes in the economy are very important. In fact, some observers think the changes in families are entirely due to changes in the economy; others believe that culture may have played a role. In a previous book, I presented my interpretation. I will present it again here, with the caveat that no one can yet be sure exactly what mix of causes and effects was at work:

> *What happened in the last half of the twentieth century, I think, was that black families responded to two developments—one was a societywide shift in values and the other was a change in the labor market that was particularly damaging to blacks. The societywide shift was the weakening of the institution of marriage, [which was, in turn,] rooted in the increasing economic independence of men and women. [The decline of marriage] also reflected a cultural drift throughout the West to a more individualistic ethos, one which emphasized self-fulfillment in personal relations. It de-emphasized the obligations people have to others—including their spouses and partners. . . .*
>
> *The second development also affected the entire nation, but it hit blacks especially hard: the economic restructuring described by Wilson and others. It appears to have decreased the growth of semiskilled manufacturing jobs, which can provide stable employment at adequate wages to people without a college degree. The greater growth of the service sector benefited black women more than black men because many of those jobs—secretaries, sales clerks, waitresses—had been labeled as women's work. The expansion of government social welfare programs may also have increased the economic independence of women and men. These changes in the labor market eroded the earning potential of black males, which in turn lessened their ability to support a wife and children.*
>
> *The way that blacks responded to these broad-based cultural and economic shifts, I would argue, was conditioned by their history and culture. . . . Faced with difficult times economically, many blacks responded by drawing upon a model of social support that was in their cultural repertoire, a way of making it from day to day passed down by African Americans who came before them. This response relied heavily on extended kinship networks and de-emphasized marriage. It is a response that taps a traditional source*

of strength in African-American society: cooperation and sharing among a large network of kin. It was also a response consistent with the general movement away from marriage in the U.S. . . . Young black mothers relied heavily on their own mothers and other kin to help care for their babies. For most, a marriage followed several years later, and not necessarily to the father of their first child. Had these adaptations not been part of African-American culture, the retreat from marriage and the increase in the proportion of births to unmarried women probably would not have been as dramatic. The increased reliance on extended kin has allowed many poor blacks to have two or three children, pay their bills, and put food on the table—and obtain emotional support as well. But it is a response that also can have costs for parents and children (Cherlin, 1992b).

The costs, as described in the previous chapter, include the difficulty of escaping from poverty until *everyone* in your network escapes.

MIDDLE-CLASS BLACK FAMILIES

Yet over the past few decades, some African Americans have managed to escape from poverty. Since the 1960s, a substantial black middle class has developed for the first time in U.S. history. A national study that followed for 15 years black children who were under age four in 1968 found that 13 percent of them lived in families whose incomes were always at least 50 percent over the poverty line. Another 8 percent lived in families that were never poor but whose incomes were close to the poverty line in at least one year (Duncan, 1991). Although these percentages are modest compared with those of white children (see Chapter 14), they are an overlooked social advance.

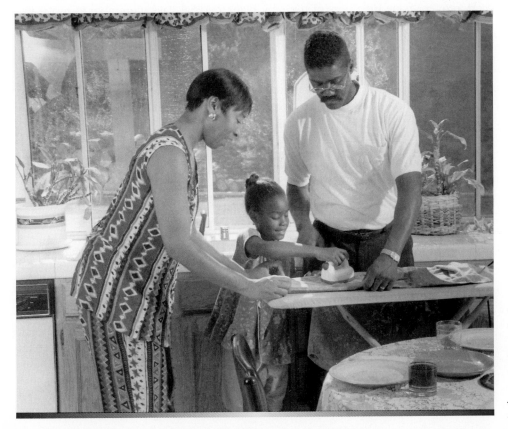

Since the 1960s, a sizable middle class has emerged among African Americans. They are often ignored in the public focus on black poverty.

The newness of the black middle class means that most of its members have working-class or lower-class origins. Their parents typically did not accumulate enough wealth to provide them with much of a nest egg or an inheritance. Consequently, they tend to have less money in assets (savings, investments, homes, cars) than comparable white middle-class people. For instance, a study in the mid-1980s found that black households had monthly incomes that were 62 percent of white incomes but that their median assets were only 9 percent of those of whites (Farley & Allen, 1987). As a result, their hold on middle-class status can be precarious. In words that only slightly overstate the case, Harriette Pipes McAdoo wrote that many black middle-class families are "only one paycheck from poverty" (McAdoo, 1988).

In a recently published study of the assets of respondents to the Census Bureau's Survey of Income and Program Participation in 1987 through 1989, Oliver and Shapiro (1995) also found much larger differences, on average, in wealth (assets) between blacks and whites than in income. Comparing college-educated blacks with college-educated whites, for instance, they found that whereas the blacks earned 76 cents for each dollar earned by the whites, blacks had assets of just 23 cents for every dollar of white assets. And if homes and cars were excluded from assets (leaving savings accounts, stocks, small businesses), black college graduates had *one cent* of assets for every dollar of white assets. Oliver and Shapiro ascribe the difference to three factors: (1) whites are more likely to inherit some wealth or borrow money for a down payment on a home or car from their parents; (2) whites can more easily obtain home mortgage loans from banks; and (3) homes in predominantly black neighborhoods don't appreciate in value as much as homes in white neighborhoods.

Moreover, many members of the new black middle class were able to move upward in part through the assistance of kin, such as siblings who helped pay for college or an uncle who provided a first job. These extended kinship ties tend to remain after a person has attained middle-class status, but the flow of assistance often reverses. The sister who has attained a job as a computer programmer may have an unemployed brother who needs a short-term loan to stave off his family's eviction from their apartment or a bright cousin from a poor family who needs financial help so he can go to college. Having benefited from the assistance of her kin on her way up the economic ladder, the computer programmer has a difficult time refusing their requests. Yet her salary may be insufficient to maintain her middle-class status as well as help all the relatives who are in need. The resultant financial pressure can create what Andrew Billingsley called "the mixed blessings of upward mobility" (Billingsley, 1992). Still, the growth of the black middle class is a success story that is too often lost in the understandable focus on the black poor.

Black churches have been a great source of social support to African Americans who have newly gained middle-class status. Throughout African-American history the church and the family have been the enduring institutions through which black families could gain the strength to resist the oppression of slavery, reconstruction, segregation, and discrimination (Berry & Blassingame, 1982). The church has served as a **mediating structure**, a midlevel social institution (other examples are civic groups, neighborhoods, and families themselves) through which individuals can negotiate with government and resist governmental abuses of power (Berger & Berger, 1983). It has been the greatest source of continuity, outside of the family, in the African-American experience. Today the church also serves as a link between the black middle class, many of whom have moved out of inner-city neighborhoods, and the black poor. Often by virtue of sanctuaries that are still in poor neighborhoods, churches provide a direct way for middle-class congregants to provide assistance to the poor (Gilkes, 1995). In some of the poorest black neighborhoods, which have lost both population and organizations over the past few decades (Wilson, 1996), churches are among the few non-governmental institutions left.

HISPANIC FAMILIES

The label "Hispanic" covers groups that are so diverse with respect to family patterns that it makes little sense to combine them, yet that is the direction public discussions have taken. It lumps together recent immigrants with citizens whose families have been in the United States for generations, and white, middle-class political émigrés with darker-skinned, poorly educated laborers looking for work. In 1990, the Bureau of the Census counted 22.4 million Hispanics, although it surely missed some who were in the country illegally. The bureau defines Hispanics as those people who answered affirmatively to the question of whether they were of Spanish or Hispanic origin or descent. If they said yes, they could then check categories for the three largest Hispanic groups in the United States: Mexican or Mexican American, Puerto Rican, and Cuban. Otherwise, they checked one of several residual "other" categories (e.g., "Other Central/South American") and could write in their exact nationality (e.g., Guatemalan).

As Figure 5.4 shows, Mexicans and Mexican Americans were by far the largest Hispanic group in 1990, constituting 60 percent of the population. Puerto Ricans constituted 12 percent, and Cuban Americans 5 percent. No other nationality had more than one million people counted in the census. Nevertheless, note that there are several other substantial groups. Salvadorans and Dominicans, for example, have

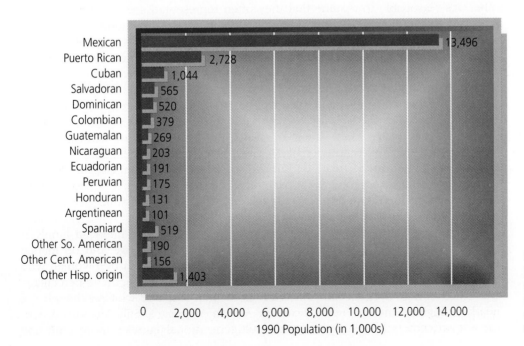

FIGURE 5.4 Hispanic population, by type of origin: 1990. (*Source:* U.S. Bureau of the Census, 1993a.)

each grown to half the size of the Cuban population. At least 100,000 people were counted from each of seven other Latin American nations. In fact, between 1980 and 1990, the smaller Hispanic populations from Central and South America grew faster than the Mexican-, Puerto Rican-, and Cuban-origin populations (U.S. Bureau of the Census, 1993a). (Several other residual categories contain people who identified themselves generally as Spanish or Hispanic, plus Caribbeans not otherwise counted, plus people who may have unintentionally not specified a nationality.)

MEXICAN AMERICANS

Mexican-American families occupy an economic level that is, on average, higher than that of Puerto Ricans and lower than that of Cubans. As was discussed in the previous chapter, Mexican poor and wealthy alike rely on kin networks for employment and support. In a country such as Mexico, where a strong central government has not always existed, kinship ties are also a way for the middle class to ensure trust and reciprocity in exchanges of money, goods, or property. Among the poor, kinship ties serve to help people shoulder the burdens of poverty. Recall that, according to anthropologist Larissa Lomnitz, the "grandfamily," the unit composed of parents, their children, their children's spouses, and their grandchildren, was the fundamental family unit in Mexico, rather than the nuclear family of parents and children (Lomnitz, 1987). Often the oldest generation lived separately but near their children and grandchildren.

Because the census does not measure kinship ties across households, we cannot directly test Lomnitz's claim. Nevertheless, the census data do suggest extensive three-generational links between Mexican-American parents, their adult children, and their grandchildren. Tabulations of 1980 data by Frank Bean and Marta Tienda showed that 28 percent of all Mexican-origin households had three or more adults, compared with 15 percent of non-Hispanic white households (Bean & Tienda, 1987). Although we don't know exactly how these adults were related to one another, it's reasonable to assume that they often represented a married couple and their parents or, alternatively, an older married couple and their adult children.

Mexican Americans also have more children than virtually any other large racial-ethnic group. Figure 5.5 shows, for racial-ethnic groups, the **total fertility rate (TFR)** in 1990. The TFR is the average number of children that women would bear over their lifetime if current birthrates were to remain the same. As can be seen, Mexican-American women would average just over three children, a substantially higher number than the TFR for non-Hispanic whites or blacks or other Hispanic groups, for that matter. Only Hawaiians match the high fertility of Mexican Americans. In part, the higher fertility of Mexican women can be explained by their lower levels of education, relative to non-Hispanic white women. But the differential remains even after controlling for educational level (Bean & Tienda, 1987). Mexican Americans also marry at a younger age than other Hispanic groups, non-Hispanic whites, and African Americans (Bean & Tienda, 1987).

This picture of a marriage-based, multigenerational Mexican-American family is tempered somewhat by statistics on childbearing outside marriage and on marital instability. Figure 5.6 on page 154 shows the percentages of unmarried women who gave birth in 1990 for the same racial-ethnic groups as in Figure 5.5. The percentage was twice as high for Mexican Americans as for non-Hispanic whites although not nearly as high as among Puerto Ricans or African Americans. Still, Mexican Americans seem centered on high-birthrate, multigenerational families more than any

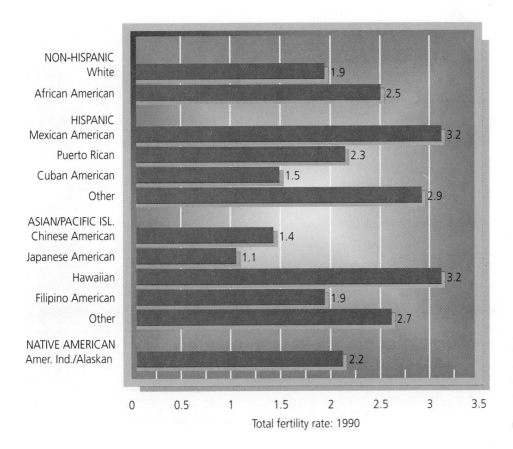

FIGURE 5.5 Total fertility rate for racial-ethnic groups in 1990. (*Source:* U.S. National Center for Health Statistics, 1993e.)

other major racial-ethnic group in the nation. Some observers have suggested that the multigenerational households persist because older parents can provide child-care assistance or shelter to their economically pressed adult children, and this is no doubt true. Even so, the Mexican-American pattern of large, multigenerational families seems culturally distinctive. Perhaps the extensive communication and movement across the long, permeable U.S.–Mexican border keep the influence of the sending country stronger than is the case among some other immigrant groups.

There has been considerable change in the family lives of Mexican-American women. The traditional image of a Hispanic family is of a male-dominated household in which women do not work outside the home. Whether or not that image used to be accurate, it certainly isn't anymore. Between 1960 and 1990, the percentage of Mexican-origin women in the labor force increased from 28.8 to 52.9 (Ortiz, 1995). (The **labor force** is defined as all people who are either working outside the home or looking for work.) It is nearly as high as among non-Hispanic white women (57.5 percent). As non-Hispanic women have moved into the labor force, so have Mexican-American and other Hispanic women.

This change doesn't necessarily mean that the norms in Mexican-American and other Hispanic families have also changed greatly. In her study of dual-earner couples, Arlie Hochschild includes a case study of a Hispanic family in California, whom she calls Frank and Carmen Delacorte, in which the wife works outside the home and the husband does a substantial amount of housework (Hochschild, 1989). Yet Frank claims to believe that the man should be the head of the household, and

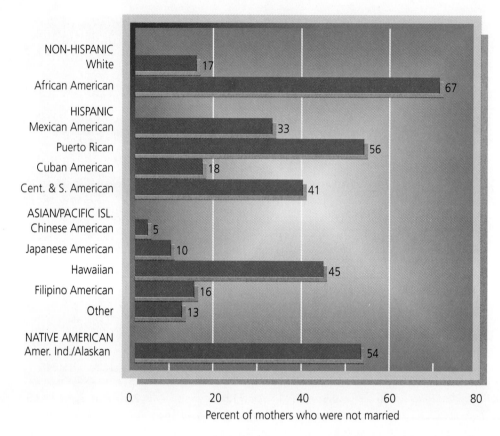

FIGURE 5.6 Percentage of women giving birth who were not married, for racial-ethnic groups in 1990. (*Source:* U.S. National Center for Health Statistics, 1993e.)

Carmen agrees with him. Carmen doesn't want to work outside the home, she said, but the family needs the money: "I'm not working to discover my identity. No way!" (Hochschild, 1989, pp. 62–63). Frank and Carmen believe that housework is women's work, but he "helps out" because of Carmen's supposed failings: Frank just happens to cook rice better than she does, he sews because she can't, he uses the ATM machine for her because she "always forgot" the password, and so forth. Thus, the Delacortes have moved toward more egalitarian gender relations without altering their beliefs in a more traditional division of labor. Other studies of Hispanic families confirm that even when husbands and wives hold traditional views they often expect that wives will work outside the home because the family needs their income (Hurtado, 1995).

PUERTO RICANS

All Puerto Ricans are U.S. citizens because the island of Puerto Rico is a U.S. territory. Consequently, Puerto Ricans, unlike all other major Hispanic groups, are free to move to the mainland if they wish, and many have done so. In 1990, 2.7 million people who identified themselves as Puerto Ricans were residing on the mainland (see Figure 5.4), whereas 3.5 million people lived in Puerto Rico. In other words, 44 percent of all people who claim Puerto Rican ethnicity live on the mainland. It is more difficult for individuals from other Hispanic groups to immigrate to the United States; they must either obtain visas, for which there may be a long wait, or find a way to enter and remain illegally. Demographers have long known that

Puerto Ricans, as United States citizens from birth, are free to move back and forth between the mainland and the island.

when the barriers to immigration are substantial, the people who manage to immigrate tend to have more education and skills than the average person in their home country. Immigration, in other words, is more selective when the barriers are high. People with greater skills are more confident that they can find decent-paying work in the United States, so they are more likely to take the trouble to immigrate. When the barriers are lower, on the other hand, immigration is less selective. We might expect, then, that Puerto Rican immigrants would tend to have less economic success, on average, than other Hispanic immigrants because Puerto Rican migration has been less selective.

Indeed, that is what the data show. Puerto Ricans are the most economically disadvantaged of the major Hispanic groups. (From here on I will be referring only to Puerto Ricans on the mainland, unless otherwise noted.) In 1993, 35 percent of all Puerto Rican family households had incomes below the poverty line, compared with 28 percent of Mexican-American family households, 24 percent of Central and South American family households, and 17 percent of Cuban-American family households (U.S. Bureau of the Census, 1997g). During the 1970s and 1980s, the economic well-being of Puerto Rican families deteriorated more than the well-being of Mexican-American families (Tienda, 1989). According to one summary, "Of all Hispanic-origin groups, Puerto Ricans have the lowest labor force participation rates, the highest unemployment levels, the highest incidence of poverty and of welfare utilization, and the lowest average levels of education" (Sandefur & Tienda, 1988). Some speculate that the economic decline among Puerto Ricans was heightened by their concentration in the New York City metropolitan area, which has undergone a loss of blue-collar jobs (Tienda, 1989).

Consistent with their lower economic standing, Puerto Ricans are second only to African Americans in the percentage of children born to unmarried mothers (see Figure 5.6). Yet many of the formally unmarried mothers are living in a partnership that they consider to be a marriage. In Puerto Rico and other Caribbean islands, a long tradition of **consensual unions** exists. These are cohabiting relationships in which couples consider themselves to be married but have never had religious or civil marriage ceremonies. From the viewpoint of the state and the Church, people in consensual unions are unmarried; but from the viewpoint of the couples and their peers, they are in a marriagelike relationship.

Among Puerto Ricans, then, there are three kinds of socially recognized unions: cohabiting unions, in which the partners do not consider themselves married; consensual unions, in which they have not undergone a marriage ceremony but still consider themselves to be informally married; and formal marriage, in which they have had a marriage ceremony and registered with the state. In a 1985 survey of Puerto Rican women aged 15 to 49 in the New York City area, the participants were asked:

> *As you know, there are various ways in which a man and a woman live in a union. Some couples legally marry, that is, they obtain a license; some couples consider themselves married but without a license; and some couples just live together and do not consider themselves married, legally or informally. I would now like to ask you some questions about your marital history* (Landale & Fennelly, 1992).

Among all women who had borne a child, 32 percent said they had ever lived in an informal marriage without a license, whereas just 13 percent said they had ever cohabited. The authors of the study report that whether or not a woman has borne a child in a union is a key factor in whether she defines it as an informal marriage or as a cohabitation. The birth of a child seems to change the social meaning of a union, making it more like a marriage (Landale & Fennelly, 1992).

Still, the tradition of consensual unions on the island of Puerto Rico cannot by itself be responsible for the increasing number of informal unions among mainland Puerto Ricans because consensual unions have been declining in frequency on the island. The deteriorating economic situation among mainland Puerto Ricans has played a major role. Among women in the same survey who had borne a child, those whose partners were employed and had at least a high school diploma were more likely to be in legal marriages (Landale & Forste, 1991). It would seem to follow that as the employment situation of Puerto Rican men has deteriorated, informal marriages and cohabitation have increased. I would speculate that—much as African Americans responded to tough times by drawing upon their tradition of strong, female-centered kin networks—Puerto Ricans have responded to tough times by drawing upon their tradition of informal marriage as a second-best substitute for formal marriage.

CUBAN AMERICANS

Most major immigrant groups today in the United States arrived in labor migrations: They came looking for higher-paying jobs. In contrast, the first waves of Cuban Americans came here in a political migration, fleeing the Communist government of Fidel Castro, who had led a successful revolution in 1959. The U.S. government allowed Cuban citizens to enter the country as political refugees. Indeed, the early migrants were drawn from the Cuban upper and middle classes, the elite that Castro's Communist party overthrew. These immigrants arrived with substantial amounts of education, skills, and capital. In addition, they were largely white in racial appearance. The U.S. government, sympathetic to their plight and wishing to isolate and embarrass Castro, welcomed them enthusiastically and provided assistance in retraining (Suarez, 1993).

Despite government efforts at resettlement, most Cuban immigrants chose to settle in the Miami metropolitan area, where a majority of the population is now of Cuban origin (Portes & Jensen, 1989). Classic sociological theories of immigration held that immigrants would adjust better and prosper more if they assimilated into the mainstream. (**Assimilation** means the process by which immigrant groups merge their culture and behavior with that of the dominant group in the host country.[11]) In the U.S. context, assimilation implies learning English, sending children to public schools, and dispersing geographically. Many Cuban immigrants chose, instead, to remain clustered in the Cuban neighborhoods of one metropolitan area, to listen to Spanish-language radio stations, to buy their food at markets owned by Cuban Americans, to eat at Cuban restaurants, and to send their children to private Cuban schools. They limited much of their lives to a large, dense, single-ethnic group, almost self-sufficient community of the type that Kenneth Wilson and Alejandro Portes have called an **immigrant enclave** (Wilson & Portes, 1980).

According to classic immigration theory, then, Cuban immigrants should have suffered. Instead, they prospered. By 1970 the median income of Cuban-American families was higher than that of any other Hispanic group or of African Americans, at 80 percent of the median income of non-Hispanic white families; and by 1980 it had reached 88 percent of the median income for non-Hispanic white families (Bean & Tienda, 1987). Portes and other observers claim that Cuban immigrants successfully used the ethnically based connections of the enclave to obtain loans to start businesses when no Anglo bank would lend to them; they also used their connections to find jobs at Cuban enterprises. (See *Families in Other Cultures: Social Capital and Immigrant Families,* on pp. 158–159.) He argues that the enclave strategy is a viable way for an immigrant group to achieve economic success.

Yet it must be remembered that these immigrants started out with a friendly reception from their hosts, arrived with substantial education and skills, received government assistance, and had white skin. These advantages were not shared by those who were part of a later wave of Cuban immigration that began in 1980, when Castro allowed a flotilla of small boats to depart from the port of Mariel. The Cuban government declared that many of the Mariel Cubans were criminals and undesirables; in addition, about 30 percent were nonwhite (Suarez, 1993). Unlike the first wave of Cuban immigrants, who arrived during an economic boom, the Mariel Cubans arrived at a time of stagnant wages and high unemployment. They were not welcomed enthusiastically or assisted, and they experienced discrimination from the earlier wave of immigrants. Later studies showed that only a small minority were criminals, mentally ill, or otherwise socially undesirable; in fact, 14 percent of Mariel refugees interviewed in 1983 and 1984 had been managers or professionals in Cuba and another 24 percent had been skilled blue-collar workers (Portes, Stepick, & Truelove, 1986). By 1992, the median income of Cuban-origin families had slipped to 77 percent of the median for non-Hispanic white families, reflecting the influx of Mariel refugees. Nevertheless, Cuban Americans remained by far the most prosperous Hispanic group, with a 1992 median family income 31 percent higher than among Mexican-origin families and 46 percent higher than that of Puerto Rican families (U.S. Bureau of the Census, 1993a).

[11]A fuller definition of assimilation can be found in Gordon (1964).

Families in Other Cultures

Social Capital and Immigrant Families

How did the number of Cuban-owned firms rise from 900 in 1967 to about 25,000 by the mid-1980s? One reason was that immigrants could use their social standing in the Cuban community in Miami to obtain the initial loans needed to start a business. In the mid-1960s, according to Alejandro Portes and Julia Sensenbrenner, a few small banks owned by South Americans hired Cuban immigrant ex-bankers. The Cubans began to make loans to their fellow immigrants that other financial institutions would have thought risky. As one Cuban banker said:

> At the start, most Cuban enterprises were gas stations; then came grocery shops and restaurants. No American bank would lend to them. By the mid-sixties we started a policy at our bank of making small loans to Cubans who wanted to start their own business, but did not have the capital. These loans of $10,000 or $15,000 were made because the person was known to us by his reputation and integrity. All of them paid back; there were zero losses. With some exceptions they have continued being clients of the bank. People who used to borrow $15,000 on a one-time basis now take $50,000 in a week. In 1973, the policy was discontinued. The reason was that the new refugees coming at that time were unknown to us (Portes & Sensenbrenner, 1993).

Whereas American banks would have required more proof that an applicant would be able to pay back a loan, the Cuban bankers relied solely on the applicant's "reputation and integrity." That reputation was established through a network of ties within the Cuban enclave in Miami. The banker might have known someone who had married the sister of the applicant and could vouch for the applicant's character. To enforce the terms of the loan, the banker relied on the humiliation and, perhaps, ostracism that would befall a person who defaulted.

In this way, Cuban immigrants were able to use their ties to a network of relatives and friends to obtain the money they needed to buy a grocery store or restaurant. Their ties were an asset to them, irrespective of their own levels of education and income. Sociologists have called this network-related asset **social capital,** by which they mean the economic advantages a person has by virtue of the structure of his or her relations with other people (Coleman, 1988). Often that structure involves kinship: People are more likely to provide money, food, or childcare to their relatives than to strangers because there is a greater likelihood that relatives will reciprocate. A casual friend has no compelling reason to reciprocate, but a relative would be shamed for

failing to do so. Just as important, people feel they can loan money to others in their networks with little risk that the loans won't be repaid. As is the case in the Mexican upper class, kinship and community ties increase people's trust that others will reciprocate for what they are given.

Many Asian immigrant groups also have used their social capital to obtain the support they need to start businesses. Among some Chinese and Japanese immigrants, for example, a group of relatives and friends was formed in which each person invested a modest amount of money into a single credit fund. Subsequently, one member was allowed to borrow the entire amount in the fund to start an enterprise, and he was required to pay it back with interest. Then the fund was made available to another member of the group, and then another. The members trusted that their loans would be repaid because of the loss of face a person who did not repay would suffer from the other members of the group. These "rotating credit associations" provided their members with an advantage not shared by outsiders—an advantage based on close kinship and friendship ties (Light, 1972).

The following figure shows the rate of business ownership—the number of firms owned per 1,000 persons for the major racial-ethnic groups in

The prosperity of Cuban Americans is derived in large part from business ownership. Cuban immigrants have become entrepreneurs, opening new businesses in far greater numbers than other Hispanic immigrants. The number of Cuban firms in the Miami area rose from about 900 in 1967 to approximately 25,000 by the mid-1980s (Portes & Jensen, 1989). The rate of business ownership among Cuban Americans in 1987 was three times higher than the rate among Mexican Americans and six times higher than among Puerto Ricans (O'Hare, 1992).

Many of the businesses were organized on a family basis. Married Cuban men were more likely to be self-employed, even after taking into account differences between married and unmarried men in education, work experience, citizenship,

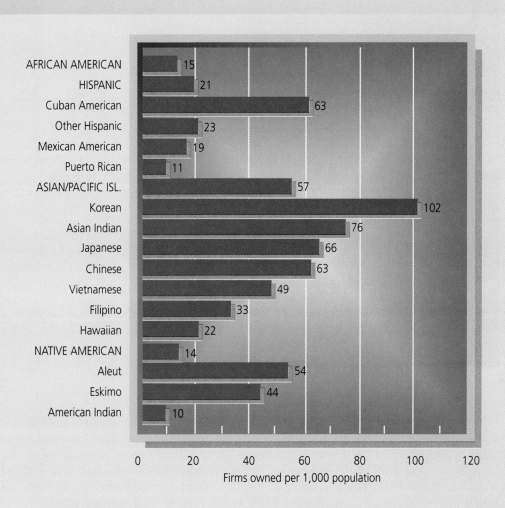

AFRICAN AMERICAN 15
HISPANIC 21
Cuban American 63
Other Hispanic 23
Mexican American 19
Puerto Rican 11
ASIAN/PACIFIC ISL. 57
Korean 102
Asian Indian 76
Japanese 66
Chinese 63
Vietnamese 49
Filipino 33
Hawaiian 22
NATIVE AMERICAN 14
Aleut 54
Eskimo 44
American Indian 10

0   20   40   60   80   100   120
Firms owned per 1,000 population

Number of firms owned per 1,000 population for racial-ethnic groups in 1987. (*Source:* O'Hare, 1992, Table 10.)

the United States in 1987. As noted in this chapter, Cuban Americans have a substantially higher rate than other Hispanics. Note that several Asian immigrant groups have rates that are just as high as or higher than the Cubans'. In contrast, African Americans and Puerto Ricans, who have neither rotating credit associations nor banks that will lend to them on the basis of racial-ethnic ties, have low rates. Koreans have by far the highest rate, 102 per 1,000 population, which implies that there was 1 Korean-owned business for every 10 Koreans in 1987.

and English proficiency. If the men had children, they were even more likely to be self-employed (Portes & Jensen, 1989). Moreover, married men living with adults other than wives in their households were less likely to be self-employed, suggesting that the conjugal family of husband, wife, and children was most congenial to business ownership. Cuban immigrants appear to have used conjugal families as a means of pooling the labor and accumulating the capital necessary to start a business. Too many adults represented a drain on capital that could be used for the business; too few children or the absence of a spouse, on the other hand, resulted in insufficient labor or outside income (as from a wife's job) for starting a firm.

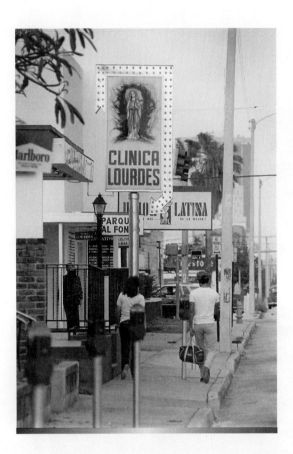

Cuban immigrants have established an economically successful enclave in the Miami metropolitan area.

Cuban Americans in the enclave, then, used their ethnic ties to obtain loans and credit from other immigrants and their family ties to start independent businesses. "Ethnic enterprise," wrote Portes and Jensen, "is, to a large extent, a family affair. Men claim ownership of the businesses, but it is frequently couples that start and consolidate them" (Portes & Jensen, 1989). Consistent with this strategy, Cuban-American families were slightly more likely to be headed by a married couple in 1980 than Mexican-American families, and far more likely to be headed by a married couple than Puerto Rican families (Bean & Tienda, 1987).

ASIAN-AMERICAN FAMILIES

Much less has been written about Asian-American families than about African-American and Hispanic families because of their modest numbers prior to the 1965 immigration act. For example, the Korean population increased from an estimated 69,000 in 1970 to 350,000 in 1980 and to 800,000 in 1990 (Min, 1993). The family patterns in the many sending nations are diverse, but, in general, Asian cultures emphasize interdependence among kin more, and individualism less, than Western culture (Goode, 1963). Asian families place a greater emphasis on children's loyalty and service to their parents than do Western families. For instance, as will be discussed in Chapter 15, a majority of elderly parents in Taiwan, Japan, China, and Korea live with one of their adult children.

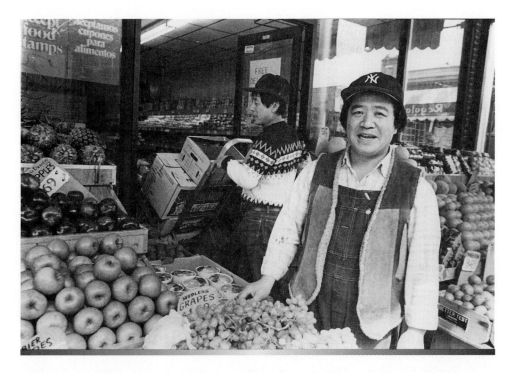

Asian immigrants, such as these Korean Americans in New York City, often pool their resources to start family-run small businesses.

These Asian ways can conflict with American ways. Two researchers, for instance, read a series of vignettes to a sample of Chinese-American immigrants from Taiwan and one of their parents in Chicago and Los Angeles. Here is one:

> *Wang Hong has to transfer three times on public transportation to get from where he lives to his office. Because of the time and inconvenience of taking public transportation, Wang Hong has tried very hard to save money to buy a car before winter. However, Wang Hong's parents have a need for money and ask Wang Hong to give them the money Wang Hong has saved.*

Both the parents and their adult children were asked to react to this vignette. The authors noted that when a similar vignette had been read to a general U.S. sample of the elderly and their caregivers, about three-fourths of both groups had thought that the child should buy the car. Yet a majority of the Chinese adult children and parents said that Wang Hong should give the money to his parents—placing obligation to one's parents over convenience of transportation (Lin & Liu, 1993).

Immigrants' families frequently pool economic resources to start businesses or to buy homes. Several Asian-origin groups have very high rates of business ownership, often accomplished by borrowing funds from kin and close friends. As for homeownership, shared residence and income pooling often help, as one Vietnamese immigrant told an interviewer:

> *To Vietnamese culture, family is everything. There are aspects which help us readjust to this society. It is easy for us because of [the] tradition of helping in the family.*
>
> *We solve problems because [the] family institution is a bank. If I need money and my brothers and my two sisters are working I tell them I need to buy a house. I need priority in this case. They say OK, and they give money to me. After only two years, I bought a house.*

Some Americans ask me, "How come you came here with empty hands and now you have a house?" I told them, it is easy for us because my brother and sister help with the down payment. Now I help them. They live with me and have no rent (Gold, 1993).

This is not to say that all Asian immigrants adjust well and prosper. The first wave of Vietnamese immigration occurred in the immediate aftermath of the Vietnam War in 1975. Like the initial Cuban influx, it was a political migration of middle-class business and military personnel who were assisted on arrival. They have been successful as a group. Yet like the Mariel immigration, a later, less-educated stream of Vietnamese immigrants escaped in overcrowded boats to refugee camps in Southeast Asia. Those who have emigrated to the United States have fewer skills, have received less assistance, and have encountered a sluggish economy. A 1984 study of some of the later immigrants found that 61 percent had household incomes of less than $9,000 (Gold, 1993). In addition, as noted earlier, government statistics on the Asian-American population sometimes include Hawaiians or Pacific Islanders, who are among the poorest racial-ethnic groups in the United States. The median family income of Hawaiians is only slightly higher than that of African Americans (U.S. Bureau of the Census, 1991e). Nevertheless, Asian Americans are a prosperous group overall. In 1993, the median family income for Asian and Pacific Islander families was $44,456, which was 8 percent *higher* than the median for white families, $41,114, an impressive achievement for a population that includes so many recent immigrants.

As Figure 5.5 shows, Chinese- and Japanese-origin women have substantially lower numbers of children, on average, than any other racial-ethnic groups except Cuban Americans, who come close. If current birthrates continue, the average number of births per Japanese-American woman would be just 1.1. Demographers have long maintained that some better-off racial-ethnic groups, such as Japanese Americans, seek to consolidate their economic gains by having fewer children and investing much time, effort, and money in their upbringing and education (Goldscheider & Uhlenberg, 1969). Moreover, as Figure 5.1 shows, Asian-American households with children were more likely to be headed by a married couple than non-Hispanic white households. The low rates of family disruption and the emphasis on marriage can also be seen in Figure 5.6, which shows that Chinese, Japanese, and Filipino families had a lower percentage of babies born to unmarried mothers than non-Hispanic whites in 1990. In Chapter 12, you will see a chart showing the low levels of divorce and separation among most Asian-American groups. In these respects, Asian-American families resemble the kinds of families in their native countries, where there is less emphasis on marriage as a means of personal fulfillment and more emphasis on the responsibilities of parents and children, and husbands and wives, toward each other (Goode, 1963). Asian-American parents still sometimes play a role in restricting their children's dating activities and helping them choose their spouses. Indeed, a study of Koreans in Los Angeles found that one-third of those who had married in the previous five years had flown back to Korea to obtain a spouse. There they were introduced to prospective partners who had been carefully chosen by parents and relatives (Min, 1993).

The extent to which these Asian-style patterns will survive through the second and third generations of Asian Americans remains to be seen. Perhaps the most important fact about the new families being formed by Asian-American young adults is that about two-thirds of them involve non-Asian spouses. Consider the trends in marriages involving Asian-American women in their twenties: In 1980,

47.5 percent of these marriages were to an Asian-American husband; but by 1990 only 33.5 percent were to an Asian-American husband (Qian, 1997). Thus, the rate of intermarriage increased substantially during the 1980s; no data is available for the 1990s. Most of the intermarriages are to non-Hispanic whites, suggesting that Asian-American family patterns after the turn of the century may be more similar to the dominant U.S. patterns.

NATIVE AMERICAN FAMILIES

Before the twentieth century, kinship ties provided the basis for governing most American Indian tribes. A person's household was linked to a larger group of relatives who might be a branch of a matrilineal or patrilineal clan (see Chapter 2) that shared power with other clans. Thus, kinship organization was also political organization. Under these circumstances, extended kinship ties reflected power and status to a much greater extent than among other racial-ethnic groups in the United States. American Indian kinship systems allowed individuals to have more relatives, particularly distant relatives, than did Western European kinship systems (Shoemaker, 1991). Even today, extended family ties retain a significance for American Indians that goes beyond the sharing of resources that has been noted among other groups (Harjo, 1993). Kinship networks constitute tribal organization; kinship ties confer an identity.

Only 43 percent of the 1.9 million American Indians in 1990 lived on or near tribal lands—if we define an American Indian as someone who identifies him- or herself as such in the census. That figure is down from 53 percent in 1980.[12] As noted earlier, a substantial share of the growth of the American Indian population in urban areas in the East and on the West Coast between 1970 and 1980 reflected a rise in the number of people who considered themselves to be American Indians; that trend may have continued in the 1980s. In addition, migration from reservations to urban areas may have accounted for some of the drop in the percentage living near tribal lands. A large number of Americans have some American Indian ancestry because American Indians have a far higher intermarriage rate than racial-ethnic groups such as African Americans. In 1990, only about 40 percent of married American Indians were married to other American Indians (Sandefur & Liebler, 1997).

American Indians remain an economically disadvantaged population. Their median family income is comparable to that of African Americans (Snipp, 1989). Consistent with their high levels of poverty, the percentage of American Indian families headed by an unmarried woman is substantial: As Figure 5.1 shows, 31 percent of Native American families with children in 1990 (including Eskimos and Aleuts) were headed by an unmarried woman. Only African Americans had a higher percentage. Consistent with these figures, 54 percent of Native American mothers who gave birth in 1990 were unmarried—a percentage comparable to Puerto Ricans and again exceeded only by African Americans. The percentage of adults who are divorced is also higher among American Indians than among the U.S. population as a whole (Sandefur & Liebler, 1996).

[12]For 1980: Snipp (1989). For 1990: U.S. Bureau of the Census (1993g). Detailed tabulations on American Indians from the 1990 Census had not yet been published when this chapter was written. Because of the small size of the Native American population, only the Decennial Census provides enough cases for detailed examination.

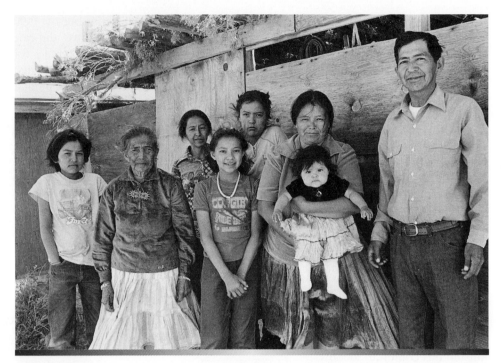

Less than half of the people who identified themselves as American Indians in the 1990 Census lived on or near tribal lands. One who does is Larry Simonson, the treasurer of the "Big Mountain People," whose family resists being relocated from their farmland.

It's likely that many of the unmarried mothers were enmeshed in kinship networks that provided assistance. Little research, however, has been done on contemporary American Indian family patterns— especially among American Indians outside tribal lands. Beyond these lands, intermarriage and shifting conceptions of American Indian ethnicity make the study of families more complex. It is increasingly difficult to talk of the "American Indian family": There always has been diversity in family patterns among Indian tribes and among persons residing on reservations versus persons not on reservations, and now an American Indian family is often a multiracial family.

RACE, ETHNICITY, AND KINSHIP

Family ties have been central to the successes and the struggles of racial-ethnic groups in the United States. All the groups that have been discussed in this chapter have relied on their relatives for support—whether that support be food for dinner or money to buy a restaurant. Their reliance on extended kinship contrasts with the nuclear family ideal among the non-Hispanic white middle class. To be sure, there are substantial differences among racial-ethnic groups in the kinds of family lives they tend to lead. Some of these differences reflect economic forces. In Chapter 4 and this chapter, we have seen similarities in the ways poor whites, African Americans, and Puerto Ricans organize family and kinship. Among these disadvantaged groups, the strongest family tie is often between a mother and her adult daughter. In what I have called women-centered kin networks, women organize exchanges of support that extend across households, linking networks of people who share their meager resources.

Nevertheless, the precise form of kinship varies from group to group, reflecting, in my opinion, long-standing cultural differences. For example, in Potter

Addition (see Chapter 4), a majority of low-income white households included both a wife and a husband. Yet even though most men were married and living with their wives, it was women who, in practical terms, ran the households and provided most of the support for other kin. The distinctive characteristic of Puerto Rican households is the consensual union, although there are also many households headed by women without live-in partners. Single-parent households, or grandmother-daughter-grandchild households, are the common form among African Americans, with young mothers often residing with their own mothers for several years. For all these groups, assistance from family members other than one's spouse or partner is crucial for subsisting from day to day.

Among many immigrant groups, family ties provide critical assistance to individuals who wish to start small businesses. Most banks will not lend money to new immigrants because they are not sure they will be repaid. Immigrants tend not to have homes or other assets that they can use as collateral to secure a bank loan. Sometimes, however, they can obtain start-up loans from members of their kinship and community networks. Those who loan the money rely upon kinship and community ties as a form of moral collateral: A borrower puts his reputation and standing among his peers on the line when he or she obtains a loan. If the borrower were to default, he or she would be dishonored before family and friends. Thus, kinship ties provide a form of social capital that immigrants can use to obtain the physical capital—money, equipment, storefronts—needed to start an enterprise. These same ties also become recruiting networks through which members of the group can find jobs.

The immigrant entrepreneurs utilize what we might call marriage-centered kin networks. These exchanges tend to connect households that are headed by husbands and wives. It is the married couple that starts and maintains the business, although other relatives may work in it. Ties to a wider network of kin provide financial assistance that the married couple is allowed to manage largely for its own benefit. In contrast, women-centered kin networks require that any surplus be shared. In this way, the kin networks of the poor allow the maximum number of people to get the resources they need to avoid becoming destitute. Thus, the two kinds of kinship networks discussed in this chapter and the previous one have different functions: Marriage-centered networks allow for the accumulation of resources by the husband-wife household, whereas women-centered networks allow for the maximum sharing of resources across predominantly single-parent households.

I would suggest that these two forms of kin networks have different strengths and limitations. The women-centered networks are superior for easing the hardships of persistent poverty. They have allowed many poor individuals to subsist from day to day. Yet they make it difficult for network members to accumulate the resources necessary to rise above poverty. The marriage-based networks, on the other hand, are superior for allowing people to be upwardly mobile by accumulating enough resources to start a business or move to a better neighborhood. Yet they make it difficult for network members to provide assistance to all kin who need it. The differences between the two networks suggest, therefore, a tension that many people with low incomes may face: helping all of one's kin who need assistance versus accumulating enough money to better the position of one's own household. Different racial-ethnic groups resolve this tension in different ways.

This is not to suggest that whether a household escapes from poverty is solely, or even primarily, a matter of kinship networks. Entrepreneurial ethnic groups such as the Cubans and Koreans were drawn from the better-educated segments of the sending countries. In 1980, for example, 78 percent of the Korean-origin population had at least four years of high school, compared with 71 percent of the white population and 56 percent of the African-American population (U.S. Bureau of the Census, 1991e). As mentioned previously, most of the early Cuban immigrants were white and therefore did not face racial discrimination. A case could be made that, although there has been discrimination against Asian Americans, it has not been as institutionalized and as pervasive as has discrimination against African Americans. Moreover, the restructuring of the economy has had a major effect on the family lives of African Americans. Still, within these constraints, family and kinship patterns appear to make a difference in the life chances of the members of racial-ethnic groups, allowing many to survive and some to prosper.

Families, however, do not operate independently of government. Despite strong sentiment in the United States against government "interference" in family life, the state does intervene importantly. Let us next examine the relationship between the family and the state.

SUMMARY

1. Immigration from Latin American and Asian countries is changing the racial and ethnic balance in the United States. The major U.S. racial-ethnic groups today are African Americans, Hispanics, Asian Americans, and Native Americans, as well as a large residual category, non-Hispanic whites. The family patterns of these groups differ substantially. Moreover, even within each group there is substantial variation in family patterns. Data on these racial-ethnic categories have become important to the enforcement of civil rights legislation, even though, in reality, many people cannot easily fit into any of them.

2. African Americans have been affected greatly by changes in the economy that have reduced the number of semiskilled and skilled blue-collar jobs. As a result, in part, of this economic transformation, the place of marriage in African-American families has declined substantially, relative to ties to extended kin such as grandmothers. The link between childbearing and marriage has also weakened, with about two-thirds of black children now born to unmarried mothers. Women's marriage prospects, in addition, have been dimmed by the toll of drugs and violence among black men. Faced with this situation, African Americans have responded by drawing upon a traditional source of support in African-American culture: reliance on exchanges among a network of kin for subsistence. Still, a significant middle-class African-American population has emerged over the past few decades.

3. Hispanics comprise several groups whose family patterns differ. The most numerous group, Mexican Americans, is characterized by high birthrates and large households. Nevertheless, Mexican-American women (and women from most other Hispanic groups) have entered the labor force in large number over the past few decades. Puerto Ricans, the poorest of the main Hispanic groups, have a relatively high number of children born to unmarried mothers. But some of the unmarried mothers are living with partners, often in consensual unions that they consider to be like marriages. Cuban Americans are the most prosperous Hispanic group, although recent immigrants have reduced the group's economic standing somewhat. Cubans tended to settle in an immigrant enclave in the Miami area, where they used the social capital of family and community ties to obtain financing for new businesses.

4. Asian-American families have married couples heading their households more than any other group, including non-Hispanic whites. They also have low percentages of children born outside marriage and low divorce rates. These characteristics probably reflect the greater emphasis in Asian cultures on the interdependence and mutual obligations of kinship. Asian immigrant families pool incomes and obtain loans from associations to start businesses at very high rates. Although some subgroups are poor, Asian-American families have a higher median income than non-Hispanic white families. A majority of young adult

Asian Americans are marrying non-Asians, meaning that Asian-American families in the future will increasingly be multiracial.

5. Kinship ties were central to the political organization of American Indian societies; even today, broader kinship ties provide a sense of identity and belonging for American Indians. Family households among American Indians have a low median income, reflecting the economic disadvantage of the group. Moreover, a relatively high percentage of family households are headed by unmarried women. Little research has been conducted on contemporary American Indian family life.

6. Two kinds of kinship networks have been noted among racial-ethnic groups. One is a marriage-based network that connects households headed by married couples. The second kind consists of households that are linked by the ties of mothers, daughters, and other female relatives, often unmarried. The two kinds of networks seem to have different strengths and weaknesses. The women-centered networks are superior for easing the hardships of persistent poverty, yet they make it difficult for network members to accumulate the resources necessary to rise above poverty. The marriage-based networks, on the other hand, are superior for allowing people to be upwardly mobile by accumulating enough resources to start a business or move to a better neighborhood, yet they limit the help received by less fortunate households.

KEY TERMS

Native American	Asian American	labor force
American Indian	non-Hispanic white	consensual union
Alaska native	union formation	assimilation
racial-ethnic group	mediating structure	immigrant enclave
Hispanic	total fertility rate (TFR)	social capital

FAMILIES ON THE INTERNET

The U.S. Bureau of the Census collects detailed statistics through its monthly Current Population Survey, its Decennial Census of Population, and other studies (**www.census.gov**). The information in this chapter on the growth of racial and ethnic minority families, household composition, and interracial families was obtained from the Census Bureau's home page. Information about rates on childbearing outside of marriage and other births is available through the U.S. National Center for Health Statistics (**www.cdc.gov/ nchswww/nchshome.htm**); and figures on work and unemployment can be obtained from the U.S. Bureau of Labor Statistics (**www.bls.gov**). The report of the federal statistical committee which decided that Americans will be allowed to choose more than one race in the 2000 Census can be found at **www.whitehouse. gov/WH/EOP/OMB/html/fedreg/Directive_15.html**; and an electronic newsletter, Interracial Voice, published by advocates of a multiracial category, is available at **www.webcom.com/~intvoice.**

CHAPTER 6

The Family, the State, and Social Policy

Consider two hypothetical families. In family A, a poor single mother struggles to raise two children. She receives cash assistance from the government and food stamps. When she or her children are sick, they visit the emergency room at the local hospital, where their care is paid for through Medicaid, the federal program of health insurance for the poor. She lives on the 15th floor of a publicly owned housing project that charges less for rent than she would pay if she rented an apartment privately. Her four-year-old goes to government-funded Head Start classes to learn skills that will be useful for school. It is obvious that family A receives a great deal of assistance from the government.

In family B, two employed, college-educated parents are raising two children. They are not receiving welfare, and they own their own home. It may seem as though they receive no assistance from the government, but they do. Their elderly parents in Miami Beach and Sun City receive Social Security checks, relieving family B of having to support them. Moreover, the couple deduct the interest payments for their home mortgage from their taxable income, which makes it easier for them to own a home. They take an income tax credit for part of the cost of the day care center their four-year-old attends, which makes it easier for both of them to hold jobs outside the home. In addition, when Mr. B was laid off from his job as a computer programmer for three months this past year, he collected federally funded unemployment compensation.

In truth, most American families, including most middle-class families, receive substantial government assistance. It has not always been the case that most families receive assistance. In the colonial era, almost no economic assistance was provided; rather, the family was viewed as an independent entity that ought not to be interfered with—a "little commonwealth" in Demos's phrase (Demos, 1970). In fact, there was relatively little government financial assistance to families throughout the nineteenth century. In the early decades of the twentieth century, however, labor unions gained enough strength to demand higher pay, shorter hours, old-age pensions, and unemployment compensation. Moreover, civic groups led by middle-class women pressed for programs to assist mothers and children in poverty, such as pensions for widows (Skocpol, 1992).

Then, in 1929 came the economic collapse of the Great Depression. The masses of unemployed workers looked to the government for assistance. Herbert Hoover, a Republican president who opposed most government involvement in the economy, was defeated in the 1932 election by Franklin Delano Roosevelt. Under Roosevelt, the federal government developed a number of programs to assist unemployed workers and their families. Among them was the **Social Security Act of 1935,** which created, among other provisions, Social Security (the system of pensions for the elderly), unemployment compensation (payments to workers who lose their jobs), and aid to mothers with dependent children. The latter program was subsequently renamed **Aid to Families with Dependent Children (AFDC).** It was the program of financial assistance to low-income, single-parent families that became commonly known as "welfare." For 61 years, AFDC was the heart of government assistance to poor mothers and children. Then in 1996 Congress passed, and President Bill Clinton signed, a bill that drastically changed the face of cash assistance to poor families. It is the ungainly named **Personal Responsibility and Work Opportunity Reconciliation Act of 1996,** which policy analysts refer to by its acronym, **PRWORA.**

In this chapter we will explore in detail the history of welfare programs between the Social Security Act and PRWORA, a period during which government assistance to poor families, and programs to compensate for families' alleged limitations, expanded greatly as the following examples (reflecting 1995 data) reveal:

- 13.6 million people (9.3 million of them children) received cash assistance through AFDC.
- 26.6 million people received food stamps, introduced in the 1960s to reduce hunger and malnutrition.
- 468,000 children were living in foster care, most having been removed from their homes by government caseworkers.
- 751,000 three- to five-year-old poor children were enrolled in Head Start, a program begun in the 1960s that attempted to provide early readiness for school[1]

---

[1] All figures in this paragraph and the following one are from U.S. House of Representatives, Committee on Ways and Means (1996), except where noted.

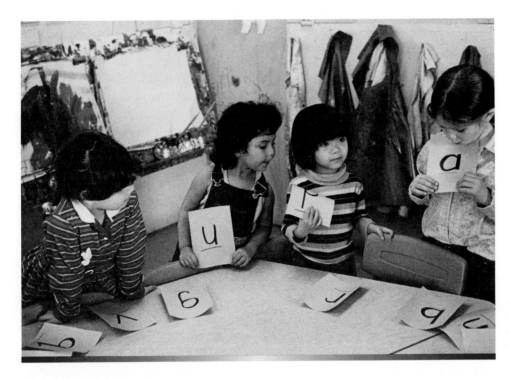

Government programs such as Head Start for preschool children provide assistance to low-income families.

As the example of family B showed, government assistance is not limited to the poor. Consider as well the following data:

- In 1991, 25.3 million retired workers received Social Security payments, which eased their children's burdens of support (U.S. Bureau of the Census, 1993g).
- In 1991, 10.1 million workers received unemployment compensation, enabling them to provide income to their families while looking for other jobs (U.S. Bureau of the Census, 1993g).
- In 1995, 6.2 million parents at all income levels deducted part of the cost of out-of-home childcare from their income taxes, a subsidy that made it easier for them to work outside the home and that cost the federal government 2.7 billion dollars in lost tax revenue (U.S. House of Representatives, Committee on Ways and Means, 1996).
- In 1995, 28 million federal income tax returns deducted the interest payments on home mortgages, a subsidy to homeowners that cost the federal government $51 billion in lost tax revenue—nearly four times as much as it spent on AFDC (U.S. Bureau of the Census, 1996e).

This list, which could be expanded, demonstrates that the government is far more involved in supporting families economically than was the case in earlier times. Extensive federal economic support is a twentieth-century phenomenon. Most government involvement is based on a concern about the well-being of children (as in the cash assistance or foster home programs) or of the elderly (as in Social Security). In other words, most government programs that affect families do so out of concern about the proper caretaking and support of dependents—people too young or too old or too ill to care for themselves. Most, therefore, reflect the perspective introduced in Chapter 1 as the public family. The great attention government pays to these issues of caretaking and dependency shows that the family is still viewed as an important source of care.

Yet many of these measures were conceived at a time when the family was different than it is today—a time when there were far fewer divorces, births outside marriage, married women working outside the home, and unmarried couples living together; a time before birth control pills allowed better control of pregnancy, before medical technology allowed fertilized eggs to be implanted in a woman's uterus, and before large numbers of gay and lesbian couples, some with children, were living openly. For example, the Social Security Act's program of aid to mothers with dependent children (the forerunner of AFDC) was originally designed to help widowed women support their children. Its designers never dreamed that, a few decades later, most of its recipients would be never-married or divorced parents.

In the wake of these changes, public support rose in the 1980s and 1990s for new laws and government policies that would assist families. Family policy had become a major political issue. In the presidential campaigns of the 1980s and early 1990s, "family values" was a prevalent theme. In the 1992 campaign, Bill Clinton promised to "end welfare as we know it" if he were elected. Much of the debate centered on two sets of issues: (1) how to respond to the growth of single-parent families and childhood poverty, such as by reforming welfare or by enforcing the child support obligations of absent fathers; and (2) whether, and how, to assist parents employed outside the home, such as by providing childcare assistance or work leave to care for infants or seriously ill relatives. By the 1990s, public interest in family issues was so intense that the covers of newsmagazines featured "underclass" families on welfare, middle-class children in day care centers, and so-called deadbeat dads who had never paid child support.

This chapter will probe these policy debates for what they reveal about the underlying themes in public discussions on the family. It will focus on the increasing public concern during the twentieth century about the family's ability to care for dependents—and on the public laws and programs that have been enacted to assist it. In order to do so, however, it is necessary first to examine more generally the often thorny relationship between the family and the state. The current debates are rooted in long-standing questions about how involved in people's family lives the government should be. More specifically, how actively should the government, through law and social policy, regulate and support the family in its care and nurturing of children, the frail elderly, and the chronically ill? And how is the government to decide what kinds of interventions are best to provide? Issues of gender roles have nearly always been central to these debates; often issues of class and race have also been important. The answers to these questions depend, in part, on ethics and morality—subjects beyond the bounds of sociology. Yet the answers also depend on social structure and social change, subjects to which a sociological inquiry can contribute.

THE FAMILY AND THE STATE

In this book, the term **state** means a government that claims the right to rule a given territory and its population and to have a monopoly of force in that territory. The term **nation** refers above all to a people with shared economic and cultural interests—people who have a sense of belonging, a common bond. The countries of the world today are most accurately described by the term **nation-state**, which combines the governmental and cultural connotations of the two words it comprises. Yet most people use the simpler term "nation" rather than "nation-state" to refer to countries, and I will sometimes follow this simpler usage. The emergence of nation-states has been the central political development in the world since the late 1400s, when monarchs consolidated territories in England, France, and Spain, breaking the power of medieval lords over their lands. Today, the nation-state system, as embodied in the United Nations, is firmly entrenched throughout most of the world.

THE WELFARE STATE

The economic system in the Western nation-states and in most others is capitalism. As noted in Chapter 3, it is an economic system in which goods and services are privately produced and sold on a market for profit. Workers offer their labor to the owners of the means of production, such as factories, and accept the highest offer of wages they receive. The owners then try to sell their products at a price high enough to yield a profit after they subtract the wages, rents, and other expenses they have paid. In its purest form, the ideology of capitalism argues that there should be no interference by government in the labor market or in the market for products. Beginning with Adam Smith, capitalist economic theorists have argued that the forces of the market—the interplay of the demand for and supply of goods—produce a socially optimal distribution of wages and prices. The market, in Smith's famous phrase, acts as an "invisible hand" that guides the economy toward an outcome that is the best for all (Smith, 1776). The socialist economic system, in contrast, is organized quite differently. (See *Families in Other Cultures:* Women Hold Up Half the Sky, pp. 174–75.)

It is but a short extension to argue that, according to capitalist economic theory, the government should not intervene in family affairs. To intervene is to disturb the workings of the invisible hand and therefore to risk doing more harm than good. For example, some critics of cash assistance to poor families argue that it discourages them from taking jobs, thereby reducing their standard of living in the long run.[2] (Others believe that the shortage of available jobs, or the need for some parents to care full time for their children, justifies cash assistance.) Yet not to intervene is to do nothing to help people in need or assist groups that might be unjustly disadvantaged in the labor market.

As noted earlier, the view that the government should not intervene in family affairs prevailed in the United States until the hardships of the Depression. Since then, the U.S. Congress has passed substantial legislation to protect workers and their families from the most harmful consequences of the labor market. In the social scientific literature on these laws and programs, authors refer to them as "social welfare" measures, and they write of the **welfare state**, by which they mean a capitalist government that has enacted numerous measures—such as Social Security, unemployment compensation, and a minimum wage—to protect workers and their families from the harshness of the capitalist system and to raise their standard of living above what wages paid in the labor market alone would do. Here the term "welfare" is used not in its common meaning of cash assistance to the poor but rather in the broader sense of the well-being of members of society. These social welfare measures expanded greatly in the 1950s and 1960s, as labor and minority groups pushed for them and as growing affluence allowed the government to raise taxes to support them.

[2]See, for example, Murray (1984).

Families in Other Cultures

Women Hold Up Half the Sky

In 1906, a peasant in Hunan province in China tried to arrange a marriage between his 13-year-old son and a 19-year-old woman. The father's objective was to exploit the labor of the woman for several years before the son was old enough for the marriage ceremony to be carried out. The son, however, was so opposed to the marriage that he ran away from home and refused to return until the father canceled it. That the father would make such an arrangement without consulting his son was not unusual in China. In all the world, China was probably the foremost example of *patriarchy*, defined in Chapter 3 as a system in which older men control their families and in which family groups are the main economic units of society. Parents routinely arranged marriages without consulting their children. Many Chinese parents crippled their young daughters with painful foot bindings in order to produce the small, deformed feet that some Chinese men found erotic. Upon marriage, a young woman went to live with her husband's family, which had nearly complete control over her.

The son of the peasant became a journalist and activist, publicizing cases in which young women had committed suicide rather than go through with arranged marriages to men they disliked. Later he led a revolutionary war that defeated the government and installed a socialist regime with himself as chairman. His name was Mao Zedong. One of his many sayings was "Women hold up half the sky" (Witke, 1967).

It is an interesting question, then, to ask what happened to the position of women in Chinese society under socialism and, more generally, what is the association between a nation's economic system and its level of male domination. *Socialism,* as stated in Chapter 3, is an economic and political system under which the state, acting in the name of the workers, owns the means of production (such as land and factories) and assigns workers to their jobs. The number and type of goods produced, and whom they are distributed to, is decided by the government rather than by the actions of a market. The question is interesting because early socialist writers believed that men's domination of women in the Western nations was caused by capitalism. Friedrich Engels, Marx's colleague, asserted that women's inferior status stemmed from men's ownership of property and women's lack of participation in work outside the home. After the socialist revolution, he wrote, women would work outside the home, the state would own the property, and women and men would become equals (Engels, 1972).

It hasn't worked out that way. To be sure, women's status has improved in many important ways in postrevolutionary China. The 1950 marriage law outlawed marriages arranged without children's consent and banned the most notorious practices, such as foot binding. The power of the lineages has been broken, so women are no longer controlled by their in-laws. They receive nearly as much schooling as men. Moreover, in the cities nearly all adult women work full-time outside the home (Whyte & Parish, 1984).

Nevertheless, substantial inequalities remain. Women tend to have lower-paying jobs, and the kinds of jobs they do in cities—services, clerical work, health care—are similar to those that are viewed as "women's jobs" in Western societies. Women also hold far fewer positions of power in the government (Whyte & Parish, 1984). The traditional Chinese preference for the birth of sons rather than daughters remains strong. As noted in Chapter 3 (see *Families in Other Cultures:* China's Missing Girls), since the government began its efforts to enforce a one-child-per-family limit on births, there have been reports of abandonment of female newborns, sex-selective abortion, and even of increased infanticide. In the countryside, most production teams are headed by men and government payments are given to the family head, almost always the male (Stacey, 1983).

Above all, the division of labor in the household remains profoundly unequal. Chinese men appear to do no more, and possibly less, housework and childcare than do Western men. What is more, since labor-saving devices such as refrigerators, gas or electric stoves, washing machines, and dryers are still not commonplace,

Chinese women must work a full day and then do the shopping, cooking, cleaning, washing, and so forth—a double burden that probably exceeds that of Western women (Whyte & Parish, 1984).

Nor does the double burden appear to be merely a vestige of the Chinese patriarchal system. Women in what was the Union of the Soviet Socialist Republics reported a similar lack of assistance from men in household labor. A visitor wrote:

> Throughout the weeks of our travels . . . we heard women complain about the double burdens of home and career in a mood of bitterness, frequent anger, and amazing candor. . . . In this nation where 92 percent of the women are fully employed, and compose 51 percent of the nation's workforce, the word we heard most frequently was *peregruzhennost,* "overburdening" (du Plessix Gray, 1990).

What, then, is the relationship, if any, between the type of economic system a nation has and the extent of male domination? After examining the Chinese case, Judith Stacey concludes that "socialism has not liberated women" because a socialist system has proved to be compatible with continued male domination (Stacey, 1983). Men still tend to control the government and to allocate resources in their own favor. Stacey concluded that a nation's system of gender relations is "relatively autonomous" from its economic system, be it socialism or capitalism. This conclusion certainly does not imply that one can ignore a nation's economic system in studying issues of gender and family. Nor does it suggest that capitalism is a necessarily benign force in shaping the relations between women and men. The evidence, nevertheless, does provide lessons for students of family and gender in the Western nations. The persistence of inequalities of gender under socialism suggests that male domination cannot be explained wholly by a nation's economic system. Rather, male domination must have a noneconomic basis as well. The Chinese and Russian cases suggest that it is a mistake for Westerners to blame their own inequalities of gender on capitalism merely because they occur in capitalist nations.

Although Chinese women have been integrated into the militia, among other social institutions, the socialist revolution did not eliminate male domination in China.

The welfare state has treated husbands and fathers differently from wives and mothers. In the terms of feminist theory, the development of the welfare state has been "gendered" (Orloff, 1993). Beginning around the turn of the twentieth century, reformers campaigned, without much success initially, for laws that would require employers to pay male workers enough so they could support their families without their wives' (and children's) having to work for wages. During the same period, women's organizations and labor unions campaigned, with more success, for protective legislation: laws to limit the number of hours women could work for wages to "protect" them from having to work too long and hard outside the home (Skocpol, 1992). Together, these different objectives for women and men supported the **family wage system**, a division of labor in which the husband earns enough money to support his family and the wife remains home to do housework and childcare. This system, which was the "breadwinner-homemaker" family, is now in decline, but an examination of its development is useful for understanding the family policy debates occurring today.

THE FAMILY WAGE SYSTEM

The moral vision behind campaigns for the family wage system specified that the family works best when men and women inhabit separate spheres (see Chapter 2): his, paid work outside the home; hers, unpaid homemaking and childrearing inside the home. This view, as has been discussed, gained in popularity in the nineteenth-century United States as industrialization moved the workplace out of the home. The family wage system was never a reality for many working-class and minority families, whose men could not earn enough to support a family. Nevertheless, it remained the dominant cultural view of the family throughout the first half of the twentieth century, and it still has advocates.[3]

The Social Security Act of 1935 followed the division of labor implicit in the family wage system. It provided old-age pensions only to persons who "earned" them by working a certain number of years in the paid labor force; originally only industrial and commercial workers were covered. The clear expectation was that these covered workers would overwhelmingly be men. In 1939, Congress passed an extension of the act that allowed widows of Social Security recipients to receive continued benefits after their husbands died. Women whose husbands were absent for other reasons, and who were still raising children, were eligible for the Aid to Dependent Children program—but only if their income was below a certain level. Congress did not anticipate that large numbers of women raising children might need assistance because they were divorced from their husbands or had never had a husband. It did not anticipate that large numbers of women would qualify for Social Security benefits themselves by working outside the home. The system presumed that, until the death of one spouse, families would consist of a husband who would *provide* for the family and a wife who would *care* for the family (Sapiro, 1990).

The act set the tone for government policy concerning the family. Throughout the 1950s, the prosperous decade in which the breadwinner-homemaker family was much celebrated, the family wage system remained the cultural ideal. During the 1960s, policymakers paid little attention to the family per se. Rather, the 1960s was the decade of the War on Poverty. Under President Johnson, Congress initiated

[3]See Carlson (1986).

Franklin D. Roosevelt signed the landmark Social Security Act of 1935, which created the Social Security system, unemployment compensation, and aid to mothers with dependent children.

and enlarged numerous programs in aid of the poor. Nevertheless, some of these programs had important effects on families. Substantial increases in Social Security benefits and the creation of a health insurance system for the elderly (Medicare) greatly improved the economic well-being of older Americans, making them more independent of their children (see Chapter 15). The number of single-parent families on the AFDC rolls rose sharply in the late 1960s as benefit levels were increased and eligibility standards loosened. The 1964 Civil Rights Act and subsequent Supreme Court decisions banned discrimination against women in hiring and in wages, thus weakening the family wage system.

FAMILY POLICY DEBATES

Still, it was not until the mid-1970s that politicians began to talk specifically about "family policy." In the meantime, the face of the American family had changed. Between the early 1960s and the late 1970s, the divorce rate doubled; by 1980, about one of every two marriages was predicted to end in divorce. More and more married women were working outside the home: By 1980, three-fifths of married women with children under age six were employed.[4] The proportion of children born outside marriage had risen sharply to 11 percent among whites and 55 percent among blacks in 1980 (U.S. Bureau of the Census, 1991e). (These proportions have continued to increase; in 1991 they were 22 percent for whites and 68 percent for blacks [U.S. National Center for Health Statistics, 1993a].) This great growth in single-parent families and in two-earner, two-parent families—which continued in the 1980s and early 1990s—undermined the breadwinner-homemaker ideal.

---

[4]The statistics on divorce and women's labor force participation are from Cherlin (1992b).

Sensing the anxiety these changes caused in some quarters, Jimmy Carter brought a family-strengthening theme to his 1976 campaign and to his presidency. Carter's defense of the family seemed as uncontroversial as endorsing Mom and apple pie. But family policy turned out to be a much more contentious topic than Carter had suspected, and it has remained a battleground ever since. For example, during the campaign, Carter promised to hold a "White House Conference on the American Family" to discuss "specific ways we can better support and strengthen our families."[5] But after a controversy over who would direct the conference, conservatives and liberals battled over whether it should be titled a conference on "the family" (meaning the breadwinner-homemaker family) or "families" (which would include dual-earner and single-parent families).

The battle over the White House conference exemplifies the first of two kinds of conflicts that were not far beneath the surface of any major public issue concerning families during most of the twentieth century: the conflict over women's autonomy—specifically, over the degree of women's economic independence from men (Cohen & Katzenstein, 1988)—and the conflict over income assistance—specifically, over providing assistance to the poor and near poor versus reinforcing their obligation to work. It is worth examining each of these conflicts.

THE CONFLICT OVER WOMEN'S AUTONOMY

What distinguishes the breadwinner-homemaker family from the kinds of families that were dominant both before it arose in the nineteenth century and after its demise began in the 1960s is the nearly complete dependence of wives on their husbands for the means of obtaining the family's needs. The means of obtaining these needs in an industrialized society is money, and in the breadwinner-homemaker family, men make it and women don't. Chapter 10 describes other kinds of families, such as the preindustrial farm family, in which both spouses worked together in a joint enterprise, and the contemporary dual-earner family. In these kinds of families, women are less economically dependent on their husbands because they help run the farm or work for wages at the office.

To be sure, full-time homemakers perform valuable labor—their washing, cooking, and sewing allow the family to get by on the husband's wages. (Put another way, their labor allows employers to pay men lower wages than they would need if they had to purchase housekeeping services.) Homemakers' care of children benefits their families and the larger society. In fact, men are dependent on women for these services, but this reverse dependence is masked by the off-the-books nature of the homemaker's work (Zaretsky, 1986). For instance, only now that many working parents have to pay someone else to care for their children do we realize how much childcare is worth. Nevertheless, male wage earners, having money, can buy services if they wish; female homemakers, lacking money, cannot—except with their husbands' consent.

Some of the advocates of the breadwinner-homemaker family believe it to be God-given or biologically designed. They argue that a strict division of labor and male dominance is natural. They believe that the moral worth of men and women depends on how well they each perform their distinct roles—husband as provider, wife as caregiver (Schlafly, 1978). Another group of advocates concedes that the breadwinner-homemaker family may not be natural in a religious or biological

---

[5]Quoted in Steiner (1981).

Now that many families with employed parents have to pay for childcare, it is apparent how economically valuable is the care that mothers provide for their own children.

sense, but they nevertheless believe it to be the most preferable form. Although they acknowledge the historical variation in families, they argue that the breadwinner-homemaker family has been the backbone of capitalist prosperity and democracy. It is said to support prosperity, in part, because it provides a small, self-sufficient unit that can move to where the job opportunities are in an industrial society; it is not tied to one city by linkages to a network of extended kin (Baumgarth, 1986).[6] It is also said to encourage prosperity by creating self-reliant individuals who can become entrepreneurs and managers. These valuable individuals, it is argued, can venture forth from the small conjugal family and then retire for rest and spiritual renewal into the domestic sphere of privacy it creates. Brigitte Berger and Peter Berger wrote that, far from being the product of the Industrial Revolution, the breadwinner-homemaker family was "one of the important *preconditions* of this technological cataclysm" (Berger & Berger, 1983).

Finally, writers such as the Bergers and others believe the breadwinner-homemaker family to be essential to democracy because it is a mediating structure (see Chapter 5) that can give individuals the support they need to resist the dictates of the nation-state. Without these mediating structures, it is argued, individuals would have loyalties only to the state. With them, individuals can join together, if necessary, to resist the great power of the national government, the freedom-limiting rules of the bureaucracy, the dictates of a totalitarian regime. In the United States, this idea can be traced back to the Bill of Rights, which protects mediating structures through "the right of the people peacefully to assemble" and the right to bear arms because "a well-regulated Militia" is "necessary to the security of a free State." Mediating structures, then, provide a setting for individual and social action. It is important that they have strong leadership in order to protect and support individuals. The two-parent family is said to be a mediating structure because the authority of the father and the emotional bonds among the members create a "countervailing power" (Glendon, 1989) that protects individuals from abuses of power by the state.

---

[6]William Goode made the more general argument that the conjugal family fits the need of industrial societies in *World Revolution and Family Patterns* (New York: The Free Press, 1963).

Until very recently, those who favor the breadwinner-homemaker family tended to oppose social welfare programs that they view as encouraging women's independence. For instance, many social conservatives have opposed legislation that would subsidize the cost of out-of-home care for the children of employed parents. They have argued that assistance to employed parents encourages more mothers to take jobs outside the home, which erodes the breadwinner-homemaker family (Gill, 1991). Some favor little or no further government action of any kind, in large part because many existing policies, as noted, were designed to support the breadwinner-homemaker family. Others support programs that would benefit families with stay-at-home wives as well as those with employed wives, such as an increase in the tax deduction any family can claim per child (Carlson, 1986).

But critics of the breadwinner-homemaker family read the tributes to the self-reliance and autonomy it produces and ask, Self-reliance and autonomy for whom? They note that the self-reliant, young entrepreneurs who venture forth from this type of family are overwhelmingly male. Women, by and large, do not share equally in the autonomy this family form creates; their talents and desires for work outside the home are stifled. To be sure, there are other rewards that some women may find attractive, such as having close interaction with children and avoiding the stresses of a paying job; but in any case they are asked to sacrifice their individuality on behalf of the male members of their families. "This family ideal," writes Barrie Thorne, "denies women individualism, equality, and full access to economic and political resources" (Thorne, 1982).

The costs to women are apparent in the transcripts of interviews with 300 middle-class married couples in 1955—perhaps the height of the breadwinner-homemaker family's popularity. The wives, according to historian Elaine Tyler May, were twice as likely as their husbands to report that they were dissatisfied with their marriages. Moreover, twice as many said they would not marry the same person if they had to do it over again. Many stayed in their marriages despite substantial strain. One wife wrote:

> *One particular source of friction: My husband is a firm believer in "woman's place is in the home"—so it is, to a degree—but I have always felt the need for outside activities and interest in community affairs because I felt mentally stagnant by not taking part in outside programs and because I feel morally obligated to take part, in view of my education and some capabilities. He takes no interest in my interests and belittles most women's groups. . . . Whatever I have done has had to be at no inconvenience to him—and often with a scornful attitude on his part* (May, 1988, p. 198).

The argument that women's own individuality is lost in the breadwinner-homemaker family was popularized by Betty Friedan in 1963. Her influential book *The Feminine Mystique* (Friedan, 1963) helped to launch the contemporary feminist movement. Feminist writers challenged the idea that only the breadwinner-homemaker family can provide a balance of autonomy and community. More fundamentally, they challenged the claim that the breadwinner-homemaker family is natural. Rather, they noted that it is unusual in historical perspective and therefore very nontraditional. They cited anthropological studies of the great variety of family forms in various societies. In the more radical critiques, some feminists argued that there is little that is "natural" about any kind of small, husband-wife-children family structure; rather, family types were said to be socially constructed—usually, it was said, in ways that allow men to dominate women (Collier, Rosaldo, & Yanagisako, 1982).

The conclusion of this body of writing is that the defenders of the breadwinner-homemaker family are asking women to pay a high price in lost autonomy to maintain a family form that is neither more natural nor more desirable than other forms. This stance translates into political support for measures that increase the economic equality of women and make it easier for mothers to work outside the home. For instance, critics of the breadwinner-homemaker family typically support laws which require that women and men who are doing comparable jobs be paid the same wages. Most would also favor greater subsidies to employed parents for their out-of-home childcare expenses and more generous work leaves to care for newborn children or seriously ill relatives (Pogrebin, 1983).

THE CONFLICT OVER INCOME ASSISTANCE

The second kind of conflict—the conflict over income assistance—is also not far beneath the surface of the debates over family policy. David Ellwood, a poverty scholar who was appointed to a high position in the Clinton administration, called this conflict the "security-work conundrum." He wrote:

> *When you give people money, food, or housing, you reduce the pressure on them to work and care for themselves. . . . The conundrum is posed most starkly in a true welfare system—one that gives money to the poor solely on the basis of their income. . . . Welfare could discourage work for two conceptually different reasons: It reduces the pressure to work and it reduces the rewards of working* (Ellwood, 1988, p. 19).

Public opinion in the United States favors assistance to the poor that enhances independence and self-reliance; there is much less support for cash assistance to people thought to be capable of working. A national survey carried out in 1994 illustrated this difference. People were asked whether they thought the country was spending "too much money," "too little money," or "about the right amount" on each of several problems. One-half of the sample was asked this question about "welfare," one-half was asked instead about "assistance to the poor." The results are shown in Figure 6.1. A majority thought the country was spending "too little" on

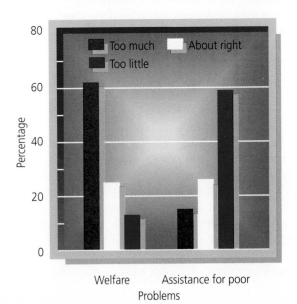

FIGURE 6.1 Percentage of persons in a 1994 national survey who supported different levels of government spending for two problems: "welfare" and "assistance to the poor." (*Source:* National Opinion Research Center, 1997).

assistance to the poor; but a majority also thought the country was spending "too much" on welfare, even though almost everyone who receives welfare is poor. As noted earlier, the use of the term "welfare" in the United States came to mean AFDC, the program of cash assistance to poor, single-parent families from 1935 to 1996.

Political scientist Hugh Heclo interprets these survey responses as demonstrating a public disinclination to provide cash assistance to working-age people. To be sure, many adult AFDC recipients are single mothers with young children, and the wisdom of requiring them to find paid work is debatable (see the discussion of PRWORA below). Perhaps the survey respondents were also thinking of the absent fathers of children receiving AFDC. In any case, Heclo notes that surveys from the 1930s onward show that never has a majority of Americans favored spending more on "welfare" or on "relief and recovery," as it was called during the Depression (Heclo, 1986). Instead, a majority believes that adults should be able to find jobs and manage economically on their own.

Since cash assistance such as AFDC is mainly available to single-parent families, critics of the program charge that it is an important cause of the growth of single-parent families over the past few decades. The evidence, however, is mixed. The most prominent critic in the 1980s, Charles Murray, noted that during the 1960s, AFDC benefit levels increased and so did the number of single-parent families. The implication is that more generous benefits encouraged more single-parent families to form. During the 1970s and 1980s, however, the value of AFDC benefits actually decreased because the cost of living rose faster than benefit levels did (Ellwood & Summers, 1986). In 1992, the average AFDC family received $136 per person per month, compared with $166 (adjusted for inflation) in 1970. This decrease was largely offset by an increase in food stamps from an average of $44 per person in 1972 to $69 in 1992 (U.S. House of Representatives, 1993). Yet although the benefit package of AFDC plus food stamps stayed roughly the same in value, the number of single-parent families continued to increase in number. Welfare, it seems, is not the whole story.

Still, it is possible that AFDC and related assistance programs reached a threshold by the end of the 1960s that supported a greater number of single-parent families. Several studies, however, suggest that these programs have probably not been the main force (Moffitt, 1990; Ruggles, 1997a). Another important contributor to the increase in single-parent families, as discussed in Chapters 4 and 5, is the growing scarcity of semiskilled manufacturing jobs that can provide people without college degrees enough steady income to support a family. Yet another, as also discussed, is the societywide cultural shift away from marriage that has occurred at all income levels.

Defenders of income assistance programs such as AFDC and food stamps argue that the social benefits of the programs exceed the costs. They note that cash assistance substantially improves the well-being of American children—one in five of whom lives in a family with an income below the poverty level. If cash assistance programs are not the main source of increases in single-parent families but are important sources of income for children, they reason, then the programs should be supported and even expanded. To do otherwise would be to punish poor children needlessly for the alleged sins of their parents (Grubb & Lazerson, 1988). It is also argued that some single-parent families are formed in circumstances—such as the end of an abusive marriage—that may improve the well-being of children. Moreover, providing single parents with enough support so that they can remain at home to spend more time caring for their children might be as good for children's well-being as compelling parents to work outside the home (Cherlin, 1995).

THE 1996 WELFARE REFORM LAW

As discussed earlier, AFDC was originally designed to support widows and their children, as part of the Social Security Act of 1935. Both AFDC and Social Security (the program that pays benefits to retirees) were created as entitlement programs by Congress. If a government program is an **entitlement**, the government is obligated to provide benefits to anyone who qualifies, regardless of the total cost of the program. For example, if I reach the official retirement age, walk into my local Social Security office, and ask to be signed up for benefits, they cannot say to me, "We're sorry, but we don't have any more money left this year. Come back next year." They *must* pay me the benefits I am entitled to. Not all government programs for low-income families are entitlements; housing subsidies, for instance, are limited: Only 31 percent of AFDC families also received housing subsidies (or lived in publicly owned housing) in 1995 (U.S. House of Representatives, Committee on Ways and Means, 1996). But starting in 1935, the government pledged to provide assistance through the AFDC program to any family that qualified (usually by having a low income, just one parent, and children under 18).

In 1950, Congress increased the AFDC benefit level in the hope that poor mothers would be able to stay home and care for their children. Starting about 1970, however, Congress passed a series of laws that encouraged, and later required, mothers receiving AFDC to take jobs and leave their children in the care of others. For instance, the Family Support Act of 1988 required recipients with no children under age three to participate in a job training and job search program. If a job was found, the recipient had to accept it or she would lose part of her AFDC benefits. The program, however, was to be phased in gradually. States were required to enroll only 20 percent of their recipients in the new program by fiscal year 1995 (Smith, Blank, & Bond, 1990).

In order to help former recipients keep their jobs, the Family Support Act required that states provide funds for childcare and Medicaid (the program of health insurance for the poor) to the women for 12 months after they became employed. Since many low-paying jobs do not provide health insurance coverage, some workers in the past have had to quit their jobs and return to the welfare rolls in order to obtain health insurance. The Family Support Act regulations removed this disincentive to work—at least for the first year of employment.

Yet "welfare" remained unpopular with the public. In a 1990 national survey, 70 percent of adults favored "reducing welfare benefits to make working for a living more attractive" (National Opinion Research Center, 1997). Bill Clinton, running against President George Bush in the 1992 election campaign, seized upon this unpopularity by promising to "end welfare as we know it." Clinton's plan required most welfare recipients to work within two years of their first welfare payments and limited cash assistance to five years. At the end of five years, mothers still on the rolls would be given government service jobs.

After winning the 1992 election, Clinton shelved his welfare plan while concentrating on his ultimately unsuccessful attempt to institute universal health insurance coverage. In the 1994 mid-term elections, the Republicans gained enough seats to take control of the House and Senate. They then proceeded to craft their version of ending welfare as we knew it (see Table 6.1). First, they ended the entitlement to welfare benefits: States would be given a fixed amount of money each year—a so-called **block grant**—which they would have to match with state funds. If a

TABLE 6.1   MAIN DIFFERENCES BETWEEN AFDC AND TANF

	AFDC	TANF
Limit on government expenditures	Government expenditures are unlimited because AFDC was an *entitlement:* The government had to provide benefits to all who qualified, regardless of the cost. The federal government and the state governments each provided about half the funds.	Federal government expenses are limited because each state receives a fixed amount of funds, called a *block grant.* States may add more of their own funds to the program, but the federal government will not provide more.
Time limit on families' receipt of assistance	Families can receive benefits for an unlimited time, as long as they continue to qualify for the program.	States can use federal funds to pay for only five years of benefits for a family. States may enforce a shorter time limit if they wish. If states want to pay for more than five years of benefits, they may do so if they use only their own state funds.
Work requirements	Twenty percent of recipients were supposed to be working (usually part-time) by 1995.	Adults are required to work within 24 months after they receive assistance. Overall, 25 percent of the families in each state were required to be working by 1997, increasing to 50 percent by 2002.

state exhausted its block-grant and matching funds, it could choose to turn away new applicants until the next year. And the amount of the block grant would not be raised until 2002 at the earliest.

Second, the Republicans embraced the five-year time limit on cash assistance but provided no government jobs afterward. People still on the rolls after five years would be cut off, period. States were free to set an even shorter time limit (and several subsequently did). Recipients also had to accept work within two years of being on the rolls or their families would lose their benefits. Less money was provided for job training and education than in the Clinton plan because Republicans didn't believe them to be effective in helping recipients obtain jobs. Twice the Republicans passed their plan and twice the Democratic president vetoed it as too tough. Then in the summer of 1996, Congress passed the plan a third time; and Clinton, facing a re-election campaign, signed the legislation.

PRWORA, the Personal Responsibility and Work Opportunity Reconciliation Act of 1996, was a stunning rollback of policies toward poor families that had stood since 1935. No longer would the government guarantee to assist every poor, single-parent family in need. No longer could such families count on receiving cash assistance as long as their incomes remained low. No longer could poor mothers stay home full-time to care for their children. The emphasis was on temporary assistance and on getting a job, any job. The legislation scrapped the title AFDC and renamed the time-limited cash assistance program **Temporary Assistance to Needy Families,** or **TANF.**

What caused such a sweeping reversal of six decades of social policy toward poor families? Three differences between the 1930s and the 1990s stand out:

1 *Attitudes toward women's roles*   First, attitudes toward women's roles had changed greatly. The goal of the legislation that created AFDC was consistent with

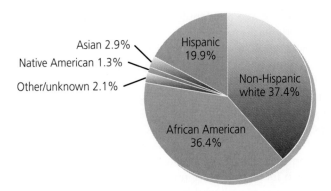

FIGURE 6.2 Race and ethnicity of parents receiving Aid to Families with Dependent Children in 1994. (*Source:* U.S. House of Representatives, Committee on Ways and Means, 1996).

the prevailing value of the era, namely, that women's place was in the home. The legislation was an attempt to extend to poor, single mothers the same role that nonpoor mothers were supposed to play. By the 1990s, however, a majority of mothers were working outside the home. It seemed less punitive to require that poor, single-mothers attempt to find jobs when the majority of middle-class mothers were employed as well. Encouraging self-reliance and independence among poor mothers seemed consistent with emerging values for nonpoor women.

   2 *Characteristics of the recipients*   Second, the characteristics of welfare recipients had also changed. No longer are most widowed; rather, the vast majority are separated, divorced, or never married. About 200 years ago, a distinction emerged in both American and British society between the "deserving" and "undeserving" poor (Katz, 1989). There was, and there remains, substantial public sympathy for the deserving poor, those whose poverty is seen as beyond their control. There has been much less sympathy for the undeserving poor, those whose poverty is perceived, whether fairly or not, as somehow their "fault" because they have failed to behave as society expects. Historically, the main category of "undeserving" poor had been unemployed, able-bodied men. Strong sentiment has always existed that they should be able to find jobs and be self-reliant. In contrast, as victims of their husbands' deaths, widows clearly fall among the deserving poor—their poverty is not their "fault." The situation of separated, divorced, and never-married mothers is less clear. Some observers wish to provide them with support as graciously as it is provided to widows, whereas many others do not. The latter group view the mothers—and perhaps even more so, the fathers of their children—as having chosen, in some sense, an irresponsible path to parenthood. Whether fairly or not, many Americans believe that people should refrain from having children until they can provide for them and are not willing to exempt the poor.

   Moreover, there is another troubling subtext to the discourse about "deservingness." Not only the marital status but also the racial composition of the AFDC population had changed since the early days of the program. As noted in the previous chapter, African-American single-parent families are heavily overrepresented among the persistently poor and, therefore, among AFDC recipients. Figure 6.2 shows the race of parents who received AFDC in 1994. African Americans, who constituted 36 percent of the AFDC rolls, were overrepresented compared with their percentage of the total U.S. population in 1994 (12 percent) and even compared with their percentage of the total population with incomes below the poverty line (27 percent) (U.S. Bureau of the Census, 1997i). Observers of the welfare debate have suggested that racial animosity may underlie some of the public opposition to welfare spending (Grubb & Lazerson, 1988; Quadagno, 1994). Both Heclo and Katz argue that whites in the 1960s came to identify antipoverty policy with African Americans because of the civil rights movement, the activities of welfare rights organizations, the black urban riots in Watts and Northern cities, and the largely black bureaucracy that arose to administer the antipoverty programs (Heclo, 1986).

3 *Concern about "dependency"*   The third reason for the policy reversal is the spread of the idea that the welfare-receiving poor had become too dependent upon public assistance. According to this line of reasoning, usually advanced by conservatives, people who receive public assistance for years and years often lose their initiative to find jobs. It is rational, Charles Murray (1984) argued, for welfare recipients to stay on the rolls: If they were to take a job, they would not only lose their benefits but also incur childcare, transportation, and clothing costs. Their new jobs probably wouldn't pay well and might not include health insurance (whereas AFDC/TANF recipients are covered by Medicaid). We have built a system, so this argument goes, that discourages people from moving from welfare to work (Kaus, 1992; Mead, 1992).

Moreover, the welfare critics state, children who grow up in this environment often become dependent on welfare themselves, thus perpetuating dependency from generation to generation. Drawing upon the work of anthropologist Oscar Lewis, who studied poor Puerto Rican families, critics claim that growing up on welfare fails to teach children the value of working hard, investing in the future, and waiting until marriage to have children. It also fails to provide them with successful role models to emulate. Of the culture of poverty, Lewis (1965) wrote:

> *Once it [the culture of poverty] comes into existence, it tends to perpetuate itself from generation to generation because of its effects on children. By the time slum children are age six or seven, they have usually absorbed the basic values and attitudes of their subculture and are not psychologically geared to take full advantage of changing conditions or increased opportunities which may occur in their lifetime* (p. xlv).

The supporters of PRWORA see it as a chance to break the cycle of dependency; hence the phrases "personal responsibility" and "work opportunity."[7]

Some social conservatives also argue that government agencies cannot do a good job of moving people from welfare to work because they are too impersonal and value-free. Rather, they maintain, religious organizations and other private agencies should take a greater role in assisting the poor, just as they did prior to 1935. (See *Families and Public Policy:* Who Should Help the Poor?)

This critical view of welfare is vigorously contested by others (mostly liberals) who believe that welfare usage is a *response* to poverty, not a cause of it. Yes, it is true, the defenders of time-unlimited welfare acknowledge, that children who grow up in families that receive welfare are more likely, as adults, to receive welfare themselves. (Although most adults on welfare did not receive it as children [Rank & Cheng, 1995]). But this association only shows that children who grow up in poverty are more likely to be poor as adults. What's being transmitted from generation to generation, according to this line of thought, is not a "culture of poverty" but rather social disadvantage: Children whose parents have less education and less income are themselves less likely to graduate from high school and obtain a good job (Rank & Cheng, 1995). In other words, poverty is the illness that public policy should treat, and welfare is only the symptom. Adults on welfare don't lack initiative,

---

[7]The word "Reconciliation" in the act's title just means that the final version was agreed upon by a House-Senate conference committee after the two bodies had passed slightly different versions.

it is said; rather, they lack the opportunity to find steady jobs paying wages that can sustain a family (Handler, 1995). Ending cash assistance after five years, it is argued, is a cruel step that will further impoverish many poor children and their parents. In truth, no one knows how many poor children will be helped and how many will be harmed by the transformation of the welfare system under PRWORA.[8]

Despite these different points of view, a Democratic president and many Democratic members of Congress joined with Republicans to enact the welfare reform law. Why did so many liberals and moderates support PRWORA? By the end of the 1980s, many liberal members of Congress had joined a new consensus that endorsed work outside the home with social support, rather than continued dependence on cash assistance, as the preferable goal for poor mothers. For one thing, they did so because so many nonpoor mothers were working outside the home. To some liberals, a program to help mothers receiving welfare obtain jobs seemed likely to increase their autonomy. In addition, many accepted the idea that persistent poverty was not just a problem of income but also of prolonged dependence on cash assistance. Finally, welfare remained deeply unpopular, and even liberal politicians were reluctant to oppose the 1996 bill, especially after it became clear that President Clinton would sign it.

PRWORA also strengthened enforcement of the obligations of absent fathers to support their children from previous unions, as had the Family Support Act of 1988. Here, too, an agreement was reached by conservatives and liberals. For conservatives, tougher child support enforcement was a way to enforce responsibility and work discipline on lower-class men. Liberals were willing to go along because stricter enforcement seemed likely to increase the economic well-being of children and their custodial parents, usually their mothers. Child support enforcement will be discussed further in Chapter 12. These developments suggest that liberals and conservatives are reaching a degree of consensus on family policy. The following section takes a closer look at the factors responsible for this emerging consensus.

TOWARD A CONSENSUS ON FAMILY POLICY?

Richard Wagner's operas are famous for their *leitmotifs,* short musical phrases repeated many times, that are associated with a particular person or idea. If you had listened carefully to the debates on family policy in the United States over the past few decades, you would have heard spoken *leitmotifs.* When the conservatives stepped onto the stage, they said, "The government should not intrude into family life." When the liberals appeared, they said, "The government should help families solve their problems." Both phrases stood for large ideas often implicit and sometimes not fully understood even by the speaker.

THE CONSERVATIVE VIEWPOINT

Consider the conservative *leitmotif.* It suggests that the family should be left alone by the government. Yet, as the earlier discussion of the Social Security Act has shown, the U.S. welfare state was constructed to support the breadwinner-homemaker family. To a large extent, its programs encouraged women to marry

---

[8]I have written a fuller analysis, "How Will the 1996 Welfare Reform Law Affect Poor Families?" in Andrew J. Cherlin, *Public and Private Families: A Reader* (New York: McGraw-Hill, 1997).

Families and Public Policy

Who Should Help the Poor?

The Reverend Eugene F. Rivers III, leader of the Azusa Christian Community, a Pentecostal church and outreach group in a poor section of Boston, has been getting a lot of ink—newspaper and magazine profiles, appearances on television specials, participation in a summit on volunteerism headed by Gen. Colin Powell, and so forth—and deservingly so. An African American and a Harvard graduate, Rivers heads one of the most successful efforts at faith-based, street-level support for inner-city black families. Every day he, his three full-time youth workers, and volunteers meet with troubled children, run after-school programs, organize fatherhood classes for young unmarried men, and lead bible study and prayer groups. In a profile of Rivers in the *New Yorker*, journalist Joe Klein (1997) wrote:

His message is that religious institutions are better equipped to deal with the problems of the poor than the government is, and that they should receive public support to do everything from crime prevention to welfare reform. It is an argument that has intensified in recent years, and has found its way to Washington. (p. 40)

And indeed it has. During the debate over welfare reform, influential voices urged a greater role for private charity, especially charities that are run by religious organizations. The claim is that government programs for the poor are too impersonal and distant (e.g., handing out checks and food stamps) to help poor people better their lives. Faith-based charities, it is said, have the personal involvement and the moral vision needed to make a difference.

The argument comes in two strengths: regular and high-test. The regular strength version suggests that more of the money the government spends on poverty programs should be channeled to religious groups that serve the poor. Supporters of this position maintain that churches are often the only important institutions still left in impoverished inner-city neighborhoods. John DiIulio, a Princeton University professor who devotes half-time to working with church groups in Philadelphia, told Klein:

When you look at the gutbucket stuff, the every day in-your-face working with troubled kids in these neighborhoods across the country, almost all of it is being done by people who are churched. (p. 42)

In addition, supporters argue that the spiritual nature of these efforts is what makes them successful. Ministries to the poor provide moral guidance and support, it is said, that is crucial to helping people become self-reliant.

The high-test version suggests that government welfare programs should be substantially cut back, or even abolished, and replaced with faith-based private charities that are not supported by government funds. Supporters of this position claim that government welfare programs have been a failure because they too easily provide assistance to the poor without making moral demands on them: Welfare agency staff don't become personally involved in poor people's lives; don't (until recently) ask applicants to work for their benefits, and don't provide a religious faith that can sustain people during the difficult climb out of poverty.

The best known advocate of the high-test version is Marvin Olasky (1992, 1997), who argued that the welfare system should be scrapped entirely and replaced by the kind of private charity that was dominant in the 1800s:

and men to be the main providers. For example, programs such as Social Security and unemployment compensation were designed with male recipients in mind. Full-time homemakers can accrue eligibility for Social Security only through marriage, and they cannot receive unemployment benefits. The income tax system also encourages the formation of breadwinner-homemaker marriages and discourages the formation of two-earner marriages. If a man earns $50,000 and a woman earns nothing, they will pay less in taxes if they marry than if they stay single. On the other hand, if a man and a woman each earns $25,000, they will pay *more* in taxes if they marry than if they stay single (Crenshaw, 1994).

Support by conservatives for the programs and tax provisions described above demonstrates that they are not opposed to all government interventions into family life. Rather, conservatives were defending a particular set of interventions that

During the nineteenth century, a successful war on poverty was waged by tens of thousands of local, private charitable agencies and religious groups around the country. . . . Thousands of eyewitness accounts and journalistic assessments show that poverty fighters of the nineteenth century did not abolish poverty, but they enabled millions of people to escape it (1997, pp. 58–59).

Their secret, he wrote, was the moral demands they made on the poor: "They saw family, work, freedom, and faith as central to our being, not just as 'lifestyle options' " (1997, p. 59).

Olasky combed historical sources to compile an impressive list of the activities of private charities. But nowhere does he present any convincing evidence of how many poor people were successfully reached by all of this activity. As Olasky acknowledges, "the platoons of the greatest charity army in American history often were small" (1997, p. 58). Did they reach 10 percent of the poor, or 20 percent, or 50 percent? Olasky has no way of knowing; he provides no statistics to support his contention that private charities "enabled millions of people to escape" poverty.

Moreover, critics of Olasky's position make the following points. First, they note that private charities depend on government support: 22 percent of the budgets of the one hundred largest charitable organizations in 1993 came from federal, state, or local government (Blank, 1997). For some religious-based charities that aid the poor, the figure was higher: 65 percent of the budget of Catholic Charities, which provides food and shelter services to the poor, was from the government. One of Rev. Rivers's three youth workers, for example, is paid for by the city of Boston. Consequently, Olasky's critics argue, government agencies and private charities work in partnership rather than in competition. To withdraw government support of these agencies, the critics say, would devastate their abilities to help the poor.

Second, the critics argue that private donations could not compensate for the loss of government programs. Economist Rebecca Blank (1997) estimates that to replace AFDC (now TANF), Food Stamps, and Supplemental Security Income (a program for the disabled and the elderly poor), every one of the 258,000 churches, synagogues, and mosques in the United States would have to raise an additional $350,000 per year—and spend that money entirely on the poor. It is inconceivable, she writes, that this much money for the poor could be raised.

The regular strength version of the argument for involving faith-based private charities draws less opposition, in part because the government, as noted, already provides subsidies to charitable organizations. Nevertheless, the government sets limits on the religious content a charity can impose on its recipients while aiding them with government funds. Observers who worry about maintaining the separation between church and state oppose dropping these limits.

But across the ideological spectrum, there is increased recognition of the important role played by faith-based private charities. Referring to the despair among the residents in African-American ghetto neighborhoods, Rev. Rivers told Klein:

> What's happened is that hope has died, and secular liberals can't speak to the death of hope. They don't have the grammar or the vocabulary for it. We do. (p. 48)

were consistent with their vision of the family. The Depression-era and 1950s roots of these programs lie so far in the past that the government's role can seem almost invisible. It's understandable, then, that a politician might mistakenly believe that the government has had no role in shaping the contemporary family.

In fact, conservative groups have advocated government intervention when court rulings and legislation have undermined their vision of the family. After the 1973 Supreme Court decision known as *Roe* v. *Wade* struck down restrictions on abortion, grassroots conservative organizations joined with religious groups to campaign for restrictive state laws and for a constitutional amendment banning abortion. The anti-abortion forces succeeded in passing legislation that prohibited the use of federal funds for performing abortions, thus restricting poor women's ability to obtain them (Tribe, 1990).

THE LIBERAL VIEWPOINT

As for the liberal *leitmotif,* it suggests a desire both to use government to assist families and to help all families equally. Actually, the kinds of measures advanced by liberals tend to help married couples in which wives are employed outside the home and single parents more than they help breadwinner-homemaker couples. This also is no coincidence. By and large, liberals, a political category in which there is a large overlap with feminists, believe that the breadwinner-homemaker family is at best no better than other family forms or at worst a form that unjustifiably restricts the autonomy of women.

In the 1980s, for example, liberals worked for the enactment of government programs that would provide employed parents with assistance in finding and paying for out-of-home care for their children. Many liberal advocates of childcare legislation recommended that the government make available vouchers that low- and moderate-income parents could give to their childcare providers, who in turn could exchange them for money. Also recommended were subsidies to childcare providers to improve the quality of care. Women who stay home full-time to take care of their own children would receive no benefits from these vouchers or subsidies.

In the family policy opera, liberals charge that conservatives, having set up the rules in their favor, are now saying that it's not fair to change them. Conservatives, in turn, accuse liberals of feigning support for all families while pushing measures that are unfair to breadwinner-homemaker families. Conservatives ask what the justification is for new spending programs that favor one kind of family over another. Liberals reply that the present set of programs already favors one form, and they are merely trying to restore a balance.

A PRACTICAL COMPROMISE

Yet in the late 1980s and early 1990s, a pragmatic consensus was sometimes reached between conservatives and liberals that resulted in the enactment of significant legislation. The Family Support Act of 1998 and PRWORA in 1996 are two such examples. Perhaps the foremost example of the consensus, however, is the expansion of the **Earned Income Tax Credit (EITC).** Introduced in the 1970s, the EITC provides a refundable tax credit to low-income families with children in which at least one parent is employed. Even if the family earns so little that its members owe no taxes, they still receive a check for the value of the credit from the government if they file their tax returns. Essentially, the EITC is an income subsidy for parents who earn low wages. Conservatives like it for two reasons. First, it goes only to families in which a parent is employed; in the policy jargon, it targets the "working poor," those who earn barely enough (or not enough) to stay above the poverty line. (For a family of four, benefits are phased out at income in the low $20,000s.) An unemployed single parent is not eligible. Therefore, the EITC reinforces the obligation to work. Second, it applies not only to dual-earner, two-parent families but also to breadwinner-homemaker families because a family qualifies even if only one parent works outside the home. It therefore appears neutral toward wives working outside the home.

Liberals, on their part, like the EITC because it provides income assistance to many low-income families. Liberals also realize that there are relatively few breadwinner-homemaker families among the working poor (who can't afford a stay-at-home parent), so that, in reality, most of the money goes to two-earner families and to employed single parents. Finally, liberal members of Congress in this era realized that a program of tax credits for the working poor went as far as they could convince conservatives to move with regard to income assistance. The EITC was increased substantially as part of the 1988 welfare legislation and again in 1990. Then, as part of President Clinton's 1993 budget legislation, it was increased yet again and its upper income limit was raised so that more families were eligible.

With regard to gender and public policy, PRWORA also has moved conservatives and liberals closer together. Although PRWORA is certainly a public policy victory for conservatives, it has undermined their claim that government should not support mothers who work outside the home. In requiring work and providing childcare subsidies for TANF recipients, the Republican majority tacitly conceded that it is acceptable for the government to assist mothers who are employed. To be sure, the assistance is limited to poor, single mothers on welfare, but it will be hard for conservatives to hold the line. In 1997, at least two states with Republican governors announced plans to provide childcare subsidies to nearly all poor parents with jobs, whether they were on welfare or not.[9]

Moreover, an important childcare bill had passed Congress in 1990 only because a number of conservative members of Congress adopted a more pragmatic attitude than they had in the past toward women working outside the home. For instance, Republican Senator Orrin Hatch of Utah braved criticism from within his party to become a cosponsor of the childcare legislation. He told his supporters that, although he might wish otherwise, women were in the labor force to stay and their children needed assistance. In addition, in 1993, President Clinton signed into law a bill requiring large employers to provide their employees with 12 weeks of leave to care for newborns or deal with other family emergencies.

These developments suggest that, at the end of the century, the conflict over women's autonomy, so long a part of family policy debates, is moving toward a partial resolution: Many conservatives are reluctantly accepting the legitimacy of government programs to assist working mothers. So far this assistance has been limited to mothers with low incomes, but the general principle of government assistance to working mothers has been established. Given the large number of families with mothers who are employed, I think it is likely that such assistance will be broadened in the early twenty-first century. Many liberals, for their part, are reluctantly accepting the principle that assistance to the poor should not be unconditional but rather should be accompanied by attempts to make the poor self-sufficient. This is a significant retreat from their political position over the past several decades. It suggests that further assistance to low-income families is likely to take the form of services (e.g., job training, Head Start) and subsidies (e.g., childcare) rather than cash.

In the meantime, millions of poor families must cope with the time limits and work requirements that PRWORA has imposed. It is the greatest social experiment with poor children and their parents that the federal government has undertaken. Despite the assurances of its supporters and the warnings of its detractors, its results are hard to predict. Those concerned with family policy will be tracking the results over the next decade.

---

[9]The two states were Illinois and Wisconsin.

SUMMARY

1. The government is far more involved in supporting families economically than was the case a century or two ago. Most U.S. families receive some form of government assistance. Because of the great changes in the family over the past few decades, family policy has become a major political issue.

2. The nation-state is a way of organizing people that has spread around the world. It involves a government that claims the right to rule a territory and a group of people in that territory who have common economic and cultural interests. In the twentieth century, the United States and other Western nation-states have enacted numerous social programs that provide support to workers and their families. These "welfare state" measures soften the hardships of the labor market. In neither capitalist nor socialist nation-states has gender equality been achieved. In the United States, the programs were initially designed under the assumption that husbands would work full-time for wages and that wives would (and should) do domestic work in the household full-time. Congress did not anticipate that large numbers of wives would work outside the home or that divorce and childbearing outside marriage would become more common.

3. In the United States, politicians did not begin to talk specifically about "family policy" until the mid-1970s. When they did, they found it a topic of much disagreement and debate. Two kinds of conflicts characterize most debates about family policy. The first is a conflict over women's autonomy, specifically over the degree of women's economic independence from men. Defenders of the breadwinner-homemaker family, which restricts women's economic independence, argue that it is the preferable family form. Critics note that the benefits of this family form go disproportionately to men, whereas a high cost in autonomy is paid by women. The second kind of conflict is over income assistance, specifically over providing assistance to the poor and near poor versus enforcing their obligation to work. Critics of "welfare" programs such as AFDC argue that they reduce work effort and contribute to the formation of single-parent families. Defenders of AFDC (and its successor, TANF) note that the evidence of its harm is mixed, whereas it clearly lifts the incomes of poor children.

4. The Personal Responsibility and Work Opportunity Reconciliation Act of 1996 (PRWORA) illustrates issues of both income assistance to the poor and women's autonomy. Changes in women's employment since midcentury made a program to require employment among AFDC recipients more acceptable. Changes in the characteristics of AFDC recipients—their marital status, their race—reduced public sympathy for providing them with income assistance. The belief spread among policymakers that the welfare-receiving poor had become too dependent on public assistance, although the evidence on this point is contested.

5. In debates over family policy, conservatives often say that they want to keep the government from intruding into family life. But the government has already intervened in family life; social welfare legislation from the 1930s through the 1950s was designed to support the breadwinner-homemaker family. Liberals tend to propose measures that would benefit married couples in which wives are employed outside the home and single parents more than they would benefit breadwinner-homemaker families. Conservative legislators tend to resist these proposals.

6. Beginning in the late 1980s, a pragmatic consensus has been reached that has allowed several pieces of legislation to be enacted, including multiple expansions of the Earned Income Tax Credit, the Family Support Act of 1988, childcare legislation in 1990, family leave legislation in 1993, and PRWORA in 1996. Conservatives are reluctantly accepting the legitimacy of government programs to assist mothers who work outside the home. Liberals are reluctantly accepting the principle that assistance to the poor should not be unconditional.

KEY TERMS

Social Security Act of 1935
Aid to Families with Dependent
    Children (AFDC)
Personal Responsibility and Work
    Opportunity Reconciliation Act
    of 1996 (PRWORA)

state
nation
nation-state
welfare state
family wage system
entitlement

block grant
Temporary Assistance to Needy
    Families (TANF)
Earned Income Tax Credit (EITC)

FAMILIES ON THE INTERNET

For information on PRWORA and other welfare reform issues, the best place to start is **http://welfare-info.org**, the home page of the Welfare Information Network, which describes itself as "a clearinghouse for information, policy analysis, and technical assistance on welfare reform." It contains links to the complete text of PRWORA (it's massive) and several summaries and analyses of the bill by both liberal (e.g., Children's Defense Fund) and conservative (e.g., Heritage Foundation) organizations. A page entitled "Selected Welfare Reform Related Data" provides links to a large amount of statistical data on poverty and welfare in the United States. A page entitled "Welfare Related Web Sites" provides links to over 100 other sites.

PART THREE

Sexuality, Partnership, and Marriage

In this part, we move from a focus on the effects of larger social structures—gender, class, race, ethnicity, government—on families to a consideration of how intimate family relationships are built from the ground up. These three chapters examine the emotional satisfactions and difficulties that people experience as they come to love someone and to form partnerships and marriages. In other words, the focus now shifts mostly to the private family. This is not to say that social structure disappears. On the contrary, family relationships are formed, maintained, and dissolved in a social context that must be considered. Nevertheless, the emphasis in this part is on how contemporary family relations provide intimacy, love, personal fulfillment, and cooperation.

Chapter 7 discusses the emergence of the modern concept of sexuality, which is about a century old. It then traces the great changes in sexual attitudes and practices over the past few decades. In addition, it examines the emergence of a gay and lesbian subculture.

Attention then shifts in **Chapter 8** to the formation of partnerships. Courtship and dating are examined, as is cohabitation and its relationship to the process of becoming married. In addition, the chapter discusses the issue of childbearing among unmarried teenagers.

Chapter 9 examines the interaction between spouses and between cohabiting partners. It discusses how marriage changed to a companionship in the early 1900s and how it has recently changed again to a more independent kind of partnership. In addition, the chapter reviews the many studies in both the sociological and psychological traditions that try to determine what characteristics lead to successful marriages. It then concludes with a discussion of the transition to parenthood.

CHAPTER 7

Sexuality and Love

WHY MAUD CHOSE ELMER OVER ROBERT

Between 1882 and 1884, Isabella Maud Rittenhouse was courted by several suitors. Maud's diary, discussed by Steven Seidman, reveals that two stood out (Seidman, 1991). The first was Robert Witherspoon, a handsome, charming, educated, cultivated man, to whom Maud was powerfully attracted. The other was Elmer Comings, a rather plain-looking and socially awkward man who was, nevertheless, hard-working, reliable, and responsible. Today, the choice between them would be easy: 9 out of 10 Mauds would pick Robert, the object of romantic love, over unexciting Elmer. The real Maud, however, chose Elmer. Her reasoning shows how different was the relationship among sex, love, and marriage in the Victorian era than it is now.

To Maud and to most other nineteenth-century women and men, marrying someone because of strong romantic feelings was considered risky. Passionate, romantic love was thought to be a base emotion that faded away quickly, leaving little support for the couple. Far longer lasting was a spiritual love in which the partners joined together in a moral, uplifting marriage. The spiritual relationship rested upon a deep knowledge of each other and a sense of mutual obligation. Spiritual love was "true love," a union not only of the heart but also of the soul and the mind. Strong sexual attraction was equated with "romantic love," a dangerous emotional state that was hard to control. True love was much to be preferred.

There were practical reasons, rooted in the structure of nineteenth-century society, why people thought this way. The general standard of living was far lower than it is today, and most married women did not work outside the home. In order to have a comfortable life, it was crucial for a woman to marry an economically reliable, hard-working man. Correspondingly, a man needed to marry a woman who would raise children and manage a home competently. Feelings of romantic love could tempt a person to choose passion over partnership. Indulging in passion was a luxury most nineteenth-century people could not afford.

And so Maud decided that her romantic love for Robert was immature and that she could not overlook some lapses of character. She wrote that he had "beauty of feature and charm of tongue with little regard for truth and high moral worth"; whereas Elmer, "though not graceful . . . and handsome . . . [had an] inward nobility in him." Maud was well aware that she was rejecting romance when she rejected Robert: "If I do marry [Elmer] it will be with a respectful affection and not with a passionate *lover* love."[1] Moreover, Maud knew that, unlike Robert, Elmer did not share her knowledge of and interest in the arts and literature: "All the time I am planning to bring him up to a standard where I *can* love him." Thus, she girded for the task of marrying Elmer. Fortunately for her—although not for Elmer—she broke off the courtship when Elmer entered into some suspicious business dealings that cast doubt on his character. But even in ending the courtship, Maud relied on practical and ethical considerations rather than on her feelings.

This separation between romantic love and sex, on the one hand, and marriage, on the other hand, was typical of the cultural tradition of the Western nation-states prior to the twentieth century. One historian studied the detailed writings on marital sexual activity by 25 medieval theologians and found that only 2 of them ever addressed the subject of love (Flandrin, 1985). Sexual relations that were too passionate were thought to be immoral and to compete with a person's worship of God. Sensual pleasures were for the love affairs a person had outside of his or her marriage—never sanctioned by theologians but tolerated, in practice, for men only. St. Jerome, quoting the Roman philosopher Seneca, wrote:

---

[1]All quotations are from Seidman (1991).

A prudent man should love his wife with discretion, and so control his desire and not be led into copulation. Nothing is more impure than to love one's wife as if she were a mistress. . . . Men should appear before their wives not as lovers but as husbands (Aries, 1985a).

This separation between erotic love and marriage evaporated during the twentieth century. Both Seneca and Maud would be surprised to read the 1987 treatise *Super Marital Sex: Loving for Life,* the author of which states, "Super marital sex is the most erotic, intense, fulfilling experience any human being can have" (Pearsall, 1987). More surprising still would be the increase in sexual activity outside the context of any kind of long-term relationship, the emergence of an open homosexual subculture, and the public display of sexually oriented goods, services, performances, and advertisements. How did we get from there to here? And what are the implications of these changes for family and personal life as we enter the twenty-first century? These are the questions to be explored in this chapter.

THE EMERGENCE OF SEXUAL IDENTITIES

Although sex isn't new, sexual identities are. By a **sexual identity**, I mean a set of sexual practices and attitudes that lead to the formation in a person's mind of an identity as heterosexual, homosexual, or bisexual. Most people in our society today could give a clear and immediate answer to the question "Are you heterosexual or homosexual?" Our sexual identity, in turn, becomes an important part of our sense of who we are. Furthermore, we see this as "natural"—everyone, we assume, has a sexual identity.

Yet the question "Are you heterosexual or homosexual?" would have stumped Americans until the late nineteenth century. Not only the terms "homosexual" and "heterosexual" but also the idea of "being" homosexual or heterosexual had not yet been invented. There were only two categories of sexual activities, the socially approved (sexual intercourse within marriage, in moderation, and undertaken mainly to have children) and the socially disapproved (all other activities, including acts between persons of the same sex, masturbation, oral sex regardless of the genders of the partners, and so forth). To perform any of the latter was sinful, but such behavior did not define a person as having a particular sexual identity. Moreover, one's sexual acts played a smaller role in defining one's sense of self. The concept of a sexual identity requires a self-consciousness and self-examination that was not prominent until the late nineteenth century.

That sexual identities only recently emerged as a concept suggests that they are socially constructed. The categories we use (for instance, homosexual versus heterosexual) are defined by the society we live in. This is not to say that biological predispositions play no role in sexuality; many believe them to be a part of the story, too (Schwartz & Rutter, 1998). But whatever predispositions do exist are shaped and labeled according to social norms and values. Moreover, as the story of Maud, Elmer, and Robert shows, these norms and values are, in part, a response to the way society is organized—such as how women and men divide their labor—and to economic factors such as its standard of living. The social norms and the organization of late-eighteenth- and nineteenth-century middle-class society in the United States, for example, may have supported more intimate same-sex friendships than is the case today. (See *Families in Other Cultures:* Was Alexander Hamilton

Families in Other Cultures

Was Alexander Hamilton Gay? And Other Irrelevant Questions

In April of 1779, Alexander Hamilton wrote to John Laurens, with whom he had served in the American Revolution:

> Cold in my professions, warm in [my] friendships, I wish, my Dear Laurens, it m[ight] be in my power, by action rather than words, [to] convince you that I love you. I shall only tell you that 'till you bade us Adieu, I hardly knew the value you had taught my heart to set upon you.

In September, after almost giving up hope of receiving a letter from Laurens, Hamilton wrote of his joy at finally receiving one:

> But like a jealous lover, when I thought you slighted my caresses, my affection was alarmed and my vanity piqued. I had almost resolved to lavish no more of them upon you and to reject you as an inconstant and an ungrateful———. But you have now disarmed my resentment and by a single mark of attention made up the quarrel (Katz, 1976).

Nor were famous American men the only ones who wrote intimate letters to other men. Karen Hansen tells the story of Brigham Nims, who lived for most of his life on his family's farm in New Hampshire, married, and had three children. In the 1830s, prior to marrying, Nims worked in a box factory in Boston for two years, where he struck up a close friendship with J. Foster Beal. They corresponded for a few years afterward. In one passage, Beal writes:

> can not forget those happy hours [th]at we spent at G. Newcombs and the evening walks; but we are deprived of that privilege now we are separated for a time we cannot tell how long perhaps before our eyes behold each other in this world.

In a later letter, Beal reminds Nims of the time Beal nursed him through an illness:

> I guess you have forgot all about you being at Boston last Sept. when you was so sick, and I took care of you, doctored you up, even took you in bed with myself; you will not do as much, as, to write me (Hansen, 1989).

Upon discovering these accounts, it is the instinct of the contemporary reader to immediately consider whether the relationships were homosexual. Yet historians argue that such a question represents the myopia of a person steeped in twentieth-century culture peering back at another time. The categories of homosexual and heterosexual did not yet exist, and therefore nineteenth-century people did not need to fit into them. Whether or not Hamilton's intimate friendship ever involved a sexual act was not its defining feature. As historian Jonathan Katz notes, even if many of the phrases in these letters were merely rhetorical flourishes, it is striking how easy it was for men to use language that today would be seen as indicating a sexual relationship.

In fact, what seems so different about these relationships is the seeming ease with which two same-sex individuals could engage in intimacies, such as sharing a bed or declaring their love for each other, without

Gay? And Other Irrelevant Questions.) The emergence of sexual identities is a key to understanding the changing relationships among sex, love, and marriage that have occurred during the late nineteenth and early twentieth centuries.

THE COLONIAL ERA TO 1890: SPIRITUAL LOVE AND SEXUAL RESTRAINT

Over the centuries, religious doctrine has powerfully shaped standards of acceptable sexual behavior. Prior to the American Revolution, religious authorities preached that sexual intercourse was appropriate only within marriage and only for the purpose of having children. The laws of the Massachusetts Bay Colony forbade, on penalty of death, most other sexual acts, including rape, adultery, and sodomy—which encompassed acts of penetration between two persons of the same sex, acts between men and animals, and acts other than vaginal intercourse between a man and a woman. Few people, however, were actually executed. One of the unfortunate was 18-year-old Mary Latham, hanged in 1645 after she admitted to having had sex with 12 men and calling her elderly husband a cuckold—

these acts' marking the relationship as sexual or asexual. (Indeed, Hansen tells us that sharing a bed was not uncommon among the working class in nineteenth-century Boston because of the lack of space.) A broad range of affection and intimacy was open to same-sex friendships in a way that, for most men at least, it is not today.

The best-known study of same-sex intimacy in the late eighteenth and nineteenth centuries is Carroll Smith-Rosenberg's "The Female World of Love and Ritual" (Smith-Rosenberg, 1975). Smith-Rosenberg explored the "separate sphere" of middle-class women and found that they often formed deep emotional bonds of friendship with other women. Immersed in a network of female kin and friends, women helped one another in crises such as childbirth, helped to prepare one another for weddings, and spent long hours together talking. Some of their correspondence seems, by today's standards at least, to have a romantic and even erotic tone. Smith-Rosenberg writes of Sarah Butler

Wister and Jeannie Field Musgrove, who first met as teenagers during a summer vacation, attended boarding school together for two years, and formed a lifelong intimate friendship. At age 29, Sarah, married and a mother, wrote to Jeannie, "I shall be entirely alone [this coming week]. I can give you no idea how desperately I shall want you." Jeannie ended one letter "Goodbye my dearest, dearest lover" and another "I will go to bed . . . [though] I could write all night—A thousand kisses—I love you with my whole soul."

The point of studying exchanges such as these, as Smith-Rosenberg herself argued, "is not whether these women had genital contact and can therefore be defined as heterosexual or homosexual." Rather, the point is that these women lived in a social context that allowed them the freedom to form a friendship that was quite intimate without the friendship's being labeled as anything more than that. Middle-class women's bonds could be loving and sensual without necessarily

being sexual; it is likely that even if they were, the sexual acts would not be seen as the defining characteristic of the relationship. The social context allowed women more flexibility in creating intense emotional ties than is the case today, when we tend to think that close, sensual same-sex relationships must be "homosexual."

Smith-Rosenberg believes that the creation of a separate sphere for middle-class women established the conditions that allowed such close friendships to flourish. But the correspondence between Nims and Beal suggests that some men may also have established intimate friendships. How unusual Nims was we cannot know. Other than the two years he spent in Boston, he worked on the farm. Hansen argues that rural men, who did not leave home to work in a factory every day, did not experience as strict a split between the worlds of women and men. Perhaps, she suggests, they had a more fluid conception of gender that allowed them to be intimate friends with other men.

someone whose wife has committed adultery. Another was William Hacketts, convicted of having sex with a cow, who was hanged in a public square just after he watched the execution of the cow (D'Emilio & Freedman, 1988).

Even among married couples who were trying to have children, sex was approved only in moderation. The Puritan minister Cotton Mather warned married couples of the dangers of "inordinate affection" (D'Emilio & Freedman, 1988). But after about 1750, as noted in Chapter 2, young adults began to play a greater role in choosing their spouses. The growth of commercial capitalism provided sons with employment alternatives to the family farm; they no longer needed to wait to marry until they were given land by, or inherited it from, their fathers. As this change occurred, parents' influence over whom their children married declined. More so than parents, young adults tended to choose spouses on the basis of affection and mutual respect (although not necessarily passion or romantic love). Gradually, it became more acceptable for married couples to engage in sexual intercourse solely for the pleasure it gave them. But they were warned to exercise restraint; medical experts cautioned that excessive sexual activity caused illnesses ranging from

Adultery was seen as a shameful act in the 1700s, although more so for women than for men.
In Nathanial Hawthorne's novel, The Scarlet Letter, *Hester Prynne was forced to wear a scarlet "A" for adultery.*

depression to loss of vision to insanity. A widely read 1865 text by Dr. William Acton stated, "Too frequent emission of the life-giving fluid, and too frequent sexual excitation of the nervous system is . . . in itself most destructive" (Acton, 1865).

Then, in the nineteenth century, the growth of wage labor in factories separated the worlds of husbands, who typically worked outside the home, and wives, who typically didn't. The two domains came to be seen as "separate spheres": hers, the home and children; his, the wider world beyond. In the doctrine of separate spheres, women were said to be the guardians of virtue and morality. Consequently, women's sexual instincts were labeled as spiritual rather than carnal. It was part of the wife's role to limit the sexual passions of her husband and to balance the spiritual and physical sides of their union. By showing sexual restraint at the wife's request, the couple could focus on their love—for marital love was seen as a spiritual condition, quite separate from erotic desires. The common wisdom was that wives were better suited than husbands to maintaining sexual restraint because of their lesser desires. Dr. Acton wrote, "The majority of women (happily for them) are not very much troubled with sexual feelings of any kind. What men are habitually, women are only exceptionally" (Acton, 1865).

This denial of women's sexual feelings has been seen as a part of the sexual repression of the Victorian era (so named for Queen Victoria, ruler of Great Britain and Ireland from 1837 to 1901) (Marcus, 1964). It was not a natural condition but rather the result of the way young women and men were socialized. Yet the ethic of sexual restraint may have been useful to women. Historian Carl Degler argued that because childbearing was so dangerous, it was in wives' interest to limit the frequency of intercourse with their husbands. Their supposed lack of erotic interest gave them some measure of control over pregnancy (Degler, 1980).

1890 TO 1960: ROMANTIC LOVE AND SEXUAL GRATIFICATION

As described in Chapter 2, a series of economic, demographic, and cultural changes occurred during the early decades of the twentieth century. Foremost among them was a rising standard of living. In more and more families, people earned enough money to meet their basic needs for food, shelter, clothing, and so forth. No longer facing crises of subsistence, they could focus on the quality of their emotional lives. Moreover, as industrialization and urbanization grew, married couples saw that children were costlier than in previous generations: Instead of laboring in the farm fields from an early age, children needed to stay in school so that they could obtain good jobs when they reached adulthood. Consequently, instead of benefiting from their children's labor, parents had to support them while they studied. As a result, couples had fewer children and invested more financial resources in each one (Stern, 1987). Women who reached adulthood in the late 1890s bore four children on average, whereas women who reached adulthood 20 years later bore about three (Cherlin, 1992b). Declining birthrates meant that married couples would eventually enter a stage in which they were no longer caring for young children—a stage in which they could focus their attention on their personal lives.

Connecting Romantic Love and Marriage   These changes produced, among other things, the rise of the private family. Young couples began to see marriage as a means of self-fulfillment, to be obtained not through restraint and spirituality but through romantic love and sexual gratification. The notion began to spread that husbands and wives should be companions who attend unselfishly to each other's needs, including their sexual needs. In a major shift, women's sexual needs were acknowledged. Indeed, by the 1920s, young women were displaying their sexual nature publicly in ways that shocked their parents' generation. Cosmetics sales, for example, rose from $14 million in 1914 to $141 million in 1925 (D'Emilio & Freedman, 1988). The dance hall and the movie theater provided nighttime commercial activities that promoted romance.

Moreover, public discussion of sexual matters grew, as the writings of European and American intellectuals on the subject became popular. For instance, the British author Havelock Ellis challenged the Victorian ethic of sexual restraint in a widely read series of books published at the turn of the century. Ellis argued that sexual activity within marriage was "all that is most simple and natural and pure and good." He asked, "Why . . . should people be afraid of rousing passions which, after all, are the great driving forces of human life?" What the world needed, he wrote, was "not more restraint but more passion" (D'Emilio & Freedman, 1988). Sigmund Freud, the founder of psychoanalysis, put forth the stunning thesis that our sexual drives and needs are an unconscious, fundamental force that shapes our personalities from childhood onward.

All these developments strengthened the connection between sexual expressiveness and romantic love, on the one hand, and marriage, on the other hand, during the first half of the twentieth century. No longer was love within marriage primarily a spiritual ideal; rather, sexual gratification and romance became a central indicator of your love for your spouse, which became, in turn, an increasingly important indicator of the health of your marriage. Thus, an enjoyable sex life and a romantic attraction came to be seen as necessary components of a successful marriage. Prior to 1900 a marital sex life that was *too* satisfying was spiritually suspect. One hundred years later, there is no such thing as too much sexual satisfaction, as the readers of *Super Marital Sex* can attest.

The meaning of romantic love itself remains elusive. It is clearly bound up with sexual attraction, but it encompasses more than that. It usually leads to a desire for an intense, close relationship that will endure indefinitely. Some authors distinguish between **passionate love**, the sexually charged attraction at the start of many love relationships, and **companionate love**, the affection and partnership felt in a love relationship of long duration. Susan and Clyde Hendrick write:

> If passionate love is the flame that consumes two people at the beginning of their relationship, then companionate love is the glowing embers that endure when the dramatic flame has subsided. Sexual attraction, intense communication, and emotional turbulence early in a relationship give way (if the relationship is to endure) to quiet intimacy, predictability, and shared attitudes, values, and life experiences later in the relationship (Hendrick & Hendrick, 1992).

Gender Differences in Romantic Love

Women and men may experience romantic love differently. Several authors argue that women more often use practical criteria in addition to romantic love in choosing a spouse, whereas men rely more on romantic criteria such as physical attractiveness. In particular, women are said to pay attention to a man's potential for holding a steady job, earning a good salary, and remaining faithful and loyal. A national survey confirms this difference, in general, as will be noted in the next chapter. Unmarried women aged 19 to 35 in the survey were less willing than comparable men to marry someone who was unlikely to hold a steady job, who earned much less, or who was more than five years younger. Men, on the other hand, were less willing to marry someone who was not good-looking or was older (South, 1991).

Evolutionary psychologists would argue that these differing preferences reflect the reproductive strategies that men and women have evolved: women valuing support and commitment in men; men valuing evidence (physical attractiveness, younger age) that women can bear children.[2] Perhaps there are some echoes of our hunter-gatherer past in these patterns. But sociologists would point to other reasons. Arlie Hochschild, for example, has argued that women have these preferences because they are financially dependent on men; even when married women work outside the home, they tend to earn less than men. Therefore, writes Hochschild, the choice of a spouse is more important to them in material terms. Yet because our culture places such an emphasis on love in marriage, and because of their own desire for love, women feel they must come to love the men they choose. In order to do so, according to Hochschild, women spend more time managing their feelings of love, by which she means being aware of one's feelings, working on them, and consciously shaping them. Women, she suggests, more often do the "feeling-work" of willing themselves to love someone (Hochschild, 1983). It is the kind of work Maud set for herself when she wrote of Elmer, "All the time I am planning to bring him up to a standard where I *can* love him."

[2]See Chapter 1.

1960 TO THE PRESENT

The ideological and material currents of the first half of the twentieth century also undercut the justification for limiting sexual activity to marriage. Before this century, when sex was viewed primarily as a way of producing children, it was important to limit it to the only socially approved arrangement for rearing children, namely marriage. Men guarded sexual access to their wives through a double standard that punished women more harshly than men for engaging in premarital sex and **extramarital sex**—sexual activity by a married person with someone other than his or her spouse. Yet as the idea of sex for personal pleasure spread during the twentieth century, the rationale for restricting sex to married couples weakened. Through the 1950s, moralists were successful in limiting sexual intercourse to engaged or married persons, especially among middle-class women. But beginning in the late 1960s, sexual activity prior to marriage rose to unprecedented levels. Moreover, in the 1970s, unmarried, middle-class young adults began to live together openly, a previously unheard-of arrangement except among the poor. Rates of cohabitation rose so high that about half of young adults in the 1990s are likely to live with a partner before marrying.[3]

The changes in the late 1960s and 1970s are reflected in the answers that women in a 1992 national survey of adults' sexual activity gave to the question of how many sex partners they had had by age 30. Among women who had entered adulthood in the 1950s, two-thirds had had only one partner. Clearly, having sex just with one's husband was the norm. Only a daring few had many sex partners: 3 percent reported five or more (Laumann, Gagnon, Michael, & Michaels, 1994). In fact, although there are few numbers in the historical record, virtually every historical study suggests that through the 1950s, a majority of women had first intercourse only after they were engaged to be married (Rothman, 1984).[4] Women's sexual needs still were thought to be less than men's, and women were still seen as the guardians of virtue—which in this case meant abstinence until marriage. Yet among women who entered adulthood in the 1960s, just 46 percent reported only one partner by age 30; and 18 percent reported five or more. The proportion reporting only one partner by age 30 fell further to 36 percent among women who entered adulthood in the 1970s, whereas the proportion reporting five or more rose to 22 percent.

The changes have been less dramatic for men, reflecting the decline of the sexual double standard. This decline is evident from questions about sexual activity that were asked between 1988 and 1991 in the General Social Survey (GSS), an annual, national survey of the adult population of the United States. At the close of the interview, the interviewee was handed a three-minute supplementary questionnaire and envelope. The supplement noted the public health need for information about sexual partners and asked the interviewee to fill out the form and then to seal it inside the envelope. Figure 7.1 shows the number of sexual partners in the past 12 months reported by never-married women and men in the four annual surveys combined. Never-married women were just as likely as never-married men to report having had at least one sexual partner. Just 23 percent of never-married women and 21 percent of never-married men said they had not had sex in the previous 12 months. The major difference that remains is that men were more likely to report having two or more sex partners in the past year (Michael, Laumann, & Gagnon, 1992).

[3]See Chapter 8 for evidence on the trends discussed in this paragraph.
[4]See the discussion at the beginning of Chapter 8.

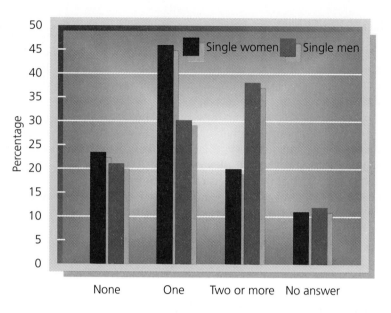

FIGURE 7.1 Number of sexual partners in the past 12 months, for single (never-married) women and men in the United States, 1988–1991. (*Source:* Michael, Laumann, & Gagnon, 1992.)

Premarital Sex   Some of the increase in sexual activity before marriage has occurred during adolescence. Figure 7.2 displays the findings of a series of national surveys of adolescent girls since 1970. Among unmarried girls aged 15 to 19, the percentage who had ever had sexual intercourse rose dramatically during the 1970s. There was a more modest rise between 1979 and 1988, and the most recent figure, from 1995, shows a slight decline. Still, sexual activity in the 1990s was far more common than in the early 1970s. Little is known with precision about the sexual activity of teenage boys prior to 1980, but at midcentury the rates of sexual activity appear to have been much higher for boys than for girls (Darling, Kallen, & VanDusen, 1984). Since 1980, sexual activity has increased among boys, although the rate of increase was lower for boys than for girls. Consequently, by 1995 the gap between boys and girls had narrowed: 55 percent of unmarried teenage boys aged 15 to 19 and 48 percent of unmarried teenage girls aged 15 to 19 had had sexual intercourse (Sonenstein, Ku, Lindberg, Turner, & Pleck, 1997; U.S. National Center for Health Statistics, 1997d). Coupled with a rising age at marriage, this increase in sexual activity among adolescents led to a greater proportion of teenage pregnancies and births occurring outside marriage. (The causes and consequences of these pregnancies and births will be discussed in the next chapter.)

During the 1980s, the increase in sexual activity before marriage was greater among the middle class than among the poor, and greater among whites than among blacks. Premarital pregnancies have long been more common among young adults from low-income families, who have less to gain economically from waiting until marriage to have children. Among African-American young adults, as noted in Chapter 5, marriage has declined sharply, leading to a greater proportion of births occurring outside marriage. Recently, however, class and racial differences in sexual activity have narrowed because of increases among the middle class and among whites.

For instance, from 1982 to 1988 there was little change in the percentage of 15- to 19-year-old women from low-income families who had ever had sexual intercourse: 56 percent in the earlier year, 57 percent in the later year. Yet among comparable women from families with incomes at least twice the poverty level, the proportion who had had intercourse increased from 40 percent in 1982 to 50 percent in

FIGURE 7.2 Percentage of never-married, 15- to 19-year-old girls who had ever had sexual intercourse, 1971–1995. (*Sources:* U.S. National Research Council (1987); Forrest & Singh (1990); and U.S. National Center for Health Statistics (1997d), Table 19. For 1971, 1976, 1979, and 1982, percentages are for girls residing in metropolitan areas only. The 1988 and 1995 percentages are for all girls. However, the 1982 percentage, which is available for both groups, is nearly identical whether or not nonmetropolitan girls are included.)

1988.[5] The same study showed that the increases for white young women were greater than the increases for black young women. The increasing propensity for middle-class individuals to have sex outside marriage seems to be moving middle-class sexual patterns toward patterns long-established among the poor and near-poor.

Marital and Extramarital Sex   Given the increases in sexual activity outside marriage, you might expect that married persons would be increasingly likely to have extramarital sex. Indeed, widely read books published in the 1960s and 1970s, such as *Open Marriage* (O'Neill & O'Neill, 1972) argued that marital relationships could coexist with, and perhaps even be enriched by, openly acknowledged extramarital affairs. Yet **sexual monogamy**—having just one sex partner—is still the rule rather than the exception among married persons. Consider trends in public opinion. There is no doubt that the American public has become more tolerant of sexual activity among persons who have not yet (and may never be) married. Almost every year since 1972, the GSS has asked people their opinions about both premarital and extramarital sex. Between 1972 and 1996, the proportion who agreed that *premarital* sex was "always wrong" or "almost always wrong" declined from 48 percent to 33 percent. During the same period, however, the proportion agreeing that *extramarital* sex was "always wrong" or "almost always wrong" increased from 84 to 93 percent.[6]

Moreover, when the GSS in 1988 through 1991 asked its respondents about their sexual behavior, 98 percent of married women and 95 percent of married men said that they had had no sex partners other than their spouses during the previous 12 months (Greeley, Michael, & Smith, 1990). Clearly, most married couples adhere to the norm of monogamy almost all the time. Indeed, in the 1992 survey of adults' sexual activity, over 90 percent of women and over 75 percent of men said that they had never had another sex partner during the duration of their marriages, giving rise to wry newspaper headlines such as "Study Sees Marital Fidelity Rampant" (Laumann et al., 1994).

The emphasis on sexual gratification for both partners in marriage, new in the twentieth century, has provided wives and husbands with the potential for greater

[5]The data are from the 1982 and 1988 rounds of the National Survey of Family Growth. Low-income families were those with incomes that were less than twice the poverty level (Forrest & Singh, 1990).

[6]The question on extramarital sex was first asked in 1973; for both questions I have excluded "Don't know" and "No answer" responses (Davis & Smith, 1996).

Most married people are monogamous. About 90 percent of women and 75 percent of men report never having had another sex partner during their marriages.

intimacy and emotional satisfaction. And access since the 1960s to modern methods of contraception, such as the birth control pill, has allowed individuals to separate sex-as-pleasure from sex-as-reproduction. Especially for women, whose sexual desires were often denied or ignored prior to the twentieth century, the legitimation of sexual gratification can be considered an advance. "Twenty years ago," wrote three feminist authors in 1986, "the woman dissatisfied with sex was made to believe she was lacking something; the woman who selfishly advanced her own pleasure was made to worry about being less than normal" (Ehrenreich, Hess, & Jacobs, 1986). Now it is taken for granted that both women and men should receive pleasure from sexual activity. The three authors praise the acceptance of *"pleasure*—perhaps especially sexual pleasure—as a legitimate social goal" (Ehrenreich et al., 1986). Yet observers have also noted that the emphasis on sexual satisfaction can create its own tyranny, since couples may believe that unless their sex lives are continually fulfilling there is something wrong with their marriages. For example, much popular literature about sex has focused on the simultaneous orgasm as the sexual ideal, leading some people to believe that their sex lives are lacking unless this ideal is regularly achieved (D'Emilio & Freedman, 1988). Lillian Rubin interviewed working-class wives who felt obligated to have orgasms as regularly as possible less out of their own needs than out of their husbands' need to feel manly. "I rarely have climaxes," one woman told Rubin,

> *But if it didn't bother my husband, it wouldn't bother me. I keep trying to tell him that I know it's not his fault, that he's a really good lover. . . . But it scares me because he doesn't believe it, and I worry he might leave me for a woman who will have climaxes for him* (Rubin, 1976).

University of Oklahoma law professor Anita Hill testified before Congress in the 1991 confirmation hearings for Supreme Court Justice nominee Clarence Thomas. Hill's assertion that Justice Thomas had sexually harassed her received widespread attention and has led to more open, public discussion of the issue of sexual harassment.

Most women, however, don't always have orgasms: In the 1992 survey, only 29 percent of the women reported that they always had orgasms with their primary sex partner during the previous year (Laumann et al., 1994).

The Commercialization of Sex   In addition, after 1960, sexual activity became a larger part of people's lives in several ways. It pervaded social life through images in the media and through a mushrooming sex industry. Historians John D'Emilio and Estelle Freedman described the post-1960 period as a time of "the commercialization of sex, and the sexualization of commerce" (D'Emilio & Freedman, 1988). The commercialization of sex is visible in the sexually oriented magazines, X-rated movie theaters, and so-called adult bookstores that have appeared since the Supreme Court, in a series of decisions, struck down many laws against obscenity. (See *Families and Public Policy:* Feminism and Pornography.) It is also visible in the more explicitly sexual themes treated in prime-time television programs. The sexualization of commerce is visible in advertisers' use of erotic images to sell products—such as half-naked male models wearing designer blue jeans or beer-drinking young men frolicking with bathing beauties.

What is more, public discussions about sexual matters have become much more frank. When Anita Hill testified before Congress concerning her allegations of sexual harassment against soon-to-be Supreme Court Justice Clarence Thomas in 1991, a fascinated nation followed every word of her sometimes graphic testimony

Families and Public Policy

Feminism and Pornography

Americans are used to thinking of political and social debates in terms of liberals versus conservatives, or Democrats versus Republicans. But sometimes people's positions on issues don't divide along liberal or conservative lines. Such is the case in recent debates about pornography, which have divided feminists, most of whom are politically liberal, for the past two decades.

Pornography is hard to define—indeed, that's part of why it's such a divisive issue. Supreme Court Justice Potter Stewart said famously that, although he couldn't define it, "I know it when I see it" (*Jacobellis* v. *Ohio*, 1964). Everyone agrees that part of the definition is "sexually explicit material." To that phrase various judges, activists, and moralists have added descriptions such as "degrading or abusive to one of the participants," depicting sexual conduct in a "patently offensive way," and "lacking in serious literary, artistic, political or scientific value." These are, however, subjective criteria on which not everyone agrees.

When the modern feminist movement emerged in the 1960s and 1970s, two of its goals were to end men's exploitation of women and to give women more control over their own lives. As activists and writers in the movement confronted pornography, they split into two camps (Schwartz & Rutter, 1998). The first camp, the anti-pornography feminists, argued that pornography was an important aspect of men's exploitation of women. The second camp, which came to be known as the libertarian feminists (or sometimes "free-expression" feminists), argued that overly broad restrictions on sexually explicit material would interfere with women's control over their own sex lives.

Studies show that men use pornography more than women do. In the General Social Survey, a nationally representative survey of adults that has been repeated every year or two since 1972, 29 percent of men say they have seen an X-rated movie in the previous year, compared with 17 percent of women. The belief is widespread among the public that explicit sexual materials may contribute to sexual assault: 50 percent of the men and 67 percent of the women interviewed by the General Social Survey agreed with the statement that sexual materials "lead people to commit rape." Social scientific studies do suggest a link between the use of sexual materials depicting violence and men's sexual aggression; but studies of the effects of nonviolent sexual materials are inconsistent and inconclusive (Berger, Searles, & Cottle, 1991).

In 1983, two of the leaders of the antipornography feminists, writer Andrea Dworkin and law professor Catherine MacKinnon, persuaded the Indianapolis City Council to pass an ordinance that would allow women who considered themselves victims of acts relating to pornography (such as a woman who was forced to take part in a pornographic performance or, more controversially, a woman who was sexually assaulted by a man she believed was motivated by viewing or reading pornographic materials) to sue the alleged pornographers for violating her civil rights (Berger et al., 1991). The ordinance defined pornography as "graphic sexually explicit subordination of women" that met one of six criteria, such as "women are presented as sexual objects who enjoy pain or humiliation" or as "sexual objects who experience sexual pleasure in being raped."

That pornography consists of women's "subordination" is central to the antipornography feminists' position. Writers such as Dworkin argue that pornography aids in men's oppression of women because it encourages them to treat women as

on television. In the mid-1990s, charges of sexual harassment in the U.S. armed forces led to a series of court-martials and resignations that were heavily covered by the news media. AIDS has also contributed to this frankness, as will be discussed later in this chapter.

The spread of sex and sexuality has also had its foes. In the 1970s, a grassroots movement of social conservatives organized to defend what they called the "traditional" family—by which they meant the breadwinner-homemaker family—and to oppose sexual activity outside marriage and deplore homosexuality (Cherlin, 1988). As mentioned in Chapter 1, conservative groups fought a losing battle to have the dehumanized objects to be exploited (Dworkin, 1985). It sometimes depicts sexual violence and suggests that women may even enjoy it. But Dworkin and MacKinnon go further: Even when it is not violent, they argue, pornography can violate women's civil rights if it encourages men to dominate women rather than to treat them as equals. The last of six criteria in the Indianapolis ordinance stated that pornography included materials in which "women are presented as sexual objects for domination, conquest, violation, exploitation, possession or use, or through postures or positions of servility or submission or display."

Should a sexually explicit but nonviolent film in which women are shown as sexual objects for domination be able to trigger a civil rights lawsuit? Questions such as this one led some feminists to criticize the Indianapolis ordinance as being too broad (e.g., Manning, 1991). The critics believed that one of the great victories of feminism was the liberation of women's sex lives from the control of men. In most societies of the past (and some today), men had controlled women's sex lives because men wanted to control childbearing. The only way a man could be certain that a woman was carrying his child

was to block that woman's sexual access to other men. Even within marriage, women were often taught that sex was a duty rather than a pleasure. The greater sexual freedom of American women today, including unmarried women and lesbians, is important to preserve, argued the libertarian feminists; and that sexual freedom includes the right to watch or read material that could be considered pornographic. Women are not merely victims of oppressive male sexuality, it is said; rather, much of women's sexual activity and even pornography is consensual (Duggan, Hunter, & Vance, 1985).

Challenged in court by many organizations, including libertarian feminists, the Indianapolis law was ruled unconstitutional by a federal court in 1984, and the Supreme Court let the ruling stand without comment in 1986 (*American Booksellers Association* v. *Hudnut,* 1984). The federal court judge ruled that the prohibition on speech (taken here to encompass books and films) was too broad and therefore violated the First Amendment to the Constitution, which protects freedom of speech. A higher court judge, affirming this ruling, stated that "inexorable" (inevitable) harm to women had not been proved (Berger et al., 1991).

Yet the issue continued in other forms in the 1990s, most notably concerning the Internet. In 1996 President Bill Clinton signed the Communications Decency Act, which forbade anyone from displaying "indecent" materials on the Internet without first setting up an age-screening mechanism to keep minors out of the area. In June 1996, a Philadelphia court struck down the law as "impermissibly vague" (*Reno* v. *American Civil Liberties Union,* 1996) and the Supreme Court upheld the decision in 1997. Although the issue was debated in terms of harm to children more than harm to women, a libertarian feminist group, Feminists for Free Expression, was among the opponents who submitted briefs to the court. The Act was "the biggest censorship issue of 1996," their year-end report said (Feminists for Free Expression, 1997).

Antipornography feminists are not, of course, the only groups opposing the availability of sexually explicit materials. Many religious organizations and conservative groups have supported restrictions on sexual materials. But the debate within the feminist community shows that on social issues, those with a particular political leaning—in this case liberals—don't always speak with one voice.

singular form "family" rather than the plural form "families" in the title of the 1980 White House Conference on Families. In the late 1970s, entertainer Anita Bryant led a movement to oppose the extension of antidiscrimination statutes to cover sexual preference, and the issue has been on and off state and local legislative agendas ever since. Throughout the 1980s, conservative members of Congress argued that the best way to stop teenage pregnancies was to encourage abstinence. In the 1980s, Republican presidential campaigns successfully incorporated a theme of "family values," which became a code phrase for the breadwinner-homemaker family. In 1993, Republican opposition forced newly elected President Bill Clinton to retreat from his campaign promise to allow gay men and lesbians to serve openly in the U.S. armed forces. In 1997, the Promise Keepers organizers sponsored a Washington, D.C. rally at which several hundred thousand men pledged to be good, traditional fathers and husbands.

Sexuality and Marriage: An Overview   In sum, there have been three eras in the attitudes toward sexuality and romantic love in the United States. Before about 1890, sexual attraction and romantic love were thought to be inappropriate bases for choosing a spouse. Moreover, even within marriage, sexual expression was thought to be an activity best done in moderation. From about 1890 to about 1960, in contrast, sexual attraction and romantic love were increasingly viewed as not only appropriate but, in fact, crucial criteria. Within marriage, people increasingly valued the emotional fulfillment they could obtain through sex and romantic love. The idea of a sexual identity, based on one's attitudes and practices, passed into common usage. Still, sexual expression outside marriage continued to be seen as illicit.

In the most recent era, the positive value given to sexual expression and gratification has continued and even increased. In addition, sexual activity has become defined even more as a private matter. In 1965, for example, the Supreme Court ruled that a state law prohibiting the use of contraceptives violated marital privacy by allowing police to search the "sacred precincts of marital bedrooms" (*Griswold* v. *Connecticut,* 1965). In 1972, the Court, using similar reasoning, overturned laws prohibiting the sale of contraceptives to unmarried persons (*Eisenstadt* v. *Baird,* 1972). The rationale for these laws had been that sexual activity was carried out in order to have children and that the state had an interest in seeing that married couples did, in fact, have children and that unmarried persons did not. In this way, the state could promote and control the reproduction of the population. By the time of these court decisions, however, sex had become primarily a means of individual fulfillment. Therefore, the rationale for state intervention had weakened.

This changing view of sexual activity is part of the broader growth of individualism during the twentieth century. In the post-1960 era, cultural changes were spurred, in part, by the increasing economic independence of women, which made it possible for young adult women to postpone marriage without postponing intimate sexual relationships. In turn, young men were able to initiate sexual relationships with women without making a commitment to support them. (Women's economic independence will be discussed in more detail in Chapter 10.) The changes in sexual behavior were also guided greatly by the availability of more effective means of contraception, notably the birth control pill.

Within marriage, as noted above, the changes have increased the possibility of mutually and personally fulfilling sexual relations. Our culture has rejected Dr. Acton's old warning that too strong a focus on sexual activity is "most destructive" and has accepted instead Ellis's view that what the world needs is "not more restraint but more passion." Yet the cultural and economic changes of the past few decades have undercut the rationale for restricting this passion to marriage. It is no longer necessary to be married to have a regular, satisfying sex life. Consequently, the changes in sexual activity have weakened the role of marriage as the core of family life in the United States. Marriage must now compete with singlehood and cohabitation—an increasingly common form of sexual union that will be discussed in the next chapter.

THE CREATION OF A GAY AND LESBIAN SUBCULTURE

The twentieth-century acceptance of sexual activity for reasons other than having children also weakened the justification for limiting acceptable sexual activity to opposite-sex couples. If sex was now a personal matter, the purpose of which was pleasure, then one might question why sexual acts between two men, or two women, shouldn't also be acceptable. During the 1950s, mainstream moralists supported the popular ideal of marriage and childbearing in part by harshly criticizing all the alternatives—especially homosexuality. Public vilification and persecution of homosexuals were intense in the 1950s before weakening in the 1970s.

A HISTORICAL OVERVIEW

In fact, Americans defined heterosexuality in part by mounting a public campaign against homosexuality beginning in the late nineteenth century. Recall from Chapter 2 (see also the *Families in Other Cultures* essay in this chapter) that in the nineteenth century many women formed strong, deep friendships, reinforced by the separate sphere in which they lived. These friendships were assumed to be spiritual and carried no stigma, although some of them may have had a sexual component (Smith-Rosenberg, 1975). To a lesser extent, men were allowed to express love in a friendship without stigmatization (D'Emilio & Freedman, 1988). Certainly, there are examples from antiquity of attraction to the same sex without stigma: In much of ancient Greece and Rome, men were allowed, even expected, to desire sex with other men or boys as well as with women (Aries, 1985b). The Greek biographer and historian Plutarch wrote:

> The noble lover of beauty engages in love wherever he sees excellence and splendid natural endowment without regard for any difference in physiological detail. The lover of human beauty [will] be fairly and equally disposed toward both sexes, instead of supposing that males and females are as different in the matter of love as they are in their clothes.[7]

Yet although the Greeks had words for specific sexual tastes, they had no general term comparable to "homosexuality" (Weinrich & Williams, 1991). In fact, no such term existed in Western societies until the nineteenth century.

Then, toward the end of the nineteenth century, an influential body of medical literature began to describe not merely homosexual acts but homosexual persons—distinctive individuals who were seen as suffering from a psychological illness that altered their sexual preference. Their supposedly unnatural condition was labeled "homosexuality," and it was said to pervade their personalities. They were no longer just men or women who engaged in sexual acts with a same-sex partner; they were homosexuals—seriously ill people (Foucault, 1980). In contrast to them, the same writers defined a "normal" sexual preference for the opposite sex as "heterosexuality." Heterosexuals were seen as mentally healthy as opposed to sick. This was the way sexuality entered our everyday language and our consciousness: as a means of organizing people into two contrasting sexual identities, one viewed as normal and one disparaged as diseased.

---

[7]Quoted in Boswell (1982).

In the nineteenth century, women formed strong, intense friendships with other women, some of which may have had a sexual component. This 1891 photo shows photographer Alice Austen (left) and her three friends who formed "The Darned Club."

The medical model remained dominant until 1973, when the American Psychiatric Association removed homosexuality from its list of mental disorders (Silverstein, 1991). The model stigmatized homosexual people and served as a basis for prejudice and discrimination. But the very force of the critique also created a group identity for individuals who had previously had none. Much as the ideology of separate spheres created conditions that allowed for social and political action by women's groups, so the discourse on homosexuality as an illness created conditions that ultimately provoked social and political actions by homosexual persons. "Homosexuality began to speak in its own behalf," wrote Michel Foucault, "to demand that its legitimacy or 'naturality' be acknowledged, often in the same vocabulary, using the same categories by which it was medically disqualified" (Foucault, 1980). But that is getting ahead of the story.

In the early twentieth century, the growth of cities and the spread of wage labor allowed homosexual men and women to leave their families and communities and establish an underground sexual subculture. This anonymous, marginal world, however, was still small. Then, in 1948, Alfred Kinsey, a zoology professor at the University of Indiana, published the results of thousands of interviews with men about their sexual behavior. Kinsey's dry, statistical book with 173 figures and 162 tables, often referred to as the **Kinsey Report**, became an immediate bestseller. His findings on homosexuality shocked the country: Half of all men in his sample, he reported, acknowledged having had erotic feelings toward other men; one-third had had at least one sexual experience with another man; one out of eight had had sexual experiences predominantly with other men for at least three years; and 4 percent had had sexual experiences exclusively with other men (Kinsey,

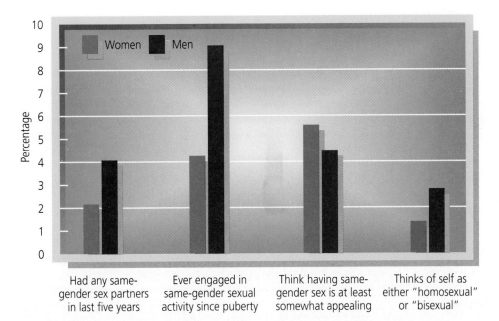

FIGURE 7.3 Prevalence of four measures of same-gender sexual activity, U.S. adults, 1992. (*Source:* Laumann, Gagnon, Michael, & Michaels, 1994, Tables 8.1 and 8.2.)

Pomeroy, & Martin, 1948). Kinsey concluded from his study that sexual orientation was a continuum running from exclusively heterosexual behavior to a mixture of heterosexual and homosexual behavior to exclusively homosexual behavior. Thus the book contained two far-reaching conclusions. First, the proportion of men whose experiences were predominantly homosexual was higher than most had imagined. Although Kinsey gave a range of figures, the one that came to dominate public discussion was that 10 percent of males were "more or less exclusively homosexual" for at least three years between the ages of 16 and 55 (Kinsey et al., 1948). Second, the even larger numbers of men with some homosexual experience or feelings suggested that homosexuality or bisexuality was not an abnormal condition but rather was within the range of normal sexual behaviors.

Although Kinsey's general conclusions still stand, his figures are not representative of the U.S. population now, and probably not then either. His study was based entirely on interviews with volunteers, the vast majority of them white, well educated, young, and from the Midwest and Northeast. In 1992, researchers at the University of Chicago directed the first, detailed survey of a large, random sample of the U.S. adult population (3,432 persons aged 18 to 59) on sexual activity (Laumann et al., 1994). (Although the researchers strongly defend their methods, some observers have expressed skepticism about the possibility of doing a survey on sexual behavior. See *How Do Sociologists Know What They Know? Asking about Sensitive Behavior.*) The survey measured sexual orientation in several ways, four of which are shown in Figure 7.3. Each person was asked whether he or she had had any same-gender partners in the last five years; the set of two bars on the left shows that 2.2 percent of women and 4.1 percent of men said yes. Later in the survey, the subjects were asked to fill out a questionnaire and place it in a sealed envelope, without the interviewer's ever seeing the answers. Several of the questions asked about oral sex, anal sex, or other sexual practices with someone of the same gender. The second set of bars in Figure 7.3 shows the percentages of women and men who said they had ever engaged in any of these practices at any time since puberty. (Further questions indicated that

How Do Sociologists Know What They Know?

Asking about Sensitive Behavior

How do sociologists collect information on people's behaviors and attitudes? For the most part, they ask them. The most common way of doing so is through the random-sample survey (see Chapter 1). Typically, a survey research organization will be hired to randomly select households and to ask the occupants a list of questions. In 1992, the National Opinion Research Center, one of the leading academic survey research organizations, asked a random sample of 3,432 adults detailed questions about their sexual activities and preferences. Researchers from the University of Chicago, who had written the questions, tabulated the results and published *The Social Organization of Sexuality* (Laumann et al., 1994). Several of their findings are presented in this chapter.

But can those findings be trusted? After all, the interviewers were inquiring about some of the most private and sensitive aspects of behavior. Biologist Richard Lewontin, writing in the *New York Review of Books* (Lewontin, 1995a), ridiculed the sociologists for believing the responses of

their subjects. His scathing critique, and the subsequent exchange of letters between social scientists and him, addressed the limits of survey-based sociological research.

Lewontin's main objection is that sociologists can't be sure that people tell the truth when asked about their behavior, especially when the topic is as sensitive as sexuality. Some people may lie, while others may not even admit the truth to themselves. Lewontin also pointed to a discrepancy in the data: Men reported 75 percent more sexual partners in the previous five years than did women. A few complexities aside, the average number of sexual partners of men and women should be almost the same. The authors examine this discrepancy and conclude that the most likely cause is that men exaggerate or women understate the number of partners when asked. Writes Lewontin: "If one takes the authors at their word, it would seem futile to take seriously the other results of the study" (1995a, p. 29).

The authors responded that although they "readily admit that we were not always successful in securing full disclosure," they "spent a

great deal of time worrying about how we could check the reliability and honesty of our respondents' answers" (Laumann et al., p. 43). They used techniques such as asking similar questions at different points in the interview to see if a person's responses were consistent. For some sensitive questions, the respondents were given a form to fill out that they could return in a sealed envelope. The researchers asked their interviewers to evaluate whether the respondents appeared to be responding frankly, and 95 percent were judged to be frank. Then they compared the answers given by the "frank" respondents with the answers of the other 5 percent. They found few differences. For instance, less-than-frank women and men were just as likely to report having more than one sex partner in the past year (pp. 564–68).

Lewontin was not appeased. For him, the sex survey is an example of sociology reaching for knowledge that is beyond its grasp. When they accept self-reports of sensitive behaviors and statistically analyze them, he argues, sociologists are trying too hard to imitate the natural sciences.

nearly half of the 9 percent of men who answered positively had experienced a same-gender sexual act before age 18 but not since then.)

The survey also inquired about people's sexual preferences. The third set of bars displays the percentages who thought "having sex with someone of the same sex" was either "very appealing" or "somewhat appealing." These responses show that, whereas fewer women than men said they had actually engaged in same-gender sexual activity, the percentage of women who found it at least somewhat appealing was comparable to (indeed, slightly greater than) the percentage among men. Finally, the respondents were asked, "Do you think of yourself as heterosexual, homosexual, bisexual, or something else?" As the last set of bars shows, less than 3 percent of men and less than 2 percent of women said that they considered themselves homosexual or bisexual.

Note that the percentages who consider themselves homosexual or bisexual are substantially lower than the percentages who have ever had a same-gender sexual

Without adequate ways to measure information such as sexual behavior, and above all without the possibility of performing experiments, he maintains, sociology is limited:

> [Sociologists] are asking about the most complex and difficult phenomena in the most complex and recalcitrant organisms, without that liberty to manipulate their objects of study which is enjoyed by natural scientists. In comparison, the task of the molecular biologist is trivial. . . . Like it or not, there are a lot of questions that cannot be answered, and even more that cannot be answered exactly. There is nothing shameful in that admission (Lewontin, 1995b, p. 44).

Lewontin's argument must be taken seriously by sociologists. There are indeed limits on how much sociologists can learn about human behavior; and random-sample surveys and statistical analyses can't surmount these limits. For some problems, sociologists might be better off abandoning surveys and turning to the kind of intensive, long-term field observations that anthropologists and some sociologists do—even though the findings from field studies aren't

necessarily representative of the population under study.

Does it follow that we should reject all findings from the study of sexual behavior because it is likely that men exaggerated, or women understated, the number of partners? This is a matter of judgment. My answer would be no. For one thing, the results of the 1992 survey are likely to be more reliable than Kinsey's results, which have dominated discussions of sexual orientation for decades. As noted elsewhere in this chapter, Kinsey's sample is far less diverse and representative than is the Chicago researchers' sample.

In addition, some comparisons among different groups represented in the 1992 sample are likely to be valid even if the individual responses aren't entirely accurate. For instance, in one chapter the authors divide people into groups according to their responses to nine statements about sexuality (for example, "premarital sex is always wrong"). They find that, based on these statements, people's beliefs about sexuality can be classified into a few groups: "traditional," "relational," and "recreational." These groups

differ greatly in their composition according to gender, race and ethnicity, age, and other characteristics. The researchers then discuss the implications of these social divisions for public debates on sexuality. (The chapter is reprinted in abbreviated form in the reader that accompanies this textbook [Cherlin, 1998].) These conclusions are likely to be valid unless people in some of the groups are more likely to reply truthfully than people in others. While this is a possibility, it seems unlikely to be a large enough problem to undermine the conclusions.

We should be wary of pushing survey research techniques beyond the limit of their usefulness. The 1992 survey pressed on that limit. The more sensitive the material and the more subjective the questions, the more skeptical readers should be. Nevertheless, we needn't dismiss the contributions of survey research to understanding sensitive issues. We should seek to supplement surveys with other, more intensive forms of data gathering. And we should recognize that there may be some questions about society that are beyond the capability of sociology to answer.

experience or who find same-gender activity at least somewhat appealing. Numbers such as these suggest that a smaller group of women and men are regularly and exclusively homosexual; but a larger group have at some point had homosexual experiences or have at some point felt homosexual attraction. The researchers concluded, as did Kinsey, that homosexuality is multidimensional and that no single number can adequately represent its prevalence. Nevertheless, all the relevant percentages in the 1992 survey are considerably lower than comparable percentages reported by Kinsey in 1948.

Other American and European surveys have produced similar findings. In the GSS from 1989 to 1991, about 5 percent of men and 3 to 5 percent of women reported ever having a same-gender partner, and only about 1 percent of men and women reported sexual behavior exclusively with their own gender (Michael et al., 1992). In a 1991 survey of American men aged 20 to 39, 2 percent said that they had had any same-gender sexual activity during the previous 10 years (Billy, Tanfer,

Grady, & Klepinger, 1993). European surveys have produced similar findings. A 1990–91 national survey in Great Britain found that 6 percent of men reported "any homosexual experience" (however the person defined it), and 4 percent reported one or more homosexual partners ever (Johnson, Wadsworth, Wellings, Bradshaw, & Field, 1992).[8] A 1991–92 national survey in France reported that 4 percent of men and 3 percent of women reported at least one occurrence of sexual activity with persons of the same sex during their lifetimes (Spira et al., 1992). To be sure, all these figures—including those in the 1992 University of Chicago survey—are likely to be minimum estimates, since some people probably did not divulge homosexual behavior, despite efforts to assure confidentiality.

Although the Kinsey Report badly damaged the model of homosexuality as an illness, the 1950s actually saw an increase in discrimination against homosexuals. Two factors contributed to this reversal. First, Americans turned inward toward marriage and childrearing after World War II, marrying younger and having more children than before or since in the twentieth century. The strong cultural support for the breadwinner-homemaker family also translated into renewed criticism of homosexuality—or any other reason for not marrying. Unmarried adults were sometimes suspected of being homosexuals and, implicitly, of being unable to live a proper adult family life. Second, the anti-Communist extremists of the late 1940s and early 1950s, such as Senator Joseph McCarthy, charged that homosexual people in government were security risks. According to their reasoning, homosexual people were vulnerable to blackmail by Communist spies, who would threaten to disclose their sexual identities unless they divulged government secrets. In 1950, a Senate committee investigating the employment of "homosexuals and other perverts" in government warned that homosexuals lacked "moral fiber." "One homosexual," the committee wrote, "can pollute a Government office" by enticing "normal individuals to engage in perverted practices" (D'Emilio & Freedman, 1988). Just after Dwight D. Eisenhower became president in 1953, he signed an executive order barring homosexual men and women from all federal jobs. This action spurred many states and localities to enact similar measures and fed something of a national panic about homosexuals (D'Emilio & Freedman, 1988). Overall, it was as if the increased emphasis on heterosexual marriage in the 1950s required defining and defaming its opposite—in this case, homosexuality. Moreover, homosexual people became lightning rods for the fear of communism.

THE GAY POLITICAL MOVEMENT

The political liberalism of the 1960s improved the climate for homosexual people, and the civil rights movement and women's movement provided models for political organizing. Activists in the growing homosexual communities in cities such as New York and San Francisco urged the adoption of a positive, affirmative homosexual identity. The term "gay" began to be employed to mean not just a sexual orientation but an entire lifestyle, an open subculture with its own dress, social life, sexual mores, and community institutions. "Being gay," wrote the editor of a gay newspaper in 1975, "is more than just being attracted to members of the same sex. Being gay includes the affirmation and celebration of our varied lifestyles" (Seidman, 1991). The popularity of the term "gay" signified that homosexual women and men were transforming themselves from people labeled merely by

[8]No figures were presented for women.

their sexual preferences to a social group with its own subculture and its own claims to equal citizenship and equal treatment.

Many authors date the emergence of the gay political movement to the **Stonewall riot**, which occurred in the aftermath of a police raid on a gay bar, the Stonewall Inn, in the heavily gay Greenwich Village area of New York City in 1969. Influenced by other 1960s protest movements, a gay liberation movement formed in the aftermath of the riot. It urged homosexual people to develop a public identity, and it linked an end to discrimination against homosexual people with the radical social changes urged by other groups of the New Left. Lesbians found common ground with radical feminists in denouncing male dominance. By the mid-1970s, the movement had scaled back its more radical demands, but it continued to urge that homosexuality be defined as a positive, worthwhile style of life. Through encouraging gay individuals to "come out" to friends and relatives by announcing their sexuality and to be visible at public events such as gay pride marches, the movement helped to enhance the senses of selves of gay men and lesbians. It also had some success in overturning state laws and in the removal of homosexuality from the list of mental disorders. Yet, even in the early 1990s, nearly half the states had laws against sexual acts between two persons of the same sex, although these laws were rarely enforced. In 1986, the Supreme Court affirmed the conviction of a Georgia man who was arrested in his bedroom while having consensual sex with another man. The decision, *Bowers* v. *Hardwick,* means that states may still enforce laws that declare gay and lesbian sex illegal (Rivera, 1991).

In the early 1990s, the rights of homosexual people remained a contentious political issue. Immediately upon assuming office in 1993, President Bill Clinton attempted to keep a campaign promise by ordering the military to allow homosexual people to serve. The order caused so much controversy that the president was forced by Congress to accept a compromise that allowed homosexuals to serve only as long as they did not divulge their sexual orientation or engage in homosexual behavior. Moreover, in a number of cities and states, citizens fought bitterly over ballot initiatives that would limit or expand the legal rights of homosexual people. In the latter half of the 1990s, controversy flared over the possibility of legalizing marriage for gay and lesbian couples. (See Chapter 1.)

THE ORIGINS OF SEXUAL ORIENTATION

Some of the people who oppose gay and lesbian civil rights believe that homosexuality is a lifestyle choice—one they themselves find objectionable. Thus, the political disputes center, in part, on the right of individuals to freely choose their sexual orientation without suffering discrimination as a result. Yet evidence is emerging that there may be a substantial biological component to sexual orientation (LeVay & Hamer, 1994). In one study, researchers examined the genetic material of pairs of brothers, both of whom were gay. Thirty-three of the 40 pairs had identical material at the end of the X chromosome, which in men is one of the two so-called sex chromosomes, the last of the 23 pairs of chromosomes found in every human cell. The probability of this similarity's occurring by chance, the authors reported, was less than 1 percent. Since a male always inherits an X chromosome from his mother (and a Y chromosome, the other sex chromosome, from his father), the study suggests that this likely biological influence operates through a person's maternal kinship line (Hamer, Hu, S., Magnuson, Hu, N., & Pattatucci, 1993). Still, more studies need to be done to confirm the findings from this one group.

Another study recruited gay men and lesbians, each of whom had a same-sex sibling who was an identical twin, a fraternal twin, or an adopted sibling. The researchers then ascertained the sexual orientation of the subjects' twins or adoptive siblings. Identical twins have identical genetic material; fraternal twins share, on average, half their genetic material; and adopted siblings share no genetic material. Consequently, if homosexuality were partly biological in origin, one might expect the greatest similarity of sexual orientation among the identical-twin pairs and the least similarity among the adoptive-sibling pairs. If homosexuality were not at all biological in origin, one might expect no difference in the similarity of sexual orientation among the three groups of siblings, since both siblings in every pair had been raised in the same home by the same parents. The authors found that, among the men, 52 percent of the identical twins, 22 percent of the fraternal twins, and 11 percent of the adoptive brothers were homosexual, which supports the biological model (Bailey & Pillard, 1991). Similarly, among the women, 48 percent of the identical twins, 16 percent of the fraternal twins, and 6 percent of the adoptive sisters were homosexual (Bailey, Pillard, Neal, & Agyei, 1993).

These studies are not without limitations (Byne, 1994). Both teams of researchers recruited subjects by placing advertisements in publications aimed at homosexual readers; it is possible that the kinds of people who responded to the advertisements are not representative of the general population of lesbians and gay men. Moreover, the twin study assumes that parents treat fraternal twins (and adoptive siblings) as similarly as they treat identical twins. If parents treat identical twins more similarly, such as by dressing them alike, it is possible that their treatment accounts for some of the greater similarity in identical twins' sexual orientations. In addition, even if there are biological influences, it is unlikely that a trait as complex as sexual orientation would be determined at a single genetic site on a chromosome.[9] Rather, several genetic sites, as well as levels of sex hormones, might be involved.

In addition, these studies suggest that sexual orientation is *not* completely genetically determined. After all, about half the identical twin pairs—who shared the same genetic material—had different sexual orientations. Clearly, something about the twins' environments influenced them differently. As is the case with gender differences, any biological effects probably operate not by determining a person's sexual orientation but rather by creating predispositions toward one orientation or the other. Social and cultural factors then further influence sexual orientation. But unlike gender differences—where substantial evidence exists of the different treatment boys and girls receive from parents, peers, schools, and the like—there is little evidence that parents or peers treat children who will grow up to be gay or lesbian differently than they do other children. Moreover, the general failure of psychiatrists and psychologists to change the sexual orientation of gay and lesbian clients who wish to do so has undermined the credibility of the psychoanalytic explanation for homosexuality, which emphasizes unresolved issues of identification with one's parents (Haldeman, 1991). Nor is there much evidence that children and adolescents learn homosexual behavior from adults. So, although social and cultural factors clearly play a role in sexual orientation, no satisfactory theories have been advanced to explain their role.

The biological studies (including one in which autopsies showed that a region of the brain involved in sexual response was smaller in gay men than in

[9]Hamer et al. make this point in "A Linkage between DNA Markers."

heterosexual men [LeVay, 1991]) have been controversial, in large part because of their political implications. Some observers argue that if homosexuality is not a lifestyle choice but rather an inherent, immutable part of an individual's personality, there is little justification for restricting the legal rights of gay men and lesbians. Other gay advocates argue that the studies are less consequential because civil rights should not depend on whether a person's style of life is of cultural or biological origin. And some opponents of legal rights for homosexuals, noting that there is evidence of biological influences on behaviors such as alcoholism, argue that a person needn't give in to biological predispositions if they are undesirable or objectionable to others.[10]

To be sure, research into the biological origins of sexual orientation need not have political significance. Rather, its purpose could be the same as that of most of the research discussed in this book—to increase our understanding of why people behave as they do in their family and personal lives. The great variation from society to society in the ways that sexual orientation is structured—the *berdache* tradition among Native Americans, the open acceptance of homosexual relations among the ancient Greeks and Romans, the mental illness model of the United States in the first half of the twentieth century, the recent emergence of an open lesbian and gay subculture—shows that social forces are an important part of the explanation for the behaviors and attitudes that emerge. But it seems likely that biological forces are also part of the story.

THE AIDS EPIDEMIC AND SEXUALITY

Gay men were the first group in the United States to be hit hard by the AIDS epidemic, but they are not the only group affected. **Acquired immune deficiency syndrome (AIDS)** is caused by the **human immune deficiency virus (HIV)**, which can be spread through the exchange of blood or semen, typically during sexual contact or during the sharing of hypodermic needles by injection drug users. (It can also occur through blood transfusions, although the testing of donated blood has minimized the latter risk in the United States and many other countries.) Even though exchanges during heterosexual sex can also spread the virus, the primary source of sexual transmission in the United States has been between males. The reason for this predominance isn't clear; in Africa, in contrast, heterosexual sex has been the primary route of transmission, as will be noted later.

Until recently, the medical wisdom had been that people infected with HIV invariably progress to AIDS and then invariably die. Most medical treatment had aimed at prolonging the time from infection with HIV until AIDS symptoms appeared and then prolonging the period until death. But in 1996, the prognosis for people with HIV improved dramatically. A new class of drugs, called protease inhibitors, when used in combination with two (or more) older anti-viral drugs, vastly improved the medical condition of many people (Altman, 1997). As Figure 7.4 shows, AIDS deaths dropped 22 percent between 1995 and 1996. The new treatment has raised hope that many people with HIV will be able to live indefinitely with the infection. However, the treatment has not worked in every case, and it is too soon to know how long its beneficial effects will last. Moreover, it is expensive and requires close medical supervision (see below).

[10]Examples of the positions noted in this paragraph can be found in Angier (1993).

FIGURE 7.4 Number of deaths due to AIDS in the United States, for non-Hispanic whites, non-Hispanic blacks, and Hispanics, from 1985 and before, through 1996. (*Source:* For 1985 and before, and through 1990, U.S. Bureau of the Census [1996e]; For 1991–1996, U.S. Centers for Disease Control and Prevention [1997]. Changes in the definition of AIDS cause some discontinuity in the annual number of deaths.)

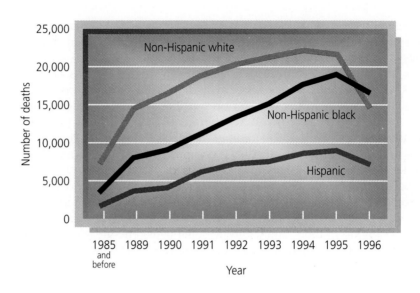

SEXUAL BEHAVIOR AND AIDS

By mid-1997, 612,000 cases of AIDS had occurred in the United States (U.S. Centers for Disease Control and Prevention, 1997). As of the end of 1996, 345,043 people had died of AIDS (U.S. Bureau of the Census, 1997i; U.S. Centers for Disease Control and Prevention, 1997). That is seven times as many people who died during the Vietnam War.[11] Gay men are heavily overrrepresented in these totals: 47 percent of all the AIDS cases that have occurred can be traced to a category that the U.S. Centers for Disease Control and Prevention (1997) calls "men having sex with men." Since the mid-1980s, AIDS has increasingly spread through the population of injection drug users: 21 percent of all cases were traceable solely to injection drug use and another 6 percent to men who had sex with other men and who injected drugs. Whereas gay men with AIDS are mainly non-Hispanic whites, injection drug users with AIDS are mainly poor African Americans and Hispanics. Moreover, the vast majority of persons who have been infected with HIV by heterosexual contact—often with infected drug users or persons from regions or countries where AIDS is prevalent, such as Africa or Haiti—are African Americans or Hispanics.[12]

Figure 7.4 shows the result of the shifting composition of deaths from AIDS. From the beginning of the epidemic through 1995, there were more deaths to non-Hispanic whites than to non-Hispanic blacks or Hispanics, reflecting the early dominance of transmission through homosexual contact. However, the ethnic and racial composition of deaths has changed greatly, as transmission due to drug use and heterosexual contact has grown. In 1996, for the first time, more blacks died of AIDS than non-Hispanic whites. Thus, year by year, AIDS has been shifting from a disease of gay white men to a disease of poor Hispanics and blacks, particularly drug users and their sex partners.

---

[11]47,366 U.S. soldiers died in the Vietnam War (U.S. Bureau of the Census, 1993g).

[12]Among all cases of AIDS reported by June 1997, 65 percent of those traceable solely to male homosexual contact were non-Hispanic white; among cases traceable solely to injection drug use, 79 percent were African American or Hispanic; and among cases traceable to heterosexual contact, 79 percent were African American or Hispanic (U.S. Centers for Disease Control and Prevention, 1997).

Nevertheless, the virus has also appeared in the nonpoor heterosexual population, although not in large numbers. About 9 percent of all adult AIDS cases have occurred through heterosexual contact with someone other than an injection drug user. What is more, the percentage of cases due to heterosexual contact has been increasing (due in part to decreases among gay men): It was 14 percent from July 1996 through June 1997 (U.S. Centers for Disease Control and Prevention, 1997). Moreover, HIV appears to be transmitted from men to women much more efficiently than from women to men (Padian, Shiboski, & Jewell, 1991). In the early 1990s, heterosexual transmission spurred the government (in a way that homosexual transmission in the early 1980s did not) to fund a number of national surveys of sexual behavior and attitudes in order to ascertain the number of persons engaging in "high-risk" behavior and to monitor behavioral and attitudinal trends.

One definition of high-risk behavior is having heterosexual sex with two or more partners without using condoms. Among men aged 20 to 39 who had ever had heterosexual intercourse in 1991, 25 percent had had two or more partners during the previous 18 months, including 4 percent of married men, 45 percent of never-married men, and 52 percent of formerly married men (Billy et al., 1993). Men who reported having had two or more partners were more likely to report having used condoms recently (within the previous three or four weeks); yet among men with four or more partners, only half had used condoms recently. Among men who responded that they had had a "one-night stand" in the previous four weeks, just 62 percent had used condoms (Tanfer, Grady, Klepinger, & Billy, 1993). As for women, a 1988 national survey of women aged 15 to 44 collected information on the number of sex partners during the previous three months. Among unmarried women (either never married or formerly married) who had had sex at all during the three months, 10 percent had had multiple sex partners. And among this latter group, only about one-third had used condoms (Kost & Forrest, 1992). Thus, many women and men with multiple sex partners do not use condoms.

SOCIAL NETWORKS

"Social diseases" was the sanitized term used in polite company a few decades ago to refer to sexually transmitted illnesses, and AIDS is indeed a social disease. Almost all infectious diseases, of course, are spread from person to person. In order to spread, HIV requires a **social network**, a group of people who are linked through interaction with one another. In the case of HIV, the specific interaction is sexual contact or the sharing of contaminated needles. It's not necessary that each person in a network interact with—or even know—all the others, although that sometimes happens. Rather, what matters is that a path, however direct or circuitous, can be traced from any person A to any person B. The contrast between the spread of AIDS in the United States and Africa illustrates how different kinds of social networks can produce very different outcomes.

The United States   In the United States, HIV infection at first spread primarily through homosexual contact. In the early 1980s, the high concentration of gay men in cities such as San Francisco and New York provided brutally efficient social networks for the sexual transmission of a virus no one yet knew about. Then injection drug users provided a second network. Persons who belonged to both of these networks—gay men who were also injection drug users—probably provided

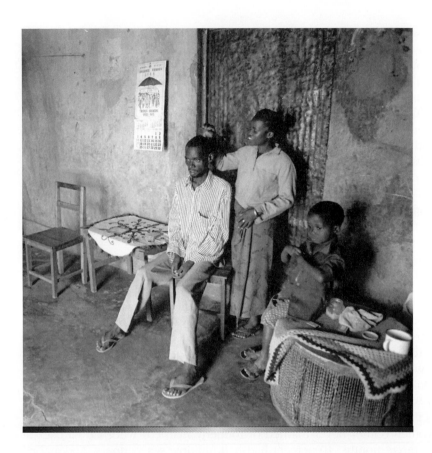

Sub-Saharan Africa has the highest concentration of people with AIDS, such as this man in Rwanda.

the crucial link from one to the other. In turn, injection drug users may have been the link, through their sex partners, to a third network, heterosexuals who have had more than one sexual partner.

Efforts to educate gay men about safe sex practices have been effective in slowing the spread of HIV infection, as evidenced by the decline in deaths among non-Hispanic whites in Figure 7.4. For injection drug users, efforts have been less successful. Campaigns to educate addicts about the dangers of sharing needles have been unsuccessful, and a debate has emerged about the morality of starting public programs to allow users to exchange used needles for clean ones.

Africa   Sub-Saharan Africa is the region of the world with the most severe AIDS problem. A United Nations study of 15 African nations estimated that, by 1995, AIDS had caused 1.5 million more deaths than would have occurred without it. If no progress is made in combating AIDS, the study concluded, by 2005 it will have caused an additional 4.3 million deaths (United Nations, 1995; Adetunji, 1997). In Africa, HIV has been transmitted primarily through heterosexual intercourse from the start of the epidemic. Medical researchers are not sure why heterosexual transmission is so much more common in sub-Saharan Africa than in Western nations. One possibility is the greater prevalence of sexually transmitted diseases that cause genital ulcers, which can be sites of infection. The highest prevalence of HIV infection has occurred in areas where relatively few men are circumcised, and uncircumcised men may be more susceptible to genital ulcers, through which HIV can be transmitted during heterosexual intercourse (Caldwell & Caldwell, 1993). But most experts also believe that African social structure and culture, and the social networks they have created, have played a large role.

Before the European colonization of Africa, men in most African societies sought to have two or three wives and many children. In order for this system to work, men had to postpone marriage for perhaps 10 years beyond the age at which their sisters married, or else older men could not accumulate so many wives. Consequently, this system produced a large group of young men who had no sexual access to wives. Moreover, in many societies husbands traditionally abstained from having sex with wives who were breast-feeding babies, and in some societies women were expected to abstain from sex altogether when they became grandmothers. So husbands were commonly denied sexual access to their wives for long periods. Societies developed ways to satisfy the sexual demands of the large proportion of men without current sexual access to wives. These included discreet liaisons between young men and the young, junior wives of their fathers and brothers; sexual acts between unmarried young men and women that stopped short of complete intercourse; extramarital lovers; and commercial sex (Caldwell, Caldwell, & Orubyloye, 1992).

Moreover, patterns of migration during and after the colonial period created cities with excesses of males. Rural men, seeking work, temporarily migrated to urban areas or mining towns, often leaving their wives behind. As a result, prostitution flourished in the cities and towns. In addition, some men began relationships with urban "outside wives," women who were informal substitutes for the older tradition of more than one wife. Most men would visit home at least once a year and have sex with their wives, thus creating sexual networks involving a smaller number of women in the cities and a larger number throughout the adjacent rural areas.

Both of these characteristics of African societies—the development of alternatives when sexual access to wives is blocked and the use of prostitution and informal relationships to satisfy the sexual demands of labor migrants to cities—created sexual networks that could facilitate the heterosexual spread of a virus such as HIV. For example, 61 percent of a sample of prostitutes in Nairobi in 1985 tested positive for HIV infection, and each of them averaged 1,440 clients per year (Larson, 1989). So it appears that a large number of men are having sex with a small, heavily infected group of prostitutes. Some of these men then establish relationships with unmarried women in Nairobi; others return to their home villages, where they can spread the virus to wives and lovers. From that point on, wives and lovers can spread the virus further through extramarital liaisons.

Networks and Policy   By contrasting the social networks in the Western nations with those in Africa, we can see how the culture and social structure of an area can influence the course of an epidemic. Nonsocial factors, of course, also play a role—as in the presumed higher risk of transmission in Africa due to genital sores from widespread venereal diseases. But a focus on social networks can help health workers and political leaders to determine what actions might slow the epidemic. For example, urging gay men to practice safe sex and drug addicts to exchange used needles for new ones are extremely useful steps in the United States but would be of relatively little value in Africa. Granted, just because a policy would slow the spread of AIDS doesn't mean it will be enacted. Rather, what to do about the spread of AIDS is a contentious political issue in the United States (and also in Africa).

THE POLICY RESPONSE IN THE UNITED STATES

In the United States, the public policy response to AIDS was slow in starting. In the early 1980s, when the disease was confined mainly to gay men in large cities, notably New York and San Francisco, there was little government response. Some activists believe that little was done because AIDS was perceived—inaccurately, it turned out—as a disease that affected only gay people. President Ronald Reagan didn't make his first speech on the subject until 20,000 people had died. As a result of this neglect, too many individuals engaged in unprotected sex for too long, and too few efforts were made to educate the public and to develop an effective medical treatment. It wasn't until the late 1980s, by which time over 50,000 people had the disease and it had begun to infect heterosexuals, that a large-scale response began (Shilts, 1988).

Even then, there was much disagreement about how to respond. The dilemma is that AIDS places two sets of principles at odds: (1) individual freedom versus the collective interest; and (2) discouraging unpopular behavior versus trying to limit its consequences. As for the former, gay rights groups had fought for sexual freedom in the 1970s, had achieved something close to it in large cities, and were reluctant to give it up. In the 1970s, a growing number of bathhouses and sex clubs provided settings for impersonal gay sex. Moreover, an affirmative attitude toward gay sex became a centerpiece of the gay liberation political movement. Consequently, even when the link between unprotected sex and HIV transmission became apparent to public health officials, calls for the closing of the bathhouses were resisted by some gay political leaders and by the sex industry (Shilts, 1987).

Social conservatives and some public health professionals advocated widespread testing for HIV in the collective interest of identifying infected persons to prevent contact with them. Gay advocates argued, however, that mandatory testing would impose an unacceptable restriction on individual freedom because it would allow organizations such as the military or insurance companies to identify gay men and exclude them from membership or coverage. Nevertheless, Congress allowed the armed forces to institute HIV tests and exclude those who tested positive. Mandatory testing had widespread public support: Among respondents to the General Social Survey (GSS) in 1989 to 1991, 62 percent supported permitting insurance companies to test applicants for the AIDS virus and 89 percent favored mandatory testing before marriage (Davis & Smith, 1996). The public, however, did balk at segregating or quarantining people with AIDS; for example, 74 percent of the GSS respondents opposed prohibiting students with HIV from attending public school.

As for the second clash of principles, many social conservatives genuinely felt that homosexual relations—and even heterosexual relations outside marriage—were morally wrong and should not be condoned. Their response to the AIDS epidemic was to urge chastity for the unmarried and monogamy for the married (D'Emilio & Freedman, 1988). In contrast, other interest groups argued that, even though sex outside heterosexual marriage might be objectionable to some people, the threat AIDS posed to health required accepting its existence and urging people to limit risky behavior and to use condoms. By the late 1980s, the latter view had prevailed, as exemplified by the explicit brochure Surgeon General C. Everett Koop sent to every home in the United States in 1988. Public opinion also backed forthright measures: 86 percent of the GSS respondents supported a government information program to promote safe sex practices such as the use of condoms, and 88 percent favored the teaching of safe sex practices in sex education courses in public schools.

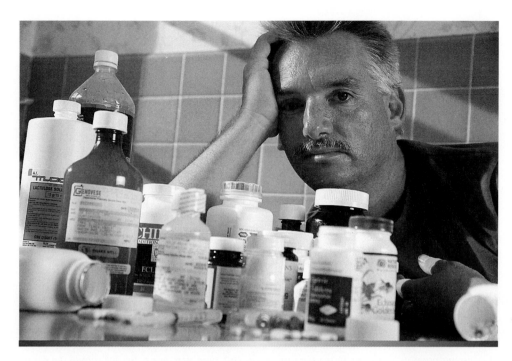

Combinations of new drugs have proven effective in controlling HIV infection.

    The development of effective drug therapy has produced a new policy question: Should all persons with AIDS have equal access to the new drugs—and at what cost? They are very expensive—well over $10,000 per year—and they require expensive medical supervision and blood testing. Most middle-class people belong to health insurance plans through their employers that cover the expenses of treatment. But the United States has tens of millions of people who have no health insurance coverage; in 1996, 41.7 million were without coverage for the entire year (U.S. Bureau of the Census, 1997i). Many are in working-class families where wage earners have jobs that do not provide health insurance. The cost of the AIDS treatment is far more than they could afford. Some of the poor—including families that are receiving what used to be called Aid to Families with Dependent Children and is now called Temporary Assistance to Needy Families (see Chapter 6)—are covered by the government's Medicaid program of health insurance. But not all state Medicaid plans include sufficient funds for treating with the new drugs those who are infected (Groopman, 1997). As a result the poor and near-poor have limited access to the new treatments. Statistics show that in 1996, death from AIDS declined by 33 percent for non-Hispanic whites, but only by 20 percent for Hispanics and 13 percent for African Americans—reflecting, at least in part, the greater access to the new treatments among non-Hispanic whites (U.S. Centers for Disease Control and Prevention, 1997).

    The response to AIDS shows that public health issues involving sexual activity often involve more than technical and medical considerations. The social context of a sexual issue can determine what action, if any, the government takes. Prevailing moral values influence public opinion about whether the affected persons are worthy of assistance—whether they are blameless or, in some sense, to blame for their health problems. Concerns about individual freedom determine how restrictive the public response will be. These social and political conflicts influence the nature of the response.

AIDS AND SEXUALITY

Beyond how, and to whom, the disease spreads, another question is what AIDS has done to sexuality—to our sexual identities, and to our attitudes and practices about sex. The AIDS epidemic has made sexuality more of a public issue than it has ever been. It is true that for several decades now, the commercialization of sex has made erotic images increasingly public. But AIDS has made the mechanics of sex itself—the organs and orifices involved, the same-sex and different-sex varieties, the kinds of contraceptives—a topic of unprecedented public discussion. As discussed earlier, as recently as the 1960s, some states had laws that prohibited even married couples from using contraceptive devices. Yet in 1988, just two decades after these laws were declared unconstitutional, C. Everett Koop, then the surgeon general of the United States, sent a brochure to every household in the nation explaining the connection between AIDS and sexual activity and urging everyone—not just married couples—to use condoms. In response to the spread of AIDS, adolescents were informed about anal intercourse, pieces on safe sex appeared regularly in the media, and condoms were advertised on television. In this discourse, sex was seen less as a means of personal gratification than as an issue of public health. Koop wrote:

> *Some of the issues involved in this brochure may not be things you are used to discussing openly. I can easily understand that. But now you must discuss them. We all must know about AIDS. Read this brochure and talk about it with those you love* (U.S. Centers for Disease Control, 1988).

Married couples who have no outside sex partners, however, are at virtually no risk of HIV infection. Therefore, by focusing attention on safe sex practices, health workers and educators have unavoidably communicated the message that sex outside marriage is acceptable, or at least tolerable, and can be publicly acknowledged—indeed, must be publicly acknowledged given the gravity of the risk to people's health.

Family planners have been urging for decades that we accept sexual activity outside marriage and encourage the use of contraceptives to avoid unwanted children and to stop sexually transmitted diseases. They have urged that contraceptives be made available to American teenagers to reduce pregnancies. Doing so, however, would require a tacit acceptance of teenage sexuality, a step many Americans have been unwilling to take. AIDS has broken this deadlock. The epidemic, said Marian Wright Edelman of the Children's Defense Fund, has accomplished "what one million teenage pregnancies couldn't do: get us talking about sex" (D'Emilio & Freedman, 1988). The talk has had results; national surveys reveal that the proportion of sexually active adolescent boys who use condoms at first intercourse rose from 55 percent in 1988 to 69 percent in 1995 (Sonenstein et al., 1997). And the increase has been greater among boys who reported receiving AIDS education or sex education (Ku, Sonenstein, & Pleck, 1992). In fact, from the standpoint of family planning advocates, the small silver lining in the great gray cloud of AIDS may be the increased use of condoms by boys and unmarried men.

Moreover, the AIDS epidemic raised the profile of gay men and, by extension, lesbians. Public health campaigns demystified and explained homosexual sex. This explicit consideration implied a certain level of tolerance of homosexuality among the heterosexual majority. The origins of homosexuality and the political rights of lesbians and gay men were the subject of numerous feature stories in newspapers and magazines.[13] Yet until the mid-1990s, there was little change in the percentage of the population that accepted homosexual sex. In the GSS between 1973 and 1991, a constant 80 percent of the population, give or take one or two percentage points, agreed that homosexual sex is always wrong or almost always wrong (Davis & Smith, 1996). In the early-to-mid 1990s, the aforementioned ballot initiatives and battles over gay men in the military suggested deep divisions in public sentiment. The attention due to AIDS, therefore, seemed to have led to greater frankness and discussion about homosexuality but not much greater public acceptance. Very recently, however, there are signs that attitudes may be changing: In the 1993 and 1994 GSS rounds, 71 percent agreed that homosexual sex is always wrong or almost always wrong; the percentage agreeing fell to 66 percent in the 1996 round (Davis & Smith, 1996).

Among the adult heterosexual population, AIDS has also brought a greater frankness about sex. Yet there have been only modest changes in sexual behavior. As noted earlier, for instance, condom use has increased; yet many people with multiple sex partners do not use condoms regularly. Perhaps the changes have not been greater because the spread of HIV through the non–drug-using heterosexual population, despite the apprehension of public health experts and the example of Africa, has been limited. For reasons not clearly understood, then, AIDS in the United States has largely remained a disease of gay men, mostly white, and drug users and their partners, mostly black or Hispanic. The social composition of the victims AIDS has killed may explain why the public response to the disease was slow in coming and, some would argue, inadequate.

SUMMARY

1. The idea that individuals have a coherent sexual identity, involving a preference for either opposite-sex or same-sex partners, did not exist until the late nineteenth century. Before then, religious doctrine and civil laws forbade numerous sexual practices, but there was no sense that a person who broke the law had a fundamentally different personality than people whose sexual behavior was conventional.

2. During the nineteenth century, a separation still existed between spiritual love, which was seen as a proper basis for marriage, and romantic love, which was seen as a poor basis for marriage. It gradually became acceptable for married couples to engage in sex for pleasure, but only in moderation.

3. During the twentieth century, marriage came to be seen as a means of self-fulfillment through romantic love and sexual gratification. After about 1960, sexual activity by unmarried persons became more acceptable and much more widespread. Among unmarried adolescents, the percentage who had ever had intercourse rose substantially. And whereas unmarried women in the past had abstained from sexual relations outside marriage more than men, by the 1990s the difference in unmarried women and men's sexual activity had narrowed dramatically. The changes also have been greater for the nonpoor rather than the poor. Still, opposition to extramarital sex remains strong, and most married persons limit their sexual activity to their spouses.

4. After 1960, the growth of the sex industry and of erotic themes in the media, as well as more frank public discussion of sexual issues, resulted in sexuality's becoming a more pervasive aspect of society. The rise of nonmarital sex weakened the role of marriage as the core of family life in the United States.

[13]See, for example, Gelman (1992); Henry (1993); Mathews (1993).

5. A body of medical literature in the late nineteenth and early twentieth centuries defined homosexuality as a psychological illness that pervaded the personalities of certain men and women, who were labeled homosexuals. Heterosexuality was defined, in contrast, as a mentally healthy attraction to the opposite sex. This illness model of homosexuality remained dominant until the 1970s, although it was undercut by evidence that homosexual behavior, in various degrees, was widespread in the population. A small percentage of men and women engage in regular homosexual activity, but a larger number have ever had at least one such experience. In the 1970s, a gay political movement developed, and it urged a positive homosexual identity and an end to prejudice and discrimination. Recent studies suggest that sexual orientation may have a biological component as well as social and cultural components.

6. The AIDS virus spread rapidly through the gay male community in the early 1980s. Beginning in the mid-1980s, it spread into the population of injection drug users and their sex partners. As a result, the proportion of African Americans and His-panics among all AIDS cases grew to the point that, by 1996, for the first time, more blacks died of AIDS than non-Hispanic whites. Nevertheless, AIDS also has spread into the nonpoor heterosexual population, although in smaller numbers. The virus spreads through social networks, and, in the United States, networks of gay men and of injection drug users and their partners have been the main source. In Africa, heterosexual networks, sometimes involving informal liaisons and prostitutes, have been the major source of spread. The study of social networks can identify useful public policies to prevent further spread. Yet effective policies are often controversial because they involve clashes of values, notably between individual freedom and the collective interest and between discouraging unpopular behavior and trying to limit its consequences. AIDS has led to a more frank, public discussion about sexual activity. The discussion itself is an acknowledgment that sexual activity (or at least heterosexual activity) outside marriage is now publicly tolerated, perhaps even accepted.

KEY TERMS

sexual identity
passionate love
companionate love
extramarital sex
sexual monogamy

Kinsey Report
Stonewall riot
acquired immune deficiency syndrome (AIDS)

human immune deficiency virus (HIV)
social network

FAMILIES ON THE INTERNET

The Sexuality Information and Education Council of the United States (**www.siecus.org**), an organization that favors the dissemination of information about sexuality and sex education in schools, maintains a web site with a great deal of information about sexuality issues. For a conservative perspective, consult the web site of the The Traditional Values Coalition (**www.traditionalvalues.org**), which opposes gay rights and sex education that does not stress abstinence. Concerning the feminist debates about pornography, you can find the free-expression position defended by Feminists for Free Expression (**www.well.com/user/freedom**). For the anti-pornography view, consult the Andrea Dworkin web site (**www.igc.org/womensnet/ dworkin**). The National Campaign to Combat Internet Pornography (**www.nccip.org**) is an organization working to restrict access to pornographic materials on the Internet. Finally, for answers to questions about sexuality and sexual health, consult Go Ask Alice (**www.cc.columbia.edu/cu/ healthwise/alice.html**), a site maintained by the Columbia University Health Services.

CHAPTER 8

Paths to Family Formation

"Love and marriage, love and marriage," crooned Frank Sinatra, "go together like a horse and carriage. Let me tell you, brother, you can't have one without the other." As a commentary on love and marriage during the 1950s and early 1960s, Sinatra's song was on the mark. Yet not long after it was recorded, the way in which Americans fall in love, marry, and form families was beginning to undergo a change so massive that the song would soon sound hopelessly outdated. In the 1950s and early 1960s, sexual intercourse, marriage, and childbearing were indeed bound together like a horse and carriage, perhaps even more so than in previous decades. The little we know suggests that a majority of women and many men first had sexual intercourse with the person they would marry—and often only after their marriages began (May, 1988). The sexually adventurous in the first half of the century were largely those who began intercourse just after they were engaged. "Engagement," wrote historian Ellen Rothman, "functioned like the safety net under the trapeze artist: It did not eliminate missteps and falls, but it minimized the cost of mistakes" (Rothman, 1984).

The feared misstep was pregnancy, which led to a hasty marriage. If a woman who wasn't even engaged became pregnant, the consequences for her and her partner were severe. The phrase "shotgun wedding," with its evocation of the woman's angry father forcing her partner to marry her at gunpoint, conveys the moral tone of the first half of the twentieth century. Children born outside marriage were considered illegitimate—another term that now has a somewhat dated ring. In the 1950s, more than 70 percent of babies conceived by unmarried white women were made legitimate by a marriage before the baby's birth (O'Connell & Moore, 1980). In contrast, only 34 percent were legitimated by a marriage in the period 1985 to 1989 (U. S. Bureau of the Census, 1991b; more recent figures are not available).

Moreover, as noted in Chapter 2, young adults in the 1950s married at earlier ages than at any other time in the twentieth century. Half of all women were married by age 21 (Schoen, Urton, Woodrow, & Baj, 1985), leading to the expression on college campuses "Ring by spring or your money back." And once married, they had children sooner than their mothers' generation (Ryder, 1980). It was as if the entire process of marrying and having a first child had been compressed and standardized into one rapid assembly-line operation. Just as homes were being mass-produced in the burgeoning suburbs, so too were the families that would occupy them. For almost everyone, becoming an adult meant getting married and having children and doing so rather quickly (Modell, Furstenberg, & Strong, 1978; Modell, 1989). But times have changed, and the changes have made the study of family formation more complex.

This chapter will examine the increasingly diverse ways in which young adults find partners and begin to create their own families. It will begin with a brief review of the changing rates of marriage, childbearing outside of marriage, and cohabitation. It will then focus on the influences a person's social environment—her or his parents, friends, neighborhood, race, social class, and so forth—has on the process of family formation. For although young people in the Western nations typically choose their own partners, their choices are influenced by their social worlds. Or, paraphrasing Marx, we might say that young adults make their own families, but they do not make them just as they please.[1] The influence of parents, who are still a factor, albeit a weakening one, in family formation will be discussed first. Then, courtship and dating, two important phenomena that may nevertheless have passed their peaks, will be examined.

The process of finding a spouse occurs in what social scientists call the marriage market, about which there are theory and evidence that will be considered. The chapter will explore the question of who marries whom—what are the characteristics of men and women who are likely (or unlikely) to choose each other as marriage partners? Afterward, the rise of cohabitation and its relationship to marriage will be discussed. Indeed, because of the rise of cohabitation, this chapter will focus not only on marriages but also on *unions,* and in particular marital unions and cohabiting unions. I define a **union** as a stable, intimate relationship between two people who live in the same household but may or may not be married. All these topics, however, are more appropriate for young adults who proceed directly to cohabitation or marriage than for the growing proportion

---

[1]Marx made this famous statement not about families but rather about how "men make their own history." See Marx (1959).

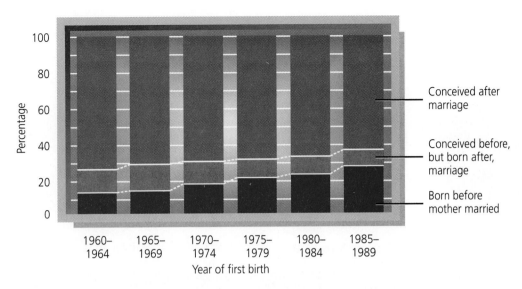

FIGURE 8.1
Percentage of first births (1) conceived after the mother married, (2) conceived before marriage but born after the mother married, and (3) born before the mother married, 1960–1964 to 1985–1989. (*Source:* U. S. Bureau of the Census, 1991b. Data is for women aged 15 to 34.)

who have a child prior to living with a partner. Consequently, the chapter will close with a consideration of the causes and consequences of childbearing prior to forming a union.

CHANGING TRENDS IN FAMILY FORMATION

Beginning in the mid-1960s, sexual activity, marriage, and childbearing began to drift apart. It became common for young adults to have sexual intercourse prior to marriage, often many years before, as discussed in the previous chapter. During the same period as early sexual activity was increasing, early marriage was decreasing. In fact, between the mid-1950s and the mid-1990s the age at which half of all first marriages occur rose by four years for both women and men (U.S. Bureau of the Census, 1996b). Because of this enormous jump, ages at marriage—which were at twentieth-century lows in the 1950s—are higher today than at any other time in the twentieth century. Teenage marriage, for instance, has plummeted: In 1960, 32 percent of 18- and 19-year-old women had married, compared with 8 percent in 1995. Among women aged 20 to 24, the vast majority in 1960—72 percent—had married, whereas the vast majority in 1995—67 percent—had not married. Even among 25- to 29-year-old women in 1995, 35 percent had not married. Thus, far more young women now remain single throughout late adolescence and early adulthood. The changes have also been dramatic for men: nearly half—47 percent—of 20- to 24-year-old men in 1960 had married, compared with just 19 percent in 1995 (U.S. Bureau of the Census, 1975; U.S. Bureau of the Census, 1996c).

Earlier sexual activity and later marriage set the conditions for a sharp rise in the proportion of first births to unmarried women after 1960. The upward trend in the percentage of children born to unmarried women is apparent in Figure 8.1. Each bar of the figure shows, for a five-year period, the percentage of first children that were (1) born before the mother had ever married; (2) conceived before the mother had ever married but born after she had married; and (3) conceived after the mother had married. The percentages are shown for women 15 to 34 years old in each period.[2]

---

[2]The trend is even more striking for teenagers. In 1960–1964, 17 percent of first births to 18- and 19-year-olds occurred to mothers who had never married; the corresponding figure in 1985–1989 was 59 percent (U.S. Bureau of the Census, 1991b).

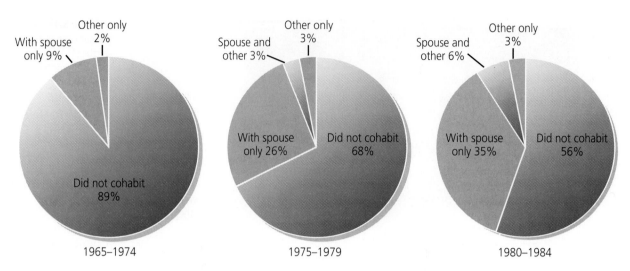

FIGURE 8.2 Percent cohabiting before first marriage, for persons marrying in 1965–1974, 1975–1979, and 1980–1984. (*Source:* Bumpass & Sweet, 1989.)

As can be seen, 29 percent, or nearly 3 in 10, first births in 1985 to 1989 (the latest period for which complete information on time of conception is available) occurred to unmarried women. Another 1 in 10 was conceived before marriage. Just 6 in 10 were conceived after a marriage had begun. By 1995, 32 percent of all births occurred to unmarried women (U.S. National Center for Health Statistics, 1997a).

Also complicating the picture was the great rise in cohabitation, commonly called living together, that began about 1970. Before the 1960s, cohabitation was found mainly among the poor and near-poor. With little in the way of resources to share and little prospect of leaving money or possessions to their children, the poor have less reason to marry, and for many cohabitation has served as an acceptable substitute for legal marriage. But beginning around 1970, the proportion of all young adults who lived with someone prior to marrying increased sharply. Figure 8.2 shows the dramatic increase across three groups of marriages: those begun in 1965–1974, 1975–1979, and 1980–1984. Premarital cohabitation went from being the experience of a few to being commonplace. According to a 1995 national survey, 47 percent of ever-married women under 30 had cohabited before they married.[3] Thus, it appears that about half of young adults will live with a partner (usually, but not always, their future spouse) before marrying. Cohabitation on a large scale is so new that no one knows for sure how it will affect the formation of families.

Clearly, then, the old, uniform, marry-then-have-sex-then-have-children path to family formation must compete with several other paths today. To understand these contemporary alternatives, we need first to step back and study the changing nature of the process that leads, for most people, to marriage. In the preindustrial Western nations, the choice of a marriage partner for a son or daughter was of great significance to the parents and other kin. Parental influence was therefore substantial—and continues to be in many developing countries today. However, parental influence was rarely strong enough in the preindustrial Western nations to dominate the choice of a spouse. Parents often had veto power and frequently

[3]These are my calculations using data from the National Survey of Family Growth, Cycle V, 1995.

made suggestions and introductions, but considerable latitude was granted to young adults. They found partners through the process we know as courtship. Then, in the twentieth century, a new form of courtship—dating—was invented by young adults. Its rules and rituals became ever more elaborate through midcentury and then entered a period of decline.

PARENTAL INFLUENCE

In the United States, about 9 out of 10 young adults, whether they live with someone or not, eventually marry. Most believe that they alone selected their spouses, free of interference from outsiders. Yet that is an overstatement because parents and peers can play a role. For example, John Finley Scott argued in a classic 1965 article that, despite appearances to the contrary, parents still influenced their children's marriage choices in subtle but important ways (Scott, 1965). Scott studied the sorority systems that had expanded on most campuses. (He could easily have extended his analysis to fraternities.) He noted that each sorority, under the guidance of its alumnae, tended to take in members who were similar to one another in their class, religious, and ethnic backgrounds. In addition, he wrote, parents encouraged their daughters to join sororities that matched their backgrounds. As a result, Jewish students joined predominantly Jewish sororities, daughters of well-to-do Protestant families congregated with others with this background, and so forth. The sorority members then socialized primarily with fraternities made up of young men from the same class, religious, and ethnic backgrounds. By seeing that their children joined the appropriate sorority, parents increased the likelihood that their daughters would choose marriage partners from their own social group. Yet they did so in a way that maintained the illusion that the marriage choice was totally their daughters' own.

Parental influence was more direct in most societies historically, and it is still more direct in some developing nations today. For instance, in rural villages throughout the developing world, parents who have land or wealth to pass on to their children are especially likely to have a voice. (See *Families in Other Cultures: Parental Influence on Marriage in Thailand*.) In India and Pakistan, it is still common for parents, even prosperous city dwellers, to play the dominant role in the choice of their children's spouses. When I visited New Delhi, India, in 1985, a friend, knowing of my interest in the family, suggested I buy the Sunday edition of *The Times of India*. On page 2 I found classified advertisements under the heading "Matrimonials for Brides"; on page 4 were more ads under "Matrimonials for Grooms." For example:

> *High status business Sindhi family of Jaipur highly connected seeks suitable match for their two daughters both fair, homely, non-working, sophisticated, cultured, convent educated, 24 | 152 B.Sc. (Hon.) Diploma in textile designing & interior decoration, 22 | 167 M.Sc. early decent marriage, only well placed similar status families of well settled grooms caste no bar. Write Box 96825 Times of India, New Delhi-2.*

Here a well-to-do family advertises for husbands for their two daughters, one aged 24 and 152 centimeters (60 inches) tall and one aged 22 and 167 centimeters (66 inches) tall, making clear their ethnic origin (Sindhi), complexion (fair), and home (Jaipur). The daughters are college-educated but aren't working outside the home and apparently don't plan to. ("Homely" here means good in the home, not bad-looking.) And the parents are looking for matches only with sons of other

Families in Other Cultures

Parental Influence on Marriage in Thailand

In Angthong province, about 70 kilometers from Bangkok, Thailand, lies a land of rice fields, canals, and houses sitting on stilts 10 feet off the ground. When I visited there in 1985, the fields were dry and green. But during the rainy season, the canals flood and inundate the land, providing the necessary irrigation for rice growing. The families that owned these rice farms were relatively well off as peasants go: They had large, sturdy homes, plenty of food, electricity, and even some appliances. One household had a refrigerator sitting in the middle of the floor. At the movie theater in the market town, attendance was down, we were told, because too many families had VCRs. Traditionally, among these farm families, one of the daughters would remain in the home, take in a husband, and inherit the farm. Farm-owning parents were usually involved in helping their children select spouses because the future of their property—or of someone else's property that their sons might inherit through marriage—was involved. Unlike in some other Asian societies, such as China, Thai parents have never had sole control over whom their children marry, but often the decision is a joint one.

In fact, it is common for parents to exert a greater influence on their children's marriage choices when more wealth or land is involved.

In Angthong province, a survey carried out by my Thai collaborator showed that parents who did not own land had less influence over their children's marriage choices (Cherlin & Chamratrithirong, 1988). In fact, young adults whose parents were landless laborers were much more likely to "elope"—run away temporarily to a nearby village and then return, begging forgiveness from the woman's parents. On the face of it, parents have less influence over an elopement than over a planned wedding ceremony. Yet some of the poorest parents may have tacitly given their approval to an elopement, for it provided a face-saving alternative to an expensive ceremony, which many could not afford.

In another part of Thailand, an anthropologist found that the larger the size of the parents' farm, the more likely daughters were to be influenced by their parents' preferences about whom to marry. About two-thirds of married women from wealthier landowning families said that they and their parents had made the decision jointly or that their parents had made the decision for them. Among the poorest families only about one-third of married women reported any parental influence. Villagers often described wealthier families as "choosy" or "demanding" concerning marriage partners for their children (Podhisita, 1984). They were choosy because

they owned land they could pass along to their children. This legacy made their children more attractive as marriage partners, which encouraged the parents to find good matches—perhaps to the children of other well-off families. Moreover, in order to protect their children's legacy, they took care to ensure that their sons- or daughters-in-law would be reliable, competent workers. In other words, they were choosy because there was more at stake than was the case among poor, landless families. Even today, Thai villagers say that they pick spouses primarily on practical, not sentimental, grounds; although attractive looks and a good personality are appealing, they say it's more important that a prospective spouse have a reputation as a good, hard worker (Podhisita, 1984).

On the same trip, I also visited Slum Klong Toey, one of the oldest and largest squatter settlements in Bangkok. In this vast maze of pathways, I walked on wooden slats raised a few inches above pools of fetid water. Most dwellings were small one-room shacks of tarpaper, tin, or wood in which entire families lived. Although most had electricity, sanitary conditions were poor. The men sought work as porters, drivers, or similar kinds of unskilled laborers. A survey of the settlement revealed that one-third of the couples were cohabiting—living together without ever having a

high-status families. It is likely that the daughters themselves would have the right to refuse a particular offer. Americans, who are steeped in a more individualistic tradition, sometimes express surprise that young adults today would accept so much parental involvement. But many of my Indian and Pakistani acquaintances were pleased to leave most of the work of finding a spouse to their parents, who knew them well and spared them the anxiety their Western friends suffered over dating and courtship.

marriage ceremony. In contrast, a similar survey of the rice-farming villages in Angthong province found that only 7 percent of the couples were cohabiting. Living together without marrying was more common in the squatter settlement not because of loose morals but rather because there was nothing to inherit or acquire through marriage; it mattered much less who was morally or legally bound to whom.

The survey was also conducted in a prosperous, although not wealthy, established neighborhood in Bangkok. Parents had more influence over their children's marriages than in the squatter settlement, undoubtedly because there were once again more resources involved—not farmland but businesses, education, and savings. So it is not the case, then, that parents simply have more control over their children's marriages in "traditional" rather than "modern" settings. Prosperous Bangkok neighborhoods were more "modern," in terms of industrialization and urbanization, than Angthong province; yet similar proportions of young adults reported that their parents were involved in their choice of marriage partners. The case of Thailand suggests that landowning and prosperous urban parents can retain their influence over their children's marriages as nations develop economically; poor parents probably had less influence even before economic development.

In Thailand and other less-developed countries, prosperous urban and rural families have more influence over their children's choice of marriage partners than do poor families.

In general, parents take control of the matchmaking process when the choice of whom to marry is too important to them to be left to their children alone. In the past, as discussed in Chapter 2, a good marriage and many children were crucial to the survival of the household. A son who would inherit the farm needed a wife to help him and to have children who would provide more help. A woman needed to marry a man whose parents owned land, or whose relatives owned cattle, or who would inherit a trade. It is probable that throughout human history practical considerations have dominated the search for a spouse. I think it likely that only within the past 100 years in the Western nations—and within the past few decades in newly developed nations—has the standard of living improved so much that young adults have had the luxury of paying more attention to a partner's personality than to his or her industriousness or family worth.

Parental influence also erodes when children can find ways of making a living that don't depend on their parents' resources. In eighteenth-century Austria, the heir to the farm had no other good sources of income and couldn't marry without his father's permission. Often permission wasn't granted until the father retired. A folk song of the time expressed the frustration of the unmarried son:

> *Father when ya gonna gimme the farm,*
> *Father when ya gonna sign it away?*
> *My girl's been growin' every day,*
> *And single no longer wants to stay* (Berkner, 1972).

But as wage labor spread, sons could find paying jobs away from the farm, and they gained greater independence from their parents. Sometimes the transformation in marriage practices can occur with startling speed. This has been the case in the rapidly industrializing nations of East Asia, where strong parental influence has been eroded over a generation or two. (See the *Families in Other Cultures:* World Revolution and Family Patterns, in Chapter 16.)

In the American colonies, the influence of parents seemed to decline in the mid- to late 1700s. Recall from Chapter 2 that historian Philip Greven found that prior to the late 1700s, sons in Andover, Massachusetts, married at later ages than their fathers. The later marriage occurred, he argued, because sons had to wait until their fathers turned over control of the family farm. By the late 1700s, when commercial capitalism began to provide alternative job opportunities, the marriage ages of sons declined (Greven, 1970). Similarly, Daniel Scott Smith found evidence in the records of Hingham, Massachusetts, that, prior to 1700, daughters were more likely to have married in the order of their birth (i.e., the eldest married before the second eldest). This pattern suggested that parents were finding husbands for their daughters one at a time. After about 1750, marriages out of birth order became more common (Smith, 1973). Smith took this as evidence of a decline in parental influence.

COURTSHIP AND DATING

ANGLO-AMERICAN COURTSHIP

By the 1800s, then, most young adults in the United States at least shared with their parents the responsibility for choosing a spouse. Indeed, young adults from the lower economic classes probably had substantial autonomy because there was little property for parents to worry about. (Among the upper classes, parents undoubtedly retained a stronger role.) Young people went about finding a spouse through courtship, a process that had been developed in Europe. **Courtship** is a publicly visible process with rules and restrictions through which young men and women find a partner to marry. The words *publicly visible* emphasize the important role of the community—and, in particular, parents—in

In the nineteenth century, young women and men went about choosing spouses through a publicly visible, and publicly supervised, process of courtship.

watching over, and participating in, the courting a young adult does. For instance, in early modern Britain, the first stages of courtship occurred mainly outdoors, in plain view of peers and kin (Gillis, 1985). By and large, it was acceptable for casually acquainted young men and young women to be seen together only at public events such as festivals, games, or dances, and even then only in groups. At dances young people changed partners so frequently that no couple spent too much time together.

The words *rules and restrictions* emphasize the close adherence to well-established ways of acting. British courtship, for example, followed a carefully prescribed path from "talking" to "walking" in public places and then to "keeping company." Only when the couple became more serious did they begin seeing each other outside public, group settings. Typically, they moved on to night visiting, whereby a young man would call upon a young woman at her home. At first, there was little intimacy and privacy in these formal visits. Suitors often brought along a male friend to ease the potential awkwardness and embarrassment of the situation. The young woman's parents would be present in the home, although they might discreetly retire to bed. If the visits continued, a certain amount of kissing and fondling was permitted, but nothing more. Until a couple became betrothed (engaged), they were not allowed much privacy or sexual intimacy.

According to historical studies, American courtship, like British courtship, retained this basic character through the mid-1800s. (The historical studies, unfortunately, tell us little about the poor, African Americans, or immigrants, who left few diaries and letters.) The first phase of courtship still took place at out-of-home events such as picnics, sleigh rides, and church socials. In a later phase, young men called at the homes of young women. Yet there were subtle changes over time. Most notably, the role of love increased. In the 1500s and 1600s, love was an emotion people distrusted in selecting a spouse. To be sure, it was desirable to choose a partner whom you might grow to love after you were married, but more practical considerations—inheritance of land, strength, health—should guide your choice. By the 1800s, however, young adults wanted to love their partners before they married them (Rothman, 1984). Even so, love had a different meaning than it has today, as Maud Rittenhouse's diary showed. Young people were wary of passion, which was seen as wild and uncontrollable and therefore dangerous as a basis for a long-term relationship. Love was defined more in terms of sympathy, openness, candor, and understanding than of passion. Thus, Maud rejected her romantic love for Robert in favor of responsible Elmer.

This centuries-old system of courtship met its demise after 1900. Its decline in the United States was linked to great social and economic changes: migration from rural areas (and from overseas) to cities, the rise of industrial capitalism, higher standards of living, and the lengthening of adolescence. As more and more people moved to cities and worked in factories and offices, the number of potential partners and the places where they could meet grew. Consequently, it became harder for parents to monitor and oversee the process. And as standards of living rose, it became possible for young adults to keep some of their earnings or to receive allowances from their parents. Thus, young people began to accumulate a key resource: spending money. The city provided plenty of places to spend it, most notably the movie theater and the dance hall. Rising standards of living also allowed many families to buy an automobile. This marvel of technology let young couples wander far from home; it also gave them a private place for necking (kissing) and petting (touching below the neck). As a result, courtship, in the words of historian Beth Bailey, went from "front porch to back seat" (Bailey, 1988).

Finally, a new view of the teenage years arose: They were seen as a time during which teens needed to develop their personalities and capabilities free of the pressures of the adult world. In an influential 1904 book, psychologist G. Stanley Hall popularized the term "adolescence" for this newly recognized stage of life (Hall, 1904). Attention to adolescence emerged as child labor laws restricted how much younger teenagers could work and as more prosperous middle-class families no longer needed their children to work. Moreover, it arose as changes in the economy made it clear to parents that children needed at least a high school education in order to obtain better-paying jobs. Consequently, adolescence was embodied most clearly in the high school, which removed teenagers from the world of adults. Not until the early decades of the twentieth century did a majority of teenagers enroll in high school. College enrollments also increased early in the century and then skyrocketed after World War II. The high school and college years gave adolescents a protected time in which they could create and participate in their own subculture, relatively free of parental involvement.

THE RISE (AND FALL?) OF DATING

What evolved, then, after the turn of the twentieth century was a new system of courtship based on dating. Although some might think that dating has been around for a long time, it was rare until 1900 or so, and the term was not even used until then. The spirit of the change was captured in a 1924 short story in *Harper's* magazine. A man comes calling at the home of a young woman, expecting to spend the evening in her parlor. But when she opens the door, she has her hat on—a clear sign that she expects to go out.[4] As the story suggests, suddenly a young man was expected to take a young woman somewhere on a date—which meant he had to spend money. A firm rule of the dating system was that the young man paid the expenses. In return, he enjoyed the company of the young woman. Dating placed courtship on an economic basis. Young men provided goods such as movie tickets or restaurant meals in exchange for companionship and, often, necking and petting. Through these rules, argues Bailey, dating shifted the balance of power in courtship from women to men (Bailey, 1988). Under the old system, women received men in their own homes, at times they chose, and usually with their parents nearby. (During a girl's first season of receiving callers, her mother might initially invite the young men.) Now the evening was initiated and controlled by males, and it depended on cash earnings, which favored men over women.

Dating also shifted power from parents to teenagers and young adults. The movement of activity away from public gatherings and the home made it much harder for parents to influence the process. Rather, adolescents became oriented toward the dating system of their peer group—the other adolescents in the local school or neighborhood. With the triumph of dating, courtship moved from a parent- and other-adult-run system to a peer-run system where the participants made the rules and punished the offenders.

By the 1920s, sexual activity was more common, although intercourse was still rare. Some parents were alarmed at the apparent spread of necking and petting, which became a central part of the youth culture of dating. Popular accounts warned of the spread of "petting parties" among high school students, and adults sought unsuccessfully to stop them (Rothman, 1984). Colleges wielded parentlike authority through residence and visiting rules. Sometimes their efforts at control verged on the comic: In 1947, the dean of Northwestern University decreed that any mixed group of more than two people listening to the Michigan-Northwestern football game on the radio must register as a "party" and have an appropriate number of approved chaperons (Bailey, 1988).

Nearly all the efforts to control sexual activity centered on women. For although men initiated attempts at necking or petting (which they were expected to do in the dating culture), no one blamed them. Instead, it was seen as women's responsibility to stop them; if a young man wasn't stopped, it was his date's fault. Girls who complained of boys' advances were asked to consider whether they might somehow be encouraging them. Consistent with the cult of true womanhood, young women were seen as the repositories of virtue and morality; it was their responsibility to tame the wild impulses of men, who couldn't stop themselves. The author of a 1945 courtship manual for women wrote, "a man is only as bad as the woman he is with."[5]

Some observers complained that dating had become a crass competition for status among high school and college students, in which the objectives were popularity rather than finding a partner to marry. Personality and physical attractiveness, not openness and understanding, had become the most valued characteristics, it was said. Willard Waller argued in 1937 that dating on college campuses was so unrelated to finding a partner that it was merely "thrill-seeking behavior" rather than true courtship. College students, he wrote, had fallen under the spell of a "rating and dating complex" in which prestige was enhanced by good clothes,

---

[4]This story is cited in both Rothman (1984) and Bailey (1988). It is cited by Bailey as Black (1924).
[5]Quoted in Bailey (1988).

The dating system probably peaked in the 1940s and 1950s, when college enrollments rose and young adults married at earlier ages than at any other time in the twentieth century.

dancing skills, and dating popularity (Waller, 1937). Elements of Waller's critique rang true, but Rothman has argued that less exploitative relationships coexisted with rating and dating on campus and were common among the larger number of youths who didn't attend college (Rothman, 1984). There also were some racial and ethnic variations. Among African-American youths in the 1920s, for instance, the dating system appears to have been less elaborate and less entrenched, with relative sexual freedom for boys but not for girls (Modell, 1989). And because African Americans married at earlier ages, on average, than whites during the first half of the twentieth century, relationships between young black women and men were more directly tied to marriage (Cherlin, 1992b).

The dating system probably had its heyday in the 20-year period—1945 to 1965—after World War II. Throughout the period, college enrollments rose sharply and most young adults at least completed high school. Postwar parents had grown up in the dating system, and so there was less parent–child disagreement about it than had been the case in the 1920s and 1930s. At the same time, young people in the 1950s may have started to date earlier than their parents.[6] In a national survey of high school students conducted in 1960, about two-thirds of all boys and three-fourths of all girls stated that they had begun to date by grade 9; virtually all had dated by grade 12 (Modell, 1989).[7]

[6]Both Bailey and Rothman suggest that adolescents began to date at younger ages in the 1950s. But when a random sample of Detroit-area women in 1984 was asked to recall when they had begun to date, there was little difference in the responses of those who had married before the war versus after the war; see Whyte (1990).
[7]The data came from the Project Talent survey of 4,000 high school students nationwide.

What did alarm adults was the growth of "going steady," in which a boy and girl agree to date only each other. Previously common only among older, seriously involved couples, going steady was found in the 1950s among very young couples as well. According to the 1960 high school survey, a majority of 10th-grade girls and 11th-grade boys had gone steady at least once; two-thirds of the girls had done so by 12th grade (Modell, 1989). Adults, most of whom had not gone steady as adolescents, feared that adolescents were settling down too soon and that going steady, by withdrawing the couple from the dating competition, would prevent adolescents from finding an appropriate partner. They also feared it would lead to more premarital sex. Yet their fears proved groundless; rates of premarital intercourse did not rise sharply until a decade or two later. Whereas teenagers saw going steady as security, adults saw it as a premature commitment. And in the early-marrying postwar period, adolescents who went steady were, in fact, more likely to marry early—although their spouse was not necessarily a high school sweetheart. When the 1960 national sample of high school students was reinterviewed in 1971, 59 percent of the girls who had gone steady by 12th grade had married before age 21 compared with just 27 percent of those who had not gone steady (Modell, 1989).

Many of these concerns about dating seemed less important by the 1970s and 1980s, for by then the dating system had become less closely connected to marriage. As the average age at marriage soared into the mid-twenties, steady dating in high school seemed more and more remote from serious attempts to find a spouse. What's more, cohabitation, perhaps a new stage of courtship, became a common event in young adults' lives prior to marriage. Also, the sharp rise in premarital intercourse for teenage boys and girls demonstrated that the dating system was increasingly ineffective in holding sexual activity to petting. Adolescents may have begun to socialize more often in larger, mixed-sex groups (Modell, 1989). To be sure, dating remained a part of youth culture, but it became less formal and less tied to marriage. And the old limitations on sexual activity were greatly weakened.

THE SOCIOLOGY OF COURTSHIP

Waller's scathing critique of dating is still the best-known attempt by sociologists to dig beneath the surface of the courtship system. He also noticed a power imbalance in dating relationships: The partner who is less interested in the relationship has more power because he or she could more easily leave it. This, Waller wrote, is the **principle of least interest**. His insight presages later, more general principles advanced by sociological exchange theorists such as Richard Emerson and social psychologists such as Harold Kelley. In an interaction, according to Emerson, the person who has fewer alternative sources of satisfaction is dependent on the other person. It seems reasonable to conclude that, in a relationship, the more interested partner cannot as easily find equally satisfying alternatives. Therefore the more interested partner becomes dependent, and the less interested partner gains some power over her or him (Emerson, 1972).[8]

After midcentury, sociologists devoted less time to critiques and more time to developing general "theories" of courtship. These so-called **courtship stage theories** attempted to describe the stages of courtship that young adults must follow if

---

[8]See the discussion below of Harold H. Kelley's related concept of the comparison level for alternatives among partners in a relationship.

TABLE 8.1 STAGE THEORIES OF COURTSHIP			
STAGE	REISS'S WHEEL THEORY OF LOVE	MURSTEIN'S STIMULUS-VALUE-ROLE MODEL	LEWIS'S PREMARITAL DYADIC FORMATION FRAMEWORK
Initial	Rapport: ease of understanding and communication	Stimulus: physical attractiveness, reputation, etc.	Perceiving similarities: common background or interests
			Achieving pair rapport: ease of communication, etc.
Intermediate	Self-revelation: revealing values and beliefs	Value comparison: self-disclosure; search for common values	Inducing self-disclosure: revealing values and beliefs
Final	Mutual dependency: developing reliance on each other	Role: assessing compatibility of marital roles	Role-taking: ability to place oneself in other's role
	Intimacy need fulfillment: does relationship meet need for closeness and intimacy?		Achieving interpersonal role fit
			Achieving dyadic crystallization: commitment, identification as a couple

their relationship is to result in marriage. In their attempt to identify the basic stages of the courtship system and the functions these stages fulfilled, their work was similar to the dominant theoretical tradition in postwar American sociology, the functionalism of Talcott Parsons and others.[9] That is, the theorists tried to describe the set of rules that governed how people went about finding a spouse and then to explain why this way of finding a spouse worked well for the young adults and for society.

The stage theories of courtship all defined plausible sequences of events that begin with initial attraction, proceed to openness and self-disclosure, and move to mutual dependence. Table 8.1 presents the stages in three of the best-known theories of this type: Ira Reiss's wheel theory of love, Bernard Murstein's stimulus-value-role model of marital choice, and R. A. Lewis's premarital dyadic formation framework (Reiss, 1960; Murstein, 1970; Lewis, 1972).[10] The stages can be thought of as a sequence of questions that must be answered positively if a marriage is to result. The basic questions in the initial stage of these models are as follows: Is s/he someone I might be interested in? Can we get along well together? In the initial stage, my interest might be stimulated by someone's physical attractiveness; class, ethnic, or religious background; or earning power. How well we get along might be determined by how easy I find the other person to talk with or by the reaction I get from the other person when I open up about my interests, values, and beliefs. The basic question in the intermediate stages is: Can we help and support each other? I answer it by observing whether I've come to depend on and provide support to the other person in ways that meet my needs. The question in

[9]For Parsons' writings on the family, see Parsons (1942) and Parsons and Bales (1955).
[10]For a more comprehensive discussion of sociological theories of courtship, see Cate and Lloyd (1992).

the final stage is whether the relationship meets my expectations for intimacy and support—is it enough? If my partner and I answer all these questions affirmatively, we may make a long-term commitment to each other.

Although these models have a certain commonsense validity, they have limitations as social scientific theories. It is not clear, as others have observed, just what specifically constitutes a stage, how many there are, and how an observer can tell when a transition has been made from one stage to the next one.[11] The theories assume that a great deal of verbal communication occurs; consequently, they are more useful for studying relationships between highly educated, verbal persons than between less-well-educated individuals. These theories also ignore external events. If, for example, jobs are not available because of an economic depression, all the compatibility and emotional support in the world may not be enough to induce a couple to marry. (Marriage rates declined in the Great Depression of the 1930s for this reason.) Moreover, the stage theories apply best to a dating situation in which committed couples are expected to go directly from dating to engagement and marriage and in which sexual intercourse is restricted to engaged or married couples. That was the usual situation in the 1950s and early 1960s. But the introduction of the birth control pill, the great increases in premarital intercourse, the difficult employment situation of young men, the increasing economic independence of women, and the sharp rise in cohabitation have all changed the nature of the relationship between unmarried partners.

In fact, upon reviewing this body of research, one has the sense that the sociological study of dating and courtship in the 1960s and 1970s was overtaken by events and is no longer the most useful way to study the close relationships young adults form. Indeed, an interdisciplinary group of researchers has been developing frameworks for studying close relationships that are more broadly conceived.[12] These approaches see relationships as more fluid, more prone to ups and downs and unexpected changes than the stage theories suggest. They study the individuals (both separately and as a couple), their social networks, and the environments they live in. In their theoretical approach, they assume that individuals make rational choices about relationships based on the costs and rewards they would bring. The benefits might include companionship, sexual satisfaction, or a partner's income, whereas the costs might include a partner's excessive drinking or periods of unemployment.

Moreover, these choices are said to depend, in part, on an individual's **comparison level for alternatives**—the level of satisfaction that a person thinks she or he could find in other relationships. It represents the ease with which a person in a relationship (or considering one) could find equally satisfying partners (Kelley, 1979).[13] A person with a lower comparison level for alternatives has fewer attractive options outside the relationship. She or he may be more likely to accept someone who isn't beautiful or whose income isn't substantial. Therefore, she or he is more likely to enter a relationship with a plain-looking partner or with someone whose income is mediocre. Once in a relationship, this person is less likely to leave it than is someone with a higher comparison level. The emphasis on alternatives harks back to Waller's principle of least interest: The person with more alternatives is less committed to the relationship and, according to Waller, has more power within it.

[11]This critique is developed in Cate and Lloyd (1992).
[12]See, for example, Kelley et al. (1983).
[13]The concept was first developed in Thibaut & Kelley (1959).

INDEPENDENT LIVING

The dating and courtship model assumes that most young adults will be living in their parents' homes and receiving at least some supervision from them. Historically, that was the case: At the start of the twentieth century, a lower standard of living, a shortage of housing for single people, and the predominant values of the time precluded almost all young adults from living independently of their parents until they married. Even at midcentury, many young adults did not leave home until they married. But since then, an increasingly larger percentage of single young adults have moved into apartments or homes, either by themselves or with roommates. In 1950, 15 percent of 18- to 24-year-olds were unmarried and living independently of their parents; by 1980 the comparable figure was 26 percent (Goldscheider, 1997).

The trend toward independent living reflected the generally rising standard of living during the twentieth century. One hundred years ago, most single young adults helped support their families by turning over their wages to their parents; today it is common—even expected—for young adults to keep their wages. In addition, the rise in independent living was consistent with the broader growth of individualism in the twentieth century, which uncoupled sexual activity from marriage for young adults (see Chapter 7). The increase in divorce also spurred independent living: Studies have shown that adolescents whose parents divorce, and in particular those whose parents divorce and remarry, leave home sooner than adolescents whose biological parents remain married (Cherlin, Kiernan, & Chase-Lansdale, 1995).

In addition, since midcentury the average age at first marriage has risen substantially (see Chapter 2). Consequently, it has become common for young adults to set up an independent household years before they marry. But young adults who live independently are more likely to return to their parents' homes than are young adults who marry. (Usually, married young adults will only return if their marriages dissolve). Frances Goldscheider (1997) calculated that, since the 1950s, the odds that a young adult who left the parental home would return have increased by more than 50 percent. Parents whose children move out have learned to expect that the children may move back in if, for example, they lose their jobs. Some of the unmarried, independent young adults are, in fact, cohabiting, as will be discussed later in the chapter. But cohabiting relationships have higher rates of dissolution than do marriages, and young adults who end cohabiting relationships are more likely to return home than are young adults who end marriages (Goldscheider & Goldscheider, 1994).

WHO MARRIES WHOM

At midcentury, for most young adults, dating and courtship led directly to marriage. Today, many will live with a partner before marrying. Others will have a child prior to marrying and then live with or marry someone else. Later in this chapter, the increases in cohabitation and in births to teenagers outside marriage will be discussed. It is still the case, however, that about 90 percent of whites and 70 to 75 percent of African Americans are projected to marry eventually (see Chapter 5). What kinds of people they marry, and how their social and economic environment affects their choices of spouses, has been a topic of much social scientific research. The literature describes the type of bargain that most prospective spouses used to make at midcentury: Men specialized in work for pay and women specialized in unpaid work at home. Among the poor, that bargain usually was not possible; rather, it was necessary to pool the earnings of both the husband and the wife (and often the children also) to obtain enough money to live on. Recent studies suggest that the bargain has now changed for the nonpoor too.

THE MARRIAGE MARKET

When sociologists and economists study who marries whom, they often make an analogy with the labor market, in which people seeking employment look for employers who will hire them at an acceptable wage. In the **marriage market**, unmarried individuals (or their parents) search for others who will marry them (or their children). Instead of an acceptable wage, the searchers require that a partner have an acceptable set of desired characteristics, such as a college education, good looks, a pleasant disposition, and so forth.

There are three components to this market model of marriage. The first component is simply a group of people who are actively looking for a spouse at the same place at the same time. They constitute the *supply* of men and women who are in the marriage market. The second component is *preferences*. Each person has an idea of his or her own preferred characteristics in a spouse. Some people may care more about good looks, others more about personality or earning potential. A person will try to find a mate who ranks as high as possible on the characteristics she or he prefers. And that same person will probably have a minimum set of characteristics that she or he will accept. The third component is *resources*. These are the characteristics a person possesses that are attractive to others. In a sense resources are the flip side of preferences: Resources are what I have that a partner might want; preferences are what I want a partner to have.

So people who are looking for spouses, who have preferences about the qualities they want, and who have resources to offer create a marriage market. To be sure, it is difficult in real life to decide just who is looking for a spouse and who isn't. Moreover, this depiction of searchers as rational, calculating individuals who tote up the pluses and minuses of prospects is at odds with the popular image of people falling in love with each other. Clearly, the market metaphor can't explain everything about who marries whom. Nevertheless, in the aggregate, the behavior of unmarried persons resembles that of job searchers enough that the metaphor is useful.[14]

Sometimes preferences and resources are so incompatible that the market can't provide acceptable spouses for all who are looking. The most extreme case occurs when there is a great imbalance in the number of men and women. Demographers define the **sex ratio** as the number of males in a population compared with the number of females. Frontier areas, such as the nineteenth-century American West, are often heavily populated at first by male migrants. Because the sex ratio was so high in the American West, many of these settlers could not find spouses. Some contracted through the mail with matchmakers who, for a fee, sent mail-order brides out west. In most instances, though, the marriage market is local. Men and women find spouses in their communities through friends, family, college, or work.

More recently, attention has been drawn to a shortage of black men with good jobs in central cities. As discussed in Chapter 5, marriage rates have dropped

---

[14]The job search analogy has been carried furthest by Oppenheimer (1988).

dramatically for African Americans. One explanation is that decent-paying industrial jobs—making steel or cars or television sets—have moved to suburban plants or to firms in developing countries, so that men without college educations (and African-American men are less likely to have attended college) have a harder time finding a job that can support a family. Therefore African-American women, so this argument goes, can't find enough employed African-American men to marry (Wilson, 1987). Recent studies have indeed found that women's marriage rates are lower in areas where more men were unemployed, although the effect has not been large enough to fully explain racial differences in marriage patterns.[15] As Chapter 5 noted, high levels of homicide, imprisonment, and drug use also remove some black men from the marriage market.

In most marriage markets, men tend to be older than the women they marry. This custom was important in agricultural societies, in which children provided needed labor. Since a woman's capacity to bear children declines with age, it was advantageous for men and their relatives to prefer younger women, who could bear more children. In many preindustrial Asian societies, age differences were commonly 5, and sometimes 10, years. A family could make a better match for a young daughter; her value in the market decreased as she grew older. In preindustrial Europe, where land was more limited, very large families were not as advantageous. Consequently, young men and women both married later, and the age gap was perhaps three to five years, on average (Hajnal, 1982).

Now that the average married couple has only about two children, there is no longer a strong biological reason for wives to be younger than husbands. Single men still typically pay more attention to physical attractiveness, which may be a marker for the youth and health of a person, than single women.[16] This preference reflects the high value placed on women's attractive appearance in our society. A 1986 research study that provoked a national uproar demonstrated that marriage probabilities still decline as women age (See *Families and Public Policy: The "Harvard-Yale Study"*). Nevertheless, the age gap should be eroding, and government statistics—although not up-to-date—suggest that it slowly is. In the United States in 1970, the bride was older than the groom in 12 percent of all first marriages; by 1988, 20 percent of brides were older.[17]

THE CHANGING MARRIAGE BARGAIN

In fact, over the past several generations, at least, men have placed a greater emphasis on the physical attractiveness of their spouses than women; conversely, women have placed a greater emphasis on the earning potential of their spouses (Buss, 1985). This difference fit the predominant marriage bargain at midcentury, in which men worked outside the home and women specialized in home work and emotional support. It is the bargain hailed in the writings of Parsons and his associates in the 1950s, as noted in Chapter 1. It is also the bargain implied by the theory of the division of labor advanced by economist Gary Becker, whose theoretical work since the 1960s pioneered the economic approach to studying the family.[18]

---

[15]See, for example, Lichter, Le Clere, and McLaughlin (1991).

[16]See Figure 8.3 and the associated discussion later in the chapter.

[17]For marriages in which neither the bride nor the groom had been married previously. Personal communication from Barbara Wilson, U.S. National Center for Health Statistics.

[18]See Becker (1991).

Becker drew his model from the theory of international trade, under which each country is said to have a "comparative advantage" in producing particular goods relative to other countries. For example, a poor, underdeveloped country with land and farmers but few schools and factories might be able to produce grain more "efficiently" (meaning cheaply) than tractors. In contrast, a developed country such as the United States, with its assembly-line factories and skilled workers, may be able to produce tractors (and other manufactured goods) more efficiently than grain. If so, according to the theory, each country will benefit if the underdeveloped country specializes in producing grain, some of which it can trade for tractors, and the developed country specializes in producing tractors, some of which it can trade for grain. Becker's application of this model to the family is straightforward: If women are more "efficient" at housework and childcare relative to earning money—either because they are better at caring for children or because they tend to be paid less than men—and men are more efficient at earning money rather than at housework and childcare, both will benefit if the wife specializes in housework and childcare and the husband specializes in paid work outside the home. Consequently, the model predicts that in the marriage market women will search for good providers and men will search for good homemakers. We might call this the **specialization model** of the marriage market.

Becker and his followers rarely examined any evidence on whether women actually are more efficient in housework and childcare than men. Nor did they explain why women might earn less in the labor force, except to suggest that women's wages are lower because they spend more time caring for children and therefore invest less in their careers. Rather, these social conditions—women are better at homemaking, men get paid more—were taken as given and not subject to much change; so was a cultural climate in which it was expected that married women with children should stay at home. In addition, Becker's theory assumes that the husband and wife are producers of a joint enterprise—their home and family—and that their preferences are identical. That is to say, a particular division of labor that makes the husband happier will make the wife equally happier.[19] Yet studies of the internal economy of the family suggest that husbands' and wives' preferences aren't identical.[20] Nevertheless, the predictions of the model fit the typical outcome of the marriage market at midcentury.

More recently, however, a number of studies have shown that the specialization model no longer fits the marriage market well. A set of questions in the 1987–1988 National Survey of Families and Households (NSFH) allows us to gauge the marriage preferences of women and men in the United States. Figure 8.3 (see page 254) displays the answers of unmarried white men and women aged 19 to 35, as analyzed by Scott South. Each person was asked to rate his or her willingness to marry someone with a particular characteristic on a scale of 1 to 7, with 7 indicating the most willing. The average scores are shown for five characteristics. The gender differences are as one might expect: Women are more willing to marry someone five or more years older, whereas men are more willing to marry someone five or more years younger. Women are more willing to marry someone who is not good-looking. Men are more willing to marry someone who is earning much less.

But note that neither women nor men are especially willing to marry someone who is not likely to hold a steady job. To be sure, women are less willing than

---

[19]Some more recent work allows for different preferences among husbands and wives. See Thomas (1990).
[20]See Chapter 10.

Families and Public Policy

The "Harvard-Yale Study"

As will be discussed in Chapter 9, there is concern among politicians and social commentators about a perceived decline of marriage. Do Americans care about getting married any more? A famous incident in 1986—well after the divorce rate had peaked (see Chapter 12) and the marriage rate had fallen—suggests that most do. On February 13, 1986, a reporter from the Stamford, Connecticut, *Advocate* called sociologist Neil Bennett at Yale University in New Haven. She told him she was writing a Valentine's Day article on love in Fairfield County and asked if he had any information on the state of marriage. The request seemed innocuous enough at the time, but the news story that followed ignited a public uproar that revealed Americans' ambivalent feelings about marriage and the family.[1]

Professor Bennett and his colleagues David Bloom, then at Harvard, and Patricia Craig at Yale had been studying the rates at which black and white women with varying levels of education married. As part of the project, they had developed projections of the proportion of young, single, college-educated women who would eventually marry. Bennett retrieved some results from a discussion paper and read them to the reporter. Current marriage behavior, he said, implied that white women who were college graduates and still single at age 30 would have only a 20 percent chance of ever marrying; those who remained single until age 35 would have only a 5 percent chance; and at age 40 the chance would be a mere 1 percent.

Recognizing a good story, the reporter incorporated Bennett's projections into her article, which ran on page one the next day. An Associated Press reporter read the story and sent a dispatch over their national wire. The next day Bennett's figures were printed in newspapers across the country.

The reaction was spectacular. The "Harvard-Yale Study," as it came to be known, struck a nerve among single women everywhere. It seemed to show that for young female professionals, marriage postponed too long was marriage forgone. Bennett's findings were discussed on talk shows, analyzed in opinion columns, and noted on the network news in a crescendo of public attention that peaked on June 2 when, in an apparent first for social science, a graph drawn from the collaborators' discussion paper appeared on the cover of *Newsweek*. Its downward slope showed, in the magazine's memorable words, that a 40-year-old woman's probability of marrying was so low that she was "more likely to be killed by a terrorist."[2]

Subsequently, demographers at the U.S. Bureau of the Census produced somewhat higher estimates of the probability of marriage for college-educated women: 58 to 66 percent for those single at age 30, and 17 to 23 percent for those single at age 40. These more optimistic results, reported in the newspapers in August, were greeted with a collective sigh of relief by anxious commentators. During the following year or two, Bennett's group and the Census Bureau demographers debated who had the better estimates. It is likely that the true percentages will prove to be higher than Bennett's original figures but lower than the Census Bureau's figures.

Yet to analyze the Harvard-Yale Study in terms of its statistics is to miss the main point. Ultimately, the entire sequence of events will be remembered not for the debate over the precise numbers reported in the study but rather for the depth of the public reaction. After all, we live in a society in which a large majority of young adults have sexual relations prior to marriage (Forrest & Singh, 1989; Sonenstein, Pleck, & Ku, 1989). It is a society in which, as noted elsewhere in this chapter, about half of all young adults live with a partner before marrying and more than 3 out of 10 children are born to an unmarried mother. Therefore, it was surprising to find, in a

men; but even men are more willing, on average, to marry someone who is not good-looking or who is older, than they are willing to marry someone who is unlikely to hold a job. South's analyses also showed that black men were even less willing to marry a woman with poor economic prospects. Among African-American couples, low incomes have long made two-job marriages acceptable and often necessary (Cherlin, 1992b).

The specialization model predicts that women with less education and lower earnings will be *more* likely to marry than better-educated, higher-earning women.

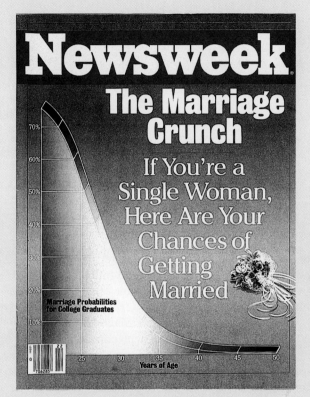

FIGURE 8.A In 1986, *Newsweek* displayed on its cover a graph from the controversial "Harvard-Yale Study" showing that the probability that a woman will ever marry declines sharply with age.

society in which sexual relations among unmarried adults are accepted, cohabiting unions are becoming the norm, and births outside of marriage are increasingly common, that so many people cared about the probability of marriage.

As I argued in analyzing the Hawaii gay marriage case in Chapter 1, Americans seem to be ambivalent about marriage. The Harvard-Yale Study, like the gay marriage case, suggests that marriage remains important to most people despite the recent trends. It is still a valued status that most young adults want to attain, even as they have sex and cohabit prior to marrying. To be sure, it is not as necessary to be married as it was in the 1950s, when nearly everyone married and married young (see Chapter 2). But for most people it is still desirable to marry. And, as Bennett, Bloom, and Craig learned, the suggestion that it might be too late get married can cause considerable anguish.

[1]This account is drawn from my article, Cherlin (1990).
[2]Bloom later told me that he had come across readers who had believed that line literally.

The former group, it is said, have more to gain by marrying a man who will earn money while they specialize in housework and childcare. But several studies have now found evidence that, on average, women with less education and lower earnings are *less* likely to marry than better-educated, higher-earning women. In contrast to the specialization model, it is women with higher earning potential who have higher rates of marriage, other things being equal, for white and nonwhite women, poor and nonpoor women alike (Lichter, McLaughlin, Kephart, & Landry, 1992; Qian & Preston, 1993; Oppenheimer, Blossfeld, & Wackerow, 1995; Oppenheimer

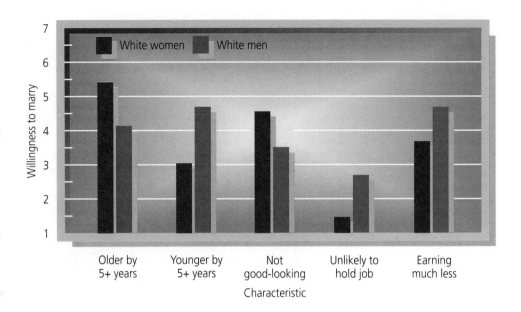

FIGURE 8.3

Willingness to marry someone with a given characteristic, for unmarried women and men ages 19 to 35: (*A*) Older than you by five or more years. (*B*) Younger than you by five or more years. (*C*) Not "good-looking." (*D*) Not likely to hold a steady job. (*E*) Earning much less. (*Source:* South, 1991.)

& Lew, 1995; McLaughlin & Lichter, 1997.) One study compares data for young adults in the 1970s and 1980s and finds that the specialization model was supported in the earlier decade not the later one (Sweeney, 1997); so perhaps the model did hold as recently as the 1970s.

It appears, then, that the marriage bargain now includes the preference, for most couples, that both spouses will contribute to the family's income. Why has this change occurred? In part, it reflects the greater acceptance of married women's work outside the home (see Figure 4.4). In addition, it reflects the prolonged stagnation of men's wages since the early 1970s. As noted in Chapter 4, there has been a decline in the wage levels of young men without a college education. Valerie Oppenheimer has argued that this decline has reduced the willingness of young adults to marry. In one paper, she and her co-authors (Oppenheimer, Kalmijn, & Lim, 1997) present evidence that young men with low earnings and a pattern of what she terms *stopgap employment*—short-term, often part-time jobs (such as fast-food worker) that aren't part of a career path—are less likely to marry than are men with better economic prospects. Her article implies (although it doesn't present direct evidence) that an increase in stopgap employment—and the delay it causes young men in attaining steady work at higher wages—may be a factor in the rising age at marriage.

MARITAL SIMILARITY

The now-fading difference in the importance men and women placed on the earning capacity of their spouses was an exception to the general rule that people have a strong tendency to marry others with similar social characteristics. These characteristics include education, race, and religion (Buss, 1985). Sociologists refer to this as marital homogamy; I will use the plain term **marital similarity**, which adequately captures the meaning. In the United States in the twentieth century, marital similarity has increased for some characteristics and decreased for others. In the 1920s, according to a recent estimate, a Protestant person was 47 times more likely to marry a Protestant than a Catholic person was to marry a Protestant, other things being equal. Yet, by the 1980s, a Protestant person was just four times more likely to marry a

Most people still marry others whose characteristics, such as racial-ethnic identity, are similar to theirs.

Protestant than a Catholic person was to marry a Protestant, reflecting a decline in the religious similarity of spouses (Kalmijn, 1991a). (These estimates were limited to white Christians because the number of blacks and Jews was too small for analysis.) In contrast, men and women—especially college graduates—are more likely to marry someone with a similar amount of education than was the case 50 years ago (Mare, 1991; Kalmijn, 1991). My guess is that college students today would think it much more acceptable to marry a college-educated person of a different religion than a high school graduate of the same religion. Yet early in the century it was more common for a college-educated person to marry a less educated person of the same religion than to marry a college-educated person of a different religion.

These and other studies suggest the decreasing importance in the marriage market of characteristics that people are typically assigned at birth, such as religion and father's occupation (Kalmijn, 1991). Correspondingly, there has been an increase in the importance of characteristics that people achieve through their own efforts, such as education (although a person's education depends in part on how much education her or his parents have). Cohabiting unions exhibit the same tendencies in exaggerated form: In the NSFH, cohabitors were even more likely than married persons to have chosen a partner with the same education and less likely to have chosen one with the same religion (Schoen & Weinick, 1993). Sociologists have long theorized that as Western societies have developed—as they increasingly comprised wage labor, markets for goods and services, individualistic values, and loyalties beyond the family—the importance of characteristics society assigns to people has decreased and the importance of characteristics people can achieve on their own has increased. In other words, it matters less in what circumstances you were born and more what you manage to accomplish. Trends in marital similarity largely, but not completely, fit this model. The notable exception is intermarriage between African

Americans and other groups, which is dampened by the historic racial barrier in the United States. Even in this case, however, intermarriage is increasing. In 1990, 96 percent of African-American wives were married to African-American husbands (down from 99 percent in 1980); and 92 percent of African-American husbands were married to African-American wives (down from 95 percent in 1980; Qian, 1997).

COHABITATION

But it is no longer adequate to study marriage versus singlehood as if they were the only two statuses young adults can choose. Rather, an examination of how people pick partners in the United States must now include **cohabitation**, a living arrangement in which two adults who are not married to each other and who have a sexual relationship share the same house or apartment. To judge from the number of cohabiting couples', at least half of young adults and many older adults approve of, or at least tolerate, cohabitation. This represents a great change in attitudes from the 1950s and early 1960s, when few middle-class Americans tolerated cohabitation. It's not possible to provide evidence from opinion polls to back up that statement, because no pollster in the 1950s ever thought to ask Americans whether they approved of couples' living together outside marriage. Had the question been asked, however, the vast majority would have disapproved.

As noted earlier, cohabitation has long been a common arrangement among people with few resources to share. In the United States and elsewhere in the developed world, the sharp differences in living arrangements between the poor and the nonpoor began to lessen about 1970. Cohabitation increased enough to be noticeable among young middle-class adults. At the time, many observers, long oblivious to the lives of poor people, thought these middle-class cohabitors were inventing a new way of living. Indeed, cohabitation did increase dramatically among

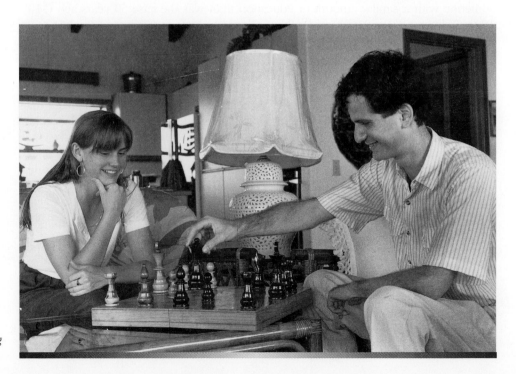

One of the greatest social changes in family patterns over the last few decades has been the rise of cohabitation, which before 1970 was common only among the poor.

the middle class after 1970. But it increased among the poor as well (Bumpass, Sweet, & Cherlin, 1991). The difference between today and the 1960s is that cohabitation is now much more common throughout society. In 1995, the Census Bureau estimated that there were about 3.7 million households in the United States maintained by two opposite-sex persons who were not married to each other and who had no other adults in the household. (There also were about 1.7 million such households maintained by two same-sex persons.) In contrast, there were only about a half million such households in 1970 (U.S. Bureau of the Census, 1993d, 1996c. So great has been the increase in cohabitation that it has compensated in large part for the postponement of marriage. That is to say, far fewer young adults marry today by their mid-twenties, but the proportion of young adults who live in either kind of union—marital or cohabiting—has declined much less.[21] Moreover, cohabitation has become more common among older adults as well. For instance, the percentage of previously married people (divorced, separated, or widowed) who cohabit is higher than the percentage of never-married people who cohabit. In addition, a surprisingly large proportion of cohabiting couples have children present in the household: In the NSFH, 22 percent of never-married, cohabiting persons interviewed said that children from one partner's prior relationship were present. Another 16 percent said that they and their current partner had had children. Births to cohabitors are now too numerous to ignore; by one estimate, one-fourth of all children who are born to unmarried women are born to a cohabiting couple. Yet we know very little about the lives of children and parents in these families and about how they differ by social class.

Why has this transformation in living arrangements occurred? The change has technological, economic, and cultural roots. The technological change is the improvement in birth control, especially the introduction of the birth control pill in 1960, and the legalization of abortion in 1973. These developments reduced the risks of unintended pregnancies and births. As for the economic change, young women are investing more time and effort in establishing job skills and experience. Consequently, an early marriage may interfere with their educational or career plans. In addition, the stagnant earning prospects for young men may encourage some to cohabit rather than marry because cohabitation involves less commitment and responsibility (Oppenheimer, 1994).

The cultural change involves the greater acceptance and practice of sex outside marriage and the reduced moral stigma of living with a partner without marrying. More generally, it involves the greater emphasis on self-fulfillment as the criterion for judging personal relationships. Happiness in marriage, as noted in Chapter 1, is now culturally defined more in terms of individual satisfaction and less in terms of how well one performs a role such as parent or spouse than was the case at mid-century. This ethic of self-fulfillment also lends itself to cohabitation. By definition, either partner can leave a cohabiting relationship without legal approval if he or she is dissatisfied in any way. Cohabitation is a way of forming a union that minimizes a person's loss of independence.

A SUBSTITUTE FOR MARRIAGE?

By and large, cohabitation is not a long-term substitute for marriage in the United States. About half of cohabiting couples either break up or marry within $1\frac{1}{2}$ years, and 9 in 10 do so within 5 years. And when cohabiting relationships

---

[21]The figures in the remainder of this paragraph are from Bumpass et al., (1991).

end, 60 percent result in marriage and 40 percent in a breakup (Bumpass et al., 1991). Moreover, if cohabitation were an acceptable, long-term substitute for marriage, we would expect that few cohabiting women would marry when they became pregnant because they wouldn't feel the need to. Yet among cohabiting white, never-married women in the NSFH who became pregnant, 63 percent married prior to the birth of their child (Manning, 1993). Apparently, a majority of pregnant cohabiting white women don't think cohabitation is a satisfactory arrangement for raising children.

In this respect, cohabiting couples in the United States differ from their counterparts in some European countries. In Sweden, for example, nearly all couples cohabit before marrying; the time until marriage or breakup is longer than here; and about half of all births occur to cohabiting, unmarried women. The situation in France is somewhere between the extremes of the United States and Sweden. Cohabiting relationships last longer, on average, than here but shorter than in Sweden. Half of the cohabiting persons in a 1985 French national survey responded that they "do not think about marriage." When they were shown a list of supposed advantages of marriage, only "the good of the children" was cited by a majority as a reason to marry. The authors of the French study concluded that cohabitation was a "neutral" phase of life, one in which the partners are keeping their options open and in which neither is thinking much about marrying or having children (Hoem & Hoem, 1988; Leridon & Villeneuve-Gokalp, 1989).[22] I think it unlikely that the United States will follow the Swedish pattern; cohabitation has been a long-standing living arrangement there. But it is possible the United States could move in the direction of France, where cohabitation lasts longer and the link between it and marriage seems weaker.

Still, among African Americans, cohabiting relationships tend to last longer and to lead to marriage less often. After four years, 38 percent have ended in marriage, compared with 67 percent among whites. African-American households are also more likely to include children; in the first month of cohabitation, children are present in 40 percent of black households but only 8 percent of white households (Manning & Smock, 1994). Thus, cohabitation among African Americans comes closer to being a long-term substitute for marriage than is the case among whites. The weaker connection of cohabitation and marriage among African Americans than among whites is consistent with the smaller role of marriage, in general, in African-American family life.

PART OF THE MARRIAGE PROCESS?

Is cohabitation among never-married adults best viewed, then, as

1 Just another, more-intimate form of single life?
2 A stage in the process of becoming married?
3 A distinct arrangement, unlike either being single or being married?

Evidence can be marshaled in favor of each of these three interpretations. All are facets of cohabitation in the United States. In support of interpretation 1, cohabitors seem quite similar to single people on a day-to-day level. Rindfuss & VandenHeuvel (1990) note, for example, that among college-age young adults, those who are

---

[22]The French and Swedish cases are compared with that of the United States in Cherlin (1992b).

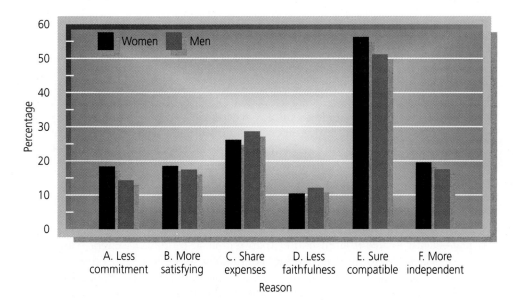

FIGURE 8.4 Percentage of cohabiting women and men under age 35 who agreed that each of the following statements was an important reason to them "why a person might *want* to live with someone of the opposite sex without being married": (*A*) It requires less personal commitment than marriage. (*B*) It is more sexually satisfying than dating. (*C*) It makes it possible to share living expenses. (*D*) It requires less sexual faithfulness than marriage. (*E*) Couples can be sure they are compatible before marriage. (*F*) It allows each partner to be more independent than marriage. (*Source: Bumpass, Sweet, & Cherlin, 1991.*)

cohabiting are nearly as likely to be enrolled in college as are those who are living without a partner. In contrast, those who are married are much less likely to be enrolled. This pattern suggests that cohabitors behave more like singles when they make decisions about continuing their education. Moreover, neither singles nor cohabitors have made a long-term commitment to stay with their partners, but married persons have. Nor do cohabitors appear outwardly to be more committed to the institution of marriage than singles: In the NSFH there was virtually no difference between the percentage of singles and cohabitors who agreed with the statement "It's better for a person to get married than to go through life being single" (Bumpass et al., 1991).[23]

Yet in other ways cohabitation does seem like a stage in the marriage process, even though the partners have not made a permanent commitment to each other. When never-married cohabiting persons in the NSFH were asked if they had marriage plans, 50 percent said they had "definite plans" to marry their partner and an additional 31 percent said they "think they will marry" their partner (Bumpass et al., 1991).[24] The cohabiting couples in the NSFH were also presented with a list of "reasons why a person might *want* to live with someone of the opposite sex without being married." They were then asked which of the reasons was important to them. The results are displayed in Figure 8.4. As can be seen, few cohabitors chose reasons pertaining to lower personal commitment, greater sexual satisfaction, less sexual faithfulness, or greater independence than in marriage. Rather, the only reason that was chosen by a majority was "Couples can be sure they are compatible before marriage."

One way to resolve the tension between interpretation 1 (it's like being single) and interpretation 2 (it's part of the marriage process) is to use the concepts of **manifest functions** and **latent functions**. Robert Merton first coined these terms to

[23]Among persons under age 35, 36 percent of cohabiting, never-married persons agreed with that statement, compared with 34 percent of noncohabiting, never-married persons.

[24]Still, the partners disagreed about their plans in about one-fifth of the unions in which at least one person planned to, or thought he or she would, marry his or her partner.

argue that social actions often serve two kinds of purposes: the publicly stated, acknowledged ones, which he called manifest functions, and the unacknowledged, unstated ones, which he called latent functions (Merton, 1968). The latter, he argued, may be as important as the former. One might argue that cohabitation has a manifest function that has little to do with marriage, namely providing a way to increase the emotional and sexual satisfactions to be gotten from intimate relationships. If you observe cohabiting couples who have recently moved in together, you will probably find men and women who devote little time to thoughts of marriage, except when a stray sociologist wanders in and asks about it. Nevertheless, if you pay a return visit a few years later, you are likely to find that they have married; and if they haven't, they probably won't be together any longer. The latent function of their cohabiting relationship was to assess the compatibility of a potential spouse. If the assessment proved positive, a marriage resulted; if not, a breakup occurred. That few would have acknowledged this function early on makes it no less real—it just makes it latent rather than manifest. Indeed, its latent nature may make it easier to perform: If cohabitors continually reminded each other that their every move was being evaluated, their relationship might become strained.

If the latent function of cohabitation is to be a part of the marriage process, as I am arguing, just what role does it play? Who makes use of it, and how? First, young women who are in a strong economic position seem to be using it to learn whether their male partners will be good earners—and possibly whether they will share equitably in the housework. A study that followed a national sample of high school graduates for 14 years showed that young single women with high earnings were more likely to cohabit than they were to marry. In contrast, young single men with high earnings were more likely to marry than to cohabit (Clarkberg, 1997). It is as if women with the highest—and therefore most attractive—earning potential were using these resources to establish a cohabiting relationship in which they could find out more about their partners. In particular, women can determine whether men seem to be steady wage earners and whether they will share the work at home. In this way, cohabitation may benefit the search process that young women with strong marriage market positions undertake.

As for interpretation 3 (unlike being either single or being married), cohabiting relationships are different from marriage in several ways—yet unlike singlehood, they *are* partnerships. Women and men in cohabiting relationships are more egalitarian in their attitudes about sharing housework (Brines & Joyner, 1993). For instance, one study using the NSFH found that married women, on average, do six hours more housework per week than do cohabiting women—but that married men do no more housework than cohabiting men (Shelton & John, 1993). Women who move from cohabitation to marriage, then, pay a "penalty" in housework that their husbands don't share. This penalty may make cohabitation an attractive alternative to marriage, at least in the short term, to women who value an equitable division of labor at home. Moreover, about 10 percent of whites and about 25 to 30 percent of African-American women never marry. About half of those who never marry have had a cohabiting relationship by their forties, which for some may be a substitute for marriage.[25]

The growth of cohabitation could also provide an alternative to marriage for men who do not highly value commitment, and a way for them to receive the benefits of

---

[25]For instance, I used data from the 1995 National Survey of Family Growth to estimate the percentage of never-married women, aged 35–44, who had had at least one cohabiting relationship: 44 percent for whites and 49 percent for blacks.

a regular sexual relationship without having to marry. Akerlof, Yellen, and Katz (1996) maintain that the introduction of effective birth control methods and legal abortion—coupled with the acceptance of sex outside of marriage—have benefited men because they can obtain a sexual relationship without the risk of an unwanted birth. This scenario only holds if men, on average, value long-term commitment in relationships less than women do (otherwise women would benefit just as much from nonmarital sexual relationships). The biosocial, or evolutionary, view of gender differences suggests that men may, on average, care less about commitment than women do (see Chapters 1 and 3). Alternatively, gender theorists in sociology might argue that men are socialized into valuing commitment less. If either view is true, cohabitation may be to men's advantage in this regard.

UNION FORMATION: A SUMMING UP

The process by which young adults find long-term partners has changed greatly since the middle of the twentieth century (see Table 8.2). In the 1950s, nearly everyone married, and they married at younger ages than before or since. Young single people spent less time searching for a partner than they do now. They may not have needed to do as much searching given (1) the advantageous labor market position of young men during the economic boom of the 1950s and 1960s; and (2) the expectation that married women would stay home and raise children

TABLE 8.2 CHANGES IN UNION FORMATION SINCE THE MID-TWENTIETH CENTURY		
	1950s	**1990s**
When do sexual relations begin?	For a majority of women and many men, sexual relations began only after engagement or marriage.	Sexual relations typically begin many years before a union is formed.
What happens when premarital pregnancies occur?	Usually led to a hasty marriage because childbearing outside of marriage was highly stigmatized.	Much less likely to lead to marriage because childbearing outside of marriage is more acceptable. Still, many cohabiting couples marry when a pregnancy occurs.
Who cohabits?	Cohabitation is common only among the poor; it is not considered respectable among the nonpoor.	About half of all young adults will cohabit before they marry. It has become an important part of the process of finding a marital partner.
Who marries and when?	About 95 percent of whites and almost 90 percent of African Americans married; average age at marriage was younger than in any other decade.	90 percent or less of whites will marry, and only about 70 to 75 percent of African Americans will marry. Typical ages at marriage are several years older than in the 1950s.
What is the economic bargain?	Men typically exchanged their earning power for women's housework and childrearing effort. Middle-class and working-class married women rarely worked outside the home.	Men and women typically pool their earnings and achieve economies of scale (i.e., only one mortgage to pay for). Women with higher earning potential are more likely to marry.

(Oppenheimer, 1988). Cohabitation was held in such disrepute that it was not an option except among the poor. Childbearing outside of marriage was highly stigmatized, and a pregnancy often led to a forced marriage. Most young women and many men did not have sex until they were engaged or married.

As we enter the twenty-first century, nearly all these conditions have changed. The typical age at marriage is much higher than at midcentury; and the proportion of people who never marry has grown. Young people typically spend more time searching for a partner. They do so in part because the earning potential of young men without college degrees has eroded and in part because cohabitation has emerged as an accepted, or at least tolerated, alternative living arrangement. About half of all young adults cohabit prior to marrying. It provides a way for them to enjoy some of the benefits of a partnership without committing to marriage. Childbearing outside of marriage is much less stigmatized, and far fewer nonmarital pregnancies lead to a hasty marriage. Most young adults begin to have sex many years before they marry; and better birth control technology and legalized abortion make it easier for them to do so.

Given all this change, one might reasonably ask: What *is* the marital bargain these days, and why do most people still eventually marry? The marital bargain is based more on a pooling of joint earnings than on an exchange of men's earnings for women's housework and childcare. Men are still required to be good, steady earners in order to be acceptable as spouses; but increasingly women are required to be good earners as well. Although women still provide more of the housework and childcare, the marital bargain typically calls for men to do more work at home than was the case at midcentury. Women with higher earning potential may be using their economic attractiveness to strike a bargain that results in a more equitable distribution of work in the home.

Why do most people still marry? Perhaps the only advantage marriage offers over cohabitation is that it requires a public commitment to a long-term, possibly lifelong, relationship. What's different about marriage, in other words, are social norms, such as the expectations of friends, relatives, and religious congregants about how married people will behave, and the legal rights and privileges reserved for spouses and married parents. This long-term public commitment is still attractive to most people. It allows individuals to invest emotionally in each other with less fear of abandonment. It also maximizes the chances that both parents will live together while their children are being raised—which is why pregnancy and childbirth are the events that lead many cohabiting couples to marry. Nevertheless, despite these advantages, it is clear that marriage does not hold as privileged a position in our family system as it did in midcentury. The gains to marriage, relative to alternatives, are perceived to be lower on average today than they were 40 or 50 years ago.

CHILDBEARING WITHOUT A PARTNER

An increasing proportion of adolescents and young adults bear or father a first child before either cohabiting or marrying. Thirty-nine percent of first births in 1995, nearly two out of five, occurred to unmarried women—those who had never married or who were separated, divorced, or widowed. Making the transition to motherhood without a husband is now the predominant experience for African-American women: 78 percent of black first births occurred to unmarried women in 1995. But recently the figure has been rising more rapidly among

Why do some cohabiting couples choose to marry? A common reason is pregnancy or the birth of a child.

whites: 33 percent of white first births occurred to unmarried women in 1995.[26] Although stories in the media tell of middle-class, unmarried women in their thirties having children of their own or of lesbians having children, these kinds of first births are still rare in the aggregate. Rather, first-time, unmarried mothers tend to be young: 49 percent are teenagers; another 33 percent are aged 20 to 24; and only 18 percent are 25 or over.[27] Moreover, some first-time, unmarried mothers in their twenties and thirties are cohabiting with men. As noted earlier, one-fourth of all babies born outside marriage are born to cohabiting couples. Fewer unmarried teenage mothers, however, are cohabiting; instead, the great majority are living with their parents or other relatives (Parish, Hao, & Hogan, 1991). It is these unmarried teenage mothers who have been the focus of most of the studies of childbearing outside marriage.

THE TEENAGE PREGNANCY "PROBLEM"

Most people have read or heard something about the teenage pregnancy "problem," but few people have a good understanding of exactly what the problem is. About one out of ten 15- to 19-year-old women in the United States becomes pregnant each year. Nearly half these pregnancies are ended by an abortion,[28] leaving 512,115 births in 1995.[29] Despite widespread talk about an "epidemic" of

[26]Unpublished figures supplied by the U.S. National Center for Health Statistics; and U.S. National Center for Health Statistics (1997a).

[27]Unpublished tabulations provided by the U.S. National Center for Health Statistics.

[28]For 1988, James Trussell estimates 850,000 pregnancies to young women aged 15 to 19 and 400,000 abortions. See his article, Trussell (1988).

[29]This figure includes 12,242 births to girls under the age of 15 and 499,873 births to girls aged 15 to 19. See U.S. National Center for Health Statistics (1997a).

teenage childbearing, this is a lower number of births than was the case 10 or 20 years ago. In fact, the birthrate for teenage girls decreased steadily from the 1950s to the mid-1980s before turning upward at the end of the 1980s (U.S. National Research Council, 1987; U.S. National Center for Health Statistics, 1991a). It has since declined for most of the 1990s. That is to say, the probability that a teenage girl will have a baby in a given year has gone down, not up, over the past few decades.

Then what is the problem? Marriage, or rather the lack of it. Marriage among teenagers has decreased faster than birthrates have. A pregnant 18- or 19-year-old who got married in 1960 would have had plenty of company—31 percent of all 18- to 19-year-old women were married. But to marry at those ages today is to stand out: Just 7 percent of 18- to 19-year-old women were married in 1995. Because the age at first marriage has risen even faster for blacks than for whites, married black teenagers are even rarer: Only 1 percent of black 18- to 19-year-old women were married in 1995 (U.S. Bureau of the Census, 1996c).

In addition to their lower likelihood of marrying, black teenagers are more likely to be sexually active than white teenagers. Nevertheless, whites are catching up, as noted in Chapter 7 (Forrest & Singh, 1990). Still, black teenagers tend to initiate intercourse at younger ages and to have more partners than white non-Hispanic or Hispanic teenagers (Sonenstein et al., 1991). Black teenagers are also less likely to use contraceptives, slightly less likely to get an abortion when pregnant, and less likely to marry before the baby's birth than whites. As a result, nearly all births to black teenagers—95 percent in 1995—occurred outside marriage. Among white teenagers, 68 percent of all births occurred outside of marriage, up sharply from 55 percent in 1990.[30]

As sexual activity among white unmarried teenagers increased and as the proportion of teenagers of all races who were unmarried rose, the consequence was a sharp rise in the proportion who were risking a pregnancy outside marriage. Teenagers can lower that risk by using contraceptives more effectively; and, as noted in Chapter 7, contraceptive usage has indeed increased among teenagers—especially in the 1980s. The percentage of teenage girls who reported using any contraceptive the first time they had intercourse rose from 48 percent in 1982 to 65 percent in 1988; for boys it jumped from 48 percent in 1979 to 88 percent in 1988 (Forrest & Singh, 1990; Sonenstein et al., 1989). What's more, the increase was due almost entirely to the use of condoms. It's likely that the greater use of condoms represents a reaction on the part of teenagers to the risk of AIDS and other sexually transmitted diseases.

But over the long run, the increased use of contraceptives has merely kept pace with the increasing numbers of unmarried teenagers who are sexually active. Consequently, the **nonmarital birth ratio**—the proportion of all births that occur to unmarried women has increased sharply for teenagers, even though the *birthrate*—the probability that a teenager (married or not) will have a birth—declined until recently. For example, in 1970 the nonmarital birth ratio for 15- to 19-year-olds was less than 1 out of 3; by 1995 it had risen to 3 out of 4 (U.S. National Center for Health Statistics, 1997a). The increased ratio is the source of public concern.

Few unmarried teenage mothers report that they intended to become pregnant; according to one estimate, about four out of five pregnancies among teenagers

---

[30]Unpublished figures supplied by the U.S. National Center for Health Statistics; and U.S. National Center for Health Statistics (1993a, 1997a).

were unintended (U.S. National Research Council, 1987). So, whereas most married couples plan the timing of their children's births, most teenagers do not. In many cases, the news of the pregnancy comes as a surprise, even a shock, to the young woman and her parents. Sociologists and psychologists have written about events in people's lives that are "off time" or "nonnormative," meaning that they occur before or after the ages in life when most people expect them and want them to happen (Elder, 1975). Individuals and their families aren't as well prepared for off-time events and may not be able to adjust to them as successfully. Most teenage pregnancies are off-time events—which is why nearly half of them end in abortions.

Yet in some low-income neighborhoods, having a first child as a teenager may be an alternative strategy for entering adulthood that is accepted by the young mothers and their families. Observational studies of low-income African-American neighborhoods show that although most young women share the cultural norm about marrying the father of their children and then supporting themselves as a family, neighborhood teenagers believe that this scenario may not be an option for them (Anderson, 1991). As they grow up, children see few lasting marriages; they see few men holding stable jobs that pay enough to support a family; and many conclude that their chances of entering the economic mainstream are small. Children also see teenage mothers whose babies have given them more status in their families and among some of their peers. They also see that parents disapprove of early pregnancies but value and accept the babies who are born (Furstenberg, 1981). Consequently, as Elijah Anderson writes of teenage girls in a poor black neighborhood he studied: "Although an overwhelming number may not be actively trying to have babies, many are not actively trying to prevent it" (Anderson, 1991). He tells of "baby clubs," in which new young mothers support one another but also compete for status by having the cutest or best-dressed baby.

Another observer, Linda Burton, studied what she called an "alternative life-course strategy" in a small, semirural black community consisting of poor, multigenerational households (Burton, 1990). In this community, the typical ages of mothers at the births of their first children were 15 to 18; and the babies were raised primarily by their mothers' mothers—the new grandmothers, who themselves had begun bearing children as teenagers and were only in their mid-thirties. Here the transition to parenthood is split into two stages. A young woman first becomes the biological mother of a child in her mid-teens, which is earlier than is typical in the United States, but she does not become a parent—in the sense of having primary responsibility for raising a child—until her daughter has a child. Thus, the transition to parenthood is not completed until a woman becomes a biological grandmother. In fact, Burton found some cases in which mothers in their thirties encouraged their teenage daughters to have babies so that the mothers, for the first time, could have the experience of raising a baby.

Burton argued that this family pattern was normative—in the sense of being accepted as proper and thought of as typical—in the community. She noted that the age differences between the generations were compressed, compared with national norms, and that caregiving skipped a generation: Not only did grandmothers care for their grandchildren, but teenage mothers cared for their great-grandmothers. Now in their fifties and sixties, the great-grandmothers were the generation who had raised the now-teenage mothers. One 19-year-old mother told Burton: "My grandmother raised me. Now it's time for me to give something back. It's O.K. if my mother raises my child for now. If she didn't, I couldn't do as much as I do for my grandmother" (Burton, 1990).

Burton's community seems more uniform in its behavior than most inner-city black neighborhoods that have been studied, but much of what she observed has also been found among some families in poor city neighborhoods. Frank Furstenberg reported that most of the black adolescent mothers he studied in Baltimore and Philadelphia lived with their parents for several years (Furstenberg, 1976; Furstenberg, 1981). For those mothers who coped successfully, family support was crucial. Grandmothers and other kin helped to care for the children until the mothers could finish high school, get a job, get married, or get stable support from the welfare office. Furstenberg concluded:

> *Most adolescent mothers do not stop being their parents' children, in the sense of requiring and receiving care and support when they, themselves, become parents. As a corollary, most of the parents are not relieved of childrearing duties when their daughters become pregnant* (Furstenberg, 1981).

WHERE ARE THE FATHERS?

As marriage among teenagers has declined sharply among whites and virtually disappeared among blacks, the roles of adolescent fathers in their children's lives also have declined. By and large, unmarried adolescent fathers contribute little to the support of mothers and children and often play modest roles in their children's lives. This is so for several reasons. First, few teenage fathers have the earning power necessary to make a substantial contribution to a mother and child. Most are in school, working at low-wage jobs, or unemployed. Second, given that support from the father is unlikely, the mother's parents may prefer not to share the child with him and his kin. Furstenberg reports that the parents of the teenage mothers he observed often negotiated with the fathers' families over how much support the fathers' kin would provide and how much access to the child they would have (Furstenberg, 1981). Third, some teenage young men prefer to be free of responsibility for children they have fathered and to be able to pursue other young women (Anderson, 1989).

Nevertheless, some teenage fathers do provide support to their children and visit them frequently, but little is known about how this life transition affects them. We do know that boys who hold stereotypically macho attitudes about male roles feel less upset about getting girls pregnant. One national survey found that teenage boys who agreed with statements such as "A guy will lose respect if he talks about his problems" and "Men are always ready for sex" were more likely to say they would be pleased if they "got a girl pregnant now" (although the majority of boys said they would be "very upset" if that happened). Boys from poor neighborhoods, African-American boys, and boys who had already impregnated girls were also more likely to say that making a girl pregnant would make them feel pleased and "like a real man" (Marsiglio, 1993).

Observational studies of poor neighborhoods confirm the existence of a male street culture that emphasizes sexual conquests and that leads to pregnancies outside marriage. For example, Anderson observed that the teenage boys in the neighborhood he studied gained status with peers for sexual conquests and for fathering babies but that the peer group also expected its members to avoid exclusive commitment to one woman (Anderson, 1991).

THE CONSEQUENCES FOR TEENAGE MOTHERS

Despite support from their parents and other kin, adolescents who bear children appear worse off later in life, on average, than adolescents who wait until their twenties to begin having children. Teenage mothers complete fewer years of schooling, have jobs that pay less, are more likely to be dependent on public assistance payments, and are less likely to have stable marriages. The more difficult issue to resolve is whether these differences are due to having a child as a teenager per se or to the kinds of impoverished backgrounds common among teenage mothers. In 1968, demographer Arthur Campbell surveyed the evidence and wrote the most frequently quoted assessment of the consequences of teenage childbearing outside marriage:

> *The girl who has an illegitimate child at the age of 16 suddenly has 90 percent of her life's script written for her. She will probably drop out of school; even if someone else in her family helps to take care of the baby, she will probably not be able to find a steady job that pays enough to provide for herself and her child; she may feel impelled to marry someone she might not otherwise have chosen. Her life choices are few, and most of them are bad* (Campbell, 1968).

Campbell was writing at a time when marriage ages had just begun their steep rise and the problem of teenage pregnancy was just beginning to be noticed. His statement downplayed the possibility that some of the supposed negative consequences of teenage childbearing might have been caused by the poverty of many of the families of the teenagers who became pregnant (Luker, 1996). (See *How Do Sociologists Know What They Know:* Selection Effects and Teenage Childbearing.) From the standpoint of the 1990s, it is clear that the statement exaggerates the (still very real) difficulties teenage mothers face. Consider school enrollment: Campbell's article appeared at the close of an era when many schools had expelled pregnant girls as a matter of policy. We now know that the majority of girls who bear a child before graduating from high school will eventually graduate.

The effects of pregnancy on high school graduation are smaller than Campbell thought because some teenage mothers get help from other family members that allows them to stay in school. Others are forced to drop out but later—sometimes much later—return to school and obtain a high school diploma or its equivalent. In 1984, Furstenberg and two collaborators, Jeanne Brooks-Gunn and S. Philip Morgan, reinterviewed about 300 women who had been in Furstenberg's original Baltimore study of adolescent mothers 22 years earlier (Furstenberg, Brooks-Gunn, & Morgan, 1987). Five years after the original interview, only 51 percent had graduated from high school, and few of the dropouts were enrolled in school. But by the 22-year reinterview, 67 percent had graduated from high school or received a general equivalency diploma—still fewer than among nonmothers, but an improvement. About one-third of the mothers who had not graduated at the 5-year mark had done so by the 22-year mark (Furstenberg et al., 1987).

Nor are teenage mothers doomed to a life on welfare. There is ample evidence that their family incomes are indeed lower and that they are indeed more likely to rely on public assistance later in life than women who do not have children as teenagers (U.S. National Research Council, 1987). In the Baltimore study, 70 percent of the young mothers eventually received welfare. But within three years, more than half of those who had received welfare had left the rolls; by the 22-year interview,

How Do Sociologists Know What They Know?

Selection Effects and Teenage Childbearing

Many teenage mothers were poor before they became mothers; it is therefore a mistake to blame childbearing outside marriage for all their economic difficulties. This may seem an obvious point, but for a long time after Arthur Campbell's article was published, it was overlooked. In the 1990s, however, several studies have been published that question Campbell's logic (Geronimus, 1991; Geronimus & Korenman, 1992; Hotz, McElroy, & Sanders, 1996). The heart of their argument is that having a baby as a teenager poses few penalties for young women who are already poor, because they are likely to remain poor regardless of whether they bear children or not. This latter point is an example of a **selection effect,** the principle that whenever individuals sort, or "select," themselves into groups nonrandomly, some of the differences among the groups reflect preexisting differences among the individuals. Selection effects frequently complicate the interpretation of data that sociologists collect.

For example, suppose we want to know whether teenage mothers grow up to be poor at a higher rate because of the effects of (1) having a child as a teenager or (2) coming from low-income families. To truly settle this issue, a truth-seeking but cold-blooded social scientist would want to conduct the following experiment: Obtain a list of all families with teenage girls in the United States and then assign at random some of the girls to have children and others to remain childless until their twenties. Because of the random assignment, teenage childbearing would be about as likely to occur in middle-class families as in poor families. In this way, the social scientist could eliminate family background as a cause of any differences that emerge between teenage mothers and nonmothers.

In the real world, of course, teenage pregnancies don't occur randomly; rather, they are more likely to occur in families that were poor before the teenager gave birth. The teenage childbearers are self-selected,

in a sense, from less-fortunate families. It is very difficult to separate out the selection effect of family background from the true effect of having the baby per se. Recent studies suggest that some of the apparent effect of teenage childbearing is indeed a selection effect—in other words, teenage mothers probably would grow up to have somewhat lower incomes even if they had waited until after age 19 to have children. But some studies still suggest that the economic circumstances of teenage mothers remain worse after the selection effect is accounted for.

One way to reduce the problem of the selection effect is to compare pairs of sisters, one of whom had a child as a teenager and one of whom didn't (Geronimus & Korenman, 1992). The logic of this comparison is that a pair of sisters were raised in essentially the same environment, so that differences between them are unlikely to be caused by differences in their parents' incomes or their upbringings. To be more specific, if the teenage mother is less likely to graduate from high

two-thirds had left the rolls. In fact, at the 22-year reinterview their incomes varied widely: One-fourth were on welfare, one-fourth had family earnings of less than $15,000 (equivalent in purchasing power to about $19,000 in 1990 dollars), one-fourth had family earnings between $15,000 and $25,000 (equivalent to about $32,000 in 1990 dollars), and one-fourth had family earnings of $25,000 or more (Furstenberg et al., 1987).

Although teenage mothers are more likely to marry early than childless teenagers, their marriages are often brittle. In the Baltimore study, half of all the early marriages had dissolved by the 5-year reinterview, two-thirds by the 22-year reinterview. Most mothers had married at some point, and many cohabited with a partner, but the great majority of the marriages and partnerships had ended. Early marriages are, in general, less stable, perhaps because the spouses are less mature or because they cannot yet tell who will make a suitable long-term partner. The school than her sister who postponed childbearing, the difference cannot be due to the kind of family in which the teenage mother grew up because her sister grew up in the same family. (This logic assumes that parents treat all their children the same, which isn't strictly true.)

For example, in one large, national study, 54 percent of the teenage mothers eventually graduated from high school. Among comparable teens who hadn't had children, 86 percent eventually graduated from high school—a 32 percent increase. But when the researchers examined just pairs of sisters in the study, one of whom had had a child as a teenager and one of whom hadn't, they found only an 18 percent increase in high school graduation among those who had postponed childbearing (Hoffman, Foster, & Furstenberg, 1993). Apparently, there were some unmeasured ways—possibly connected with poverty—in which the families of the teenage mothers and their sisters differed from the families of other young women in the survey. Comparing the teenage mothers with their sisters produced a smaller estimate of the gains to postponing childbirth. Nevertheless, an 18 percent difference in high school graduation is substantial. Consequently, even after controlling for the selective nature of families in which a teenager had a child, a noticeable difference in the likelihood of graduation still existed.

Another study examined differences between teenagers who gave birth to children and teenagers who became pregnant but experienced miscarriages (Hotz et al., 1996). The logic behind this comparison is that miscarriages are more-or-less random events that can be considered "natural experiments," beyond the control of the teenagers affected. The study found few differences between the two groups of teenagers, which suggests that having a child did not have a large effect on the teen mothers' lives.

More generally, sociologists need to use caution in interpreting differences between groups when individuals can choose which group to belong to. For example, suppose that the earnings of college graduates in a city are $10,000 higher, on average, than the earnings of high school graduates in the city. It would seem logical to conclude that if the high school graduates had gone to college, their earnings would be $10,000 higher. But the individuals in this city who had the most to gain from college—those with the most ability and motivation—were most likely to choose to go to college. The high school graduates probably would have gained less from college had they attended; their earnings might be only $5,000 higher if we could have intervened in their lives and sent them to college.

Economic and social statisticians have developed statistical techniques that can adjust for bias due to the selection effect in some, limited circumstances (Winship & Mare, 1992). Still, it is often a problem that researchers need to consider before making comparisons between groups.

small minority of Baltimore teenage mothers who had managed to attain lasting marriages were in far better economic situations (Furstenberg et al., 1987). Because it usually brings a male worker's income to a family, marriage is one of the most important routes out of poverty for single mothers. It is, unfortunately, a difficult route for teenage mothers to follow.

So it appears that teenage mothers do not have 90 percent of their life's script written for them. Although they are substantially disadvantaged in education, income, and employment, there is much variation in how their lives turn out. Some are able to return to school and eventually to obtain a diploma and a good job. Most avoid long-term dependence on welfare. Still, even if only 25 percent of their life's script is written, teenage childbearing is a serious problem for young women. It is also a serious problem for the children of the teenage mothers, a topic that will be addressed in Chapter 14.

SUMMARY

1. Since the 1950s and early 1960s, the close connection among sexual intercourse, marriage, and childbearing has weakened. Rates of sexual intercourse among unmarried teenagers have risen sharply since 1970. Young adults now marry a few years later, on average, than in the 1950s and early 1960s, and many cohabit with a partner prior to marrying. The process of forming a family is less uniform and more complex than it was at midcentury.

2. Parents' involvement in finding marriage partners for their children is greater when they have more resources, such as land or investments, to protect; when they control the means children can use to make a living; and when the addition of spouses and children to a family is of crucial importance to the well-being of the larger family unit. In the United States, since the mid- to late 1700s, young adults have had substantial autonomy in choosing a spouse, although parents still have some influence.

3. In the United States and other Western nations, young adults for centuries went about finding a spouse through the publicly visible process of courtship. Courtship declined in the United States after 1900 due to migration to large cities, growing affluence, and the emergence of adolescence as a protected time between childhood and adulthood. The rise of dating after 1900 placed courtship on an economic basis and transferred power from young women (and their parents) to young men. Theories of courtship and dating have emphasized the greater power of the person who has less interest in, or more alternatives to, the relationship. The heyday of dating was probably 1945 to 1965; during the 1970s and 1980s, it became less closely connected to marriage as the average age at marriage rose and cohabitation became more common.

4. The marriage market model, widely used by social scientists, consists of individuals who are searching for a spouse in the same geographic area, who have a set of preferences concerning the type of person they wish to find, and who have a set of resources to offer to others. The market can be disrupted by an extreme imbalance in the sex ratio or by a shortage of people with critical resources such as a good earning potential. The predominant marriage bargain

at midcentury—the specialization model of marriage—often involved a husband who traded earnings for childcare and housework performed by a wife. Theoretical writing emphasized the gains each spouse received from specializing in either market or home work. This model of marriage no longer fits the market; in particular, there is evidence that both men and women now prefer partners with a greater earning potential. Most people marry others similar to themselves, but compared with earlier in the century, young adults today are more likely to marry someone with similar education and less likely to marry someone of similar religion.

5. Prior to 1970, cohabitation was largely found among the poor. Since then, it has expanded greatly among young adults at all income levels. It is now an important part of the union formation process. Among whites, most cohabiting unions lead fairly quickly to either marriage or a breakup; among blacks, cohabiting unions are less likely to end in marriage. Some observers believe cohabitation to be an extension of the single life, a way of gaining the benefits of a union without making a commitment to it. Others believe it functions in practice as a stage in the process of finding a spouse; still others consider it a distinct arrangement unlike being either single or married. There is some evidence for each of these ways of viewing cohabitation.

6. The union formation process has changed greatly since midcentury. Sexual relations typically begin well before a person's first union. Premarital cohabitation is widely accepted. Having a first child outside of marriage is much less stigmatized than in the 1950s. Young adults take longer to find partners to marry and more of them never marry than at midcentury. And both women and men appear to prefer partners who can contribute a steady flow of income to a marriage. Still, marriage offers a public, long-term commitment that remains attractive to most young adults.

7. The proportion of teenage births that occur outside marriage has risen sharply over the past few decades because of the decline in marriage among teenagers. Most pregnancies outside marriage are unwanted, but, in some low-income neighborhoods, bearing a child—or fathering a child—may be one of the few ways that teenagers

can gain status and respect among their peers and families. Few unmarried teenage fathers contribute much to the support of their children. Bearing a child as a teenager makes it harder for a young woman to lead a successful adult life in several respects: schooling, employment, wages, and marriage. Yet some of these observed disadvantages occur because teenage mothers tend to come from disadvantaged families and not because of having a child per se.

KEY TERMS

union
courtship
principle of least interest
courtship stage theories
comparison level for alternatives

marriage market
sex ratio
specialization model
marital similarity
cohabitation

manifest function
latent function
nonmarital birth ratio
selection effect

FAMILIES ON THE INTERNET

On adolescent pregnancy and childbearing: Child Trends, Inc., a nonprofit, nonpartisan research organization that studies children, youth, and families, maintains a fact sheet on adolescent pregnancy and childbearing, Facts at a Glance, that is updated annually. It is the most up-to-date concise source of information on the topic (www.childtrends.org). The U.S. Department of Health and Human Services maintains a web site, Youth Info, that provides links to a number of reports, speeches by agency officials, and a statistical profile of American adolescents (www.youth.os.dhhs.gov). The Alan Guttmacher Institute, a research center devoted to family planning issues, has much relevant information about adolescent pregnancy and childbearing, birth control, and abortion (www.agi-usa.org).

CHAPTER 9

Spouses and Partners

"Nine years ago I gave for the first time a course on the family," wrote Professor Ernest Burgess of the University of Chicago in 1926. Among all the literature in the field, he found "not a single work that even pretended to study the modern family as behavior or as social phenomenon. It has been studied as a legal institution but it had not been studied as a subject of natural science . . . in the way in which the biologist studies the potato bug" (Burgess, 1926).[1] Many scholars, he asserted, had studied laws and beliefs about the family, but few had studied how family members actually behaved toward one another. Moreover, Burgess realized that in the decades preceding his article, married couples in the United States had gained greater privacy and had sought increased emotional satisfaction through their

[1]Burgess's major articles can be found in Cottrell, Hunter, & Short, (1973).

relationships. Consequently, Burgess urged sociologists to study the family as a "unity of interacting personalities." As Burgess's influence spread through his writings and the research of his students, **marital interaction**—how wives and husbands behave toward each other—became the potato bug of the sociology of the family. Expanded to include interaction among opposite-sex and same-sex cohabiting couples, it will be the subject of this chapter. Chapter 10 will continue the discussion, with a focus on how work and power shape interactions.

TWO MARITAL TRANSITIONS

In 1945, Burgess elaborated his views in a widely cited textbook. Here is the first paragraph of the preface:

> *The central thesis of this volume is that the family in historical times has been, and at present is, in transition from an institution to a companionship. In the past the important factors unifying the family have been external, formal, and authoritarian, as the law, the mores, public opinion, tradition, the authority of the family head, rigid discipline, and elaborate ritual. At present, in the new emerging form of the companionship family, its unity inheres less and less in community pressures and more and more in such interpersonal relations as the mutual affection, the sympathetic understanding, and the comradeship of its members* (Burgess & Locke, 1945).

Burgess meant the family-as-institution and the family-as-companionship to be seen as ideal types. Introduced by Max Weber, the *ideal type,* as noted in Chapter 4, is a hypothetical model that consists of the most significant characteristics, in extreme form, of a social phenomenon. *Ideal* is used not in the sense of best or perfect but rather in the sense of a pure, distilled form—so pure that it probably doesn't exist in reality. The ideal type is useful for understanding social life, even though any real example of the phenomenon may not have all the characteristics of the ideal type. Thus, Burgess cautions that purely institutional and purely companionship families exist "nowhere in time or space." Moreover, the companionship form "is not to be conceived of as having already been realized but as emerging" (Burgess & Locke, 1945).

As Chapter 2 suggested, family life in preindustrial Western nations was, indeed, guided more by law and custom than by affection and emotional stimulation. The local government in Plymouth Colony, you will recall, kept a close watch over the conduct of family members. Parents seem to have played a greater role in selecting a spouse for their children than was the case in later centuries. In general, husbands and fathers had greater authority than they do today: Religion and law certified the father as the head of the family, with broad powers over his wife (whose property he could sell) and his children (who remained with him in the event of divorce). In addition, the marginal existence of poor farm families and the modest standard of living of most urban families made the family's survival a higher priority than the personality development of the members.

In the twentieth century, an increasing proportion of men and women came to value family life for the personal, emotional satisfaction they could gain from it. In the terms of Chapter 1, Burgess's model reflects the rise of the private family—a process that began a few hundred years ago in the more prosperous classes but became widespread only after 1900. Not until this century was the average standard of living high enough to allow family members to focus on their own personal fulfillment rather than on their daily subsistence.

Margaret Sanger (1883–1996), shown here about to testify before a U.S. House of Representatives committee in 1932, led the early twentieth-century campaign for birth control (a term she invented) at a time when sending contraceptives— or even information about contraceptives— through the mail was illegal. Sanger was arrested in 1915, after circulating a pamphlet entitled Family Limitation. *Public support was strong enough, however, that the government decided not to prosecute. She was arrested again and jailed briefly in 1916, after opening a birth control clinic in Brooklyn, New York, but she continued her crusade to make contraceptives freely available to women.*

THE COMPANIONSHIP MARRIAGE

In the late nineteenth and early twentieth centuries, companionship and sexual fulfillment became more important to a successful marriage. The sexual prudery of the Victorian era may have been overstated, but restraint of sexual passion seems to have been highly valued. For instance, the percentage of brides who became pregnant before their marriages decreased from 1800 to 1870 (Smith & Hindus, 1975). Until the twentieth century, sexual relations in marriage (and there was relatively little sexual activity outside marriage except among couples who were engaged) were seen more as a means of producing children than as a way to personal fulfillment. Historian Elaine Tyler May claims that nineteenth-century writers thought it immoral and dangerous for a married couple to have sexual relations more than once or twice a month (May, 1980). But after the turn of the century, progressive writers argued that an active sex life was central to a happy marriage. Birth control advocates, such as Margaret Sanger, fought for greater availability of contraceptives, an essential condition for removing the link between sexual relations and childbearing (Mintz & Kellogg, 1988).

In the 1920s, Robert and Helen Lynd conducted a famous study of life in Muncie, Indiana, which they selected as a typical American town and called "Middletown" (Lynd & Lynd, 1929). The Lynds reported that, compared with the 1890s, young adults were more likely to view romantic love as the only valid basis for marriage. In this new romantic climate, they noted, women were more concerned with "youthful beauty." Throughout the country, mass production and rising incomes made fashionable clothing affordable. Advice columnist Dorothy Dix told her readers that "good looks are a girl's trump card." And she counseled, "Dress well and thereby appear fifty percent better looking than you are. . . . Make yourself charming" (May, 1980). This emphasis on sexual allure was new: Prior to the twentieth century, a young woman needed to convince a suitor that she could be a good partner, but it was less important that she be attractive. Although a young man expected that his wife would bear children and that their sexual relations would be pleasurable, he didn't necessarily expect much emotional fulfillment from sex. Nor did he necessarily expect a close friendship to develop with his wife. However, by the 1920s or 1930s, as May concluded, a young man wanted "both excitement *and* domesticity in a wife" (May, 1980).

These changes ushered in what we might call, following Burgess, the **companionship marriage**, with its emphases on affection, friendship, and sexual gratification, in contrast to the **institutional marriage**, with its emphases on male authority, duty, and conformity to social norms. When looking back on Burgess's work, however, one must keep in mind that the "modern" companionship marriage that he saw emerging in the 1920s and 1930s was the single-earner, breadwinner-homemaker family that flourished in the 1950s—not the dual-earner family that emerged only in the last half of the twentieth century. Nineteen hundred thirty was the end of a three- to four-decade period during which companionship and emotional satisfaction had become central to more and more middle-class families. The husband and wife in the companionship marriage ideally adhered to a sharp division of labor (he working outside the home, she working inside the home). Nevertheless, they were supposed to be each other's companions—friends, lovers—to an extent not imagined a few generations earlier. Young women were seen increasingly as needing higher education, not so they could establish a career but rather so they could be stimulating conversationalists and adept homemakers. By midcentury, large state universities around the country enrolled hundreds of thousands of bright young women who majored in home economics or consumer science and joked that what they really hoped to get at college was an "MRS." degree.

Marriage patterns were somewhat different among African Americans in the first half of the century. Because of discrimination and lack of economic opportunity, African-American men often did not have the strong earnings record necessary to claim the authority and duty of a husband; consequently, the institutional marriage was never as strong. Statistics show that from the beginning of the twentieth century African Americans were more likely to end a marriage if there were serious difficulties than were whites (Preston, Lim, & Morgan, 1992). A comparison of the life histories of whites and blacks in the South in 1938 and 1939 collected by the Federal Writers' Project found that African-American women were more likely to leave abusive marriages than were white women (Pagnini & Morgan, 1996). Although the higher rate of divorce may reflect cultural differences, it also may reflect the lower economic benefits for women of being married. Among African Americans, then, the transition from institution to companionship was less well defined.

THE INDEPENDENT MARRIAGE

In the 1960s, the breadwinner-homemaker marriage began to lose ground as both a cultural ideal and a demographic reality. It was gradually overtaken by family forms that Burgess had not foreseen, particularly marriages in which both the husband and the wife worked outside the home. Although women continued to do most of the housework and childcare, the roles of wives and husbands became more flexible and open to negotiation. Moreover, an even more individualistic perspective on the rewards of marriage took root. When people evaluated how satisfied they were with their marriages, they thought more in terms of individual satisfaction, as opposed to the mutual satisfaction gained through building a family. Recall the two national surveys of mental health described in Chapter 1, one of which was carried out in 1957 and the other in 1976 (Veroff, Douvan, & Kulka, 1981). These surveys detected a shift in the criteria people use to evaluate whether they were satisfied with their lives. When people in the 1957 survey were asked to rate their life

FIGURE 9.1 Percentage of magazine articles containing at least one of three themes about marriage: self development, flexible and negotiable roles, and communication and openness, 1900–1979. (*Source:* Cancian, 1987).

satisfaction, their thoughts turned to the social roles they played, such as spouse or parent. For example, in the 1950s, the editors of *McCall's* magazine wrote of a "new and warmer way of life," through which people would become fulfilled "not as women alone or men alone, isolated from one another, but as a family sharing a common experience" (Friedan, 1963)[2] Men who felt they were good workers and good providers tended to be more satisfied, as did women who felt they were good mothers and supportive wives. In other words, in 1957, people often used criteria external to themselves to decide how satisfied they were with their lives.

But by 1976, people were more likely to use internal criteria. When asked how satisfied they were, the people in the 1976 survey responded in terms of their own sense of personal fulfillment, emotional satisfaction, and self-development. It mattered less how well they were performing the roles society expected of them, such as earning money, raising children, or working hard on the job. It mattered more how much they enjoyed their jobs, how much emotional satisfaction they were getting from their marriages, how gratifying their sexual relationships were, and how pleased they were with the ways their lives were changing and developing. Being a good citizen or a responsible parent was less important; being emotionally satisfied was more important. Feeling that you were meeting your obligations to others was less central; feeling that you had opportunities to grow as a person was more central.

Francesca Cancian documented the changing beliefs about marriage by studying popular magazine articles offering marital advice in every decade between 1900 and 1979 (Cancian, 1987). She identified three themes that characterized beliefs about the post–1960-style marriage. The first was "self-development," the belief that each person should develop a fulfilling, independent self instead of merely sacrificing oneself to one's partner. Second, roles within marriage should be flexible and negotiable; and, third, communication and openness in confronting problems are essential. She then tallied the percentage of articles in each decade that contained one or more of these three themes. The results are presented in Figure 9.1. As the

[2]Cited in Mintz and Kellogg (1988).

How do Sociologists Know What They Know

Archival Research

Both Francesca M. Cancian's study of the changing content of women's magazines from 1900 to 1979 (Cancian, 1987) and Deanna L. Pagnini and S. Philip Morgan's study of biographies of African Americans and whites collected in the 1930s by the Federal Writers' Project (Pagnini & Morgan, 1996) are examples of **archival research.** This term refers to research that uses printed or written documents stored in libraries or other data archives. Historians rely on archival research of necessity because the written records of events are often the only information they have. Sociologists sometimes use this method, too, especially when they want to study social change by examining the past and comparing it with the present.

For each five-year period, Cancian selected eight articles listed in *Reader's*

Guide to Periodicals under the heading "marriage," from large-circulation magazines addressed primarily to women, such as *Ladies' Home Journal, McCall's,* and *Reader's Digest.* She recorded codes for each article according to its "dominant themes," and then tallied the codes by decade to see whether the themes had changed over time (see Figure 9.1). Pagnini read all 1,170 life histories that were collected by the Federal Writers' Project in 1938 and 1939 in the South and stored at the Southern Historical Collection at the University of North Carolina at Chapel Hill. Every time she encountered material on marriage or nonmarital childbearing, she prepared an excerpt that had no identifying information except an identification number. Later, Pagnini and Morgan analyzed the content of each excerpt (e.g., whether a woman who had an abusive marriage had left it) without

knowing the race of the person whose excerpt they were examining. Only after the excerpts had been examined did they use the identification numbers to assign the proper race to each excerpt. (If you are interested in the biographies that the Federal Writers' Project collected, you can view some of them through the web site of the Library of Congress [Lcweb2.loc.gov/ wpaintro/wpahome.html] and search their contents through key words such as "marriage" or "divorce.")

Archival research presents many challenges. The best archival researchers know these limitations, face them squarely, and take pains to minimize them. First, it is difficult to know how representative the materials are. For instance, did the articles Cancian selected represent the views of American women at the time? Cancian forthrightly acknowledged this limitation:

reader can see, the presence of these themes rose in the 1920s but then declined through the 1950s. After 1960, however, these themes rose to new heights. Assuming the content of these magazines reflects cultural beliefs about love and marriage, there is indeed evidence of a shift toward a more independent conception of marriage (Cancian, 1987).[3] (On the use of historical records by sociologists, see *How Do Sociologists Know What They Know? Archival Research.*) If the 1950s were the peak of the companionship marriage, we might then call the emerging post–1960 form the **independent marriage,** with its emphases on self-development, flexible roles, and communication about problems. Cancian called the change in meaning that accompanied the transition to the independent marriage a shift "from role to self" (Cancian, 1987).

EXPLAINING THE TRANSITIONS

Why, over the past century, did the shifts from the institutional marriage to the companionship marriage and then to the independent marriage occur? Both transitions— from institutional to companionship and from companionship to independent—

[3]Cancian, also argues that a more interdependent style of marriage may arise, one which combines the mutual support of the companionship marriage with the greater equality and role sharing of the independent marriage.

The intended audience of the magazines seems to come from a higher social class in the earlier decades, and the content of the articles partly reflects the policies of editors and advertisers and the attitudes of the writers. Nonetheless, the magazines seem to provide a fairly valid measure, since my findings are consistent with the other sources of data described in this chapter (pp. 173–174).

Pagnini and Morgan frankly noted that the life histories gathered in the South overrepresented poor whites and included many blacks:

> While these could be termed limitations in that they do not statistically reflect the class, marriage, and geographical distribution of the Southern population, we would label them as strengths. So often in historical work we are not able to find materials about the working class or blacks; to have both is an advantage (p. 1702).

Another difficulty in archival research is determining how accurate the information is. For instance, the biographies of the Southerners are told through the words of the writers, who determined what questions to ask and what words to write down. Moreover, the subjects were recalling events that took place, in some cases, decades earlier. Pagnini and Morgan claimed that they could make a virtue out of this necessity:

> Thus, we must be aware that we are dealing with subjective perceptions and selected events . . . For those interviewed, we have memories and perceptions of what was important to these individuals and their families. We stress that for our purposes this is what we seek—there are superior sources that simply record the events themselves. Our goal here is interpretive . . . (p. 1702).

It is also difficult to know how to analyze the information. What categories should one use and how does one tell if a record fits in the category? For instance, how does a scholar reading women's magazines determine whether an article conveys a tone of self-sacrifice or self-fulfillment toward marriage? Cancian had pairs of people read and code each article independently. She set rules for interpreting the content of the magazines and refined the rules until both coders in each pair agreed on 85 percent of the coding for a particular article.

Archival research does not necessarily provide a representative picture of social history. But it is one of the only tools we have. If social scientists recognize the limitations of archival research, inform their readers about them, and take care to minimize them, the written record can provide an enlightening window on the past.

were consistent with the long-term rise in the value Americans and citizens of other Western nations place on individualism. During the first transition, people were able to focus more on the satisfaction they derived from the small conjugal unit of spouses and children, as opposed to their membership in larger kinship groups or communities. Wives and husbands focused on the pleasures of companionship and affection and on the satisfactions of raising children together and performing their respective roles as homemaker or breadwinner. Yet there was little to prevent people from eventually pushing individualism one step further—to their own personal growth, to the development of their own adult personalities, to their own feelings of fulfillment. Once they began to do so in the 1960s, pressures rose to make marital roles more flexible and negotiable and to focus more on the individual concerns of the spouses. The second transition then ensued. In addition, both transitions had economic roots. When most people's standard of living was so low that they had difficulty earning enough money for food and shelter, few had time for personal fulfillment. People needed to pool earnings and housework with spouses and children in order to subsist, and marriage was therefore more of an economic partnership. The rising standard of living during the twentieth century gave more people the luxury of focusing on their own feelings of satisfaction. They did so first in the context of the companionship marriage, focusing on the satisfactions of having one's spouse as a friend and raising children together. Moreover, the movement of women into the labor force during the century gave women more opportunities for independent living, even though their wages have remained well below men's. Their greater economic leverage could be used to demand more satisfaction from marriage. Their jobs also gave them a life outside the home. Women as well as men could now think in terms of their own individual development through adulthood.

To be sure, this description fits middle-class families better than others. Even among them, the companionship and independent marriages still represent ideal types, not fully achieved. For the poor, personal fulfillment has remained a luxury, and marriage of any kind has become less common and more brittle. Yet the sharply rising incomes of the 1950s and 1960s did bring a level of prosperity to the working class that it had not seen before. Assisted by veterans' benefits, millions of blue-collar workers and their wives and children were able to buy homes in the suburbs. Many of them followed the breadwinner-homemaker norm. Even in working-class families where wives worked for pay, it was common for the husband and wife both to think that it would be preferable for her to stay home if finances allowed (Rubin, 1976). Then, in the 1970s and 1980s, the incomes of young working-class men fell due to the restructuring of the economy. Having wives work for pay became an unavoidable necessity to most young couples. Whether this change caused a more independent form of marriage to emerge among the working class is unclear. On the one hand, more working-class wives have independent sources of income; on the other hand, growing financial pressures may have limited the focus on personal development that has characterized middle-class marriages.

RELIGION AND MARRIAGE

Organized religion in the United States has always supported marriage, and it continued to do so throughout the transitions to the companionship and independent marriages. In recent decades, one of the greatest changes in the influence of religion on family life has been the convergence in the practices of Catholic and Protestant families (Thornton, 1985). The numbers of Catholics surged in the United States during the late nineteenth and early twentieth centuries, as large numbers of immigrants from heavily Catholic countries in Southern and Eastern Europe (e.g., Italy, Poland) arrived. The teaching of the Catholic church is that marriage is a sacrament that can be dissolved only by annulment (a decree by the Church that a marriage was never valid). Moreover, the primary purpose of marriage, the Church teaches, is to bear and rear children, and all forms of artificial birth control and abortion are forbidden. In the first half of the twentieth century, Catholic families had more children, used birth control methods less, and had lower divorce rates than did Protestants. But by 1980, these differences had been greatly reduced. Among young Catholics aged 18 to 29 in a 1979 survey, 95 percent approved of birth control, and 89 percent approved of remarriage for divorced people (D'Antonio, 1985). Personal autonomy has replaced obedience to religious authority as the main determinant of family-related behavior among American Catholics.

Whereas Catholics have been changing greatly in their attitude toward religious authority, fundamentalist Protestants have changed much less (Thornton, 1985). They now constitute a distinctive subgroup in terms of family life: Compared with other religious groups, they are less likely to divorce, they have the highest birthrates, they have the lowest rates of married women working outside the home, and they have the most conservative attitudes toward gender roles (Ammerman & Roof, 1995). Although there is variation among fundamentalist families, they tend to hold to a more literal interpretation of the Bible, which leads them to view husbands as the authority in the home.

More generally, churches and synagogues remain strong supporters of marriage. (The link between church and marriage is less central among African-American churches because, while supporting marriages, these churches have historically reached out to the larger percentage of single-parent families [Gilkes, 1995].) And among married persons, those who are active religiously describe themselves as somewhat happier with their marriages, although it is not clear that religious activity causes the greater happiness (Booth, Johnson, Branaman, & Sica, 1995). In recent years, churches have been an expanding base for counseling, educational programs, and other attempts at "marriage-strengthening" (Stanley, Markman, St. Peters, & Leber, 1995). For example, some educational programs teach communication skills to engaged or recently married couples so that they will be better equipped to discuss and resolve problems that may arise.

INTERACTION IN NONMARITAL UNIONS

After 1960, there was less reason to restrict intimate relationships to marriage of any form. Rather, single women and men could find emotional and sexual fulfillment in nonmarital relationships to a much greater degree than previously. Beginning in the 1960s, as chronicled in Chapters 7 and 8, the proportion of young adults who engaged in premarital intercourse increased sharply, and cohabitation prior to (or after) marriage grew from the frowned-upon behavior of a fringe to the accepted behavior of a majority. The introduction of improved contraceptive methods in the 1960s, particularly the birth control pill, reduced the risk of unintended pregnancy, and the greater availability of abortion after the 1973 Supreme Court decision *Roe* v. *Wade* made it easier to terminate an unintended pregnancy. These changes allowed intimate relationships to thrive outside marriage in a way they had never done before; marriage was simply less necessary.

COHABITING COUPLES

In many respects, cohabiting relationships are even more independence-oriented than contemporary marriages. For example, marriages appear to be more likely to end in divorce when both spouses work outside the home than when only one does (see Chapter 12). But among cohabiting couples, unions are *less* likely to disrupt when both partners work for pay and their earnings are more equal, according to one study (Brines & Joyner, 1993). The authors suggested that cohabiting couples are more inclined to judge the worth of their relationship in terms of equity and fairness rather than in terms of fixed roles such as breadwinner and homemaker. An emphasis on equity and fairness suggests that flexibility, negotiation, and communication about problems would be a larger part of cohabiting relationships than of marriages. Cohabitors are even less focused on children, because fewer of them already have children or plan to have children in the near future (Rindfuss & VandenHeuvel, 1990). Friends and relatives don't expect that the relationship will last for life and aren't surprised if it doesn't. In all heterosexual and most homosexual cases, no wedding ceremony—or gay or lesbian alternative ceremony—has been held. A partner need take no legal action to end his or her relationship or to start another one.

As a result, both heterosexual and homosexual cohabiting couples seem to break up at higher rates than legally married couples. Philip Blumstein and Pepper Schwartz followed a sample of gay and lesbian and heterosexual cohabiting couples and married couples for 18 months. At the beginning of the period, all the groups were similar in their opinions of whether their relationships were likely to continue. But by the end of the period, only 4 percent of the married couples had broken up, compared with 22 percent of the lesbian couples, 17 percent of the heterosexual cohabiting couples, and 16 percent of the gay male couples (Blumstein & Schwartz, 1983). So the rate of dissolution was four to five times higher for all the nonmarried groups than for married couples. If this difference in rates were to hold over 36 additional months, about half of all the nonmarried couples would have broken up, as opposed to less than 20 percent of all the married couples. Opposite-sex and same-sex cohabitation seems to be a continuation, even an enhancement, of the movement toward a greater emphasis on individualism in intimate partnerships.

GAY AND LESBIAN COUPLES

Gay and lesbian couples, about whom relatively little has been written, seem concerned with the issue of self-development versus commitment to a partner in ways that are similar to the concern of heterosexual couples. Many gay and lesbian activists have sought legal changes that could secure rights and benefits for homosexual couples that are similar to the rights and benefits of married couples. (See *Families and Public Policy:* Domestic Partnerships.) Although there are no adequate data, studies suggest that a large majority of lesbians and a substantial

Lesbian and gay couples face many of the same relationship issues as cohabiting heterosexual couples.

proportion of gay men—perhaps even a majority—have steady relationships (Peplau, 1991). In many, though not all, cases, these steady relationships involve living together. Studies that have compared gay, lesbian, and heterosexual couples find no significant differences in love or relationship satisfaction. When a sample of homosexual and heterosexual couples were asked what were the "best things" and "worst things" about their relationships, a panel of raters who were given the written comments could not tell which comments came from homosexuals and which came from heterosexuals (Peplau, 1991).

Kath Weston, an anthropologist who studied lesbian and gay couples in San Francisco in the 1980s, reported a concern about excessive "merging." The problem, she wrote, is to avoid becoming so united with and dependent on your partner that you lose your independence and can't develop as a person. This language is similar to the way many married persons talk about the need to maintain a growing, independent self. Moreover, in their paid work and home lives, lesbian and gay couples fit the model of the independent marriage well: They tend to rely less on a division of labor than do heterosexual couples. Instead, they seem to split the domestic chores more equitably and flexibly, with partners sharing various tasks such as cooking and cleaning (Seidman, 1991).

The term "family" may carry different connotations for lesbians and gay men than for heterosexuals. Among married heterosexuals, the primary family unit is usually the wife, husband, and children—the conjugal family. "Family" can also mean the larger group of relatives including grandparents, brothers and sisters, and so forth; but these kin are usually of lesser importance than one's spouse. Weston argues that among gay and lesbian couples in San Francisco, the primary meaning of "family" encompasses not only one's partner but also a network of close friends. In fact, friends may be more central to your "family" than a partner because of the high likelihood that you and your lover will eventually dissolve your partnership. Weston cites a common adage that friends last, while lovers are simply "passing through" (Weston, 1991). The families of many of the people she studied consisted fundamentally of networks of friends and lovers who provided social and emotional support for one another. Family, she was often told, means having people you can count on—people who are "there for you." Thus the term "family" referred to a more or less stable group of people who served as a support network for one another. A partner might be integrated into this network, and he or she might remain in the network even if the partnership ended. A family of this kind seems similar to the kinds of kin networks African Americans often construct. As described in Chapter 5, many low-income blacks belong to families in which the marriage bond is less important, and the ties to a network of kin are more important, than in the dominant white middle-class model of family structure. What counts in these networks is whether a person offers regular support to others, not what her or his genealogical position is on a family tree.

Nevertheless, the heavy reliance on friends rather than biological kin is a distinctive feature of the family networks of gay men and lesbians. The relationships between gay people and their parents and siblings vary greatly, depending on whether they have come out and what the reactions of the blood relatives were to the announcement. What gay people must do is create a family from the relationships they can retain with biological kin, the close friends they have, and their present and former partners. One person told Weston, "Gay people really have to work to make family" (Weston, 1991). In contrast, most heterosexuals have a biological family they can take for granted and another family they acquire through

Families and Public Policy

Domestic Partnerships

Getting married is not only a way for couples to express their love and commitment to each other but also a way for them to obtain important practical and financial advantages not available to couples who cohabit or live apart. In most nations the law has long recognized marriage as a privileged relationship in which the spouses have special rights and responsibilities. Here is a partial list of rights and responsibilities that married couples have but cohabiting couples, in most jurisdictions in the United States, do not have:

- They can include each other as beneficiaries on pension and annuity plans offered by their employers, and they can purchase health insurance for each other through their employers.
- They can file a joint income tax return, which may reduce their tax liability.
- They can receive Social Security survivors' benefits if their spouse dies, and they can inherit from each other even when there is no will.
- They are jointly responsible for their children, and each can give legal

permission to schools, doctors, and the like, for trips, operations, and so forth.
- They can adopt children together.
- In the event of a divorce, they are both normally entitled to either custody or visitation rights.

This list reflects the view, virtually unchallenged until a few decades ago, that marriage constitutes the only legitimate context for the raising of children. It also reflects the ideal, prominent in the first half of the twentieth century, that families should have one wage earner (the husband), who should be able to provide health insurance, survivors' benefits, and so on, to his wife.

Yet social changes have made the granting of rights solely to married couples debatable. For instance, about 8 percent of all births in the United States occur to women who are cohabiting with the fathers of their children.[1] Cohabitation itself is so common that some observers question the rationale for denying cohabiting couples similar rights to those married couples have. They argue that there is little difference between a cohabiting couple raising children and a married couple raising

children—and that the former ought to have the same rights and receive the same benefits as the latter. Others favor retaining the privileged place of marriage for any of several reasons: because of a moral or religious belief that heterosexual marriage is the only proper setting for having and raising children; because of a pragmatic belief that marriage provides a more stable two-parent setting than cohabitation; or because of a wish to avoid further spending by government or business that would be triggered by treating cohabitors like spouses.

Cohabiting heterosexual couples, at least, can avail themselves of these benefits by marrying. Lesbian and gay couples cannot. No U.S. jurisdiction recognizes marriage between people of the same sex. As noted in Chapter 1, a lawsuit that could result in legal same-sex marriage in Hawaii is working its way through that state's courts. And in response, the U.S. Congress passed the Defense of Marriage Act (Public Law 104-199) in 1996, which decreed that a state need not recognize a marriage license granted to a same-sex couple in another state. It is not clear whether the Defense of Marriage Act would withstand a challenge to its constitutionality because

marriage (although people in stepfamilies must also do the work of constructing a family—see Chapter 13). The families woven together by lesbians and gay men are another example of created kinship—the kind of kinship people must work to construct. "There's a way of doing it gay," another person remarked to Weston about family ties, "but it's a whole lot harder, and it's less secure" (Weston, 1991).

MEASURING MARITAL SUCCESS

Although Burgess drew eclectically from several theoretical traditions, he was most influenced by the symbolic interactionism developed by Mead and others at the University of Chicago (Cottrell et al., 1973). He saw marriage as a situation in

Article IV, Section I of the Constitution states, "full faith and credit shall be given in each State to the Public Acts . . . of every other state."

Whereas the early gay liberation movement—like the heterosexual New Left—endorsed sex outside conventional relationships as a political alternative to heterosexual marriage, the movement in recent years has placed increasing emphasis on securing legal rights and benefits for gay and lesbian couples (Weston, 1991). In part this change is a reaction to the greater risk of acquiring HIV (the virus that causes AIDS) in nonmonogamous relationships, and in part it reflects a more favorable view among homosexual and heterosexual liberals toward long-term family relationships than was prevalent in the late 1960s and early 1970s.

Over the past decade or so, a number of cities and counties have instituted ways for couples, whether heterosexual or homosexual, to register as "domestic partners," a kind of legal middle ground between marriage and cohabitation. In some places, domestic partners obtain minimal new rights, such as the right to visit an ill partner in a hospital (which was particularly desired by gay rights organizations due to the AIDS epidemic). In other places, such as New York City, municipal workers can obtain health insurance benefits for their domestic partners. Many of the companies and municipalities that offer benefits to unmarried partners restrict the offer to same-sex partners on the theory that heterosexual employees can marry if they wish to receive comparable benefits. So far, the costs of providing these benefits have been lower than expected because many gay or lesbian employees have partners who obtain benefits through their own jobs and because some employees find that coming out as gay isn't worth the extra benefits. New York City at first estimated that its plan would cost an additional $40 million to $75 million, but by 1994 the cost was only $4 million (Steinhauer, 1994).

The extension of rights and recognition to gay and lesbian partnerships has often been controversial. A number of local and state initiatives have been on ballots in recent years. Social conservatives believe the benefits to be an unwarranted endorsement of a form of family life they morally oppose. Advocates of domestic partnerships, and of the more radical step of legalizing gay marriages, argue, in contrast, that these steps would allow gay men and lesbians to openly live the conservative lifestyles of committed, monogamous couples. The debate reflects the weakening role of marriage in the institution of the family. Although still dominant, heterosexual marriage is no longer the only acceptable way for couples to live together. Rather, heterosexual cohabitation is broadly tolerated. This toleration is so recent, however, that there is little consensus on the rights and responsibilities heterosexual partners should have toward each other and toward the children in their households. Toleration of gay and lesbian partnerships would seem to be a logical next step. Yet it is a leap that many heterosexuals still cannot make. The extension of legally recognized domestic partnerships—and even marriage—to lesbian and gay couples is likely to remain a contentious public issue into the beginning of the twenty-first century.

[1]About 30 percent of all births occur outside marriage. And of these 30 percent, about one-fourth occur to women who are cohabiting with the fathers of their children. One-fourth of 30 percent is about 8 percent. (See Chapter 8.)

which two people construct shared meanings by interacting with each other. He and his students attempted to discover the characteristics of people, and of their relationships, that lead to successful interactions and therefore to successful marriages. This approach immediately posed the question: What is a successful marriage? More than half a century after this research tradition began, there is still no definitive answer to this question. One could define success in terms of happiness; indeed, the most frequently asked survey question on the topic is "Taking all things together, how happy would you say you are with your marriage these days?" One could also define success in terms of adjustment: accommodation to each other's needs, lack of conflict, agreement on important issues. Or one could define success simply by how long the marriage lasts. Even though these criteria overlap, they are different. I might be unhappy with my marriage but adjusted to it,

Families in Other Cultures

Love and Marriage in Japan

Is love necessary for a lasting marriage? Most Americans would say yes, of course. But marriage in other cultures suggests a different answer. Consider Japan: Marriages among the older generation, especially in rural areas, were stable but often loveless. In 1996, Yuri Uemura, an elderly woman in the town of Omiya told a *New York Times* reporter, "There was never any love between me and my husband. But, well, we survived" (Kristof, 1996). In 40 years, she said, her husband had never told her he liked her, never held her hand, never given her a present, never said "thank you," and never shown affection in any way.

Yet their marriage endured, as did most others. Until the 1980s, Japan had one of the lowest rates of divorce in the developed world. Love, however, was not the main ingredient keeping couples together. In part, strong social pressure kept couples together. Becoming divorced was shameful, a sign of individual weakness or moral failing. Marriages were also held together by a strict division of labor. Women were responsible for nearly all of the housework and

childrearing. Japanese men did, and still do, much less housework and childcare than men in Western countries such as the United States. National studies of time use in Japan from 1965 to 1990 show that husbands do only 10 percent of the housework and childcare (Tsuye, 1992; see Chapter 10 for figures for U.S. husbands).

Marriages in Japan were also held together by low expectations for love and companionship. Japanese adults viewed marriage more in terms of social roles, such as mother or wage earner, than in terms of pleasurable relationships between the wife and husband. A woman's primary family role was as mother to her children rather than as companion to her husband (Hsia & Scanzoni, 1996). With expectations low, married couples did not experience the kinds of crises Americans do if one spouse's affection for the other falters.

But marriage in Japan is changing. Women's roles are becoming more varied. Between 1965 and 1990, the proportion of married women aged 20 to 54 who were paid employees in nonagricultural industries rose from 15 to 41 percent

(Tsuye, 1992). Attitudes about women's roles are also changing. A series of national opinion surveys in Japan from 1972 to 1990 have asked women and men whether they agree with the statement that "the external world is for men and the domestic world is for women." In 1972, 83 percent of women and 84 percent of men agreed; but by 1990 just 25 percent of women and 35 percent of men agreed (Tsuye, 1992). Moreover, young adults, particularly in cities, expect more companionship from their spouses.

In these ways, Japanese marriages have become more like Western marriages, which are based on a less-strict division of labor, a larger role for married women outside the household, and more love and companionship. But these changes have also helped to produce a sharp increase in divorce. Between 1980 and 1994, the percentage of Japanese marriages that are projected to end in divorce increased from 20 percent to 29 percent (Yamamoto & Kojima, 1996). While still lower than the projection of about 50 percent in the United States, the rising divorce rate has prompted concern in Japan.

or my spouse and I might be poorly adjusted but never consider divorce because of our religious beliefs. Westerners often assume that love is the key to a lasting marriage; but marriages in non-Western countries such as Japan suggest other models (see *Families in Other Cultures:* Love and Marriage in Japan). The most common approach to the problem of definition is to combine questions on all these aspects into a single index of marital success; this is the approach Burgess's collaborators eventually settled upon in posthumous editions of his textbook (Burgess, Locke, & Thomes, 1971).

Research on marital interaction has produced hundreds of articles that report on the characteristics of successful and unsuccessful marriages. Among the more interesting results are the following: Marital success often depends less on how often (or whether) an activity occurs than on people's perception of whether the frequency

Japanese marriages have become more like Western marriages, with a greater emphasis on love and companionship. Here, three young men present their name cards to young women at a meeting arranged by a matchmaking service.

Attitudes have changed among the older generation as well. "The other day, he tried to pour me a cup of tea," Mrs. Uemura said of her husband (Kristof, 1996, p. 12). "It was a big change. I told all my friends." Yet as divorce has become more acceptable, there has also been a surge of divorces among older, traditional married couples, according to reports from demographers (Tsuye, personal communication). In support of this observation, national data show that the average age of people at the time of divorce has been increasing (Yamamoto & Kojima, 1996). Apparently, the reduced stigma of divorce has led some couples in long-term, relatively loveless marriages to break up.

The changes in Japanese marriage over the last few decades suggest that love and companionship do not keep couples together. In fact, the divorce rates in societies in which marriage is primarily a working partnership are generally lower than in societies in which marriage is defined in terms of love and companionship. Once marriage becomes a companionship rather than a working partnership, people who are dissatisfied with the level of love and closeness in their marriages feel justified in obtaining a divorce. As a result, Western-style marriages, while emotionally satisfying to each spouse, also lead to a higher rate of divorce.

(or occurrence) is consistent with what they wish. For example, there is little association between the frequency of sexual intercourse in a marriage and the satisfaction partners express with that marriage. Partners express more dissatisfaction when the level of intercourse differs from what they would like whether it is more frequent or less frequent (Burgess et al., 1971). Similarly, whether or not the wife is working outside the home is not as important to satisfaction as whether or not the husband is supportive of her employment (Glenn, 1990). Results such as these suggest that the fact of disagreement between spouses is itself a stronger predictor of marital success or failure than the substance of what they disagree on. According to this logic, if marriages had thermostats that controlled their temperatures, there would not be a single temperature that was best for all of them; rather, what would matter would be whether the husband and wife could agree on the temperature.

In addition, many studies show a *U*-shaped pattern of marital quality over the life course, with the quality declining when children are born and then rising when the children are older (Glenn, 1990). This does not mean that having children is bad for a marriage; rather, it shows that the first few years of parenthood are a difficult and demanding period during which there is less time for other satisfying activities. That many parents have more than one child suggests that the rewards of raising children outweigh these temporary declines in marital satisfaction. The transition to parenthood will be discussed later in this chapter.

Studies have also demonstrated that wives and husbands don't necessarily agree on the success of their marriages. In the first early study to use a reasonably representative sample of marriages, the correlation between husbands' and wives' ratings was 0.36, meaning that one partner's responses accounted for only about 13 percent of the variation in the other partner's responses (Locke, 1951). This discrepancy is important because many research projects have asked questions of just one person per couple. Finally, the literature also contains numerous findings about characteristics that predict marital success, many of them unsurprising, at least in retrospect: higher education, a longer period of engagement, regular church or synagogue attendance, marriage after the teenage years, and so forth. Yet questionnaires based solely on these findings have generally had only modest success in predicting marital quality over time. The questionnaires that show better predictive ability include a much wider range of questions.[4]

OBSERVING COMMUNICATION

Psychologists and communications specialists have developed another approach to studying marital interaction, based on the following logic: Instead of merely asking a couple (or, worse yet, just one member of the couple) how they get along, why not observe them directly? And if the amount of disagreement is a critical factor in marital success, why not observe them while they are in conflict? Most sociological studies of marital interaction have been based solely on long questionnaires that the subjects fill out. Numerous questions—sometimes well over 100—on various aspects of marital success are presented, such as "When disagreements arise, do they generally result in: you giving in, your spouse giving in, neither giving in, or agreement by mutual give-and-take?" Or "How frequently do you and your spouse get on each other's nerves around the house?"[5] Even though any single question is an incomplete and imperfect measure of marital success, the statistical theory is that if you combined the answers to many similar questions, you can obtain a reliable scale of marital success.

But this method assumes that the subjects' reports are an accurate reflection of both their behavior and their spouse's behavior. Although most people try to answer honestly, it is possible that their memories and perceptions about the relationship are inaccurate. Psychologist John Gottman began a series of laboratory studies in which he and his colleagues videotaped couples discussing mutual problems and then studied in great detail the sequences of communications

---

[4]The better questionnaires include questions on a number of more social psychological domains, such as conflict resolution, realistic expectations, and attitudes of family and friends; see, for example, Larsen and Olson (1989).

[5]With minor modifications, these items are taken from the marital adjustment questionnaire presented in Burgess et al. (1971).

Married couples in distress exhibit cycles of anger and accusation, with one person's display of negative feelings leading to an expression of negative feelings by the other.

between them (Gottman, 1979). He then noted differences in communication between couples whose marriages seemed to be distressed (according to low scores on a Burgess-like marital success questionnaire) and those that seemed nondistressed (according to high scores).[6] Viewing the videotapes over and over, trained raters coded each phrase a person uttered according to its verbal content and non-verbal emotion.

Gottman and his colleagues found that nonverbal behavior—the feelings the couple showed—was a better predictor of whether or not a marriage was distressed than verbal behavior—what they said. Although distressed couples showed just as much positive feelings as nondistressed couples, they showed more negative feelings. In addition, distressed couples were more likely to reciprocate each other's negative feelings. That is, when the researchers examined the sequence of communications, they found that among distressed couples a negative gesture or tone of voice on the part of one spouse was more likely to lead to a negative gesture or tone of voice on the part of the other, which in turn was more likely to lead to yet another. So among distressed couples, one person's anger or impatience was more likely to touch off a cycle of bad feelings, whereas among nondistressed couples one person's sarcasm or smirk might elicit merely attention and concern.

Moreover, there was a gender difference in how couples reacted during these negative cycles. Among distressed couples, husbands tended to withdraw emotionally from conflict more than their wives, whereas wives attempted to engage their husbands in continuing discussions. This difference is consistent with the complaints, common among couples seeking counseling, that the wife sees her husband as withdrawn and aloof and the husband sees his wife as overly emotional

---

[6]In some studies, the investigators compared couples who were seeking marital counseling with couples who answered an advertisement for couples who thought their relationship was "mutually satisfying." Note that, using either criterion, couples in the middle of the distribution of distress or satisfaction were not studied; Gottman (1979).

and even nagging (Markman & Kraft, 1989). In another study, Robert Levenson and Gottman attached devices to each spouse that measured changes in physiological arousal: heart rate, blood pressure, perspiration, and body movements. Increases in these measures of arousal proved to be better predictors of marital satisfaction than were the observational measures (Levenson & Gottman, 1983). When these couples were reinterviewed three years later, the researchers found that the more aroused a person had been in the earlier study, the more his or her marital satisfaction had declined (Levenson & Gottman, 1985).

Gottman and Levenson speculate that men may be more aroused physiologically under extreme stress and that their problem-solving ability may suffer as a result. In other words, as men enter an argument, the "fight-or-flight" response of increased heart rate, blood pressure, and perspiration occurs to a greater degree and then dissipates more slowly than is the case among women. Less able to argue coolly, according to Gottman and Levenson's line of reasoning, men attempt to withdraw from the argument, which frustrates and angers their wives, who attempt to pursue the point further (Gottman & Levenson, 1987). It is an intriguing hypothesis, but relevant evidence is as yet modest. Sociologists would add that there are other reasons why men may withdraw and women may engage during arguments, most notably that men are socialized to hide and suppress their feelings, whereas women are socialized to express them.

In any event, negative cycles of anger and accusation, leading to the husband's attempted withdrawal and the wife's pursuit, seem to be a central part of the distress of unhappy marriages. One strategy, then, for strengthening marriages would be to teach better communication and problem-solving skills. Behavior-oriented psychologists such as Howard Markman and his collaborators have developed programs that attempt to do so. These interventions teach couples many techniques, such as establishing separate problem-discussion and problem-solution phases in any dispute (in the former phase feelings are expressed but no resolution is expected); allowing either person to stop the action if she or he agrees to discuss the issue in the not-too-distant future; and establishing clear rules about alternating between speaking and listening (Markman, Floyd, Stanley, & Storaasli, 1988).

As promising as behavior modification approaches such as this one may be, they assume that the problems couples face can be overcome if their communication skills are good enough. "Interaction seems to us to be the litmus test of a marriage," wrote Levenson and Gottman. "On a day to day basis, the quality of interaction defines the quality of a marriage" (Levenson & Gottman, 1985). Sociologists wouldn't deny the importance of interaction, but they would suggest that married couples' problems are often due to external factors, such as poverty or unemployment. Unless these external difficulties are resolved, sociologists would suggest, many couples will be unable to improve the quality of their marriages. Not so, say some of the communications specialists. "It is not the lack of money that causes marital problems," wrote Mary Anne Fitzpatrick, "but rather how the couples communicate and negotiate with each other about their economic difficulties" (Fitzpatrick, 1988). The truth must be somewhere in between. Undoubtedly, there are some couples who would remain in conflict even if they hit the lottery. On the other hand, couples with more money have fewer economic difficulties to argue about, which is one reason why higher-income couples are less likely to divorce (Sweet & Bumpass, 1987). Both the psychologists' microperspective on interaction and the sociologists' macroperspective on the external social world contribute to our understanding of what makes marriages work.

IS MARRIAGE GOOD FOR YOU?

Do individuals benefit from being married? A substantial body of literature shows that married men appear advantaged compared with unmarried men in many ways and that, to a lesser extent, married women seem advantaged as well. But it is difficult to know whether marriage *causes* these differences.

For example, married men and women live longer, on average, than do unmarried men and women. A recent study estimated that married men and women who are age 48 have a greater-than-80-percent chance of reaching age 65, whereas never-married and divorced men and women have a less-than-70-percent chance of living that long (Waite & Lillard, 1995). A number of studies have found evidence that married men have substantially better health then unmarried men, in terms of general life satisfaction, depression and anxiety, and treatment for psychiatric difficulties. The same relationships hold for women, but the differences between the married and the unmarried are smaller. (See Gove, Style, & Hughes, 1990, for a review.)

There are two possible reasons for these findings:

1 *Being married actually causes people to feel better and live longer.* Waite (1995) suggests two ways that marriage might be good for one's physical and mental health. First, it may deter people from undertaking risky behavior. Married men and women are less likely to drink and drive, abuse alcohol or drugs, and get into serious arguments (Umberson, 1987). Marriage may provide people with a

Married people seem advantaged compared with unmarried people in several ways, but the advantages appear greater for men than for women.

sense of responsibility to children and spouses that leads them to take fewer risks. In addition, marriage may provide a partner who monitors a person's health closely and urges a healthier lifestyle. Second, married people have higher incomes and more wealth (Smith, 1994), in part because of economies of scale (two people can share a home or a car). A higher standard of living eases stress and makes people less likely to abuse alcohol or drugs.

2 *Mentally and physically healthier people are more likely to get married and to stay married.* As women and men choose partners, we would expect them to favor the healthy and the happy over the troubled and the ill. So there should be *positive selection into* marriage: People with positive qualities are more likely to enter into it. Recall the discussion in Chapter 8 of the selection effect on teenage childbearing: Young women who have children as adolescents are not a random sample of all adolescents. Similarly, people who marry are not a random sample of all adults; rather, they represent the most attractive 90 percent of the population in the marriage market. Moreover, people with poorer mental health have marriages that are more troubled and are therefore more likely to divorce. So as couples age, there is *negative selection out of* marriage: People with negative characteristics are more likely to leave it. Because of selection into and out of marriage, we would expect currently married individuals to be physically and mentally healthier even if what goes on in a marriage has nothing to do with it.

Because sociologists cannot randomly assign some people to marry and others to stay single and then study them, we cannot say definitively whether being married actually causes people's health and mood to improve or whether we are merely witnessing a selection effect. But the findings for men, at least, are so strong and consistent across a number of studies of different domains of life as to suggest that some of the advantages shown by married men are caused by the marriage relationship itself. And it is quite possible that there are some benefits for women as well. If the effects of marriage were purely due to selection, we would expect that as people get older, the difference between the married and unmarried would increase—because the unmarried group would be composed more and more of unhealthy individuals who never married or who divorced. But data on death rates and treatment for mental illness do not show a gap between the married and the unmarried that increases with age (Gove et al., 1990).

That the effects are often stronger for men suggests that marriage may benefit men more than women. Recall from Chapter 8 that when cohabiting couples marry, women's time spent in housework increases, but men's does not. For many women, this increase constitutes a housework penalty that they must pay for marrying. Moreover, as Chapter 15 will show, women are enmeshed in support networks with other women—mothers, sisters, grandmothers—much more than men are. In contrast, men tend to rely heavily on their wives for social support. Unmarried men, then, have fewer social resources to draw upon than do unmarried women, and they therefore have more to gain from marrying. Finally, marriage has played a crucial role in defining what it means to be an adult male in our society (Nock, 1998). Chapter 3 presented theories of gender suggesting that men define themselves by separating from their birth family more than women do (Chodorow, 1978). Marriage has been the culturally approved way for men to achieve this separation in adulthood. It leads to noticeable changes in their public behavior: Married men spend more time with relatives or at religious services and events, and less time with friends and at bars or taverns, than they did before they married

Having a new baby can change the relationship of a married couple, sometimes causing stress but also bringing satisfaction.

(Nock, 1998). It is the way that men in American society have taken on the culturally prescribed roles of wage earner, father, and public citizen.

THE TRANSITION TO PARENTHOOD

CHILDREN AND MARITAL SATISFACTION

Because humans have had children since the evolution of the species, you might think parents would adjust easily to the presence of a newborn child. In fact, some do. But others find, often to their surprise, that the adjustment is difficult. The birth of a child can change the relationship between a wife and husband in ways that cause psychological stress and reduce their satisfaction with their marriage. Numerous studies show that parents of infants and toddlers report lower levels of satisfaction with their marriages after their first child is born than beforehand. But it is not clear how to interpret this drop. For one thing, marital satisfaction tends to decline from its peak during the honeymoon period regardless of whether a child is born. A few recent studies have found that childless couples experience a similar drop in marital satisfaction over time.[7]

Moreover, the same parents who tell social scientists that their marriages are less satisfying also report that having a child is a deeply moving and gratifying experience. A study reported that "romance" scores among new parents decreased but "partnership" scores increased (Belsky, Spanier, & Rovine, 1983). Another found that fathers reported a sense of "being more of a family" and mothers reported that their overall life satisfaction seemed to increase (Grossman, Eichler, & Winikoff, 1980).[8] Indeed, if parenthood were uniformly grim, it would be hard to explain why 80 to 90 percent of all adults have children.

---

[7]These studies are summarized in Glenn (1990).
[8]Cited in Entwisle (1985).

Having a child, then, has effects that seem to both increase and decrease parents' satisfaction. During the last half of the twentieth century, as was just discussed, people's sense of life satisfaction has depended less and less on how well they perform their social roles and more and more on their own sense of personal fulfillment. This is a shift toward the kind of satisfaction that is associated with the rise of the private family. Parenthood, in contrast, has always provided the kind of satisfaction associated with the public family: pleasure in the performance of a socially valued role (in this case, raising children). Becoming a parent increases most people's sense that their lives are satisfying and meaningful because of their commitment to others—their children. But parenthood can also interfere with the newer, self-oriented kind of satisfaction. The time and effort required to care for a small child can interfere with the parents' feelings of romance, intimacy, and sexual gratification.

Some of the adjustment difficulties of parenthood, therefore, are peculiarly modern. One hundred years ago, married couples were less concerned about achieving self-fulfillment, so children's interference with their parents' lives was perceived as less of a problem. Today, however, children can simultaneously lower a parent's sense of marital satisfaction and raise his or her sense of broader life satisfaction. In addition, parenthood disrupts the employment of mothers far more than was the case at the beginning of the century. Although it was common for young, single women to work, most women expected to stop working outside the home after they had children. Today, half of all mothers return to paid employment within a year of the birth of a child. Yet mothers who work outside the home still do most of the childcare and housework. How to mix employment and parenthood is a major issue for many couples, and its ramifications will be examined in the next chapter.

Moreover, new parents have less experience in childrearing than was the case prior to industrialization in the West—and still is in developing countries (Weisner, 1987). When birthrates were high and families worked in joint agricultural enterprises, older siblings often supervised and cared for younger siblings. While growing up, older and middle siblings—especially girls—learned how to carry, feed, discipline, and nurture a young child. Today, in contrast, weekend baby-sitting is the closest many young adults get to caring for a child until the day they bring one home, crying and fussing, from the hospital.

NEW BABY CARE AND GENDER ROLES

It's far easier for a married couple to have an egalitarian division of labor before they have children than afterward. Even couples who have shared household tasks more or less equally often find that the birth of a child introduces a sharper division of labor. For example, Ralph LaRossa and Maureen Mulligan LaRossa studied 20 white, middle-class couples just after they had their first or second child (LaRossa & LaRossa, 1981). When asked who was caring for the new baby, every couple said the husband was "helping" the wife, but not one said the wife was helping the husband. Clearly, the wife had major responsibility in all cases. The authors note that the father distanced himself from the role of parent by, for example, holding the newborn infant awkwardly at first. His feelings of incompetence were often reinforced by the anxious behavior of wives and grandmothers, who were ready to step in as soon as he or the infant seemed uneasy. In contrast, the mother embraced the role of parent by holding the newborn confidently and discouraging assistance from others. In addition, as other studies show, some new mothers are reluctant to encourage fathers to take on a large role. One mother told the Cowans, "I love seeing the closeness between him and the baby . . . but if he

Although the proportion of fathers who share in the care of their young children has increased, mothers still do most of it.

does well at his work *and* his relationship with the baby, what's my special contribution?" (Cowan & Cowan, 1987). Through these strategies of "role distancing" (by the father) and "role embracing" (by the mother) just after the birth, couples begin to define a division of labor in which primary care is the mother's responsibility.

When fathers do help, they tend to play with the baby. Play, as the LaRossas point out, is a self-contained interaction, easier to postpone for a few minutes and easier to stop, as opposed to more urgent and messy tasks such as changing diapers. It is likely to arouse smiles and laughter from the child. Fathers' physical, arousing play gives their children experience with a range of emotions; it can also help children learn to regulate their own emotions appropriately—a skill that helps them form friendships with other children (MacDonald & Parke, 1984).[9] But when it's time for a feeding or a bath, the father usually hands the baby back to the mother. There are some exceptions—fathers who do a greater share of the care or even divide the responsibility equally.

Studies show that the transition to parenthood is somewhat different for working-class couples. In one of the few studies to examine social class differences, Doris Entwisle and Susan Doering followed 120 white couples, half blue collar and half white

[9]Cited in Chase-Lansdale and Vinovskis (1993).

collar (according to their fathers' and husbands' occupations) from six months before their first births to six months after. They found that blue-collar husbands tended to defer to their wives in childcare matters more than white-collar husbands. The latter group rated their fathering behavior as more successful if they thought their infants were happy and content when they cared for them, whereas the blue-collar husbands seemed to see the infants' happiness as their wives' concern, not theirs. Blue-collar husbands, in other words, tended to view themselves as caretakers' helpers; if the caretakers (their wives) were satisfied with how much they helped, so were they. Middle-class men, in contrast, viewed themselves as bona fide caretakers and were more independent, even though their wives still did more care. If their babies seemed satisfied with their performances, so were they (Entwisle & Doering, 1981). Entwisle and Doering suggest that the differences in men's behaviors were consistent with other studies of class differences in personalities. Blue-collar men, who must follow orders on the job, tend to be more conformist—indeed, they are often socialized that way by their blue-collar parents (see Chapter 14)—whereas middle-class men, who must often show initiative and flexibility, are more self-directed.

One of the few studies to look both at blacks and whites and at unmarried mothers suggests that the findings for white, married couples don't necessarily apply to other groups. Philip Morgan and Linda Waite reported that, in a national sample of high school seniors who were followed for seven years, white women who married and then gave birth did, indeed, become less egalitarian in their attitudes toward women's and men's family roles, just as numerous smaller studies have shown. But unmarried women—and unmarried African-American women in particular—who gave birth became *more* egalitarian in their attitudes. The authors speculate that unmarried mothers, who often can't stay home to raise their children, become aware of the limits of the mother-homemaker role and are more likely to reject it. They assert, in addition, that young African-American women may have a difficult time finding a man who has a stable job and can support a family (Morgan & Waite, 1987). (See Chapter 5.)

MARRIAGE AS AN ONGOING PROJECT

Whereas in earlier times what mattered most in a marriage was how well you and your spouse carried out your duties, now what matters most is whether the marriage helps you to achieve a more fulfilling sense of self, to grow as an individual, or to experience a greater level of personal satisfaction. Ann Swidler writes of changes in idealized views of love in Western society, which she calls "love myths." The nineteenth-century myths defined love as a spiritual, moral matter in which sexual restraint was valued—the kinds of myths that made Maud choose Elmer. But the current love myths, Swidler argues, define love as part of a quest for fulfillment and identity (Swidler, 1980). Unlike in the past, the quest doesn't end when you find a marriage partner; on the contrary, it involves a continuing effort to find a better personal life through an evolving relationship. It also implies a new model of adulthood. In the old model, you developed an identity in young adulthood, found a partner compatible with that identity, got married, and then further personality development stopped. Now there is a cultural imperative to keep changing and developing your identity throughout adulthood in order to maintain or, better yet, increase your sense of personal fulfillment.

Developing a satisfying sense of self through love and sexual expression, then, becomes an ongoing project throughout adulthood. To carry out this project, a married

Married people sometimes seek a more satisfying personal life by attempting to change their relationship through open and honest communication.

person must be able to communicate openly and honestly with his or her spouse about thoughts and feelings. Consequently, communication and understanding become highly valued qualities in today's love myths. But suppose one partner isn't satisfied and then decides he or she can't develop his or her sexual life adequately within the relationship. Or suppose one partner feels he or she has gotten all the personal benefits out of the relationship that are possible. Then, given the new emphasis on self-fulfillment and self-development as the standards by which to judge intimate relationships, there is little reason for the unsatisfied partner to stay in the relationship. On the contrary, the emphasis on self-fulfillment encourages him or her to leave.

In this way, the new love myths devalue qualities such as commitment, trust, and permanence (Swidler, 1980). And herein lies an important reason for the sharp rise in the divorce rate in the United States and other Western nations in the 1960s and 1970s. The cultural changes surrounding love and marriage have made it more acceptable for a person to leave a relationship if he or she feels personally dissatisfied. One is no longer expected to keep a marriage together for the sake of the children—although the presence of young children does lower the odds that a couple will separate (Cherlin, 1977). This emphasis on self-fulfillment and development in marriage has placed high expectations on the relationship. Only in the twentieth century has marriage had to bear such a heavy responsibility for personal happiness, and the institution may not be able to match the expectations spouses now have. To be sure, there are other important causes of the post-1960 rise in divorce, foremost among them the increasing economic independence of women. (This topic will be examined in detail in Chapter 12.) Nevertheless, the cultural changes in the way people evaluate love and marriage have certainly played a significant role.

The increased emphasis on self-development in marriage has been criticized as creating shallow, potentially exploitative relationships in which each partner seeks what is best for his or her own development—but not what's best for the marriage and for their children. Yet there is also a positive side to this form of marriage. Communication and negotiation may allow couples to attain greater intimacy than if they were forced to retain their initial way of relating. Although it is easy to criticize the excesses of the search for a more fulfilling personal life, the ability of couples to increase their satisfaction through communication and openness may revitalize some marriages. Until recently, argues Swidler, our culture of love suggested that the only problem was finding someone to marry—that, once married, there was nothing else to worry about. It was as if adult life were unchanging and unproblematic once you married and found a job. But that is not so. Adult life today, for many, does involve changes in one's experiences outside the home. The recent cultural shifts, Swidler writes, allow for "a search for models of self and models of love that are compatible with continuing growth and change . . . rather than giving moral meaning only to the dramatic moment of the shift from youth to adulthood" (Swidler, 1980).

In the independent marriage, wives and husbands need not be locked into roles that are set when they marry. The emphasis on communication and flexibility allows them to renegotiate the marital bargain if they wish. In contrast, the roles of wives and husbands in the companionship, breadwinner-homemaker marriages were restrictive and, to a much greater extent, nonnegotiable. Husbands were often opposed to their wives' having an active life outside the home. They frequently refused to do housework and childcare. Although the husband's role relieved him of work in the home, it also denied him the opportunity to be deeply involved in his children's lives. The more flexible roles of the independent marriage allow men to develop greater involvement with their children. They also allow women to pursue a rewarding work life outside the home. In these ways, the independent marriage holds out the possibility of a fuller life for both spouses and a more equal partnership. Whether the emergence of the independent marriage is favorable for children is another issue, which will be examined in Chapter 14. Moreover, even for the spouses, the possibilities are not always realized: Few fathers share childcare and housework equally, and power imbalances remain a feature of many marriages, as the next chapter will show.

SUMMARY

1. Writing in the first half of the century, influential sociologists such as Ernest Burgess argued that the nature of the family was changing. Where once it was held together by community pressure and the authority of the family head, now it is held together more by mutual affection and companionship. Burgess urged sociologists to study the interaction between these new marital companions, who sought emotional satisfaction in fulfilling the roles of spouse and parent and in building a family. The companionship marriage that Burgess saw emerging was the single-earner, breadwinner-homemaker family that flourished in the 1950s. It was overtaken, beginning in the late 1960s, by the independent marriage, in which the spouses were increasingly concerned with personal growth and self-fulfillment.

2. Nonmarital intimate relationships have also become more common in the last few decades, due to an increase in sexual activity outside marriage, improved contraceptive methods, and a greater social acceptance of unmarried couples. Cohabiting relationships tend to be even more independence-oriented than contemporary marriages. Roles are more flexible and negotiable, and rates of dissolution are higher. Gay and lesbian couples seem concerned about the same issue of self-development versus commitment to a partner that concerns heterosexual couples. In addition, they must put together a family from networks of close friends and whatever ties they can retain with biological kin. The varied networks they build are an example of created kinship—the kind people must work to construct. Some gay and lesbian activists are pressing for laws and regulations that recognize gay couples and provide them with the same benefits married couples obtain. A number of localities have passed domestic partnership laws that grant

unmarried couples, whether same-sex or opposite-sex, some of these benefits.

3. There are several ways in which one could define a successful marriage, such as happiness, adjustment, or how long it lasts. Researchers have tended to combine these definitions into a single index of marital success. The large body of research on marital interaction has produced numerous findings on the differences between successful and unsuccessful marriages. For example, the way marital life is organized—whether the wife works outside the home, how often the couple has sex—is less important than whether the spouses agree or disagree about it. And wives' and husbands' reports on the success of their marriages don't always agree.

4. Psychologists and communications specialists have developed a research tradition of directly observing married couples during disputes and coding in great detail what is said and how it is said. Distressed couples tend to show a pattern in which one spouse's expression of negative feeling sets off a cycle of negative feelings between them. In addition, husbands tend to withdraw emotionally during disputes, whereas wives attempt to engage their husbands in continuing discussion. This difference could be due to different physiological responses, to the differential socialization of girls and boys, or to relational personality differences between men and women.

5. A substantial body of literature shows that married men appear advantaged compared with unmarried men in many ways and that, to a lesser extent, married women seem advantaged as well. There are two possible reasons for these findings: First, being married may actually cause people to feel better and live longer; and second, mentally and physically healthier people may be more likely to get married and to stay married. Both explanations are plausible, but it is likely some of the advantages shown by married men (and possibly married women) are caused by the marriage relationship itself.

6. The birth of a first child interferes with the romance and intimacy of a marriage but also produces feelings of broader life satisfaction. It frequently produces a sharper division of labor, with the wife doing more of the childcare. Men distance themselves from the role of caretaker, whereas women embrace it. Working-class husbands tend to see themselves as assistants to their wives, whereas middle-class men tend to see themselves as more directly involved in care, even if their wives do substantially more of it.

7. In the independent marriage, the relationship between the spouses is often seen as an ongoing project open to negotiation and change. Wives and husbands seek changes over time in order to develop a more satisfying sense of self. This emphasis on self-fulfillment has made it more acceptable for a person to leave a marriage if she or he feels personally dissatisfied. Still, the independent marriage allows for changes that can revitalize a marriage and for the development of a more equal partnership.

KEY TERMS

marital interaction	institutional marriage	independent marriage
companionship marriage	archival research	

FAMILIES ON THE INTERNET

Several cities now allow unmarried couples, opposite-sex and same-sex, to register and receive limited benefits similar to those enjoyed by married couples. New York's information is displayed at **www.columbia. edu/cu/gables/dpinfo_nyc/dp.brochure.html**; Seattle's is at **www.pan.ci.seattle.wa.us/seattle/leg/clerk/ dpr.htm**. A compendium of information for gay and lesbian couples is available at the web site of the Partners Task Force for Gay and Lesbian Couples, **www.buddybuddy.com/toc.html**.

There are several sites devoted to marriage enrichment or enhancement, such as **www.more-fun.com/ relationships**. Helpful information on the transition to parenthood can be found at **www.parentsoup.com**.

Power, Conflict, and Disruption

Power imbalances and conflict between women and men have a public significance beyond the immediate family context. That is to say, the consequences of conflict and of inequalities in power span both the private family, where they affect the quality of emotional support, intimacy, and cooperation, and the public family, where their social consequences are played out on a larger scale. Inequalities in power affect the division of housework and childcare and contribute to acts of violence against women. Conflict between spouses can also lead to separation, divorce, and remarriage.

Chapter 10 examines the connection between the world of work and the balance of power and authority in the family. It begins with a consideration of the meaning of power and authority, as sociologists have used the terms, and how they apply to the family. Then the chapter examines the movement of married women into the labor force and the consequences of this change for family life.

Chapter 11 considers the most extreme exercise of male power and dominance: violence against wives and partners. In addition, violence by parents of either gender against children is discussed. After a brief review of the history of domestic violence, the chapter summarizes what we know about it today. The most important theories that can explain domestic violence are presented, followed by an examination of sexual aggression and violence in dating relationships and a discussion of public policies.

Marital conflict, these days, often leads to divorce. About one of every two marriages in the United States, at current rates, would end in divorce. **Chapter 12** probes the causes and consequences of this high level of marital dissolution. The process that divorcing couples experience is examined, as are the consequences of divorce for both children and adults.

A majority of divorced persons remarry. Yet remarriage, as **Chapter 13** shows, can bring its own difficulties for adults and children. The chapter describes the new kinds of family relationships and kinship networks that form after remarriages. Then it discusses why children whose parents are remarried seem to fare no better than children in single-parent families.

CHAPTER 10

Work and Families

"After I started earning money," a billing clerk who is married to a forklift operator told a sociologist, "my husband showed me more respect" (Hochschild, 1989). She is not alone. In a Mexico City shantytown, a wife who did piecework at home and worked as a maid told an interviewer:

> *Now that I get my own money, I feel better, less short of money. . . . Before I used to ask him for everything. [He gave her a daily allowance.] I obey and respect him, but I feel I also have some rights . . . before he used to shout at me if he thought I was spending too much on the children, or did not give him the food he wanted. Now I tell him: "with the small salary you earn and you go and spend it on drinking with your friends. Look at me, I am also earning, and I do not buy anything for myself, but all I get I put in the house." It is not fair* (Benería & Roldán, 1987).

An American woman who earned far less than her husband, on the other hand, complained to her interviewers:

> *Gordon still has to have the last word on everything. We get annoyed with each other over that, but when I start to push back, he reminds me just who supports me and the children. He doesn't always bring that up, but if I start to win an argument or make more sense about something we should do, I think he gets frustrated and so he gives me his big final line which is something like, "If you're so smart, why don't you earn more money?" or how dumb I am 'cause if I had to go out and support myself I'd be a big fizzle* (Blumstein & Schwartz, 1983).

The marriages of all these women demonstrate, as numerous studies have shown, that wives have less power when they earn substantially less money than their husbands.[1] To be sure, lower earnings are not the only reason why wives typically have less power in marriages. Both wives and husbands may have been socialized to expect that the husband should be the head of the household, the person who makes the final decisions. This expectation certainly was one of the tenets of the breadwinner-homemaker family, and it is still endorsed by some couples today.

This chapter claims, nevertheless, that earnings and employment are an important part of the story of husbands' greater power and authority. Why do lower earnings translate into less power? Paula England and George Farkas argue that the investments of time and effort that a wife typically makes in the home—raising the children, providing emotional support to her husband, keeping in touch with the husband's relatives, and so forth—cannot easily be transferred to a new marriage. Rather, they are **relationship-specific investments,** efforts that are valuable only in a person's current relationship. That is to say, if a wife initiates a divorce, keeps custody of the children (as is usually the case), and wishes to remarry, she will likely find that the children—in whom she has invested much time and effort—lower her attractiveness to prospective husbands. Her efforts to nurture and support her first husband and her ties to his family also won't do her any good in the marriage market. If she doesn't wish to remarry, her income will probably be lower than before she divorced. Husbands, in contrast, tend to invest time and effort in their jobs, accruing, if they are fortunate, seniority, promotions, and wage and salary increases. These job investments can more easily be transferred to another marriage, because prospective wives will value the increased earnings (England & Farkas, 1986).

In other words, husbands and wives who work outside the home make investments in earning power that could be used in any marriage, whereas household investments can be used only in their current marriages. Wives who do not work outside the home would consequently have fewer alternative partners than their husbands, should they divorce and wish to remarry. According to social exchange theory, if person A needs the income partner B provides and values being married, and if person A has fewer alternative sources of partnership (because her investments of time and effort aren't as transferable), then A is said to be dependent on B. The degree of dependency is greater the more A needs the income and the fewer her alternatives are—which implies, in this case, that wives with little job experience and lower earning potential are more dependent. And the more A is dependent on B, the theory states, the greater is B's power over A (Emerson, 1972). He can use his greater power to shape his family's daily life and to control key decisions.

[1]For a review, see England and Farkas (1986).

This chapter will explore differences in power and authority between wives and husbands and the consequences of those differences in their daily lives. It will look historically at family power prior to the twentieth century. As will be noted, the most important twentieth-century development in family power has been the movement of married women into employment outside the home. How that movement has altered— or failed to alter—wives' and husbands' roles in the family will be discussed. Finally, the chapter will conclude with an examination of changes in the workplace that have been advocated in the wake of the great increase in wives and mothers who are employed.

POWER AND AUTHORITY

THE MEANING OF POWER

A large research literature exists on marital power, in which the word "power" is used loosely in two different senses. These parallel the distinction that sociologists make between two ways in which a person or group of people can dominate others: power and authority (Gerth & Mills, 1946). *Power,* as defined in Chapter 4, is the ability to force a person to take an action—or to accept another person's actions—even if he or she doesn't want to and resists. It is the "possibility of imposing one's will upon the behavior of other persons" (Bendix, 1960), whether or not one actually exercises this power. For example, in some societies a man can take a second wife even if his first wife objects.

Sometimes widespread cultural beliefs and values lead some people to accept the domination of others. When a group of people acknowledges the right of others to supervise and control their behavior, sociologists say that those in command are in **authority**. In distinguishing between power and authority, the key words are "acknowledged" or "accepted." I have authority over an aspect of your life if you acknowledge and accept it. The great sociologist Max Weber wrote of "patriarchalism" (most people now use the term *patriarchy,* defined in Chapter 3)—meaning a social system based on the domination of husbands and fathers over wives and children—in so-called "traditional" societies. Here, wrote Weber, the right of the husband to be dominant is supported by long-standing, widely held norms and values that both women and men accept. Therefore, Weber asserted, the patriarch rules through "traditional authority." A farm wife might accept the authority of her husband as part of the natural and correct order of society. But male authority isn't just a preindustrial phenomenon. When Adlai Stevenson told the Smith graduates in 1955 that their place in politics was to influence men through the role of housewife (see Chapter 3), he was repeating a widespread cultural belief that even many educated women themselves agreed with at the time. Many women in the audience that day must have accepted Stevenson's statement as part of the natural order of family life.

In practice, however, it is often difficult to distinguish between power and authority. Your power over me may be latent—under the surface, hidden—most of the time, but it may be real nonetheless. For instance, if you have power over me, I may refrain from doing something I know you don't like—which means that you will obtain the results you want without having to flex a muscle or withhold a penny (Komter, 1989). If a wife knows her husband adamantly opposes her working outside the home and if she fears his anger, she may not even raise the issue of taking a job. An observer might not notice the wife's latent desire to work out-side the home and the husband's power over her.

Moreover, persons in power may grant limited authority to their subordinates. I would argue that this often occurs in family life. During the nineteenth century, men accepted—even promoted—the authority of wives over moral and domestic matters. Yet wives' access to opportunities in the emerging world of paid work was limited. Today, wives often have substantial authority in the home because husbands—who do less domestic work—accept their wives' authority in this sphere. Still, most husbands retain substantial power, based on their greater earning power, and they still retain substantial authority, based on widely held, though changing, beliefs about what is proper behavior for women and men.

THE FAMILY'S INTERNAL ECONOMY

We also tend to assume that, although income is earned by individual husbands, wives, and children, it is used for the benefit of the whole family. In our own thinking about families, and in much of the academic literature, we usually ignore how income is distributed once a family member earns it. In economic writing about family income, for example, it is almost always assumed that everyone in the family has the same preferences about how to spend their income—as if the family were a single person with one set of preferences and earnings.[2] In contrast, a growing number of sociologists who study family power and authority write of the **internal economy** of the household. They mean the study of what happens to income inside the household: how much income gets allocated to meet each member's needs and whose preferences shape how income is spent.

For example, a number of studies in developing countries report a difference in how husbands and wives allocate their incomes, with husbands sometimes spending more of their income on personal consumption and leisure pursuits. Among poor farm families studied in South India, women contributed 90 to 98 percent of their income to food, clothing, and other expenses basic to the sustenance of their families, but men contributed only 70 to 74 percent of their income. Another Indian study showed that whereas children had higher levels of nutrition when their mothers had larger vegetable gardens and cash earnings, their nutritional levels improved less when their fathers' earnings increased.[3]

Nor is this imbalance in how income is spent confined to developing nations. In a study of British married couples in 1983, Jan Pahl found that if the incomes of the wife and husband increased by the same amount, 28 percent of the wife's increase would be spent on housekeeping expenses, on average, compared with 16 percent of the husband's increase. The husbands were more likely to spend part of their income on leisure, most commonly drinking and gambling (Pahl, 1989).

In nearly all the above cases in South India and Britain, the husbands' earnings exceeded the wives' earnings. The ability of husbands to hold back more income for personal consumption would seem to be a clear example of male power over women concerning family finances. But often this power shades into authority; that is to say, most wives accepted the idea that their husbands were entitled to more leisure spending because the men were steadily earning most of the family's income. "You can't deny a man when he's earning," one English woman told an interviewer (Pahl, 1989). Yet when wives had their own earnings, they were more likely to protest.

---

[2]That is to say, the husband and wife have a single, joint utility function. See Becker (1991).
[3]These two Indian studies are cited in Blumberg (1991).

All the members of a family in India join in plucking saffron flowers. Studies in developing countries such as India show that when women control some of the family's income, they are more likely than men to spend it on food, clothing, and other necessities.

POWER AND MODES OF PRODUCTION

With these ideas in mind, what can be said about the power and authority wives have historically had relative to husbands in different modes of production? The evidence is inconsistent at times, making it hard to draw definitive conclusions for every situation. Men's power has exceeded women's power—and has often far exceeded it—in almost every historical setting. That is to say, family and kinship systems are run by males almost everywhere. This discussion, then, addresses the issue of relative levels—of the degree of authority and power in family matters that wives in one society have relative to wives in other societies.

THE FAMILIAL MODE OF PRODUCTION

With the development of settled agriculture, perhaps 9,000 years ago, a way of life emerged in which families produced most of the food and goods they needed to survive. In Chapter 2, I called this arrangement the familial mode of production. At first, people used wooden digging sticks to turn the soil. The next great technological advance, perhaps 6,000 years ago, was the introduction of a metal digging stick: the hoe. It dug more deeply, unearthing more nutrients, uprooting more weeds, and therefore increasing crop yields (Huber, 1991). In many, if not most, hoe cultures, women did the hoeing and cultivation of food crops. Ester Boserup, in her influential book about women's roles in economic development, referred to hoe culture as a "female farming system" (Boserup, 1970).

In Africa, the major area in which a hoe culture still exists, men still control much of the wealth and power, but women are relatively more independent than in other agricultural societies. The major responsibilities for men, according to Boserup, were hunting, felling trees for farmland, and warfare. But these tasks have become less important over time, so that men's productive roles have declined compared with women's roles. Women not only grow most of the food, they market it. In much of Africa, women and immigrants such as Indians or Lebanese dominate the business of trading and marketing. Anthropological and

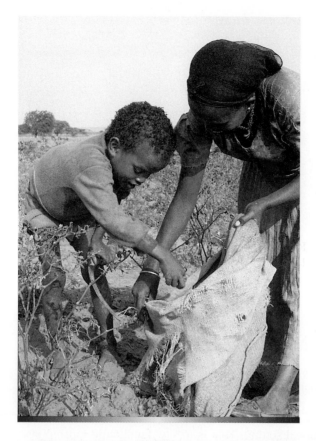

An Ethiopian mother and child harvest chili peppers in Ethiopia. In Africa, women have more responsibility for food growing and marketing than in most other developing regions.

historical studies paint a picture of wives who often have an independent economic base and who sometimes become economic entrepreneurs (Guyer, 1988).

Hoe cultures have survived in Africa because the soil is typically too thin to benefit from the next great innovation in agriculture: the plow. Able to dig deeper, the plow unearths even more nutrients and allows the same soil to be reused indefinitely—in contrast to the hoe, which exhausts the soil and forces farmers to shift from plot to plot. The introduction of the plow greatly increased crop yields. Yet, because the metal plow is heavy, men nearly always do the plowing. Therefore, Boserup refers to plow-based agriculture as a "male farming system."

The shift from hoe to plow, and from female to male food cultivators, generally restricts the autonomy of women, Boserup argues. They have much less control over the production and distribution of food. In addition, the introduction of the plow changes patterns of land inheritance. In many African hoe cultures, land is held jointly by the lineage or tribe, rather than being individually owned. A family moves on to new land when the current soil is exhausted. But in the plow culture, land tends to be owned by families—or more precisely by the male heads of families—who remain on the land and then pass ownership on to the next generation. In most such societies, the inheritance rules favor sons, although women can sometimes inherit property (especially if a family has no sons surviving to adulthood).

Consider, for example, the family of Jean-Baptiste and Rosalie, who were studied in 1861 by an associate of the French sociologist Frédéric Le Play.[4] They lived

[4]The report on this family is presented and discussed by Meyering (1990).

on a 10-acre farm in the province of Aisne with their 15- and 13-year-old sons. Two older daughters had already married and left home. The family produced most of the food they needed and grew a cash crop, hemp, the fibers of which they sold to ropemakers. During the planting season, Jean-Baptiste and his sons spread manure, plowed, and sowed the land. In the harvesting season, the whole family (including the two daughters before they were married) helped to cut, gather, and thresh the rye grain that the family used for bread and to cut and separate the hemp fiber from the stem. In the winter the family prepared the hemp fiber for sale: Jean-Baptiste cleaned and straightened it while Rosalie rolled the coils and assembled them into 5-kilogram bundles.

Rosalie also had primary responsibility for preparing the family's food, washing clothes, tending the vegetable garden, and caring for the barnyard animals (two cows, two pigs, eighteen chickens, and six rabbits). When Rosalie's children were young, her mother cared for them when she worked in the fields. When they were old enough to work in the fields, Rosalie cut back on fieldwork. Nonetheless, she still spent so much time in the fields that, unlike many other wives, she bought the family's clothes rather than making them. In addition, she sold excess food produce at local markets.

As Jean-Baptiste and Rosalie's family illustrates, in the familial mode of production there is always a clear difference in the tasks men and women do. Nevertheless, there is no question that both the wife and the husband are doing valuable, productive work. Jean-Baptiste couldn't get along without Rosalie's labor—which is why many widowers remarried quickly after their wives died. No one would think of calling Rosalie a "housewife"; no teenager would ask her sons "Does your mother work?" Yet today in common English, we often restrict the word "work" to mean working for a wage or salary outside the home, which excludes what's done in and around the home. We restrict the definition of work to mean **production for exchange value**—work for wages outside the home, or production in the home of goods or services that can be sold—rather than **production for use value**—work that produces goods and services used within the home, such as cooking food and caring for children. Yet this is a rather time- and place-bound usage, most applicable to the middle-class families in the nineteenth- and twentieth-century West who invented the housewife. It obscures the fact that important work always goes on in the household, whether or not it brings in cash.

Still, farm wives such as Rosalie had less power and independence than their husbands. Granted, they typically managed the provision of food and all or part of the family budget (Tilly & Scott, 1978). Thus, they had considerable authority within the family over daily food consumption and expenditures. Of their economic role, Thomas Tusser wrote in 1562: "husbandrie weepeth, where huswiferie sleepeth" (Pahl, 1989).[5] Yet overall control of family finances usually remained in the husband's hands. What's more, the farm wife was legally subordinate to her husband. For instance, under English law until 1882, a husband had complete control over the income and personal property of his wife, and he could dispose of it any way he wished. At the time of their marriage, the husband and wife became one legal person—and that person was effectively the husband. A married woman could not enter into a business partnership or make contracts without her husband's participation (Hall, 1990). The law also punished women more heavily than men for committing adultery and tolerated physical beatings of wives. A wife was

---

[5]By "husbandrie" Tusser here means husbandry, the management of domestic affairs on a farm by men.

important enough to the household that it would be unwise for her husband to alienate her or to go too far in mistreating her; nevertheless, he had substantial, if latent, power over her.

THE LABOR MARKET MODE OF PRODUCTION

Chapter 2 described how the introduction of the labor market mode of production changed the nature of the Western family. Initially, husbands and older children worked for wages and contributed them to a common family fund, under the control of the male head. In 1862, another of the French families studied by LePlay's associates—Constant, his wife, Madeline, and their five children, aged 6 to 20—lived in the province of Upper Rhine (Meyering, 1990). Constant and his two sons, both teenagers, worked in the same small factory weaving cotton cloth 13 hours a day. Nearly all the boys' earnings—30 to 40 percent of the family's total income—went into the family fund. Constant's earnings accounted for about 40 percent of the family's total income. The eldest daughter was a domestic servant in another local household, which relieved her parents of the burden of supporting her; the two youngest daughters, aged 10 and 6, were in school. The family also rented a room in their house to a weaver they knew.

Until 1858, when her sons were old enough to work in the factory, Madeline had worked at home winding bobbins (reels of thread) on a piece-rate basis. Now her contribution consisted of unpaid but essential work preparing food, caring for the children, cleaning the house, and making, mending, and washing the family's clothes. Like Madeline, most wives specialized in production for use value, although some earned money for work done at home such as taking in lodgers or doing laundry for wealthier families. Most husbands specialized in production for exchange value. A number of writers have proposed that greater power accrues to family members who produce for exchange value than to those who produce primarily for use value. This proposition is, in fact, the core of Friedrich Engels' analysis, more than a century ago, of the source of inequality between women and men; and related propositions have been stated frequently by others since then. Whereas men are compensated with money for their work, women's valuable work of raising children, which creates the next generation of the labor force, is unpaid. Under socialism, Engels wrote, childcare would be performed by public agencies and all women would work outside the home. Once this happened, Engels (and presumably his collaborator Karl Marx, who wrote nothing directly on the subject) believed, male domination would fade away: "The supremacy of the man in marriage is the simple consequence of his economic supremacy, and with the abolition of the latter will disappear of itself" (Engels, 1972). Socialist nations have not, however, eliminated male domination. (See *Families in Other Cultures:* Women Hold Up Half the Sky, in Chapter 6.)

In nearly all societies, wives' ability to produce goods and services for exchange is limited because they must also carry out household and childrearing tasks. These tasks, as noted above, create investments in children and husbands that would not be transferable to other marriages. Even when wives do work for pay, they may be required to turn over their income to their husbands or fathers. But where wives have control over earnings from production for exchange, so this argument goes, they have more power. Their earnings give them the stature to speak their grievances. (See *Families in Other Cultures:* "I Also Have Some Rights," on pp. 312–313.)

FROM SINGLE-EARNER TO DUAL-EARNER MARRIAGES

By the mid-twentieth century, the wives in most working-class and middle-class families, who did not work outside the home, had also withdrawn from informal sources of income such as keeping lodgers or taking in laundry. They had withdrawn because of increases in men's earnings and because of reduced demand for home services such as lodging. Teenage and young adult children stayed in school longer and worked fewer hours, often keeping for personal use most of what they did earn. The two-parent family usually had only one paid worker—the husband. As described in Chapter 2, the 1950s were probably the high point of the single-earner, two-parent family in the United States. Many commentators refer to this breadwinner-homemaker family as the "traditional" family, but the history of women's work demonstrates how atypical the single-earner family was.

MARRIED MOTHERS ENTER THE LABOR FORCE

Figure 10.1 below shows the low levels of married women's work outside the home at midcentury and the great changes since then. The two lines show the percentage of married women with children who were in the labor force for every year since 1948. Government statistical agencies consider someone to be in the labor force if he or she is working for pay outside the home or looking for such work. In 1948, only about one-fourth of married women whose youngest children were at least six years old (and therefore in school) were in the labor force, as were only about one-tenth of married women with children under age 6. The graph shows the steady increase in labor force participation since then. The expansion of the service sector of the economy caused an increase in the demand for workers to fill the kinds of jobs that had been gender-typed as women's work: secretaries, salesclerks, nurses, and so forth (Oppenheimer, 1970). As a result, the wages of these jobs increased, attracting more women to take them (Butz & Ward, 1979; Smith & Ward, 1985).

FIGURE 10.1 Labor force participation rates of married women with children under age 18, by age of youngest child, 1948–1996. (*Sources:* U.S. Bureau of Labor Statistics [1988]; U.S. Bureau of the Census [1993g]; U.S. Bureau of the Census [1997i].)

"I Also Have Some Rights"

Sometimes it is easier to recognize inequalities of power in a social setting different from one's own. Consider the relations between wives and husbands in poor Mexico City neighborhoods studied by Lourdes Benería and Martha Roldán (1987). Like nineteenth-century wives, married women in industrializing nations today often contribute to the family's income through means other than a job outside the home. Sociologists who study national development distinguish between the **formal sector** and the **informal sector** of a nation's economy. The formal sector consists of jobs that meet legal standards for minimum wages, are relatively long-lasting and secure, include fringe benefits such as contributions to social security or health insurance, often have possibilities for advancement, and are sometimes unionized. In contrast, the informal sector consists of temporary or casual jobs that

sometimes offer illegal subminimum wages, have little security, little possibility for advancement, and no fringe benefits. In the United States an example of a formal sector job would be a computer programmer at a large corporation; an informal sector job would be a seamstress at an illegal sweatshop in the garment district in New York City. The distinction is useful even though, in practice, it is sometimes hard to draw a line between the two sectors.

In industrializing nations, the informal sector is far larger than in the United States and, in fact, is an important part of the way production is organized. Established firms in the formal sector often let out work to subcontractors, who hire workers on a temporary basis, sometimes in violation of laws about wages and working conditions. By subcontracting, firms save money because they pay lower costs, evade labor laws regarding fringe benefits and hours, and

avoid the fixed costs of directly hiring more workers (such as constructing more space at the factory). Some of the subcontracts involve labor that can be done on a piecework basis at home; and like Madeline and her bobbins in nineteenth-century France, married women today do much of it.

Precisely because it can be done at home, piecework is acceptable even to husbands who would not want their wives to work outside the home. It allows husbands to feel that they are still the main earners in the family and yet to obtain the benefits of a higher family income. It allows wives to combine working for pay with the care of younger children, which is almost always seen as their responsibility. What is more, older children can help with the piecework, thus increasing the family's income even more. Thus, piecework by wives fits with the dominant ideology about what husbands and wives should do in many industrializing nations.

At first, the rate of participation increased faster among those whose children were in school. Because women began childbearing at relatively younger ages in the 1950s and early 1960s and rarely had more than three or four children, they were still in a prime working age when all their children reached school age. With school to use as a childcare center and less childrearing effort necessary at home, many women with school-aged children reentered the labor force. Since the 1970s, the rate increased faster among those with at least one preschool-aged child. As a result of these changes, 77 percent of all married women with school-aged children, and 63 percent of those with preschool-aged children, were in the labor force in 1996, although a majority were working part-time (Spain & Bianchi, 1996). In fact, the increase has been greatest in recent years among mothers of very young children, so much so that 59 percent of all married women with children under age 2 were in the labor force in 1996 (U.S. Bureau of the Census, 1997i).

Several factors contributed to the increase in married women's labor force participation. During the twentieth century, the service sector of the economy expanded greatly. The **service sector** consists of the workers who provide personal services such as education, health care, communication, restaurant meals, legal representation, entertainment, and so forth. Many of the jobs in the service sector had

Doña Goya was a 33-year-old married woman interviewed by Benería and Roldán. As a teenager, she labored at times as a childcare worker and domestic for several families. After she married, she stopped paid work and she and her husband—who was steadily employed as a factory worker—moved in with her parents. Like most working-class families in their neighborhood, they accepted the idea that men should be the main earners of the family and women should be the main caregivers. After having six children, Doña Goya began to take in washing and to work as a domestic in the neighborhood. After her 10th child, she began to do piece-work at home, assembling toys with the help of 8 of her 10 children. She also continued to work as a laundress and domestic. Her assembly work was brought to her home by a middle person who had obtained a subcontract from a toy company. Whereas her husband worked in the formal sector, albeit for wages that were insufficient to support a family, Doña Goya and her children supplemented the family's income by working in the informal sector and by unpaid childcare and household work.

This division of labor between formal sector employment for married men and informal sector employment for married women is common in Mexico City, state the authors of the study. Because formal sector employment is more secure, pays more, and has more benefits, this division virtually ensures that most married women will remain economically dependent on their husbands. Benería and Roldán found that husbands exercised control at a number of points in the process of spending income. Many husbands, first of all, gave their wives allowances without telling them how much their wages were. Second, husbands often kept back some money for personal spending. The wives were expected to meet all of the family's expenses without asking for further contributions. And in all cases, the wives contributed their entire earnings to the family pot.

Still, in those cases in which women contributed a substantial proportion of the household's income, they did report more power over family decision making. Thus, the Mexico City woman quoted at the beginning of this chapter said that, because of her relatively large earnings, "I obey and respect him [her husband], but I feel I also have some rights." Most women like her, Benería and Roldán found, had won the right to answer back when their husbands demanded that they do something and to make their views known to their husbands, as long as they did not embarrass their husbands publicly. These may seem like minor victories, but for the women involved, they were significant changes that bolstered their self-esteem and offered some protection from abuses of power by their husbands.

come to be stereotyped as women's work; these jobs usually required some education but paid less than men's work. Examples include secretary, nurse, and elementary school teacher. As the demand for these kinds of jobs increased, wages increased (although they remained lower than men's wages) and more married women were drawn into the labor force (Oppenheimer, 1970).

In addition, as the population shifted from farms to cities, each generation (except for the parents of the baby boomers) had fewer children. There was no longer a need for lots of child labor to help on the farm; moreover, the rising wages of women in the labor force meant that women who stayed home were passing up more and more income (Butz & Ward, 1979). As a result, parents' preferred strategy was to have fewer children and to invest more resources in each—to pay for college education or job training courses, for example. This strategy reduced the number of years in which young children would be present in the home and therefore freed married women sooner from childcare, the major responsibility that had kept them out of the labor force. Moreover, the decline in the wages of men without college educations since the early 1970s (see Chapter 4) has motivated many wives to take paying jobs. Finally, the high divorce rate of the past few decades (a result, in part, of women's greater economic independence) made it increasingly

Families and Public Policy

The Abortion Dilemma

"The hardest family problems for governments to deal with," wrote Gilbert Steiner, "are those that involve choices between incompatible goals or values, each of which has merit, each of which commands responsible and consequential support" (1981, p. 49). The quintessential such family problem is abortion. It has been the most bitterly contested and divisive of issues in our society. It is also an issue that starkly contrasts two visions of women's roles: one that emphasizes childbearing and mothering versus one that emphasizes autonomy and employment.

From the late 1800s to the early 1970s, access to abortion was restricted in the United States, generally available only when physicians certified that it was necessary to save the life of the mother. In the 1960s, feminist groups began to demand access to abortion as a woman's right—thereby making abortion a political issue. With the fertility rate falling to about two births per woman, on average, and with life expectancy lengthening, childrearing no longer lasted most of a woman's adult life.

Pro-abortion-rights activists, who prefer to be called "pro-choice," sought to control the timing and numbers of the children they bore. They did so, in part, on behalf of poor women who simply wanted to limit how many children they would have. Yet the pro-choice advocates, as Kristin Luker (1984) has written, also shared a "world view" in which women and men are equal and deserve equal opportunity to work outside the home. Legal abortions, by helping women to plan when to have children, would help them obtain equal opportunity.

Their cause was aided immensely by a 1973 Supreme Court decision, *Roe* v. *Wade* (1973). In this case, the Court ruled that women had the constitutional right to terminate a pregnancy by abortion during the first trimester and that in the second trimester the state may regulate access to abortion only for reasons reasonably related to the mother's health. *Roe* made abortions legal, but it also spurred the formation of a strong, national movement against abortion. The "pro-life" forces, as the anti-abortion movement came to be known, view human life as beginning at conception

and therefore oppose abortion except to save the life of the mother. According to Luker (1984), they share a world view in which women and men are fundamentally different and women's primary role is to raise children.

Both sides claim to be defending the family. For example, in a 1977 congressional debate, Senator John C. Stennis of Mississippi said, "I believe that on this matter of abortion, abortion at will or by choice, whatever it may be called . . . is an attack on the family" (Steiner, 1981, p. 61). In contrast, Representative Millicent Fenwick argued that access to abortion strengthens families by enabling them to avoid the strain of raising unwanted children: "Some of these people are mothers trying to protect their children . . . and they are trying to work out some kind of a solution to a difficult life" (Steiner, 1981, p. 61).

Both sides are, in fact, defending the family, but it's not the same family. Senator Stennis sees abortion rights as threatening a family in which a woman's highest duty and responsibility is to bear and raise children. In fact, many pro-life activists are homemakers who view abortion rights as

---

risky for married women to leave the labor force and let their job skills deteriorate. Given the low amount of child support payments that most divorced women receive (see Chapter 12), they need to be able to rely on their earning power.

This great movement of married women into the labor force is one of the most important changes in American family life in the second half of the twentieth century. It has profoundly altered women's and men's lives. It has affected the balance of power between women and men, as will be discussed in this chapter. It has been instrumental in the shift from the companionship marriage to the independent marriage, as described in the previous chapter. It has provided the backdrop for debates on issues such as abortion, about which women whose identity is bound up in home and childrearing tend to disagree with women who value working outside the home. (See *Families and Public Policy:* The Abortion Dilemma.) To be sure, the change has been less pronounced for women from poor or minority undermining the validity of the lives they have led. In the other camp, pro-choice activists champion a newer vision of the family in which women choose whether and when to have children and whether to have a life beyond the domestic sphere.

Abortion rights also vary by class, because the biggest victory for the pro-life forces was the passage of legislation in 1976 that prohibited the use of government funds to pay for abortions. Since most poor women receive medical care through the government program Medicaid, the law makes it difficult for them to obtain an abortion. Supporters argue that the ban on the use of public funds is morally justified because abortion is repugnant to many taxpayers. Nevertheless, the ban made abortion a class-related issue because middle-class women have an easier time finding the funds to pay for an abortion than do poor women.

In her 1984 study of the politics of abortion, Luker found "complacency" among the pro-choice faction after *Roe*. But that complacency vanished as Presidents Reagan and Bush nominated pro-life judges to fill vacancies on the Supreme Court. Then in the 1989 case, *Webster* v. *Reproductive Health Services*, a divided Court upheld some restrictions on abortion in a Missouri law. More important, the Court nearly overturned *Roe*, with four members clearly leaning in that direction.[1] Justice Harry Blackmun, who wrote the majority opinion in *Roe*, wrote in *Webster*, "Today, *Roe* v. *Wade* and the fundamental constitutional right of women to decide whether to terminate a pregnancy, survive but are not secure" (Tribe, 1990).

With this wake-up call, pro-choice activists once again mobilized; rallies were held, leaders spoke out, and a march on Washington was organized. Pro-choice support was strong enough that the Republicans did not use opposition to abortion as a major theme of the 1992 presidential campaign, even though President Bush had established a strong pro-life position. The issue that seemed most winning for the pro-choice side was not women's independence but rather privacy: the claim that restrictions on abortion violated personal privacy—the same grounds the Court had used in deciding *Roe*. It appeared that a majority of voters felt strongly enough about family privacy that they were not willing to make an exception for restrictions on abortion. After President Clinton won the 1992 election, he appointed seemingly pro-choice judges to fill Supreme Court vacancies, making it likely that *Roe* would not be overturned during his terms in office.

In 1998, 25 years after *Roe* v. *Wade*, public opinion remained split. A national sample of adults was asked, "Is abortion more of an issue involving a woman's ability to control her body or an issue involving the life of a fetus?" Forty-four percent said it was an issue of a woman's ability to control her body, the position more often taken by those who favor women's working outside the home. Forty-five percent said it was an issue involving the life of a fetus (Goldberg, 1998), the position favored by those who see women's childrearing role as central. As we enter the twenty-first century, abortion is still an issue that deeply divides Americans in ways that reflect different views of women's lives.

[1]*Webster* v. *Reproductive Health Services*, 109 S. Ct. 3040 (1989).

backgrounds, who have always had a greater need to work. For example, census statistics show that in 1975, when only 35 percent of white married women with preschool-aged children were in the labor force, 55 percent of comparable African-American women were. Still, labor force participation has increased sharply among African-American women as well: By 1996, 76 percent of married African-American women with preschool-aged children were in the labor force (compared with 62 percent of whites) (U.S. Bureau of the Census, 1997i).

THE CURRENT SITUATION

By the 1990s, it was common for married women to remain at work outside the home from young adulthood to retirement. Moreover, the post-1960 rise in divorce and childbearing outside marriage created a large number of unmarried

FIGURE 10.2 Labor force participation rates for U.S. women by age, 1970 and 1990. (*Sources:* Bianchi & Spain [1986], Figure 5.1; U.S. Bureau of Labor Statistics [1991]).

mothers who needed to provide their own incomes. This increasingly continuous labor force participation can be seen more clearly in Figure 10.2 above. For two time points 20 years apart, 1970 and 1990, the figure displays the percentage of women who were participating in the labor force, according to the women's ages. In 1970, the percentage of women in the labor force was higher for women in their early twenties than for teenagers; but then it dropped among women in their mid-twenties and early thirties, which are the most common years for having small children at home. The percentage then rose again to a second peak among women in their forties, whose children tend to be older. Therefore, the second peak reflects women who returned to the labor force after their children entered school. This double-peaked pattern typifies a society in which many women enter the labor force before marriage, drop out while raising young children, and then enter again. Yet by 1990 the dip between the peaks is gone; rather, the graph has a single, high plateau for women between about 25 and 50, reflecting women's higher and more-continuous levels of work outside the home throughout the prime working years of adulthood.

Despite women's increased attachment to the labor force and rising wages, it is still the case that they earn substantially less, on average, than men. From 1960 to about 1980, the average woman who worked full-time, year round, earned about 60 cents for each dollar earned by a comparable man.[6] To be sure, women have worked outside the home less, on average, than men have during their adult lives, so they have accrued less seniority, on-the-job training, and so forth. Yet differences in job experience appear to account for only about one-fourth to one-half of the gap (England & Farkas, 1986). A substantial proportion reflects a more complex process involving employer discrimination and the resultant way that parents socialize their daughters. (See *Families and Public Policy:* The Earnings Gap, in Chapter 3.)

Since 1980, however, women's average earnings have increased faster than men's, reaching 74 cents for each dollar a man earned in 1996 (U.S. Bureau of the

---

[6]This figure represents the ratio of women's median earnings to men's median earnings, for year-round, full-time workers; U.S. Bureau of the Census (1997f).

The number of women in professions such as law increased greatly in the 1980s.

Census, 1997f). Women's earnings rose relative to men's in the 1980s and 1990s because some women workers were doing better economically and some men were doing worse. As for women doing better, demographers Daphne Spain and Suzanne Bianchi note that in the 1980s, women born during the baby boom were finishing school and entering the labor force. Conversely, the mothers of the baby boomers were exiting the labor force to retire. Since the mothers had married at early ages and had children soon after marrying, they had received less education than their daughters and spent less time working outside the home prior to having children. As a result, their earning potential had been limited. In contrast, their daughters had received more education, postponed marriage and childbearing, and spent more time in the labor force before having children—all of which had increased their earning potential. Well-educated women moved into professional occupations in unprecedented numbers: Women's share of law school degrees rose from 5 percent in 1970 to 41 percent in 1990, and their share of medical school degrees rose from 8 percent to 33 percent during the same period. So in the 1980s and 1990s, as the baby boom daughters replaced their mothers in the labor force, the average earnings of college-educated women increased (Spain & Bianchi, 1996).

Yet that is only half the story. Earnings did not rise much for baby boom daughters without college educations, most of whom were clerical and service workers such as secretaries, bank tellers, or cafeteria workers. The men they tended to marry—baby boom sons without a college education—saw their incomes decline as skilled blue-collar jobs became scarce. Therefore, the ratio of women's earnings to men's earnings rose among the less-well-educated not because women were earning substantially more but rather because men were earning substantially less. The rising ratio demonstrates how important wives' earnings have become in maintaining the standard of living of working-class and lower-class married couples (Bianchi & Spain, 1996).

Among African Americans, the ratio of women's earnings to men's earnings has long been higher than among whites. In the first half of the twentieth century, discrimination severely limited job opportunities for both black women and men, but black women were hired as household workers for white families—jobs that may have been demeaning but were at least available and steady. In 1940, 60 percent of all black women in the labor force were private household workers. Beginning in the 1960s—a decade of civil rights legislation and economic prosperity—employment opportunities for African Americans improved. The improvement, however, was greater for black women, who took advantage of the expanding opportunities in service sector occupations, than for black men. By 1990, just 2 percent of black women were household workers (Bianchi, 1995). What is more, young black women were earning virtually as much, on average, as young white women. Because black men's economic progress (like the progress of less-well-educated white men) lagged behind, the median earnings of black women rose to 89 cents for every dollar earned by black men in 1992, compared with 70 cents for every dollar among whites (Spain & Bianchi, 1996). Black women, then, are approaching earning parity with black men.

WIVES' POWER AND AUTHORITY

The increased labor force participation of married women, and the growth of women's incomes relative to men's, should translate into increased marital power for wives—at least according to the theory outlined at the start of this chapter. In the vast majority of two-parent families with mothers who are employed, the husband is also working outside the home. The most famous American study of wives' employment and marital power was conducted in 1955. The authors, Robert Blood and Donald Wolfe, asked a sample of married women in the Detroit area "who usually makes the final decision about" each of eight common household decisions, including what car to get, whether to go on a vacation, and how much the family can afford to spend on food. Wives who were employed were more likely to make the final decisions themselves or to jointly make the decisions with their husband than wives who were not employed (Blood & Wolfe, 1960).

Daily decisions of the kind Blood and Wolfe studied may reflect authority more than power. Consider more recent information that comes from a study of more than 3,000 married couples in the late 1970s by Philip Blumstein and Pepper Schwartz. The higher the wife's income, the more likely she was to have "more say about important decisions affecting [their] relationship" and the more likely she was to see herself as "running the show in [their] relationship." But a wife's income did not have as much effect on whether her husband was more likely to "give in to [her] wishes when one of us wants to do something the other does not want to do." As the authors note, the last measure is closer to the sociological definition of power than the first two (Blumstein & Schwartz, 1991). Their findings,

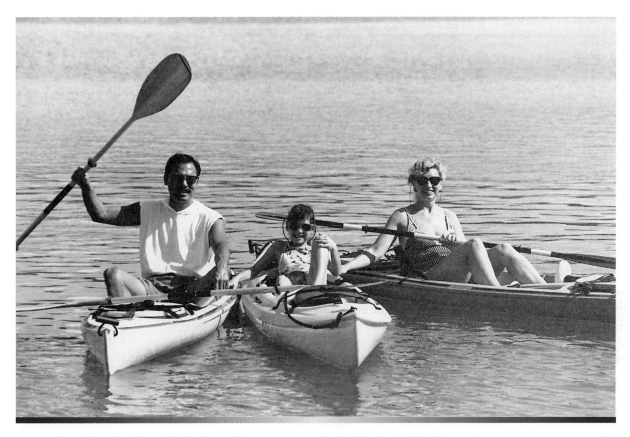

Wives who are employed outside the home have more power in family decisions such as where to go on vacations.

then, suggest that wives' earnings may boost their authority to make daily economic decisions more than their power to win disputes with their husbands. Moreover, husbands still do much less household work and childcare than their wives. It seems unlikely that employed wives want to do so much more work in the home. Instead, men seem to be retaining enough power to resist doing as much domestic work as their wives do.

THE STALLED REVOLUTION?

In fact, a number of studies have reported that, at least until recently, husbands hardly increased the number of hours they spend on housework or childcare as their wives moved into the labor force. Several surveys in the 1960s and 1970s asked married men and women to record or recall the amount of time they spent on various household tasks during a typical day or week. The results of these time-use studies showed that husbands whose wives were employed outside the home did not spend more time doing household work.[7] Yet the *proportion* of household work done by husbands did increase when their wives were employed (a finding also reported by Blood and Wolfe). The reason: Wives who were employed

[7]The studies are summarized in Pleck (1985).

sharply reduced the time they spent on household work. The major accommodation, then, that married couples were making to the wife's employment was to have her do less, rather than to have him do more. Wealthier dual-income couples often pay someone else to do much of the household work and childcare that wives traditionally would have done (Hertz, 1986).

Nor are there pronounced social class differences in the proportion of household work done by husbands. There is a certain image of the working-class husband as doing less around the home, perhaps exercising more power in the household to compensate for having less power in the workplace. But a comparative study involving national surveys of dual-earner couples in the early 1980s in both the United States and Sweden found no difference in the proportion of housework done by husbands in different social classes in the United States and little difference in Sweden (Wright, Shire, Hwang, Dolan, & Baxter, 1992).

What often differs by class is how couples talk about the wife's and husband's contribution (Hochschild, 1989). It is common in working-class families for the couple to define what the husband does around the house as "helping out" the wife, whereas middle-class couples talk about husbands' taking responsibility for household tasks. In addition, it is common for working-class couples to define the man as the main earner, even if his wife's wages are an important source of income. This way of thinking allows couples to retain the breadwinner-homemaker ideal even as their actions contradict it. The husband can continue to consider himself a successful earner who merely needs his wife's help. Similarly, he can view his housework and childcare as merely helping his wife do her tasks. A factory worker told Ellen Israel Rosen that she needs to "help out her husband" financially. In addition, she said, "My husband helps me a lot too. That's one thing I told him. If you want me to help you out then you'll have to help me. That way we can help each other. So far it's been working pretty good" (Rosen, 1987).

The seeming intransigence of husbands in dual-earner families regarding household work has puzzled and disappointed many observers. Arguing that the current period is a transitional phase in American family life, Arlie Russell Hochschild wrote of a "stalled revolution," in which wives have moved into the labor force but husbands have not yet adjusted. The result, she asserted, is that employed wives work a "second shift" of household tasks and childcare. In addition to the burden this situation imposes on wives, she wrote, the stalled revolution may hurt men, whose wives "cannot afford the luxury of unambivalent love for their husbands" (Hochschild, 1989). For example, one woman she interviewed, whose husband retreats to the basement to work with his tools every night while she does housework, expressed her resentment indirectly by losing interest in sex:

> When I was a teenager, I vowed I would never use sex to get my way with a man. It is not self-respecting, it's demeaning. But when Evan refused to carry his load at home, I did, I used sex. I said, "Look, Evan, I would not be this exhausted and asexual every night if I didn't have so much to face every morning" (Hochschild, 1989).

Yet most of the available time-use information about husbands and wives was collected in the late 1970s or earlier. It was in the 1980s, as we have seen, that women's earnings began to rise relative to men's. Especially if Hochschild is right that this is a transitional phase, husbands may have begun to do more household work in the 1980s and 1990s. There is, however, little data that reliably shows trends in household work over time. The only set of comparable national time-use

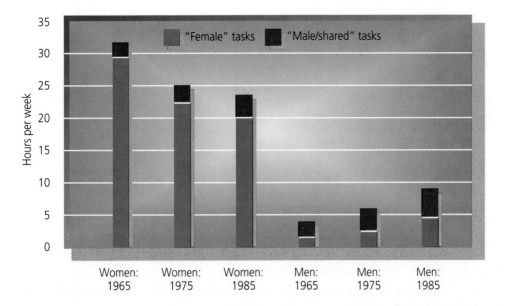

FIGURE 10.3 Time spent doing household tasks, for women and men aged 18 to 65 with children under age 5 living in their household, 1965, 1975, and 1985. *Note:* "Female" tasks are cooking, meals and cleanup, cleaning house, and laundry and clothing care. "Male/shared" tasks are outdoor work, home repairs, garden and pet care, and paying bills. (*Source:* Robinson [1988].)

surveys was carried out under the direction of John Robinson in 1965, 1975, and 1985. Figure 10.3 shows the hours per week spent in household work, on average, for men and women who had children under age 5 in their households in 1965, 1975, and 1985 (Robinson, 1988). The researchers divided their list of questions about household work into typically "female" tasks (cooking, meals and cleanup, cleaning house, and laundry and clothing care) and "male/shared" tasks (outdoor work, home repairs, garden and pet care, and paying bills).

Looking at the figure, one is struck first by how much higher the bars are for women than for men, reflecting the imbalance in the division of household labor. One also sees that between 1965 and 1985, women's hours declined by a larger amount than men's hours increased, which shows that couples have cut back on the total amount of time they spend doing household work. Nevertheless, the figure does show modest increases in men's time spent in household work. According to the findings on which Figure 10.3 is based, men in households with children under age 5 were doing 10 percent of the household work in 1965 and 18 percent in 1975, although most of this rise occurred because women sharply decreased their time. Between 1975 and 1985, however, men's share rose further to 29 percent; more of this rise was caused by men's increased time than by women's decreased time.

Consequently, the figure shows progress toward a more equitable household division of labor, although how much progress depends on whether you view the glass as still 71 percent empty or 29 percent full. The fact remains that much of the change since 1965 reflects women's doing less rather than men's doing more: Women still do far more household work than men. On the other hand, men have begun to change. Whether that change has continued between 1985 and the time you read this book is a crucial question; but there's not much data on it. Bits of information suggest some change; for example, in a national sample of married women and men interviewed in 1980 and 1992, 33 percent of wives report a decrease in their share of housework, and only 19 percent report an increase (Amato & Booth, 1997). If—and it is a big if—the time spent by men and women in household work has continued to change at the same rates as during the 1975–1985 period, then by 1995 men would have been doing 40 percent of the household work in families with children under age 5—and most of the post-1985 change would reflect men's increased time.[8] A 60/40 split still wouldn't mean equal effort, but it would represent substantial progress over the 90/10 split of 1965.

Since the 1985 survey, the percentage of married women with young children who are employed outside the home has continued to rise, which has put pressure on more husbands to help out at home. In addition, studies show that men's involvement in household work and childcare is becoming more accepted culturally. In 1979 and 1989, a national sample of men were asked the question "Would you respect a man more, less, or about the same if he decided to stay home and take care of the children while his wife worked?" The proportion who would respect a man *more* increased from 6 to 17 percent, whereas the proportion who would respect a man *less* decreased from 39 to 19 percent (Pagnini & Rindfuss, 1993).

Nevertheless, surveys indicate that behavioral changes are still limited (Galinsky, Bond, & Friedman, 1993). In a 1992 national survey of employed women and men, how much each partner does depends on who was asked. For instance, 43 percent of men in dual-earner marriages or partnerships reported that they shared childcare equally with their wives or partners, but only 19 percent of women in dual-earner families reported equal sharing. As for cooking and cleaning, men in dual-earner marriages or partnerships did more than men whose partners were not employed, yet women still did far more, on average, than men. Eighty-one percent of women in dual-earner families said they took major responsibility for cooking, and 78 percent said they took major responsibility for cleaning. Even according to men's reports, their employed wives and partners took major responsibility for cooking 69 percent of the time and cleaning 63 percent of the time. Moreover, women who earned more than half the household's income still took responsibility for cooking, cleaning, and shopping more often than their husbands or partners. Employed wives still do substantially more of the housework than their husbands.

OVERLOAD AND SPILLOVER BETWEEN WORK AND FAMILY

The imbalance in the amount of housework and childcare done by employed women and employed men has led to concerns about employed women having too many roles with conflicting demands—what is sometimes called **role overload**. In addition to being a worker, the roles can include spouse, parent, and sometimes caregiver to other relatives. The 1992 survey of employed women and men found that two-thirds were living with a spouse or partner, 42 percent had children under age 18 at home, and 8 percent were providing care to an elderly or other adult relative (Galinsky et al., 1993). Does adding paid employment to the demands a married woman typically faces from spouse, children, and others lead to an overload? That depends crucially, according to research, on whether or not she wants to work outside the home and on whether or not she receives support from her husband.

[8]Here I am projecting 1995 percentages based on the rates of change shown by men and women with children under the age of 5 between 1975 and 1985. Men would be expected to increase their time from 9 hours to 13.5 hours; women would be expected to decrease their time from 22.5 hours to 20.3 hours. The 1975 and 1985 figures are taken from the bottom row of the table "Children's Hour" in Robinson (1988).

One study was based on a national telephone survey done in 1978, in which wives and husbands were asked about employment, support from their spouses, and childcare arrangements. They were also asked 12 questions designed to measure depression (for example, "How many days in the past week have you felt . . . depressed? cheerful? lonely? like not eating? like you can't shake off the blues?," etc.) (Ross, Mirowsky, & Huber, 1983). For wives, the lowest levels of depression were found among two groups: those who were not employed and preferred housework *and* those who were employed and preferred a job to housework. The highest level of depression was found among women who may have felt trapped at home—those who were not employed but who preferred a job to housework. Husbands reported lower levels of depression except in marriages where the wife was employed despite the husband's preference that she stay home.

When the researchers asked employed women specifically about childcare arrangements, they found sharp differences in depression levels, as shown in Figure 10.4 (Ross & Mirowsky, 1988). Among employed married women with children under age 12, by far the highest depression levels occurred among those who reported some difficulty in arranging childcare *and* whose husbands did not share the childcare equally at home. These are the women who are most vulnerable to role overload—they work outside the home, they get little childcare help from their husbands, and they have trouble arranging adequate childcare while they are at their jobs. In contrast, the lowest levels were reported by women whose husbands shared the childcare equally at home and who found no difficulty arranging for care while they worked. Having a husband who shared childcare at home reduced depression levels even among women who had difficulty arranging for care while they were at their jobs. So a husband's sharing of childcare had a strong impact on his wife's psychological well-being.

More broadly, research has *not* found a clear relationship between the number of roles a person must manage and the degree of distress she or he experiences (Thoits, 1992). In fact, there is some evidence that people with multiple roles (including nonfamily roles such as being involved in the activities of a religious organization) may in some cases have better mental health than people with fewer roles (Thoits, 1986). It may be that multiple roles increase a person's sense of

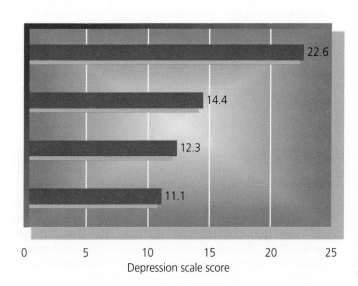

FIGURE 10.4
Depression scale scores for married women who are employed outside the home and who have children under age 12, by difficulty in arranging childcare and by whether the husband shares the childcare equally. (*Source:* Ross & Mirowsky [1988].)

meaning and purpose in life and therefore improve mental health. Or it may be that mentally healthier people join more organizations, are more likely to marry, and have busier lives. One researcher suggested that a combination of roles may cause distress mainly when it differs from the normal, expected combination for a person of a particular gender and age (Menaghan, 1989). For example, being a mother who works outside the home may have been more stressful in the 1950s and 1960s, when there were fewer social supports for such people, than it is today.

SPILLOVER

Another motif in the research literature is that stressful events in one part of a person's daily life often spill over into other parts of her or his life. **Spillover** can occur whether or not the person experiences role overload. In other words, a bad day at even an enjoyable job can cause a parent to come home and behave angrily toward his or her children. In an influential article in the late 1970s, Joseph Pleck argued that spillover involving work and family operates in opposite directions for employed men and employed women. The demands of family life—a school vacation, an ill child—are permitted to intrude into women's jobs more than into men's jobs, he wrote, because supervisors and coworkers expect that when a family emergency arises, mothers rather than fathers will be called upon to deal with it. In contrast, according to Pleck, the stresses of work are permitted to intrude on family life more for men than for women. Because men's jobs are often seen as more demanding and more central to the family's well-being than are women's jobs, it is more acceptable, for example, for husbands to miss school concerts because of business trips than it is for employed wives to do so (Pleck, 1977).

It may also be more acceptable for husbands to come home from work irritable or preoccupied than it is for wives. Wives are often cast in a more supportive role, even though their daily lives may be stressful. One woman talked about her husband to two researchers:

> He takes a lot of crap [at his job]. He gets very few rewards for what he does, and people are not very facilitating there. So it's up to me when he comes home to try and fill that need and make him feel good about himself. And yet, I am not getting any reverse back (Pearlin & McCall, 1990).

Wives may serve to buffer husbands from further stress at home more than husbands do for them. One woman in the same study said that when she sees her husband come home troubled, she tells her children, "Dad has a lot on his mind. If you want to ask him for something, wait until later" (Pearlin & McCall, 1990).

Men also appear more likely to withdraw from their families in reaction to a stressful day at work. One author suggests that the male professionals he studied view displays of stress at home as signs of failure in meeting work responsibilities. Men may instead act weary, which is more acceptable because it can be seen as a sign of hard work, or they may tune out their wives and children. But worries are hard to hide, and withdrawal can lead to irritability and anger, as in this case:

> A situation that is perfectly normal and next to nothing—something happens with a kid—I may go into a tailspin over it. I might boil up or boil over. Norma will then fly up and say, "You are not treating them fairly." And then it will come out that at that particular point I was up to my eyebrows with the damned business and I just wasn't relaying that. In fact, I was keeping it in (Weiss, 1990).

For many blue-collar workers, the important causes of stress may be low pay, dirty or dangerous work, or dehumanizing treatment by supervisors. Blue-collar men, some studies show, bring their troubles home in ways similar to middle-class men who have had a bad day at the office. Tired and irritable, blue-collar men sometimes withdraw from their wives and children in the evenings (Mortimer & London, 1984). Low-wage jobs also increase a couple's need for a second income. Consequently, a higher proportion of working-class wives than middle-class wives work outside the home (although the difference is narrowing).

CHILDCARE

One surprisingly common way in which dual-earner working-class couples manage childcare is to work different shifts. In the National Survey of Families and Households, one-fourth of all dual-earner married couples had at least one spouse working an evening, night, or rotating shift. Husbands who were home when their wives were working did more cooking, cleaning, and washing than husbands who were never home when their wives were working (Presser, 1994). The increase in nonday-shift and weekend work isn't due solely to couples' childcare needs. The growth of the service sector of the economy is also responsible. Nevertheless, when asked why they were working evening or night shifts, a majority of married women in a Census Bureau survey said the main reason was that their hours made it easier to care for their children or other relatives (Presser, 1989).

In fact, it appears that wives and husbands in many of these split-shift couples are sharing the childcare (Presser, 1989). How best to care for the children of employed parents is a topic that will be discussed in later chapters. Some observers view staggered-shift parent care as a good solution to the childcare problem. Other things being equal, parents arguably provide better care in most instances than nonrelatives. But split-shift childcare sharing is not without its difficulties. Employed wives, who still tend to accommodate their working hours to their spouse's needs more than their husbands do, may be forced to turn down better jobs or work fewer hours so that they can be available when their husbands aren't home. Couples working different shifts may have little time for each other, and their marriages may suffer. One repair worker told Lillian Rubin:

> I usually get home about forty-five minutes or so before my wife has to leave for work, so we try to take a few minutes just to make contact. But it's hard with the kids and all. Most days the whole time gets spent with taking care of business—you know, who did what, what the kids need, what's for supper, what bill collector was hassling her while I was gone—all the damn garbage of living. It makes me nuts (Rubin, 1994).

Single parents, of course, do not have the luxury of relying on a spouse to provide care, regardless of when they work. Yet never-married, separated, or divorced mothers are even more likely to work nonday, weekend, or rotating shifts than married mothers, perhaps because of their more limited education or work experience (Presser, 1989). With few commercial childcare providers offering evening, night, or weekend care, single mothers must often rely on their own mothers or other relatives. Here again, one could argue that, as caregivers, grandmothers are superior to nonrelatives. Many of the grandmothers, however, are themselves working or are caring for their own aging parents (see Chapter 15); providing care may be a strain on them. Some single mothers, with no one to rely on, attempt to care for their children themselves while working. Nationally, 8 percent of all preschool-aged children with employed mothers were cared for by the mothers themselves. For example, a mother might earn money by caring for the children of several other employed mothers as well as her own children.

More generally, single parents often have no one with whom to share the burdens of the day, and unless they live with their mothers or other relatives, there is no one to buffer them from the demands of their children when they come home from their jobs. Moreover, employed single mothers are sometimes in a precarious financial situation. I will describe in Chapter 12 how the economic status of many women plummets after a divorce. The lack of money may force them to reduce their standard of living, move to a new neighborhood, or otherwise disrupt their daily lives. Single parents are sometimes successful in constructing new support networks made up of other single parents, friends, and kin. Still, it seems likely that overload and spillover are a greater problem for employed single parents than for employed married parents.

UNEMPLOYMENT

Most of the studies of spillover between work and family assume that adults in the family who want to work outside the home can find and keep a job. Yet unemployment also creates stress. Research dating back to the Great Depression suggests that unemployment is more likely to cause marital problems among couples whose marriages were already shaky before the husband or wife lost a job (Komarovsky, 1971). More recently, a Boston area study of 82 families in which the husband had recently lost his job found that spouses who rated their marriages as satisfactory prior to the job loss were less anxious and depressed afterward (Liem & Liem, 1990). The Boston study, an Iowa study of 76 rural families, and a few others like them provide some insight into the process by which job loss leads to family problems. At the first interview, the unemployed husbands in the Boston study were more depressed and anxious than a matching group of employed husbands, but their wives were not more depressed or anxious than the wives of employed husbands. Four months later, however, the wives were experiencing more depression and anxiety. The authors speculate that many husbands become upset soon after the job loss and begin to act irritably and angrily toward their wives and children. Most wives are not as upset initially, but as their financial concerns grow and their husbands' behavior worsens, they often develop psychological symptoms. The Iowa study showed similarly that economic strain leads husbands to behave in a hostile way toward their wives—as well as to reduce their warm, supportive behavior. The husbands' hostility and lack of warmth, in turn, lead wives to feel less positively about their marriages. If the wives then respond with hostile behavior, their husbands' satisfaction with the marriage also declines (Conger et al., 1990).

On the whole, the available studies suggest that it is not as much the absence of supportive behavior as the presence of angry, irritable, hostile behavior that triggers these declines in the quality of the marriage. The results are consistent with laboratory observations that cycles of negative behavior from husband to wife and back are central to escalating marital conflict (see Chapter 9). The studies also suggest that spouses with fewer prior psychological problems and more social support from kin and friends are more likely to weather the storm of unemployment. Finally, working-class and middle-class families show similar distress when a parent loses his or her job, despite their differing economic circumstances. Working-class families, who typically have few financial reserves, experience the more immediate economic consequences, but they report receiving more support from kin and friends than do middle-class families. Among the latter group, losing a job, as has happened to executives during the recent waves of corporate "downsizing," means losing status and social identity (Liem & Liem, 1990).

TOWARD THE RESPONSIVE WORKPLACE?

To judge by the concerns of workers and, increasingly, of corporate managers, the strict separation of paid work and family life—to the extent that it ever existed—is breaking down. When employed women and men in the 1992 survey who had been at their current jobs for less than five years were asked how important various factors were in their original decisions to take their jobs, 60 percent said that the job's effect on personal and family life was very important and 46 percent said that family-supportive policies at the job were important. In contrast, only 35 percent said that wages and salary were important. Moreover, one-quarter to one-third of those without access to flexible working hours said they would switch jobs or sacrifice advancement in their companies to obtain flexible hours. About half without access to time off to care for sick relatives said they would trade salary or other benefits to obtain it (Galinsky et al., 1993). Clearly, family responsibilities are on the minds of many workers.

During the 1980s and 1990s, corporations began to address these concerns. They did so largely out of self-interest. By one estimate, two-thirds of the new entrants to the labor force in the 1990s are women, many of whom will have family responsibilities (O'Connell & Bloom, 1987). Employers who wish to recruit and retain good workers realize that they must make their jobs attractive to people who are caring for children—and to the growing number who are caring for elderly parents. Most large firms now have some personnel policies to help employees with family responsibilities (Glass & Estes, 1997). Small firms are much less likely to offer family-friendly policies for several reasons:

- They typically do not invest as much time and money training new workers, so they don't have as much to lose if employees quit because of family-related problems.
- They don't have the volume of workers necessary to make services such as on-site childcare cost-effective.
- Because of their lower sales revenues, they cannot pass along the costs of the policies to consumers as easily as large firms can.

Consequently, a two-tiered class system is developing: Larger firms, which tend to have better-paying, steadier jobs and better-educated workforces, offer better policies to help workers achieve balance between the demands of work and family; smaller firms, which tend to have lower-paying, less-steady jobs and less-well-educated workforces, provide less help. So middle-class, well-educated managers and professionals and better-paid blue-collar factory workers are much more likely to be offered assistance with family demands than are less-advantaged workers, such as the part-time and temporary "contingent" workers noted in Chapter 4 or low-paid service workers (Kingston, 1990). In fact, many of the contingent jobs that are being created lack any fringe benefits such as health insurance, pension contributions, sick leave, and vacation days.

Even among large firms, much of the assistance is limited, such as establishing information and referral offices to match parents with childcare openings. Cash benefits are usually limited to salary reduction plans that allow workers not to pay taxes on the part of their earnings (up to a limit) they spend on childcare. Yet these plans are of more value to higher-paid employees—who can afford to have the extra earnings withheld from their paychecks by their employers and who pay a greater percentage of their incomes in taxes—than to working-class employees.

One of the most common, and most widely used, employee benefits is **flextime**, a policy that allows employees to choose, within limits, when they will begin and end their working hours. For example, a company might allow its employees to begin work anytime between 7:00 and 9:00 A.M. and to leave anytime from 3:00 to 5:00 P.M., as long as they work eight hours. Studies suggest that this is the family-friendly policy workers use the most (Galinsky, 1992; Hochschild, 1997). In 1991, 15 percent of all workers who usually work full-time said they had flexible schedules, up from 12 percent in 1985. Again, middle-class employees benefit more than working-class employees: the more prestigious the occupational category, the more likely workers are to have flextime. For example, 22 percent of managers and professionals had flextime, compared with 11 percent of service workers (U.S. Bureau of the Census, 1993g). Employed parents use flextime to match their work schedules to the school or day care schedules of their children. Flextime doesn't necessarily increase the amount of time parents can spend with their children, but it does allow them to avoid stressful conflicts between childcare and job responsibilities.

To be able to spend more time with their children, especially when they are infants or when they are sick, employed parents need other options. One of these is **parental leave**, time off from work to care for a child, with a guarantee that the employee can have her or his job back when she or he returns. Many employers have been reluctant to grant parental leave automatically because they have feared it would hurt their productivity and cost too much. Most Western European nations require corporations to provide parental leave; yet in this regard, as in many family policies, the United States lags behind. France, by comparison, provides 33 months of unpaid leave. Germany allows 36 months and pays workers on leave the equivalent of about $400 dollars a month for the first 16 months (Dumon, 1992). Sweden provides over a year of leave at 90 to 100 percent of the worker's salary (Haas, 1992). Nevertheless, a modest parental leave bill was enacted by Congress and signed by President Clinton as one of his first acts in office in 1993. It required companies with 50 or more employees to offer unpaid leaves of up to 12 weeks to employees with newborn babies or seriously ill children or other relatives. Employers must allow employees to return to their jobs at the end of the leave. Because the leave is unpaid, it is likely that middle-class workers will take it more than will workers with low incomes.

Other innovations are as yet less common. These include part-time work with fringe benefits and job sharing. Whether significant numbers of part-time jobs with fringe benefits will be created remains to be seen. In job sharing, two people split the time and duties of a full-time position usually held by one person. Unlike part-time positions, which are often in low-status occupations, shared jobs presumably can be on a higher level—and therefore more appealing. The small number of existing shared jobs tend to be in such professions as teaching, psychology, and social work. Few have been created in for-profit corporations (Kamerman & Kahn, 1987).

But even when innovations such as part-time jobs with benefits and job-sharing are offered, most workers don't take them. In fact, Americans are working longer hours than they did a few decades ago (Schor, 1992). Hochschild (1997) studied

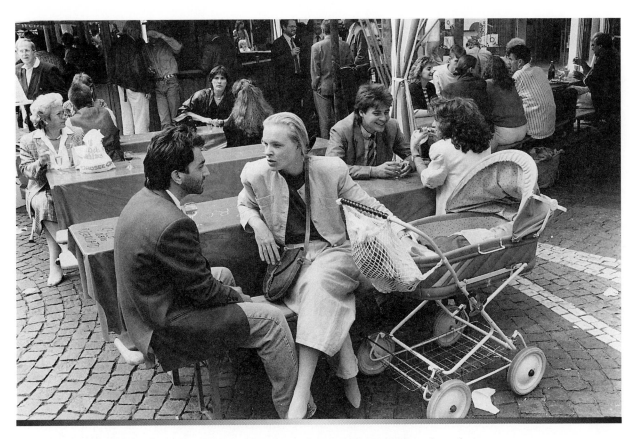

In European countries such as Germany, workers can take partially paid leaves from their jobs to care for a baby.

the employees of a large corporation and found that family life is so hectic for working parents that some of them retreat into their work. Especially for women, who do the majority of housework and childrearing, combining work with family life makes for a busy home life. Ironically, then, some workers are finding the workplace to be a haven from overburdened home lives. But others work long hours because they are afraid of being laid off or passed over for promotions. Even at Hochschild's plant, downsizing and restructuring led to the layoffs of many workers and expectations of faster production for the remaining workers.

Overall, there has been progress in making the workplace more responsive to workers' family needs. The least progress, however, has occurred in occupations that don't pay well. Yet workers in low-paying jobs need assistance *more* than those who are better paid. For instance, a 1990 survey showed that, among mothers who were paying for care and had a child under age 5, those earning less than $15,000 spend 23 percent of their incomes for childcare, whereas mothers earning more than $35,000 spent just 7 percent of their incomes for childcare (Hofferth, 1992). Future changes in the nature of work could widen the gap between poor and nonpoor. Visionaries write that as the economy turns to information processing rather than manufacturing, computer-assisted communication could allow large numbers of workers to do their jobs from home.[9] Such a shift, it is proposed, could

[9]Galinsky (1992), for example, writes of the "anytime-anyplace office."

make it easier for family caretakers to mesh the demands of family and job. Already, 24 percent of workers in the 1992 survey said they were regularly allowed to work at home. Yet changes such as these are easier to imagine in professional and clerical jobs than in lower-paying part-time service jobs such as janitors and waiters. It may be more of a challenge, therefore, to provide a responsive workplace for workers at the low end of the occupational distribution than at the high end.

In addition, the responsive workplace will become more of a reality only if men continue to increase their share of childcare and domestic work. Unless they do, family-friendly reforms will continue to be seen as primarily a "woman's issue." If they do, more male managers of corporations will pay attention to the topic. There are signs that the corporate culture is recognizing that many men wish to increase their involvement in their families. By the 1990s, even a staid business magazine such as *Fortune* could publish an issue with a man and his children on the cover under the headline "Can Your Career Hurt Your Kids? Yes, Say Many Experts. But Smart Parents—and Flexible Companies—Won't Let It Happen" (*Fortune,* 1991). Such a cover story would have been unthinkable 10 years previously. Nevertheless, changes in men's attitudes toward housework and childcare, as we have seen, have so far outstripped changes in what they actually do. There is no guarantee that men will soon drop their resistance and do more.

Corporate efforts, although increasing and important, are unlikely to meet the demands of employees for assistance in caring for children and the elderly. To the extent that they do, they will benefit middle-class employees and those in large firms more than working-class employees or those in small firms. These conclusions led advocates of the so-called **responsive workplace**—meaning a work setting in which job conditions are designed to allow employees to meet their family responsibilities more easily—to urge that corporate initiatives be supplemented by government assistance targeted at low-income workers (Kamerman & Kahn, 1987). In the 1990s, pressure from working parents prompted Congress to enact legislation providing childcare assistance, beginning with a 1990 bill. The 1996 welfare reform law (see Chapter 6) also included childcare assistance funds for parents who left the welfare rolls to take jobs. In 1997, President Bill Clinton held the first White House Conference on Child Care, and, sensing the popularity of the issue, he included a call for increased government assistance in his 1998 State of the Union address. It seems likely that government will do more to help working parents find and pay for childcare in the years ahead.

SUMMARY

1. By power, sociologists mean the ability to force someone to take an action even against her or his will; by authority, they mean the acknowledged right to supervise other people or to act on their behalf. The kinds of work women and men do are related to wives' and husbands' authority and power in the family. In general, working for pay outside the home increases a person's power in the family; therefore, wives who work outside the home tend to have relatively more family power. Moreover, the money family members earn does not necessarily benefit all members equally. Men are more likely than women to hold back part of their income for personal consumption. Women tend to devote more of whatever they earn to the family's subsistence.

2. Women's work differs in two kinds of agricultural societies: hoe cultures and plow cultures. In hoe cultures, women often have the major responsibility for food production and distribution, and therefore they tend to have greater family power and authority than women in plow cultures.

There is, however, substantial variability in women's power and authority, and in all cases, husbands retain substantial power over wives. The only region that still has hoe-based agriculture is sub-Saharan Africa, and women there are relatively more independent economically than in other regions of the developing world. In plow cultures, men do most of the cultivation in the fields. Still, women have extensive responsibilities for producing food and other goods and for rearing children; their contributions are essential to the family's subsistence

3. With the introduction of wage labor, men's and women's work roles changed—although men's changed more than women's. Husbands began to work for exchange value, trading their labor for wages in factories or shops. Wives mainly worked for use value in the home, although they often earned money at home by producing goods on a piecework basis or by taking in lodgers or by doing laundry. Where wives had control of earnings from production for exchange, as in the Mexico City study, they tended to have more power in the family.

4. As men's wages rose, more wives withdrew from earning money altogether, leading to the growth of single-earner families. In the second half of the twentieth century in Western societies, however, married women have entered the labor force in large numbers as the service sector of the economy has expanded, so that a majority of married women with children, even small children, are in the labor force. The rise of the service sector and the long-term decline in fertility are two important reasons why the increase in labor force participation occurred. Women still tend to earn less than men, in part because they have less labor market experience but also because employers tend to pay women less than they pay men who do comparable work. Women's earnings rose relative to men's in the 1980s and early 1990s because well-educated women workers were faring better and less-well-educated men were faring worse.

5. Until recently, fathers had not increased the amount of household work and childcare they do, despite the greater employment of mothers outside the home. Instead, the major response has been for employed women to decrease the amount of household work and childcare they perform. A series of time-use studies conducted between 1965 and 1985 suggests that men may have begun to do more, and attitudes have become more approving of men's doing more. Still, employed married women do substantially more household work and childcare than their husbands, regardless of social class.

6. Women who are employed and who, as is typical, do more of the household and childcare tasks than their husbands can experience role overload. Among employed women, the least depressed are those who can arrange childcare without great difficulty and whose husbands share in the care. Difficulties at work can spill over into home life, leading to withdrawal from the family or to irritable, angry exchanges. One increasingly common way that working-class couples are managing childcare is to work split shifts, which provides children with parental care but can strain marriages. Unemployment also causes strain, especially in marriages where there are prior problems.

7. Workers are concerned about how to mesh their jobs with their family responsibilities, and corporations and government have begun to respond. Large corporations are increasingly providing limited assistance such as childcare information and referral offices. Fifteen percent of workers report having flexible working hours. These and other reforms so far have benefited middle-class workers and workers at large corporations more than workers in low-paying jobs and at small corporations. In response to worker demand, government childcare assistance has increased.

KEY TERMS

relationship-specific investment	formal sector	flextime
authority	informal sector	parental leave
internal economy	service sector	responsive workplace
production for exchange value	role overload	
production for use value	spillover	

FAMILIES ON THE INTERNET

To examine the voluminous information on the Internet about women and work outside the home, it is probably best to rely on one of the World Wide Web search engines that have a subcategory which includes this topic. For instance, log onto **www.yahoo.com/society_and_culture/**, and then, in the search window enter "women and careers." You will see links to organizations, data, new stories, and other resources.

There is, if anything, even more information about abortion on the Internet. Two well-known groups at opposite ends of the debate are the pro-choice National Abortion Rights Action League (**www.naral.org**) and the pro-life National Right to Life Committee (**www.nrlc.org**). Although the positions of these two organizations are black and white, much of the debate takes place in the gray middle, where people are ambivalent. To get a sense of the middle, you again could use a search engine. For example, log onto **www.yahoo.com/society_and_culture** and enter "abortion" at the search window.

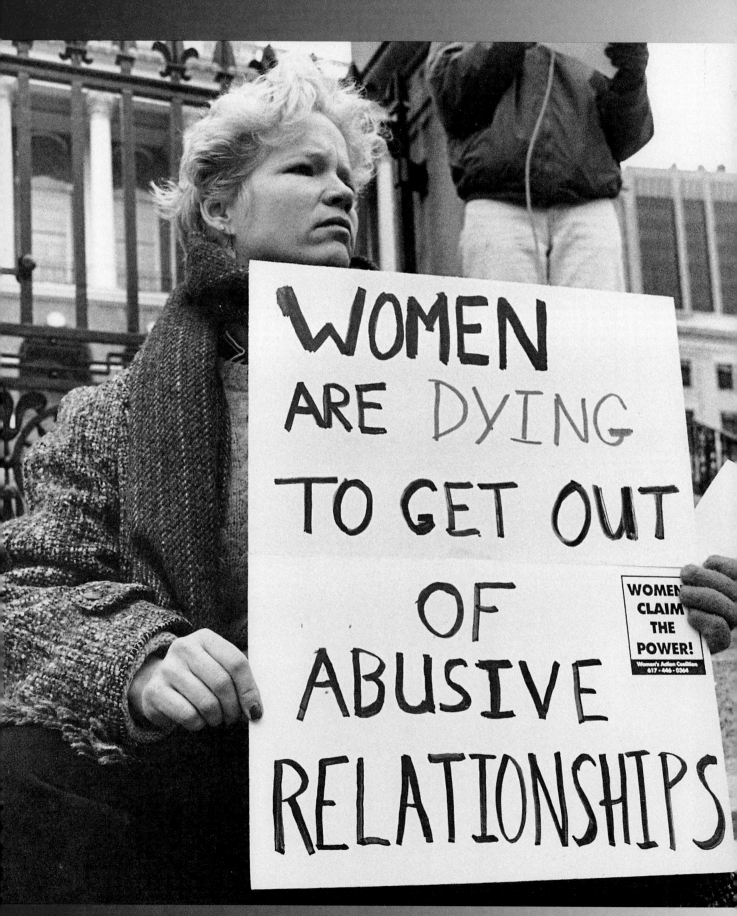

Domestic Violence

In 1996, the body of 4-year-old Nadine Lockwood was found in her mother's apartment in New York City. She had been starved to death. Prior to her death, a police detective and a city caseworker, acting on tips that the child was being abused, had separately visited the home. Neither found any evidence of abuse. Consequently, the case was closed, even though Nadine's mother had been known to the city's child protective agency since 1989, when her first child was born addicted to cocaine, and then two years later, when Nadine was born addicted to cocaine. Nadine's death—and the death in 1995 of six-year-old Elizabeth Izquierdo, who was beaten to death by her mother after several visits by caseworkers—led to demands that child protective service workers be more aggressive in removing children from potentially abusive parents ("Starving a Child to Death," 1996). Yet removing children from their homes has its own risks, as when children separated from their families drift through the foster care system.

The problem is that the public hears about child abuse or marital violence mainly through sensational cases, such as Nadine's and Elizabeth's deaths or O. J. Simpson's trial for the murder of his former wife. A few decades ago, even social scientists ignored **domestic violence,** which will be defined in this chapter as violent acts between family members or between women and men in intimate or dating relationships. Not a single article on the topic appeared in *Journal of Marriage and the Family,* the major scholarly journal in the field, between its founding in 1939 and 1969 (O'Brien, 1971). Now, however, hardly an issue appears without one. In fact, the increase in research has been so sudden and so massive that it requires an explanation. It wasn't spurred by an increase in domestic violence because there isn't much evidence of an increase, at least until recently, as will be noted later. Rather, its rise reflects the increased political power of the feminist movement, which views domestic violence as an important barrier to women's equality, and the increasing cultural emphasis on individualism in marriage and family life. To appreciate what has occurred, it is necessary first to examine the history of domestic violence as a social problem.

DOMESTIC VIOLENCE IN HISTORICAL PERSPECTIVE

The recent attention to highly publicized cases of child abuse and wife battering is not the first outpouring of public concern about domestic violence. Rather, the history of domestic violence in the United States shows short periods of public attention separated by longer periods of neglect. The periods of attention have had less to do with the prevalence of violence than with the power of various political and social groups (Pleck, 1987).

EARLY HISTORY

In the New England colonies, the Puritans believed that it was the responsibility of the government to enforce moral behavior, even if that meant intervening in the affairs of the family. And moral behavior excluded violent acts by husbands against their wives. The well-known minister Cotton Mather told his congregants that for "a man to Beat his Wife was as bad as any Sacriledge. Any such a Rascal were better buried alive, than show his Head among his Neighbours any more" (Pleck, 1987). Friends, neighbors, and fellow churchgoers watched over a family's conduct in ways we would view today as nosy, if not meddlesome. In 1641, the Massachusetts Bay Colony enacted the first law against wife beating in the Western world, according to historian Elizabeth Pleck; it also prohibited parents from exercising "any unnatural severitie" with their children (Pleck, 1987).

How strictly this law was enforced, however, is unclear because the number of persons actually charged with wife beating was small. The Puritans must have felt the tension between respecting the integrity of the family and intervening to protect women and children from abuse. After the Puritans, government officials in most eras were even more reluctant to intervene. Indeed, the history of the issue of domestic violence is, in large part, a story of conflict between the goals of preserving the family unit and of protecting women and children. When intervention was seen as shoring up the family (as among the Puritans), it received broader support; when it was perceived as undermining men's authority and contributing to divorce, it received less.[1]

A peak of concern occurred in the late 1800s, when the child protection movement arose. In 1874 the first society for the prevention of cruelty to children was founded; 40 years later there were 494 of them. Pleck argues that the growth of these societies, usually started by leaders of the local social elite, reflected a desire to control the behavior of the unruly, growing immigrant and working-class populations. In addition, I think, the growth came at a time when attitudes toward children were evolving from seeing them as economic assets to seeing them as emotionally rewarding beings to be nurtured (Zelizer, 1985). (See Chapter 2.) Still, leaders of the movement were careful to reassure parents that their authority to discipline their children, even by occasional physical punishment, was not in question. The founder of the New York Society for the Prevention of Cruelty to Children assured nervous supporters that he favored "a good wholesome flogging for disobedient children," although he wished to protect children from "undue parental severity" (Pleck, 1987). And the few organizations that sought to help battered wives had to fight suspicion that they were encouraging the breakup of the family.

THE TWENTIETH CENTURY

The Political Model of Domestic Violence   During the twentieth century, two ways of thinking about domestic violence have emerged. The first is what might be called the *political model* of domestic violence—political not in the sense of Democrats and Republicans but rather in the sense of the relations of power and authority between men and women. Historian Linda Gordon has argued that domestic violence has been a politically constructed problem in two senses:

> *First, the very definition of what constitutes unacceptable domestic violence, and appropriate responses to it, developed and then varied according to political moods and the force of certain political movements. Second, violence among family members . . . usually arises out of power struggles in which individuals are contesting real resources and benefits. These contests arise not only from personal aspirations but also from changing social norms and conditions* (Gordon, 1988).

The struggles are usually about men's power to control the behavior of women. Resorting to force is a way for a husband to compel his wife to behave as the husband wishes. Traditionally, social structure has supported men's control over women through law and social custom. Laws that allowed husbands to use physical force against their wives are an example: The term "rule of thumb," for instance, comes from a rule in old English law that a husband was allowed to hit his wife with a stick no thicker than his thumb (Gelles & Cornell, 1990). The political

---

[1]This paragraph, and the next several, draw heavily from Pleck (1987).

Wife beating was permissible until the twentieth century in many Western societies; old English law allowed a man to beat his wife as long as he used a stick no thicker than his thumb.

model implies that domestic violence is deeply rooted in laws and customs that reinforce male dominance and is unlikely to be ended without political action by women's groups and their allies.

The Medical Model of Domestic Violence　　The second way of thinking is the *medical model,* under which domestic violence is seen as an illness and a source of injuries. In contrast to the political model, the main concern is not with relations of power but rather with illness and well-being. Health and social welfare professionals who have campaigned against child abuse, for example, have focused attention on the physical and mental harm that children suffer from physical and sexual violence. Some have argued that both the victims and the perpetrators of violence suffer from various "syndromes," illnesslike complexes of symptoms, injuries, and attitudes, that need to be treated. The professionals point to links between being violent and such personal problems as a history of abuse as a child, alcoholism, or mental illness. The medical model therefore conceives of the problem as though it can be solved by the intervention of health and social welfare professionals, much as they might attack schizophrenia or tuberculosis.

The first two decades of the twentieth century were a time when domestic relations courts, which treated family disputes more as social welfare cases than as criminal cases, were established throughout the states. But the issue of domestic violence was relatively quiescent until 1962, when pediatrician C. Henry Kempe and his colleagues, troubled by X-ray pictures of broken bones in children and reports of maltreatment, published an article entitled "The Battered Child Syndrome" (Kempe, Silverman, Steele, Droegemuller, & Silver, 1962). Kempe and his colleagues brought the medical model of domestic violence to the public's attention. In their view, child abuse was centered on a "syndrome" of repeated violence and inadequate parenting. This perspective created sympathetic concern not only for the blameless victims but also for the abusers, who seemed to be fighting a mental illness that needed treatment. In these ways the "syndrome" attracted broad public interest; within five years, every state had enacted laws that required medical personnel to report suspected cases of child abuse.

Still, there was little attention paid to wife beating until the mid-1970s, when feminist groups succeeded in making violence against women into a political problem. A decade earlier, the feminist movement had undergone a major revival, boosted by the parallel growth of the civil rights movement and the anti–Vietnam War movement. Some feminist groups focused on combating rape. Part of their strategy was the formation of services for rape victims, such as hot lines, crisis centers, and legal support. The issue of rape led organizers to the issue of sexual and physical violence directed toward married women. The movement's fundamental goal was not to treat the injuries of the victims or ease the personal problems of the perpetrators—valuable as those steps might be—but rather to remove the social supports for male violence, such as a reluctance to prosecute alleged offenders. Consequently, activists worked for changes in the law, funds for crisis centers and shelters for battered women, and the rejection of social norms that tolerated violence directed at women. With feminist influence at a high point in the 1970s, political pressure for action grew. By the end of the 1970s, nearly every state had enacted laws to protect women from violence through a mixture of support services, requirements that physicians report suspected cases, and tougher criminal procedures.

The increased emphasis on individualism in family life in the 1960s and 1970s—part of the growing focus on the private family—also helped the victims of domestic violence (Carp, 1991). The individualistic ethnic justified efforts to support battered wives who wanted to end their marriages and to support the removal of children from abusive parents. It undermined the legitimacy of allowing husbands to control their wives' behaviors by the use of force. Nevertheless, the tension between preserving two-parent families and helping victims of abuse soon reemerged. In 1980, liberals in Congress proposed legislation to provide support services for victims of domestic violence. Conservatives argued that the bill would wrongly commit the federal government to intervene in private, family matters, and they maintained that its remedies, by assisting women who wanted to leave their husbands, would hasten the breakdown of the two-parent family. Despite this opposition, supporters of the bill were able to secure modest funding in compromise legislation. Meanwhile, President Reagan closed the newly founded Federal Office of Domestic Violence. The debate over how the government should help spouses and children cope with domestic violence continues to this day; I will return to it at the end of the chapter.

WHAT DO WE KNOW?

In this mixture of concern, apathy, and debate, one important question often gets lost: How much domestic violence is there? We know little about how much violence there was in the past. The official records of court proceedings can tell us only about the rare instances when abuse came to the attention of the legal system. Consequently, it's impossible to know whether domestic violence has increased, decreased, fluctuated, or stayed the same over the past few hundred years—or even over the past 50 years. For the very recent past, medical records provide an estimate of the more severe forms of violence, although an unknown number of battered victims may not be treated. A 1984 study found that domestic violence led to an estimated 21,000 hospitalizations and 28,700 emergency room visits a year.[2] In 1992, of murders where the relationship between the victim and the killer was known, about 10 percent involved the killing of a spouse or ex-spouse and almost 6 percent involved the killing of a boyfriend or girlfriend (U.S. Bureau of Justice Statistics, 1994b).

WHAT CONSTITUTES DOMESTIC VIOLENCE?

To go beyond these medical reports, one must have a set of criteria about exactly what acts constitute domestic violence. Unfortunately, there is little consensus about those criteria among either the public or academic researchers. Consequently, it's not possible to state a single, precise definition. In fact, one article reviewed 30 research reports on marital violence published between 1980 and 1988 and found that only 5 of the reports even included a description of how abuse was defined (Geffner, Rosenbaum, & Hughes, 1988). From the perspective of the medical model, the main criterion that defines domestic violence is injury, in the case of physical abuse, and sexual penetration, in the case of sexual abuse. Domestic violence, according to this viewpoint, is relatively clear-cut: It is synonymous with the broken bones in Dr. Kempe's X-rays or the cuts and bruises a woman displays as she enters a hospital emergency room.

From a political perspective, however, violence can be defined more broadly as including minor injuries or even the threat of serious injury. That is to say, a slap in the face may not injure a woman, but she may see it as a threat that harsher blows will follow if she does not accommodate her husband's or partner's wishes. Even a verbal threat of physical harm may make her submit to an unwelcome demand or an unwanted sexual advance. Under this broader definition domestic violence could include not just serious injuries but also attempts to coerce women through minor violence such as slapping or through the threat of injury. Critics of this kind of definition would suggest that it confuses serious harm with much less serious consequences and makes the problem so broad as to be unmeasurable. Supporters of this definition would suggest that the narrow medical model misses the point, which is to work toward ending men's domination over women through the use or threat of superior physical force.

Many studies measure both moderate and severe acts of violence and make distinctions between them. The only national surveys specifically on domestic violence were conducted in 1975 and 1985 by Murray Straus and his colleagues (Straus, Gelles, & Steinmetz, 1980). In 1975, they supervised interviews with 2,143 married or cohabiting adults who had children between ages 3 and 17 living with them. A similar, somewhat larger survey was carried out in 1985. In both surveys, the persons being interviewed were asked to think of situations during the past year when they had had disagreements or had been angry with a specified family member. Then they were asked how often they had engaged in a list of acts, eight of which were violent: (1) threw something at the other person; (2) pushed, grabbed, or shoved; (3) slapped or spanked; (4) kicked, bit, or hit with a fist; (5) hit or tried to hit with something; (6) beat up the other; (7) threatened with a knife or gun; and (8) used a knife or gun. In their statistical analyses, the authors differentiate between "overall violence," which includes all eight categories, and "severe violence," which includes categories 4 through 8.

---

[2]This was a study by the Centers for Disease Control cited in Gelles (1987).

MARITAL VIOLENCE

Data from the 1985 survey concerning violence by husbands (and male partners) toward their wives (and female partners) are displayed in Figure 11.1. Keep in mind the limitations of this study: The answers don't tell how long the incident lasted, whether the victim was injured, or what the circumstances were. The results may underestimate violence because separated and divorced couples, who are more likely to experience violence than married couples (Stark & Flitcraft, 1988), were excluded and because respondents may not admit to being violent. Nevertheless, the survey provides the best information on the incidence of violence over a one-year period. The figure shows that the less severe acts were fairly common. About 9 percent of husbands reported that they had pushed, grabbed, or shoved their wives in the previous year, and about 3 percent had slapped or thrown something at their wives.

The percentages admitting to severe violence were smaller. Nearly 1 percent of husbands, for example, admitted to beating up their wives, and about 0.5 percent admitted to threatening them with a gun or knife. When the authors combined the answers to categories 4 through 8, they found that 3 percent of husbands admitted to having carried out at least one act of severe violence toward their wives in the previous year. If this estimate is accurate (and it is likely to be low, if anything), about 1.6 million wives in 1985 had been victimized by severe violence.

The authors also compared the 1975 and 1985 results and found that severe violence by husbands toward their wives appeared to decline over the period (from 4 percent to 3 percent), as did severe violence by parents toward children; other forms of violence stayed about the same. Yet the number of serious incidents in the two surveys is small enough that it is hard to judge whether the declines are real. In any case, the surveys contradict the idea that there is an "epidemic" of spreading severe violence. To be sure, the current levels are disturbing. But most likely, what has changed over time is not the prevalence of domestic violence so much as the amount of attention we have paid to it. (See *How Do Sociologists Know What They Know?* Advocates and Estimates: How Large [or Small] Are Social Problems?)

There have been a few statewide surveys of violence against women that use varying definitions of abuse or that simply ask women whether they have been abused. Reviewing these studies, two authors conclude, "We can safely estimate that between 20% and 25% of the adult women in the United States have been

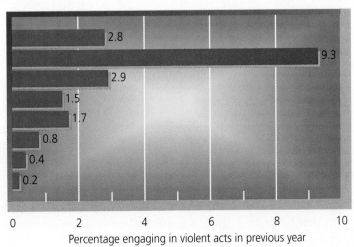

FIGURE 11.1 Acts of violence by husbands against their wives in the previous year, 1985. (*Source:* Straus & Gelles, 1986.)

How Do Sociologists Know What They Know?

Advocates and Estimates: How Large (or Small) Are Social Problems?

In February of 1997, the U.S. Department of Justice released studies showing that (1) the number of rapes reported to police had dropped in 1995 to the lowest rate per person in a decade; and (2) the number of people who said they were raped or sexually assaulted in the annual National Crime Victimization Survey had dropped by 44 percent from 1993 to 1995 (Butterfield, 1997). This was good news—except to some advocates for victims of rape and sexual abuse. Professor Mary Koss told the *New York Times* that reports showing a decrease in rape "upset me because it lessens the sympathy for rape victims" and makes them even less likely to come forward (Butterfield, 1997, p. A1). She disputed the new figures: "The Justice Department looks at the

incidence of rape year by year, but many mental health experts believe it is common sense to look at prevalence, over a lifetime," as if this criticism somehow meant that a sharp decrease in the annual rate was meaningless.

Professor Koss was acting no differently than many advocates for (and against) social causes when they describe the scope of the problem they care about. As a general rule, advocates for social causes tend to use the broadest definition of the problem, whereas opponents tend to use the narrowest. Consider homelessness (see Chapter 4). In the 1980s, advocates for the homeless repeated an estimate by activist Mitch Snyder that two to three million people were homeless. When government officials or academic researchers produced far lower estimates, they were sharply

criticized. Then Snyder was asked about the basis of his estimate in a television interview, and he replied:

> Everybody demanded it. Everybody said we want a number . . . We got on the phone, we made a lot of calls, we talked to a lot of people, and we said, "Okay, here are some numbers." They have no meaning, no value (Jencks, 1994, p. 2).

Christopher Jencks later estimated, based on his analysis of several studies, that the homeless population grew from about 100,000 in 1980 to about 200,000 in 1984 and about 400,000 in 1987–1988 (Jencks, 1994). If he is correct, homelessness increased substantially in the 1980s, which should be worrisome to anyone concerned about poor families. But the size of the problem seems to

physically abused at least once by a male intimate" (Stark & Flitcraft, 1988). In the 1985 survey, Straus and his colleagues found that, combining all eight categories of violence, 28 percent of couples reported that an act of violence had occurred at least once during their marriage (Gelles & Cornell, 1990).

Men and Women as Perpetrators   The 1975 and 1985 national surveys also found that married women reported doing about as many acts of violence toward their husbands as their husbands did toward them. This does not mean, however, that wives are just as violent as husbands. Recall that the surveys did not ask who started the violence, what injuries resulted, or how many incidents occurred. (Nor did the researchers ever interview both spouses. Each man and each woman came from a separate household.) Given the general size and strength differences between women and men, it is highly likely that men initiate most of the incidents of severe violence. Many of the severely violent acts of wives are probably committed in retaliation or self-defense. Strength differences also imply that a husband's punch is likely to produce a more serious injury than a wife's punch. Yet the survey did not differentiate between a first blow by a husband that breaks his wife's nose and a retaliatory punch by his wife that lands harmlessly on his stomach. Although each counted as one act of violence, their implications are different. This is not to deny that in a small number of marriages the wife may be the aggressor, but in most instances she would be the victim.

be much smaller in scope than advocates suggested early on.

Nor is the tendency to define the magnitude of a problem in a way that's consistent with one's view of the problem limited to liberals and feminists. In 1995, three conservatives published an analysis of welfare benefits in every state. Welfare benefits, they argued, were so generous that they destroyed the incentive to work; therefore, welfare benefits should be sharply limited (Tanner, Moore, & Hartman, 1995). The benefit levels they reported were startlingly high. For example, in Maryland, the "full package" of welfare benefits was equivalent to $22,000 per year—so high that a worker would have to earn $11.00 per hour to match them. But the "full package" included $5,864 of housing assistance, even

though only one-fourth of welfare recipients in Maryland received such assistance; $1,028 for the value of the food given to pregnant and nursing mothers and their young children under another program that most recipients don't receive; and other such benefits. When the package was restricted to Aid to Families with Dependent Children, food stamps, and Medicaid, it was reduced to $12,124.

This is not to say that any of the advocates described here are distorting the data or lying. There is more than one way of defining most social problems. It is probably true, for example, that rape and sexual assaults are still underreported in government surveys, as advocates would claim. So the problem is larger than official statistics show. It is difficult to find all of the homeless, who hide themselves in

the abandoned buildings and alleyways of low-income neighborhoods; consequently, Jencks's estimate could be too low. And housing assistance is worth money to those welfare recipients fortunate enough to receive it. So just focusing on cash benefits to the poor is too restrictive.

My point is only that, as a consumer of social statistics, you should always ask yourself what the biases are of the people who are presenting you with the numbers. If they have a strong stake in convincing you that the problem is large in scope, they will probably choose an expansive definition of it. If they want to convince you the problem is not serious, they'll usually choose a much narrower definition. Evaluate not only their numbers but also their social and political arguments with this tendency in mind.

Responses to the National Crime Victimization Surveys of 1987 to 1991 also suggest that women are the victims of domestic violence far more often than men. The surveys asked a national sample of adults whether they had been the victims of rape, robbery, or assault and, further, whether the perpetrator had been a relative or intimate partner (spouse, ex-spouse, boyfriend, girlfriend), an acquaintance, or a stranger. Women reported that 33 percent of the rapes, robberies, and assaults they had experienced were committed by a relative or intimate partner, whereas among men, relatives and intimates had committed just 5 percent. Moreover, women who had been victimized by relatives and intimates were more likely to have been injured than women who had been victimized by acquaintances or strangers. For instance, 42 percent of women who had been victimized by relatives or intimate partners reported receiving medical or hospital care, compared with 22 percent of women victimized by strangers (U.S. Bureau of Justice Statistics, 1994a). The statistics paint a picture in which women face a much higher risk of being injured by someone they know well than men.

Social Class   Although domestic violence affects all social classes, several studies report substantially higher rates of domestic violence among low-income couples than among higher-income couples.[3] Part of this difference, however, may reflect a

[3]For a summary, see Stark and Flitcraft (1988).

greater reluctance of middle-class individuals to admit to violence or a greater vigilance toward poor families by social welfare agencies. Still, it appears that there is at least a modest association between lower social status and violence against spouses and partners (Stark & Flitcraft, 1988). There are theoretical reasons to expect this association: More than two decades ago, William Goode suggested that men with more income and education have additional resources besides force that they can use to control the behavior of their wives (Goode, 1971). This relationship between social class and violence against wives also holds in developing countries: A Bangkok, Thailand, survey found that men with more income, education, and prestigious occupations were less likely to have hit, slapped, or kicked their wives (Hoffman, Demo, & Edwards, 1994). In addition, the frustrations of poverty and unemployment create stress that may lead some men to beat their wives. Studies show that unemployed men have rates of assault on their wives that are nearly double the rates for men who are employed (Gelles & Cornell, 1990).

Sexual Assault   What is more, there is evidence that in severely violent marriages, many incidents include forced sexual acts. In one random sample of women in San Francisco, most of the women who acknowledged sexual assaults by their husbands also acknowledged physical assaults (Russell, 1982). The idea of marital rape—that husbands cannot force their wives to engage in sex against their will—is recent and still controversial. Until very recently, laws against rape have specifically excluded sexual relations between a husband and wife, and in the 1980s several states even broadened that exclusion to cover cohabiting couples (Frieze & Brown, 1989). The long-accepted legal principle is that, by marrying, wives give their consent to sexual intercourse and their husbands may demand it by force if necessary. Some advocates of family privacy and the traditional authority of the husband still agree with that position. But as attitudes toward physical violence in marriage have changed, forced sexual acts have come into question.

The leading studies of **marital rape** have defined it as sexual assault by a husband accompanied by physical force or the threat of physical force (Pagelow, 1988). In one study of a random sample of 930 women in San Francisco who had ever been married, 14 percent reported that they had been raped by a husband or ex-husband according to this definition (Russell, 1982). Moreover, nearly three-fourths of the women who reported that their husbands had raped them also reported that their husbands had beaten them. The typical sexual incident, then, does not take place in a happy home in which an otherwise nonviolent husband forces his wife to have sex. Rather, it appears to take place in a troubled, violent home, and the sexual assault may be a deeply upsetting part of the violence. In a study of battered women in Pittsburgh, one-third of whom reported forced sexual intercourse with their husbands, whether a woman was victimized by sexual violence was a better predictor of whether she wanted to leave her marriage than whether she was victimized by physical violence alone (Frieze, 1983). Once laws are in place against physical violence between husbands and wives, then, the case for laws against forced sexual acts between husbands and wives is strengthened. Notwithstanding the difficulty of establishing whether a forced assault occurs, it seems likely that legal changes prohibiting sexual violence in marriages will continue to occur in the 1990s.

Some people wonder why more wives who are abused don't leave their husbands. In part, they don't leave for economic reasons. Many are dependent on their husbands for financial support and are unsure of their ability to find jobs that

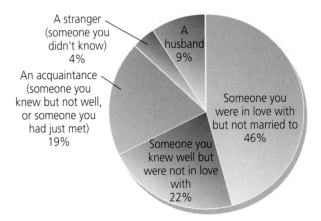

FIGURE 11.2 Women's relationships to the persons who forced them to have sex, U.S. women aged 18 to 59, 1992. (*Source:* Laumann, Gagnon, Michael, & Michaels, 1994, Figure 9.3.)

can support themselves and their children. Studies show that women with few economic resources—little education, no job skills—are less likely to leave an abusive husband. If a woman has few resources and no kin willing to take her in for more than a short time, she may decide to stay with her husband and hope that the assaults stop. In addition, the repeated battering can lead to a lowered self-image, a feeling that one is not worthy of better treatment and cannot control what will happen. Such women may feel unable to protect themselves against further assaults (Gelles & Cornell, 1990).

More generally, 22 percent of all adult women in the 1992 University of Chicago survey of sexual activity said that they had been forced to have sex by a man at least once in their lives (Laumann, Gagnon, Michael, & Michaels, 1994).[4] White women reported somewhat higher rates than black women, who in turn reported somewhat higher rates than Hispanic women. College-educated women were as likely to report forced sex as women who had not attended college. Reports were lower among Catholic women than among Protestants or those with no current religious affiliation. Most people knew the man who had forced them to have sex, often very well, as Figure 11.2 shows. The category chosen by nearly half the women was "someone you were in love with but not married to."

As for the consequences of forced sex, women who had been forced to have sex during their lives were somewhat more unhappy in the previous year (20 percent said they were not happy in the previous year, compared with 12 percent of women who had never been forced). Moreover, women who had been forced to have sex had engaged in more sexual activity but seemed to have enjoyed it less: They were more likely to have had more than 10 sex partners in their lifetime (21 percent versus 6 percent); more likely to have ever received or performed oral sex or to have had anal sex or group sex; and more likely to have masturbated in the past year. Yet they also were more likely to report that sex was not pleasurable in the past year (34 percent versus 18 percent), that they lacked interest in sex and were unable to experience orgasms, and that they had emotional problems that interfered with sex. It is difficult to know what is cause and what is effect in these reports—some of the women's sexual difficulties could have occurred before the

[4]Table 9.7. The 22 percent figure combines information obtained from the face-to-face portion of the interview and from the self-administered questionnaire, which the subjects placed in a sealed envelope without the interviewer's seeing the answers.

incidents of forced sex. Nevertheless, the responses suggest a troubling association between forced sex, on the one hand, and an unsatisfying yet more frequent and varied level of sexual activity, on the other hand (Laumann et al., 1994).

CHILD ABUSE

Hitting children is the most tolerated form of family violence. Indeed, the vast majority of parents have spanked or slapped their children (Steinmetz, 1987). Although it is difficult to make historical comparisons, the Puritans' view that children's wills need to be broken (see Chapter 2) suggests that the use of physical force against children may have been more prevalent in colonial times than ever since. Physical force was probably more common a century ago—no one today could imagine the head of a children's welfare organization announcing his support for flogging.

Even if we grant parents the right to spank or slap, at some point physical force shades into physical abuse. As with violence between spouses and partners, there is no single definition of exactly what constitutes **child abuse**. The definition that earns the greatest consensus among child welfare professionals is serious physical harm (trauma, sexual abuse with injury, or willful malnutrition) with intent to injure—although it is difficult to determine whether there has been intent to injure (Starr, 1988). There is less consensus about other possible forms of abuse, many of which adults would find disturbing, such as sexual abuse without injury or various forms of neglect (e.g., leaving young children home by themselves all day). The 1985 national survey of married or cohabiting adults with children found that 2 percent had kicked, bitten, punched, or beaten up their children during the previous year. (This percentage excludes parents who had hit their children with an object such as a stick or a belt.) I think that most people would view repeated kicking, punching, and beating as child abuse (Straus & Gelles, 1986).

Further information comes from several national surveys of child welfare professionals. In 1980, 1986, and 1993, the National Incidence Study of Child Abuse and Neglect (NIS) interviewed a broad range of professionals who serve children; they were asked whether they had seen children who appeared to be abused or neglected (Westat, Inc., 1981; Sedlak, 1991; Sedlak & Broadhurst, 1996). In a separate 1993 study, child protection officials in each state were asked about the numbers and characteristics of cases of child abuse and neglect that had been reported to them. Although all of these surveys miss children who were not seen by professionals or reported to state agencies, they still provide some of the best recent information. Figure 11.3 shows the percentage of substantiated cases (i.e., verified as accurate by state or local agencies) in 1993 that fell into each of five categories, according to the reports of the state child protection officials.

Nearly half the reports were of parental neglect rather than abuse. The NIS surveys of professionals found that more than half of the neglect cases referred to educational neglect, which typically means that the children weren't attending school regularly and that their parents were not making much effort to have them attend. The remainder of the cases of neglect referred to physical neglect, which usually means that children were left unattended or poorly supervised by their parents. Note that less than half of all cases referred to physical or sexual abuse, the kinds of child-related domestic violence that are of greatest public concern.

The surveys also suggest that child abuse was not equally likely in all families. Rather, it was more likely to occur in low-income families, in single-parent families, and in families in which the husband did not have a full-time job (Steinmetz,

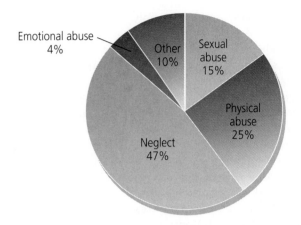

FIGURE 11.3
Substantiated cases of child abuse and neglect, 1993. (*Source:* McCurdy & Daro, 1994.)

1987). The 1993 NIS found that, compared with children in families with incomes of $30,000 or more per year, children in families with incomes below $15,000 were 22 times as likely to experience some form of maltreatment (Sedlack & Broadhurst, 1996). To be sure, some of this social class difference could merely reflect a greater tendency of doctors, nurses, social workers, and neighbors to report poor families for suspicion of neglect or abuse (Hampton & Newberger, 1985). Even so, a review article concludes, "Child abuse *is* class related" (Starr, 1988).

As was the case with spouse abuse, there is good theoretical reason to think that the hardships of poverty might lead distressed parents to have less patience with their children or at least to be more neglectful. In fact, neglect appears to be more closely associated with poverty than does abuse: Low-income families were nine times more likely to have been involved in educational or physical neglect than other families, according to the professionals' reports, compared with four to six times more likely to have been involved in physical or sexual abuse (Besharov & Laumann, 1994). It is poor families that are more often forced to leave a child unattended while adults work or who have little faith in the present system of education and therefore don't make sure their children attend school.

The state child protection officials' reports indicate a low prevalence of child sexual abuse, but social surveys find a higher rate. In the 1992 survey of sexual activity, the adult subjects were asked, "Before you [reached puberty] did anyone touch you sexually?" (Laumann et al., 1994). Seventeen percent of the women and 12 percent of the men said yes. Among the women, nearly all the touching had been done by men (63 percent) or adolescent boys (28 percent) rather than by women. Men, however, were most likely to report touching by adolescent girls (45 percent), followed by men (23 percent) and adolescent boys (15 percent). Nearly all the incidents for both sexes had involved touching genitals, with a minority reporting vaginal, oral, or anal sex.

The interviewers also asked who did the touching (Laumann et al., 1994). Among women, the most common responses were an older relative (29 percent) or a family friend (29 percent); even more men named a family friend (40 percent). As for cases of sexual abuse that would fit the usual legal definition of **incest**—sexual relations between a child and her or his parent, brother, or sister—16 percent of women who had been touched named a father or brother. Thus, our best estimate is that, overall, about 3 percent of adult American women (that is, 16 percent of the 17 percent who reported touching by anyone) had experienced incest as children.

As for abuse at preschools or schools, only 3 percent of the women who were touched and 4 percent of the men reported that a teacher had done the touching. Despite attention in the media to alleged incidents of sexual abuse of children in day care centers, less than 1 percent of all substantiated cases of child abuse in 1992 occurred in day care or foster-care settings (McCurdy & Daro, 1994).

Studies also suggest that women who are abused sexually before puberty have earlier and riskier sexual careers. Women in the 1992 survey who reported that when they were children they were sexually abused by a person at least four years older than they were were more likely to have first intercourse before age 16, to have 11 or more sexual partners as adults, to acquire a sexually transmitted infection in their lifetime, and to report a later experience of forced sex (Browning & Laumann, 1997). A survey of over 10,000 adolescent girls in a midwestern state found that girls who had been sexually abused had twice as many sexual partners during the past year than did girls who had never been abused (Luster & Small, 1997). Christopher Browning and Edward Laumann argue that sexually abused girls absorb a model of sexual relationships, a "sexual script" (Gagnon & Simon, 1973), on which future sexual relationships may be based; lacking alternative models, they may be "eroticized" to be more receptive to early sex and may associate sex with power inequalities or social isolation. "Adult-child sexual contact, for women," the authors write, "seems to provide access to sexuality without cultivating the emotional and cognitive skills to manage sexual experiences" (Browning & Laumann, 1997, p. 557).

Rising Abuse or Rising Reports?   In 1993, according to the state child protection officials, about three million reports of suspected cases of child abuse and neglect were made to state or local government officials (McCurdy & Daro, 1994). This compares with slightly over one million reports in 1980 and about 150,000 reports in 1963 (Besharov & Laumann, 1994). No one, however, believes that there is 20 times as much child abuse and neglect now as in 1963. In fact, it's not clear whether there has been any increase. The state laws passed after the Kempe article was published clearly increased the number of cases of suspected abuse that doctors and nurses reported to government authorities. In the 1980s, the expansion of reporting requirements to include other professionals such as teachers, as well as a general rise in public consciousness about child abuse, resulted in further increases in the number of reported cases. People seem to be increasingly likely to report a family to the authorities if they suspect maltreatment. Of the three million cases that were reported in 1993, enough evidence existed to substantiate only about one million (McCurdy & Daro, 1994). (States now investigate each reported case to see whether there is evidence of maltreatment.) Even the latter figure includes repeat reports on the same child; when repeats are eliminated, about 800,000 substantiated reports remain.

Still, there may have been an increase in child abuse and neglect in the late 1980s and early 1990s. The 1993 NIS survey reported a 42 percent increase in the number of physically abused children and an 83 percent increase in sexually abused children since the 1986 NIS (Sedlak & Broadhurst, 1996). An increase of this magnitude between 1986 and 1993 would be significant and troubling—if it really reflected more abuse. But experts caution that it is impossible to tell whether this is the case (Donnelly, 1994; Besharov & Dembosky, 1996). Between 1986 and 1993, reporting systems continued to broaden in many states. It is possible that the increase occurred solely because professionals were looking ever more closely at children for signs of abuse and were more likely to file reports. Nevertheless, the period from the mid-1980s to the early 1990s is one in which the well-being of children in low-income families has deteriorated on several dimensions and the number of children in foster care has soared (see Chapter 14). It could be that an increase in abuse and neglect has also occurred.

Poverty or Abuse?   Not surprisingly, studies show that children who are physically or sexually abused often experience greater emotional problems, including depression, aggression, low self-esteem, troubled relationships with peers, and many others. Not all abused children, of course, show all—or even any—of these problems. Furthermore, it is unclear what proportion of the problems these children display are the result of their abuse, as opposed to other difficulties (Emery, 1989). Many abused children, for example, grow up in families that are troubled by poverty and unemployment. Consequently, some of the problems that abused children show would probably have occurred even if they hadn't been abused. In fact, Douglas Besharov, the first director of the National Center on Child Abuse and Neglect, argues that child protective workers sometimes overreact to families in which the real problem is poverty, not maltreatment. When they remove a child from his or her parents in cases of neglect without physical or sexual abuse, Besharov maintains, workers often make his or her problems worse. Such children are usually sent into the foster-care system, which has its own problems and is not a clear improvement over living at home. (See *Families and Public Policy:* Foster Care, on pp. 350–351.) Besharov and Lisa Laumann advocate, instead, that more social services be focused on assisting the parents of these children (Besharov & Laumann, 1994).

Is there a "cycle of abuse," in which adults who were abused as children are more likely to abuse their own children? One review of the literature estimated that about 30 percent of persons who were abused as children become abusers when they reach adulthood, compared with about 5 percent among persons who were not abused. Those who were abused as children but managed to avoid repeating the behavior were more openly angry about the abuse, were more likely to have been abused by just one parent, and were more likely to have had a supportive relationship with the nonabusing parent (Kaufman & Zigler, 1987). If this estimate is accurate, two conclusions can be drawn: (1) Adults who were abused as children are indeed more likely to become abusers; but (2) most adults who were abused as children do not become abusers. The effect of abuse on children is to raise the risk of undesirable consequences, including becoming an abuser, yet many children do not experience these consequences.[5]

ELDER ABUSE

Another kind of domestic violence that has drawn public attention is **elder abuse**. It is, however, a problem without a clear definition. One definition, which reflects the emphases in public discussions, is physical abuse of elderly persons by nonelderly persons—typically their children or other caretakers in their children's generation. Yet the only large, random-sample survey on the topic found that the most frequent abusers of the elderly were their spouses. In this study of 2,020 elderly persons in the Boston area, 2 percent reported that they had been the victims of physical abuse

---

[5]The literature on domestic violence (e.g., Gelles & Cornell, 1990) also discusses so-called "hidden" victims, such as parents, siblings, and elders. Yet, by definition, it is difficult to accurately estimate how many such people are victimized.

Families and Public Policy

Foster Care

Foster care—the removal of children from their parental home and their placement in another home—is a program with few admirers and many critics. Like abortion policy, foster-care policy involves a difficult choice between two worthy goals, in this case protecting the integrity of the family unit and protecting children from physical and mental harm. In most circumstances, the children are removed without their parents' permission after a child welfare worker investigates a report of abuse or neglect. Consequently, foster care embodies the most severe form of state interference between parents and children—seizing the children against the parents' will. Because child welfare workers tend to be middle-class and the affected children tend to be poor, it is sometimes criticized as a class-based intrusion into family life (Liss, 1987). Because it substitutes state-directed care for parental care, it is sometimes criticized as antifamily (Berger, 1986). Because it fails to return many children to their families in a timely manner, it is criticized for warehousing children from problem families, rather than helping the

parents provide better care (Steiner, 1981). Yet few would disagree that children should be protected from some parents—the drug-addicted, the physically or sexually abusive, for instance—who are not fit to raise them.

In the late 1970s, when about 500,000 children were living in foster care, a policy consensus formed: Alarmed by the numbers of children in care, both conservatives and liberals agreed that child welfare workers should place a higher priority on helping troubled parents keep their children and care better for them. If a foster-care placement was needed, greater efforts should be made to return the children to a permanent home—either by sending them back to their parents or, if absolutely necessary, by putting them up for adoption. Congress codified this consensus in the Adoption Assistance and Child Welfare Act of 1980.[1]

The new consensus worked as intended for several years. The number of children in foster care declined to about 275,000 in 1983 through 1985 (*The Crisis in Foster Care*, 1990). Then, suddenly, the numbers rose sharply to 340,000 in 1988 and to

442,000 in 1992 (Toshio, 1993).[2] By 1996, it had returned to the 500,000 level (Kilborn, 1997). The new law, it appears, was overwhelmed by a huge, unexpected wave of children at risk of harm. The wave was greatest in large cities such as New York and Chicago, and the largest percentage increases in foster care occurred among newborns and infants, many of whom were low-birth-weight or otherwise impaired babies born to mothers who had had little or no prenatal care (Wulczyn & Goerge, 1992).

Many observers have speculated that at least some of this rise was the result of the rapid spread of crack cocaine usage during the same period (U.S. House of Representatives, 1993). Women in poor neighborhoods have used crack more than they had used earlier addictive drugs such as heroin. The legacy of crack appears to include much larger numbers of babies born with drug-induced impairments or abandoned at birth in hospitals. It is unlikely, however, that crack is the whole story. A rise in homelessness among families also occurred during the late 1980s and early 1990s. Consequently, some parents were not able to provide basic shelter and security to

at least once since they had reached age 65. In three-fifths of these cases, the abuser had been the elderly person's spouse (Pillemer & Finkelhor, 1988). Although spouse abuse is as regrettable among the elderly as among the nonelderly, there's no need to characterize the elderly version as a separate problem. To be sure, a small number of elderly persons are assaulted by their children or other younger adults. The victims of this kind of abuse tend to be mentally or physically impaired persons who are dependent on their caretakers (Gelles & Cornell, 1990). Although public programs to reduce such assaults may be worthwhile, there is no convincing evidence that such assaults are as common as assaults against spouses or children. In the Boston-area survey, only nine elderly persons, or less than 0.5 percent, said a son or daughter had ever abused them physically.

their children, and child protective workers are more likely to remove a child from a homeless family than from one in a home (Rossi, 1994; Jencks, 1994).[3]

Coupled with the rise in reported cases of child abuse, the surge in abandoned and drug-impaired infants led some experts to call for seizing more at-risk children from parents (Ingrassia & McCormick, 1994). More important, highly publicized cases such as the deaths of Nadine Lockwood and Elizabeth Izquierdo, described at the beginning of the chapter, caused a public outcry against child protective workers who were seen as too slow to remove children from potentially abusive families (Sexton, 1996). Thus, the pendulum of professional and public opinion has swung back to the 1970s, before the movement toward keeping families intact reached its peak.

Yet neither option—vigilance and early removal of children perceived to be in danger, or increased efforts to help troubled parents so that they can keep their children—has worked well. The foster-care system was designed on the basis of assumptions about families that no longer hold. It as-

sumed that the family problems leading to foster care were temporary—as when a mother became ill with a disease such as tuberculosis and needed six months or a year to recuperate. It assumed that large numbers of mothers who did not work outside the home could be found to care temporarily for children whose parents couldn't care for them. It didn't anticipate the shortages, now occurring, of suitable and willing foster parents (*The Crisis in Foster Care*, 1990). It didn't foresee families sleeping in homeless shelters and drug-addicted newborns abandoned in nurseries. In addition, it probably ignored levels of child abuse that today would be unacceptable.

The heart of the problem is that there still are no good alternatives to parental care for children. Long-term foster care, with children frequently shuttled from family to family, is problematic. Yet abusive or neglectful parents also harm children. One recent innovation is to place children in the homes of relatives and pay them. This so-called "kinship care" option preserves some of the child's family bonds and seems preferable to care by non-relatives, but it is not without problems. Relatives may have more diffi-

culty than strangers in restricting visits by abusive parents. Moreover, they tend to keep children for a longer period of time than other foster parents; yet they are sometimes reluctant to adopt the children for fear of angering the parents (Wulczyn & Goerge, 1992). Thus, kinship care can conflict with the goal of finding a permanent home for foster children. Moreover, foster parents typically receive substantially more money per child than parents do under Temporary Assistance to Needy Families (the newly renamed cash welfare program—see Chapter 6), creating a possible incentive for families receiving TANF to place the children in kinship foster care. The only real, long-term hope is to prevent more children from being abused and neglected. That would require an assault on poverty, unemployment, and family breakup. Meanwhile, the quandary of what to do about abusive and neglectful parents and their children continues.

[1]Public Law 96-272.
[2]The APWA's estimate for 1993 is 464,000.
[3]A small but growing number of children in foster care, estimated at about 1,000 in 1990, were born to mothers with AIDS and have tested positive for the HIV virus that causes AIDS. See *The Crisis in Foster Care*.

EXPLANATIONS

Why do people abuse their spouses, partners, or children? According to the political model of domestic violence, assaults against spouses and partners arise, in part, from power struggles between men and women. Men have an advantage in these struggles because of their greater physical strength, on average, and because of a social system that often reinforces male dominance. During the many thousands of years humans spent as hunter-gatherers, male strength was central to the life of bands. Men defended the band's territory against intrusions by other bands, and men armed with spears hunted animals. It is likely that men used their strength to compete for women and to dominate them. Later, in larger social groups, men were often able to shape laws and norms—such as the belief that the husband should be the head of the household—to their advantage so that they didn't need to use force to achieve their ends. The system of male dominance that still appears to some extent in virtually every society today is based in part upon the use of, or the threat of the use of, force against women.

But most men, despite their advantage in strength and despite cultural beliefs, don't hit their wives. In addition, both men and women abuse their children. Consequently, the general notion of male dominance isn't useful in explaining why some husbands are violent and others are not or why parents abuse their children. Many other explanations have been proposed, most of which have some plausibility. These explanations are often referred to as "theories" of domestic violence, although most of them are just collections of related propositions. Some of these perspectives emphasize psychological factors, whereas others emphasize social structural factors. At the present time, we don't know enough to tie them together into a single, coherent explanation. When Richard Gelles and Murray Straus, two leaders in the field, were asked to write an essay integrating theories of domestic violence, they presented propositions and outcomes from 13 so-called theories (Gelles & Straus, 1979). Instead of mechanically discussing all 13, let me focus on the ones I think are the most important.

SOCIAL LEARNING PERSPECTIVE

The explanation that is probably cited the most draws upon the **social learning perspective** developed by social psychologists. According to this perspective, individuals learn behavior they will later exhibit by observing what others do and seeing the consequences of these actions. Thus, children from violent homes are said to learn by observation and personal experience that aggressive or violent behavior is an acceptable and often successful way of controlling others and getting what you want (Bandura, 1973). In fact, a number of studies do show that children who grow up in homes characterized by domestic violence are more likely, as adults, to act violently toward their spouses and children. (All children may, to some extent, learn that violent behavior is acceptable through watching the pervasive violence in television programs and films.)

For example, respondents in the 1975 national survey were asked whether, as children, (1) they had ever observed either of their parents hitting the other and (2) whether their parents had hit them as teenagers. Among men who had neither seen hitting nor been hit, 1 percent committed acts of severe violence against their wives. Among men who had been hit by their parents, the corresponding figure was 3 percent. It was 6 percent among men who had observed their parents hitting each other, and it rose to 12 percent among men who had both observed their parents hitting each other and had been hit themselves (Kalmuss, 1984).

This pattern of findings can be interpreted in two ways. The glass-half-empty interpretation is that men are far more likely to beat their wives if they had witnessed hitting or had been hit by their parents. This interpretation shows why the social learning perspective does help us to understand why some men are violent. The glass-half-full interpretation is that the vast majority of men who had witnessed hitting or had been hit by their parents do *not* beat their wives. This second interpretation shows the limitations of the social learning perspective as an explanation for violent behavior: It doesn't explain why most people who have been exposed to violence are not themselves violent.

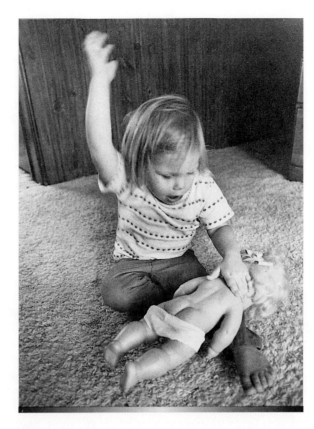

According to the social learning perspective, people learn violent behavior by observation and experience in their own families while growing up.

FRUSTRATION-AGGRESSION PERSPECTIVE

An alternative explanation is derived from the **frustration-aggression perspective**. Here the central idea is that aggressive behavior occurs when a person is blocked from achieving a goal, such as when economic inequalities cause men and women to work for low wages, high unemployment rates make it hard to find a job, or racial discrimination limits the opportunities of people from racial-ethnic groups. When these conditions occur, it is said, the person may displace his or her frustration and anger onto a safer target—such as his or her spouse or children. These targets are safer than employers or strangers because there is less chance of being arrested, being hit hard in return, or losing one's job. In contrast to the social learning approach, violent behavior is not viewed as directed toward a specific end, such as dominating a wife. Rather, violence is seen as an emotional outburst of displaced anger, usually by a man. So this perspective suggests that, regardless of what people have learned about violence as children, they will be more likely to act violently if they are frustrated by forces they feel are blocking their ability to get a job, move out of a dangerous neighborhood, or attain other important goals. Consequently, the frustration-aggression approach helps us to understand why domestic violence is somewhat more common among the lower social classes, whose members are more likely to be blocked from attaining their goals (but who may also be more likely to have grown up in violent homes).

The frustration-aggression approach raises the question of where a person's basic tendency to act violently (when blocked or frustrated) comes from, other than social learning. Chapter 3 reviewed evidence which suggests that men's greater aggressiveness, compared with women's aggressiveness, may be partly of biological origin. Gelles and Straus argue, in contrast, that aggression is learned behavior; in fact, they reject the idea that there is any biological influence on domestic violence.[6] Yet a national study of armed services veterans found that husbands who had higher levels of testosterone—the male sex hormone—were more likely to have hit or thrown things at their wives (Booth & Dabbs, 1993). The possibility of biological influences is not presented here to excuse the behavior of violent men. Most people can (and do) control their urges and predispositions. Even in the testosterone study, 71 percent of men in the group that had the highest levels of the hormone did *not* hit or throw things at their wives—just as most men who come from violent homes do not beat their wives. Still, men with a greater biological predisposition toward aggression might be more likely than others to beat their wives and their children if they are frustrated and angry about events occurring outside the home.

SOCIAL EXCHANGE PERSPECTIVE

A third explanation draws upon the **social exchange perspective**. This explanation proposes that people calculate whether to engage in a particular behavior by considering the rewards and costs of that behavior and the rewards of alternatives to it. The model here is that of the rational actor. It suggests that a man may decide whether to beat his wife by considering the rewards (he can control her; he can let out his anger and frustration at the rest of the world) against the costs of violence (she might seek a divorce) and the rewards of not being violent (she will continue to do much of the childcare and contribute the paycheck from her job). This approach helps to explain why wives are more likely to be the victims of violence if they don't work for wages; in that case, the costs of violence to the husband (she might seek a divorce) are lower and the rewards of not being violent (she will contribute earnings) are lower because the wife is not employed. The social exchange perspective is also consistent with cross-cultural evidence that severe violence against women is less common in societies in which women have more economic independence. (See *Families in Other Cultures:* Wife Beating in the Developing World.) Moreover, it also helps to explain the greater violence against women among the lower social classes. Men with more income can influence their wives' actions by exchanging money for the desired behavior. With money they can get the same rewards poorer men must use force to obtain, but without incurring the high costs of force—such as the possibility that the wife will seek a divorce.

SEXUAL AGGRESSION AND VIOLENCE IN DATING RELATIONSHIPS

Spouse and child abuse are not the only aspects of violence between men and women that have received attention of late. As courtship and dating have changed, so have attitudes toward the use of coercion to obtain sexual intercourse. During the 1980s, researchers and clinicians introduced the study of sexual aggression by men against women whom they were dating and against acquaintances. There are

[6]See Gelles and Straus (1979), footnotes 7 and 8.

at least two reasons for the lack of attention to this problem before 1980. First, the rates of sexual activity among unmarried young persons were substantially lower prior to the 1970s; consequently, the incidence of acquaintance rape was probably lower also (although there are no satisfactory data). Second, young women tended to be blamed for their dates' improper sexual advances (see Chapter 8). As the practice of blaming the victim began to weaken and as rates of sexual activity increased, researchers brought forth study after study showing significant amounts of sexual coercion, including forcible rapes that were rarely reported to the police.

PREVALENCE

Yet adequate national data on the prevalence of sexual aggression among acquaintances still do not exist. Figure 11.2 showed that acquaintances (defined as "someone you knew but not well" or "someone you had just met") were named in 19 percent of the incidents of forced sex reported by women in the 1992 survey of sexual activity. Overall, then, we can estimate that 4 percent of all adult American women (that is, 19 percent of the 22 percent who reported forced sex by anyone) have experienced forced sex by an acquaintance. Most other studies include only college students, who can be interviewed by professors with modest research budgets. One of the best and largest college studies involved questionnaires answered by 6,159 students, about equally divided between women and men, in a random sample of 32 colleges across the country in the fall and winter of 1984–1985 (Koss, 1988). Women were asked to respond to 10 questions about being the victims of sexual aggression of increasing severity. The first question was "Have you given in to sex play (fondling, kissing, or petting, but not intercourse) when you didn't want to because you were overwhelmed by a man's continual arguments and pressure?" Parallel questions were asked about giving in to sex play "because a man used his position of authority . . . to make you" and "because a man threatened or used some degree of physical force . . . to make you." The researchers labeled positive answers to any of these three questions as "sexual contact." Affirmative answers about giving in to sexual intercourse because of a man's continual pressure or position of authority were labeled "sexual coercion." And affirmative answers to questions about attempted sexual intercourse because of force, drugs, or alcohol were labeled "attempted rape" if intercourse did not occur or "rape" if it did. Men were asked 10 parallel questions about whether they had ever initiated any of these behaviors.

SEXUAL AGGRESSION

Figure 11.4 shows the percentage of female college students in the study classified by the most severe form of sexual aggression they had experienced. At one extreme, nearly half had not experienced any form of sexual aggression. But at the other extreme, 15 percent, or nearly one in six, had experienced rape, and another 12 percent had experienced attempted rape. Responses to further questions showed that 84 percent of the rapes had involved a man who was known to the woman and 57 percent were dates. Women who had experienced rapes thought their assailants had been drinking or using drugs in 77 percent of the cases; moreover, women admitted drinking or using drugs themselves in 55 percent of the cases. Only 27 percent thought the event was "definitely a rape"—even though it objectively met the legal criteria for a rape in many states and just 8 percent had reported the event to the police.

Families in Other Cultures

Wife Beating in the Developing World

In Santiago, Chile, in late 1986, a hospital emergency room and two clinics treated 2,618 women for assault. Of these, 1,884 had been assaulted by family members, usually their husbands. A study of bodily injury cases in Bogotá, Colombia, hospitals found that 20 percent were women who had been assaulted by their husbands or partners.[1] Studies such as these demonstrate that domestic violence is not restricted to the United States and other developed countries. In fact, it is a widespread phenomenon found throughout the nonindustrial and developing world. Although good studies are limited, some generalizations can be made about the conditions under which domestic violence is more prevalent.

Anthropologist David Levinson examined the massive Human Relations Area Files for information on domestic violence in 90 preliterate and peasant societies. The HRAF archive, created by anthropologist George Murdock in the 1940s, now contains hundreds of thousands of pages of documents, mostly field reports from anthropologists, on societies around the world. Murdock's idea was to create a data archive that would allow scholars to make cross-cultural comparisons of human culture and behavior. Levinson used a diverse sample of societies including the Iroquois and Hopi tribes of North America, the Pygmy and Zulu societies of Africa, the Okinawans of Asia, and the Yanoama people of the Amazon jungle in South America (Levinson, 1989). He found that wife beating occurred in 85 percent of the societies. In a majority of the societies where wife beating occurred, it was sometimes severe enough to cause permanent injury or death.

People in the societies advanced three main reasons for wife beating, Levinson found. The first was sexual jealousy: Violence was seen as punishment for adultery or for the suspicion that one's wife had been unfaithful. The second reason was "for cause": A husband could beat his wife if he had what was culturally understood as a good reason, typically her failure to perform her duties or to treat her husband with the respect he expected. An ethnographer's report in the HRAF archive on the Truk of Oceania states:

> Wife beating is quite common but appropriate only if there is a good "reason." When a woman violates the proscriptions on "haughty behavior" or is disobedient, her husband may beat her with no fear of interference from her relatives. However, if a husband beats his wife too frequently, or if the beatings are too severe, the woman's relatives will "pity her" and will cause a separation (Swartz, 1958).[2]

The third and most common reason, predominating in 39 societies, was beating "at will": the belief that it is a husband's right to beat his wife for any reason or no reason at all.

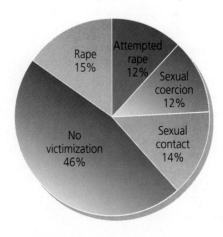

FIGURE 11.4 Highest degree of sexual aggression ever experienced by female college students in the United States, 1984–1985. (*Source:* Koss, 1988.)

Rape 15%
Attempted rape 12%
Sexual coercion 12%
Sexual contact 14%
No victimization 46%

The most interesting question in the HRAF study is what characteristics differentiate societies where wife beating is common from societies where it is unusual or absent. Levinson found that the extent of economic inequality between the husband and the wife made a difference. Wife beating was more likely to occur in societies in which men controlled the allocation of food or cash to the members of the household; it was more likely where women could not amass or control wealth, as by earning an independent income or owning a dwelling; and it was more likely where men had the final say in household decision making. Where men's economic power over women was greater, they had little to lose by alienating a wife or her kin through excessive violence because the wife controlled fewer resources. Therefore, husbands had less incentive to restrain their violent impulses (Levinson, 1988). In addition, wife beating was less common where female work groups, which could provide support to abused wives, existed.

What of the larger societies that have undergone economic development and urbanization in recent decades? Several authors have suggested that urbanization and development might increase levels of domestic violence initially. The increase supposedly would occur because traditional social controls would break down as urbanization and industrialization proceeded; then, as newer social controls were developed, domestic violence might decrease again. This line of reasoning implies that levels of domestic violence should be lower in rural societies untouched by industrialization than in industrializing societies (Gelles & Cornell, 1990). Yet evidence for this proposition is slim. A recent study compared responses of rural and low-income urban respondents to a survey in Papua New Guinea, one of the few developing countries that has relevant survey data (Morley, 1994). Samples of rural villagers and urban dwellers were asked whether they had hit their spouses, as well as other questions about their attitudes toward domestic violence. In contrast to the idea that development boosts violence, hitting was slightly more common among the rural villagers. Moreover, fewer urban residents thought that it was a "husband's right" to hit his wife. Rebecca Morley, the author of the Papua New Guinea study, suggests that wife beating may emerge as a clearly defined "social problem" in urban areas, in contrast to its greater acceptance in rural areas (Morley, 1994). This greater awareness and attention may create the perception of an increase, even if the underlying rates of wife beating remain the same.

[1]Cited in United Nations Centre for Social Development and Humanitarian Affairs (1989).
[2]Cited in Levinson (1989).

PERPETRATORS

The college men were far less likely to report initiating a rape (4 percent) or an attempted rape (3 percent). The lower figures probably represent a mixture of underreporting, multiple rapes by some, and rapes committed by nonstudents. Most (88 percent) of the men who answered affirmatively to questions about forced intercourse that seemed to indicate a rape responded that it "definitely was not a rape"; moreover, these men perceived the woman's refusal as less clear than the women in the sample perceived it. Seventy-four percent said they had been drinking alcohol or using drugs, and 75 percent said the woman had been. Forty-seven percent said they expected to engage in similar behavior again.

Nationally, 55 percent of all the rapes reported in the National Crime Victimization Surveys of 1987 to 1991 were committed by someone the victim knew. Only about half these rapes had been reported to the police; in 18 percent of the cases the victim didn't report the rape to the police because she was afraid of reprisals from the offender, and in another 35 percent of the cases the victim didn't report the rape because she considered it to be a personal or private matter (U.S. Bureau of Justice Statistics, 1994a). The younger the rape victim (and the victim is under age 18 in more than half of all rapes), the more likely the rapist is to be a family member. One Justice Department study of rapes that were reported to the police in several states found that 16 percent of the rapes had occurred to girls under age 12, and virtually all these rapes had been committed by family members or acquaintances ("Report Cites Heavy Toll," 1994).

Other studies suggest that young men who commit sexual aggression against acquaintances are more likely to show hostility toward women and to believe that men are supposed to be more dominant and women more subordinate (Lundberg-Love & Geffner, 1989). The men also show greater physiological arousal when presented with rape scenarios in psychology experiments, are more likely to consider violence against women acceptable, and are more sexually active than men who don't commit sexual aggression. In contrast, there are relatively few differences between women who have been victims of sexual aggression and those who haven't (Cate & Lloyd, 1992).

The circle of friends a person has also makes a difference. At one large university, researchers found three distinct peer groups. In the first, neither the women nor the men had initiated or been victimized by sexual aggression; in the second, some of the women had been victimized but the men in the group had not been the aggressors; and in the third, women had been victimized and men had been aggressors. The peer groups in this latter category included students who used alcohol and drugs more often, tended to live in dormitories, fraternities, and sororities (as opposed to at home), and placed a higher value on the social aspects of going to college (Gwartney-Gibbs & Stockard, 1989). What can't be determined from these studies is whether belonging to an aggressive group changes a young man's behavior or whether young men who are already aggressive for other reasons join such groups.

PHYSICAL ASSAULT

Physical assault, whether or not sexual aggression occurs, also appears to be common among dating couples. A national sample of 250 never-married persons who had dated someone six or more times in the past year was asked about the incidence of physical violence in that dating relationship. The interviewer read a list of nine types of violence, ranging from "minor aggression" ("threw something," "pushed, grabbed, or shoved," "slapped") to "severe aggression" ("kicked, bit, or hit," "beat up," "used a gun or knife"). Thirty percent chose answers showing that they had inflicted minor aggression on their dating partners at least once in the previous 12 months, and 11 percent reported inflicting severe aggression. Violence was more likely to be inflicted, the survey demonstrated, by persons who reported trying to control their partners' actions ("I make him/her do what I want," "If I don't like what s/he is doing I make him/her stop"). Moreover, the survey suggested that people who were better at what sociologists have called "taking the role of the other" experienced reduced levels of violence. Specifically, persons who said they could imagine the other person's point of view and put themselves mentally in the other person's place ("When something affects him/her, I feel it too," "I understand his/her feelings quite well") were less likely to inflict violence or to have violence inflicted on them (Stets, 1992).[7]

---

[7]The subjects were between the ages of 18 and 30.

Another study compared rates of physical assault in a college student sample to national figures for cohabiting and married couples. The authors reported that dating couples had rates of physical assault (15 percent in the previous year) that were a bit lower than for married couples (20 percent), but that cohabiting couples had noticeably higher rates (35 percent) than either dating or married couples. The authors speculate that disagreements about controlling the other partner's behavior may be important. In dating relationships, they argue, the partners expect to have less control, so they may not become as angry about a lack of control. On the other hand, married couples may agree to a high level of control. In the middle, say the authors, are cohabiting relationships, where there may be more disagreement about the amount of control a partner can expect (Stets & Straus, 1989). Their argument is intriguing, but it may also be that people who choose to cohabit have personalities and backgrounds that predispose them to violence more than those who don't cohabit.

DOMESTIC VIOLENCE AND PUBLIC POLICY

In the epilogue to her book on U.S. social policy against domestic violence since the Puritans, Pleck wrote:

> *The history of social policy against domestic violence has been one of persistent, even inherent conflict between protecting the victim and preserving the family, and the gradual development of alternatives within and outside the family for victims of abuse* (Pleck, 1987).

Since the mid-1970s this often dormant conflict has surfaced again. Yet there is a subtext to the protect-the-victim versus preserve-the-family discourse. Public policies that protect the victim restrict men's use of their superior physical force and

Violence occurs in nonmarital relationships as well. This woman had been thrown against the bathtub and knocked unconscious by her boyfriend. Nevertheless, she refused to press charges and her boyfriend was released the next day.

therefore decrease the power of men over women. That is why feminist groups have worked so hard to bring the problems of battered women to the public's attention, to create crisis centers, shelters, and support services, and to modify the law in nearly all states. Wrote Gordon, "Defining wife-beating as a social problem . . . was one of the great achievements of feminism" (Gordon, 1988).

Because liberals tend to favor equality between men and women more than conservatives, more liberals than conservatives favor policies such as the following: state intervention in marriages in which husbands use severe physical or sexual violence against their wives; continued growth of support services for victims in crisis; and more assistance for battered women who wish to leave their marriages (such as childcare, job training, and tougher child support enforcement). But although the liberal, protect-the-victim activists have been succeeding recently, a conservative, preserve-the-family movement has also emerged since the mid-1970s. Conservatives are more likely than liberals to support male-headed two-parent families. Since this family form has traditionally been dominant (although it is becoming less so), conservatives have an interest in preserving the family status quo. That is one reason why many conservatives disapprove of state intervention in families, except in the most extreme cases, and why, in part, they believe that what occurs in a family is the private business of its members. Conservatives have not had much success on these issues recently; their most notable triumph was delaying and reducing federal funds in the early 1980s. They did not have much success in the 1990s in part because of legislation that was passed in the wake of the O. J. Simpson case. For example, within days of Simpson's arrest in 1994 on charges of murdering his former wife, the New York State Legislature passed a bill that required the police to arrest suspected perpetrators of domestic violence whether or not the victim is willing to press charges. Within two months, the U.S. House of Representatives had approved nearly all the provisions of the Violence Against Women Act, which had first been introduced, without success, six years earlier.

Other recent developments, mentioned earlier, also seem to have assisted the liberals. For instance, the cultural emphasis on independence and self-fulfillment implies that an unhappy spouse should be able to leave her or his marriage. These values are inconsistent with the notion that a woman should stay in an abusive marriage. Moreover, the increasing economic independence of women provides them with earning power that they can use to gain more authority in marriage or to live independently of men. In addition, the deteriorating earnings of young men, especially those without a college education, reduce their attractiveness to women and therefore make it less likely that women they abuse will remain with them. Unless there is a reversal of these trends, liberal policy positions seem likely to continue to prevail.

Still, it can be challenging to translate the protect-the-victim policy into effective programs. Consider the spread since the early 1980s of mandatory arrest policies in domestic violence complaints. This approach was influenced by an experiment conducted by the Minneapolis police force in 1981 and 1982. When responding to domestic violence complaints, the police randomly assigned the offender to one of three treatments: arresting him, ordering him to leave the home for eight hours, or trying to mediate the dispute. The results, based on subsequent arrest records and interviews with the victims, showed that arresting the suspect resulted in the lowest level of repeat violence (Sherman & Berk, 1984).

Intrigued officials at the Department of Justice decided to support replications of the experiment in other cities. But many state governments—eager to take action

"I hate you for beating my mother," this boy shouted as his father was arrested in Minneapolis in 1987. The Minneapolis police were pioneers in testing a mandatory arrest policy in cases of domestic violence.

against the problem—legislated mandatory arrest policies without waiting for the results of the replications. Unfortunately, when the experimental results from the other localities were published in 1992, they showed that arrests were effective only for suspects who were employed. Arrests of suspects who were unemployed did not reduce subsequent violence; in fact, in some localities unemployed suspects were more likely to commit subsequent attacks if they had been arrested. The experiments seem to show that arrest deters only men who have something to lose by going to jail—namely, their jobs and their incomes. For men with little to lose, the arrest may do little good and may even spur the suspect on to further violence.[8] If these results are valid, there is no uniform policy conclusion to be drawn from them: A suburb with a low unemployment rate might find a mandatory arrest policy effective in combating domestic violence, but a central city police force in a high-unemployment area might find mandatory arrests counterproductive.

Even so, the results certainly don't suggest dropping arrests as an option for police officers. Rather, they suggest that mandatory arrest policies, such as New York State's post-Simpson law, may impose rigid practices that don't work as well as more flexible programs. Altogether, these recent results illustrate the difficulty of designing programs to address spouse abuse. Similarly, the problems of the foster-care system (refer to *Families and Public Policy:* Foster Care) illustrate how difficult it is to devise policies that protect children from abuse without disrupting their family lives and placing them in problematic settings outside their homes. Research and debate over how to respond to domestic violence are likely to continue throughout the 1990s, although public attention will probably fade when the

[8]Three articles reporting the results of the replications were published in Sherman and Smith (1992), Pate and Hamilton (1992), Berk, Campbell, Klap, and Western (1992). See also the comments and replies in the December 1993 issue (vol. 58, no. 6) of *American Sociological Review.*

next celebrity-problem-of-the-year appears. Still, the changes in public policy have been substantial, and more are likely. In the current period of high divorce rates, greater gender equality, and rising individualism, the image of the bruised and battered woman has led most Americans to approve of government efforts to help her escape her husband. It is hard to imagine returning to a time when men could hit their wives with impunity or parents could boast of giving their children a good wholesome flogging.

SUMMARY

1. The history of domestic violence as a social issue shows cycles of concern and neglect throughout U.S. history. The Puritans, who took a strong stand against domestic violence, passed the first Western laws against it. A second period of activity occurred in the late 1800s, and a third period began in the 1960s. Both a medical model and a political model have been used as ways of thinking about domestic violence. The current interest and activity are largely a result of political and social action by feminist groups and by health and social welfare professionals.

2. There is no reliable evidence of trends in domestic violence before the mid-1970s. Between 1975 and 1985, the level of severe violence by husbands toward wives appears to have declined, or at least to have remained steady. Still, a 1985 national survey found that about 3 percent of husbands admitted to engaging in one or more acts of severe violence against their wives in the previous year. Although wives also engage in violence, evidence suggests that they are far more often the victims than the aggressors. Sexual violence is often linked to physical violence; studies show that forced sexual acts are frequently a part of a violent marriage. Cross-cultural studies show that assaults against wives occur in most societies. Societies with less violence against women tend to be more egalitarian and to encourage intervention in family disputes.

3. Physical abuse of children has probably decreased in the long term, but surveys continue to show abuse by parents. Among cases that are reported to government agencies, nearly half referred to educational or physical neglect; 40 percent referred to physical or sexual abuse. Neglect and, to a lesser extent, physical abuse are somewhat more common among low-income families. Reports of child neglect and abuse have risen greatly in recent decades, but this may reflect more complete reporting rather than an increase in the actual rates of neglect and abuse. Some of the cases of neglect may reflect the constraints of poverty rather than abusive parents. Severely neglected or abused children are sometimes placed in foster care, a system with many critics and few admirers. After declining in the late 1970s and early 1980s, foster-care rolls rose dramatically in the late 1980s and 1990s. There is a continuing debate about whether foster-care policies should emphasize preserving families or protecting children.

4. Assaults against spouses and partners arise, in part, from power struggles between men and women. Men have an advantage in these struggles because of their greater physical strength, on average, and because of a social system that often reinforces male dominance. But most men do not hit their wives, despite these advantages, so other explanations need to be advanced to explain why some men are violent and some are not. The social learning approach proposes that children from violent homes will learn that violent behavior is an acceptable and often successful means of controlling others; consequently, they will be more likely as adults to use violence against their spouses and children. The frustration-aggression approach emphasizes that individuals who are blocked from attaining a goal may displace their frustration and anger onto their spouses and children. The social exchange approach proposes that people calculate the rewards and costs of violent behavior and the rewards of the alternatives to it. It suggests that women who have more economic resources will be less often victimized, as comparative studies of other cultures indeed show.

5. Although adequate data do not exist, studies suggest substantial amounts of sexual aggression and violence by men toward women they are dating and toward acquaintances. According to one national survey, about 4 percent of adult U.S.

women have experienced forced sex by an acquaintance. Men who commit sexual aggression are more likely to show hostility to women, to be more easily aroused by rape scenarios, to be more sexually active, and to belong to sexually aggressive peer groups. Eleven percent of dating couples in one national study reported severe physical aggression. Persons who tried to control the behavior of the other partner, or who were less able to imagine the other person's point of view, were more likely to be physically abusive. Physical assault may be more common in cohabiting relationships than in dating relationships or in marriages.

6. Liberals and conservatives disagree over the desirability of early and extensive state intervention in cases of domestic violence. The fundamental issue is the tension between preserving the family and helping the victims. Liberals, who tend to emphasize helping the victims, generally favor more equality between men and women. Conservatives, who tend to emphasize preserving the family, generally favor the continued dominance of the male-headed, two-parent family. Liberal activists have been more successful in pushing their agenda in the 1990s.

KEY TERMS

domestic violence	incest	social learning perspective
marital rape	elder abuse	frustration-aggression perspective
child abuse	foster care	social exchange perspective

FAMILIES ON THE INTERNET

Several sites offer information and links on child abuse: The National Clearinghouse on Child Abuse and Neglect Information (www.calib.com/nccanch) provides statistics, reports, and answers to frequently asked questions. The National Committee to Prevent Child Abuse (www.childabuse.org) offers information on steps you can take to work with organizations to prevent child abuse. As for foster care, the Kids Campaign web site of the Benton Foundation provides a page with information and links to organizations (www.kidscampaigns.org/fostercare/ issues/foster.html). The Family Violence Prevention Fund (www.fvpf.org) offers facts, personal stories, organizational resources, and even a "celebrity watch" that keeps you abreast of the latest domestic violence problems of your favorite Hollywood stars and sports figures. The Yahoo search engine web site maintains a page with comprehensive links to numerous organizations and articles on domestic violence (www.yahoo.com/society_and_culture/crime/crimes/domestic_violence).

CHAPTER 12

Divorce

INTRODUCTION

What if you and your spouse-to-be had to sign a pledge, enforceable in court, to undergo marriage counseling before you wed and to undergo more counseling if you ever wanted a divorce? And what if you waived the right to divorce without your spouse's consent, except after a 24-month waiting period? Would that lower the chances that you would ever divorce? The Louisiana state legislature is betting that it would. In 1997, the legislature passed a bill creating a new, optional form of marriage they named "covenant marriage." When applying for a marriage license, couples who choose covenant marriage sign a document in which they pledge to follow the restrictive rules outlined above (Jeter, 1997). Other state legislatures are considering similar proposals.

Covenant marriage is a reaction to the high level of divorce in the United States and to a perception that recent changes in divorce laws have been, in part, responsible. In the 1970s and 1980s every state instituted a version of so-called "no-fault" divorce, which allows one partner to obtain a divorce after a short waiting period, even if the other partner doesn't want one. But, as will be noted below, it's not clear whether the liberalized divorced laws helped cause the high level of divorce or whether the laws were a reaction to it. What is clear is that the United States has the highest rate of divorce of any developed country. The probability of a marriage ending in divorce doubled between the early 1960s and late 1970s. At current rates, about half of all American marriages begun since the late 1970s will end in divorce (Cherlin, 1992b). (See *How do Sociologists Know What They Know?* Measuring the Divorce Rate.)

Divorce has not always been common in the United States and Western Europe. In fact, we know the name of the first person to obtain a divorce in England: John Manners, also known as Lord Roos. We know his name because the only way for someone to obtain a divorce in England prior to 1858 was to ask Parliament to pass an act granting him one. (Few women were granted divorces.) Lord Roos, whose wife had given birth to a child fathered by another man, introduced a bill in the House of Lords in 1669 that dissolved his marriage and left him free to marry again. From that time until 1858, a grand total of 325 divorces was granted by Parliament (Phillips, 1991). All were granted to wealthy persons, because a common person could not hope to get his or her case taken up by Parliament.

Disagreement with the Church of England on matters such as divorce was one reason why the Puritans left for North America (Phillips, 1991). Many of the American colonies legalized divorce. Still, it was frowned upon and granted under only a few conditions, such as adultery and desertion. The divorce rate crept upward, slowly at first, so that by the mid-nineteenth century, about 5 percent of all American marriages ended in divorce. From then on the rate of divorce moved upward at increasing speed. In 1892, there were about 22,000 divorces; in 1992, there were that many each week.[1]

The young adults who entered college in the mid- to late 1990s are members of the first cohort to grow up after this latest great surge of divorce. (About 40 percent of American children who grew up in the 1980s and early 1990s experienced the breakup of their parents' marriages [Furstenberg & Cherlin, 1991].) When two childless adults divorce, the breakup, although emotionally painful, is straightforward. Having concluded their legal business, the ex-spouses need not, and often do not, see each other again. When children are involved, however, a clean break is not in their interest. Even though divorce severs the family ties between the husband and wife, it does not sever the ties between each parent and the children. In the majority of cases, the mother keeps custody of the children, forming a single-parent family that may endure for years. The

---

[1]The 1892 figure is from Jacobson (1959). In 1992, 1.2 million divorces occurred; U.S. National Center for Health Statistics (1993c).

Henry VIII (1491–1547), King of England, broke with the Catholic Church so he could divorce Katherine of Aragon and marry Anne Boleyn.

father's relationship—typically reduced to regular visits, or less—is problematic. Indeed, many divorced fathers fade from their children's lives. Nevertheless, a modest but growing number of fathers are obtaining custody of their children, either by themselves or jointly with their wives.

Moreover, for many adults and children, a divorce does not signal the end of the changes in their family lives. A substantial proportion of parents will remarry, often after a period of cohabiting with their spouse-to-be. Remarriage after divorce further complicates adults' and children's lives. It introduces a stepparent into the child's family but doesn't subtract a biological parent—unlike remarriage after a parental death. It can bring a bewildering network of quasi relatives that extends over several households. In short, it necessitates another major adjustment for adults and children who may have struggled to adjust to postdivorce, single-parent life. In addition, almost half of all children whose custodial parents remarry will witness a *second* divorce before they reach the age of 18 (Bumpass, 1984).

These developments have greatly altered American family life. They have also been a source of concern. What do we know about the causes and consequences of the recent rise in divorce? About the effects of remarriage on stepparents and stepchildren? How are divorce and remarriage altering the nature of the family? These are the questions to be pursued in this chapter, on divorce, and in the next chapter, on remarriage and stepfamilies.

THREE ERAS OF DIVORCE

Far from requiring an act of Parliament or permission from a state legislature, divorce is now easy to obtain in most Western nations. It was not always so. The law and public opinion have changed dramatically over the past two centuries, greatly altering the way in which marriage is viewed. It is useful to think of three historical eras of divorce.

How Do Sociologists Know What They Know?

Measuring the Divorce Rate

A newspaper reporter calls a sociologist who does research on divorce and asks, "What's the most recent statistic for the divorce rate in the United States?" "In 1996," the sociologist replies, "about 20 out of every 1,000 married women divorced." "Twenty out of a thousand," she responds, "No way! That's tiny. The divorce rate has got to be much higher than that."

"Well," says the sociologist, "another way of saying it is that about half of all marriages would end in divorce at current rates." "Great," the reporter replies, "and what year is that for?" "It's not for a year," the sociologist tries to explain, "it's a projection based on this year's rates . . ." But he can tell that the reporter is losing patience fast. She wants a figure and a year, not a lecture in demogra-

phy, and she's writing a story on a deadline.

In fact, it's hard to answer the question, "what's the current divorce rate?" in a way that is both precise and meaningful. The difficulty is that the most meaningful statistic describes the proportion of all current marriages that will end in divorce, but it's impossible to know that proportion until everyone who is now married has grown old and died. So sociologists try to estimate this lifetime figure, but their estimates are just educated guesses. The precise statistic is based on the number of divorces in the most recent year for which data are available, but it doesn't tell us much about people's experience with divorce.

The 20-out-of-1,000 rate is the precise statistic; it represents the number of divorces in the United States divided by the number of mar-

ried women (U.S. National Center for Health Statistics, 1997b). It includes women who have been married for many years as well as those who married only recently. It gives the probability that a married woman would have become divorced in 1996: 20/1,000, which is equivalent to 2/100, or 2 percent. So in 1996, 2 percent of married women obtained divorces.

This does indeed sound like a very low figure, given all of the public concern about divorce. No wonder reporters are unhappy with it. It is a *cross-sectional rate*, meaning a rate at one point in time. It provides a snapshot of the experiences of married American women during a single year. In 1997, the 980 of every 1,000 married women who didn't divorce in 1996 were still at risk of divorcing, and another 20 or so did. In 1998,

THE ERA OF RESTRICTED DIVORCE

England's law before 1858 was one approach to divorce taken during what I will call the **era of restricted divorce**, which characterized the Western nations until the middle of the nineteenth century. In nearly all the countries, according to historian Roderick Phillips (1991), it was very difficult to obtain a divorce.[2] Still, the European countries differed from one another in how restrictive their divorce laws were according to what religion was most prominent in each country. Catholic countries, such as France, followed the Catholic Church's position that divorce was forbidden. Only if Church officials granted an **annulment**—a ruling that a marriage had never been properly formed in the first place—could a couple dissolve their marriage. Annulments could be granted only in situations such as a marriage between relatives of too close a degree or one in which the spouses had never had sexual intercourse. Protestant countries (except for England) were more liberal, typically granting divorces in cases of adultery or desertion. Several of the American colonies were more liberal still. Most of the colonies recognized the grounds of adultery and desertion; some also allowed divorces on the ground of extreme violence by a husband.

[2]The historical material in the next few paragraphs draws upon Phillips (1991). The eras and their titles are mine.

yet another 20 obtained divorces, and so on, year after year, into the future. So although the average woman married in 1996 had a 2 percent chance of becoming divorced *in 1996,* she had a far higher chance of becoming divorced *over the rest of her married life.*

Just how high her lifetime chances are, we cannot know with certainty. But let us conduct the following thought experiment: Suppose the risks of divorce in 1996 were to stay the same, for every age group, for the next few decades. That is to say, suppose that a woman in her thirties 10 years from now would have the same risk of divorce as did women in their thirties in 1996 and that a woman in her forties 20 years from now would have the same risk as did women in their forties in 1996, and so on. Now think of a hypothetical young woman

in her mid-twenties who married in 1996. We could fast forward her through time and calculate her risk of divorce at every age throughout her lifetime—because we are assuming that these risks will remain the same as those observed in 1996. Then we could sum these risks. The result would be a measure of her lifetime probability of divorce.

When sociologists do this calculation, they find that the lifetime probability of divorce for a young woman marrying today is about 50 percent. I write "about" because the exact answer depends on some of the technical assumptions in the calculations, and different sociologists make different assumptions. It's important to recognize that this figure is just a projection of current risks into the future. In fact, it is unlikely that divorce risks will stay the same for the next few decades. It

is true, as Figure 12.1 suggests, that the risks of divorce have not changed much since 1980. But as the figure shows, the 1950s, 1980s, and 1990s are the only decades since the Civil War in which divorce risks have remained more or less stable. They could start changing again tomorrow.

The utility of the lifetime estimate, then, is not that it will prove accurate 40 years from now—it may not—but rather that it indicates the underlying force of divorce that is implied by the behavior of married people today. The lifetime estimate, in other words, answers an important *what if* question: What if the risks of divorce at each age stayed the same as they are now; what lifetime level of divorce would these current risks imply? This is the question most newspaper readers want an answer to, even if the answer is necessarily uncertain.

Nevertheless, divorce remained rare everywhere. Its rarity, in large part, reflected the strong male dominance in marriage. Most divorces were granted on grounds of the wife's adultery, but very few wives were granted divorces on grounds of the husband's adultery. In fact, as mentioned earlier, few divorces were granted to women at all. Adultery was the main ground used by men for divorce not just because of sexual jealousy but also because of men's concern about who would farm their land and inherit their property. If, for example, a farmer's wife gave birth to a child fathered by another man, the child might have a claim on the farmer's land—especially if the farmer was unaware that he was not the father. Thus, divorce in this era was very difficult to obtain and, when obtained, was usually invoked because a man wished to ensure that his wife would not bear a child by another man. Marriage, for both men and women, was primarily an economic partnership—a means of pooling labor in order to grow enough food, or to make enough money, to subsist. Its romantic aspects were decidedly secondary, if only because making a living took so much effort. One reason why wives were valuable to husbands was that they could bear children, who were a major source of labor. It was important to husbands, as heads of households, to control that labor by controlling sexual access to their wives.

It is inconceivable, however, that marital breakup in this era was as rare as the low frequency of divorce implies. Although divorce was usually unavailable to the landless and the poor, separation without divorce must have been commonplace. Contemporary studies of families around the world demonstrate that the legalities of coupling and uncoupling—obtaining a legal marriage or a legal divorce—are less important in the poorer classes, where little money or property is involved (Goode, 1982). Cohabitation without marriage and separation without divorce are much more common. Moreover, the African slaves in the American colonies, as noted in previous chapters, were denied access to legal marriage or divorce. Thus, a considerable amount of separation and desertion must lie hidden beneath the history of formal divorce in the era of restricted divorce as well.

THE ERA OF DIVORCE TOLERANCE

The middle of the nineteenth century marked the beginning of the **era of divorce tolerance**, which lasted in the United States until 1970. During this period, it gradually became easier to obtain a divorce. As the doctrine of separate spheres, with its emphasis on domesticity for women, became more widespread, legislatures and courts grew more sympathetic to cases in which husbands' conduct toward their wives was reprehensible. Most jurisdictions in the United States added as grounds for divorce behaviors such as habitual drunkenness or failure to provide for one's wife. In the twentieth century, legislatures added less specific offenses such as "mental cruelty." These new grounds made divorce more accessible to mistreated wives.

Just as the doctrine of separate spheres was important to changes in divorce laws, so too was the shift in how marriage was viewed. Marriage in the nineteenth and twentieth centuries underwent a gradual change from an economic partnership first and foremost to an emotional partnership based on love and companionship—from an institution to a companionship, in Burgess's memorable phrase. As this transition was made, the failure of a marriage to involve love and companionship came to be seen as a valid reason for divorce. Figure 12.1 shows the annual divorce rate for the United States from 1860 (the earliest year for which statistics exist) until 1996. It shows, for example, that about 2 of every 1,000 married

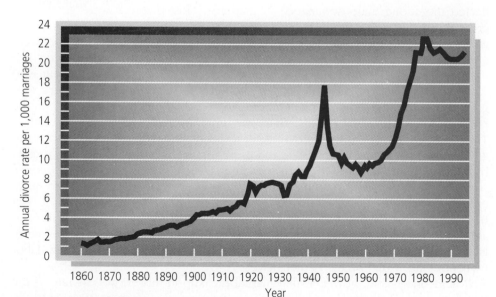

FIGURE 12.1 Annual divorce rate, United States, 1860–1996. For 1860–1920: divorces per 1,000 existing marriages. For 1920–1996: divorces per 1,000 married women age 15 and over. (*Sources:* for 1860–1988, Cherlin [1992b]; for 1989–1996, U.S. National Center for Health Statistics [1993b, 1995, 1997b].)

couples in 1880 obtained a divorce that year, whereas about 20 of 1,000 couples obtained a divorce in each of the most recent years.

The divorce rate rose substantially in the late 1800s and early 1900s. According to demographic estimates of lifetime divorce experience, 8 percent of all marriages begun in 1880 eventually ended in a divorce, compared with 12 percent of marriages begun in 1900 and 18 percent of marriages begun in 1920 (Preston & Mc-Donald, 1979). Divorce was transformed from a rare privilege granted mainly to wealthy men, in the previous era, to a common, if still frowned upon, occurrence increasingly available to women. In fact, Phillips reports that more than two-thirds of divorces in the United States between 1880 and World War I were granted to women. During the same period, divorce caused great concern among social reformers in the United States—not unlike the concern expressed today (O'Neill, 1973). Organizations such as the National Divorce Reform League encouraged legislatures to make divorce laws more restrictive (see Chapter 2).

Still, the annual rate of divorce kept rising, as can be seen in Figure 12.1. The steady rise through the first half of the twentieth century was broken only by two spikes in the years after World Wars I and II and a dip during the Great Depression years. The spikes were caused by the disruption and pent-up demand for divorce that had built up during each war. The dip occurred not because marriages were happier during the depths of the Depression but rather because many unhappy couples couldn't afford to get divorced. After World War II the annual rate of divorce fell somewhat, reflecting the home- and family-oriented ethos of the 1950s baby boom years. Then, in the early 1960s, a sharp rise began. By the late 1970s, about 20 of every 1,000 married couples were getting divorced each year—a rate that has not changed much since then (Cherlin, 1992b). (There have long been some non-Western societies with even higher divorce rates than ours. See *Families in Other Cultures:* Divorce among the Kanuri, on the following page.)

As recently as the 1960s, in order to obtain a divorce, a person had to prove that her or his spouse had done something wrong—and not just anything wrong, but rather one of a short list of specific wrongs: adultery, desertion, nonsupport, mental cruelty, and so forth. In truth, however, an increasing number of people were seeking divorces not because the other spouse had committed a terrible act but rather because the divorce seeker was unfulfilled by the marriage, unsatisfied emotionally, and trapped in a relationship that no longer seemed worth maintaining. Often, the other partner, feeling angry and alienated, consented to the divorce. Self-fulfillment, as has been discussed in earlier chapters, has become a dominant, perhaps *the* dominant, criterion for evaluating marriages. As a result, a divorce hearing was often a sham, in which one partner would "prove," with the tacit cooperation of his or her spouse, that some nonexistent or overblown wrong had occurred. In reaction to this situation, sentiment grew for eliminating altogether the idea that one spouse had to be at fault for a divorce to be granted.

THE ERA OF UNRESTRICTED DIVORCE

The first major laws to eliminate fault were implemented in the United States in 1970, ushering in the **era of unrestricted divorce**, in which a divorce has been available virtually without restriction, except for a waiting period, to any married person who wants one. In that year California became the first jurisdiction anywhere in the Western world to eliminate fault grounds for divorce and to replace them with **no-fault divorce**, the granting of divorce simply for marriage breakdown

Families in Other Cultures

Divorce among the Kanuri

What if a society had a divorce rate that made ours look low? What if every marriage ended in divorce and some individuals divorced many times? What would such a society look like, and how would it function? It turns out that there have been many societies in which divorce was more common than it is in the United States and other Western countries today. Some of the recent ones were Islamic societies, for, under traditional Islamic law, divorce was easy for a man to obtain. He needed only to say "I divorce thee" three times and he and his

wife were thereby divorced. Now, a wise man did not abuse this power, and social pressure may have existed to settle disputes short of divorce. It was much more difficult for a woman to obtain a divorce, but if she was really unhappy, she could often provoke her husband into giving her one.

The Kanuri of northeastern Nigeria were a high-divorce-rate Islamic society until the 1960s, at least (Cohen, 1971). When anthropologist Ronald Cohen studied six different sites, he found that 68 to 99 percent of all marriages had ended in divorce. Men would say "I divorce thee" only once

to establish a divorce because they believed it possible for a man to remarry a woman whom he had divorced, and that could not happen if the declaration had been repeated three times. Men were allowed to have up to four wives, although only the wealthier half had more than one and few had more than two.

Although frequent, male-initiated divorce among the Kanuri was part of a system of strong male dominance, divorce also served the interests of women at times. Girls' first marriages were arranged by relatives shortly after puberty. A young girl was frequently

due to "irreconcilable differences" (Glendon, 1987). Coming several years after rising divorce rates had begun to clog the courts, no-fault divorce was hailed as the way to bring the law into line with changes in societal attitudes toward divorce. It reflected the belief that a person should not be forced to continue in a marriage that she or he found to be personally unacceptable. Such an individualistic view of the marriage bond would have outraged the American colonists and their Western European contemporaries; yet in 1970 it carried the day. It was consistent with the shift noted in Chapter 9 from the companionship marriage to the independent marriage. England, where a century earlier only Parliament could authorize the end of a marriage, also added no-fault grounds to its divorce law in 1969. By the end of the 1980s, virtually every Western nation and every state in the American union had adopted some form of no-fault legislation. England, France, Germany, and other countries required that if only one partner wanted the divorce, and children were involved, he or she had to wait several years before it was granted. In contrast, the typical U.S. state required a waiting period of one year or less (Glendon, 1987). Divorce had changed from a way for wealthy men to protect their property from heirs fathered by other men to a way for the average person to improve her or his own sense of well-being. In the most liberal no-fault states and nations, it had become something close to an individual right.

FACTORS ASSOCIATED WITH DIVORCE

Given the current high level of divorce, two questions arise about its causes: First, on an aggregate level, why did the divorce rate virtually double in the 1960s and 1970s? Second, on an individual level, what factors place a person at greater risk of experiencing a divorce? Let us examine these questions in turn. Table 12.1 (see p. 374) provides a summary of the factors associated with divorce.

sent to be the wife of an older, prosperous man, whom she was expected to obey. A divorce allowed her to escape this marriage. Moreover, divorced women had much more independence than married women. The latter were often secluded in the household, whereas divorced women could move about freely. Cohen writes of the divorced woman, "she can entertain lovers, visit with relatives, and no man has a right to order her about."

In this patriarchal system, children remained with the husband after a divorce. Consequently, most children experienced being separated from their mothers. The Kanuri dealt with this problem in part by enlarging the role of the father's sister. Because Kanuri kinship is patrilineal (descent is reckoned along the male line only), the father's sister is part of his kinship group. It was believed, therefore, that she might treat the man's children better than a new wife brought into the household to replace the departed one. As a result, many children were raised for a time by their paternal aunts. In cases of frequent, rapid divorce, the paternal aunt might be the only stable female figure in the lives of the children of the household.

It was no accident, then, that the sister of the emir, the ruler of the society, was one of three female relatives who had a noble title (the others were his mother and his senior wife). She had a warm, maternal image. For example, she was the head of an organization that provided hospitality to strangers who came to town. Her membership in the royal family served to institutionalize the role of the paternal aunt as mother surrogate. In this way, the Kanuri managed the problem of mother loss that was inherent in their high-divorce-rate society.

THE SOCIETYWIDE RISE

You might think that the introduction of no-fault divorce would boost the divorce rate. There is some evidence that a surge of divorces occurred during the first few years after a state enacted no-fault legislation (Nakonezny, Shull, & Rodgers, 1995). The surge may have been a "backlog effect" (Rodgers, Nakonezny, & Shull, 1997) of couples in unhappy or troubled marriages who were quick to take advantage of the new, liberalized rules. It is unclear whether, after the initial surge, no-fault divorce had a lasting effect on the number of divorces; several studies suggest that it did not (Schoen, Greenblatt, & Mielke, 1975; Wright & Stetson, 1978; Peters, 1986).[3] Whereas no-fault laws began to spread through the 50 states in the 1970s, the divorce rate, as Figure 12.1 shows, had begun to increase substantially several years earlier. These facts suggest that no-fault divorce was more a consequence of the trend toward more divorce than a cause. Its introduction is an example of how changes in family law in the contemporary United States have often followed, rather than preceded, changes in behavior and values. In this instance, the social changes were the greater emphasis on personal fulfillment as a criterion for whether a marriage should continue and the greater economic independence of women from men.

Cultural Change   Previous chapters have examined the growing place of personal fulfillment in marriage, and an extensive discussion will not be presented here. Cultural critics claim that this emphasis erodes bonds of obligation and trust. As a framework for thinking about relationships, it is alleged, the emphasis on personal fulfillment results in a vocabulary that is rich in ways of thinking about individual well-being but impoverished in ways of thinking about commitment (Bellah,

---

[3]For similar findings from the Netherlands, see van Poppel and de Beer (1993).

TABLE 12.1   FACTORS ASSOCIATED WITH DIVORCE

SOCIETYWIDE FACTORS:

No-fault divorce legislation	State no-fault divorce laws produced an initial surge of divorce in the 1970s, but it is unclear whether no-fault laws have had a lasting effect.
Cultural change	A greater emphasis on personal fulfillment made divorce a more acceptable option for people who felt unfulfilled by their marriages.
Women's employment opportunitites	Women's growing employment opportunities led to a rise in the number of wives working outside the home. Employment gave wives greater economic independence, which made divorce a more attractive alternative to an unhappy marriage.
Men's employment opportunities	As young men's economic opportunities decreased since the early 1970s, their reduced earning potential may have caused stress in marriages.

INDIVIDUAL FACTORS:

Low income and unemployment	Divorce is more common among people with lower incomes. Lack of money can cause strain and tensions in a marriage.
Age at marriage	People who marry as teenagers have a higher rate of divorce. They may not choose partners as well as those who marry later.
Race and ethnicity	African Americans have higher rates of separation and divorce than most other groups. Low income and unemploment, as well as a lesser emphasis on marriage in African-American kinship, may contribute.
Cohabitation	People who cohabit prior to their marriage have a higher rate of divorce. They may have a weaker commitment to marriage than do people who marry without cohabiting first.
Parental divorce	People whose parents divorced are more likely to end their own marriages in divorce. They may model their behavior on their parents' marriages, or they may have a genetic tendency toward having problems in intimate relationshps.
Spouse's similarity	People who marry people who are similar to them in characteristics such as religion have a lower rate of divorce. Such couples may be more compatible in their values and interests.

Madsen, Sullivan, Swidler, & Tipton, 1985). For instance, numerous books, articles, lecture series, courses, and support groups exist on self-actualization or self-development or human potential, but much less intellectual activity is centered on maintaining personal responsibilities and obligations to others. Put another way, a focus on personal fulfillment represents a shift toward the concerns of the private family as against the concerns of the public family. Under these circumstances, divorce becomes a more acceptable option for people who feel personally unfulfilled; indeed, *not* divorcing in the face of personal dissatisfaction comes to need justifying. Still, there's little direct evidence to show just how large a factor cultural change has been in the rise in divorce since the 1960s.

Women's Employment   In most cases, women do not earn as much as men nor do they typically earn enough to fully support themselves and their children.

Nevertheless, the average wages earned by women rose substantially between 1950 and 1980; this rise, in turn, spurred the great increase in married women's movement into the paid labor force (Smith & Ward, 1985). Wives' employment theoretically could have contrasting effects on divorce.

- *Income effect.* Women's employment could lower the likelihood of divorce because the increase in the family's income could relieve financial pressures and thereby reduce tension in the marriage. Moreover, the job could increase the wife's self-esteem and make her more satisfied with her life in general.
- *Economic opportunity effect.* On the other hand, employment could raise the likelihood of divorce by providing an opportunity for the wife to support herself independently of her husband. This opportunity would make divorce a more attractive alternative for women who were unhappy with their marriages. The economic opportunity effect would even operate for wives who were not themselves working outside the home. They might be more likely to divorce if they lived in areas in which the employment prospects for women were good.

Research suggests that the economic opportunity effect is more powerful than the income effect. Historian Steven Ruggles (1997b) examined the individual records from the censuses of 1880, 1910, 1940, 1980, and 1990. In each census, he found that women were more likely to be divorced or separated if they lived in areas where it was common for married women to work outside the home. He interprets these findings to mean that women who have greater opportunities for paid employment are more likely to be divorced or separated. And he notes that between 1880 and 1990, employment opportunities for women have increased dramatically. Numerous studies show that married women who work outside the home are more likely to divorce than married women who do not, although it is unclear whether this association is due to the mere fact of working outside the home, to the number of hours worked, or to the level of wages earned (Greenstein, 1990). Commentators throughout the twentieth century have noted the relationship between women's paid employment and divorce.[4]

Nevertheless, women by no means initiate all divorces; a wife's income might also make a husband feel less guilty about asking for a divorce. A woman's independent income facilitates divorce; equally unhappy couples in which the wife is not employed might not be able to divorce as easily. It is also possible that the chain of cause and effect works the opposite way; at least one study suggests that a woman who thinks her marriage is in trouble may be more likely to take a job outside the home in case the marriage fails (Johnson & Skinner, 1986). Moreover, the cultural change toward self-fulfillment could be the driving force behind both the greater number of women working outside the home *and* the greater number of divorces.

Men's Employment   Since the early 1970s, the employment opportunities for men without college educations have been declining, as noted in Chapter 4. Oppenheimer (1994) argues that the economic opportunity effect has worked in reverse for men. That is, divorce has risen not just because women's economic opportunities have *increased* but rather because young men's economic opportunities have *decreased,* leading to greater stress in marriages and more divorces. Despite the increase in married women's employment, our society still expects that husbands

---

[4]For a review of these studies, see Cherlin (1992b). Some recent studies have not found strong associations of women's employment and divorce (Tzeng & Mare, 1995).

earn a steady income. When they do not, Oppenheimer argues, their marriages are subject to greater stress and a higher risk of divorce. Still, Oppenheimer's view cannot explain the long-term rise in divorce rates prior to the early 1970s because men's economic opportunities were improving during most of the late nineteenth and early twentieth centuries (Ruggles, 1997a).

INDIVIDUAL RISK FACTORS

There are many other social and economic factors that seem to increase or decrease an *individual's* likelihood of ever experiencing a divorce but have not contributed to the recent, *societywide* increase. Consider teenage marriage: As will be noted below, people who marry as teenagers have a greater likelihood of divorce than those who postpone marriage. Yet the societywide average age at marriage has been increasing since the 1960s. Consequently, we can rule out teenage marriage as a cause of the societywide rise in divorce. The list of individual risk factors includes the following.

Low Income and Unemployment　　Divorce is more likely if the husband is unemployed. In fact, it is more likely among families with low incomes, regardless of employment, than among families with higher incomes. Some middle-class observers, aware of the sharp rise in divorce among middle-class families, are surprised to learn this. During the 1960s and 1970s, the divorce rate rose sharply among families in all social classes, but at all times the rate has been greater among families with lower incomes (Cherlin, 1992b). The simple reason is that lack of money can cause problems and tensions in any marriage. Also, recall evidence from Chapter 10 on the strain that unemployment places on a marriage: It can lead to depression and then to hostile and irritable behavior by the husband, who is failing to fulfill his traditional responsibility as a provider. His behavior, in turn, can provoke anger and depression in his wife and children.

Age at Marriage　　In addition, as noted above, people who marry as teenagers have a higher likelihood of divorce than people who wait until their twenties. Teenagers probably cannot choose partners as well as older persons can. In part, they are not mature enough. Compared with people in their twenties, teenagers may not know as well what kinds of persons they will be as adults and what their needs in a partner will be. Even if they do have a good sense of their emerging selves, they will have a more difficult time picking an appropriate partner because it is hard to know what kind of spouse an 18-year-old will prove to be over the long run. Moreover, teenage marriages are sometimes precipitated by an accidental pregnancy, and it is known that a premarital birth raises the likelihood of divorce. It does so partly because it brings together a couple who might not otherwise have chosen to marry each other. It also may be more difficult, on a practical level, for a couple to make a marriage work if a young child is present from day one. Still, earlier marriage cannot be an explanation for the post-1960 rise in divorce because age at marriage increased after 1960.

There is some evidence that the divorce rate is also higher for people who marry for the first time at an unusually late age, such as over 35 (Sweet & Bumpass, 1987). Late first marriage could be a sign of some personality factors that make them less attractive as marriage partners, or it could be that people who marry late (especially women, who tend to marry men who are older than they) have a restricted pool of eligible partners and must compromise in their selection. In either case, most of the evidence is based on data from 1980 or earlier, when marriage ages were generally lower than in the 1990s. As more and more people postpone marriage until their thirties, the distinctiveness of late marriers will fade and the association between late marriage and divorce may diminish.

Moreover, people with less education have a greater probability of ending their marriages in divorce. Yet much of this effect occurs because people with less education tend to marry earlier—soon after high school, for example, rather than soon after college (Sweet & Bumpass, 1987). After taking into account age at marriage, the most distinctive group is high school dropouts, who in some studies show the highest probability of divorce. Demographers have speculated that dropouts may be less persevering in marriage as well as schooling, but the evidence is slim (Glick, 1984).

Race and Ethnicity   African Americans have substantially higher rates of marital separation than most other racial-ethnic groups; about one-half of the marriages of black women end within 10 years (Sweet & Bumpass, 1987). Although lower income, unemployment, and lower educational level are important sources of this racial difference, these factors alone cannot account for it. For example, among college graduates in 1980, 44 percent of black women who had married 10 to 14 years earlier had already separated or divorced, compared with 23 percent of comparable non-Hispanic white women (Sweet & Bumpass, 1987). Indeed, at every level of education, black women are more likely to have separated. It is likely that the lesser emphasis in African-American culture on marriage, relative to extended kinship ties, also plays a role, as discussed in Chapter 5. African Americans, who can rely more heavily on mothers, grandmothers, and other kin, have less need to stay married; they also have an alternative source of support if a marriage ends.

In addition, black women who separate from their husbands are considerably less likely to obtain a legal divorce, and again the differences are not due solely to economics or education. Within three years of separating, 55 percent of black women had obtained a divorce, according to the 1980 Census, compared with 77 percent of Mexican-American women and 91 percent of non-Hispanic white women. What these statistics imply is that black women have a higher likelihood of separating from husbands, but they turn these separations into divorces at a much slower pace. Perhaps their lower expectations of remarrying, which will be discussed in the next chapter, provide less motivation to obtain a legal divorce.

Figure 12.2 compares the prevalence of divorce among 13 racial-ethnic groups in the United States, according to the 1980 Census. Comparisons this fine-grained can be made only by using the computer files from the large, decennial census, and no one has yet constructed a similar chart from the 1990 data. For women who had married for the first time 10 to 14 years prior to 1980, the bars show the percentages that had separated or divorced by the 1980 Census. As can be seen, Native Americans have the second-highest percentage of couples who had separated or divorced. To what extent this reflects their high levels of poverty versus other factors is not clear. The figure also demonstrates the great diversity of the ethnic groups often lumped together as Hispanic. Puerto Ricans have the third-highest percentage of separated or divorced couples. Yet Cubans have a lower percentage than non-Hispanic whites, and Mexicans have a lower percentage than any other major racial-ethnic group except Asians. The Asian groups are still made up heavily of recent immigrants from countries with low divorce rates; whether they will retain their distinctively low rates of dissolution in subsequent generations remains to be seen.

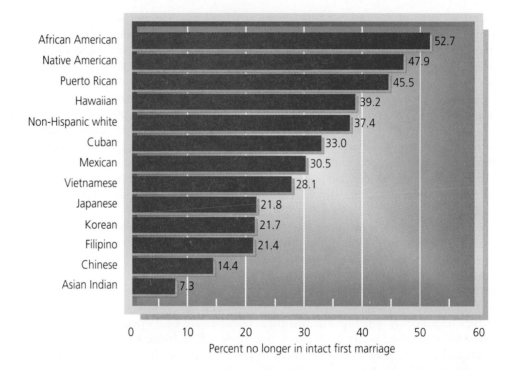

FIGURE 12.2
Percentage of women who had separated or divorced by 1980, among all women who had married for the first time 10 to 14 years earlier, by racial-ethnic group. (*Source:* Sweet & Bumpass [1987].)

Personal and Family Background   The personal and family histories people bring to a marriage also matter. Since married couples who live together prior to marriage have already had, in a sense, a trial run at marriage, we might expect that they would have a lower divorce rate than couples who did not live together before marrying. Just the opposite, however, is true: Couples who cohabit have higher divorce rates. Researchers have found that people who will not cohabit before marriage often have a stronger commitment to marriage and family life than those who will. Consider a study in which a national sample of high school seniors in 1972 was asked a series of questions about personal and family values and then was followed through 1986. Those who responded in 1972 that "finding the right person to marry and having a happy family life" was "very important" were substantially less likely to cohabit prior to marrying than those who responded that it was "not important." So were those who responded that "living close to parents and relatives" was important. Individuals who participated actively in church-related activities were also substantially less likely to cohabit prior to marrying (Clarkberg, Stolzenberg, & Waite, 1993).

Results such as these suggest that people who cohabit prior to marrying are a self-selected group who differ from noncohabitors in their attitudes toward personal relationships and family life. The cohabiting individuals carry these values with them when they marry, and, as a result, they are more likely to divorce than married people who did not cohabit. In addition, some evidence suggests that the experience of cohabiting itself, with its lower level of commitment than marriage, may change an individual's values and contribute to a higher likelihood of divorce (Thornton, Axinn, & Hill, 1992).

It appears that persons whose parents are divorced are more likely to become divorced themselves, although the reason for this association isn't clear.[5] Adult

[5]These and other findings on the determinants of divorce are discussed in White (1990).

children may model their behavior in marriage after their parents' failed marriages, or they may learn destructive habits such as physical abuse. Another possibility is genetic linkage, and a recent study of 1,500 same-sex pairs of twins indeed suggests that there may be genetic factors that affect a person's likelihood of maintaining a lifelong marriage. The researchers compared the marriage histories of identical twins, who share the same genetic material, and fraternal twins, who share, on average, half their genetic material. They found that if a person was an identical twin, and her or his twin was divorced, the odds of that person's also being divorced were nearly six times higher than if his or her twin had not divorced. If a person was a fraternal twin, the corresponding odds were only two times higher. Thus, the divorce-related behavior of identical twins, who are genetically closer, was more similar than the divorce-related behavior of fraternal twins. The authors maintain that these results imply a genetic predisposition that affects relationship quality, although they caution that the genetic mechanism is likely to be far more complicated than a simple "divorce gene." In addition, even if there were a genetic mechanism, it could not account for the nineteenth- and twentieth-century increases in the nation's divorce rate because, as noted in earlier chapters, evolutionary genetic changes occur far more slowly (McGue & Lykken, 1992).[6]

Finally, people who marry people who are similar to them are, in general, less likely to divorce, probably because the couples are more compatible in their values and interests. For example, Catholics married to Catholics and Protestants married to Protestants are both less likely to divorce than Catholics married to Protestants (Lehrer & Chiswick, 1993). People who are far apart in age also have higher divorce probabilities than people who are closer in age, particularly if it is the wife who is much older (Carter & Glick, 1976). (If the wife is older, the marriage goes against the social norm of older men marrying younger women.) We don't know exactly why; it may be that a large age difference, especially if the wife is much older, indicates that one or both of the partners had personal characteristics that made them less desirable on the marriage market.

THE PROCESS OF DIVORCE

The unmaking of a marriage occurs in many stages over a period of time that often begins well before the couple separates and that extends well after they are granted a divorce. A number of observers of the process of divorce have attempted to describe its different aspects.[7] Here are the four major aspects.

THE EMOTIONAL DIVORCE

Separating from a spouse is a difficult process for nearly all the people who go through it, notwithstanding the fact that at least one spouse initiated the process and is presumably better off because of it. In instances of clear fault, such as wife battering, drunkenness, or desertion, the cause is obvious and both spouses are usually

[6]As in all twin studies of this genre, the researchers assumed that parents treat fraternal twins as similarly as they treat identical twins, so that the home environment of fraternal twins is as similar as the home environment of identical twins. If this is not so, the greater similarity of identical twins' divorce behaviors could reflect not only their greater genetic similarity but also their more-similar home environment.

[7]See, for example, Bohannan (1971b). Bohannan also writes of the "community divorce" involving changes in friends and community and the "psychic divorce" involving regaining autonomy; these aspects are included elsewhere in the discussion.

aware of it. In the many more instances in which one or both spouses are unhappy and unfulfilled, the causes are murkier, and neither spouse, at first, may be aware of the true situation. Typically, though, one person becomes dissatisfied first and begins the process of ending the marriage. Diane Vaughan, who interviewed people about the process, calls this person the **initiator** (Vaughan, 1990). The initiator has the advantages of being the first person to know that there is a chance of separation, of preparing emotionally for it, and of using the threat of leaving in order to demand change. The threat is similar to what Willard Waller, writing in the 1930s about courtship, defined as the "principal of least interest": the party that is less interested in maintaining the relationship has the advantage in bargaining (Waller, 1938).

The initiator begins to express discontent, but without clearly and directly stating that he or she is unhappy with the marriage. Instead, the initiator may try to change the other partner's behavior or the relationship—as by having a baby or urging the partner to change jobs or take up a new interest. One person told Vaughan:

> Somehow I had misjudged her—who she was and what she was capable of. Maybe I thought she was someone she was not. . . . She needed something of her own, some friends of her own. . . . I encouraged her to get out in the world and get involved (Vaughan, 1990).

If these efforts are unsuccessful, the initiator begins to invest more energy and emotion outside the relationship. At some point, the initiator declares his or her dissatisfaction with the relationship to the partner. Only then, in many cases, does the partner realize the seriousness of the situation. The confrontation can bring about efforts by the spouses to reconcile their differences or to alter the relationship to their joint satisfaction.

> I was very upset, hurt, crying, but at the back of my mind I thought well, maybe this too will pass if I continue to play—play, that's an interesting choice of words—play this open, warm, loving type of person, that maybe I'll get her back, still, and not be too angry or hostile at her (Vaughan, 1990).

Sometimes these efforts, perhaps aided by marital counseling, succeed and the separation is averted. If they fail, it is likely that the couple will separate, sometimes with the thought that it is temporary.

Often, however, the initiator has decided by that time that he or she doesn't want the marriage to continue.

> Even at that point, at initial separation, I wasn't being honest. I knew fairly certainly that when we separated, it was for good. I let her believe that it was a means for us first finding out what's happening, and then eventually possibly getting back together (Vaughan, 1990).

The "temporary" separation announces the breakup to the couple's world. There may be an attempt to reconcile, but by this time the initiator's heart is usually not in it. Even if the initiator is making a good-faith effort, it may not be possible for the partner to regain a sense of trust in the initiator (Weiss, 1975). A final separation then occurs.

In his studies of newly separated persons, Robert Weiss noticed the persistence of their feelings of attachment to their partners, even among initiators. **Attachment,** a concept Weiss borrows from the literature on infants, is a bonding to another person that produces feelings of security, comfort, and ease when the other person is present or nearby. Weiss found that feelings of attachment persisted for months—sometimes years after a person separated, long after feelings of anger had replaced feelings of love. The persistence of attachment caused "separation distress": the person focused his or her attention on the estranged spouse and experienced discomfort that the spouse was no longer accessible (Weiss, 1975).

Weiss estimated that it took his subjects two to four years to recover fully from the separation. The first phase of recovery—after the old pattern of life had been destroyed but before the separated person had successfully integrated a new pattern—was a time of stress, often accompanied by disorganization and depression. Another writer called this first phase "crazy time" (Trafford, 1982). According to Weiss, it lasts about a year, after which time there is a longer period in which the person has put together a new pattern of life but is still vulnerable to setbacks. One man who had been the initiator of his separation told Weiss:

> *I had quite a bit of guilt over the whole thing happening, and as a result of that I was really bogged down with it. . . . I can remember the first four months of separation were just horrendous. . . . It was four months of bouncing off the walls. I couldn't eat. I couldn't sleep. I could not work. . . . And a friend of mine said, "Hey, get hold of yourself. Get some sleep." I saw a doctor who prescribed some antidepressants or something. I started to eat again, started sleeping. And then once I started eating and sleeping I started to rebuild. The first thing was my job. And then all the other things just fell into place* (Weiss, 1975).

Eventually, most people adjust emotionally to the separation. As life moves on, people become less preoccupied with their former spouses. In fact, one study of divorced persons found that their adjustment was significantly higher when they were less preoccupied with their ex-spouses. Those who were more likely to disagree with statements such as "I can't stop thinking about my ex-spouse," "I am curious about what my ex is doing," and things "trigger thoughts about my ex-spouse" answered positively to questions about emotional well-being (Masheter, 1997).

THE LEGAL DIVORCE

In addition to ending their emotional relationship, the couple must end their legal relationship. If there are no children, the separation agreement mainly specifies any continuing payments that one agrees to make to the other and divides up their property and assets. In the past, the important property, if any, has consisted of savings, homes, automobiles, and so forth. Increasingly, though, the most valuable property a person owns is intangible. This "new property," as it is sometimes called, consists of personal intangible assets, created during the marriage, from which one spouse will continue to benefit. It may include a professional license or educational credential, such as a medical school degree that allows a person to practice as a physician. Or it may include retirement benefits that one spouse has accrued for old age. As long as the couple remain married, they will share the rewards of these assets, but if they separate, only one spouse will benefit from them.

Consider a 1979 case in Kentucky, *Inman* v. *Inman*. The couple met when they were both undergraduates planning to attend medical school. After their graduations, Ms. Inman took a job as a biologist to pay for Mr. Inman's medical school expenses, with the understanding that after he received his medical degree she too would attend medical school. Instead, the couple separated a year after Mr. Inman graduated. Ms. Inman asked the court to award her compensation for her husband's medical degree, arguing that she had financed it in the expectation of joint benefits but that now the benefits would accrue only to him. The court ordered Mr. Inman to reimburse her for the costs of medical school plus inflation and

Nearly all married couples need legal assistance to complete their divorces. The procedure is much more complex if children are present than if the couple has no children living at home.

interest (Weitzman, 1985). Still, there is no consensus in legal rulings about what exactly constitutes marital property, how to value it, and how to distribute it. In the event of a divorce, asks legal scholar Robert Levy, is the wife of an inventor entitled to a share of his future royalties on patented inventions? If so, how much? To date, the law has provided little consistent guidance, Levy concludes, on matters of marital property such as this (Levy, 1989).

Although wives may request maintenance payments—known as **alimony**—from their ex-husbands, few couples now agree to it and few judges order it. As women have moved into the paid labor force, the legal system has come to assume that they can be self-supporting following a divorce, perhaps after some temporary financial assistance from the ex-husband. This assumption, however, may not hold for wives who have been out of the labor force for many years—a point I will return to shortly.

When children are present, the legal situation is more complex. There is first the matter of custody: Who will have responsibility for the children, and where will they live? **Legal custody** refers to having the right to make important decisions about the children and to having legal responsibility for them. **Physical custody** refers to where they actually live. In the United States in the past, the two kinds of custody were usually merged; the father typically had custody in both senses prior to the mid-nineteenth century, the mother, after that. Family law throughout much of the twentieth century was based on a presumption that maternal custody was better for young children; indeed, custody was awarded to the mother in about 85 percent of the cases (Weitzman, 1985). In most states, however, that presumption has been replaced with the rule that the court should decide according to the "best interests of the child"—a standard that formally favors neither parent. Nevertheless, it is still the case today that in the majority of divorces, mothers have both legal and physical custody. (It is also the case that in a majority of divorces, fathers do not want physical custody.)

Increasingly, though, state laws are moving toward a presumption in favor of **joint legal custody**, which means that both parents retain an equal right to make important decisions concerning the children (as opposed to sole legal custody, in which one spouse can make the decisions without consulting the other). A decree of joint legal custody is essentially a decree that the parents' responsibilities toward their children have not changed; despite the divorce, they both remain responsible. In California, which has led the move toward this kind of custody, two-thirds of a sample of more than 1,000 divorce cases in the mid-1980s resulted in joint legal custody. In practice, however, joint legal custody didn't mean much in this sample; legal scholar Robert Mnookin and psychologist Eleanor Maccoby found that fathers who had joint legal custody didn't see their children more often than fathers whose ex-wives had sole legal custody, nor were the fathers more involved in decisions about their children. The researchers concluded that joint legal custody is valuable mainly as a symbol of the father's continuing responsibility for his children (Maccoby & Mnookin, 1992).

In a growing but still small number of cases, divorcing couples are agreeing to **joint physical custody**, under which the children spend substantial time in each household—perhaps alternating on a weekly basis. Joint physical custody, however, requires a great deal of cooperation between the ex-spouses, who must transport children back and forth, share clothing, coordinate schedules, and so forth. Many—perhaps most—divorcing couples cannot manage this much cooperation. To jump ahead briefly to the effects on children, the California study shows that joint physical custody can work very well for the children when the parents voluntarily choose it and can cooperate. But if the parents are still angry and warring with each other, the children tend to feel caught in the middle. For example, a parent may attempt to extract information about the private life of the ex-spouse from the children, which often causes stress and anxiety. The researchers urge judges not to impose joint physical custody on parents who don't want to undertake it (Buchanan, Maccoby, & Dornbusch, 1991).

THE COPARENTAL DIVORCE

Regardless of state laws, the reality is still that most children remain in the care of their mothers most of the time. This imbalance persists because it carries forward the typical childcare situation in two-parent families—namely, the wife does most of the care. It is difficult to get fathers involved in care after the divorce because most of them were not intensively involved before. In fact, the level of contact between fathers and their children after divorce is stunningly low. Figure 12.3 shows the amount of contact between children and their fathers, for children who were living with their mothers and whose fathers were living elsewhere. The pie charts are based on responses of the mothers of these children in the 1987–88 National Survey of Families and Households (Seltzer, 1991). There are separate pie charts for children whose parents were married when they were born—the group of main concern in this chapter—and children whose parents were not married when they were born. About one-third of the children of previously married parents had seen their father either once in the past year or not at all. Among the children of never-married parents, the comparable figure climbed to about half. Only about one-fourth of the children of previously married parents had seen their fathers once a week or more often during the past year.

Why do so many fathers fade from their children's lives after a divorce? For some, visits to the children may be a painful reminder of the life they left behind,

FIGURE 12.3 Amount of contact between children and fathers, for children who were living with their mothers and whose fathers were living elsewhere, according to the National Survey of Families and Households, 1987–1988. (*Source:* Seltzer [1991].)

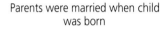

Parents were married when child was born

Parents were not married when child was born

triggering feelings of guilt or sadness. Others may be investing their emotional energy in new families formed by remarriage. In addition, Frank Furstenberg and I have speculated that many fathers, when they were married, may have related to their children only indirectly, through their wives. They tend to see parenting and marriage as a package deal; when the wife is removed, they have difficulty connecting directly to their children (Furstenberg & Cherlin, 1991).

Even when fathers do remain involved, conflict between the parents tends to diminish over time. Still, the parents don't necessarily cooperate in rearing the children. Advocates of joint legal custody had hoped it would encourage more ex-spouses to practice **coparenting**, in which the divorced parents coordinate their activities and cooperate with each other in raising the children. Coparenting does occur, but more commonly the parents gravitate toward a more detached style: They talk as little as possible, avoid meeting each other, send messages through their children, rendezvous at restaurant parking lots to exchange them, and go about their parenting business separately. Rather than coparenting, this dominant style might be called **parallel parenting**, in recognition of the separate tracks the two parents follow in their dealings with the children (Furstenberg & Cherlin, 1991). One and a half years after they had filed for divorce, the California couples' most common style of parenting was conflicted: lots of arguments, threats, and distress (although there were many cooperative parents, too). When the parents were reinterviewed two years later, the most common style was "disengaged": little conflict and little cooperation; in short, parallel parenting (Maccoby & Mnookin, 1992).

THE ECONOMIC DIVORCE

Many fathers seem to fade from their children's lives in part because they will not or cannot contribute to their children's support. Figure 12.4 displays the sad story of the child support pyramid. The figures are from a 1991 Bureau of the Census study of the 6.6 million separated, divorced, or remarried mothers who had children under the age of 21 who were living with them and whose fathers were absent from the household. The base of the pyramid represents all these women.

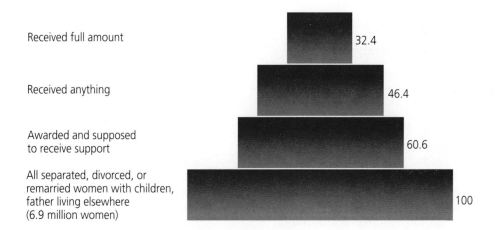

Received full amount   32.4

Received anything   46.4

Awarded and supposed
to receive support   60.6

All separated, divorced, or
remarried women with children,
father living elsewhere   100
(6.9 million women)

FIGURE 12.4 The child support pyramid: award and receipt of child support payments to women with children under the age of 21 living in their households who have fathers living elsewhere, 1991. (*Source:* U.S. Bureau of the Census [1995].)

Moving up the pyramid, we can see that less than two-thirds had been awarded child support payments and were supposed to receive them in 1991. (Most of the rest had not been awarded child support payments for various reasons, such as inability to find the father.) Only about half had actually received any child support money in 1991, and only about one-third had received the full amount that was due. Among those who had received anything at all in 1991, the average amount was $3,212, or about $268 per month (U.S. Bureau of the Census, 1995). (The situation was even grimmer for the 3.3 million mothers who had never married the fathers of their children; just one-fifth had received any child support payments in 1991, and the average amount they received was $1,721, or about $144 per month.)

Many mothers, therefore, are hit with a financial double whammy when they divorce. First, they lose their husbands' income, which typically exceeds theirs by a substantial margin. Second, only about half receive any money in child support payments. As a result, the average mother's standard of living is reduced by about 30 percent in the first year after she separates from her husband. In contrast, the average father's standard of living *rises* about 15 percent—because usually he is supporting only himself (Hoffman & Duncan, 1988).[8] One woman told Terry Arendell:

> *My husband really liked good food and always bought lots and the best. So when he left, it was really hard to cut the kids back. . . . Now there's often no food in the house, and everybody gets really grouchy when there's no food around. . . . We've lost $150 a month now because my husband reduced the support. It gets cut from activities—we've stopped doing everything that costs, and there's nowhere else to cut. My phone is shut off. I pay all the bills first and then see what there is for food. . . . I grew up playing the violin, and I'd wanted my kids to have music lessons—piano would be wonderful for them. . . . But lessons are out of the question* (Arendell, 1986).

Sometimes women and children fall into poverty because of the breakup. For instance, a government survey followed thousands of households for 28 months beginning in 1984, including many in which fathers left the household during the study. Among the children whose fathers left the household, 19 percent had been living below the poverty line even before the breakup had occurred. But the loss of a father nearly doubled the proportion of children who were living in poverty

[8]Hoffman and Duncan demonstrate convincingly that the widely cited figures in Weitzman (1985)—namely, that women's standard of living falls 73 percent and men's rises by 42 percent—are almost certainly too high and, in fact, are inconsistent with other figures in Weitzman's book.

Enforcing Child Support Obligations

Children in single-parent families would benefit if every absent parent knew he or she would have to pay child support. This has been the goal of several new laws that were enacted in the 1980s and 1990s. Since 1994, for example, all parents who have been ordered by the courts to pay child support have had their payments deducted automatically from their paychecks. Moreover, states are now required to adopt guidelines for the amount of child support a parent should pay, according to income and number of children; judges must follow these guidelines or state in writing why they didn't (Cherlin, 1993).

In fact, toughening child support enforcement has been one of the most popular family policies among both conservatives and liberals. Conservatives favor tougher enforcement because making fathers pay is consis-tent with their belief that parents should take responsibility for the well-being of their children. (Although the law applies equally to absent mothers who owe child support payments, in practice the vast majority of payments are collected from fathers and distrib-uted to mothers.) The new measures send a message to fathers that they can leave their marriages, but they can't leave their children. Conserva-tives hope that the measures will deter men from fathering children they can't, or don't intend to, sup-port. Liberals favor tougher measures because more economic support will be provided to children in low-income single-parent families.

The steps taken so far, however, will help middle-class single parents and their children more than poor sin-gle parents and their children. Middle-class single mothers, most of whom are divorced, can obviously identify the fathers of their children, and these fathers are likely to have jobs. Many poor single mothers, in con-trast, were never married to the fa-thers of their children. In some cases, they do not know who the father is; in other cases, the father may deny paternity; and in still other cases, the mother may not wish to identify the father because she does not want him to be a continuing part of her and her child's life.

The 1996 welfare reform act (see Chapter 6) contains a number of addi-tional proposals to strengthen the sys-tem. For instance, it provides more support for programs to establish pa-ternity in hospitals at the birth of the children, and it penalizes welfare recip-ients who fail to cooperate. It requires employers to send the names of newly hired employees to state and federal agencies that will match the names against lists of parents who have not paid child support obligations. It allows states to deny occupational and

---

to 36 percent by the end of the study. Moreover, the proportion whose mothers relied on Aid to Families with Dependent Children doubled from 9 to 18 percent just after the separation, and the proportion whose mothers were receiving food stamps jumped from 10 to 27 percent just after the separation (U.S. Bureau of the Census, 1991a). Because of statistics such as these, there have been several at-tempts to increase the amount of child support fathers pay. (See *Families and Public Policy:* Enforcing Child Support Obligations, above.)

The inequity is worst for older women who have been out of the labor force for many years and whose husbands initiate their divorces. They married their hus-bands under the terms of the breadwinner-homemaker bargain: They were to raise the children and do the housework while their husbands worked for pay outside the home. Over the years, whatever skills they had developed that might land them a paying job deteriorated. Then, after perhaps 15 or 20 years of marriage, their husbands left. They turned to a legal system that, in an effort to treat men and women equally, expects divorced mothers to become self-supporting soon after their marriages end. It is a system that increasingly allows either spouse to end the marriage unilaterally, that rarely grants alimony, that often orders hus-bands to pay only modest levels of child support, and that, until recently, did a poor job of enforcing its support orders. It is a system that seems to assume it is driver's license renewals to parents who fail to pay (U.S. Administration for Children and Families, 1996).

Nevertheless, the weakness of this approach is that if the absent parent has little income, the children will still get little or no support. To remedy this problem, Irwin Garfinkel and others have proposed a **child support assurance system** (Garfinkel, 1992). Under this system, the state would guarantee that a mother would receive the child support awarded to her, up to a maximum of perhaps $2,500 per year for one child and $500 to $1,000 for each additional child. The state would then endeavor to collect court-ordered support payments from the father, but, crucially, it would pay the mother the guaranteed benefit even if it didn't—unless she was already receiving welfare benefits, which are now called Temporary Assistance to Needy Families (TANF).

If the state collected money from the father and the mother was not receiving TANF, she would receive the entire amount collected. If the state collected money from the father but the mother was receiving TANF, the state would hold back an amount equivalent to the TANF payments. Thus, the child support assurance system is designed to provide financial support to children in single-parent families, to lower TANF costs (assuming more money can be collected from the fathers of children on TANF), and to provide a strong incentive for women to leave the TANF rolls and take a job (because they would then receive the support payments the government collected). Its advocates claim that its overall cost to the government would be modest because the TANF savings would largely offset the cost of the assured benefits.

Still, many conservatives are wary of an assured minimum benefit. They

fear that the benefit, by giving single mothers a guaranteed source of income, albeit modest, might encourage more divorce and more childbearing outside marriage. They would rather rely solely on ever-tougher enforcement. Yet it is unclear how much support can ever be collected from fathers who are chronically unemployed or earn little. An approach that relied only on enforcement, therefore, would be likely to leave some single parents and their children without any support payments. Some conservatives are willing to pay this price to avoid the possibility of encouraging the formation of more single-parent families and to limit the overall cost of government aid to the poor. This political split reflects the broader disagreement, discussed in Chapter 6, between conservatives and liberals over the issues of women's economic independence from men and assisting the poor versus reinforcing their obligation to work.

dealing with upper-middle-class dual-career families in which wives have well-paying professional or managerial jobs. But even in upper-middle-class families, most women's earnings are substantially lower than their husbands' incomes. No wonder that, in one national study, 31 percent of women whose families had above-average incomes before their separations saw their standard of living drop by more than half in the first year (Duncan & Hoffman, 1985).

Although most single-parent families are headed by mothers, the number of single-father families has been growing rapidly. Between 1980 and 1996, the number of single fathers living with their own children under 18 more than doubled from 616,000 to 1,628,000. These families now constitute 18 percent of all single-parent families with children (U.S. Bureau of the Census, 1997i). In addition, there are perhaps 800,000 custodial fathers who have remarried and therefore are not counted in the single-father total (Meyer & Garasky, 1993).[9] Adding in the remarried fathers would bring the total number of custodial fathers, single and married, to about 2.5 million. Single fathers tend to have higher incomes than single mothers because men's wages are typically higher than women's. However, single

[9]The authors, using another government survey, estimate that remarried, custodial fathers constitute about 40 percent of all custodial fathers. The remaining figures in this paragraph are all taken from Meyer and Garasky.

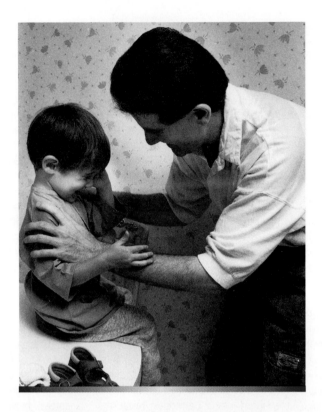

The number of single-father families has been growing, although most children still reside with their mothers after a parental divorce.

fathers tend to have lower incomes and less education than married fathers. A 1989 Census Bureau survey of single fathers found that 18 percent had incomes below the government poverty line and another 21 percent had incomes less than twice the poverty line. Yet few single fathers are granted child support awards, since most have higher incomes than their ex-wives. Nevertheless, some single fathers with low incomes may need assistance from their former wives.

About 4 percent of all children in 1995 lived in single-father families (U.S. Bureau of the Census 1996c). Our mental image of the single-father family is the divorced dad living alone with his children. However, only one-fourth of single-father families consist of divorced men living alone with their children. Of the rest, most are sharing their households with mothers, sisters, or new girlfriends, who may be doing much of the childcare (Eggebeen, Snyder, & Manning, 1996). Yet the census counts them as "single-father families" as long as the mother of the child is not in the household.

THE EFFECTS OF DIVORCE ON CHILDREN

At least one partner chooses to divorce in every case of marital disruption. Presumably, then, at least one partner's well-being is enhanced by the divorce. But children do not choose that their parents divorce. It isn't necessarily true that their well-being is enhanced by their parents' divorce. In fact, there are good reasons to think that their well-being should be, in many cases, diminished. They lose the benefit of having both of their parents living in the same household with them. They must go through an emotionally difficult process of adjusting to the breakup.

Frequently, they must cope with continuing, bitter conflict between their parents. They often feel the consequences of a sharp fall in family income. Here is a description of their experiences.

THE CRISIS PERIOD

Psychologists P. Lindsay Chase-Lansdale and E. Mavis Hetherington have written that the first year or two after the parents separate is a **crisis period**, during which both the custodial parent and the children—nearly all of whom are intensely upset when they learn of the separation—often experience difficulties (Chase-Lansdale & Hetherington, 1990). After the breakup, the custodial parent (typically the mother) is often angry, upset, and depressed. One consequence, according to observers, is the "diminished parenting" that often occurs during the crisis period (Wallerstein & Kelly, 1980). Distracted, distressed parents may have difficulties providing the daily mixture of emotional support and moderate, consistent discipline that psychologists called "authoritative parenting" (see Chapter 14). Instead, parents seem to be emotionally distant and preoccupied, prone to ignore misbehavior or to lash out with harsh discipline. For example, a child misbehaves, prompting the harried, depressed parent to respond angrily. Her response can set off more negative behavior: A toy is thrown on the floor or a bowl of cereal is knocked off the table. The parent responds even more angrily, further provoking the child.

In this way, the parent and child are drawn into what Hetherington and others call "coercive cycles," in which the parent's and child's responses aggravate the situation. Hetherington found that acting-out behavior and coercive cycles are more common among boys than girls (girls show fewer outward problems, although they may be holding in feelings that will erupt years later). After a year or two, however, many custodial parents have reorganized their lives and begun to manage their anger and depression enough to provide a more supportive and structured routine for their children (Hetherington, M. Cox, & R. Cox, 1978).

Moreover, as discussed earlier, the frequent decline in the family's standard of living, brought about by the withdrawal of the father's income and partial or nonexistent support payments, creates an additional source of distress for the recently separated parent and her children. In a recent study of families with young children, interviewed before a separation and about one year afterward, boys were showing more behavior problems in families whose incomes had dropped below the poverty line (Morrison & Cherlin, 1995). A number of studies do show that children's distress is greater during the crisis period than afterward, as parents begin to adjust to the divorce.

Several other factors are at work in making life difficult for children after the breakup, increasing the chances that they will be upset and misbehave. The situation of each child usually involves some combination of the following factors.[10]

Loss of a Parent   Most of the early articles on the impact of divorce on children addressed the consequences of having the father leave home. Following a Freudian model, the writers theorized that a boy would have difficulty adopting the adult male role if he could not see how his father behaved and if he was not subject to his father's authority. However, a major review of the research literature in 1973 found little evidence to support this viewpoint (Herzog & Sudia, 1973).

[10]This list draws upon (but is not identical to) the categories in Amato (1993).

Being exposed to continual conflict between their parents can harm children, whether the parents are married or divorced.

Nevertheless, many observers believe that the loss of a parent, of either gender, will make the tasks of the remaining parent more difficult for other reasons. For instance, if a teenager protests when a parent tells him he can't go to a party Friday night, it helps if a second parent is around to back up the first one. In other words, the tasks of monitoring and supervising the behavior of children may be more difficult if only one parent is present. Several studies do show that if a second adult, such as a grandmother, is present in the household, children seem to behave better and do better in school.[11]

Parental Conflict   Continuing conflict between the parents harms their children's well-being, especially if the parents use the children as pawns in their battles. When parents fight, children tend to become fearful and distressed—whether the parents are married or divorced. In fact, studies show that children in two-parent families wracked by intense conflict are more depressed and show more behavior problems than children in divorced families (Peterson & Zill, 1986). After the breakup, children have fewer problems if their parents can cooperate or at least engage in parallel parenting. A recent study found evidence that if parents are still fighting after a divorce or separation, their sons show *more* behavior problems if they see the nonresident parent regularly than if they see him or her less often. Conversely, if there is little conflict between the parents, the sons show *fewer* behavior problems if they see the noncustodial parent regularly. (No differences were found for daughters (Amato & Rezac, 1994).)

It's important to recognize that the conflict that harms children can begin before the breakup. Divorce is not just an event that happens the day a parent moves out; rather, it is a process that typically begins much earlier. In a research project that I carried out with several collaborators, we examined the records of thousands

[11]See for example, Dornbusch et al. (1985).

of British and American children who had been followed from age 7 to age 11 (Cherlin et al., 1991). We focused on children whose parents had been married at the beginning of the study and watched as they split over time into two groups: those whose parents divorced and those whose parents stayed together. Not surprisingly, the children whose parents divorced were showing more behavior problems and were doing worse in school. But then we looked back to the start of the study, before anyone's parents had been divorced. We discovered that children whose parents would later divorce were *already* showing more behavior problems and doing worse in school than children whose parents would remain together. This finding suggests that some of the trauma of divorce begins before the separation, as unhappy parents begin to move apart. In addition, it suggests that the problems that children exhibit after a divorce might have occurred to some extent even if their conflicted parents had remained together.

Multiple Transitions   Apart from exposure to the parents' distress and conflict, the breakup forces children to adjust to jarring transitions. The first, of course, is the departure of a parent from the home. This is not necessarily the last transition, however. The financial settlement between the parents frequently requires that the family's house be sold. As a result, children must often move to a new neighborhood, begin classes at a new school, and make new friends. One study found that two-fifths of divorced mothers move during the first year after the divorce—a majority of them because they are forced to do so by a falling income (McLanahan, 1983). Many divorced mothers move in with their parents temporarily while they make the transition to single parenting (Goldscheider & Goldscheider, 1994).

Other adults will probably move in and out of the child's household. A majority of single parents remarry, and, as will be discussed in Chapter 13, two-thirds of remarriages are preceded by a period of cohabitation. Moreover, as noted earlier, half of all children whose parents remarry will witness a second divorce before they reach age 18. More will be said about remarriage shortly; for now I will suggest that the cumulative stress of these multiple transitions may cause difficulties. For instance, one national study found that the number of family transitions a young woman had experienced was a stronger predictor of whether she would bear a child before marrying than the number of years she had spent in a single-parent family (Wu & Martinson, 1993).[12]

AFTER THE CRISIS PERIOD

After the crisis period, the majority of children resume normal development. Still, a study by Hetherington and W. Glenn Clingempeel found that, five years after the disruption, about 25 to 30 percent of young adolescents were displaying serious behavior problems, as opposed to less than 10 percent of young adolescents who were still living with both parents.[13] The researchers found that the problems of some boys in the crisis period had persisted; in addition, girls were now displaying as many problems as boys. Early adolescence is a time when tension between parents and children can increase as the children try to become more independent. It is possible that this task is more difficult for children whose parents have divorced. According to the Hetherington and Clingempeel study, single mothers monitored

---

[12]See also Capaldi and Patterson (1991).

[13]By "serious" behavior problems, I mean scores on a checklist of behavior problems that were high enough to indicate that some clinical help might be needed. See the commentary by Maccoby (1992).

their children's behavior less closely and engaged in more arguments with them than did married mothers. Moreover, the researchers speculated that children who are just coming to terms with their own burgeoning sexuality may have a more difficult adjustment when they must confront intimate relationships between a parent and that parent's new boy- or girlfriend or spouse.

LONG-TERM ADJUSTMENT

Less is known about the long-term effects of experiencing a parental divorce. One widely read study by Judith Wallerstein and Sandra Blakeslee reported that, 10 years after a parental divorce, young adults showed pervasive unhappiness and loneliness; moreover, young adult women frequently experienced fear and anxiety at the prospect of making an emotional commitment to a man (Wallerstein & Blakeslee, 1989). Yet the study was based upon families that had voluntarily come to Wallerstein's clinic for counseling and therapy soon after the breakup. Although she screened out children who had seen a mental health professional, many of the parents had extensive psychiatric histories.[14] In addition, there was no comparison group of young adults from nondisrupted families, many of whom also may be anxious about making a commitment to a partner.

Rather than Wallerstein's gloomy picture, the long-term view seems to encompass both a glass-half-full and a glass-half-empty perspective. Consider studies based on national surveys by Sara McLanahan which show that, even after adjusting for parents' education, race, number of siblings, and place of residence, children who live in a single-parent family (whether with a divorced parent or a never-married parent) are more likely to drop out of high school, to have a child as a teenager, and to be "idle"—out of school and out of work (McLanahan, 1994). Her estimates imply, for instance, that 29 percent of those who grow up in single-parent families may drop out of high school compared with 13 percent of those who grow up in two-parent families. How large is this difference? On the one hand, it implies that the chance of dropping out of high school more than doubles for children from single-parent families—a substantial effect that seems worthy of concern. That's the glass-half-empty perspective. On the other hand, 7 in 10 children from single-parent families *do not* drop out of high school. That's the glass-half-full perspective. Moreover, McLanahan notes that even if all children lived in two-parent families, the nation's dropout rate would be at most 33 percent lower. She writes:

> *If all children lived in two-parent families, [dropping out of high school], teen motherhood, and idleness would be less common, but the bulk of these problems would remain* (McLanahan, 1994).

When parents divorce, or when single parents raise children outside marriage, their children run a higher risk of experiencing undesirable events (such as dropping out of school) in young adulthood and beyond. Nevertheless, most children from single-parent families will not, as a consequence, experience such problems.

A long-term study of the effects of parental divorce on the mental health of over 10,000 British children born in 1958 provides similar conclusions (Cherlin, Chase-Lansdale, & McRae, 1998). At age 33, the mental health of persons whose parents had divorced was somewhat worse, on average, than among persons whose

---

[14]See the appendix to Wallerstein and Kelly (1980).

parents had stayed together. However, the majority of persons from divorced families were not showing signs of serious mental health problems. In addition, some of the difference in mental health between the divorce and no-divorce groups had been visible in childhood behavior problems at age 7, before any of the parents of these individuals had divorced. Some of the seeming effect of divorce at age 33, then, probably reflected long-term difficulties of the individuals that would have occurred even had their parents stayed together.

It is possible that some of long-term difficulties of individuals whose parents divorced are due to the poor quality of the parents' marriages, rather than to the divorce itself. A study by Paul R. Amato and Alan Booth (1997) attempted to disentangle these two possibilities. The study began as telephone interviews with a nationally representative sample of married couples in 1980. The interviewers asked their respondents multiple questions on marital quality, including marital happiness, marital interaction (e.g., "How often do you eat your main meals together?"), marital conflict ("How many serious quarrels have you had in the past two months?"), and divorce proneness (e.g., "Has the thought of getting a divorce or separation crossed your mind in the last three years?"). The researchers divided all of the families into two groups, low conflict and high conflict, using all of the information. Then in 1992 all of the children who had lived with their parents in 1980 and who were now age 19 or older were interviewed.

The investigators report that offspring who experienced high marital conflict in 1980 were doing *better* in 1992 if their parents had divorced than if they had stayed together; on the other hand, offspring from low-conflict families were doing worse if their parents had divorced. This finding confirms the oft-stated but rarely substantiated belief that if family conflict is severe, children may benefit from a divorce. But the researchers caution that only a minority of the divorces that occurred were in high-conflict marriages (such as marriages with physical abuse or frequent serious quarrels). For that minority, the consequences of experiencing continuing conflict between their parents probably would have been worse than the consequences of the divorce. But the majority of offspring who experienced parental divorce probably would have been better off if their parents had stayed together.

Do the effects of a parental divorce carry over to an individual's own marriage? Information from the National Survey of Families and Households suggested the following picture: People whose parents divorced seemed just as happy with their marriages, on average, as did people whose parents did not divorce. However, people whose parents divorced were more likely to think that their marriages were in trouble, as if they were more sensitive to signs of marital strain. And among all people who reported their marriages as less than very happy, persons from divorced families were more likely to argue frequently and to shout or hit while arguing, as if repeating the conflictual style they may have learned or inherited from their parents (Webster, Orbuch, & House, 1995).

Overall, the still-evolving research literature on the effects of divorce on children suggests the following conclusions (Cherlin, 1992b):

- Almost all children experience an initial period of intense emotional upset after their parents separate.
- Most resume normal development without serious problems within about two years after the separation.
- A minority of children experience some long-term problems as a result of the breakup that may persist into adulthood.

From the glass-half-empty perspective, we can conclude that divorce may cause a substantial percentage increase in the number of individuals who may need the help of a mental health professional or who may not obtain as much education as they should or who may be unemployed more often than they should. As a society, we should be troubled by this development. From the glass-half-full perspective, however, it seems that most individuals do not suffer serious long-term harm as a result of their parents' divorce. We need to keep both perspectives in mind when considering the effects of divorce.

As noted, a divorce is not the end of the changes faced by many single parents and their children. A majority of the parents will either live with another partner, marry one, or do both. The next chapter explores the determinants and consequences of remarriage. I will postpone an overall discussion of the effects of divorce until the end of that chapter.

SUMMARY

1. There have been three eras of divorce in the modern history of the Western nations. During the first era, which lasted until the middle of the nineteenth century, divorce was very difficult to obtain. It was granted mainly to landowning and wealthy men, usually to ensure that an adulterous wife would not bear a child who would have a claim on the man's property. During the second era, divorce was increasingly available in cases of reprehensible conduct but was still frowned upon. The third era began in 1970, when California implemented the first law that eliminated the need to prove a fault to obtain a divorce. This change symbolized the availability of divorce in response to one spouse's demand, with few restrictions other than a waiting period.

2. The most important causes of the rise of divorce in the current era are the increased emphasis on self-fulfillment as the central criterion for judging marriages and the greater economic independence of women. There are other factors associated with divorce, even though they cannot explain the recent rise. Couples with low incomes are more likely to divorce than those with higher incomes. People who marry as teenagers are more likely to divorce. In addition, African Americans have a high rate of divorce, as do Native Americans. The divorce rate for Hispanics varies greatly, with Puerto Ricans having the highest rate and Mexican Americans the lowest. Asian Americans have the lowest rates of all. People who cohabit and then marry have a higher probability of divorcing than people who marry without cohab-

iting first. It is possible that a genetic predisposition sometimes causes difficulty in maintaining relationships. Finally, people who marry others who are similar to them in characteristics such as age and religion are less likely to divorce.

3. The process of divorce proceeds on many levels. On an emotional level, one spouse must initiate the separation; when it occurs, both spouses typically feel great distress at first. Legally, they must divide up tangible and intangible property and determine custody arrangements for the children. States have been moving toward a presumption in favor of joint legal custody. A small but growing number of cases also result in joint physical custody. Many fathers see their children infrequently after a divorce. In families in which fathers do maintain an involvement, the dominant style of parenting is a detached, low-conflict, low-cooperation mode that can be described as parallel parenting. Typically, the incomes of mothers and children fall after a divorce because of the mothers' lower wages and because most men pay little in child support. There have been several recent attempts by government to increase the amount of support fathers pay.

4. Divorce has several different kinds of effects on children. First, one parent, usually the father, leaves the household, depriving the child of a role model and the remaining parent of someone to support her and to help monitor and supervise the children's behavior. Second, during the crisis period following the separation, the custodial parent is often upset and angry; consequently, it can be

difficult for her to maintain the children's daily routine and to provide emotional support and consistent, moderate discipline. In addition, the custodial parent and her children must often cope with a substantial fall in family income. Third, the child may suffer if he or she is caught up in continuing conflict between the former spouses; the conflict and its negative effects may have preceded the separation. Fourth, the sheer number of family transitions, each requiring children's adjustment, may overwhelm the children's abilities to cope.

5. The long-term picture of children's adjustment to divorce suggests that a minority of individuals have difficulties that may be caused, in part, by the divorce, such as a higher risk of dropping out of high school, having a child before marrying, or having mental health problems. These effects are worthy of concern. Nevertheless, the studies also suggest that most children whose parents divorce will not experience serious long-term problems as a result.

KEY TERMS

era of restricted divorce
annulment
era of divorce tolerance
era of unrestricted divorce
no-fault divorce
initiator

attachment
alimony
legal custody
physical custody
joint legal custody

joint physical custody
coparenting
parallel parenting
child support assurance system
crisis period

FAMILIES ON THE INTERNET

Although there are numerous web sites about divorce, most are devoted to practical information for people about to divorce, or in the process of obtaining a divorce, or dealing with postdivorce issues such as modifying the legal agreement. Balanced overviews are harder to find. In addition to dispensing practical advice, **www.divorce-online.com** reprints a large number of articles on divorce-related topics such as whether to toughen divorce laws and how divorce affects children. For a sampling of articles that endorse the idea of stricter divorce laws, see **www.smartmarriages.com**. For supportive information about divorce, see **www.divorcesupport.com**.

CHAPTER 13

Remarriage and Stepfamilies

In 1979, when Danny Henrikson was a year old, his parents divorced. Danny's mother, Nancy, was awarded custody of his eight-year-old brother, Jay; his three-year-old sister, Joie; and him. Nancy soon married James Gable, and then in 1982 she died. The children's father, Gene Henrikson, agreed that Gable would retain custody of the children. Henrikson moved from Michigan to New York and rarely visited or called his children. Gable, on the other hand, was a devoted stepfather who worked continually with Danny to overcome a learning disorder. In 1983, Jay, who was then 12, visited his father in New York. Upon his return, Jay told Gable that he wanted to live with his father. Gable consented and transferred custody of Jay to Henrikson in New York. Then, at the end of 1985, Henrikson filed a court action seeking custody of Danny and Joie.

At this point, Danny was seven and had lived in Michigan with Gable since he was one. Gable fought the transfer, arguing that it was in Danny and Joie's best interests to remain in the home where they had been, by all accounts, raised well. The trial judge ruled in Gable's favor, writing, "the length of time the children have lived in a stable, satisfactory environment and [the] desirability of maintaining continuity . . . is weighed very strongly on behalf of the Gables." Henrikson, however, appealed to a higher court. In 1987, the Michigan Court of Appeals reversed the decision and awarded custody to Henrikson. Yes, the appeals court judges wrote, an established custody arrangement shouldn't be changed unless doing so is in the best interests of the child. However, another presumption also applied:

> *When the dispute is between the parent or parents and . . . a third person, it is presumed that the best interests of the child are served by awarding custody to the parent or parents* (Henrikson v. Gable, 1987).

After seven years of being Danny's dad, James Gable was not a parent, in the eyes of the court; rather, he was a "third person." Gene Henrikson, who had moved to New York and had hardly stayed in contact with Danny, was the parent. The appeals court clearly felt that the biological parents remain the legal parents, even if they have little to do with their children; whereas stepparents, even if they have raised the children since infancy, are still the legal outsiders.

THE INCOMPLETE INSTITUTION

David Chambers, the legal scholar who unearthed this case, notes how little standing the law gives to the relationship between stepparents and stepchildren. In most states, the stepparent has no legal obligation to contribute to the support of the stepchildren, even if he has lived with them for years and the nonresident biological parent has paid nothing. And if the stepparent and the custodial parent get divorced, the stepparent has no further obligation to support the stepchildren, even if he had been supporting them informally for years. When judges must choose between stepparents and biological parents, observes Chambers, their decisions vary widely from case to case and jurisdiction to jurisdiction:

> *The incoherent pattern of outcomes and the murky and inconsistent discussions of the governing rules almost certainly reflect our society's conflicting and unresolved attitudes about stepparents* (Chambers, 1990).

(See *Families and Public Policy:* The Rights and Responsibilities of Stepparents, on pages 400–401.)

The conflict and lack of resolution are even broader. About 20 years ago, I published an article entitled "Remarriage as an Incomplete Institution" (Cherlin, 1978). Curious about the complex families formed when divorced people remarry, I had reviewed the research literature and interviewed a number of remarried couples in Maryland. In all of them, at least one spouse had children from a previous marriage living in the household. Sometimes both did, but more often the father's children, if any, lived with his former wife. Some of the families also had a mutual child from the new marriage. What I found were people who were working hard to create a coherent family life. Every day they faced issues and problems that people in first marriages never dream of, such as, Does a stepfather have the authority to discipline his stepchild if the child does something wrong? What should a child call the woman his father married after he divorced the child's mother? Where is the "home" of a child who spends four days a week living with his father and three days living with his mother?

These daily problems often cut to the heart of more fundamental questions: What is a family, and what are its boundaries? Who is a relative and who is not? What obligations do adults and children sharing the same household owe to one another? People in first marriages rarely think about these questions because our culture provides us with a set of social roles (patterns of behavior associated with positions in society—in this case, parent, spouse, and child) and social norms (widely accepted rules about how people should behave) that address them. These roles are so ingrained that we take them for granted—we know, for example, who our relatives are; we know what a parent is. The widely accepted, taken-for-granted character of the roles and rules of family life is what makes the family a social institution. Recall that a social institution is a set of roles and rules that define a social unit of importance to society.

But stepfamilies create situations in which the taken-for-granted rules and the well-established roles don't apply. Consequently, stepfamilies must create their own rules, their own shared meanings, through a long and sometimes difficult process of discussion, negotiation, and trial and error. In other words, as I argued in my article, life in stepfamilies is incompletely institutionalized in our society. The lack of shared meanings can create problems for parents, stepparents, and children. Negotiation and bargaining take time and effort and can cause bruised feelings. To be sure, stepfamilies offer the possibility of creating useful new roles that have no counterparts in first marriages (such as the trusted "intimate-outsider" roles some stepparents play—see below). Still, institution building is difficult work and takes its toll in stepfamilies.

There are other reasons why we might expect the tasks of family life to be more difficult for stepfamilies than for families formed by first marriages (White, 1994). In terms of social networks, individuals in stepfamilies have ties to different sets of individuals, such as biological parents living elsewhere or children living with another parent (see below). The pull that these networks exert can undermine attempts to strengthen the unity of the stepfamily. In addition, stepparents who join families well after the stepchildren were born do not have the investment of time and effort that the parent already has made; therefore, the role of stepparent may be less central to their identities. Finally, evolutionary psychologists would note that parents pass on their genes to children, whereas stepparents do not pass on genes to stepchildren (Popenoe, 1994). Therefore, they would predict that stepparents would express less warmth and support toward stepchildren, on average, than biological parents, as research on stepfamilies confirms (Hetherington & Jodl, 1994). Despite these limitations, many stepfamilies are successful. How parents and stepparents put their families together, what these families look like, and how they are changing the very nature of family and kinship are the subject of this chapter.

THE DEMOGRAPHY OF REMARRIAGE AND STEPFAMILIES

There's nothing new about remarriage per se, but until recently most remarriages followed the death of one of the spouses. The decline in adult death rates in the twentieth century and the increase in divorce, however, have changed the balance: Currently in the United States, 9 in 10 of all remarriages follow a divorce rather than a death (U.S. National Center for Health Statistics, 1991a). Widows and widowers tend to be older persons, not parents caring for young children, and the probability of remarrying is lower for widows and widowers than it is for divorced persons. For the balance of this chapter, the term "remarriage" refers to remarriage

Families and Public Policy

The Rights and Responsibilities of Stepparents

Until recently, the legal rights and responsibilities of stepparents with regard to their stepchildren in American and English law could be summed up easily: There weren't any. Even if stepparents had resided with their stepchildren for many years, they had no obligation to support them or to care for them in any way. And even if a stepparent had provided most of the care of the stepchildren for years, the biological parent would still retain custody of the children if the marriage ended. The lowly status of the stepparent extends back hundreds of years in English common law. Under common law, a remarriage did not create any legal link between the stepchildren and their stepparent. "It was as if," British legal scholar Stephen Cretney writes, "the remarriage had never happened" (Cretney, 1993).

As noted elsewhere in this chapter, 9 in 10 remarriages are formed as a result of divorce rather than widowhood. Children typically reside with a custodial parent, usually their mother, and a stepparent, while a second biological parent resides elsewhere. Consequently, the traditional body of law gives the biological parent who resides outside the home legal priority over the stepparent who lives with the children. So sweeping is this priority that the judge in the Henrikson case was only following standard legal precedent when he gave Danny's biological father in New York custody over the objections of a stepfather who had lived with him for years.

The judge's decision stems from a time in which the custody of children was treated fundamentally as a matter of the ownership of property. For children were indeed seen as property a few centuries ago—not because they were unloved but rather because they were valuable sources of labor for a family. A man who remarried after his wife died wanted to protect his children from the claims of his new wife's family. His children were an important asset. Today, however, our conception of children has changed, and we view them primarily in terms of the emotional and financial investments parents make in them and the emotional gratification parents receive. When courts consider custody and support cases, they usually base their decisions on the standard of what is in the best interests of the child. And it is not clearly in the best interests of children to be removed from homes in which they have been given good care, even if the caregiver was not a biological parent. This is why many people find judges' decisions in cases such as *Henrikson* v. *Gable* troubling.

Slowly, the law concerning stepparents is changing. In England, the Children's Act of 1989 allows stepparents to assume some responsibilities and gives them the right to petition the court under a number of circumstances (Cretney, 1993). Although the stepparent does not have legal responsibility for the child, if he or she is caring for the child, he or she may do what is reasonable to promote the child's well-being. If the marriage between the parent and the stepparent ends, the stepparent

after divorce. Because of the increase in divorce, more than 4 in 10 weddings in the United States involve a remarriage for the bride, the groom, or both (U.S. National Center for Health Statistics, 1991a).

DECLINING MARRIAGE RATES

Eighteenth-century poet and critic Samuel Johnson once said that remarriage is the triumph of hope over experience. Recently, the triumph is occurring less often. Until the 1960s, the remarriage rate and the divorce rate went up and down in parallel—when the divorce rate increased, so did the rate of remarriage. It seemed that divorced people weren't rejecting the ideal of being married, they were just rejecting their own first marriages and trying again. Starting in the 1960s, however, the annual rate of remarriage (the number of remarriages in a given year divided by the number of previously married persons aged 15 and older in the population) fell even though the divorce rate began to rise. The fall has continued ever since.

may request that the children live with him or her. (The judge, of course, need not grant this request.) Should the biological parent die, the surviving biological parent has the right to take the children, as happened in the Henrikson case, but the stepparent may ask the court to let the children remain with him or her. Still, the stepparent has no recognized legal status.

In the United States, the practices of the courts seem to be evolving slowly in the direction of recognizing some rights and responsibilities for stepparents. With respect to custody, all states give biological parents priority, but many states allow a third party, such as a stepparent, to obtain custody if parental custody would be detrimental to the well-being of the child.[1] In some states, it is now easier for a stepparent to adopt a stepchild, even over the objections of the noncustodial parent. Adoption can occur if, for instance, the noncustodial parent hasn't made child support payments or visited the child for a year or more.[2] Stepparents even have won

custody in a few special circumstances. In one case, upon the breakup of the marriage of a stepmother and a biological father, the stepmother was given custody of a child who had lived with them. The child was deaf, and the court was impressed by the educational efforts made on his behalf by the stepmother during the marriage.[3]

In another case a stepmother, Mary, was granted custody of her stepson, Brendan, over the objections of the biological mother, following the death of the biological father. Brendan, age 12, had been living with Mary and his biological father prior to the father's death. Although residing in a different state, Brendan's biological mother had visited him regularly. Nevertheless, he told the court he wished to continue to live with his stepmother. The court found that a "mother-son relationship developed" between Brendan and Mary. Furthermore, it held that "the superior right of a natural parent to custody of his or her child is not absolute but only one of several

factors looked to in determining best interests of the child."[4]

I think it is likely that this slow evolution will continue, as parenthood comes to be defined partly in terms of what parents actually do for children, not just whether they are biologically related. This is not to say that the claims of resident stepparents should always win over the claims of biological parents living elsewhere. Yet, given the number of stepparents who are caring for children, it seems time to recognize the importance of their contribution and to provide them with some of the rights and responsibilities that until now have been reserved for biological mothers and fathers.

---

[1]See, for example, California Code, Section 4600, and Massachusetts Code, Section 208.28. I thank Elizabeth Scott for providing me with much of the information about recent case law in this and subsequent paragraphs.
[2]*In the Matter of J.J.J.*, 718 P. 2d 948 (Alaska 1986).
[3]*In re Marriage of Allen*, 626 P. 2d 16 (Wash. App. 1981).
[4]*In re Marriage of Carey*, 544 N.E. 2d 1293 (Ill. App. 2 Dist. 1989).

At current rates, only about two-thirds of separated and divorced women will ever remarry; the corresponding figure for men is about three-fourths.[1]

Some divorced persons are more likely to remarry than others. Some have a greater desire to remarry. For example, one study found that women who married in their teens or early twenties are more likely to remarry than women who married later. The authors speculate that women who married young may have less experience in, and less of a preference for, living independently.[2] Other women may be less attractive to potential spouses. Women who have three or more children, for instance, have a lower likelihood of remarrying, probably because they have a harder time finding a partner who would want to move into their household. Given

---

[1]Based on the 1985 data, Bumpass, Sweet, and Martin (1990) estimated that 72 percent of recently separated women would remarry. But remarriage rates have declined further since then. A 1992 Census Bureau report suggests that the true figure may be closer to two-thirds (U.S. Bureau of the Census, 1992c). The most recent estimate for men—78 percent remarry within 10 years—is from 1980 Census data and is probably too high now (Sweet & Bumpass, 1987).
[2]All the findings in this paragraph are from Bumpass, Sweet, and Martin (1990).

402 Power, Conflict, and Disruption

the norm that wives should be younger than their husbands, older women face a shrinking marriage market. They are expected to marry from the diminishing pool of older single men, whereas men can choose from the expanding pool of younger women. Consequently, women who divorce at a younger age are more likely to remarry than those who divorce at an older age. What is more, the greater financial independence of some older divorced women, who may be more established in their jobs, may make them less interested in remarrying.

In addition, remarriage is far more likely among non-Hispanic whites than among Hispanics or African Americans. According to one estimate from 1980 Census data, about half of all non-Hispanic white women will remarry within five years of their separation, compared with one-third of Mexican-American women and one-fifth of African-American women.[3] These differences occur, in part, because remarriage rates are lower for the poor than for the nonpoor. With few assets or little property to pass on to children, people with low incomes have less need for the legal protection marriage brings. Yet lower incomes don't account for the entire difference. The low remarriage rates for African Americans are also consistent with the lesser place of marriage in the African-American family. Recall that fewer African Americans ever enter a first marriage and that they take longer to do so than whites. This explanation doesn't apply to Hispanics, whose rates of first marriage are more similar to those of non-Hispanic whites. It is likely that the Catholic Church's opposition to remarriage influences the behavior of this heavily Catholic group.

Remarriages are somewhat more likely to end in divorce than first marriages. Among women, about 37 percent of remarriages have dissolved after 10 years, compared with about 30 percent of first marriages (Sweet & Bumpass, 1987). The difference is concentrated in the first several years, during which time people in remarriages have substantially higher rates of divorce than people in first marriages. In my article, I hypothesized that the lack of institutionalized rules and roles might cause conflict in remarriages that would lead to divorce. Such conflict would be more likely, I thought, in remarriages in which stepchildren are present because of the increased complexity they bring to the family unit. Frank Furstenberg, Jr., and Graham Spanier, among others, have suggested an alternative reason for the difference in divorce rates. Remarried people, they argued, have demonstrated that they are willing to resort to a divorce when their marriages are unsatisfactory, whereas some people in first marriages may be very reluctant to do so. Consequently, these authors assert, remarriage involves a select group of people who may differ from first-time marriers in their propensity to divorce (Furstenberg & Spanier, 1984). Their argument is an example of what was called a selection effect in Chapter 8: the idea that two groups differ because certain kinds of people select (or are selected into) one group more than the other. For example, the claim here is that people who are prone to divorce tend to select the remarried group, whereas people who are averse to divorce select the first-marriage group.

Another variation of this selection argument is that persons in remarriage may not be as skilled in choosing a compatible partner or holding a marriage together. For example, Teresa Castro Martin and Larry Bumpass found that a majority of remarried people had begun their *first* marriages as teenagers (Martin & Bumpass, 1989). They speculate that a teenage first marriage may be a sign of personality characteristics or other difficulties that make it harder for a person to select a good

---

[3]Sweet and Bumpass (1987). More recent statistics are not available, but it is unlikely that the racial-ethnic differentials have changed much.

spouse or maintain a marriage. (We know that first marriages begun in the teenage years have a high divorce rate.) In any case, they found that the greater number of teenage first-time marriers in the remarried population accounted for much of the higher divorce rate among the remarried. Another recent national study reported that a teenage first marriage (a measure of the selection of particular kinds of people into remarriage) accounted for portions of the higher divorce rate among the remarried as did the presence of stepchildren (a measure of stepfamily complexity) (Booth & Edwards, 1992).

INCREASING COHABITATION

The overall decline in remarriage, however, is deceptive. As remarriage rates have declined, cohabitation among the formerly married has increased. Consequently, the number of cohabiting couples in which at least one partner was formerly married has increased. Figure 13.1 illustrates the change. The bars on the left-hand side represent the situation around 1970. Forty-nine percent of persons had remarried within five years after they separated from their spouses. In addition, some had cohabited with a partner without marrying. When those who cohabited without remarrying are added to those who remarried, the sum is the number who were ever in a union—marital or cohabiting—within five years of separating. As can be seen, 58 percent had ever been in a union in 1970. By 1984, the pattern had changed. Only 42 percent had remarried within 5 years of separating, reflecting the drop in the remarriage rate. But the percentage who had ever been in a union had *increased* from its 1970 level to 62 percent in 1984. In the interim, cohabitation had become so widespread among the previously married that its increase had more than compensated for the decrease in remarriage (Bumpass, Sweet, & Cherlin, 1991). Divorced persons today, in other words, are not less inclined to live with someone; rather, they have substituted cohabitation for remarriage. At least 60 percent of remarried people live with a partner—usually, but not always, their future spouse—before they remarry (Bumpass & Sweet, 1989).

In some postdivorce cohabiting relationships, children from previous marriages are present. In the past, households such as these have not been counted as stepfamilies

FIGURE 13.1 Percent who remarried within five years, and percent who were ever in union within five years, for persons separating around 1970 and around 1984, according to the National Survey of Families and Households. (*Source:* Bumpass, Sweet, & Cherlin [1991].)

because the potential stepparent is not married to the biological parent of the would-be stepchild. From the child's perspective, however, it may not matter whether his or her parent and live-in partner are married. In both cases, the child's relationship with his or her parent's partner is similar to that of a stepchild and stepparent. Nor may it make a difference to the child whether his or her parent was ever married previously. Suppose that a never-married woman gives birth to a child and several years later cohabits with a man other than the father. Suddenly her child must live in the same household as a man who is like a stepfather.

REDEFINING STEPFAMILIES

The rise of cohabitation among parents with children from previous relationships has led some sociologists to suggest that the definition of stepfamilies be enlarged to include cohabitation as well as remarriage. Let us, then, define a **stepfamily** as a household in which:

1 Two adults are married or cohabiting, and
2 At least one adult has a child present from a previous marriage or relationship.

This definition does not require that the adults be married. Data from the 1987–1988 National Survey of Families and Households shows that under this

A stepfamily is a household in which two adults are married or are cohabiting and at least one has a child present from a previous marriage or relationship.

broad definition, one-fourth of stepfamilies involved cohabiting couples (Bumpass, Raley, & Sweet, 1995) rather than remarried couples. In fact, a majority of children first entered stepfamily life through cohabitation rather than marriage; in many instances, the cohabiting parent subsequently married the live-in partner.

This definition also does not require that the child's parent ever have married. It allows for the increasingly common case in which a woman gives birth to a child outside of marriage and later lives with or marries someone other than the father. This path is particularly common among African Americans: About two-thirds of African-American stepfamilies, under this definition, were preceded by a nonmarital birth rather than a divorce (Bumpass et al., 1995). So this definition encompasses the kind of stepfamily, formed with little connection to marriage, that has become widespread among low-income and minority populations.

This way of conceptualizing stepfamilies is still new. Nearly all of the research on stepfamilies has been conducted within a framework based on divorce and remarriage. In part, that is because most of the research has been conducted on middle-class families. We know little about stepfamily life among the poor and near-poor. Throughout most of this chapter, then, the discussion will pertain more to stepfamilies formed by divorce and remarriage than to stepfamilies formed by nonmarital childbearing and cohabitation.

THE NEW EXTENDED FAMILY

Mother, father, children: These are the building blocks of the conjugal family—the family unit based on first marriage. One of the taken-for-granted aspects of family life in the Western nations is that children are born into conjugal families and that the parents and children in the conjugal family live in the same household until the children grow up. Until the last few decades, that assumption was justified. More recently, the increases in divorce, childbearing outside marriage, and remarriage have rendered it problematic (see Chapter 14). Divorce splits the conjugal family into two households—one that typically contains a custodial parent (usually the mother) and the children and a second that contains the noncustodial parent (usually the father). In the case of a nonmarital birth, the conjugal family is never even formed.

Remarriage can bring a multitude of ties across households, creating what Furstenberg has called "the new extended family" (Furstenberg, 1987). Consider one set of family ties studied by Anne Bernstein (1988) and diagrammed in Figure 13.2. It is centered on the marriage of Carin and Josh, who reside in household 2. They have a mutual child, Alice. Josh used to be married to Peggy, with whom he had two children, Janet and Tim, who live with Peggy in household 3. Carin used to be married to Don, with whom she had two children, Scott and Bruce, who still live with her. Her former husband, Don, then remarried Anna and had two more children, Ethan and Ellen, who live with Anna and him in household 1. Here is how 13-year-old Bruce described his family (you are allowed to look at the chart while reading this):

> *Tim and Janet are my stepbrother and sister. Josh is my stepdad. Carin and Don are my real parents, who are divorced. And Don married Anna and together they had Ethan and Ellen, my half-sister and -brother. And Carin married Josh and had little Alice, my half-sister* (Bernstein, 1988).

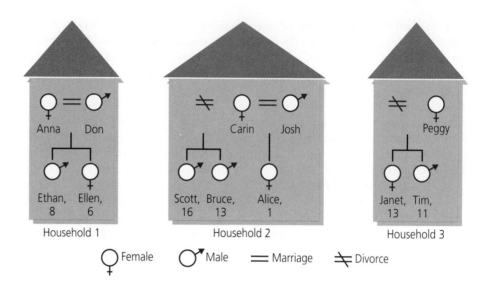

FIGURE 13.2 Bruce's stepfamily. (*Source:* Bernstein, 1988.)

SOME DEFINITIONS

How are we to make sense of this admixture? How many families are involved? What are their boundaries? The relationships spill over the sides of households, with children providing the links from one to the next. Let me suggest that there are two ways to define families in this context. The first is to focus on a household, even though ties extend beyond it. The advantage of this strategy is that we are used to thinking of families as being synonymous with households because we are used to thinking about first-marriage families. I have previously defined a stepfamily as a *household* that contains a parent with children from a previous union and that parent's current partner. The children from the previous union are the stepchildren, and the current partner is a stepparent. The household can be even more complex: Both partners may have children from previous unions, and they also may have a new, mutual child from the current union. But the defining criterion is that they all reside in the same household. Although there are three households in Figure 13.2, only household 2 contains a stepfamily according to our definition. Household 1 has no children from previous unions living there, and household 3 has children from a previous union and their biological parent but no current spouse or partner.

The second way to define families is to ignore household boundaries and to focus instead on the human chains that extend from one household to another like intertwined strands of DNA. The bonds of the chains, the forces that hold the strands together, are children from previous unions. They link a divorced woman and her new partner with her ex-husband and his new wife. Anthropologist Paul Bohannan called these pathways "divorce chains" (Bohannan, 1971a). But if our interest is the links to quasi relatives that stepfamilies bring, it is probably more accurate to refer to them as **remarriage chains**, paths that link individuals across households through the ties of disrupted unions and new unions. Bruce was describing his remarriage chain. On one end, it begins with Anna, his father's current wife, and their children, Ethan and Ellen. Bruce sees them when he goes to Anna's house to visit his father, Don. Through Don and then Bruce, the chain continues into household 2, where it comprises Bruce's brother, Scott, his mother, Carin, his stepfather, Josh, and their mutual child, Alice. In addition, Josh's children from his first marriage, Janet and Tim, are included because they come to Bruce's house to visit their father. So Bruce's chain extends from Anna to Tim. Note, however, that Bruce doesn't mention Peggy, whom he rarely sees because he has no parents to visit in Peggy's household. In contrast, if Tim were asked about his family, he would obviously include Peggy. On the other hand, he probably doesn't see anyone in household 1 very often and wouldn't include them.

In fact, if you asked the people in the figure who was in their family, you likely would get a different answer from almost every one of them. To be sure, Bruce and Scott would probably name the same chain, as would Janet and Tim, and Ethan and Ellen. Otherwise, each person has his or her own distinctive chain. Consequently, the only way to specify the members of a remarriage chain is to define it in reference to a particular person—not a household. The stepfamily becomes a node, a switching point, that routes the chains to their various destinations.

Remarriage chains can serve as support and exchange networks, as ex-spouses and new spouses give and request favors. Family therapist Jamie Keshet describes the chain of a single mother named Marge, whose mother needed surgery. Marge wanted to spend two weeks with her mother, who lived in another state, after the surgery (all parenthetical material is in Keshet's account):

She called her former husband, Peter, to see if he could take the children for that time (Peter is a resource for her). Peter talked with his second wife, Jessica, and they agreed. . . . Jessica had two children from her first marriage. She called her ex-husband, Ron, to see if he could switch his visitation weekend so it would come after Peter's kids had gone, rather than in the middle of their stay. (Ron is a potential resource for Jessica and Peter in helping them have time alone together.) Ron agreed but found himself thinking, "I am expected to change my plans because my ex-wife's second husband's ex-wife's mother is ill" (Keshet, 1988).

This system depends on the cooperation of all involved and can easily be disrupted. In extended-kin networks centered on conjugal families or "blood" relatives (see below), people might extend favors based on goodwill and a sense of shared purpose. In remarriage chains that sense of goodwill is limited, and decisions are more likely to be made using the calculus of self-interest. Ron is annoyed, but he will agree this time because he may need to ask Jessica for a similar favor in the future.

DOING THE WORK OF KINSHIP

Some links in the chains are weaker than others, and some fail entirely to form. When Americans think about kinship, they think about people related either through "blood" or through marriage. **Blood relatives** are people who share common ancestors: parents and children, uncles and aunts, nephews and nieces, grandparents and grandchildren. In theory, this network of blood relatives spreads out to an almost limitless number of people: second cousins (two people whose parents were first cousins), third cousins, and so forth. It spreads out on both the maternal and paternal sides, which is why anthropologists classify the Western countries as having **bilateral kinship,** a system in which descent is reckoned through both the mother's and father's lines (as opposed to kinship systems in which relatives are counted only on the mother's side or only on the father's side). Yet if I were to draw my family tree, I would include very few second cousins and no third or higher-order cousins because I don't know them. A friend of mine whose mother was estranged from her family never saw many of her maternal kin; her family tree includes many more relatives on her father's side than on her mother's side.

As these examples suggest, the mere existence of a blood tie does not make a relative. In American kinship, people must establish a relationship to consider each other kin. Having a relationship means seeing each other regularly, corresponding, and/or giving or receiving help—somehow making repeated connections. If there is no relationship, even a blood relative may not be counted as kin. Now, it's true that almost everyone considers their parents and their children to be relatives even if they haven't seen them in a long time. But you would understand what someone meant if she said, "My father left home when I was three and I never saw him again; I don't consider him part of my family." And you might not consider a cousin whom you last met when you were a child to be a relative.

Stepparents and Stepchildren   To be a relative, then, you must do the work of creating and maintaining kinship. Among parents and children, this happens almost automatically—so much so that we rarely think about it. But among stepparents, it does not happen automatically. For one thing, a stepparent in a remarriage or cohabiting union that has followed a divorce or a nonmarital birth does not replace the stepchild's nonresident parent, as was the case when most remarriages followed a death. Rather, the stepparent adds to the stepchild's stock of potential kin. If both biological parents are still involved in the stepchild's life, it's not clear what role the stepparent is supposed to play. Our society provides few guidelines, few norms. In the terms of my article, the role of the stepparent is incompletely institutionalized.

The "new extended family" after remarriage can be seen at events such as this graduation ceremony that both the mother and the stepmother attended.

In fact, there is great variability in how stepparents and stepchildren view one another. In a 1981 national survey, children aged 11 to 16 and their parents were asked whom they specifically included in their family. Although only 1 percent of parents failed to mention their biological children, 15 percent of those with stepchildren in the household failed to mention them. Among children, 31 percent of those in stepfamilies failed to mention the stepparent who was living with them, and 41 percent failed to mention a stepsibling (Furstenberg, 1987).

What, then, determines how stepchildren and stepparents view one another? A key factor is how old the child was when the stepparent joined the household: The younger the child, the more likely he or she is to consider the stepparent to be a "real" parent (Marsiglio, 1992). The evidence isn't precise enough to establish an age cutoff. I would speculate that if the stepparent arrives during the preschool years, it is possible to establish a parentlike relationship; but if the stepparent arrives later, it is much more difficult. Research shows that children establish strong bonds of attachment to their parents, whom they rely on for security, within their first year or two. After the preschool years, it appears to be more difficult for children to form such strong bonds of attachment (Parkes & Hinde, 1982). It may be, then, that a child cannot develop the same kind of attachment to a stepparent who arrives when the child is past the preschool years. A second factor is how frequently the stepchild sees his or her nonresident parent; the less frequent their interaction, the easier it is for a stepparent to take on a parentlike role (Marsiglio, 1992).[4] A third factor is the quality of the relationship between the stepparent and the biological parent in the home. The more satisfactory that relationship, the more authority the stepparent has to take on a parental role.

Twenty years ago there was no agreed-upon word by which a stepchild could call his or her stepparent. In recent years, it has become increasingly common for stepchildren to use the stepparent's first name. If this usage becomes widespread, it would serve to institutionalize a role for the stepparent that is neither parent nor stranger, but somewhere in between. A child doesn't (usually) call a parent by his or her first name, nor does the child use the first name of a stranger. Rather, the first-name usage suggests a role for the stepparent that is akin to that of a kindly uncle or aunt—a relative whom you like and who can give you support, but not someone who has the authority to discipline you.

Stepgrandparents and Stepgrandchildren   There is even greater variability in how more distant stepkin relate to the stepchildren. When Frank Furstenberg and I carried out a national study of grandparents, we asked them about relationships with stepgrandchildren. Once again, the younger the children had been when the grandparents had acquired them by virtue of an adult child's remarriage, the more the grandparents reported feeling that the children were like biological grandchildren. One stepgrandmother, who had not acquired her stepgrandchildren until they were teenagers, was asked what they called her:

> *Harriett. I insisted on that. They started by calling me Mrs. Scott. . . . But from the beginning, you realize, these children were in their teens, and it was hard to accept somebody from an entirely different family, and they didn't know me from Adam. . . . Now if they were smaller—you know, younger—it would have made a difference* (Cherlin & Furstenberg, 1992, p. 158).

---

[4]See footnote 3 of Marsiglio (1992).

It also made a big difference whether the stepgrandchildren were living with the grandparents' adult children (as when a son married a woman who had custody of children from a previous marriage) or were living most of the time in another household (as when a daughter married a man whose children lived with his former wife except for every other weekend and a month in the summer). Within these constraints, the closeness of the relationship depended on how much effort the stepgrandparents and their adult children put into creating the relationship. Being a steprelative depends on doing the work of kinship.

BUILDING A STEPFAMILY

After divorce, single parents and their children establish, often with some difficulty, agreed-upon rules and new daily schedules. They work out ways of relating to each other that may differ from the predisruption days. A daughter may become a special confidante to her mother. A son may assume new responsibilities, such as taking out the garbage, washing the car, and performing other tasks that his father used to do. Put another way, single parents and children create a new family system. Then, into that system, with its shared history, intensive relationships, and agreed-upon roles, walks a stepparent. No wonder that it can be difficult for the members of the stepfamily to adjust to his or her presence.

The adjustment can take years to complete. One family therapist argues that the average stepfamily takes about seven years to finish the process (Papernow, 1988). That's a very long time, considering that more than one-fourth of all remarriages break up within five years (Martin & Bumpass, 1989). At the start, the stepparent is an outsider, almost an intruder in the system. At first, the stepparent may view himself or herself naively as a healer who will nurse the wounded family back to health (Papernow, 1988). But his or her initial efforts to help out may backfire: A stepdaughter may resent the intimacy and support a new stepfather provides to her mother; a son may not wish to relinquish certain responsibilities such as washing the car to a well-meaning stepfather who thinks he is just doing what fathers are supposed to do. As Furstenberg and I wrote, "stepparents quickly discover that they have been issued only a limited license to parent." The wiser ones among them accept the limits of their job description and bide their time (Furstenberg & Cherlin, 1991, p. 85).

Family therapists seem to agree that for a stepfamily to be successful, the remarried couple must build a boundary around themselves and work together to solve problems. Their own marriage, rather than the custodial parent and child relationship, must become the dominant subsystem within the stepfamily (Keshet, 1988; Papernow, 1988).[5] To do so, they must reserve time for each other, even if that means sometimes deferring the demands of others. The task of the remarried couple is to create a shared conception of how their family is to go about its daily business. They cannot rely on generally accepted norms, as adults in first marriages can, because few norms exist. They must draw the blueprints themselves and then construct the family.

During this process, it can be harder to be a stepmother than a stepfather. Prior to the twentieth century, most stepmothers moved into a household in which the children's mother had died—a position in which they were sometimes resented. (See *Families in Other Cultures:* The Origins of the Wicked Stepmother, on

[5]See also Spanier and Furstenberg (1987).

pages 412–413.) In the typical remarriage chain today, the children live with their biological mother and a stepfather; they visit their biological father and his new wife, their stepmother. Consequently, the typical stepmother does not live with her stepchildren; rather, she must establish a relationship during the visits. She is usually dealing with children whose primary tie is to their biological mother, with whom she must compete. In contrast, stepfathers compete with noncustodial fathers, many of whom, as has been discussed, see little of their children. Moreover, in the minority of cases in which the children live with the stepmother and the biological father, other difficulties can arise. In these atypical cases, the children may have been subject to a custody battle, or they may have been sent to live with the father because the mother couldn't control their behavior (Ihinger-Tallman & Pasley, 1987). And mothers who are noncustodial parents visit their children and telephone them more often than noncustodial fathers, creating competition with the stepmother (Furstenberg & Nord, 1985).

Stepfathers, in other words, can often fill a vacuum left by the departed biological father. Stepmothers must crowd into the space already occupied by the biological mother. Moreover, stepmothers may judge themselves according to the culturally dominant view that a mother should play the major role in rearing children; if so, they may fall short of these high standards. Stepfathers, in contrast, may hold themselves to the lower standard that a father is supposed to provide support to the mother but let her do most of the hands-on childrearing. If so, they may feel satisfied with their role performance, even if they are doing less than many dissatisfied stepmothers (Keshet, 1988).

Low-income and racial-ethnic families sometimes face a different set of issues. David Mills describes the dynamic he has seen among stepfamilies that began when an unmarried teenager bore a child. The child was often raised partly by the mother and partly by the grandmother, who may herself have given birth to the mother as a teenager. Although the families Mills studied were white, this intergenerational family system has also been noted among poor African-American families (Burton, 1990). Mills found that there were frequent conflicts between the mother and the grandmother over how to raise the child. Sometime later, a stepfamily is formed when a man who is not the father of the child moves into the household as the mother's partner, or when the mother and child move in with him. In either case, this new stepfather soon faces situations in which he is urged to side with either the mother or the grandmother in their disputes about the child. If he criticizes the mother, he directly jeopardizes his relationship with her. But if he criticizes the grandmother too harshly, Mills observes, the mother may defend her and begin to reject him. Mills argues that this kind of tension makes it difficult for a stepfather to remain in an intergenerational family system for very long (Mills, 1988).

I don't want to leave the impression that stepfamily life is an interminable struggle. Most stepparents report that they are happy with their roles and their new families. In the 1981 survey, a large majority of parents and children in stepfamilies rated their households as "relaxed," "orderly," and "close," and less than one-third found them "tense" or "disorganized." Nevertheless, the ratings of persons in stepfamilies were slightly but consistently less positive than the ratings of persons in two-biological-parent households (Furstenberg, 1987). Studies suggest that there is a wide variation in the roles stepparents play. For example, in the National Survey of Families and Households, stepfathers were asked to agree or disagree with the statement "A stepparent is more like a friend than a parent to stepchildren." One-third agreed, half disagreed, and the rest were neutral (Marsiglio, 1992). Those

Families in Other Cultures

The Origins of the Wicked Stepmother

"It is, perhaps, too much to expect that the second wife of a working man should have the same affection toward her husband's children by a former wife as towards her own," wrote Dr. Barnardo, a nineteenth-century English philanthropist and child welfare advocate. "But case after case has come before us in which the jealousy of a stepmother has led to the most cruel treatment of the little folks committed to her charge."[1] The good doctor was repeating a charge against stepmothers that is hundreds, if not thousands, of years old. For further confirmation, just ask Cinderella or Snow White. Where did this view of stepmothers come from, and how does it relate to stepmothers today?

The prefix "step" in Old English signified a family relationship caused by death. In fact, "stepchild" originally meant "orphan," and "stepmother" can be rendered as "one who becomes a mother to an orphan." The common meaning of stepmother, however, was a woman who married a man whose wife had died (Oxford English Dictionary, 1989). The term has long had the connotations of cruelty, neglect, and jealousy. Pliny the Elder wrote in the first century A.D., "It is far from easy to determine whether she [Nature] has proved to man a kind parent or a merciless stepmother." Leonardo da Vinci, perhaps cribbing from Pliny, asked of Nature, "wherefore art thou thus partial, becoming to some of thy children a tender and benignant mother, to others a most cruel and ruthless stepmother?" Shakespeare had the Queen say in Cymbeline that

"you shall not find me, daughter, after the slander of most stepmothers, evil-eyed unto you."[2] Numerous fairy tales contrast the wicked, jealous stepmother to the kindly but unfortunately deceased mother.

These connotations are rooted in the reality of stepfamilies in preindustrial societies. Because of the amount of labor it took to provide food, clothes, and shelter and to raise children, a family needed two parents in order to subsist. Yet it was common for a parent to die before her or his children reached adulthood. In particular, women faced a substantial risk of dying in childbirth. If a mother of small children died, her husband had no choice but to remarry quickly. Alone, he simply could not farm the land, perform household tasks, and care for his children. If he attempted to do so, he might be risking his children's lives. Moreover, the strong patriarchal norms of preindustrial Western society discouraged him from even trying. Rather, economic necessity and social norms led him to remarry after a short period of mourning—often within several months (Mitterauer & Sieder, 1982).

Under these circumstances, the husband's remarriage choices were often limited. It was common for a second or third wife to be considerably younger than the husband; indeed, sometimes decades younger. These large age differences and the patriarchal norms sometimes led the husband to treat his second wife as if she were a child rather than a spouse (Mitterauer & Sieder, 1982). The young stepmother was relatively powerless before the older husband. In addition, she had little authority over

the older children in the household, who could be roughly her age.

The stepmother's best strategy for gaining some power within the household was to bear and raise her own children. They would at least be bound to her by the typical emotional bonds between mother and child. As her biological children grew, she would be able to influence their actions; and in her old age, they would be more likely to provide for her. This strategy is not confined to the past or to stepmothers. Anthropologist Margery Wolf discovered a similar strategy among women in rural Taiwan in the 1950s and 1960s (Wolf, 1972). In the strongly patriarchal Chinese society (where the Cinderella fairy tale may have originated a thousand years ago [Bettelheim, 1976]), a young wife typically moved into the household of her husband and his parents. She was subject to the authority of her husband and her mother-in-law, and she sometimes had infrequent contact with her parents. A central way in which she gained power was to raise her own children, over whom she would have influence. At least one of her sons was likely to remain in her household and eventually to bring in a young wife of his own. When he did so, his mother herself attained the relatively powerful status of mother-in-law.

If a powerless young stepmother in the European past followed the strategy of gaining power through raising her own loyal children, she might reasonably favor them over her stepchildren. One could imagine her desire to advance her biological children's interests within the household and her jealousy over the advancement of her stepchildren. One could also imagine

The negative image of the wicked stepmother dates back to fairy tales such as Cinderella.

that her stepchildren would be angry at her and resent her biological children. And one could imagine the appeal of a story in which the stepmother wants her biological daughters, not her stepdaughter, to meet the prince at the ball. From household dynamics such as these, the malevolent image of the stepmother may have been formed.

Today, as noted earlier, the vast majority of remarriages are formed as a result of divorce rather than widowhood. If there are stepchildren, they probably live for most of the week with their biological mother, who, unlike the situation in the past, is still

alive. The age difference between spouses in remarriages, although greater, on average, than in first marriages, is probably smaller than in the preindustrial past. Husbands and wives relate to each other as emotional equals more than in the past. The most direct route for wives to gain power in the household is not to raise loyal children but rather to work for pay outside the home (see Chapter 10). In all these ways, stepmothers today face a situation so different from the past that perhaps we shouldn't even use the same term. In fact, the French have dropped the old, pejorative term for stepmother, *marâtre,* and

replaced it with *belle-mère,* literally "fine" or "beautiful" mother, a term which also means "mother-in-law." French scholars of the family lament the absence of a prefix, such as "step," with which to precisely label relationships brought about by remarriage. But the *belles-mères* of France may be fortunate that, unlike their Anglo-American counterparts, they no longer have to bear the stigma of an outmoded, archaic term.

[1]*Day and Night,* May 1885, p. 74. Cited in Cretney (1993).
[2]The quotations from Pliny the Elder and da Vinci are cited in Bartlett (1980). The quotation from Shakespeare is cited in Cretney (1993).

stepparents who manage to integrate into the stepfamily successfully often play a valued role that is somewhere between that of a parent and that of a trusted friend—what Papernow calls an **"intimate outsider"** (Papernow, 1988). Teenage stepchildren, for example, may feel close enough to them to discuss issues that are too highly charged to discuss with their biological parents, such as sex, drugs, or their feelings about their parents' divorces. One such stepmother told Papernow:

> *Mary calls me her "motherly friend." Sometimes I think of myself as her mentor. I'm the one who helped her decide she could be an architect.*
>
> *She confides deeply in me, and it is such an honor and a pleasure to be so intimately involved in guiding her life, and yet to be seen as someone with enough distance that she can trust me not to take what she says personally. It is worth all the struggle to have this relationship with her* (Papernow, 1988, p. 81).

THE EFFECTS OF REMARRIAGE ON CHILDREN

Twenty years ago, I thought that remarriage would improve the overall well-being of children whose parents had divorced. For one thing, when a single mother remarries, her household income usually rises dramatically because men's wages are so much higher, on average, than women's wages. One national study found that 8 percent of children in mother–stepfather households were living below the poverty line, compared with 49 percent of children in single-mother households (Bachrach, 1983). Consequently, if a decline in the standard of living hurts the well-being of children in single-parent families, an increase after the mother remarries should improve it. In addition, the stepparent adds a second adult to the home. He or she can provide support to the custodial parent and back up the custodial parent's monitoring and control of the children's behavior. A stepparent can also provide an adult role model for a child of the same gender.

Despite these advantages, many studies now show that the well-being of children in stepfamilies is no better, on average, than the well-being of children in divorced, single-parent households. To be sure, most children in stepfamilies do not demonstrate serious problems (Amato, 1994; Hetherington & Jodl, 1994). Still, both groups of children show lower levels of well-being than children in two-biological-parent families. For example, psychologists Mavis Hetherington, Glenn Clingempeel, and several collaborators studied about 200 white households, divided into three groups: nondivorced, two-parent households; divorced, single-mother households in which the mothers had been divorced for about four years, on average; and stepfamilies that had just formed (four months' average duration) and in which the wife was the biological parent and the husband the stepparent. The sample was not selected randomly but rather recruited by such means as advertisements, examining marriage records, and sending notices to community organizations. All households had at least one child between 9 and 13 years of age; these early adolescents were the main focus of the study. Households were evaluated using multiple methods, including personal interviews with the parents and children, standardized tests given to the children, and videotaped family problem-solving sessions. Evaluations were conducted three times: at the start of the study, again about a year later, and yet again another nine months later (Hetherington & Clingempeel, 1992).

At all three evaluations, the children from both the single-mother and stepfamily households were not doing as well as the children in the nondivorced households. For example, all the mothers were asked which items on a list of behavior

A parent's remarriage means a new period of adjustment for a child such as this young ring bearer, whose siblings and would-be stepmother tried to convince him to march down the aisle.

problems applied to their early-adolescent child. Scores above a certain level on this widely used behavior problems checklist are said to indicate serious difficulties that might warrant referral to mental health professionals. Even at the last assessment, about 25 to 30 percent of the children in the single-mother and stepfamily households were above this cutoff level, as opposed to 10 percent or less of the children in nondivorced households; there was little difference between the former two groups (Maccoby, 1992).

A national health survey of 15,000 children in 1981 produced similar results. On average, children in stepfamilies and in single-parent households both received higher scores on a checklist of behavior problems than children in nondivorced, two-parent households. When parents were asked about the need for psychological help for their children, 3 percent of nondivorced parents said that their child needed help or had received help in the previous year, compared with 10 percent in single-mother households and 10 percent in mother–stepfather households. Children in both of the latter groups were more likely to have repeated a grade in school than children from nondivorced households. On all these indicators, there was little difference between the children in single-parent households and in stepfamilies (Zill, 1988).

There is conflicting evidence as to whether children of different ages or genders adjust differently to the arrival of a stepparent. Several studies conducted mostly with younger children have found that girls had a more difficult time adjusting to the presence of a stepfather than boys did adjusting to a stepmother.[6] Some of the authors speculated that girls tend to form close bonds to their divorced mothers and that these bonds are disrupted by the arrival of a stepfather. In support of this idea, at least two studies found that daughters showed *poorer* adjustment when their mothers and stepfathers reported greater cohesion and bonding in

---

[6]See, for example, Bray (1988); Hetherington (1987).

their marriage; conversely, they showed better adjustment when there was less co-hesion in the marriage (Brand, Clingempeel, & Bowen-Woodward, 1988; Bray, 1988). It is as if daughters' sense of well-being falls at least temporarily when their mothers turn some attention and affection toward their new husbands.

However, the 1981 national health survey showed few differences by gender. Neither did Hetherington and Clingempeel's recent joint study find differences be-tween the early-adolescent girls and boys in their study, despite the expectations of the authors, each of whom had reported gender differences in previous studies. Instead, Hetherington and her associates now suggest that the transition to adoles-cence for both girls and boys is a difficult time in which to adjust to a remarriage (Hetherington & Jodl, 1994). This is a time when children must come to terms with their own burgeoning sexuality. For this reason, it may be disconcerting to have an adult sexual partner of the parent move into the house—especially one for whom the traditional incest taboos do not hold.[7] Moreover, this is also a time when children begin to establish their own identity and independence. In addi-tion, the sheer number of family transitions might impair the adjustment of chil-dren in stepfamilies. Having coped with a divorce, and possibly with the introduc-tion of a live-in partner, these children must now cope with another major change in their family system. Some studies, as noted in the previous chapter, have found a relationship between the number of family transitions a child has experienced, on the one hand, and behavior problems and subsequently having a baby before marrying (Wu & Martinson, 1993).[8] Finally, children and parents with certain, un-known personal characteristics that impair family cohesion could be self-selecting into the population of divorced and remarried families.

Only one finding about the long-term effects on children of having lived in a stepfamily is well established. Children in stepfamilies—particularly girls—leave their households at an earlier age than children in single-parent households or two-parent households. They leave earlier either to marry or to establish indepen-dent households prior to marrying. An analysis of a large, six-year, national study of high school students showed this pattern for girls (Goldscheider & Goldschei-der, 1993). In a British study, 23-year-olds who had left their parental homes were asked the main reason why they had left. Demographer Kathleen Kiernan re-ported that those who had lived in stepfamilies were substantially more likely to have said that they had left due to "friction at home" than those who had not lived in stepfamilies (Kiernan, 1992). Again, the differences were greater for girls. An analysis of the National Survey of Families and Households found that girls who had lived in a stepfamily were more likely to have left home by age 19 to marry or to live independently than girls who had lived with single parents or with two parents; the differences were much weaker for boys. If a girl had also lived with stepsiblings, her likelihood of leaving home by age 19 was even higher (Aquilino, 1991).

That tensions between stepchildren and their parents and stepparents lie be-hind the early home leaving is suggested by interviews in 1980 and 1983 with a national sample of currently married people. Those who had stepchildren in their households reported more family problems involving children. The authors hy-pothesize that one way these problems are resolved is by encouraging, or arrang-ing for, the stepchildren to leave the household. During the three years between

[7]In most states, it is legal for a stepfather to divorce his wife and marry his wife's daughter. See Glendon (1989).
[8]See also Capaldi and Patterson (1991).

interviews, 51 percent of all the teenage stepchildren had left the households, compared with 35 percent of all the teenage biological children. Some may have chosen to move in with their other parent, some may have been forced to do so, and some may have left to go to school, establish their own residence, cohabit, or marry (White & Booth, 1985). If this effect is indeed more pronounced for girls, it suggests that the "friction" in the household may be due to the disruption of the mother–daughter bond or to the presence of the mother's male sexual partner, whose relationship to the daughter is ambiguous.

DIVORCE AND REMARRIAGE: SOME LESSONS

What can be learned from these two chapters on divorce and remarriage? The evidence we have reviewed suggests three themes. First, the emphasis on personal fulfillment, the growth of women's economic independence, and the worsening economic prospects for young men since 1973 have made marriage more fragile. There is simply less glue holding couples together than there was a half century ago. Second, divorce, remarriage, nonmarital childbearing, and cohabitation are increasing the frequency with which people create their own kinship ties out of the many possibilities available to them—rather than accepting the set of relatives that automatically come with first marriages. These efforts, like the efforts of poor people in creating sharing networks and of gay men and lesbians in constructing friend-based ties, are changing the nature of kinship. Third, the increases in single-parent families and stepfamilies have altered many children's lives, causing short-term distress, increasing the risk of long-term harm, but leaving the majority relatively unscathed. Let us consider the implications of the developments.

THE PRIMACY OF THE PRIVATE FAMILY

The first theme, it seems to me, is this: The transformation of divorce from a highly restricted device used by wealthy men to protect against unwanted heirs, to a frowned-upon but tolerated option for disastrous marriages, and finally to an individual right for anyone whose marriage isn't personally fulfilling, represents a triumph of the private family. The changes in divorce law mirror changes in the way marriage has been viewed. Once it was an economic partnership in which sentiment was secondary and men were the masters of their homes. The public functions of marriage were dominant: reproducing the population (which wasn't an easy task given widespread disease and poverty), educating children, preparing them for their adult roles, and caring for the ill and the elderly. This is not to say that people didn't find their marriages satisfying, but satisfaction was likely to come primarily from keeping a family alive and fed, from passing one's craft on to one's children, or from marrying a daughter into a good family.

Those days are gone. With the rise of the private family in the twentieth century, marriage is now primarily an instrument of individual fulfillment, a means of personal growth, an expression of romantic love. As such, it is much more fragile, more vulnerable to crises, than ever before. When men and women each specialized in certain tasks and pooled their labor, their economic partnership tied them together. Now that the division of labor is less pronounced and men and women are more economically independent of each other, marriage is held together mainly by the bonds of sentiment.

It is easy to criticize the narcissistic excesses of the search for personal fulfillment in marriage. But as even some radical critics have understood, the expansion
of private life has been a great social advance (Zaretsky, 1986). It is an advance
that the standard of living of most people in our society is high enough that they
need not concern themselves daily with sustenance. It is an advance that they no
longer need to labor 12 hours a day on the farm or in the factory. It is an advance
that they have the time to pursue gratifying intimate relationships and that they
have the luxury of marrying purely for love.

The changing nature of marriage has also been an advance for women. Once
unable to sever a marriage unless they were subject to terrible cruelty, women
(and men) now have the ability to divorce unilaterally. This option must provide
them with greater leverage against the worst excesses of husband dominance. Nor
do they need to marry as much as their ancestors did. Yet the gains for women
have come at a price. A half century ago, when divorce was more difficult to obtain and stigmatizing to live with, wives who specialized in rearing children could
be reasonably sure that their husbands would not abandon them. It was safe for
them to withdraw from the labor market and let their earning power atrophy because their husbands, according to the bargain, would have to provide for them.
Today they no longer have that protection. Choosing to be a homemaker is far
riskier than it was in the 1950s. Just ask any of the older, divorced women who
lived up to their part of the breadwinner-homemaker bargain only to see their
husbands leave them.

A central contradiction of the current era of divorce, then, is that the law assumes that husbands and wives are economic equals, when in fact they still are
not. To be sure, women's wages have increased enough that life as a single parent
is much more feasible than it was a few decades ago. Still, if a woman chooses to
end her marriage, she must often accept a steep drop in her standard of living, like
a nun taking a vow of poverty before entering an order. And if a woman chooses
to stay home and raise children, she cannot count on the lifetime support of her
husband.

Men, however, are not the winners in every divorce. They, too, pay a cost
under the new regime. The men who have gained the most are those who care
the least about their children. Divorce law allows these men to walk away from
their wives and children for a modest monthly fee; sadly, many do. The men who
pay the highest price are those who care the most about being a daily part of their
children's lives—for they no longer have the guarantee that if they fulfill their hus-
bandly responsibilities, their wives will remain with them. On the contrary, if their
wives initiate a divorce, they know they are likely to lose custody of their children,
or at best to share it.

What, then, would we expect prudent women and men to do to protect themselves in the current system of unilateral divorce? A woman would be wise to develop good labor market skills in young adulthood and to maintain a connection to
the labor market throughout her childrearing years. In fact, the trends in married
women's employment are consistent with this strategy. A man who cares about living
with his children would be wise to spend a substantial amount of time on childrearing throughout his marriage. That way his claims to his children will be far stronger
in a custody dispute, should one arise. Although men seem to be doing somewhat
more childrearing, this strategy isn't much in evidence. Perhaps men, on average,
don't care as much about rearing their children as women do. Perhaps their resistance to household work is still too strong. Nevertheless, given the costs of the new

system, we are likely to see continued investment by married women in developing job skills and careers and increased investment by men in caring for their children.

NEW KINSHIP TIES

Divorce, nonmarital childbearing, cohabitation, and remarriage are altering kinship in two fundamental ways that aren't yet fully appreciated. First, they are breaking the correspondence between family and household. Until recently, the unchallenged family unit in Western nations was the conjugal family of husband, wife, and children residing in the same household. At some points in the life cycle of the family they might welcome elderly parents, or young servants and apprentices, into their household. To be sure, the conjugal family members had many relatives living in other households. There was, however, a clear demarcation between the members of one's own household, who were the core of the family system, and those beyond the household's boundaries, who were the periphery. The correspondence between family and household is so deeply ingrained that we take it for granted. For example, our entire government apparatus for collecting statistics on "families" actually surveys households. The official Bureau of the Census definition of a family is two or more people living in the same household and related by blood, marriage, or adoption. Tell that to Bruce. This dinosaur of a definition is unlikely to survive for very long. But what will replace it is unclear. Statistically, we may have to give up the idea that we can count families simply by knocking on doors. We may have to accept that a family can be defined only in reference to a person, not a household.

Second, the rise in divorce, nonmarital childbearing, cohabitation, and remarriage is increasing the importance of what I have called created kinship, the ties that people have to actively construct, as opposed to assigned kinship, the ties that people automatically acquire at birth or through first marriage. In this regard, kinship after divorce and remarriage is similar to the extended kin networks among low-income and racial-ethnic populations and to the efforts of gay men and lesbians to form alternative families. In all these situations, individuals find it in their interest to build their own family ties. Being a father or a mother was once a status assigned to a person automatically at the birth of his or her child. To be sure, people have children through their own efforts; nevertheless, one does not have to do anything else to be a parent, nor can one easily resign from the post. Being a grandparent was ascribed similarly. All that is still the case when children are born to, and raised by, two married parents.

The creation of stepfamilies, though, adds a number of other potential kinship positions. Whether these positions are filled depends on the actions of the individuals involved. The most obvious positions are stepfather and stepmother. This chapter has described the wide variation in the roles stepparents play. Some are parentlike figures who are intensely involved with their stepchildren. Many others are more like friends or uncles and aunts. Others, particularly stepparents who don't live with their stepchildren every day, are more distant. In all cases, how much like a family member a stepparent becomes depends in large part on the effort he or she puts into developing a close relationship with stepchildren and also on the stepchild's actions. Intergenerational ties to stepgrandparents are even more dependent on individual action; they range from no contact to a kinlike role, depending in large part on the investment the stepgrandparents make.

Yet the challenge of created kinship is as follows: Kinship ties that can be created by people's actions can also be ended by lack of action. In contrast, it is much harder to end assigned kinship ties. Therefore, created kinship ties are more likely to change over the course of one's life than assigned kinship ties. Created ties may even change from year to year, as a stepparent moves into or out of the household or as contact diminishes with a stepgranddaughter who moves out of state. Just as containment within one household made families easy to spot, so, too, assignment at birth and first marriage made kinship easy to track. Now, family and kinship require new mental maps that can change from year to year. We are just beginning to draw them.

THE IMPACT ON CHILDREN

There is, finally, the important question of the effects of divorce and stepfamily life on children. I would argue that the effects are neither minor nor massive. On the one hand, the evidence suggests that most children who experience these events do not have serious, long-lasting problems because of them. Still, it must be said that we have not studied this topic long enough and intensively enough to reach a definitive conclusion. Evidence might come in over the next several years that changes this picture. Right now, however, the evidence suggests that divorce and stepfamily life do not inevitably scar children. On the other hand, it is clear that a minority of children do experience lasting problems that appear to be caused by divorce and remarriage. Some of these problems might have occurred even if the children's families had remained intact. Other problems, though, seem clearly linked to the disruption and its aftermath.

Let us suppose, for the sake of argument, that 10 percent of children from two-parent homes will grow up to have serious mental health problems as adults. Further, let us suppose that the prevalence of serious mental health problems is twice as high—20 percent—among children from maritally disrupted homes. A little algebra will show that if 4 in 10 children experience marital disruption (as current levels imply), the overall rate of serious mental health problems in the population would rise to 14 percent when this generation reaches adulthood.[9] An overall rise from an expected 10 percent (if there were no divorce in the population) to 14 percent may not seem like much. But it would require a 40 percent expansion of mental health facilities around the country and the training of 40 percent more mental health professionals. At current population levels, it would alter the lives of an additional three million people in each generation. It would mean that about 1 in 7, rather than 1 in 10, adults might need clinical help. In sum, it would mean a significant decline in mental health.

Consequently, even if only a minority of children will experience long-term problems, we should be troubled by this possibility. Some people might wish to work toward reducing the divorce rate. Although that is a worthy goal, it is unlikely to succeed (see Chapter 16). If the divorce rate can't be reduced much by government activity, we might wish to assist divorcing parents and children. We might promote conflict-resolution strategies for divorcing couples, urge that children be kept out of conflict, and provide guidelines on how to minimize the impact of divorce. We might wish to enforce child support obligations and guarantee custodial parents a minimum benefit. We might wish to encourage support groups and services in schools. In sum, we might take whatever steps we can to reduce the negative effects of divorce and remarriage on children.

[9]$(.40 \times .20) + (.60 \times .10) = .14$, or 14 percent.

SUMMARY

1. Remarriages that involve children from a previous marriage create situations in which well-established rules about everyday family life don't apply. In that sense, remarriage is incompletely institutionalized.

2. Most remarriages today occur following a divorce rather than a death. Remarriage is more likely among non-Hispanic whites than among Hispanics or African Americans. The rate of remarriage among divorced persons has fallen since the 1960s, but a rise in cohabitation among the divorced has compensated for the fall. Remarriages are somewhat more likely to end in divorce than first marriages because of the complexity of stepfamilies and the self-selection of people who are prone to divorce into the remarried population.

3. Stepfamilies have traditionally been defined in terms of remarriages that follow divorce; but the growth of nonmarital childbearing and cohabitation suggests an expanded definition that includes households in which two adults are married or cohabiting and at least one of them has a child present from a previous marriage or relationship.

4. Remarriage can bring ties across households if children from previous marriages or unions are involved. One way to define a family in this context is to focus on a household that contains a parent with children from a previous union and that parent's current partner. A second way is to identify remarriage chains, paths that link individuals across households through the ties of disrupted union and new unions. Remarriage chains can serve as support and exchange networks, although cooperation is less assured than in other kinds of kin networks.

5. Americans reckon kinship through "blood" or marriage. But even among potential blood relatives, a personal relationship must be established in order for the kinship bond to be recognized—except among the closest of kin, such as parents and children. Stepparents and other steprelatives must do the work of creating and maintaining relationships in order to be recognized as kin. There is great variability in how successful steprelatives are at becoming like kin. The stepparent role most commonly seems to become something between a parent and a stranger, perhaps a kindly uncle or aunt.

6. Stepparents must enter a family system that has been created by the custodial parent and her children. The key task for the adults in the household is to establish their own relationship as the center of the family system. Working with little guidance, they must create a shared conception of how their family is to run. It can be harder to be a stepmother than a stepfather during this process; for several reasons, stepmothers face more competition from biological mothers than stepfathers do from biological fathers. In low-income households, however, stepfathers must sometimes enter a family system in which there is some tension between a young mother and her mother over how to raise the young mother's child. Stepparents who meet these challenges can play valuable and unique roles in their stepchildren's lives.

7. Many studies now show that the well-being of children in stepfamilies is no better, on average, than the well-being of children in divorced, single-parent households. Both groups show lower levels of well-being than children in two-biological-parent families. Some studies have found a more difficult adjustment during early adolescence. Several studies now show that children in stepfamilies leave home earlier than children in other family arrangements, and this difference seems to be more pronounced for girls.

8. Divorce, nonmarital childbearing, cohabitation after divorce, and remarriage have altered family life in important ways. First, marriage is now more fragile and vulnerable to crises because of the emphasis on personal fulfillment and the economic independence of women and men. Second, the nature of kinship is being altered. The correspondence between household and family is breaking down. And people are constructing kinship ties rather than accepting the kinds of ties that are assigned to couples who marry for the first time. Third, these family forms are causing many children short-term distress and increasing the risk of long-term harm but leaving the majority without serious long-term problems.

KEY TERMS

stepfamily

remarriage chain

blood relatives

bilateral kinship

intimate outsider

FAMILIES ON THE INTERNET

There are a number of organizations of stepfamily members and helping professionals on the Web. The Stepfamily Association of America (**www.stepfam. org**) is one of the oldest and largest associations that provide education and support to stepfamilies. The site has a digest of facts about stepfamilies, with references, and articles that provide advice to step-parents. The Stepfamily Association of Illinois (**www.parentsplace.com/readroom/stepfamily/ index.html**) maintains a large site with numerous educational and advice-giving pages.

PART FIVE

Links across the Generations

Ending a marriage or starting a remarriage are just two of the ways that adults' actions can affect the lives of children. How adequately parents are meeting their overall responsibilities for raising children is a topic of much discussion and concern. In addition, working-age adults bear most of the responsibility for supporting and taking care of the elderly. The increasing number of elderly persons raises the question of whether family care will continue to be adequate. In the terms of this book, the issue is whether the public family is meeting its caretaking responsibilities for children and the elderly and, if it isn't, then why not.

Chapter 14 examines the care of children by their parents. No public issue involving the family has received more attention in recent years than the well-being of children. The chapter begins by asking two questions: What are parents supposed to do for children? And what might prevent parents from doing what they are supposed to do? It then evaluates the complex question of whether children's well-being has declined.

In **Chapter 15,** the focus shifts from the young to the old. The chapter first reviews the substantial changes that have occurred in the lives of the elderly during the twentieth century. It subsequently examines levels of contact, affection, and assistance between the elderly and their adult children. Then it discusses whether changes in health, income, and intergenerational relations have led to greater or lesser well-being among the elderly.

CHAPTER 14

Children and Parents

On her midyear report card in 1993, Crystal Rossi, a seventh-grader in Brooklyn, New York, got a 65 in social studies and failing grades in English, math, science, foreign language, and physical education. She is 12 years old, white, and lives with her mother and stepfather. Her father lives a few blocks away. "The classes are boring," she told a *New York Times* reporter (Manegold, 1993). "Kids who study are all nerds. Who'd want to be like that? Everybody makes fun of them." An assistant principal told the reporter, "We have already sent the family an 'at risk' letter. She's on a decline."

Crystal said she wants to be a lawyer because "you get to talk back to people" and "you make a lot of money." But she has never met one. In fact, if Crystal were to graduate from high school, she would be the first person in her family to

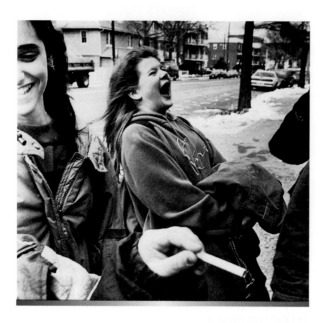

Crystal Rossi laughs with friends outside her junior high school in Brooklyn, New York, in 1993.

do so. Her mother tells her to do her homework but conceded to the reporter that she rarely checks to see if it is done. Threatening to send Crystal to her room doesn't do much good: She and her sister share a television, VCR, radio, Nintendo system, and their own telephone line.

On the streets—and even in the school's halls—Crystal faces crime, violence, and drugs. She has tried alcohol and cigarettes but not, she says, marijuana, LSD, or crack. Still, she knows kids who have tried them all: "Everybody drinks," she said. "They drink and do acid in the park." She has friends who have joined one of the two girls' gangs, Bitches on a Mission and Five Million Hoodlums. "They can protect you," she told the reporter. "They can keep you safe."

Crystal talks tough but is vulnerable underneath. "I'm always nervous," she confided. "I get nervous over nothing. And then I'll get a really big headache. . . . Sometimes I can't even sleep. I stay up all night and then I'm too tired to get up in the morning."

Lafayette Rivers was 10, and his brother Pharoah 7, when a reporter first met them in a largely black public housing project in Chicago (Kotlowitz, 1991). Their high-rise building sat in a neighborhood vacated by middle-class whites and blacks alike. Their parents had separated, and their father—steadily employed but addicted to drugs—rarely showed up. Shootings were an almost daily occurrence; sometimes children were killed in the crossfire. When the reporter asked Lafayette what he wanted to be, he replied, "If I grow up, I'd like to be a bus driver." *If* I grow up—Lafayette wasn't sure he would.

Given the horrible violence in his neighborhood, his fear was perfectly understandable. His mother certainly thought so—she had recently begun paying $80 per month out of her public assistance check for burial insurance for Lafayette, Pharoah, and her younger triplets. Her three eldest children had already been in drug-related trouble with the law. A 20-year-old daughter worked occasionally as a prostitute to support her drug habit. A 19-year-old son had been imprisoned for burglary. A 17-year-old son had been selling drugs since he was 11.

When they heard gunfire outside their first-floor apartment, Lafayette and Pharoah knew to run into the hallway and dive onto the floor. During the summer of his ninth year, Pharoah developed a stammer that worsened as the shooting wore on. He listened to classical music on the radio, he said, because it relaxed him. During one incident, as bullets whizzed by the apartment, a stuttering Pharoah asked his mother to make them stop. Then he fainted. In his quest for safety and peace, he would sit on the lawn of a calm condominium three blocks from the project until someone shooed him away.

Rachel, 14, lives a life of privilege that Crystal, Lafayette, and Pharoah see only on television. She resides in an exclusive neighborhood of an Eastern city and attends an expensive private school. It is taken for granted that she will attend college. Yet she is drifting toward trouble. Some nights, she sneaks out of the house where she lives with her mother, a lawyer, and her stepfather, a pharmacist, to rendezvous with boys. She and her girlfriends smoke marijuana and drink together, occasionally stealing liquor bottles from their parents' cabinets. She has a difficult relationship with her biological father, whom she visits once a month. Her grades aren't good, and her teachers are worried about her.

The Crystals, Lafayettes, Pharoahs, and Rachels are all too common in the United States. More than one in five children lives in poverty (U.S. Department of Health and Human Services, 1997). One in nine 15- to 19-year-old girls becomes pregnant every year (U.S. Department of Health and Human Services, 1997). Firearm homicide is the leading cause of death for black teenage males (Federal Interagency Forum on Child and Family Statistics, 1997). About 4 in 10 children will witness the breakup of their parents' marriage before they reach 18, and perhaps 1 in 10 will witness a divorce, a remarriage, and a second divorce (Bumpass, 1984). Grim statistics such as these have led to a growing sense of concern about the well-being of American children. Is their quality of life deteriorating? Is our society failing to meet their needs?

Much of that concern centers on the family. Some critics charge that the institution of the family is not providing children with the care, supervision, and discipline they need to become well-adjusted, productive adults—that it is failing in perhaps the central responsibility of the public family. If one agrees with that charge (and not everyone does), it leads to another important question: To what extent are larger social forces such as the restructuring of the economy, racial discrimination, and the cultural drift toward individual autonomy and self-fulfillment undermining the ability of the family to raise children well? These are difficult questions, about which observers have strong, conflicting opinions. Although this chapter can't provide definitive answers, it can introduce you to the extensive social scientific evidence that scholars and policymakers have produced in recent years.

WHAT ARE PARENTS SUPPOSED TO DO FOR CHILDREN?

First, however, we need to ask what it is that parents are supposed to do for their children. For the first several years of life, at least, families provide the main setting in which children's fundamental needs are met. What are the lessons children need to learn from their families, and how are those lessons shaped by social forces such as class, race, and gender? What behaviors by parents provide the best foundation for children's development?

SOCIALIZATION

Virtually all children are raised in a family of some kind. Parents, and sometimes other adult relatives, supply most of the love, nurturing, and care that children need in order to develop a basic sense of trust in other human beings. They also train young children in the skills they need to become more autonomous, such as walking, dressing, and feeding themselves. Later they provide the guidance, support, and discipline children need in order to become competent members of their society. In other words, family members socialize their children (see Chapter 3 for a definition of socialization). Indeed, families are the major source of primary socialization—the settings for the first lessons children learn about their society.

Socialization begins early in life. Consider the acquisition of language. Learning to talk not only allows children to communicate with others, it also carries important lessons about their society. A French child learns two words for *you:* Siblings and friends are called *tu,* and parents and other adults are called *vous.* Thus the child learns which relationships are characterized by equality and intimacy and which are characterized by respect and social distance. A Japanese girl learns to show deference to men by addressing them differently than she does women. At a conference I attended in Tokyo, a female Japanese professor was criticized by a male colleague—in Japanese. She replied to him in English. When asked later why she responded in English, she said that, had she chosen Japanese, she would have had to use the "respect language" a polite woman must employ when addressing a man. In English, she could fight back as a linguistic equal.

Socialization also involves teaching children norms and values. **Norms** are widely accepted rules about how people should behave. **Values** are goals and principles that are held in high esteem by a society. The norms and values may be those of

Japanese mothers carry their children with them more than American mothers, which is one reason why Japanese children learn to depend on other people more, and to act individually less, than American children.

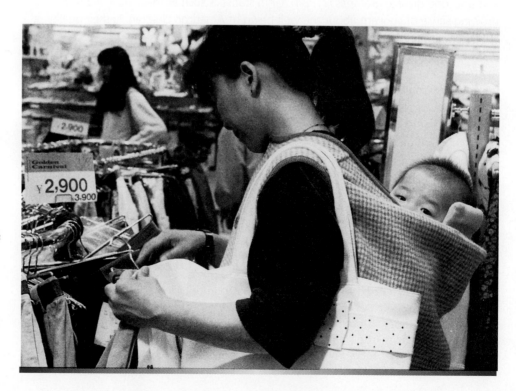

the dominant culture in the society, of a subculture, or of both. Families begin this process; schools, churches, peer groups, and even the media carry it on. For example, Japanese children learn to place a higher value on loyalty to the group in situations where an American child would learn to value independent action. Their greater dependence on others begins in the first few years of life. Japanese mothers tend to wean their children from breast-feeding later than American mothers. They also carry their children on their backs when they go shopping and often sleep with them (Preston & Kono, 1988). Childrearing manuals in Japan urge parents to emphasize the child's dependence on the family. A leading manual discounts the importance of teaching a baby to eat vegetables or any particular kind of food; rather, its author stresses the importance of teaching the baby to eat with the family and to share the same food (Boocock, 1991). Japanese preschool teachers seem to be more lenient than American teachers in allowing rough play and noise, but the Japanese teachers treat a child's reluctance to participate in group activities as a more serious problem. A reluctant child will experience more pressure to join the group in a Japanese setting than in an American preschool (Boocock, 1991).

SOCIALIZATION AS SUPPORT AND CONTROL

As parents socialize their children, they act in two broad ways (Peterson & Rollins, 1987). First, they provide emotional support—love, affection, warmth, nurturing, or acceptance. Emotional support shows children that parents care about their actions. It makes children feel more positively about themselves. Because children want to continue receiving such support, they try to act in ways they think will please their parents. Second, parents exercise control—they seek to limit or change children's behavior. Sometimes parental control is coercive, consisting of the use or threat of punishment or force. But control also may be inductive, that is, based on setting consistent limits, explaining the reasons for these limits to the child, requesting that the child comply, and praising her or his compliance. Parents may also exercise control by threatening to withdraw their love if the child does not behave well.

Numerous studies have examined the ways in which parents combine various aspects of support and control. In what is probably the most influential analysis, psychologist Diana Baumrind distinguished among three styles of parental behavior (Baumrind, 1971). In the **authoritative style**, parents combine high levels of emotional support with inductive control. Children are provided with warmth and affection and with firm, consistent discipline. But the discipline is moderate and is based on requests and explanations rather than on the use of force or punishment. Baumrind and others claim that authoritative parenting produces children who are more socially competent—meaning that they have higher self-esteem, cooperate better with others, develop a better moral sense, and are more independent (Peterson & Rollins, 1987). The two other styles of behavior, it is claimed, produce children who are less competent and who may show more behavior problems, anxiety, or depression. In the **permissive style**, parents provide support but exercise little control over their children by any means. And in the **authoritarian style**, parents combine low support with coercive attempts at control. The implication of this research tradition is that children are socialized best when parents set clear standards, enforce them consistently but without harsh punishment, and provide substantial emotional support. One can spare the rod without spoiling the child, it seems, but setting no limits on children's behavior is virtually as bad as relying solely on the stick.

SOCIALIZATION AND SOCIAL CLASS

Several studies show strong differences between working-class and middle-class parents in how they socialize their children. In Chapter 4, social class was defined as an ordering of all persons according to their degrees of power, privilege, and prestige. Middle-class families were defined as those with secure, comfortable incomes that allow them to live well above subsistence, whereas working-class families were defined as those whose incomes provide only for the minimum needs for a decent life. In much of the literature on social class and socialization, class is defined according to the occupation of the father. Families are said to be working class if the father (or the mother, if no father is present) holds a blue-collar job such as a laborer, mechanic, factory worker, or truck driver. Correspondingly, families are said to be middle class if the father holds a white-collar job such as office worker, manager, accountant, or lawyer. As Chapter 4 noted, this focus on the father is an oversimplification; nevertheless, the literature is well worth examining.

Beginning in the 1960s, Melvin Kohn pioneered a line of research showing the connections between the conditions a person experiences on the job and his or her childrearing values (Kohn, 1969). Working-class employees, for the most part, are closely supervised, work with physical objects (trash, trucks, bricks), and perform simple tasks repetitively (as on an automobile assembly line). It is important for workers in these jobs to obey their supervisors and to accept the discipline of doing repetitive tasks. In contrast, middle-class workers are less closely supervised, usually work with data (e.g., as would computer programmers) or people (as would personnel managers), and perform a variety of tasks (as would physicians). Middle-class jobs encourage more independence than working-class jobs and often reward creativity and individual initiative.

When working-class and middle-class parents are asked to select the most important characteristics that children should have, their preferences reflect their occupational positions. Working-class parents are more likely to select obedience to authority, conformity, and good manners, whereas middle-class parents are more likely to select independence, self-direction, curiosity, and responsibility (Alwin, 1990). Working-class parents emphasize the kinds of characteristics their children would need if they were to enter blue-collar jobs. To work on an assembly line for 40 years requires obedience and conformity; someone who is creative and independent might have a harder time tolerating the job. In contrast, to be a successful manager requires independence and initiative.

Thus, each class socializes its children to fill the same positions their parents have filled. Because of his or her conformist upbringing, a child from a working-class family may be less successful as a manager than a self-directed child from the middle class. In this way, socialization by parents both is influenced by and helps to perpetuate the social class divisions in the United States and similar developed societies. Some authors believe that schools often fulfill a similar function. Working-class children, it is argued, are more likely to be assigned to nonacademic tracks in which discipline and rote learning are emphasized, whereas middle-class children are assigned to college preparatory tracks in which creativity and initiative are emphasized (Bowles & Gintis, 1976).

Kohn's model assumes that occupational conditions affect people's values and ways of thinking. It is possible that the effects run in the opposite direction: People who value independence may try harder to find jobs that provide independence.

Or some underlying characteristic—such as intellectual ability—may influence both a person's preference for independence and the type of job she or he obtains. Kohn's later research, in which people were monitored over time, suggests that the effects run both ways: Jobs' conditions affect people's ways of thinking, and their ways of thinking affect the kinds of jobs they obtain in the future (Kohn & Schooler, 1978).

These social class differences in childrearing values have existed since at least the early decades of the twentieth century. Nearly half a century after the Lynds took up temporary residence in Muncie, Indiana, to write *Middletown* (Lynd & Lynd, 1929), a team of sociologists returned to Muncie to see what had changed and what had not (Caplow, Bahr, Chadwick, Hill, & Williamson, 1982). The Lynds had asked 143 married mothers to select, from a list of 15 qualities of children, the three qualities they thought most important in childrearing. In 1978, the study team asked the same questions of 333 married mothers in Muncie. The list included qualities reflecting both conformity (strict obedience, loyalty to church, good manners) and self-direction (independence, tolerance, curiosity). Figure 14.1 shows the results, which were tabulated by Duane Alwin, for "strict obedience" and "independence"; the other qualities showed a similar pattern (Alwin, 1988).

The figure shows the percentage of mothers who selected each characteristic as one of the three most important. For instance, more than 40 percent of both the working-class and "business-class" mothers interviewed in 1924 selected "strict obedience" as one of the three most important characteristics. (The Lynds' "business class" is similar to the "middle-class" definition used in this chapter.) Two conclusions can be deduced from the figure. First, in both the 1920s and the 1970s, business-class mothers were somewhat less likely to think obedience was important and, by larger margins, were more likely to think that independence was important. So the class differences in childrearing values do exist; moreover, they seem to be long-standing and not just the result of recent social change.

Second, between the 1920s and the 1970s, *both* working-class and business-class mothers have come to place less importance on obedience and more on independence. In other words, during the twentieth century there has been a shift in emphasis among all mothers away from encouraging conformity and toward

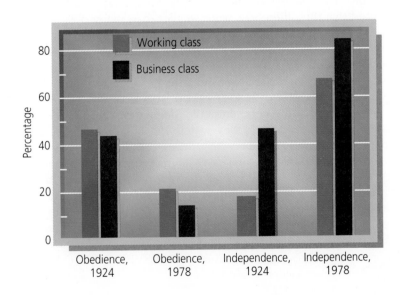

FIGURE 14.1
Percentage selecting characteristics as one of the three most important emphases in childrearing, by class, Middletown data, 1924 and 1978. (*Source:* Alwin, 1990.)

encouraging self-direction.[1] We know that educational levels in the population increased during the century; in the 1920s, a typical blue-collar worker would not have finished high school; by the 1970s, he or she probably would have. The typical white-collar worker would have gone from being a high school graduate to a college attender. As the level of education increased, it may be that parents became more adept at manipulating data and mastering complex logic—the kinds of skills that are said to lead toward a greater emphasis on self-direction. Kohn wrote that "education provides the intellectual flexibility and breadth of perspective that are essential for self-directed values and orientation" (Kohn, 1969).

Alternatively, I would add, the rising value that American (and, more generally, Western) culture has placed on individual autonomy in the twentieth century may explain the historical trend. As noted elsewhere in this book, the rise in divorce, the increase in cohabitation, and the decline in fertility are among the trends that suggest an increased cultural emphasis on individualism. Alwin makes a similar argument: He suggests that secularization—the decline of moral values linked to religion—may have affected parents across class lines and therefore caused the historical drift away from conformity. In support of the latter proposition, he reports that the percentage of mothers who selected "loyalty to church" also declined among both the working class and the business class between the 1920s and the 1970s.

These studies and others like them show that there are indeed social class differences in the ways in which parents socialize their children. These differences affect, and are affected by, people's occupational experiences. Parents stress values that are consistent with the occupations of people in their social class. In this way, they transmit the class inequalities of their generation to their children's generation. Nevertheless, parents in both working and middle classes have drifted during this century toward a greater emphasis on the importance of autonomy and self-direction.

SOCIALIZATION AND GENDER

Chapter 3 presented evidence that parents socialize their daughters differently than their sons; here that discussion will be briefly summarized. Although an early review suggested that the differences were smaller than many observers had thought (Maccoby & Jacklin, 1974), many studies have since claimed that parents do indeed treat their daughters and sons differently (Block, 1984). The distinctions parents make may reflect, in part, biologically based differences between girls and boys (Rossi, 1984); yet parents' actions also tend to magnify and exaggerate gender differences. The emphasis in sociological studies of this process has been on the conscious social learning children do as they are rewarded for some behaviors and punished for others—and as they watch and imitate adults of the same gender. In addition, girls and boys may also develop different senses of self because of unconscious, psychoanalytic processes of merging and separating from those who were their primary caretakers as infants, who are nearly always women (Chodorow, 1978). Schools, peer groups, and the media further exaggerate gender differences, so that adult gender roles are far more distinctive than any biological differences might warrant. The stereotypical adult gender roles leave men with substantially more economic power than women (Lipman-Blumen, 1984).

---

[1]Alwin (1988) provides further evidence of this shift.

WHAT'S IMPORTANT?

Social class and gender differences do exist, then, in how children are socialized. Nevertheless, it is possible to make some general statements about what parents are supposed to do. First, they should provide support to their children. This includes material support such as food, clothes, and shelter, as well as emotional support such as love and nurturing. The need for the former is obvious: Without material support, the child is in physical danger. Yet without emotional support, she or he is likely to grow up without a sense of security or a capability for trusting and loving other people. Second, parents should provide control. They must supervise and monitor their children's behavior not only to help them avoid physical harm but also to teach children the limits of acceptable behavior. This control, developmental psychologists state, needs to be consistent, rather than varying and unpredictable, and firm but moderate, rather than explosive and punitive.

One could supplement this basic list according to one's values. Some might stress the importance of religious and ethical training—an upbringing that teaches children about the spiritual and moral side of life. Those who believe that people of both genders should undertake a wide range of behaviors that are now stereotyped as masculine or feminine—who believe, for example, that men should provide more care for children and women should have better opportunities for careers—might add that parents should encourage more **androgynous behavior** (i.e., behavior that has the characteristics of both genders) in their children. From this perspective, boys should be encouraged to be more nurturing and girls more aggressive. Similarly, those who believe that the values passed along to working-class children limit their occupational achievements might add that parents of all classes ought to encourage autonomous behavior in their children.

WHAT DIFFERENCE DO FATHERS MAKE?

Most of the research literature on parenting focuses on mothers rather than fathers. This focus is understandable because mothers do most of the childrearing in nearly all societies. Over the past decade or two, however, studies of the role of fathers in childrearing have begun to appear. The increased interest in fathers is the result of two factors:

- The feminist movement has urged that fathers share more of the tasks of childrearing with mothers. Those who urge fathers to do more have an interest in showing that fathers' involvement makes a difference.
- The growth of single-mother families due to divorce and childbearing outside of marriage has created concern about father absence (see Chapter 12). It has also generated studies suggesting that, on average, children do better in two-parent families than in single-parent families.

One unfortunate consequence of the interest in single-parent families, however, is that much of the research on fathers' influence is based on families where fathers are absent; researchers typically assume that the families' problems are a result of the absence. But this is not an adequate way to understand what it is that fathers do for children. What's needed are studies that actually examine families in which fathers are present. Of late, studies of father presence are beginning to accumulate; and they suggest that fathers do make a difference. For example, Mosley and Thomson (1995) examined information from two-parent families in the 1987–1988

National Survey of Families and Households. They found that in both white and African-American families where fathers were more involved with their children (e.g., reading, helping with homework, restricting television viewing), the children had fewer behavior problems, got along better with others, and were more responsible—even controlling for the mothers' involvement with the children and the racial and social class background of the family. Still, the quality of the literature is uneven, and it is difficult to draw firm conclusions. With that caveat, here is what the literature suggests about the difference fathers make in their children's lives:

Fathers Relate to Young Children Differently Than Do Mothers   Fathers relate to young children in part through a vigorous style of play that is often labeled "rough and tumble" in the literature. Picture a father throwing his toddler up in the air and catching her, or rolling on the floor with her, and you have the idea. Psychological studies suggest that these active play sessions help children learn to regulate their emotions (Parke, 1996). Children learn the limits of excitable behavior (e.g., no biting or kicking) and how to bring their emotions back down when it is over. These lessons, it is thought, lead them to be better playmates, to have more friends, and, in adolescence and adulthood, to have more self-control in highly charged situations.

Fathers' Influence Is Often Indirect   Fathers' influence often works through mothers rather than directly to the children. Fathers exercise this indirect influence in part through providing emotional support to mothers or backing up the mothers' authority. The better the quality of the father and mother's relationship, the better is the child's behavior and school achievement, on average (Amato, 1998). Fathers also provide income to the family—in fact, that has often been seen as their major contribution—although studies suggest that income by itself doesn't help children as much as does parental input (Mayer, 1997). Frank Furstenberg and I have speculated that one reason why some divorced fathers have difficulty relating to their children is that they are not used to interacting directly with them in a context where mothers are absent (Furstenberg & Cherlin, 1991).

Fathers' Influence on Children Shows Up in the Long Term As Well As Day-to-Day Life   Because mothers tend to be the more hands-on parent in everyday life, fathers' influence is likely to be more subtle and long-term. Consider a study of over 200 Boston-area men, who were first interviewed as schoolboys in the late 1940s and reinterviewed periodically for about 40 years. In the 1980s, John Snarey (1993) reinterviewed the men and their adult children to study the long-term effects of fathers' **generativity**— a term coined by psychologist Erik Erikson (1950) to mean concern about guiding and shaping the next generation. Using information from past interviews, Snarey rated each father's parental generativity—caring activities with children that developed or shaped their capacities, such as rocking to sleep or reading to younger children, or taking an older child to an art gallery or teaching him or her how to fish. He then asked the (now grown-up) children about their education and occupation. He found that in families where fathers had been more generative, the children had had greater educational and occupational success, even when he took into account other important characteristics of the parents and children.

Fathers' Influence on Daughters May Be Different from Fathers' Influence on Sons   Some studies suggest that fathers' involvement with daughters may be more consequential when they are adolescents than when they are younger (Hetherington, 1972). The theory

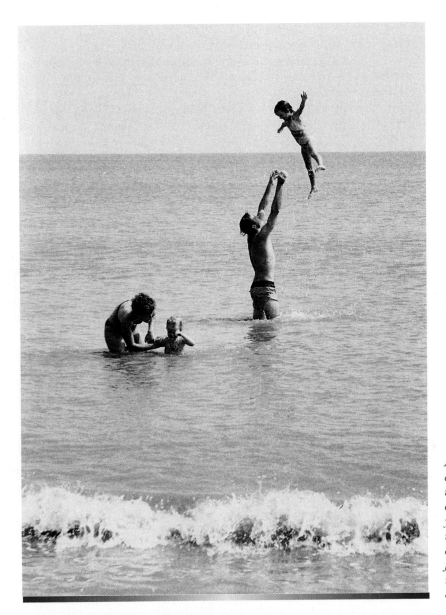

A father tosses his child into the air while a mother comforts their younger child, illustrating the different ways that fathers and mothers relate to their children.

is that adolescent girls' task is to separate from their mothers and learn to manage heterosexual relations. Involved fathers, it is said, help that process by providing safe (i.e., nonromantic) role models for their daughters (Parke, 1996). As for boys, father involvement may be more important when they are pre-adolescents, since this is the time in which they must separate from their mothers and identify as male. Indeed, Snarey (1993) found in the Boston study that fathers' generative activities prior to adolescence were important for their sons' achievements, whereas generative activities during adolescence were important for their daughters' achievements.

An Appraisal   This list is far from exhaustive; many other studies report effects of fathers on children. However, there are also many studies which have failed to find effects of fathers, and the stronger the research methodology, the less consistent are the effects. For example, studies that also control for mothers' influences and that interview both generations yield weaker evidence of the effects of fathers (Amato, 1998). This newly emerging research literature leaves the reader with two impressions: (1) fathers do have significant effects on children's development, but (2) fathers' effects are, in general, weaker than mothers' effects—especially in terms of the day-to-day behavior of children. As for the latter impression, it is hard to see how it could be otherwise: Mothers do far more of the childcare in the typical two-parent family than do fathers. One might predict that fathers' influence would be stronger in families where both parents shared the childcare responsibilities equally, but that topic remains to be studied.

Another unresolved question is whether any second adult in the household—a grandmother, a lesbian lover—can provide the same benefits to children or whether a father is needed. Some observers argue that men and women have evolved differing approaches to childrearing—as evidenced, for example, by fathers' rough and tumble play and mothers' greater nurturing—and, therefore, that a mother and father are needed (Popenoe, 1996). Many other sociologists would disagree and claim instead that fathers' behaviors aren't programmed by evolution but rather are learned from parents and peers; they would argue that the benefits of having a father rather than a different second caregiver are not proven. Unfortunately, the research evidence isn't sufficient to provide a clear answer; it may be that both evolutionary psychology and socialization contribute to shaping fathers' caregiving behaviors (Parke, 1996).

WHAT MIGHT PREVENT PARENTS FROM DOING WHAT THEY ARE SUPPOSED TO DO?

Yet even parents with the best intentions sometimes cannot care for their children and socialize them as well as they would like to. The larger society sometimes interferes, as when a parent loses a job or a family cannot climb out of poverty. The transformation of the U.S. economy over the past two decades, as discussed in Chapter 4, has hurt many parents and made childrearing more difficult. Social change also may interfere: Some observers have argued that recent changes in the organization of families make successful parenting more difficult. Among the changes causing these alleged difficulties are the great increase in the proportion of children who are cared for by someone other than a parent because their parents work for pay, the doubling of the divorce rate since the 1960s, and the increasing proportion of children born outside marriage. Newer arrangements, such as surrogate motherhood and children who live with lesbian or gay parents, have also generated interest and concern. In this section, the effects of these developments on the quality of parenting will be examined.

UNEMPLOYMENT, POVERTY, AND CHILDREARING

The literature on socialization ignores, for the most part, the family's income. "Support" in this literature means emotional support in most cases; it is as if the socialization theorists assume that all families provide children with an adequate level of income support. Of course, that is not true. On the most basic level, low income means fewer clothes and less food. It can mean being evicted from your apartment. It can mean that your children's bedroom has peeling, lead-filled paint.

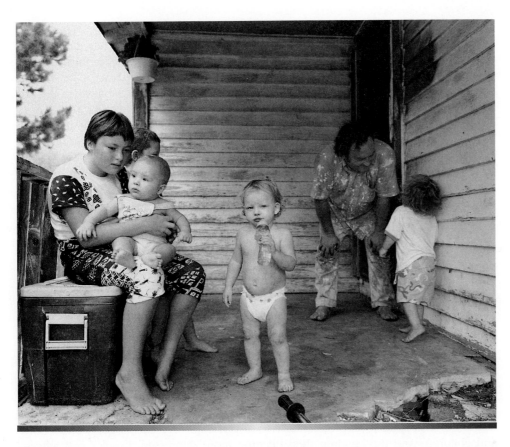

Eleven children live in poverty in this South Carolina house.

The effects of poverty on children can start before they are born. Pregnant, poor women are more likely to receive inadequate prenatal care and to engage in behaviors harmful to the fetus—such as smoking (which reduces birth weight), using drugs, and eating an unhealthy diet (Halpern, 1993).

In addition, the consequences of unemployment and poverty can be more subtle. As discussed in Chapter 10, they can change the ways parents act toward each other. They can also change the way parents and children interact. Consider the declining fortunes of agricultural communities in the American Midwest. In 1987, sociologist Glen Elder, psychologist Rand Conger, and several collaborators studied 76 families in a rural Iowa county (Elder, Conger, Foster, & Ardelt, 1992). All were white, a majority were middle class, and each consisted of a married couple and at least two children, one of whom was in seventh grade. After obtaining background information from the family members, the research team set up a video camera. While the tape rolled, they asked the parents to spend 30 minutes reviewing the history and present status of their marriage. Then they taped a 15-minute discussion in which the parents attempted to solve a problem in their marriage. They then taped one of the parents and the seventh-grader in two discussions: talking about a family activity and talking about a family problem such as doing chores or getting along with a younger sibling. Finally, they taped the other parent and the seventh-grader in the same two discussions. Over the next several months, trained raters viewed and reviewed the videotapes, coding the kinds of behaviors each person displayed, such as warmth, affection, or anger.

Unemployment   Nineteen of the fathers had lost their jobs, had had their hours cut back, or had been demoted in the preceding year. Other families had experienced a drop in income or very little growth. The researchers combined these events into a measure of how much "economic pressure" each family was facing. (Even though most of the mothers were employed outside the home, the researchers focused on fathers, who were still the main earners in nearly all the families.) Studies of families during the Great Depression had shown that men who had lost their jobs were tense and irritable in their relations with wives and explosive and punishing in their relations with their children (Liker & Elder, 1983). The tapes showed similar behavior: fathers in families under economic pressure were more irritable and hostile toward their wives and children. Their wives often replied in kind. One daughter said that at dinnertime "we are kinda cautious, like walking on hot ground or something" (Elder et al., 1992). The interviews revealed that fathers under economic pressure tended to be depressed, lacking energy and interest—moreso than their wives. One father said, "There would be some good days, but there would be more bad ones than good ones. Kind of lethargic. Oh, I know it's gotta be done, but I'll do it tomorrow. We kind of floated." Moreover, during the taped discussions, children whose fathers were more hostile and irritable were themselves more sullen, angry, and abrasive. In their interviews, these children admitted to more symptoms of depression (e.g., feeling lonely, hopeless, no interest) and aggressiveness (e.g., I am tempted to break a rule if I don't like it; I do the opposite of what a bossy person says; I yell back if I'm yelled at).

The study suggests a chain of events running from economic difficulties to children's behavior problems. The loss of a job or a drop in income causes psychological distress for the husband, who is still expected to be the family's main earner. The distress in turn leads to depression and to angry, explosive exchanges with his wife and children. And the children then become more depressed, hostile, and aggressive. It is possible, however, that causation could run the opposite way: Men who are depressed and hostile may be more likely to lose their jobs and to have children with similar characteristics. Still, the sequence proposed by the Iowa researchers is plausible and is supported by other studies (Kessler, House, & Turner, 1987).

Poverty   Studies of poor urban families show similar dynamics (McLoyd, 1990). Parents in poverty show patterns of childrearing not unlike the "authoritarian" style found among some working-class families. A parent in poverty may be depressed about job prospects, anxious about paying the bills, or angry about crime and drugs in the neighborhood. One mother receiving public assistance payments in New York City said, "Every month I have to decide which bill to pay, which doesn't give you a clear mind. You're always depressed" (Halpern, 1993). Such a parent has few psychological resources left to devote to her or his children. Instead of reasoning with the child or explaining why a certain behavior is good or bad, a depressed and anxious parent may respond to perceived misbehavior simply by threatening harsh punishment—but may then give in if the child refuses to obey. Thus, the child obtains little emotional support and receives discipline that is inconsistent, harsh, and punitive. As noted earlier, this style of parenting has been associated with diminished social competence among children. In this way, angry, depressed parents produce children who show lower self-esteem and more antisocial behavior. In fact, a 1986 national survey of young mothers found that those who had family incomes below the poverty line spanked their children more often and that the children were more disobedient, argumentative, bullying, and stubborn (McLeod & Shanahan, 1993).

It is more common among poor African-American children than among poor white children to be raised by a grandmother.

Single Mothers in Poverty   The problems are often magnified for single mothers living in persistent, long-lasting poverty. Some may be enmeshed in supportive kin networks, but others are isolated. Moreover, the kinship networks obligate hard-pressed mothers to provide assistance as well as allowing them to receive it. Studies suggest that isolated, low-income single mothers are particularly vulnerable to psychological distress. One study concluded, "the combination most productive of psychological distress is to be simultaneously single, isolated, exposed to burdensome parental obligations and—most serious of all—poor" (Pearlin & Johnson, 1977).[2] The 1986 survey found that children in persistently poor families were more anxious and depressed (McLeod & Shanahan, 1993).

Since such a large proportion of African-American children live in persistently poor, single-parent households, the distress lone mothers often experience is particularly consequential for their development. One research review suggests that poor black single mothers may be more vulnerable to psychological distress than white single mothers with comparable incomes because of the former's chronic economic difficulties (McLoyd, 1990). A higher proportion of black single mothers have never married, whereas a higher proportion of white single mothers are divorced. (See the *Families and Public Policy: Two Kinds of Single-Parent Families,* in Chapter 16.) The divorced mothers are more likely to have avoided economic problems prior to the breakup of their marriages; the never-married mothers are more likely to have lived persistently in poverty.

In addition, it is more common among poor black children than among poor white children to be raised by a grandmother—particularly among children whose

---

[2]Cited in McLoyd (1990).

mothers (and often grandmothers) were teenagers when they gave birth. In these families, teenage childbearing compresses the generations, producing grandmothers who are in their thirties and forties rather than their fifties (Burton, 1990). To be sure, many young grandmothers provide crucial support and excellent childcare. Moreover, the role of the grandmother in African-American families is stronger, in general, than in European-American families (see Chapter 5). Nevertheless, some grandmothers may not be at a life stage at which they expect to be caring for grandchildren, and they may be holding jobs themselves. Psychologist P. Lindsay Chase-Lansdale and her colleagues videotaped interactions between young African-American mothers and their children, and between grandmothers and the same children, in two kinds of families: those in which the three generations lived in the same household and those in which the grandmother lived in a separate household (Chase-Lansdale, Brooks-Gunn, & Zamsky, 1994). To the research group's surprise, the quality of parenting—by both the mother and the grandmother—was *lower* when the three generations lived in the same household. The only exception occurred when the mother had given birth in her early teens. It seems likely that a selection effect (see Chapter 8) is at work: Young mothers who have the financial and psychological resources to live on their own probably are more competent, on average, at raising a child. Mothers who have fewer resources are more likely to live with grandmothers. Joint residence is an arrangement often born of necessity. It should not be regarded as a solution to the problems of poor families.

DIVORCE AND REMARRIAGE

The most common way in which children come to live with a single parent is when their parents divorce. Chapters 12 and 13 examined the effects of divorce and remarriage on children. It was noted that in the first two years or so after the separation, most children are distressed. The custodial parent, usually the mother, often sees her income go down as the father withdraws much of his support; she may be forced to sell the family home and move to a new neighborhood. She may be so depressed and angry that she cannot provide the consistent support and supervision her children need. The children may be caught in the middle of continuing contact between the former spouses. This "crisis period" is typically a difficult time for both children and parents. Yet some of the problems that children display after a separation were present before the parents split up—suggesting that they might have occurred even had the parents stayed together.

Moreover, over the long term, as Chapter 12 noted, most children do not seem to suffer substantial harm because of their parents' divorce. To be sure, their risk of experiencing outcomes such as dropping out of school, having a child as a teenager, or receiving public assistance increases. The remarriage of a custodial parent, as Chapter 13 noted, does not appear to lower these risks—the well-being of children in stepfamilies is similar to that of children living with unmarried, divorced parents. These increased risks should be troubling to those who are concerned with children's well-being. Still, most children do not experience these undesirable outcomes; rather, most appear to enter adulthood without serious divorce-related problems. It is likely, then, that the increase in divorce has produced short-term trauma for most children and has, on average, reduced their long-term well-being moderately. I think the most prudent conclusion is that divorce is neither a benign event nor an automatic disaster for children. Over the years, most children appear to cope adequately with it and do not suffer serious harm. Yet it deserves to be a source of public concern because it adversely affects most children in the short run and a minority of children in the long run (Cherlin, 1992b).

SINGLE-PARENT FAMILIES

But what of the effects of single parenthood itself, apart from any effects of poverty or of divorce? What if, say, an unmarried middle-class woman decides, in the style of early-1990s television character Murphy Brown, to have a child? Some critics have claimed that, regardless of their income levels, single parents are hindered by the absence of a second parent. These claims are controversial because defenders of single parents counter that, given the appropriate resources, they can provide care that equals the quality of care by two-parent families (Young, 1994). There is little doubt that many of the problems single parents face can be traced to low incomes or to continuing conflicts with former spouses—and therefore could be eased by greater income support from ex-spouses or the government and a lessening of postmarital tensions. In this sense, single parents per se are capable of adequate parenting much more than critics contend. Even so, the presence of only one parent is sometimes a handicap, even after lower income is taken into account. An analysis of four national surveys found that low income, and declines in income, could account for about half the disadvantages of living in a single-parent family, such as the higher risk of dropping out of school or having a birth prior to marriage; yet half of the higher risks remained (McLanahan & Sandefur, 1994). Several studies show that single parents do not monitor and supervise their children as well as married or cohabiting parents. For instance, in a national survey of high school students, those in single-parent families were less likely to report that their parents kept close track of how they were doing in school than students from two-parent families. They were also less likely to report that their parents almost always knew where they were and what they were doing. These differences remained even after controls for the socioeconomic status of the families (Astone & McLanahan, 1991). Other studies of adolescents have found that single parents engaged in less consistent parenting and more arguments (Hetherington & Clingempeel, 1992; Dornbusch et al., 1985).

An influential 1977 study claimed that when a single mother lived with another adult, typically her own mother, the two adults could provide childrearing virtually as well as two-parent households (Kellam, Ensminger, & Turner, 1977). Yet the recent work reviewed earlier in this section suggests that mother–grandmother homes are not necessarily better than single-parent homes. In addition, far fewer single mothers are still living with their own mothers by the time their children are adolescents, even though this is the period when supervision is most difficult (Parish, Hao, & Hogan, 1991). Overall, I would draw two conclusions: First, single parents, if they have adequate incomes, usually provide good care for children. Second, it is nevertheless the case that, other things being equal, it is better for children to be raised by two parents than by one.

NONPARENTAL CHILDCARE

Because of the massive increase in the proportion of married women with children who are working outside the home, the proportion of young children who are cared for by someone other than a parent for at least part of the day has also

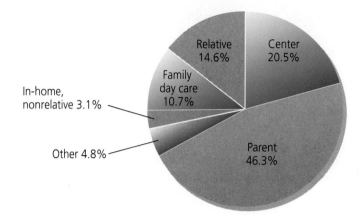

FIGURE 14.2 Primary childcare arrangements of all children under five, 1990. (*Source:* Hofferth, Brayfield, Deich, & Holcomb, 1991.)

increased dramatically. Figure 14.2 shows the primary childcare arrangements for all preschool children in the United States in 1990, according to a national survey (Hofferth, Brayfield, Deich, & Holcomb, 1991). Only about half (46 percent) of preschool children are cared for primarily by their parents during the day. Twenty percent are in a childcare center, which has been the fastest-growing kind of care. Most of the children enrolled in childcare centers have mothers who are employed, but many nonemployed mothers of three- and four-year-old children enroll them at least part of the day in a center. Another 15 percent are cared for by a relative such as a grandmother. The next most common site is the so-called "family day care" home, usually the residence of a woman who cares for several children, some of whom may be children of her own. Since many day care centers do not take children younger than two, family day care homes are a major source of out-of-home care for parents of infants (children less than 12 months old) and one-year-olds. A 1991 survey of employed mothers found that care by fathers had increased since 1990 and care by centers had decreased, perhaps due to parents' working different shifts or to a father's unemployment (U.S. Bureau of the Census, 1994c).

The increase in so-called "day care" has alarmed some observers, who worry that out-of-home care will be inferior to the care parents can provide at home. The problem is framed in terms of "working mothers," even though fathers are working outside the home, too, because in most societies women have provided more of the care of young children than men. And it is framed as a "day care" problem, even though many blue-collar parents work split shifts so that a spouse who works days can care for the children while the other spouse works evenings or nights (see Chapter 10).

Yet there is little evidence that out-of-home care causes any harm to preschool children aged 2 and over. To be sure, a grossly overcrowded center or a neglectful family day care provider can cause problems, but no study, to my knowledge, has found much evidence of harm from typical care arrangements. A National Academy of Sciences report concludes "with some certainty" that "child care participation is not inevitably or pervasively harmful to children's development. Indeed, in certain respects, children benefit from experiences in child care" (Hayes, Palmer, & Zaslow, 1990). For example, three- and four-year-old children from low-income families appear to benefit from the intellectual stimulation of a high-quality childcare center (Studer, 1991).

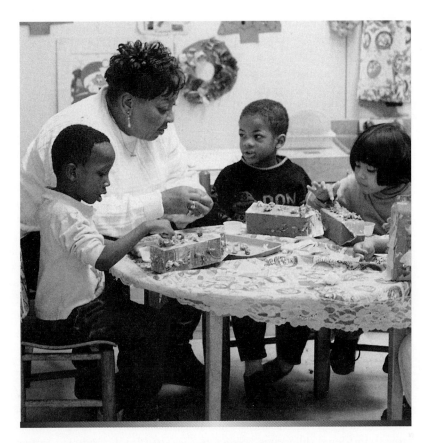

Many more young children receive out-of-home care while their parents work than was the case a few decades ago.

The remaining uncertainty is largely focused on the effects of out-of-home care for children during the first year or two of life (Cherlin, 1992a). During the 1980s, a controversial series of studies by psychologists found evidence that infants in full-time day care had less secure attachments to their mothers than infants cared for by their mothers at home.[3] A secure attachment is important for developing a basic sense of trust in others. In this context, a secure attachment means that the infant uses the mother as a secure base for exploring its environment (e.g., crawling over to new people in the room) and a haven of safety to which to return when distressed. Using the so-called "strange situation" procedure, the researchers would introduce a stranger into a room with an infant and its mother. The mother would be expected to leave and then to return. Securely attached infants, according to the theory underlying this experiment, should return to the mother without distress when she returns and then resume exploring the room. Insecurely attached infants fail to return to the mother or tend to treat the stranger as positively as the mother. The researchers found that infants cared for full-time outside the home generally showed more signs of an insecure attachment.

The meaning of the "strange situation" findings has been hotly debated by psychologists. Until recently, little information from other sources has been available on the effects of out-of-home care. In the late 1980s and early 1990s, several researchers published statistical analyses of data from a national survey of young adults that asked about their work histories and also obtained psychological

---

[3]These studies are discussed in Hayes et al. (1990).

assessments of their children. The results of their analyses, unfortunately, are contradictory: Some find detrimental effects of early maternal employment,[4] but others don't.[5]

To provide stronger evidence of the effects, if any, on infants, the National Institute of Child Health and Human Development supported a multisite study of over 1,000 infants in eight states. The families were visited several times and childcare settings were observed. The infants were assessed using the strange situation methodology at 15 months. The investigators found that, in general, use of child care was not associated with an insecure attachment to the mother, suggesting that, overall, childcare does not harm infant development. There was, however, an important exception: In families where the mother's quality of parenting was poor (e.g., she seemed detached and provided little warmth and support), the infant's attachment was worse if the parents used childcare than if the infant was cared for mainly by the mother. The investigators suggest that when infants receive adequate parenting, their attachment is not affected by childcare; but when they do not receive adequate parenting, their attachment can be damaged (NICHD Early Child Care Research Network, 1997). We can conclude that it is unjustified to proclaim that nonparental care (and, by implication, having working parents) is generally harmful to children, even to infants. It may, however, be harmful to infants who do not receive adequate parenting at home.

GROWING UP WITH LESBIAN AND GAY PARENTS

There are other living arrangements, more recent in their emergence and less common, that have consequences for children. New birth technologies, such as the fertilization of eggs outside the womb and the use of surrogate mothers, have created ethical and legal dilemmas. (See *Families and Public Policy:* Orphan Embryos and Breeder Women, on pages 446–447.) In addition, one of the newest arrangements for children is to live with an openly lesbian or gay parent and, often, that parent's partner. It is only since the 1960s that circumstances have allowed more than a rare occurrence of this kind of family. Those circumstances, which are discussed elsewhere in this book, include the following: the sharp, post-1960 rise in divorce, which encouraged more homosexual men and women who were in heterosexual marriages (often with children) to end their marriages; the emergence of an openly gay subculture in large cities, which provided a supportive environment for lesbian and gay couples; the greater tolerance of childbearing outside marriage and single parenting in general; and, most recently, an apparent increase in the number of lesbians who are becoming pregnant through insemination (usually performed by a physician) with sperm provided by a (usually anonymous) donor.

There are some theoretical reasons to expect that children raised by lesbian or gay parents might differ from children raised by heterosexuals in their sexual identities, attitudes, and behavior. As discussed in Chapter 12, writers influenced by Freud have theorized that a boy will have difficulty adopting the adult male role if he cannot see how his father behaves and is not subject to his father's authority. If this view is accurate, and if lesbian and gay parents provide boys with even fewer opportunities to interact with a heterosexual father figure than do heterosexual single parents (an assumption that has not been demonstrated), growing up with gay

---

[4]See Desai, Chase-Lansdale, and Michael (1989); Belsky and Eggebeen (1991); Baydar and Brooks-Gunn (1992).
[5]See Greenstein (1993); Parcell and Menaghan (1994).

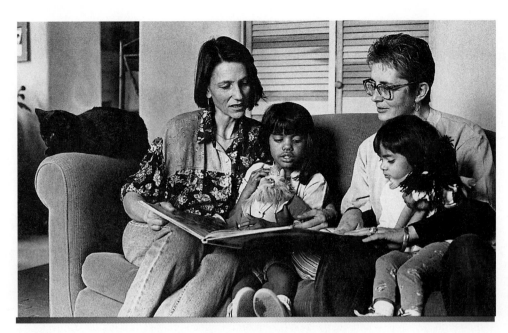

The number of openly lesbian or gay parents has increased recently.

parents should disrupt the process of heterosexual identification even more. More recently, social learning theory (Mischel, 1966), an influential perspective in social psychology, has been applied to sexual development. The basic idea is that children learn their sexual identities (and almost everything else) by imitating the adults they see. It follows, then, that the less contact a boy has with heterosexual male role models, or a girl with heterosexual female role models, the less likely it is that they will develop heterosexual identities. Moreover, social learning theory implies that children who are exposed to examples of homosexual intimacy—such as a parent and same-sex partner sharing a bed—would be more likely to manifest a homosexual orientation when they reach adulthood.

More than a dozen studies have attempted to compare children living with lesbian parents and children living with heterosexual parents—mostly heterosexual single parents.[6] Nearly all the studies have been of children born to mothers who were married and who subsequently divorced and began living openly lesbian lives. Consequently, most of the children had spent at least a few years living with their fathers in early childhood. Virtually all the mothers studied have been white, well educated, and middle class. Moreover, the studies have all been based on nonrandom samples of lesbian mothers, which means that the subjects either volunteered to be studied or were recruited through acquaintances and organizations known to the authors. They may not, therefore, be representative of lesbian mothers in general. And there are few studies of children being raised by gay fathers and their partners.

Since they volunteered to talk, it is likely that the lesbian mothers in these studies are more comfortable with their identities and more open about their lesbian lifestyle than a random sample of lesbian mothers would be. If having a lesbian mother influences a child's psychosexual development through processes such as identification and imitation, the effects should be apparent in these families, if

---

[6]For a review, see Patterson (1992).

Families and Public Policy

Orphan Embryos and Breeder Women

Sex, marriage, and childbearing: In the 1950s, they went together, as Chapter 8 showed. Then increases in sexual activity and childbearing outside marriage began to separate sex from marriage and marriage from childbearing. Now advances in birth technologies may complete the split by separating sex from childbearing. In doing so, they raise perplexing moral and political issues.

The technologies produce ways to create fertilized human embryos without sexual intercourse. Some are really not that new: **Donor insemination,** the insertion of semen into the uterus of an ovulating woman, is more than 100 years old, although it was not widely practiced until the 1960s (Isaacs & Holt, 1987). It is mainly employed as a way of inducing pregnancy in married women whose husbands have a low sperm count or other reproductive disorders. Yet with the weakening of marriage as the sole context for having children, the rationale for restricting donor insemination to married women has weakened. The number of unmarried women, including some who are lesbians, who have used the procedure to conceive children seems to be

growing, although reliable statistics are not available. **Surrogacy** goes a step further: A woman agrees to be artificially inseminated with a man's sperm, carry the fetus to term, and then to turn the baby over to the man (and typically to his wife) when it is born. The technique of *in vitro* **fertilization** involves removing eggs from a woman, fertilizing them in a laboratory dish (*vitro* means "glass") with sperm from a man, and then inserting the fertilized eggs into the uterus of a woman—either the genetic mother (if, for example, the tubes between her ovaries and uterus are blocked) or a surrogate.

If the birth of a child were to involve all three techniques, the child would have five different "parents": the genetic mother whose egg was fertilized in a laboratory dish, the genetic father who donated the sperm, the surrogate mother in whose womb the embryo was implanted and grew, and the social father and mother who took legal custody of the child at birth (Edwards, 1991). Clearly, this situation strains our understanding of what a "parent" or a "family" is. For instance, does the fact of giving birth outweigh genetic

parentage in deciding who is the mother of a child? Moralists, legislators, social scientists, and other commentators do not agree. Some states (and the United Kingdom) have outlawed surrogate motherhood. The Catholic Church has condemned all forms of reproduction that do not involve sexual intercourse. Lesbian writers, on the other hand, extol donor insemination as a way for lesbian couples to have children—an increasingly visible arrangement of unsettled legal status.

The questions raised by these technologies are legion. Consider donor insemination: If it is performed by a doctor, the law recognizes the mother's husband as the father of the child and absolves the sperm donor of all rights and responsibilities. So far, so good. But what if the mother is unmarried and inseminates herself with sperm from a donor she knows—perhaps because she can't find a doctor who will carry out the procedure? In one such case, the donor sought legal paternity and visitation rights, whereas the mother wished to exclude him and raise the child with her lesbian partner.[1] The California Court of Appeals ruled that

anywhere. In what is probably the leading study, three British researchers, Susan Golombok, Ann Spencer, and Michael Rutter, compared 37 children in lesbian households with 38 children in heterosexual, single-mother households in 1976 and 1977 (Golombok, Spencer, & Rutter, 1983). The children were all between 5 and 17 years of age, with an average age of 9.5.

The researchers examined three aspects of psychosexual development. The first was gender identity—the concept children had of themselves as males or females. All the children they studied reported that they were glad to be the sex they were and none said they would prefer to be the other sex. The second was what the researchers called "sex-typed behavior," activities that stereotypically differentiate boys and girls. They asked the mothers how often each of their children performed 14 such activities—including typically male activities, such as playing the man was the child's legal father because the insemination had not been carried out by a physician. Yet it's not clear why, medical considerations aside, the involvement of a physician ought to be the major test of who is legally a parent (Blankenship, Rushing, Onorato, & White, 1993). Other considerations might include the likelihood that the child will receive adequate financial support in the event that the mother's living situation changes or the question of whether the partner of a lesbian birth mother can claim legal rights and responsibilities toward the birth mother's child.

If embryos fertilized *in vitro* are frozen and saved for later use, other issues can arise. In 1981, a couple died in a plane crash just after the wife's eggs had been inseminated by a donor and frozen in Australia. The state legislature debated inconclusively whether the orphan embryos were the property of the estate, whether they could be implanted into a surrogate, or whether they should be destroyed. More than a decade later, the embryos remain frozen (Isaacs & Holt, 1987; personal communication from Peter McDonald, 1994).

In the most famous surrogacy case, Mary Beth Whitehead signed a $10,000 contract in 1985 to be artificially inseminated with sperm from William Stern and to then give Stern and his wife the baby at birth. After the child—known in court papers as Baby M—was born, Whitehead changed her mind and refused to yield it (Fox, 1993). The resulting court case provoked a national debate about whether such a contract was morally and legally enforceable. The New Jersey Supreme Court ruled that it was illegal and invalid because the payment violated adoption-related laws against selling babies.[2] Some observers also objected to what they see as a likely class bias in surrogacy: Middle-class people like the Sterns (a biochemist and a pediatrician) would be doing most of the buying, whereas poorer people like the Whiteheads (she did not work for pay, and her husband was a sanitation worker) would be doing the selling, creating a class of breeder women (Neuhaus, 1988). Yet some observers counter that paid surrogacy is hardly more objectionable than the customary fees that prospective parents wishing to adopt a baby pay to lawyers and agencies.

These technological advances and others still on the horizon (such as an artificial womb that could incubate a fetus until birth) may force us to redefine the boundaries of parenthood. In the legal tradition of the Western nations, paternity is defined mainly by marriage—the husband is presumed to be the father of any child born to his wife, unless there is evidence to the contrary (Fox, 1993). Today, in the case of unmarried women, paternity can be settled through testing of the DNA of the father and child. All this assumes, however, that the identity of the mother has been established and that, at least for births outside marriage, the genetic father is to be considered the legal father. These conditions aren't always met when births occur without sexual intercourse. The challenge is to find new rules that protect the varied interests of the adults and children involved and that best fit our sense of morality and justice.

[1]*Jhordan C. v. Mary K. and Victoria T.*, 224 Cal Rptr 530, 179 Cal App 3rd 386 (1986).
[2]In the Matter of Baby M, Docket No. FM.25314-86E Superior Ct. Chancery Division, Bergen County, N.J., March 31, 1987.

with construction toys, playing cops and robbers, and playing soccer, and typically female activities, such as playing with dolls, playing pretend games such as tea parties, cooking, and sewing. They also asked the children directly to name their favorite toys, hobbies, books, sports, and so forth. The result showed no significant differences between boys in lesbian households and boys in heterosexual households, nor between girls in the two kinds of households. Regardless of their mothers' sexual orientation, boys were far more likely to engage in the male activities and girls were far more likely to engage in the female activities.

The third aspect was the sexual orientation of the children. Most of the children were too young for a definitive judgment to be made, but the researchers still obtained some evidence on friendship patterns. Among the younger children, nearly all reported a best friend of the same sex. Children who were beyond puberty were questioned about romantic crushes or friendships. Six of the nine such children in lesbian families showed heterosexual interests, two showed no definite interests, and one showed homosexual interests (a girl reported a crush on a female teacher). Among eleven such children in heterosexual single-parent families, four showed heterosexual interests and seven showed no definite interests. The researchers judged that both patterns seemed typical for these age groups. Moreover, there were no significant differences in behavior problems (as assessed by both parents and teachers) and in the quality of relationships with other children (as assessed by parents' reports) for children in lesbian versus heterosexual homes.[7]

In 1991 and 1992, one of the original researchers and a collaborator located and reinterviewed 46 of the children, who were now 17 to 35, with an average age of 23.5 (Tasker & Golombok, 1995). They found that the children who had grown up in lesbian families were more open to the possibility of same-gender sexual relationships but that few of them identified as gay or lesbian. The greater openness was observable in two ways: First, 6 of 25 children from lesbian families reported at least one same-gender relationship, ranging from a kiss to cohabitation; but none of the 21 children from heterosexual families reported a same-gender relationship. Second, 14 children from lesbian families said they had considered the possibility of a same-gender relationship, compared with 3 of the children from heterosexual families. Nevertheless, only two of the children from lesbian families were currently in a same-gender relationship and identified as lesbian (both were women). In other words, growing up in a lesbian family seems to have expanded the sexual possibilities that the children considered and to have led to some short-term, same-gender sexual relationships, but it does not seem to have altered the basically heterosexual orientation of the vast majority.

It is hard to know how much confidence to place in these nonrandom studies. Nor do we know whether the situation is similar for children born to lesbian mothers through insemination by a donor.[8] But the evidence so far, such as it is, supports the conclusion that children in lesbian homes look very much like children in heterosexual single-parent homes, although they may be more open to the possibility of same-gender relationships. Most children from lesbian homes who were studied showed the kinds of behavior that one expects in children who will grow up to have a heterosexual orientation. These children also showed no greater symptoms of mental health problems than the children from heterosexual single-parent homes. In their earlier article, the British researchers concluded, "Perhaps it is the quality of family relationships and the pattern of upbringing that matters for psychosexual development, and not the sexual orientation of the mother" (Golombok et. al, 1983). I would add that the small number of children who identify as gay or lesbian, despite their upbringing in lesbian families, suggests that psychosexual development unfolds, in part, from biological predispositions that children carry with them from birth.

THE WELL-BEING OF AMERICAN CHILDREN

Now that we have studied what it is that parents should do for their children and how social changes may have aided or hindered parents' tasks, we are ready to confront what is probably the most critical question to be asked about the public

---

[7]See also Kirkpatrick, Smith, and Roy (1981); Hoeffer (1981).
[8]A recent study of these children reports similar findings but lacks a control group; Patterson (1994).

family in the 1990s: Has the well-being of children declined? It is a question that, in recent years, has often been posed and answered affirmatively by national commissions, politicians, and editorial writers. (We should also examine how children's well-being is studied by sociologists and other participants in this debate. See *How Do Sociologists Know What They Know:* Measuring the Well-being of Children.) The answer to the question depends on two further questions: (1) Compared with when? and (2) Which children?

COMPARED WITH WHEN?

The reality of children's lives in the past was harsher than the nostalgic picture that is sometimes drawn. In the early 1930s, my Aunt Rose gave birth to a son, William, the first member of my generation in my maternal family. William caught strep throat as an infant. Half a century later, when the pediatrician told me that *my* son had strep throat, I trudged to the drugstore, bought an antibiotic, and nonchalantly spooned it into him. Within two days, he was fine. But antibiotics such as penicillin had not yet been isolated when William took ill, and sulfa drugs, their precursors, were not yet in general use. William died, a victim of an illness that today is hardly more serious than the common cold. The death of an infant, though tragic, was not an unusual event in 1935; 1 in 18 babies died before its first birthday. Nearly 1 in 10 died before reaching age 15 (U.S. Bureau of the Census, 1975).

   We tend to forget how much lower the typical standard of living was in the first half of the twentieth century than it is today. One-third of all homes in the 1940s had no running water, two-fifths had no flush toilets, half had no refrigerators, and three-fifths had no central heating. The average person ate half as much beef and one-third as much chicken as has been the case in recent years.[9] Thousands of children contracted polio each year. The infant mortality rate—the proportion of children who die in their first year of life—was three times higher than it is today (U.S. Bureau of the Census, 1975; U.S. Bureau of the Census, 1997i). Just 53 percent of persons in their twenties had graduated from high school, compared with 87 percent today (U.S. Bureau of the Census, 1997e). I could go on; the point is that a nostalgic picture of a carefree childhood in the "good old days" is inaccurate. Even as late as the 1940s, life was far tougher for children in many respects than is the case now.

   Consider, for instance, trends in the income of families with children. Whether the economic situation of children has become worse or better over time depends on when you start looking. Figure 14.3 shows the percentage of children living in families with incomes below the official government poverty line from 1949 to 1996. By this standard, as the figure shows, nearly half of all children in the country were poor in 1949—a far higher percentage than is the case now. But the great economic boom of the 1950s and 1960s changed all that, as discussed in Chapter 4. By 1969, as Figure 14.3 shows, just 15.6 percent of children were living in families below the poverty line. Childhood poverty had declined for whites, blacks, and Hispanics—a rising tide of prosperity had lifted all boats. Then the post-1973 economic decline, which particularly affected the kinds of entry-level jobs for which young parents tend to be qualified, reversed the trend. By 1993, the poverty rate had risen to 22 percent—higher than in 25 years—before dropping to 20.5 percent in 1996. It was far higher among children of Hispanic origin—40.3 percent in 1996—and black children—39.9 percent in 1996 (U.S. Bureau of the Census, 1997a).

[9]These statistics are cited in Levy (1987).

How Do Sociologists Know What They Know?

Measuring the Well-Being of Children

The troubling trends in the lives of many American children have created a demand by policymakers, journalists, and other observers for better information about the well-being of children. Until the 1980s, the federal government collected relatively little information about children. Family sociologists were focused on the conjugal family of husband, wife, and children—but paid little attention to the children themselves. The rise in divorce and in childbearing outside of marriage in the 1960s and 1970s increased the demand for better knowledge about the consequences for children, and academic researchers and government agencies began to respond.

The first questions they had to consider were the following: How do you measure children's well-being in the large-scale surveys that the federal government tends to fund and

that sociologists study? And what aspects of children's lives are important for well-being? The most obvious areas are basic needs such as a child's standard of living and health. The Bureau of the Census gathers information annually about income levels and poverty of households with children. In 1981, the government fielded the first child health supplement to the National Health Interview Survey, a large, ongoing survey of Americans' health. The data from these and other government surveys are made available (with names and addresses deleted to ensure confidentiality) to sociologists who wish to analyze them.

But these indicators only tell part of the story. Sociologists and psychologists are interested in two other important domains: *cognitive* indicators of what children are learning and *socioemotional* indicators of how they are feeling and behaving. Cognitive

indicators are relatively straightforward; sociologists studying random samples of children and their families can ask permission to talk to children's teachers and to obtain test scores from their schools. For preschool-aged children, of course, there are no test scores to obtain. As a result, survey researchers interested in young children sometimes administer short tests directly to them. For example, a child might be shown a progressively more difficult series of pictures and asked to identify each one.

More difficult to measure are the socioemotional aspects of well-being. For younger children, the best strategy for survey researchers is to ask parents questions about their children's behavior. Following the work of developmental psychologists, sociologists ask parents questions about two kinds of behavior problems: externalizing problems (acting out, aggressive behavior) and

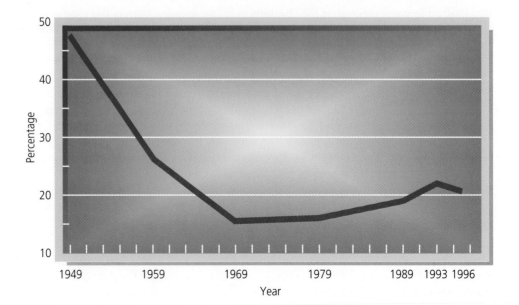

FIGURE 14.3 Poverty rates for children in the United States, 1949 to 1996. (*Sources:* for 1949–1969, Smolensky, Danziger, & Gottschalk, 1988; for 1979 and 1989, U.S. Bureau of the Census, 1993f; for 1993, U.S. Bureau of the Census, 1997i; and for 1996, U.S. Bureau of the Census, 1997g.)

internalizing problems (feelings kept inside, such as anxiety and depression). Rather than posing broad questions (e.g., Is your child anxious?), the researchers typically ask multiple questions about each of the two kinds of behavior problems. For externalizing problems, for example, they might ask whether a child is destructive, disobedient, fighting with other children, and so on; then they would create an externalizing scale for the child by assigning one point for each "yes" answer and adding up the points. The scales could be used to study issues such as the effects of divorce on children by comparing the scale scores of children whose parents have divorced with the scores of children whose parents are still married (Chase-Lansdale, Cherlin, & Kiernan, 1995).

Older children can be asked directly about problematic behavior. For instance, since 1991 a federally funded national study, Monitoring the Future, has annually asked nationwide samples of 8th, 10th, and 12th graders about drug use. To be sure, we cannot determine whether students are being fully truthful in their responses (See *How Do Sociologists Know What They Know?* Asking about Sensitive Behavior, in Chapter 7). But even so, changes in their responses from year to year are likely to represent real increases or decreases. (Between 1991 and 1997, the surveys show an 11 to 17 percent increase in the use of any illicit drug, with marijuana being the most widely used drug. [Institute for Social Research, 1998].) Other surveys have tracked trends in sexual behavior and pregnancy among adolescents (see Chapter 8).

Overall, far more information on children's well-being is available from survey research today, compared with two decades ago. In recent years, interest in indicators of children's well-being has been so high that federal government agencies have coordinated their data gathering and even produced summary reports. In 1997, for instance, a new coordinating body, the Interagency Forum on Child and Family Statistics, published *America's Children: Key National Indicators of Well-Being,* which includes graphs and tables showing trends in economic security, health, problem behavior, social environment, and education. Also in 1997, the U.S. Department of Health and Human Services published an even larger volume, entitled *Trends in the Well-Being of America's Children and Youth,* filled with graphs and tables. Both reports provide very useful information for sociologists and for students writing papers on the well-being of children, and both are available on the Internet. (See "Families on the Internet" at the end of this chapter.)

This evidence suggests that, to answer the question about the declining well-being of children, we must ask, compared with when? The well-being of American children in the first half of the twentieth century cannot be judged to be better overall than their well-being today. The period in which children's well-being was at its peak was not in the distant past but rather in the third quarter of the twentieth century—and particularly in the 1950s and 1960s. This was the era when baby boom children grew up. In many ways, neither their parents nor their children have had it so good. In this period, as Figure 14.3 showed, rates of childhood poverty declined to lower levels than before or since.

Moreover, children were less likely to spend time in a single-parent family than before or since. At the turn of the century, almost one-fourth of all children saw one of their parents die by the time the child was 15 (Uhlenberg, 1980). When this figure is added to the divorce rate, which was much lower at that time, perhaps one in three children spent time living in a single-parent household. By the 1950s, however, death rates had fallen substantially and the divorce rate was still much lower than it is today; as a result, fewer children—perhaps one in four—spent time in a single-parent family than was the case at the turn of the century. Yet by the 1970s and 1980s, the continuing decline in death rates had been overwhelmed

FIGURE 14.4 Percent of U. S. children who were living in "poverty," "frugality," "comfort," and "luxury," 1939–1988. (*Source:* Hernandez, 1993.)

by the sharp rises in divorce and childbearing outside marriage; consequently, the proportion of children spending time in a single-parent family has reached a high in the 1990s of about one in two (Furstenberg & Cherlin, 1991).

Accounts of the 1950s and early 1960s describe a generation of adults who focused on home and children more than their parents or, later, their children—perhaps in reaction to the disruptions of the Great Depression and World War II. They married at young ages, had children faster, and had more of them than the preceding or succeeding generations. They also had the luck to reach adulthood in prosperous times. Did the higher rates of marital stability and the focus on children and home provide a better environment for children? The answer is not as obvious as it may seem. The divorce rate was relatively low in part because married women's opportunities to work outside the home were restricted by social norms and employer discrimination. That restriction, in turn, caused considerable frustration and bitterness. In a set of 300 interviews with middle-class couples in 1955, the wives were twice as likely as their husbands to report that they were dissatisfied with their marriages, and twice as many said they would not marry the same person if they had to do it over again (May, 1988). It is possible that their frustration produced anger and depression that diminished their abilities to be good mothers. Yet the interviews also show that many, perhaps most, dissatisfied women tried to stifle their anger and avoid conflict so that their marriages would stay together. Consequently, it seems likely that, from the children's perspective, the marital stability of the 1950s was beneficial. This benefit was produced at a price—and wives paid that price in forgone opportunities and frustration. One can accept that the 1950s was a good decade for children without glorifying it as a golden age for all family members.

WHICH CHILDREN?

Yet it is important to note that not all children are doing worse today than in the 1950s and 1960s. For during the 1970s and 1980s, as Chapter 4 showed, the distribution of income in the United States became more unequal. Figure 14.4 shows what growing income inequality has meant for children. Demographer Donald Hernandez divided all children into four groups according to their family's income:

Relative poverty: A family income less than one-half the median family income. (The median is the point in the income distribution at which as many families have higher incomes as have lower incomes.)

Frugality: A family income above the relative poverty level but less than three-fourths of the median family income.

Comfort: A family income above the frugality level but less than 50 percent above the median family income.

Luxury: A family income at least 50 percent above the median family income.

Although these divisions and their labels are arbitrary, they can be used to follow trends over time. Using census data, Hernandez calculated the percentage of children in each group in 1939, 1949, 1959, 1969, 1979, and 1988. Each bar in the figure shows the distribution in one of these years. For example, the left-most bar shows that nearly 40 percent of children were in the "poverty" group in 1939, at the end of the Great Depression. Yet, moving down from the top of the same bar, we can see that more than 20 percent of all children were in the "luxury" category. Not all children suffered during the Depression; some were in families that weathered the storm well. It was the middle categories that were squeezed. During the next 30 years, the percentage in both the "poverty" and "luxury" groups declined, as the middle expanded. Yet since 1969, the middle has once again been squeezed: The proportion of children in the "poverty" group and in the "luxury" group *both* increased between 1969 and 1988. Children at the top of the income distribution in 1988 were doing better than they were in 1969, whereas children at the bottom were doing worse. *Which children:* The size of the group that is doing better has increased, and so has the size of the group doing worse. The number of children in the middle-income groups has been shrinking.

The bars in this figure are like photographs: They present a snapshot of all children in the United States at one point in time. Whether those same children will be poor or comfortable or wealthy the next year cannot be determined from the snapshot. In fact, a national study that has followed thousands of children and their families for more than 20 years shows that the snapshot conceals great movements of children and their families in and out of poverty over the course of childhood. Many children experience poverty for a short period. Among whites, relatively few experience it throughout their childhood; but among blacks, persistent childhood poverty is common.

Figure 14.5 shows the experiences of children in the Panel Study of Income Dynamics (PSID) who were under the age of four in 1968 and whose families were reinterviewed in each of the next 15 years (Duncan, 1991). The first set of bars on the left shows the percentage of nonblack children (whom I will call "white" for the sake of simplicity since most were, indeed, white) and black children whose families had incomes that were always at least 50 percent above the poverty line in each of the 15 years. A majority (56 percent) of white children fell into this category, compared with 13 percent of black children. The next set of bars represents children whose families were always above the poverty line but were close to the line in at least one year. Combining these two categories, we see that 75 percent of white children and 21 percent of black children never experienced poverty. The racial difference is great. Still, the figure demonstrates that a substantial number of black children are never poor. These children are often overlooked in articles about the economic situation of African Americans.

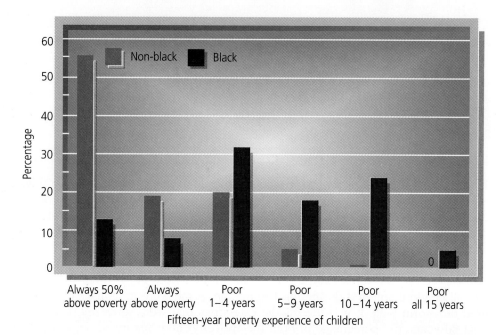

FIGURE 14.5 Fifteen-year poverty experiences of children who were under the age of four in 1968, by race. (*Source:* Duncan, 1991.)

The next set of bars represents what we might call "temporary poverty": those who were poor 1 to 4 years out of 15. About one-fifth of white children—a substantial number—experience temporary poverty. It is common to be poor for a few years. Among black children, it is even more common. But the racial differences are most dramatic in the final three sets of bars, which represent what we might call "persistent poverty," that is, being poor at least 5 of the 15 years. By this measure, only about 6 percent of white children experience persistent poverty. The modest amount of persistent poverty among whites is a great social accomplishment of the post–World War II era; before then, persistent poverty was much more likely. Yet any pleasure at that accomplishment is matched by displeasure at the situation among black children, 47 percent of whom were poor for at least five years. There are other ways of defining persistent poverty, but they all show that the percentage of white children who are affected is less than 10 percent, and often less than 5 percent (Duncan & Rodgers, 1991). Moreover, Hispanic children were included in the "white" category of the PSID analyses, which means that the rates for non-Hispanic whites are probably even smaller. The alternative definitions all show that the percentage of persistently poor black children is 30 percent or higher. *Which children:* Although many white children experience poverty at some point, persistent childhood poverty is far more common among African Americans.

As noted in Chapter 4, the PSID further indicated that children who were persistently poor were much more likely to live in single-parent families. According to the PSID study, the average black child who lived with one parent spent more than seven years in poverty—nearly half of her or his childhood (Duncan, 1991). This is not to say that family structure is the only cause of the high rates of persistent poverty among children. Many poor single mothers were poor *before* they gave birth to their children. The PSID data show that the formation of single-parent households among blacks reallocates people who were already chronically poor (Bane, 1986). In addition, black single parents tend to live in racially segregated neighborhoods with high concentrations of poverty. These neighborhoods often have high levels of crime and drug abuse, few social services, and few jobs.

One recent study found that the absence of affluent neighbors was associated with higher rates of childbearing and school dropout among teenagers, even after attempts to control for family structure and race (Brooks-Gunn, Duncan, Klebanov, & Sealand, 1993).

Information on poverty trends for Hispanic children is sketchier because government statistics were very limited until the 1970s. Even today, most tabulations display data on all Hispanic children combined; yet, as discussed in Chapter 5, there is great diversity within the Hispanic category. With this caveat, one can examine recent trends in the annual poverty rate. Between 1980 and 1995, the rate for Hispanic children increased from 33 to 39 percent, a larger increase than among either African Americans or non-Hispanic whites (U.S. Bureau of the Census, 1997g; U.S. Bureau of the Census, 1997i). It is likely that the sharp increase reflects, in part, the continuing immigration of individuals and families from low-income backgrounds.

Other indicators of children's well-being show a mixture of improvement and deterioration over the past few decades.[10] On the positive side:

- Children's parents are much more likely to have graduated from high school (especially among blacks) and to have attended college. Better-educated parents may provide more stimulating home environments, and they tend to use childrearing techniques that produce more competent children, as noted earlier. In addition, because of the decline in fertility, children have fewer siblings, which means they get relatively more attention from adults. A substantial body of research shows that children with fewer siblings develop greater verbal ability, pursue more cultural activities, and achieve more education than children with more siblings (Blake, 1989).
- Children's physical health is, in general, better than it ever has been. For example, the infant mortality rate (the proportion of children who die within 12 months of birth) is about one-third of what it was in 1960, and childhood diseases such as polio, diphtheria, and whooping cough have been nearly eradicated. A majority of all parents, including racial-ethnic group members and parents with low incomes, report their children to be in very good or excellent physical health.

But the negative side of the ledger is also full. Consider the following:

- The rate of suicide among adolescents has tripled since the 1960s. (White teenagers are more likely to commit suicide than black teenagers, although the rates of black teenagers have been increasing faster in recent years [Belluck, 1998].) In the 1980s, teenagers were the only group, except the elderly, among whom suicide rates increased (U.S. Bureau of the Census, 1993g).
- Teenage homicide rates also have tripled over the same period. At the start of the chapter, it was noted that firearm homicide is now the leading cause of death among black teenage males. Gun-related violence increased greatly in the late 1980s; just between 1985 and 1990 the rate of death due to firearm homicides tripled among black male teenagers. If the 1990 rates hold through the decade, 1 out of every 79 black men would be shot dead before the age of 25.[11]

---

[10]Except where noted, these next paragraphs draw upon Zill (1992); Zill and Rogers (1988).

[11]I calculated this estimate from the annual death rates for five-year age groups presented in Table 2 of U.S. National Center for Health Statistics (1993d).

- Scores on the Scholastic Aptitude Test taken by students applying to college declined between the mid-1960s and 1980. Verbal scores have not improved since then, although mathematics scores have increased somewhat (U.S. Bureau of the Census, 1997i). The only bright spot has been the steady progress that black and Hispanic children have shown on national achievement tests in the 1970s and 1980s; still, their achievement levels lag behind those of white children.
- Several other chapters have noted the great increases in the number of single-parent families due to divorce and to childbearing outside marriage. Because of these developments, only about 57 percent of all children were living with both biological parents in 1996. About 28 percent were living with one biological parent (either a mother or a father), and 11 percent were living with a biological parent and a stepparent.[12] These overall figures conceal large racial and ethnic differences, as noted in Chapter 5. More than half of all black children (57 percent) and 33 percent of Hispanic children lived with one parent in 1996. Moreover, 9 percent of black children lived with neither parent in 1996, compared with 5 percent among Hispanics and 3 percent among whites (U.S. Bureau of the Census, 1997e).

A SUMMING UP

Overall, I think that comparisons of the "average" child now and in the past can be misleading. As Figure 14.4 suggests, the percentage of children who are in prosperous families has increased in tandem with the percentage who are in poor families. This trend holds for blacks as well as for whites. Persistently poor children are the group that has fared the worst since the 1950s and early 1960s and that seems most distinctively and gravely deprived of a decent childhood today. The PSID data showed that persistently poor children are disproportionately black. Indeed, the racial difference is so great that, by most reasonable definitions, a majority of all persistently poor children today are African Americans, even though African Americans constitute only about 15 percent of all children. The U.S. government provides less assistance to children in low-income families than almost any other Western nation. It may be that the racial polarization between the heavily black population in deep poverty and the white majority prevents Americans from reaching out to the poor. (See *Families in Other Cultures:* U.S. Children in International Perspective, on pages 458–459.)

Persistently poor children are more likely to live in single-parent families than similar children in the 1960s (Duncan & Rodgers, 1991). To the extent that living in a single-parent family makes it more difficult to escape from poverty (as noted in Chapter 4), poor children may be experiencing hardships for a longer period of their lives. To the extent that single parents have more difficulty supervising and monitoring teenagers, children may be receiving less supervision than they need. Yet it's simplistic to blame single parents for persistent poverty. As noted earlier, many poor single mothers were poor before they became mothers. Becoming a single parent didn't make them poor—they already were. In addition, the past two decades have seen a great deterioration in the labor market prospects of young adults without college educations, which made it more difficult to start and maintain a two-parent family. One recent study estimated that, even if there had been

---

[12]I assumed that the proportion of children in two-parent families who were living with both biological parents (versus one biological parent and one stepparent) was the same in 1996 as in 1990, when it was reported in U.S. Bureau of the Census (1992c). I then adjusted the 1996 figures using this proportion.

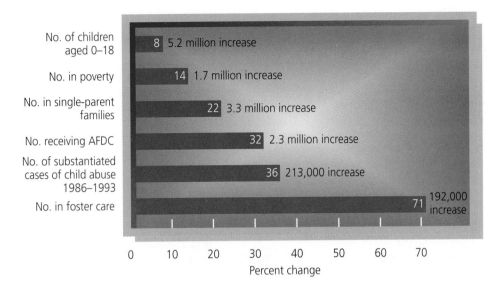

No. of children aged 0–18 — 8 — 5.2 million increase

No. in poverty — 14 — 1.7 million increase

No. in single-parent families — 22 — 3.3 million increase

No. receiving AFDC — 32 — 2.3 million increase

No. of substantiated cases of child abuse 1986–1993 — 36 — 213,000 increase

No. in foster care — 71 — 192,000 increase

Percent change (0, 10, 20, 30, 40, 50, 60, 70)

FIGURE 14.6
Percentage changes in indicators of children's well-being, 1985–1994. (*Sources: Number of children:* U. S. Bureau of the Census, 1997b. *Children in poverty:* U.S. Bureau of the Census, 1997b. *Children in single-parent families:* U.S. Bureau of the Census, 1996b, 1997b. *Number of children receiving AFDC:* U.S. Department of Health and Human Services, 1997. *Child Abuse:* Besharov & Dembosky, 1996. *Number of children in foster care:* U.S. Department of Health and Human Services, 1997.)

no increase in single-parent families since 1960, about 80 percent of today's poor children would still be poor; moreover, the gap between white and black child poverty rates would still be large (Hernandez, 1993). The growth of single-parent families hasn't helped matters for poor children, but it is probably not the major cause—and certainly not the sole cause—of the problems of poor children.

In fact, the quality of life for children at the bottom of the income distribution seems to have deteriorated even further since the mid-1980s. Figure 14.6 displays a number of changes between 1985 and 1994; the lengths of the bars show the percentage change. You can see that although the number of children grew by a modest 8 percent, the number in poverty grew by 14 percent. More troubling, the number in single-parent families grew even faster, and the number receiving Aid to Families with Dependent Children (AFDC) grew faster yet. (Between 1994 and 1997, however, the number of families receiving AFDC and its successor under the 1996 welfare reform legislation, TANF, dropped by about 30 percent. See Chapter 6.) It is hard to know exactly what lies behind these figures. It may be that some two-parent families that were already in poverty broke up into even poorer, single-parent units that applied for AFDC between 1985 and 1994. Or it may be that single-parent families that were already receiving AFDC were staying on the rolls longer. In addition, substantiated cases of child abuse increased by 36 percent between 1986 and 1993—although it is not clear whether this rise reflects greater abuse or merely increased vigilance in reporting existing abuse (see Chapter 11). Finally, the number of children in foster care rose by a stunning 71 percent (after falling in the early 1980s), with the largest increase occurring among newborns and infants. As discussed in Chapter 11, the increase in foster care may reflect the tensions of unemployed people in difficult economic times, a rise in homelessness, or the increased use of crack cocaine.

Among children from families that are not poor, I submit, the decline in well-being since the 1950s and 1960s has not been as great. A fortunate, growing minority of children live in relatively wealthy families. Although they too face an increased risk of parental divorce or teenage pregnancy, the risks are lower than among the less fortunate. (Many studies demonstrate, for example, that the higher a family's income, the lower the likelihood of divorce.) It's not at all clear that their well-being has declined; in fact, it may have improved.

U.S. Children in International Perspective

The decline in children's well-being raises the question of how well U.S. children are doing compared with children in other developed countries. The answer is not very well. U.S. children learn less about mathematics and science. They must cope with the highest rate of divorce of any Western nation (although if the breakup of cohabiting parents is included, Sweden's overall rate of family dissolution might be higher). Rates of adolescent homicide (and also adult homicide) are far higher than anywhere else. The percentage of teenage girls who give birth is higher, even among white Americans, than anywhere else. And so forth. No nation presents as pale a statistical portrait of children as the United States.

Consider poverty, for instance. Between 1982 and 1992, comparable studies of income were conducted in 18 Western countries (Rainwater & Smeeding, 1995). For each country, the study directors calculated the percentage of children who lived in low-income families, defined as families with incomes less than half of the median (or middle) family. The figure shows the percentage of children in each country who lived in families that had incomes below this level. None of the other 17 comes close to the 21.5 percent in the United States. Why do so many U.S. children live in low-income families? One possibility is the high rate of poverty among racial-ethnic groups in the United States. Yet even when childhood

poverty among U.S. whites is compared with that of whites in other Western countries, Americans still show higher rates. Another possibility is the large number of single-parent families in the United States. But even when the comparisons are restricted to children living in single-parent families in other countries, U.S. children are poorer than those anywhere else except Australia.

What really account for the difference are the more generous social welfare programs in the other countries. The governments of the other countries provide more benefits to all families, regardless of income. For example, most have a child allowance that is paid to parents solely on the basis of how many children they have. Most have unemployment benefits that are more generous and are paid for a longer period of time than in the United States. Most provide payments to parents who take a short-term leave from their jobs following childbirth. These universal benefits are popular with citizens of other countries because they are seen as aiding everyone, not just the poor.

In contrast, the United States relies more on so-called means-tested benefits, which are given only to families that fall below an income threshold. These benefits are not as generous as in the other countries. For example, the main cash benefit available to families with children is Temporary Assistance to Needy Families, which was known as Aid to Families

with Dependent Children before the 1996 welfare legislation, and which is provided primarily to single-parent families in poverty. AFDC was so unpopular that most states did not increase it to keep up with inflation; consequently, its real value declined after the mid-1970s.

Because means-tested benefits are usually less popular with voters, they tend to be less generous than universal benefits. For example, Social Security is a universal benefit in the United States because it is available to all elderly persons regardless of income. In contrast to AFDC/TANF, Social Security benefits have risen dramatically over the last few decades. The lack of universal benefits for parents of young children in the United States seems to reflect the strong individualistic ethos in this country. In the American myth, each person is supposed to make it on his or her own. The poor are often viewed as "undeserving" of help—of having failed at the task of providing for themselves and their children.

When I travel in Western Europe, I find that people have a greater sense that their fellow countrymen are deserving of assistance purely because they are citizens. The French, for example, seem to believe that every French person has a right to a minimally adequate standard of living. I find a greater sense of "weness," a feeling that we are all French (or British or German) and must assist the less fortunate—especially children. In the United States, I see a

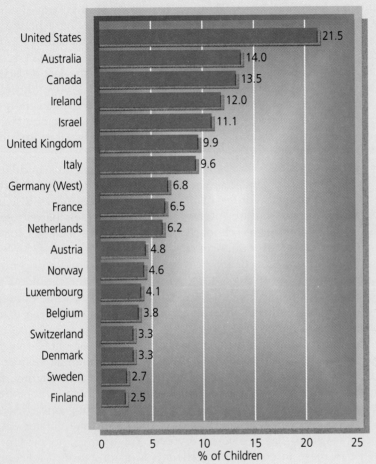

United States	21.5
Australia	14.0
Canada	13.5
Ireland	12.0
Israel	11.1
United Kingdom	9.9
Italy	9.6
Germany (West)	6.8
France	6.5
Netherlands	6.2
Austria	4.8
Norway	4.6
Luxembourg	4.1
Belgium	3.8
Switzerland	3.3
Denmark	3.3
Sweden	2.7
Finland	2.5

0   5   10   15   20   25
% of Children

Percentage of children living in families with incomes less than half of the median income for all families, 1982–1992 (*Source:* Rainwater & Smeeding, 1995).

*Poverty is defined as percent of children living in families with adjusted disposible incomes less than 50 percent of adjusted median income for all persons. Income includes all transfers and tax benefits.

greater split between "us"—the middle class—and "them" the undeserving poor. This split may well be aggravated by the ethnic and racial differences in the United States between the poor and the better off. Lingering prejudice and discrimination encourage some middle-class whites to see black or Hispanic poor people as different from them and therefore less worthy of their support. The split between us and them and the strong belief in individual initiative result in less support to poor children than in any other developed country.

It is among children from families in the narrowing middle, neither poor nor affluent, many of which have been hard-pressed to maintain their standard of living, that a judgment about trends in well-being is most difficult. My own sense is that, on average, the children in the middle have experienced a moderate, downward drift in well-being since the 1960s. They are less likely to live with two parents, due mainly to increases in divorce. They have grown up during a period of economic belt tightening by the working and middle classes. Their rates of births outside marriage are higher, their suicide rates are higher, and their SAT scores are lower. Yet there have been some encouraging reversals in the last decade or so: Drug and alcohol usage has declined substantially since 1980 (although drug usage rose somewhat in the 1990s), and SAT scores have remained more or less constant since then (U.S. Bureau of the Census, 1993g). We see among children in the middle not the alarming slide of the poor but rather a gradual erosion of some of the gains they had won during the 1950s and 1960s.

Probably the two greatest changes in the family among this middle group have been the increases in mothers who work outside the home and divorce rates. Little was said about divorce in this chapter because it was discussed in Chapter 12. Nearly all children are intensely upset when their parents separate, and their risk of dropping out of school, having a child as a teenager, or experiencing other undesirable consequences rises. These effects are troubling and worthy of serious concern. It appears, however, that most children do not suffer long-term harmful effects from divorce. Moreover, some of the problems that we blame on divorce are visible in children before their parents even separate, which suggests that some of the problems might have occurred even if the parents had stayed together.

I have argued in this chapter that having both parents (or one's only parent) work outside the home appears not to harm children after the first year or two of life; many analysts are skeptical that it causes harm at all. Consequently, there is little justification for lumping the increase in employed mothers together with clearly problematic developments such as childbearing among unwed teenagers or increased deaths by homicide and suicide. To be sure, the greater economic independence of women has facilitated divorce. Yet there is no evidence suggesting that the increase in employed mothers is a major cause of teenage pregnancy, drug use, suicide, or homicide. In fact, in the 1960s and 1970s, suicide rates were increasing for adults in their twenties and thirties as well as for teenagers—suggesting that family problems weren't the only cause of suicide. Similarly, homicide rates increased at all ages—not just among teenagers—during the 1960s and 1970s and then declined for all ages in the 1980s before turning sharply upward again (Furstenberg & Condran, 1988). Increases in teenage sexual activity have occurred during a period when sexual standards for adults have become more permissive—witness the increase in sexually explicit themes in television and film and the emergence of a sex industry supplying books, magazines, videos, and sex clubs to adults (see Chapter 7). Are we to blame employed mothers for all this?

Nevertheless, even a moderate deterioration in well-being among children in the middle is cause for concern to those who believe in the idea of progress—the idea that our society ought to be improving the lives of its citizens rather than backsliding. I think that changes in the family contributed to this deterioration, but I'm not convinced the family was the major actor. The family itself was acted upon by larger forces such as the restructuring of the economy and a cultural shift toward ever-greater individualism. Yet parents are not merely passively acted on by social forces; they must be assigned some responsibility for the consequences of their actions, such as getting divorced and having children outside marriage.

And although I am skeptical of those who claim that there is a pervasive crisis in the well-being of American children, I do think that a real crisis is occurring among children at the bottom of the income distribution. Behind the dismal statistics lie the lives of children like Lafayette and Pharoah Rivers, diving for cover during the daily gunfights and wondering if they will get to grow up. When the reporter proposed to their mother that he write a book about Lafayette, Pharoah, and other children in the neighborhood, she thought that was a great idea. Still, she warned, "But you know, there are no children here. They've seen too much to be children" (Kotlowitz, 1991).

SUMMARY

1. Families provide most of the socialization that children receive in their early years. Socialization teaches children what they need to know in order to function within their society or social group: language, norms, values, manners, customs, behaviors, rules, and so forth. Parents provide support to, and exercise control over, their children. A combination of emotional support and consistent, moderate discipline seems to produce children who are more socially competent. Working-class parents stress obedience and conformity in socializing their children more than middle-class parents; conversely, middle-class parents stress autonomy and self-direction more. Members of each social class emphasize the kinds of values that are consistent with the kinds of jobs they perform. Parents socialize boys and girls differently, so that preexisting differences, if any, are exaggerated in childhood and adult behavior.

2. Growing evidence suggests that fathers make a difference in their children's lives. Fathers often relate to young children through a vigorous style of play that is thought to help children learn to regulate their emotions. Fathers' influence on children is sometimes provided indirectly through emotional support to mothers or backing up the mothers' authority. Caring activities that fathers engage in with children may have long-term effects on the children's educational and occupational attainment. Some studies suggest that father involvement for boys may be more important in the first decade of their lives and be more important for girls in the second decade of their lives.

3. Unemployment and poverty can affect the way parents act toward each other and toward their children. Job loss or low earnings can lead a parent to be depressed and angry. Fathers in these situations are more likely to have angry, explosive exchanges with wives and children. Their children, in turn, can become more depressed, hostile, and aggressive. Single mothers who live in poverty and have little emotional support are vulnerable to a similar pattern of exchanges with their children.

4. As for parental divorce, most children seem to cope adequately after an initial period of distress, although a minority experience long-term effects. Growing up with a single parent raises the risks of some unwanted consequences, such as dropping out of school, but most children won't experience the negative consequences.

5. As for having working parents, there is virtually no evidence that children are harmed by having both their parents, or their sole parent, work outside the home after their first or second year of life. Questions remain about the possible negative consequences for infants and one-year-olds.

6. The limited evidence on children who grow up with lesbian parents suggests that they do not differ much from children with heterosexual single parents. New reproductive technology, such as the fertilization of eggs outside the womb and the use of surrogate mothers, has created ethical and legal dilemmas.

7. Children's well-being is not worse than it was during the first half of the twentieth century, but in some ways it is worse than it was in the 1950s

and 1960s, when the baby boom children grew up. The standard of living of children improved greatly from 1949 to 1969 but has worsened since then. Economic inequality has increased in the post-1969 period: The percentages of children at both the bottom and the top of the income distribution have risen, whereas the middle group has decreased in size. Studies that have followed children over time have shown that it is common for white or black children to have a temporary spell of poverty but that persistent, long-lasting poverty is heavily concentrated among African Americans.

8. Currently, only about 6 in 10 children are living with both biological parents. Positive developments in children's well-being include having better-educated parents and better physical health. Negative developments include falling college admission test scores, an increase in teenage homicide rates, and an increasing proportion of births outside marriage.

9. Comparisons between the "average" child today and the one of a few decades ago can be misleading. A growing proportion of children live in relatively wealthy settings and are doing well. At the other extreme, persistently poor children appear to have suffered the most, and there is evidence of further deterioration since the mid-1980s. Children in the shrinking middle of the income distribution may have suffered a moderate downward drift in well-being over the past few decades that eroded some of the gains of the 1950s and 1960s. The U.S. government provides less income support to families with children than almost any other Western country, which is a major reason why the percentage of children in poverty is higher than in nearly all other Western countries.

KEY TERMS

norm	authoritarian style (of parenting)	surrogacy
value	androgynous behavior	*in vitro* fertilization
authoritative style (of parenting)	generativity	
permissive style (of parenting)	donor insemination	

FAMILIES ON THE INTERNET

A great deal of information on children—especially disadvantaged children—is available on the Internet. Two reports mentioned in the "Measuring the Well-Being of Children" essay in this chapter were available in PDF (portable document format) on the Web in 1998. *Trends in the Well-Being of America's Children and Youth,* issued by the Office of the Assistant Secretary for Planning and Evaluation of the U.S. Department of Health and Human Services, was available at **http://aspe.os.dhhs.gov/hsp/trends/TOC.HTM**. *America's Children: Key National Indicators of Well-Being,* compiled by the Interagency Forum on Child and Family Statistics, could be found at **www.cdc.gov/nchswww/about/otheract/children/child.htm**. Other resources include the Child Welfare Research Institute (**www.childwelfare.com**), which provides an electronic journal, Child Welfare Review, that consists of links to numerous articles on topics such as foster care and adoption, child poverty and inequality, and child abuse. The National Center for Children in Poverty at Columbia University (**http://cpmcnet.columbia.edu/dept/nccp**) maintains a web site with several well-done on-line reports about child poverty. (Click on "Child Poverty Facts.") Finally, Monitoring the Future (**www.isr.umich.edu/src/mtf/**) is an annual survey of 8th, 10th, and 12th grade students undertaken by the University of Michigan's Institute for Social Research that includes information about drug and alcohol usage and cigarette smoking. Summary tables are available on the web pages.

CHAPTER 15

The Elderly and Their Families

In 1985, when Frank Furstenberg and I were finishing our research for a book on grandparents (Cherlin & Furstenberg, 1992), we visited a senior citizens' center in a Jewish neighborhood in Baltimore. There, we talked with a group of grandparents who told us that the new development in the neighborhood was the immigration of many families from Russia. With some envy, they described to us the relationships the Russian grandparents had with their grandchildren. One woman said:

> We have quite a few Russian friends. Now these friends, invariably the mothers are living with the sons, the daughters, with grandchildren—they're all together. I have noticed such a difference with our Russian friends, who have only been in this country four or five years—these are new immigrants. The grandchildren have great reverence for the grandparents; they live together. When they go on vacation, they take the grandparents with them! I'm just shocked! When they go out eating, they take the grandparents with them! . . . And this is such a new experience because we don't go eating with our children. They go their way, we go our way. It's a special occasion when you go out with your children—an anniversary, a birthday.

Her husband added:

> *The [Russian] grandparents are very much involved with the families of their children. They assume such a responsibility. We know a woman who was a famous surgeon in Russia, she's here in America, and she has that same feeling that she has to take care of her grandchild if the mother goes away. She's always obligated to that little girl. Now, you wouldn't find the same thing in America.*

The grandparents in the room contrasted this great degree of togetherness, respect, and mutual obligation with the weaker ties they experienced with their own children and grandchildren. After a number of these comparisons between the fullness of the grandparent–grandchild relationship among the Russian immigrants and the thinness among the Americans, one of us asked whether anyone in the group would trade places with the immigrants in order to have their type of relationship. The question was met with immediate cries of "No way!"; "No"; and "I'm satisfied." The questioner pursued the point further: "Why wouldn't you trade places? There are all these strong family ties." A woman replied, "I don't think I could live with my children," and a chorus of "No" and "No way" followed.

These American grandparents don't want to live with their children because if they did, they would lose some of the independence they prize. As will be noted later, they belong to the first generation of elderly Americans in which most persons have the opportunity for a reasonably long, healthy, comfortable, independent life. Previous chapters have shown that the kind of intimacy Americans value increasingly consists of love and affection between two independent individuals, each acting to maximize his or her own sense of self-fulfillment. This combination of affection and independence wasn't available to most elderly persons a generation or two ago—too many died prematurely or lacked the money to live on their own. In the second half of the twentieth century, however, the lives of the elderly changed dramatically for the better. Now the grandparents in Baltimore want just what their middle-aged children want: close, warm, satisfying family ties but also independence from kin. They want affection and respect from their children and grandchildren, but they do not want to be obligated to them. The price paid for strong family ties by the Russian immigrants—and by family members in developing countries around the world—is a substantial loss of independence. It is a price most Americans, old or young, are unwilling to pay.

This is not to say that all elderly persons are healthy, well-off, and independent. As the elderly population has expanded, so has the number of frail persons in need of care. The cost of the technology-driven health care provided to the increasing numbers of frail elderly has risen dramatically in recent years and has become a major problem for the nation. In addition, although the proportion of elderly persons who have incomes below the government poverty line is less than the proportion of poor among the nonelderly, it is still the case that, as of 1996, 11 percent of elderly persons were poor (U.S. Bureau of the Census, 1997g). Moreover, a disproportionately large part of the elderly population sits precariously just above the poverty line—not poor, but not by much.[1] The incidence of poverty is greater for elderly women than for men, as we shall see.

This chapter will focus on the family lives of the elderly—their interactions with spouses, children, grandchildren, and other relatives. As birthrates and death rates both

---

[1]Figures will be given later in this chapter.

decline, there are relatively more older people and relatively fewer younger people in the population. Whether society will be able to adequately meet the needs of the elderly is an issue of great importance from the perspective of the public family. Spouses and relatives, as will be demonstrated, provide most of the assistance to the elderly. Providing adequate assistance is likely to be more difficult after the turn of the century, when the huge baby boom generation begins to retire. Other changes in family life, such as the increase in women's work outside the home and the rise in divorce, may also complicate the task of caring for the elderly.

In addition, the quality of family life for the elderly is an important issue from the perspective of the private family; and here the news is heartening. The recent trends in the well-being of children are lamentable, as noted in the previous chapter, but the recent trends in the well-being of the elderly deserve at least two cheers. Programs for the elderly have been the one indisputable success of U.S. social welfare policy since the Great Depression. In fact, so successful have the programs been, and so far have both death rates and birthrates fallen, that most people fail to realize how new is the kind of life most elderly Americans are leading today—a longer, healthier life in which the elderly provide substantial assistance to their family members. In order to understand what has happened, we need to begin by looking back in history.

THE MODERNIZATION OF OLD AGE

We tend to associate grandparents with old-fashioned families—the large, rural, three-generation kind that can be seen on reruns of *The Waltons*. We have a nostalgic image of Grandma, Grandpa, Aunt Bess, Mom, Dad, and the kids sitting around the hearth, baking bread and telling stories. Correspondingly, many observers think that the role of older people in families has become less important since the farm gave way to the factory. According to this view, industrialization meant that older people could no longer teach their children and grandchildren the skills needed to make a living. Moreover, older people no longer controlled the resources—such as farmland—that gave them influence over the lives of the young. There is some truth to this perspective. But the historical facts suggest that grandparenthood—as a distinct and nearly universal stage of life—is a post–World War II phenomenon. To be sure, there have always been grandparents around, but never this many and never with so few of their own children left to raise.

MORTALITY DECLINE

First of all, a century ago—even 50 years ago—far fewer people lived long enough to become grandparents. Much of the decline in adult **mortality** (the demographers' term for deaths in a population) from preindustrial levels has occurred in the twentieth century. Only about 37 percent of all women born in 1870 survived to age 65; in contrast, about 77 percent of women born in 1930 reached age 65 (Uhlenberg, 1979; Uhlenberg, 1980). The greatest declines have occurred in the past few decades, especially for women. The number of years that the average 40-year-old white woman could expect to live increased by four between 1900 and 1940, but between 1940 and 1980 it increased by seven. For men the increases have been smaller: a gain of two years between 1900 and 1940, and four years between 1940 and 1980. The trends for nonwhites are similar, but in every decade the life expectancy of nonwhites has been lower than that of whites. In 1994, white babies had a life expectancy of 76.4 years, compared with 71.7 years for all nonwhite babies and 69.8 years for black babies (U.S. Bureau of the Census, 1997i).

A more difficult question is whether the gains in life expectancy that have been occurring recently have added healthy years or infirm years at the end of life. Have modern medicine and improved standards of living allowed the elderly more years of activity or merely more years in which they are ill or disabled? The answer appears to be that during most of the added years of life expectancy, older people have chronic illnesses that limit their activity but do not make them bedridden. They are neither fully healthy nor in need of care in a hospital or nursing home. For instance, between 1970 and 1980, life expectancy increased by 2.7 years for white women (and 4.6 years for black women), but there was no increase for white women (and an increase of only 1.1 years for black women) in the length of life expected without any disabilities (Crimmons, Saito, & Ingegneri, 1989).[2]

The decline in mortality during the twentieth century has had two consequences. First, both women and men can expect to live much longer lives than was the case several decades ago. Second, women tend to outlive men. In 1991, the average female baby could expect to live 79 years, whereas the average male baby could expect to live just 73 years (U.S. Bureau of the Census, 1997i). A century ago the sex difference was much smaller because many more women died in childbirth. So it is the case today that (1) there are many more older people in the population than there used to be, and (2) 6 out of 10 older people are women. Figure 15.1 shows the growth of the U.S. population aged 65 and over since 1900 and projections to the year 2050. Under the usual convention, which I will follow, the **elderly population** is defined as all persons aged 65 and over. This is an arbitrary cutoff point that is used because 65 has been the age at which a person could retire and receive full Social Security benefits. Most 65-year-old persons are healthy and active, however, and a recent law will gradually raise the retirement age to 67 after the turn of the twenty-first century. As can be seen, there were relatively few elderly people in 1900—about three million. In contrast, there were 32 million in 1990, and there will be an estimated 67 million in 2050 (although projections that far into the future should be seen only as educated guesses).

Moreover, as recently as 1950, according to Figure 15.1, most of the elderly were aged 65 to 74. Then, in midcentury, the proportion of the elderly who were aged 75 to 84 began to grow more rapidly, and more recently the proportion who are aged 85 or older has risen. In other words, since 1900 not only has the elderly population increased greatly but the elderly population itself has become older and older increasingly top-heavy with those in their seventies and eighties. As the older elderly population expanded, **gerontologists** (social and biological scientists who specialize in the study of aging) invented the following terms to differentiate among the aged: **young-old** for those 65 to 74, **old-old** for those 75 to 84, and **oldest-old** for those 85 and over.

The sharp decline in mortality has caused a profound change in the relationship between older persons and their children and grandchildren. For the first time in history, most adults live long enough to get to know most of their grandchildren, and most children have the opportunity to know most of their grandparents. The chances were only fifty-fifty that a child born at the beginning of the twentieth century would still have two living grandparents when he or she reached the age

---

[2]It is possible, as the authors note, that older people were more likely to report themselves as disabled in 1980 than in 1970 because of the growth of government programs that provide disability benefits.

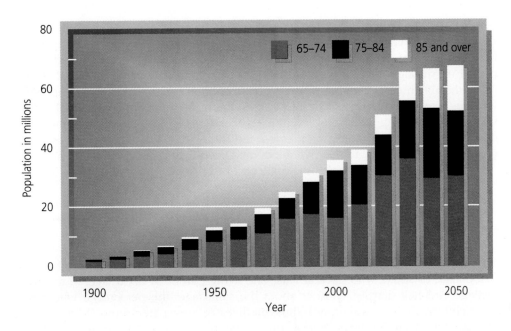

FIGURE 15.1 Actual and estimated population 65 years old and over in the United States: 1900–2050. (*Source:* U.S. Bureau of the Census, 1983.)

of 15. In contrast, the comparable chances rose to 9 in 10 for a 15-year-old in the 1970s (Uhlenberg, 1980). Currently, then, nearly all children have the opportunity to get to know at least two of their grandparents—and many get to know three or four. But children born at the beginning of the century were not nearly as fortunate.

FERTILITY DECLINE

The decline in **fertility** (the demographers' term for births in a population) is the second reason why grandparenthood on a large scale is a recent phenomenon. As recently as the late 1800s, American women gave birth to more than four children, on average (Ryder, 1980). Many parents still were raising their younger children after their older children left home and married. Under these conditions, being a grandparent took a backseat to the day-to-day tasks of raising the children who were still at home. Today, in contrast, the birthrate is much lower, and parents are much more likely to be finished raising their children before any of their grand-children are born. When a person becomes a grandparent now, there are fewer family roles competing for her or his time and attention. Grandparenthood is more of a separate stage of family life, unfettered by childcare obligations—one that car-ries its own distinct identity. It was not always so.

The combination of falling mortality and fertility rates has also altered the bonds of kinship that people have. Because birthrates have fallen, younger people tend to have fewer brothers and sisters than their parents and grandparents. So the horizon-tal bonds of kinship—those to relatives in the same generation as you—have tended to shrink. In contrast, lower mortality means that you have a much greater chance of having living parents well into your middle years than your parents or grandparents. Vertical kinship ties—those to relatives in preceding or following gen-erations—have tended to grow. The result is a kinship structure with growing links up and down the generations and withering links across them (Bengtson, Rosen-thal, & Burton, 1990). A number of gerontologists have argued that lowered mortal-ity rates are making the four- and five-generation family (e.g., my grandparents, my parents, me, my children, and my grandchildren) common.[3] Yet although there are more of these linkages than there used to be, they are still the exception rather than the rule. A recent survey in the Boston area showed that at no stage of the adult life course up through age 70 did more than 20 percent of the respondents belong to more than a three-generation linkage of kin. And the number in five-generation linkages never topped 2 percent. At all ages, the most common generational depth was three. In young adulthood, the three generations were typically my grandparents, my parents, and me; in middle age the three were my parents, me, and my children; and at older ages they were me, my children, and my grandchildren.

The authors of the Boston study, Alice and Peter Rossi, conclude:

> *The truly remarkable demographic change over the twentieth century is the impact of increased longevity on the number of years when the majority of the population may still have at least one living parent* (Rossi & Rossi, 1990).

The watershed age, they argue, is 50. Prior to age 50, there is little drop-off in the percentage of adults who have at least one living parent; at about age 50 the percentage declines sharply. (And at about the same age, the percentage who have grandchildren increases sharply.) Thus, the lives of most parents and children now overlap by about 50 years. These long, potentially rich co-biographies are the product of lower mortality.

STANDARD OF LIVING

Older people also have more money, on average, than they did a few decades ago. As recently as 1960, older Americans were an economically deprived group: 35 percent had incomes below the poverty line, compared with 22 percent of the total population. Now they have more than caught up: 10.8 percent were poor in 1996, compared with 13.7 percent of the total population (U.S. Bureau of the Census, 1997g). The main reason they are no longer disadvantaged is Social Security, the federal government program that provides retirement benefits to persons aged 62 and over. Beginning in the 1950s and 1960s, Congress expanded Social Security coverage, so that nearly all workers, except some who are employed by government, are now covered.[4] And since the 1960s, Congress has increased Social Security benefits far faster than the increase in the cost of living. As a result, the average monthly benefit has doubled in value since 1960, even after taking inflation into account (U.S. House of Representatives, 1993). Today's elderly benefited from the societywide rise in economic welfare in the 1950s and 1960s, when they were working; then, as they reached retirement, they benefited from the increase in Social Security benefits.

Still, there are sharp variations by age, race, and sex in the proportion of the elderly who are poor. Overall, older elderly persons are more likely to be poor than younger elderly persons, elderly women are more likely to be poor than elderly men, and African-American and Hispanic elderly persons are more likely to be poor than white elderly persons. For example, in 1996, 8.8 percent of persons aged 65 to 74 were poor, compared with 13.3 percent of those aged 75 and over

---

[3]See, for example, Shanas (1980).

[4]Persons between ages 62 and 65 are eligible for partial benefits if they retire; persons aged 65 and over are eligible for full benefits. However, the minimum age for full benefits will be raised gradually to 67 after the turn of the century. See Clark (1990).

The standard of living of the elderly has increased substantially since the middle of the twentieth century, in large part because of the expansion of the number of people covered by the Social Security program and the increases in Social Security benefits.

(U.S. Bureau of the Census, 1997g). Only 6.8 percent of elderly men were poor, compared with 13.6 percent of women. And 9.4 percent of the white elderly were poor, compared with 25.3 percent of the black elderly and 24.4 percent of the Hispanic elderly (of any race) (U.S. Bureau of the Census, 1997g).

Moreover, a larger percentage of the elderly than of the nonelderly have incomes that place them just above the poverty level. In 1996 14 percent of the elderly had incomes between 100 and 150 percent of the poverty level, compared with 9 percent of all persons under the age of 65 (U.S. Bureau of the Census, 1997g). This nearly poor group is in some ways more vulnerable to economic and health crises than the poor elderly. Economist Timothy Smeeding has named them the '**tweeners** because they fall between the poor, who can qualify for additional public assistance, and the middle class, who can supplement their Social Security checks with savings and pensions (Smeeding, 1990).[5] Although nearly all elderly persons are covered by **Medicare**, the government program of health insurance for the elderly, Medicare pays for less than half of the health expenditures of the elderly. Moreover, it pays nothing for nursing home care. Persons with incomes below the poverty line are also eligible for **Medicaid**, the government health insurance program for the poor of all ages, which does pay for nursing home costs. Middle-class elderly persons can afford to purchase private health insurance to pay the bills Medicare doesn't cover. But the 'tweeners typically have too much income for Medicaid and too little to buy private insurance.

It is also uncertain whether the Social Security and Medicare systems will provide the elderly of the future with the same level of benefits that today's elderly receive. Low birthrates today mean that there will be fewer workers in a decade or

[5]Smeeding defines the 'tweeners as elderly persons with incomes between 100 and 200 percent of the poverty line, but the precise cutoff is not important. By his definition, the 'tweeners constitute 20 percent of all elderly persons—and 40 percent of all elderly persons living alone.

Families and Public Policy

Financing Social Security and Medicare

The *Chicago Sun-Times* photograph published in newspapers around the country on August 19, 1989, was startling. A band of angry elderly persons, shouting and carrying placards, surrounded a car carrying their U.S. representative, Dan Rostenkowski, then the chairman of the House Ways and Means Committee. His offense had been to sponsor new legislation that *increased* the elderly's protection against long-term hospital stays by limiting the cost to individuals to a maximum of $1,370 per year (Soldo & Agree, 1988). Why were the protesters mad? Because the legislation required that the wealthiest 40 percent of the elderly pay for part of this new benefit through a surtax on their income tax liabilities. A leader of the protesters told a reporter that he did not believe that the elderly should have to pay anything for the new program (*New York Times,* 1989). Fed by questionable opposition from some advocacy groups for the elderly, the protests grew so strong that a stunned Congress repealed the legislation. The incident reinforced a stereotype—overdrawn, as most stereotypes are—of the elderly as demanding ever-greater retirement and medical benefits but refusing to contribute more to the costs of them.

That the benefits paid to the elderly have increased greatly is well known. Social Security benefits accounted for 22 percent of the federal budget in 1996—$84 billion more than all expenditures on national defense. Benefits under Medicare, the government health insurance program for the aged, constituted another 11 percent (U.S. Bureau of the Census, 1997i). The long-term worry is that, as the proportion of the population that is elderly increases, paying for the benefits will become a serious burden on the nonelderly, working-age population. The problem could become severe after 2010, when the large baby boom generation begins to retire.

There are actions that could ease this burden. Although the public pays more attention to the cost of Social Security than to the costs of Medicare, Social Security is actually in better shape. In 1983, Congress passed legislation that greatly strengthened the long-term financial status of the system. Among other things, the legislation increased the payroll taxes that workers and their employers pay into the government's Social Security trust fund. The legislation also raised the age at which people can retire and receive full benefits from 65 to 67 in 2026 (Soldo & Agree, 1988). (Although a two-year increase may seem modest, it will save money because

3 to 4 percent of 65-year-olds die within two years.) Due to the increased payroll taxes, the Social Security trust fund is collecting large surpluses that theoretically should be saved to pay for future costs. Unfortunately, politicians are finding it difficult to resist the temptation to use the surpluses to balance the federal budget today rather than to save it for the next century. Consequently, the surpluses may not provide as much help as they should.

Little has been done, however, to control the spiraling growth of Medicare payments. Three factors are contributing to the growth: the increase in the elderly population, the growing share of the elderly population that is in the old-old and oldest-old categories (and therefore at greatest risk of serious illness and disability), and the increasing cost of health care. According to one projection, Medicare expenditures will increase from about 2 percent of the gross national product (the value of all goods and services produced by the nation) in 1990 to between 4 and 8 percent of the gross national product by 2025 (Palmer, 1988). There are several options that could help contain the costs of health care. The government could raise the payroll tax that pays for Medicare, as has been done with the Social Security

two to pay Social Security taxes for the growing number of elderly. In addition, the increases in the old-old and oldest-old may strain the already costly Medicare system. (See *Families and Public Policy:* Financing Social Security and Medicare.)

Nevertheless, because of the general rise in their standard of living, older parents and their adult children are less dependent on one another economically. Family life in the early decades of the twentieth century was precarious; lower wages, the absence of social welfare programs, and crises of unemployment, illness, and death forced people to rely on their kin for support to a much greater payroll tax. Workers see one combined deduction on their paychecks for Social Security and Medicare; given the recent increases in this deduction, there could be substantial opposition to further hikes. The government could also raise the age of eligibility for Medicare and instead cover the youngest elderly through a national health insurance program. Gerontologist Robert Binstock proposed in congressional testimony in 1992 that elderly people who are better off economically could be charged larger deductibles (the amount an individual must pay for a service before Medicare pays anything) or larger copayments (the percentage of the cost of a service that the individual, not Medicare, must pay after the deductible is met) (U.S. House of Representatives, 1994). Binstock and others note the wide range of incomes among the elderly and urge that those who are better off be required to pay more of the costs of their medical care. He argued that elderly voters are not more self-centered than any other group and that they would be willing to support "sensible policy changes." Some survey research supports his view: In a 1988 random sample of area residents of Albany, New York, the elderly were less likely to support spending on retirement pensions than were middle-aged Americans (Logan & Spitze, 1996). Yet the crowds around Dan Rostenkowski's car suggest how difficult it may be to pass any bill that increases costs for even the financially fortunate elderly.

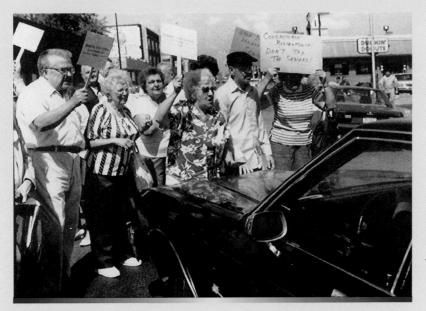

In Chicago in 1989, elderly demonstrators blocked the car of Dan Rostenkowski, who was their representative in Congress and also the Chairman of the House Ways and Means Committee. He had proposed an expansion of Medicare coverage that would have been financed in part by a surtax on the wealthiest 40 percent of the elderly.

extent than is true today. There were no such things as unemployment compensation, welfare checks, food stamps, Medicare, Social Security benefits, or government loans to students. Often there was only your family. Some older people provided assistance to their kin, such as finding a job for a relative, caring for the sick, or minding the grandchildren while the parents worked. Sometimes grandparents, their children, and their grandchildren pooled their resources into a common family fund so that all could subsist. Exactly how common these three-generational economic units were, we do not know; it would be a mistake to assume that all

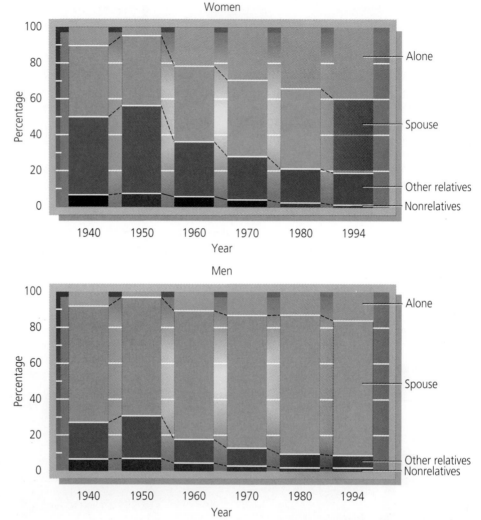

FIGURE 15.2 Living arrangements of women and men 60 years old and over in the United States, 1940 to 1980, and for women and men 65 years old and over, 1994. (*Source:* Sweet & Bumpass, 1987; U.S. Bureau of the Census, 1996b.)

older adults cooperated with their children and grandchildren at all times. Still, historical accounts suggest that intensive intergenerational cooperation was more common than it is today because it was needed more.[6]

LIVING ARRANGEMENTS

The increased independence of the elderly is clearly shown in the great changes in their living arrangements over the past half century. Figure 15.2 displays trends in living arrangements between 1940 and 1980 for persons aged 60 and over, and it also displays living arrangements in 1994 for persons aged 65 and over.[7] Living arrangements are grouped into four categories: (1) living alone, (2) living with their spouse, (3) living without a spouse but with other relatives, or (4) living with nonrelatives only. The upper panel is for women, the lower for men. Among women,

[6]See, for example, Anderson (1971); Hareven (1982).

[7]Figure 15.2 excludes elderly people who were living in nursing homes. Data for 1994 are taken from a published report from the Census Bureau's Current Population Survey, which presented information for people aged 65 and over (U.S. Bureau of the Census, 1996b).

there was a sharp increase in the percentage who were living alone—as you can see from the increasing size of the uppermost section of each bar, moving from left to right. Conversely, there was a sharp fall in the percentage who were living without a spouse but with other relatives (such as a daughter or son). By 1994 it was nearly as common for an elderly woman to live alone as to live with a husband.

This shift toward elderly women's living alone has occurred for two reasons. First, women have been outliving men by a greater and greater margin each decade, so that the number of elderly widows has grown much larger. About 7 in 10 wives survive their husbands (Treas & Bengtson, 1987), and few widows remarry because of the imbalance between the sexes. Second, an elderly widow today is much more likely to live alone than an elderly widow 40 or 50 years ago. In a Los Angeles survey, elderly persons were asked, "Would you prefer to live with your own children or in a separate residence?" Ninety-eight percent of the non-Hispanic whites, 83 percent of the blacks, and 72 percent of the Mexican Americans replied that they would prefer to live on their own.[8] The increases in the income of the elderly have allowed more of them to attain this desire. Overall, 1 of every 10 households in the United States in 1996 was maintained by an elderly person living alone (U.S. Bureau of the Census, 1997e). This represents an enormous change from midcentury, when such households were rare.

Nevertheless, Figure 15.2 shows a very different pattern for elderly men than for elderly women. To be sure, the percentage living alone has increased, as indicated by the top section of the bars, but the increase has been modest. At all times since 1940, the vast majority of elderly men have been married and sharing a household with their wife. Moreover, the proportion who were married *increased* between 1940 and 1994—as you can see by the increasing size of the next-to-the-top section of each bar. This marriage bonanza for elderly men was the flip side of the spouse drought for elderly women. Men had a higher risk of dying than women, but if they managed to live longer than their wives, their remarriage prospects were better than were elderly women's. The current generation of elderly men has been cared for by women throughout their lives—by their mothers when they were growing up and by their wives (many of whom did not work outside the home after marriage) in middle age. They continue to be cared for by women in old age. Most elderly widows, on the other hand, must continue to care for themselves or to rely on relatives living mostly in other households. And so the older years have taken on an increasingly different character for women than for men— women more likely to be living apart from kin, men more likely to be living with their wives. (The rise in divorce in early and mid-adulthood has also separated the worlds of men and women; more on that in a few pages.)

The notion that older parents should retain their independence is deeply rooted in the culture of the Western nations. Historical studies suggest that the preference for heading one's household until as late in life as possible has long been entrenched in Western Europe (Laslett & Wall, 1972). In many areas, the households were formed and maintained under the stem family system (see Chapter 2). The father eventually gave ownership of the farm to the one son who remained home (and thus formed the "stem"); he then brought in a wife. Ordinarily, the son was not allowed to marry until he was given control of the property. But older parents were often in no hurry to turn over their house and land to their son and heir, as demonstrated by the eighteenth-century Austrian folk song introduced in Chapter 8: "Father, when ya gonna gimme the farm?" A U.S. historian has documented the

[8]The study was carried out by Vern Bengtson and collaborators and is cited in Treas and Bengtson (1987).

Grandparents want "intimacy at a distance." They enjoy spending time with their children and grandchildren, but they also want to lead independent lives.

reluctance of first-generation settlers in Andover, Massachusetts, to turn over control of their property to their sons. As in the Austrian case, the young men in Andover needed their own farmland in order to marry. The reluctance of fathers to part with their land sometimes meant that sons were forced to postpone marrying until relatively late ages (Greven, 1970).

Today, of course, most children do not wait to inherit their parents' land but rather leave home to work for wages. Consequently, older parents' households are usually devoid of adult children. Still, the preference for retaining an independent household is strong. Like our Baltimore informants, most elderly persons in the United States, Canada, and Western Europe want to see their children and grandchildren often but not to live with them. What they want, according to a famous phrase, is "intimacy at a distance" (Rosenmayr & Kockeis, 1965). This trade-off between intimacy and independence has probably reduced the amount of contact the elderly have with their kin. For example, three of five elderly persons in the United States in 1900 were living with at least one (usually unmarried) child (Smith, 1979), and until recently few were living alone. But the preference that today's elderly express for living alone is genuine, and it is consistent with deeply held values of individualism in Western culture. It is not merely a rationale that the modern elderly have invented to mask disappointment at living apart from kin.

THE QUALITY OF INTERGENERATIONAL TIES

Beyond these demographic developments, what can be said about the quality of the relationships between older people and their kin today? What does it mean that so many elderly women live alone and so few elderly persons of either sex live with their children? Are they lonely and isolated? Are they a part of their children's and grandchildren's lives? Do they provide much support to their kin and receive much in return? Sociologists studying these issues often define the subject as "intergenerational solidarity." The concept is a broad one, and, fittingly, *solidarity* is a word with many connotations. When asked, a word processor pops up the following synonyms: cooperation, fellowship, harmony, unity, stability, and reliability. An unabridged dictionary defines solidarity as "an entire union of interests and responsibilities in a group," and it quotes a phrase from Joseph Conrad: "Solidarity knits together innumerable hearts" (*Webster's Third New International Dictionary,* 1976). We might say, after Conrad, that **intergenerational solidarity** refers to the characteristics of family relationships that knit the generations together.

With respect to the older parents and their adult children, three broad characteristics of intergenerational solidarity have received the most attention from social scientists. They have been given slightly different names and definitions (Rossi & Rossi, 1990; Roberts, Richards, & Bengtson, 1991; Silverstein & Bengtson, 1997). Here are the names and definitions I will use:

- *Contact* How frequently parents and children see each other and are in touch electronically through telephone calls or E-mail messages.
- *Affinity* How emotionally close parents and children feel and how much they agree on values, attitudes and beliefs.
- *Assistance* The amount of assistance, in either time, goods, or money, that parents and children provide to each other.

Contact and affinity are relevant for judging whether the elderly obtain the closeness and emotional support they wish—and whether they provide closeness and emotional support to their children and grandchildren. These are the kinds of questions included in Chapter 1 under the umbrella of the private family. Assistance, on the other hand, is relevant to the kinds of questions that arise from the perspective of the public family—specifically, who will care for the frail elderly and who will help young or middle-aged parents with problems such as amassing a downpayment for a house or coping with a divorce? Let us examine these three characteristics of intergenerational relations.

CONTACT

It might seem logical to infer that, in a society in which 1 in 10 households contains an elderly person living alone and in which few elderly persons live with their children, the elderly must be isolated from their children and grandchildren. Indeed, many observers have concluded as much. "Isolated" is a value-laden term, however, and what might seem like isolation to a Japanese grandparent (see pp. 488–489) might seem like a surfeit of contact to an American grandparent. Statistics cannot settle a matter such as this, but they can describe the patterns of contact between the elderly and their kin.

Among elderly persons in one national study who were living alone and who had living children, three-fourths lived within minutes of a child and two-thirds saw at least one of their children weekly (U.S. National Center for Health Statistics, 1986). In another national survey, about half of the elderly with children had seen at least one of them that day or the day before; four-fifths had seen a child in the last week (Shanas, 1980). Similarly, in our survey, we interviewed the grandparents of a national sample of children and asked them "When was the last time you saw any grandchild?" About half of the grandparents had seen at least one grandchild that day or the day before, and 70 percent had seen a grandchild within the last week. Just one in six had not seen a grandchild within the previous month (Cherlin & Furstenberg, 1992). Elderly persons living alone who don't have children (about 3 in 10), of course, have much less frequent contact with relatives. But overall, the amount of contact that the elderly have with their children and grandchildren is surprisingly high.

What affects the amount of contact? In our grandparent study, we found one dominant factor, so strong that it alone accounted for nearly two-thirds of the variance in contact among the families: distance (Cherlin & Furstenberg, 1992). Almost invariably, grandparents who lived near their grandchildren saw them regularly—no matter what their social class was or whether the grandparent was on the mother's or father's side. If the grandparents lived within a mile, they typically saw their grandchildren twice a week. If they lived 1 to 10 miles away, they typically visited about once a week; and at further distances the number of visits fell off rapidly.

The dominance of distance illustrates both the strength and the vulnerability of the grandparent–parent–grandchild relationship. As for its strength: When grandchildren live close by, grandparents see them regularly, except under unusual circumstances. Parents and children, with few exceptions, make sure they visit the grandparents. The pull grandparents exert when they live nearby shows how strong is the sense of obligation among adult children to keep in touch with their parents and their in-laws. This sense of obligation is usually overlaid with love, concern, and assistance, but even when it is unsupported by these props, it is often still honored. The uniformly high frequency of visiting among nearby kin suggests that the bond among grandparents, their adult children, and their grandchildren is still strong.

On the other hand, when adult children move away, grandparents' access to their grandchildren drops dramatically. To be sure, adult children who have weaker ties to their parents may be the ones who tend to move from their hometowns. Job possibilities, marriage, and many other events also enter into the decision to move. Still, from the grandparents' point of view, whether or not adult children live close by involves a large element of luck. When a son takes a job in another state or a daughter-in-law moves away after a divorce, the grandparent is rarely able to overcome this impediment to regular contact.

In addition to living close by, the grandparents in our study saw their grandchildren more frequently if they had a close relationship with the mother of the grandchild—their daughter or daughter-in-law. Middle-aged women do the work of "kin keeping" more often than middle-aged men, and studies show that their ties with older and younger generations are stronger and more consistent, on average, than men's (Rossi & Rossi, 1990). (See Chapter 4.) Finally, family culture—shared values and traditions—seems to influence contact. We found more contact among families that reported traditions of family songs, recipes, jokes, and so forth, and the Boston study reported that adults raised in more cohesive families established families in adulthood that also were more cohesive (Cherlin & Furstenberg, 1992; Rossi & Rossi, 1990).

AFFINITY

Hand in hand with the demographic and economic changes in the lives of the elderly have come great changes in the emotional content of their relationships with their children and grandchildren. During the twentieth century, there appears to have been an increasing emphasis on bonds of sentiment: love, affection, and companionship. There is no evidence that the emotional ties between parents and children have grown weaker. When Furstenberg and I asked grandparents whether grandparenthood had changed since they were grandchildren, we heard stories of their childhood that differed from the idyllic *Waltons* image. Their grand-parents, we were told, were respected, admired figures who often assisted other family members. But again and again, we heard them talk about the emotional distance between themselves and their grandparents:

> The only grandmother I remember is my father's mother, and she lived with us.

INTERVIEWER: What was it like, having your grandmother live with you?
> Terrible [laughter]! She was old, she was strict. . . . We weren't allowed to sass her. I guess that was the whole trouble. No matter what she did to you, you had to take it. . . . She was good, though. . . . She used to do all the patching of the pants, and she was helpful. But, oh, she was strict. You weren't allowed to do anything, she'd tell on you right away.

INTERVIEWER: So what difference do you think there is between being a grandparent when you were a grandchild and being a grandparent now?
> It's different. My grandma never gave us any love.

INTERVIEWER: No?
> Nooo. My goodness, no, no. No, never took us anyplace, just sat there and yelled at you all the time.

INTERVIEWER: Did you have a lot of respect for your grandmother?
> Oh, we had to whether we wanted to or not, we had to.

Grandma may have helped out, and she certainly was respected, even loved; but she was often an emotionally distant figure. This is not to say that affection was absent from the relations between young and old. But there has been a shift in the balance between respect and affection. For example, we asked grandparents who knew at least one of their own grandparents "Are you and [your grandchild] more

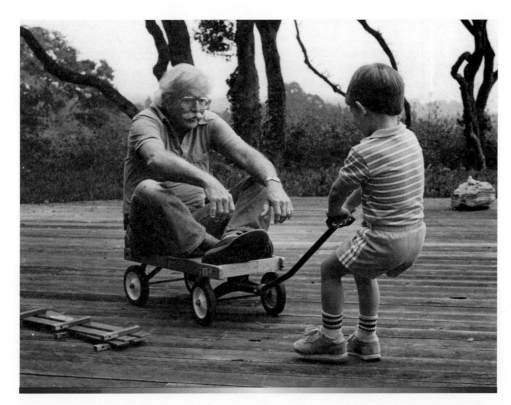

During the twentieth century, grandparents' relations with their grandchildren have increasingly emphasized love, affection, and companionship.

friendly, less friendly, or about the same as your grandparents were with you?" Forty-eight percent said "more friendly"; only 9 percent said "less friendly." Similarly, 55 percent said their relationship with grandchildren was "closer" than their relationship had been with their grandparents; just 10 percent said "not as close."

Granted, it is hard to judge the accuracy of these recollections of two generations ago. But the story that the grandparents consistently told us fits with the demographic and economic developments that have been discussed. It is easier for today's grandparents to have a pleasurable, emotion-laden relationship with their grandchildren because they are more likely to live long enough to develop the relationship; because they are not still busy raising their own children; because they can travel long distances more easily and communicate over the telephone; and because they have fewer grandchildren and more economic resources to devote to them. Earlier in the nation's history, the generations were often bound up in economic cooperation that took precedence over affection and companionship. In fact, there may be a trade-off between bonds of obligation and authority, on the one hand, and bonds of sentiment. Historian David Hackett Fischer, in his book on the history of aging in America, noted the following differences between the nation's early and later years:

> *Even as most (though not all) elderly people were apt to hold more power than they would possess in a later period, they were also apt to receive less affection, less love, less sympathy from those younger than themselves. The elderly were kept at an emotional distance by the young* (Fischer, 1978).

Conversely, in modern America:

> *As elders lost their authority within the society, they gained something in return. Within the sphere of an individual family, ties of affection may have grown stronger as ties of family obligation grew weak* (Fischer, 1978).

This increasing emphasis on affection appears to be continuing among the elderly and their children and grandchildren today.

Nearly all studies report a high level of warmth and emotional closeness among the different generations in a family (Treas & Bengtson, 1987). Nevertheless, the degree of emotional closeness between parents and children varies over the life cycle. It will come as no surprise to parents that closeness and intimacy decline as children move into adolescence. That is the life stage when children must establish their autonomy. As the children reach adulthood, closeness improves again, and it improves further as the parents enter old age and their children enter middle age (Rossi & Rossi, 1990). Moreover, there appear to be substantial gender differences in closeness. The Boston study found that in mid and later life, mother–daughter relationships are the closest, mother–son relationships are second, father–daughter third, and father–son fourth. These differences suggest once again that it is women who invest more in family ties.

The second component of affinity is agreement between the generations on values, attitudes, and beliefs. Most studies show substantial agreement between older parents and their adult children. In a 1990 survey of 1,500 adults, individuals with living parents were asked how similar their opinions were to those of their mothers and fathers. Sixty-nine percent said that their opinions were "very similar" or "somewhat similar" to their mothers' opinions. Agreement with fathers was not quite as high: 60 percent said their opinions were "very similar" or "somewhat similar" (Silverstein & Bengtson, 1997). Substantial agreement between parents and children is to be expected for two reasons (Roberts et al., 1991). First, parents socialize their children in their own values while raising them—both at home and at the family's place of religious worship. Second, parents and children often share the same social class position and therefore have similar kinds of jobs and leisure activities. As noted in the previous chapter, a person's social class position can influence her or his opinions about independence, conformity, and other values.

Nevertheless, the experiences of parents and children do diverge in ways that can cause differences of opinions. Studies suggest that individuals' beliefs are affected by the social context during their adolescence and young adulthood and that these beliefs, once formed, tend to remain throughout adulthood. For example, growing up during an economic depression may make a person frugal for a lifetime. Consequently, if the social context in which children grow up differs from the context when their parents grew up, some differences in beliefs are likely. This process is called the **cohort replacement model** of public opinion because it presumes that each successive *birth cohort* (see Chapter 2) experiences a different social environment and retains distinctive opinions throughout adult life (Alwin, 1996).

ASSISTANCE

In middle and old age, as in childhood, most people in need of assistance turn to their kin. The majority of help that the elderly and their adult children receive comes from one another. And because of lengthening life expectancy, this stage of mutual assistance lasts longer than ever before. At current rates of fertility and mortality, according to one widely cited demographic estimate, the average person can expect his or her life to overlap slightly longer with a parent over the age of 65 than with children under the age of 18 (Watkins, Menken, & Bongaarts, 1987). Here again a striking demographic statistic found its way to the cover of *Newsweek,* which announced that "the average American woman spends 17 years raising children and 18 years helping aging parents" (*Newsweek,* 1990). But *Newsweek* didn't get it quite right: Yes, adult children will provide assistance during the years when they have aging parents, but most of them also will *receive* substantial help from their aging parents as well. Until their last years, most aging parents are relatively healthy and economically independent.

In fact, until they are very old or very ill, the elderly typically give more assistance to their adult children than the children provide them (Soldo & Hill, 1993). Assistance is episodic rather than continual: Parents or children help out or give money when there is a particular need. For instance, grandparents spend much more time providing assistance to their adult children when their grandchildren are in their preschool years than when they are adolescents. Indeed, in 1991, grandparents were the primary source of childcare for 16 percent of preschool children whose mothers worked outside the home (U.S. Bureau of the Census, 1994c). As mentioned in Chapter 12, it is common for a divorced daughter to move back in with her parents temporarily after her marriage breaks up. Financial assistance also tends to occur in lump transfers rather than continual flows. Older parents might provide a child with a few thousand dollars toward the down payment on a home, or they might help a child pay for a grandchild's college tuition.

These patterns of giving assistance only when there are specific needs imply that, at any given time, most older parents and adult children are not providing much assistance to each other. In a national survey of adults with living parents, only 17 percent of the adults reported getting $200 or more from their parents, and only

Grandparents are an important source of childcare for young children whose parents work outside the home.

4 percent reported giving $200 or more, within the previous five years—excluding help with mortgage payments. Childcare is more common: About 13 percent had received baby-sitting or childcare assistance from their parents in the previous month. Giving and getting advice and support are more common still: 27 percent had received, and 25 percent had given, advice or emotional support in the previous month (Eggebeen & Hogan, 1990).

African-American and Hispanic elderly persons, who tend to have lower incomes than whites, are more likely to reside with a relative (other than a spouse) than are whites, but among those who do not coreside, there is little difference in the amount of assistance. That is to say, black or Hispanic adults and their parents who live apart are not more likely to exchange goods and services than similar whites—despite what studies of low-income people's sharing networks might lead one to expect. The researchers who have uncovered this finding speculate that many elderly poor people are not enmeshed in effective sharing networks—or else that the poor have fewer resources to share today than when many of the observational studies of kinship networks were undertaken (Eggebeen & Hogan, 1990).[9]

The kind of assistance the two generations provide to each other is complementary. According to the Boston study, adult children tend to provide more personal support, such as comfort or care during an illness, whereas older parents tend to provide more material help: a loan, part of a down payment on a house, or help with finding a job (Rossi & Rossi, 1990). This pattern allows the older generation to maintain a sense of independence, so central to American values. In reality, however, adult children also provide substantial financial support to their parents—but in such a way that no one need notice. The hidden subsidy is Social Security, the role of which in raising the living standard of the elderly was discussed earlier. I pay thousands of dollars a year in Social Security taxes, and the program sends thousands of dollars a year to my elderly parents. Yet the genius of the system is that my parents and I don't

[9]See also Hofferth (1984).

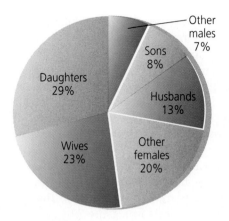

FIGURE 15.3
Relationship of informal caregivers to disabled elderly recipients of care. (*Source:* U.S. Senate, Special Committee on Aging, 1988.)

have to acknowledge this connection; we can both maintain that, as good American parents and children should be, we are economically independent of each other.

Newsweek was right, nevertheless, in using the word *woman* instead of *adult* to describe the caregiver. For here again, women are the kin keepers, providing most of the care for elderly husbands and parents. Figure 15.3 shows the relationship of the persons providing "informal"—that is, unpaid—care to disabled elderly persons in 1982; 72 percent of them were women, most often daughters or wives. Moreover, there is a rough hierarchy of caregivers. If the elderly person's spouse is alive and reasonably healthy, she or he will normally become the primary caregiver; if the spouse is not alive, an adult daughter is usually next in line; and if there is no daughter who can manage the care, another relative, such as a son or a sister, may be called upon (Gatz, Bengtson, & Blum, 1990). Since a majority of elderly women survive their husbands, this hierarchy means, in practice, that elderly women are likely to be cared for eventually by their daughters. For an unmarried elderly person, having a daughter is the key to receiving support. In a 1984 national health survey, elderly respondents were asked if they needed help with any of 13 activities of daily living and home management. If they answered affirmatively, they were asked whether or not they received help from one of their children. Among those who were unmarried and not living with a child, persons who had at least one daughter were more likely to receive help than those who had just a son or even two sons (Spitze & Logan, 1990b).

These mostly female caregivers not only assist their relatives but also perform a critical public service. Without the care that they provide, our already expensive government health care programs would be much more costly. Since Medicare does not pay for nursing home care, individuals must pay nursing home costs by spending their own money first. Only when individuals have spent most of their savings—and therefore meet the government requirements for being poor—are they eligible for Medicaid, which will then step in and pay the bills. Typically, persons of modest means who enter nursing homes—the costs of which average more than $20,000 per year—"spend down" their assets in several months and then turn to Medicaid (Palmer, 1988).[10] Public spending for nursing home care totaled about $45 billion in 1995. Individuals in care spend another $29 billion out of their own pockets (U.S. Bureau of the Census, 1997i).

Four percent of the elderly in the United States resided in nursing homes in 1995 (U.S. National Center for Health Statistics, 1997c). It is not hard to grasp the

---

[10]Palmer estimates that nursing homes costs range from $20,000 to $30,000 per year. Timothy Smeeding cites a 1984 average cost of $18,000 per year; see Smeeding (1990).

implications of the growth of the elderly population for the future demand for nursing home care. As was noted in the discussion of Figure 15.1, the oldest-old, those aged 85 and over, are the fastest-growing segment. Their numbers are expected to nearly double from about 3.8 million in 1996 to 6.8 million in 2010 (U.S. Bureau of the Census 1983, 1997i). Perhaps 40 percent of them, at current rates, will reside in a nursing home at some point during their last years (Soldo & Agree, 1988). From the public standpoint, it is crucial to hold down the number of persons who will need institutionalized care. That is precisely what family members do now.

You might think that most seriously impaired elderly persons are cared for in nursing homes, but that is not so. More are living in the community (that is, in private homes or apartments, not in institutions) than in nursing homes. Figure 15.4 illustrates this fact. In order to measure physical impairment, gerontologists have developed standard questions about the activities a person needs help with. The most common set, **activities of daily living,** or ADLs, refers to personal care, including bathing, dressing, eating, getting into and out of bed, walking indoors, and using the toilet (U.S. National Center for Health Statistics, 1987). These questions have been asked of national samples of elderly persons both in the community and in nursing homes (National Aging Information Center, 1996), allowing us to make a comparison of their degrees of impairment. Figure 15.4 compares the number of elderly persons in nursing homes with the number of elderly persons in the community who had at least one ADL limitation that lasted for six months or more in 1989. Both population are divided into two groups: those with one or two limitations in ADLs and those with three to six. The graph then shows:

- Among those with one or two ADL limitations, far more were living in the community than in nursing homes in 1989.
- Even among the most seriously impaired elderly—those with three to six limitations—slightly more were living in the community than in nursing homes in 1989.

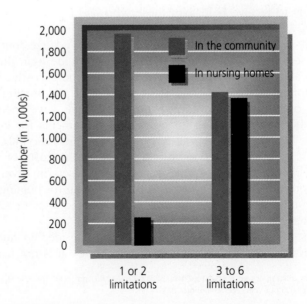

FIGURE 15.4 Elderly persons in the community and in nursing homes, by number of limitations in activities of daily living. (*Source:* National Aging Information Center, 1996.)

Women in the Middle?   About four-fifths of the care of the disabled elderly who are living in the community is provided by relatives, most of them women.[11] If these caregivers went on strike tomorrow, nursing homes would be flooded with new patients and Medicaid would pay out billions more. For instance, let us return to Figure 15.4 and suppose that most of the caregivers of the 850,000 noninstitutionalized persons with five or six limitations in ADLs quit. If, say, 500,000 of these elderly persons were forced to enter nursing homes, the bill, at about $20,000 per person, would be $10 billion per year. Of course, it is absurd to imagine that so many caretakers would quit because most are relatives who love the persons they care for and feel a sense of obligation to help. There is reason, nonetheless, to be concerned about the future availability of caregivers. The informal care system has depended on the availability and goodwill of middle-aged women. A few decades ago, most married women were not employed outside the home; presumably, they had more time to devote to caring for an aging parent. But a majority of married women now work outside the home, and the proportion will likely increase further in the next decade or two. Sons and daughters who are employed full-time give less help to, and receive less help from, their parents (Rossi & Rossi, 1990). In addition, the fall in birthrates since the 1950s means that there are proportionally fewer adult daughters per elderly parent.

Moreover, some of these caregivers may also face requests for help from their own children. A daughter, for example, might separate from her husband and wish to return to the parents' home temporarily with the grandchildren. Or the woman herself, having postponed childbearing until her thirties, might still be raising children. The specter of double demands up and down the generational ladder has led to much concern about the caregiving burden for "women in the middle" (Brody, 1981). Although concern may be warranted, few women, and fewer men, are faced with demands for care from children and parents at the same time. Most older people do not need extensive care until late in life; by that time their children are usually through raising the grandchildren. So, for a middle-aged adult, the peak years for the care of young children typically occur before the peak years of the care of older parents (Uhlenberg, 1993).

For example, a survey in the Albany-Schenectady-Troy, New York, metropolitan area found that women and men in the middle were most commonly in their early forties; even so, just 17 percent of women and 14 percent of men were spending three or more hours per week caring for children as well as three or more hours per week caring for parents. An even smaller percentage of men and women in their fifties and sixties was caring for older and younger kin (Spitze & Logan, 1990a). Being caught in the middle, then, is a brief period for most caregivers. Some people will experience it in early middle age, when they are still raising children and their parents are still alive. A few may experience it later in middle age, when divorce or unemployment produces a crisis for their adult children.

It would seem obvious that being caught in the middle would be highly stressful, as the caregiver seeks to fulfill what is expected of her as wife, employee, mother, and daughter. Some studies have indeed found a high stress level among such caregivers (Brody, Kleban, Johnson, Hoffman, & Schoonover, 1987). But it may also be the case that having a job takes a person's mind off her caregiving responsibilities, making it easier to provide care. Some recent studies have noted this "buffering" effect of one role on the stress provoked by another. One study found

[11]U.S. Senate, Special Committee on Aging (1988).

that caregivers with multiple roles—spouse, employee—experienced less stress than those mainly engaged in providing assistance (Stoller & Pugliesi, 1989).[12] The stress felt by caregivers in the middle may stem only from the care they give to frail parents, not from an overload of responsibilities. If they are employed, their jobs may provide them with a sense of fulfillment and excitement rather than strain (Epstein, 1988). This is not to minimize the difficulty of caring for an ailing parent, nor to diminish the social importance of care that adult children provide. If multiple roles do produce strain for women, who provide much of the care, one solution would be for men to assume more of the responsibility.

THE VARIABILITY OF INTERGENERATIONAL TIES

Not all families, of course, have strong intergenerational ties. Silverstein and Bengtson (1997) examined the variation in solidarity reported by adult children in a 1990 national survey. Adult daughters and their mothers were more likely to have high levels of all indicators of solidarity—contact, affinity, and assistance—than were daughters and fathers or than sons and either fathers or mothers. This finding confirms once again the central role of the mother–daughter bond in inter-generational relations. At the other extreme, adult children in the study reported low levels of all indicators of solidarity when their parents were divorced. The lack of solidarity was particularly strong between adult children and their divorced older fathers.

Other studies also show that older divorced fathers and their children, on average, have relationships that are far less close than the relationships of fathers and children from families with no divorce. In the National Survey of Families and Households, conducted in 1987 and 1988, adults were asked who, among persons not living with them, they would turn to for assistance in three situations: an emergency in the middle of the night, the need to borrow $200 for a few weeks, and the need to talk to someone about a problem. Two researchers tabulated the answers given by men aged 50 to 79 who had living adult children. About half of all the men who had been divorced did not even mention a child as someone they would turn to in any of the three situations. In contrast, less than one-fourth of never-divorced men failed to mention a child. Moreover, only 50 percent of the divorced fathers had weekly contact with their children, compared with 90 percent of never-divorced men (Cooney & Uhlenberg, 1990). Another study using the same survey found that adult children from divorced families rated the quality of their relationship with noncustodial fathers no more positively than adult children who had never lived with their fathers since birth (Aquilino, 1994). Yet another study found that if the custodial parent had remarried, thus providing the children with a stepparent, relations between adult children and the noncustodial parents were weakened further (Lye, Klepinger, Hyle, & Nelson, 1992).

The same survey indicated that adult stepchildren saw their stepfathers less often than adult biological children saw their fathers and that adult stepchildren rated the quality of their relationship with their stepfather lower. Moreover, if the marriage between the natural parent and the stepparent had ended, either because of a divorce or because the natural parent had died, the ties between an adult stepchild and stepparent often ended as well: 57 percent of the adult stepchildren in stepfamilies ended by divorce never saw their stepparent, and 46 percent of

---

[12]See also the discussion in Spitze and Logan (1990a).

adult stepchildren in stepfamilies ended by death never saw their stepparent (White, 1994). Thus, the relationship between adult stepchildren and stepparents, which in any case seems less close than between adult biological children and parents, may not even survive a divorce or death. Consequently, some elderly stepparents may not receive as much support from their stepchildren as they may need.

It seems doubtful, then, that the daughters and sons who provide so much of the care for the frail elderly will provide as much care for noncustodial fathers, never-married fathers, or stepfathers as for biological fathers they lived with continuously while growing up. And the problem will likely worsen after the turn of the century. Recall that the divorce rate doubled in the 1960s and 1970s and that the proportion of children born outside marriage rose during (and after) those decades as well. The men who will reach the age of 65 after the year 2000 will be part of the first generation to have lived most of their adult lives after the great increases in divorce and childbearing outside marriage. Chapter 12 noted that many fathers have little contact with their children after a divorce or a separation from the children's mother.

Elderly men will have to rely even more heavily on their main source of support today: their current wives. It is possible, however, that this strategy won't work as well in the future either. The women who will be reaching old age will belong to the first generation to have extensive employment histories throughout adulthood. They may have more financial resources when they retire, and some may keep working at least part-time after reaching age 65. Frances Goldscheider speculates that fewer widowed and divorced women may find it attractive to remarry an elderly man: They will have less need for financial support, and they may prefer other activities to caregiving. If divorced men aren't remarried in old age, and if they can't rely on their children, they may have no one to help them in their last, frail years. In fact, the percentage of elderly men who live with their wives, after increasing from 1940 to 1980 (see Figure 15.2), has now leveled off.[13] Research on divorce, Goldscheider writes, "has focused on women and children as the 'victims'" because of the loss of the father's income. Yet in old age, when kinship ties matter, "it is males who are at risk" (Goldscheider, 1990).

Elderly gay men and lesbians may also face challenges in obtaining support in old age. Their ability to call on others for assistance will depend on how well they have been able to construct a network of friends, partners, and biological relatives. The effectiveness of these networks is likely to vary widely. In addition, many of their ties are likely to be with people in the same generation; consequently, their access to younger adults who could provide help may be limited (Kimmel, 1992).

BUT ARE THEY *REALLY* HAPPY?

I have on several occasions given lectures about the American family to audiences of Asians, who are used to a family system in which elderly parents are expected to live with their adult children. (See *Families in Other Cultures:* The Elderly and Their Families in Japan.) Some members of the audience are surprised and dismayed to learn that most older persons in the United States, and throughout the Western nations, live apart from their children. Hands go up and I am politely asked how Americans could do such a cruel thing to their parents. I then explain, as I have in this

[13]For a comparison of 1980 and 1990, see U.S. Bureau of the Census (1991d).

Families in Other Cultures

The Elderly and Their Families in Japan

In North America and Western Europe, people are used to a family system in which most of the elderly live apart from kin. The family system in Japan, until recently at least, could hardly have been more different. In the traditional Japanese household, all children except the eldest son left home when they reached adulthood. Until their deaths, the parents lived with the eldest son and his wife in the household. Japanese culture emphasized the importance of filial piety—obeying and serving one's parents throughout one's life. As recently as 1970, 77 percent of the elderly in Japan lived with their children.

But this system is being tested by the most rapid aging of any population in the world and by Japan's continuing economic development. By world demographic standards, the Japanese birthrate plummeted overnight. As recently as 1947, the average Japanese woman bore 4.5 children; 10 years later, the average was down to 2.0. And since World War II, life expectancy in Japan has risen to the highest level in the world (Preston & Kono, 1988). This sharp fall in births and sharp increase in longevity has quickly given Japan one of the highest proportions of elderly persons of any country. And, as is well known, the Japanese economy has grown by leaps and bounds over the past few decades.

Under these changed circumstances, the proportion of the elderly who live with their children has declined. Between 1980 and 1990, for example, the proportion living with a married child decreased from 53 to 42 percent (Morioka, 1996). Although a majority of Japanese still tell pollsters that they believe it is good, in the abstract, for children to take care of their elderly parents, fewer are counting on it. For example, the proportion of married women under the age of 50 who say they plan to depend on their children in old age dropped from 65 percent in 1950 to just 18 percent in 1990 (Ogawa & Retherford, 1993). Japanese demographers are now predicting that by 2010 a majority of the widowed elderly will be living alone (Hirosima, 1997).

And many three-generation households are now formed because of a specific condition rather than because of a general commitment to filial piety. Japanese sociologists are reporting an emerging pattern of "eventual coresidence," in which the older parents live separately as long as their health allows them to; only after frailty or illness sets in do they coreside with a child (Oda, 1991). Moreover, some urban young adults are finding that coresidence with parents is economically advantageous given the very high cost of housing in metropolitan areas. Grandmothers can also provide childcare for the growing (although still modest) number of mothers employed outside the home. So the old family forms are being retained for some new reasons.

In fact, the commitment to filial piety appears to be eroding rapidly. The figure shows the responses, in surveys from 1963 to 1990, of married women under age 50 to the question "What is your opinion about children caring for their elderly parents?" As can be seen, the percentage responding that it is either "unavoidable" or "not a good custom" has increased sharply from 12 percent in 1963 to 34 percent in 1990, whereas over the same period the percentage responding that it is either "a good custom" or "a natural duty" has declined from 80 percent to 50 percent. Most of the change occurred in the 1980s. Japanese women have moved toward the view, which predominates in the Western nations, that assistance to the elderly is something to be given for specific needs rather than out of a general sense of obligation.

Moreover, the proportion of Japanese elderly who are being cared for in institutions is not as different from that in the United States as one might expect. As noted earlier in the chapter, about 4 percent of the elderly in the United States reside in nursing homes. In Japan, the figure is about 2 percent. But the average length of a

chapter, that the vast majority of older persons in the United States prefer it that way. Hands go up again, and it becomes clear that many in the audience don't believe it.

Here in the United States, as well, some observers don't believe that the elderly really are happier living apart from their children. The skeptics acknowledge that the elderly say they prefer to live apart but question whether deep down this preference is real. Hasn't there been a loss in family feeling, the skeptics ask, since the time when most elderly were living with their children? Haven't modern hospital stay for elderly Japanese is much higher than in the United States; these long stays have been labeled "social hospitalization." On any given day, 2.6 percent of elderly Japanese are in a hospital, compared with just 0.8 percent in the United States; some of the long stays in Japan may be a culturally acceptable alternative to nursing home care.[1]

The family lives of the Japanese elderly, then, are a mixture of persistence and change. Many—although no longer a majority—live with their children, sometimes with a younger son or even a daughter. General support for the cultural ideal of coresidence is still widespread. In a 1986 comparative survey, 58 percent of the elderly in Japan said it was better to live with their children than merely to meet to eat and talk, whereas in the United States only 3 percent of the elderly thought it was better to live with their children (Martin, 1989). Nevertheless, the proportion of the Japanese elderly living apart from their children has been growing, and younger parents' confidence that their children eventually will support them has been slipping. To an increasing degree, coresidence is a response to an expensive housing market, a lack of available childcare services, or an illness, rather than to the norm that parents ought to live with their children whatever the circumstances. If the housing market improves or childcare becomes more widely available, coresidence could decrease further. I think it likely that the family lives of the elderly in Japan will continue to evolve toward greater independence from their children, although older parents will probably remain more dependent on their children than in the West.

[1]The figures for Japan are from Martin (1989). I calculated the 0.8 percent figure for the United States from data in U.S. Bureau of the Census (1991e).

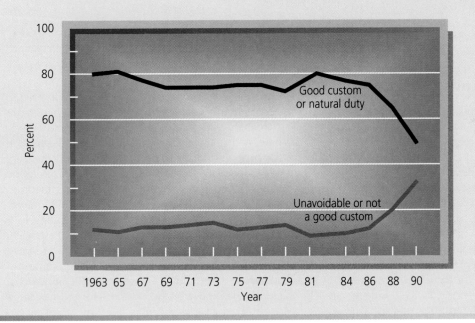

FIGURE A Responses of married women under 50 in Japan to the question, "What is your opinion about children caring for their elderly parents?" Foreground: percent responding either "a good custom" or a "natural duty." Background: percent responding either "unavoidable" or "not a good custom." (*Source:* Ogawa & Retherford, 1993.)

grandparents, in their rush to retirement villages in the Sun Belt, abandoned their bonds to their grandchildren?[14] In endorsing their independence from their busy, self-absorbed children, aren't they making a virtue out of necessity?

There is a grain of truth to these charges. There probably has been some weakening of the bonds among the generations as the elderly and their children have

[14]See for example, Kornhaber and Woodward (1981).

established separate residences. But the multigenerational households of the past were held together in part by economic hardship. Older parents and their adult children had to cooperate in order to make ends meet. As they worked for the common good, no doubt strong bonds of obligation and loyalty and trust developed. Given the chance to live separately, however, most older parents and adult children have chosen to do so. In addition, despite the growth of retirement communities in the South, there's little evidence that the elderly, as a group, live farther from their adult children than they used to (Uhlenberg, 1993).

When we asked the Baltimore grandparents why they wouldn't trade places with the Russian immigrants in order to have strong ties to their children and grandchildren, one grandmother said, simply, "It's too late." What she meant was that, given the opportunity for independence, most American grandparents had already seized it and couldn't give it up. To live with their children, they would have to adjust their daily schedules to fit their children's busy lives. It's easy to look at current living arrangements and criticize the elderly for emphasizing autonomy and personal satisfaction in their daily lives. But they are merely engulfed in the same flood of self-fulfillment that has washed over their children and grandchildren. To ask grandparents to lead a retreat to a family system that emphasizes cooperation over companionship, obligations over independence, duty over love, is perhaps unfair. This is the first generation in which most older Americans have had a choice in these matters; should they be criticized for making the same choices as everyone else?

SUMMARY

1. Although there have always been grandparents, in many ways grandparenthood is a modern experience. The life expectancy of adults has lengthened substantially during the twentieth century. The gain has been particularly sharp for women, who now live longer than men by seven years, on average. Today most adults can expect to live long enough to get to know their grandchildren; this was not the case a century ago.

2. The decline in fertility has also changed the relationships across the generations. Most adults are finished raising children by the time the children give birth to grandchildren. This means that grandparenthood is a more distinct stage of life. Moreover, the smaller number of births means that the average person has fewer kinship links to others in the same generation. At the same time, the decline in mortality means that the average person has more links to kin in preceding or succeeding generations. Most persons can expect to share about 50 years of life with living parents.

3. The incomes of the elderly have risen dramatically since the 1950s because of the expansion of the Social Security rolls, the increases in Social Security benefits, and secondarily the growth of private pensions. As a result, the elderly no longer are poorer than the rest of the population, and elderly parents are less dependent on their adult children for support. Still, women, minorities, and the very old have relatively high rates of poverty among the elderly. And many elderly persons have incomes just above the poverty line, which leaves them vulnerable to crises such as a catastrophic illness or the death of a spouse.

4. These developments, coupled with the preference of most Americans to live independently, have resulted in a significant increase in the number of elderly women who live alone. However, a large proportion of elderly men live with their wives because they tend to die first and because they have better remarriage prospects should their wives die. The elderly value their independence, even though they wish to have frequent contacts with kin.

5. Most older persons are not cut off from their kin. Rather, most have frequent contact with at least one of their grown children—especially when they live nearby. There has been a shift in the

nature of intergenerational relations in this century toward a greater emphasis on affection and companionship and a lesser emphasis on economic cooperation. There is substantial agreement between adult children and their parents regarding beliefs and attitudes.

6. The majority of help that the elderly and their adult children receive comes from each other. Except when they are ill, the elderly provide more help to their children than they receive. Most elderly men who need care get it from their wives, whereas most elderly women must rely on daughters and other relatives. The high rates of divorce of the past few decades coupled with the tendency of some fathers to have little contact with their children imply that many older men may not be able to rely on their adult children for support.

7. The majority of seriously disabled elderly persons are cared for by family members in their homes, not by nursing homes. Without the care provided by family members, the already large cost of health care for the elderly would rise much higher. The most common family caregiver, after a spouse, is an adult daughter. Yet more adult daughters are working outside the home, and the downward trend in birthrates means that fewer adult children will exist per elderly parent. There is concern, therefore, about whether family members will continue to provide as much care as they do now.

8. Some observers suggest that the greater independence of the elderly has led to a reduction in the quality of intergenerational relations. Others counter that older people and their children have chosen a style of relating—separate residences but fairly frequent contact—that both generations prefer.

KEY TERMS

mortality
elderly population
gerontologist
young-old
old-old

oldest-old
fertility
'tweener
Medicare

Medicaid
intergenerational solidarity
cohort replacement model
activities of daily living

FAMILIES ON THE INTERNET

The National Aging Information Center (**www.aoa. dhhs.gov/naic**), maintained by the Administration on Aging of the U.S. Department of Health and Human Services, offers much useful information. For instance, the data for Figure 15.4 were obtained by choosing "statistical resources" from the NAIC home page. The web page "Aging in a Social Context" (**www.gl.umbc.edu/~vdotte1/index.html**), was developed to help sociology students find information about aging, gerontology, and the political, social, and economic aspects of aging. It contains numerous links to useful articles and data sources. The U.S. Bureau of the Census (**www.census.gov**) offers a number of publications about the elderly that can be downloaded to your computer in PDF (Portable Document Format) format.

Family and Society

Where do all the great social changes of the twentieth century leave the institution of the family? That is the question to be addressed in the final part. **Chapter 16** begins by discussing the most fundamental changes in the family in the twentieth century, the lessened economic dependence of women and the weakening of marriage. The chapter then describes the emergence of a new form of kinship. It subsequently examines the implications of social change for the public family and the private family.

Any attempt to assess the overall state of the family necessarily involves the author's own interpretations. Consequently, my opinions are more prominent in this chapter than in previous ones. I have tried to clearly label my opinions as such. There is no single right answer to the difficult questions posed in this chapter; and readers are encouraged to consider what they have learned in this book and to draw their own conclusions.

CHAPTER 16

Social Change and Families

If the family wage system—the idea that employers should pay men enough so their wives would not have to work outside the home—needed a final nail in its coffin, it was hammered in by the U.S. Bureau of the Census in 1994. The bureau released a report showing a sharp increase between 1979 and 1992 in the proportion of people who worked full-time but still had an income below the poverty line. Among men employed full-time in 1992, 12 percent still had an annual income that was too little to lift a family of four out of poverty, up from 8 percent in 1979. The picture was bleakest for men without any college education, the group that has suffered the most from the restructuring of the U.S. economy. In 1992, 31 percent of full-time workers without a high school diploma, and 15 percent of full-time workers with a high school diploma but no college education, had an income below the poverty line. In both cases these percentages were about double the figures for 1979. So nearly one-third of all men without a high school diploma who work full-time, and more than one in seven with a high school diploma, don't even earn enough to support a family of four at the poverty level (U.S. Bureau of the Census, 1994b).

The decline of the family wage makes it very unlikely that the breadwinner-homemaker family will return to the dominance it enjoyed in the first half of the twentieth century. The breadwinner-homemaker family was undone first by increases in married women's employment outside the home and then, after 1973, by the decline in young men's wages—a decline that was much sharper for men without a college degree. It also was undermined by lower birthrates: If a married couple is planning to have only two children, it makes little sense for the wife to remain at home throughout adulthood. Rather, it is sensible for her to acquire job skills in young adulthood that she can use later on. Having acquired some skills and work experience, however, she is more likely to maintain a connection to the paid workforce even while raising children. Moreover, the rise in divorce and its frequent consequence, a decline in the standard of living of divorced mothers and their children, has made it risky for married women to let their ties to the labor market lapse.

To be sure, the breadwinner-homemaker family has not disappeared, but it is now far less prevalent. In 1960, as Figure 2.2 showed, 57 percent of children lived with two parents, one of whom worked outside the home and one of whom didn't; in 1989, 25 percent of children lived in such a family. Based on the most recent Bureau of the Census data, I estimate that in 1995 that proportion had dropped to 19 percent (U.S. Bureau of the Census, 1996b). It's not obvious what is replacing the breadwinner-homemaker family; we are in a period of great change, and no single family form is dominant. (Indeed, the 1950s was one of the few decades when there was one dominant form.) Rather, there is a variety of other forms, most notably cohabiting unions, dual-earner married couples, single-parent households, and stepfamilies. One might ask whether these family forms are meeting society's need to ensure that the young are being raised well and the old are well cared for. One might also ask whether the needs of individuals for love, intimacy, companionship, and personal growth are being met. In other words, one might ask how well the family is fulfilling the functions of the public family and the private family at the end of the twentieth century. That inquiry will be the subject of this chapter.

TWO FUNDAMENTAL CHANGES

First, however, it is worth reviewing the fundamental ways in which the family as a social institution has changed over the past half century. Two changes stand out: the lessened economic dependence of women on men and the weakening of marriage.

THE LESSENED ECONOMIC DEPENDENCE OF WOMEN

The decline of the homemaker role and the movement of women into the paid labor force is probably the most significant shift in the family in the past half century. It has been discussed so often in this book that there's little need to say more. Here let me emphasize one point: To some extent, the movement toward greater economic independence is a movement back toward the situation of women a century or two ago. That is to say, married women probably had less economic independence in the 1950s than they had had 50 years earlier. In the nineteenth century, rural women were an important part of the family's farm labor. To be sure, as cities expanded, most urban white married women (and many urban black married women) rarely worked outside the home. Yet urban wives earned income by taking in boarders and lodgers or by doing other families' laundry or performing other services in their homes. By the 1950s, the greater affluence of the nation had nearly eliminated boarding and lodging, and rising wages placed the washing machine and dryer within the reach of many more families. As a result, opportunities to earn money while remaining at home declined. Still, the nineteenth-century economic activity of married women kept them at home, whereas the late-twentieth-century economic activity allows them (albeit with lower earnings than men) to live apart.

THE WEAKENING OF MARRIAGE

The greatest recent challenge to the institution of the family has been the weakening of marriage. In most societies at most times, marriage has been the central organizing principle for sexual activity and childbearing. As Chapter 8 noted, marriage, childbearing, and sexual activity overlapped in the 1950s to a great extent, possibly greater than in prior times. Sexual intercourse, for the majority of women at least, was restricted to marriage (or to the men they were engaged to); consequently, few children were born outside marriage. Cohabitation was rare except among the poor. Marriage was more nearly universal than at any other time in the twentieth century. The probability that a marriage would end in divorce, although substantially higher than in the nineteenth century, was about half of what it is today. To be respectable, it was necessary to be married before living with a partner or having a child; to stay respectable, it was necessary to avoid divorce if at all possible.

Today, even though nearly 90 percent of whites and 70 to 75 percent of African Americans eventually marry, the power of marriage to regulate people's personal lives is much weaker. Cohabitation both before and after marriage has become common and acceptable to most people. Although childbearing outside marriage is still frowned upon by many, it is tolerated by most. Divorce is considered to be unfortunate but acceptable if a partner wishes to end a marriage. Lifelong singlehood, although still uncommon, is also acceptable. In general, there is a greater acceptance of nonmarried adults.

The reasons for the weakening of marriage were discussed in previous chapters. Marriage is less economically necessary than it was when most people needed to pool their labor and earnings in order to subsist. Moreover, the aforementioned lessening of women's economic dependence on men has had an important effect. Even though women's wages remain, on average, lower than men's, it is less difficult now for a woman to support herself and her children. Also, the job prospects for young men without college educations have worsened since 1973, discouraging young adults from marrying. In the realm of values, marriage is increasingly viewed as a means of personal fulfillment, with the result that many married persons believe they are justified in obtaining a divorce if they feel unfulfilled. The quest for self-fulfillment may also prolong young adults' search for a spouse or lead them to try a cohabiting relationship first. Among those who do marry, relationships are more fragile and vulnerable to crises because there is less holding them together than when marriage was more of a necessity and the gendered division of labor was more strict.

Among African Americans, marriage has long been less central to family life, compared with ties to other kin, than it has been among whites; but over the past few decades, marriage has declined in importance even more. Among poor African Americans, the connection between marriage and childbearing is especially weak. Although marriage still remains an ideal, it is far from universal, and the great majority of children, especially first children, are born outside of marriage. Even when a woman does get married, it is not necessarily to the father of her first child. The decline of marriage among African Americans was linked in Chapter 5 both to the worsening labor market position of black men and to a cultural heritage of relying on extended kin in difficult times. Hispanic groups vary greatly in the place of marriage in their family systems. Among the major groups, Puerto Ricans have the highest proportion of children living in single-parent families and Cubans the lowest. Mexican Americans display more three-generational households, suggesting the importance of extended family ties. Marriage is strongest among Asian Americans, many or them recent immigrants from societies in which marriage is nearly universal.

Still, marriage is not in danger of disappearing among Americans, and it remains the preferred form of union. (Recall that most cohabiting relationships either break up or end in marriage within a few years.) Most people choose to marry at some time in their lives, but the point is that they now have a choice. They don't have to be married in the sense that adults at midcentury did. Predictably, people spend less of their lives married and fewer children are raised by two married parents. What difference these changes mean for adults and children is a topic to be discussed below. (Social scientists have also been studying the changing nature of marriage in less developed nations; see *Families in Other Cultures*: World Revolution and Family Patterns, on pages 500–501.)

THE EMERGENCE OF CREATED KINSHIP

In turn, the decline of lifelong marriage as the organizing principle of families has led to an important change in the nature of kinship, aspects of which have been discussed in several chapters. This change has received much less attention than the decline of marriage or the movement of married women into the paid workforce. Consider, for example, the following individuals: a poor woman receiving public assistance who is raising her children by sharing what little she has with her sister who lives in the same apartment building and her mother a block away. A gay man who celebrates Thanksgiving and Christmas with a network of friends who keep in touch and help one another out. A girl who spends part of every summer vacation at her stepfather's parents' beach house yet rarely sees her biological father's parents. All are creating new forms of family life by choosing their kin from the pool of eligibles around them. In the past, you acquired your relatives at birth; then, when you married, you acquired a spouse and in-laws. There was little choice in the matter; relatives came with birth and marriage like sweet scents and thorns come with roses.

Unmarried people often create their own kinship-like ties from a mixture of relatives and friends. Here, three unrelated adults celebrate Christmas together.

CHOOSING ONE'S KIN

Today, people in a variety of settings are more likely to choose their own kin and create their own kinship networks. What all these settings have in common is that they are defined outside the boundaries of lifelong marriage. Marriage (both your parents' and your own) made kinship easy and automatic, but it also restricted the possibilities for forging alliances. People who cannot rely, or choose not to rely, on marriage construe kinship differently. They cannot take it for granted. Rather, they must do the hard work of constructing a group of kin, a broader family, they can rely on. Recall the lesbian who told Kath Weston, "Gay people really have to work to make a family" (see Chapter 9). In several chapters this new form of family making was labeled "created kinship," meaning kinship ties that people have to construct actively. The older form, based on blood relationships or first marriages, was called "acquired kinship."

Created kinship is based more on what people do for one another than on where they fit into a family tree. African Americans in Baltimore, you may remember, told Frank Furstenberg about the difference between *daddies,* who provide emotional and financial support to children, and the biological *fathers* of the children (see Chapter 5). It was the daddies, not the fathers, who became part of the mother's and child's kinship network despite their lack of a biological link. Created kinship presents the opportunity to go outside the typical boundaries of kinship in order to find love and support. It is particularly valuable to people who can't find adequate support among blood-based or first-marriage–based kin. Lesbians and gay men, for example, are sometimes rejected by their parents. They cannot legally marry, and their partnerships have a high likelihood of eventually breaking up. In these circumstances, Weston tells us, they weave together a support network of long-term friends, partners, and biological kin to whom they can maintain ties. Poor African-American women who cannot find suitable spouses exchange help not only with their mothers and grandmothers but also with close friends and even daddies,

Families in Other Cultures

World Revolution and Family Patterns

A sociologist returned from a conference in Taiwan a few years ago with a story told to him by a Taiwanese professor. The professor had begun the story by recounting an incident that had occurred when his father was a boy:

> My father and grandfather were riding in a carriage when my grandfather said, "See that little girl over there? That's the girl you are going to marry." My father never saw the girl again until his wedding day. When I was a boy, I thought my father very enlightened for allowing me to meet the woman I would marry before my wedding day. And recently, my daughter came home and asked me, "Dad, would you like to meet the man I'm going to marry?"

Taiwan is one of many societies in which the process of choosing a spouse—and indeed the very nature of marriage—changed dramatically during the twentieth century. In China, Japan, India, and elsewhere in Asia, parents used to select a son or daughter's spouse. Marriage often occurred at an early age—among girls, close to (or sometimes even before) puberty (Thornton & Fricke, 1989). Typically, the young wife would move into the home of her mother-in-law, who held considerable authority over her. In these ways, marriage was less an agreement between two individuals than a transaction between two families—the family of the groom and the family of the bride. What mat-

tered most to the parents was making a match that would help the larger family by bringing in another healthy person to work the fields or to bear and care for children.

In these Asian families, the most important family bond was often between parents and children, rather than between husbands and wives. The succession of the family line from father to son and the obligation to care for parents in their old age were primary. Yet during the twentieth century, the ties between husbands and wives grew increasingly strong. One reason for this change was the growing availability of work for wages, which gave children a way to make a living that wasn't dependent on their parents' land. They could use their economic independence to make their own decisions about when and whom to marry. In addition, the spread of schooling gave children skills that were valuable in the labor market, introduced them to new ideas, and therefore undermined further their parents' ability to control their marriages (Caldwell, 1982).

In fact, William Goode argued in an influential 1963 book, *World Revolution and Family Patterns*, that family systems worldwide are converging toward a model in which the marital bond between husband and wife, rather than the bond between parent and child, will be the core of the family (Goode, 1963). Goode cataloged the great changes that had occurred during the previous half

century in the family patterns of China, Japan, India, Arabic-speaking Islamic countries, and sub-Saharan Africa. He argued that the changes had been the result of the spread of industrialization—especially where it had brought young adults economic opportunities that their parents couldn't control. Among the related changes Goode noted were a decline in birthrates, an increase in women's holding jobs independently of male relatives, and greater sexual freedom among young adults.

What has happened since *World Revolution* was published? To a considerable extent, the trends Goode emphasized have continued in developing nations. Age at marriage has continued to rise, and more young adults have had a say in choosing whom they will marry. In Taiwan, where economic development has been rapid, 68 percent of women born in the early 1930s said that their parents had chosen their spouses, compared with just 11 percent of women born in the early 1960s (Thornton, Chang, & Lin, 1994). Moreover, the average Taiwanese woman today would give birth to 1.8 children at current rates, compared with 6.5 children at the rates prevalent in the 1950s (Freedman, Chang, Sun, & Weinstein, 1994).

Yet the prediction that all family systems would converge to a common, marriage-centered model has not proved accurate. Two developments suggest the limitations of this thesis. First, as previous chapters of this book have shown, the importance of marriage has declined in the United States and other Western nations, which Goode took as the model of the family patterns of the future. Cohabitation, childbearing outside marriage, divorce—all have increased dramatically since Goode's book was published. As he was writing about the growing dominance of the married-couple family in developing nations, it was slipping away from him in Western nations.

Second, in newly developed countries in Asia, family ties to parents and other kin often remain strong and important, even though Goode's thesis about the increasing importance of the married-couple family has proved accurate. For example, in Japan, which has undergone perhaps the fastest economic development of any nation in history, a majority of elderly people still live with one of their children, as Chapter 15 showed. In Taiwan and elsewhere, parents still play a collaborative role in choosing their children's spouses: A majority of Taiwanese young adult women report that they made their choices jointly with their parents (Thornton, Chan, & Sun, 1984). Thus, the family patterns of the developing and newly developed nations of Asia show a mixture of persistence and change, while family patterns in the Western nations have continued to move away from the married-couple model that dominated in the 1950s and early 1960s.

Family patterns in East Asia show a pattern of both persistence and change. Young couples, such as Crown Prince Naruhito and Crown Princess Masako of Japan, shown in their wedding parade in 1993, have a strong say in whom they will marry. But the Western-educated Crown Princess had to give up her career to be his wife.

creating kinshiplike relationships. A divorced mother whose ex-husband provides little child support can receive support from a live-in partner or second husband.

Yet created kinship also presents a challenge: It requires continual attention to maintain. In contrast, relations of blood and marriage are supported by strong social norms. Wives and husbands, for instance, take a public oath to support each other for better, for worse, in sickness and in health, until death (or, realistically, at least until divorce) do they part. Parents are supposed to support their young children, and adult children are supposed to assist their elderly parents. Society expects as much, and laws enforce these expectations. Moreover, evolutionary theory suggests that parents may also be predisposed to support their biological children and therefore ensure the survival of their genes into the next generation. Because of these strong supports, the relationships can be dormant for a period of time and then be reactivated. An adult daughter may be married and independent for years; then a divorce may leave her and her children in need of assistance. If she turns to her parents for support, they will usually provide it.

Lacking the strong support of social norms, legal obligations, and biological self-interest, created kinship ties must be kept active. If they are allowed to lapse, there is no guarantee that they can be revived. It is a risk, therefore, to withdraw from created kin, unless you are sure you won't be needing their help again. As Chapter 4 discussed, it is risky for poor people to withdraw from the female-centered kinship networks that many of them rely upon for support. Yet the sharing networks of the poor, although admirable in easing the hardships of poverty, may also make it difficult for the members of the networks to rise out of poverty.

THE FEMINIZATION OF KINSHIP

Because created kinship ties require continual maintenance, the system favors those who are willing to work at keeping kinship ties and penalizes those who aren't. A great deal of evidence, reviewed in earlier chapters, shows that women, on average, do much more kinship work than men. They are the ones, by and large, who run and maintain the sharing networks in poor African-American communities. They are the ones who retain the children after divorce and call upon relatives for help. Men, in contrast, seem to drift away from kinship except when they are married. Many divorced fathers, as was noted, have little to do with their children after a divorce. Many men in low-income communities have little to do with children they have fathered outside marriage. Divorced men receive comfort and support by remarrying, which they do more often than divorced women. It is unclear who provides comfort and support to the unmarried fathers in low-income communities. It seems likely that they find new partners and also rely on mothers, sisters, and grandmothers.

As marriage becomes less stable, and as kinship networks remain the work of women, more men will be left without adequate support from kin. The difference is most apparent in later life. Studies discussed in Chapter 15 suggest that stepfathers are less likely to receive assistance from their adult stepchildren than biological fathers are from their children. Moreover, once a man's remarriage ends, his relationship with his stepchildren, as befits created kinship, often ends as well. What, then, will happen to a man who divorces his first wife, sees little of his children afterward, remarries, and then divorces again? Who will care for him in his old age? The evidence suggests that he is unlikely to receive assistance from anyone—unless he marries again.

Who will provide care for elderly men who are unmarried and have not maintained contact with their children after a divorce or a birth outside marriage? It is doubtful that they will receive adequate support from their children.

Kinship, then, is becoming even more feminized than it previously was. Men's classic strategy for support is to marry and to let their wives keep up ties with relatives. This strategy worked well for men as long as most were married for life. Yet with the rises in divorce and childbearing outside marriage, men often become disconnected with kin. At first, many men gain economically because they don't share their higher incomes equitably with the mothers of their children. Yet men who become divorced may be the long-run losers in the decline of lifelong marriage and the rise of created kinship. They may be isolated unless they are remarried, distant from their adult children, and unable to forge links with other kin.

The changes in marriage and kinship reviewed so far are altering the ways in which families take care of children and the elderly. The question of how well families are managing these tasks leads to a perspective I have called the public family. From this perspective, we should ask how the great changes in families over the past few decades have affected their ability to care for the society's dependents.

SOCIAL CHANGE AND THE PUBLIC FAMILY: THE ELDERLY

As for the elderly, the data in Chapter 15 suggest that their well-being has improved in several ways over the past few decades. First, they are living longer. Indeed, most elderly persons will live long enough to get to know their grandchildren. That was not true earlier in this century, when life expectancy was substantially lower. Second, their incomes are higher, allowing, for many, a comfortable retirement. The poverty rate among the elderly, as noted, is now lower than the poverty rate for the entire population. It is also true, however, that some elderly persons remain in need. African-American older people are less advantaged today due to the same forces that affect the black working-age population. Elderly women as a group have lower incomes than elderly men. Many of these women did little work outside the home while raising children, so they accrued substantially less in Social Security and private pension benefits than do elderly men. What is more, a disproportionate number of elderly people have incomes that are above the federal poverty line but not by much.

A SUCCESS STORY

Still, the well-being of the elderly represents a success story for American social policy and family caregiving. The standard of living of the elderly has improved because the growth of government programs such as Social Security and Medicare, and of private pension plans, has increased their health and standard of living. The Social Security taxes workers pay provide an indirect transfer of income from prime-age men and women to their parents' generation. This transfer system allows the elderly to feel financially independent of their children, when in fact they are receiving subsidies from the next generation as a whole. The elderly have used their better health and increased incomes to become more independent—to remain in, or move to, their own homes and apartments, for example. By and large, their relationships with their children remain warm, and contact is frequent. This pattern of autonomy and "intimacy at a distance" appears to be the preferred pattern for both the elderly and their adult children in the United States and other Western nations. (The major exception is the Hispanic elderly, who appear to have a stronger preference for living with their children. Although few data are available, I suspect that Asian-American elderly have similar preferences.)

The support family members provide is also crucial to the well-being of the elderly. When older persons become ill or infirm, their spouses and children provide most of the care they need. It is not true that Americans place most of their frail parents in nursing homes. Even among elderly persons with serious physical impairments, family members provide the majority of the care. Family care of the elderly saves billions of dollars a year that government health insurance programs would otherwise have to pay. Thus, the contribution of adult children to the well-being of their parents' generation is still crucial. Without it, government expenditures for Medicare and Medicaid would be substantially higher.

THE CALM BEFORE THE STORM

We can conclude that there is no worsening "problem" of the public family's care of the elderly. On the contrary, this is one of the few aspects of the public family in which the situation has improved. Nevertheless, one must wonder whether we are in the middle of the calm before the storm. The individuals who will be retiring during the 1990s and 2000s will be the parents of the baby boom generation. These individuals, as noted, had more children than any other generation in the twentieth century. They will likely profit in old age from this investment in child-rearing. The chances of an elderly person living near children and grandchildren will probably rise because the elderly will have more children. For the same reason, the chances that a frail elderly person can receive help from at least one child will probably also rise. In the nation as a whole, the number of working-age persons per retired person will rise, which will increase tax payments into the Social Security and Medicare funds.

This favorable demographic situation will change sharply after about 2010, when the baby boom children themselves begin to retire. The baby boomers are

After 2010, when the baby boomers retire, the number of elderly persons per middle-aged daughter or son will increase greatly. Consequently, the elderly may not receive as much care from their families as today's elderly do.

having fewer children than any previous generation—about two, on average, compared with the average of about three in their parents' generation. Whereas about 10 percent of people who will retire in the 1990s have no children, about 20 percent of the retirees after 2010 will have no children. Fewer children will mean fewer potential caregivers. It will also mean, on a national scale, fewer working-age persons per retiree and therefore a larger tax burden on workers. Even the steps already taken to shore up the Social Security system (see Chapter 15) may not be adequate to maintain the current level of retirement benefits. Health care costs could rise sharply unless further reforms are undertaken.

Moreover, there are other trends, already under way, that are worrisome in the long run. The increase in paid work among women—who have been the main caregivers—is reducing the number of people who can devote large amounts of time to caring for the elderly without the competing demands of employment. So far, it appears that caregivers are adding the demands of elder care to their other work and family responsibilities. Whether they will continue to do so is uncertain. One could argue that they shouldn't continue to do so; rather, men should increase their caregiving. In addition, as noted earlier, elderly men may be disadvantaged by the long-run consequences of divorcing and remarrying. The increase in divorce has left many men distant from their children; it seems unlikely that their children will provide as much support for them later in life as will children who have always remained close to their fathers.

In sum, our current achievements in supporting the elderly are substantial, but they could lead to a false sense of complacency. They could also lead us to overlook elderly persons who are not doing as well even today, such as unmarried women. Currently, an elderly wife receives either one-half of her husband's benefit or the benefit her own work history has entitled her to, whichever is larger. Her husband, of course, receives his own, typically higher benefit. If her husband dies, however, the widow must choose between receiving her husband's benefit or the benefit she received before his death—she cannot continue to receive both. The government could reduce the income gap between elderly women and men by providing more generous Social Security survivors' benefits to widows (Burkhauser & Smeeding, 1994). But, to pay for this change, Social Security taxes would have to be raised or benefits to married elderly couples would have to be reduced. Neither option is politically popular. Another way to reduce the burden of Social Security costs is to increase taxes on the benefits of the well-to-do elderly. Currently they pay taxes on half their Social Security benefits. (See *Families and Public Policy:* Financing Social Security and Medicare, in Chapter 15.) Or the minimum age at which a person can retire and receive full benefits could be raised further. Yet the crowds around Dan Rostenkowski's car demonstrated how difficult it would be to reduce existing benefits to any elderly group.

Some of today's remaining problems may ease without public action. The gap in the incomes of elderly women and elderly men, for instance, may narrow when the next generation of elderly women retires; they will have worked for pay much more and accrued higher retirement benefits. Still, a prudent policymaker would anticipate the difficulties in supporting the elderly in the future and begin to confront them now. Efforts to contain the cost of Medicare will be necessary if its explosive growth is to be controlled. Some of the plans introduced in Congress during the unsuccessful attempt to reform health insurance in 1994 attempted to do so. One approach was to form large insurance-purchasing cooperatives that could bargain with hospitals and doctors for lower fees; another was to have the government itself regulate doctors' and hospitals' fees. In the end, proponents of competing plans could not agree, and no legislation was passed. Whether strong cost-containment measures will emerge from future congressional debates over health insurance remains to be seen.

SOCIAL CHANGE AND THE PUBLIC FAMILY: CHILDREN

An examination of the situation of the elderly suggests, then, that their well-being has improved, although it is not clear that the family should receive credit for it. As for children, the opposite judgment applies: Many indicators suggest that the well-being of children has declined, but it is not clear that the family should receive the blame for it. I concluded in Chapter 14 that the well-being of children in low-income families has worsened substantially since the 1950s and 1960s and that children in middle-income families have experienced a moderate decline. Yet the chapter also noted that if the comparison is extended back to 1940 or earlier, children's well-being is not worse than it used to be.

THE NONPOOR

Children in the shrinking middle—those who are neither poor nor privileged—are much better off, on average, than the poorest children, but their situation leaves little to cheer about. For one thing, they face a far higher likelihood that their parents will divorce than did children in 1960. As discussed in Chapter 12, research on the long-term effects of divorce suggests two conclusions. First, children whose parents divorce do face a higher risk of certain undesirable outcomes, such as not graduating from high school or having a child prior to marrying. Second, most children of divorce will still not experience these outcomes. I argued that the effects of divorce should be a source of concern to anyone interested in the well-being of children but that divorce does not cause the widespread devastation some observers suggest.

Divorce is likely to be followed by cohabitation and often by remarriage. One of the surprises in the recent research literature is the finding that children whose custodial parents remarry fare no better than children who remain in single-parent families. In retrospect, I think that I and other researchers focused too heavily on the beneficial effects of adding a second (usually male) income to the home and too little on the difficulties the addition of a stepparent poses to the postdivorce family system. Moreover, due to the increases in parental divorce, cohabitation, and remarriage, it has become much more common for children to live in a series of different family configurations. In fact, the effect of instability of living in a succession of different arrangements—is perhaps the key question in gauging the consequences for middle-class children of the changes in family structure. Instability is central because it is an unavoidable by-product of high divorce, cohabitation, and remarriage rates. In contrast, if we concluded that the major problem for children after divorce stems from the lack of money and downward mobility of many single parents, we could provide more financial support to single parents, as many European countries do. Similarly, we could perhaps reduce the postdisruption conflict between parents by providing mediation and counseling services. But it's hard to see how to reduce instability and the resultant movement of people in and out of the child's household, except of course by lowering the rates of union formation and dissolution.

We don't know enough yet about the process of family breakup to distinguish the effects of instability per se from other effects such as income loss or parental conflict. As noted, there are some studies which suggest that instability itself does have negative effects, yet the evidence on the importance of instability, compared with, say, parental conflict, is still inconclusive. It seems obvious that it would be more difficult for children to adjust to different family situations two or three times than to adjust once (or not at all if one's parents remain together). Yet it is possible that, were society to mitigate the other effects of divorce, most children might adjust to the new situations without major difficulty.

Another great change for children in middle-income families has been the sharp increase in the number of mothers who work outside the home. (The increase has been smaller in low-income families because it has long been more common for both parents to work for pay.) Much of the concern about the rise in mothers' employment has centered on the effects on children of being cared for outside the home while their parents work. Yet there is very little evidence that children aged 2 or over are harmed by out-of-home care. The remaining uncertainty concerns the effects of full-time out-of-home care on children in the first year or two of life. Even for these children, a recent, large study found no harmful effects in most cases. Based on what we know now, I would argue for more generous parental leave legislation that allows parents to take a temporary leave from work to care for infants and that provides partial wage replacement.

But isn't mothers' employment responsible, in part, for the increases in drug usage, juvenile crime, and other problems that have occurred? A close look at this familiar charge suggests that the evidence doesn't fully support it. As Figure 10.1 showed, the increase in married women's employment has continued, year after year, from the 1950s (actually, from much earlier) to the current day. Yet many of the indicators of children's problems, such as drug usage and arrest rates, did not increase in the 1950s, then increased sharply in the 1960s and 1970s, then leveled off. Drug usage declined in the 1980s while homicide and suicide rates moved upward again in the late 1980s. It is hard to see how a continual rise in women's employment could have produced more drug use in the 1960s and 1970s but not in the 1950s or the 1980s. Women's employment, it is true, does raise the likelihood that a couple will separate. Otherwise, it is an oversimplification to lump women's growing employment in with more problematic family trends such as teenage sexual activity and childbearing.

THE POOR

The weakening of marriage has produced what is surely the most dramatic change in the family lives of poor children, namely, the increase in the proportion who are living with just one parent. In 1995, 63 percent of poor children lived with one parent, up from 40 percent in 1969 (Hernandez, 1993; U.S. Bureau of the Census, 1996b). In sociology and social policy, the debates over changes in family structure have too often been dominated by those who see single-parent families as a sure sign of breakdown and inadequacy, on the one side, and those who defend them against all charges and even celebrate them. The classic example is the furor created by a 1965 report that Daniel Moynihan, then a Labor Department official and now a U.S. senator, wrote on black families. Alarmed by the rising numbers of single-parent families, Moynihan warned of disorganization and a "tangle of pathology." In response, a defensive and often uncritical literature arose which denied that single parents pose any problems for children except insofar as they have low incomes.[1] In all likelihood, the truth lies somewhere in between: single-parent families—and other alternative family forms—are neither as harmful nor as harmless to poor children as the extremes of the literature suggest.

There are two ways in which single-parent families are formed: through the breakup of a two-parent family and through a birth to a woman who is not living with the father of her child. Among the middle class, the breakup of two-parent families predominates, whereas among the poor, births to unmarried women also are important. The difference between these two kinds of single-parent families has implications for public policy. (See *Families and Public Policy:* Two Kinds of Single-Parent Families, on pages 510–511.) Many unmarried, poor single women were poor *before* they gave birth. Thus, it is inaccurate to say that births outside marriage "cause" the poverty of their children in any direct sense.

Still, as noted in Chapter 14, the research literature suggests that living in a single-parent family has disadvantages for children. By one estimate, about half of the undesirable consequences (e.g., a greater risk of dropping out of school) result from the low incomes that are typical of single-parent families. There are many ways this income deficit could be remedied, as will be discussed later. Yet even if the income gap could be narrowed, the other disadvantages would remain. For instance, some studies discussed in Chapter 14 suggest that single parents have more difficulty monitoring and controlling the behavior of their teenagers, even after adjusting for income. This greater difficulty arises, it seems, not because single mothers are derelict in their duties but rather because it's more difficult for one adult to control an adolescent than it is for two. If we accept that statement, another question follows: Granted that two adults are preferable, do both of them have to be parents? What about mother-grandmother households or other arrangements such

---

[1]See Rainwater and Yancey (1967). For a recent appraisal, see Wilson (1987).

as extended-kin networks, parents cohabiting with partners unrelated to their children, or lesbian or gay male couples? In principle, a parent and a second adult who is not a parent can do the job of supervision, nurturing, and control as well as two parents can. But the studies reviewed in this book suggest that, in practice, these alternative living arrangements often face other limitations.[2]

I do not make these points to reject alternative parenting arrangements or to argue that only the two-biological-parent family can provide adequate care to children. Certainly, many alternative families can and do provide adequate care. Rather, I would submit that it's simplistic to dismiss concerns about family structure with a blanket statement that all arrangements are equally good—just as it's simplistic to condemn single-parent families as inherently inadequate. Instead, it is necessary to look at the alternatives just as critically as one looks at two-parent families. When one does so, one finds some problems: Children in single-parent families tend to get less supervision and monitoring; grandmothers aren't always willing and available to provide care; supportive kin networks don't always exist; nonmarital relationships are even less stable than marital relationships. Moreover, as was noted in Chapter 12, children may have difficulty coping with multiple transitions from one type of family to another (e.g., two biological parents to single-parent to stepfamily), regardless of what kinds of families are involved.

WHAT TO DO?

One response is to urge more public support for single-parent families and other alternative family forms. But the policy problem is that public support for alternatives makes them more attractive, relative to two-parent families, and may therefore encourage the formation of more of them. Here we come to one of the major dilemmas of contemporary family policy, one which often produces a deep divide between liberals and conservatives: What mix of policies that (1) encourage two-parent families, versus (2) support single-parent families, should be adopted? The answer to this question depends on one's political and moral beliefs as well as one's reading of the social scientific evidence. Therefore, there is no single correct answer, and readers ultimately ought to make up their own minds.

Discouraging Teenage Childbearing   The issue of teenage childbearing probably produces the greatest consensus: Most people agree that it ought to be discouraged, although they don't agree on how. Studies demonstrate that teenage parents from low-income families and their children have a substantial risk of becoming, or remaining, persistently poor (although not all do). Consequently, programs to reduce teenage births are desirable if the most disadvantaged teenagers are to have an avenue of escape from poverty. Some religious, community, and school groups are attempting to reverse the increase in adolescent sex by urging abstinence. These efforts enjoy wide support, but their effectiveness is unclear. If one accepts the likelihood of continuing, substantial rates of sexual activity, an additional step is to persuade teenagers who won't abstain from sex to use contraception and to make contraceptive devices available to them. Efforts to do so are

---

[2]See Chapter 14 on recent studies that show difficulties in three-generation households of single mothers and that also show, in any case, that these households tend to dissolve by the child's adolescence. See Chapter 4 on the limits of low-income sharing networks. Chapter 14 also shows that children of lesbian parents seem similar to children of heterosexual single parents, but no comparisons have been made with children from two-parent heterosexual families.

Families and Public Policy

Two Kinds of Single-Parent Families

Not all single-parent families are alike. In particular, the kinds of single-parent families in which poor children live tend to be different from the kinds in which nonpoor children live. This difference has implications for public policy. The key distinction is that nonpoor single-parent families tend to be formed when two married parents separate and divorce, whereas poor single-parent families are frequently formed when a woman gives birth while neither married to nor living with the father. This is a generalization, of course, and is not accurate in every case. Still, in 1995, as the figure shows, a much greater share of all poor children in single-parent families was living with never-married mothers than was the case for all nonpoor children in single-parent families. For about three-fourths of nonpoor children, becoming part of a single-parent family is an event that happens suddenly when parents divorce and that often sharply lowers their standard of living. In contrast, nearly half of the poor children are born to never-married mothers, many of whom were already poor, so that their low standard of living is a fact of their existence from day one.

In fact, the closer one gets to persistently poor, young, minority children, the larger births to unmarried women loom. Among black children under the age of six living with just one parent in 1995, for example, 73 percent were living with a never-married parent and 27 percent were living with a divorced, separated, or widowed parent (U.S. Bureau of the Census, 1996c). (The figures for comparable white children were 46 and 54 percent, respectively.)

Overall, children in nonpoor single-parent families have fates that are more closely tied to marriage (and its dissolution) than is the case for children from low-income families. The link to broken marriages gives nonpoor children more resources to draw upon than poor children have. For example, although the identity of a divorced father is known, the identities of many unmarried fathers are not. This difference is a major reason why never-married single mothers receive even less money in support payments from fathers than divorced mothers. Moreover, even when the unmarried father of a poor child is identified and is willing to pay support, he is less likely to be working. (To be sure, many employed, middle-class divorced

fathers don't pay all the support they are supposed to either, as noted in Chapter 12.) Moreover, about two-thirds of divorced mothers remarry (see Chapter 13), and, by remarrying, many divorced mothers regain the middle-class standard of living their families had prior to the breakup. Consequently, even if they temporarily fall into poverty after a divorce, their spells of poverty tend to be shorter than among never-married mothers who were poor before they gave birth.

Because of all these differences, policies that rely on the existence of a broken marriage—or the contributions of a noncustodial parent—are more relevant and more likely to succeed for the middle-income group. Consider child support enforcement, a popular policy in the 1990s. Although tougher enforcement could certainly increase collections among low-income fathers somewhat, its main beneficiaries are likely to be children of divorce whose fathers hold decent-paying, steady jobs. Tougher enforcement would provide no benefits to children whose fathers are unemployed and therefore have no incomes to share.

Or consider the 1996 welfare reform legislation (see Chapter 6).

more controversial because some parents and religious organizations fear that urging contraceptive use, or making contraceptives more easily available, will encourage more teenagers to have sex. There is, however, little evidence to support that fear. Much less controversial are programs that encourage teenage mothers to continue their education. Welfare reforms passed in the 1980s require many young mothers receiving public assistance to complete high school as a condition of receiving their grant.

The research on teenage childbearing also suggests, however, that unless young adults are given a reason to hope for a better future, it will be hard to dissuade them from having children too soon. More generally, in order to improve the lives of disadvantaged children and their parents, what needs to be done is to connect

Divorced mothers often need only temporary financial assistance while they reorganize their lives, after which some will be able to find better jobs and others will remarry. The time limits on welfare receipt under the legislation will affect them less than never-married mothers. Those in the latter group tend to be younger and to have fewer skills and less labor market experience; as a re-sult, they may need a longer period of assistance before successfully entering the job market. They may need to return to high school, for example, or to receive training in job skills. Whether the legislation will provide the assistance many of these mothers need for a long enough time is an open question.

Some issues, such as health insurance, cut across these categories. The lack of affordable health insurance discourages recipients of public assistance from leaving the security of Medicaid coverage to take a job. It also hurts middle-income single mothers whose husbands no longer provided them with insurance. Often, however, single-parent families formed by births to unmarried women face different problems than single-parent families formed by divorce.

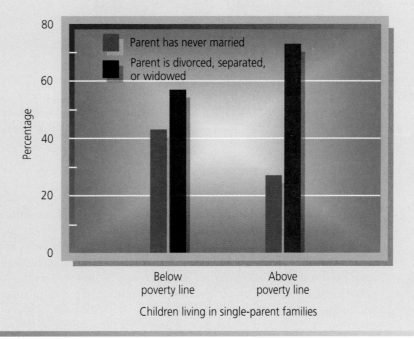

Children living in single-parent families

them to decent-paying, steady jobs. Unless that is done, public policies will do no more than ease the most extreme suffering and provide a way out of poverty for a fortunate few. Yet improving the employment picture, especially at the low-wage end, is perhaps the most difficult challenge facing government. Because firms can move their payroll funds so easily to countries with far lower wages, fewer companies are willing to pay higher U.S. wages for young unskilled and semiskilled laborers. It may be necessary for the government to subsidize wages—to pay part of the wages an employee receives—in order to generate adequate employment among less-educated and less-skilled young adults. It is also important to provide better schooling and job training so that more U.S. workers will be qualified for the higher-paying jobs that remain in the country.

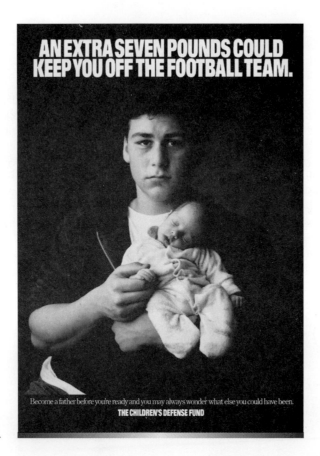

AN EXTRA SEVEN POUNDS COULD KEEP YOU OFF THE FOOTBALL TEAM.

Become a father before you're ready and you may always wonder what else you could have been.
THE CHILDREN'S DEFENSE FUND

There is widespread public support for campaigns to discourage teenagers from having children.

Encouraging Two-Parent Families   Beyond teenagers, the choice between encouraging two-parent families and supporting single-parent families is often more difficult. The majority of single mothers were married when they gave birth but then divorced. Some observers, concerned about the effects of divorce on children, advocate a campaign in which political and civic leaders urge parents to work out their differences rather than divorce. Admirable as this effort would be, it seems unlikely that it would be more effective than the unsuccessful antidivorce movement of the Progressive Era (see *Families and Public Policy:* Divorce Reform: Have We Been Here Before? in Chapter 2). That's because the increase in divorce is a response to broad economic and cultural trends that won't be easily reversed by any feasible government program. Other critics urge tougher divorce laws with mandatory counseling and longer waiting periods before one spouse can obtain a divorce without the other's consent. But there is nothing to prevent an unhappily married person from leaving his or her spouse and cohabiting with a new partner before the waiting period ends.

The main economic trend behind the rise in divorce is the movement of women into the workforce, which has increased their economic independence from men, as has been discussed many times. Few people, for good reason, would favor policies that restrict women's economic opportunities. Yet economic policies that are morally acceptable and politically feasible may not be effective in reducing divorce. For instance, there is broad support for tougher measures to compel absent fathers to pay child support (see Chapter 12). Some supporters even hope these measures will deter married fathers from divorcing their wives. Perhaps so, but the measures also would mean that divorced mothers would be more certain of receiving child support, which might encourage some married mothers to divorce their husbands. The net effect on the divorce rate is hard to predict; I suspect it would be small. A similar point could be made about increased childcare assistance: Since it would be available to single parents as well as married couples, the net effect on divorce would be unclear.

The cultural trend is increasing individualism, which has been rising in the United States at least since de Tocqueville noticed it in the 1830s but which appeared to take another quantum leap in the 1960s and early 1970s. During this turbulent time of political and social protest, the divorce rate doubled, cohabitation emerged among the middle class, and sexual activity outside marriage became more acceptable. Some people argue that cultural change can be reversed and that a concerted effort to reverse the recent rise in individualism should be mounted. The difficulty with this course of action is that the cultural changes of the 1960s and early 1970s were consistent with the economic changes that were occurring, whereas the proposed cultural reversal would be inconsistent. That is to say, the increase in women's economic independence in the 1960s and early 1970s helped to create conditions under which divorce became more of an option. What was happening in the labor market reinforced, perhaps even propelled, what was happening culturally. The proposed cultural reversal, on the other hand, would swim against the tide of women's economic independence. It is therefore less likely to be successful. Only a further, serious economic slide among the middle class, which no one desires, might undercut individualism and significantly lower the divorce rate. (The divorce rate fell during the depths of the Great Depression because fewer couples could afford to divorce.)

Assisting Single-Parent Families   Whereas government policies may do little to reduce the divorce rate substantially, the flip side of this argument is that new government policies are also unlikely to increase the divorce rate substantially. We need not hesitate then to assist single parents and their children for fear of encouraging divorce if divorce rates respond to large-scale economic and cultural changes, as I am arguing, rather than to government policies. Just as enhanced child support enforcement is unlikely to lower the divorce rate very much, it is unlikely to raise it very much. What it certainly *will* do is raise the standard of living of children in single-parent families. The same can be said for childcare assistance to low- and moderate-income families.

To be sure, the idea of expanding government assistance to single mothers and their children—or even of maintaining existing benefit levels for the poor and near-poor—is unpopular in the mid-1990s. Indeed, the Republican majority that took power in Congress in 1994 designed the restrictive 1996 welfare reform legislation. Their argument was that public assistance programs produce "dependency": a loss of work initiative and a long-term reliance on government support. Such programs are said to encourage the growth of single-parent families. These critics have a point: Studies by economists and sociologists do suggest that the availability of public assistance reduces the amount of paid work a person does and increases the probability of forming a single-parent family. But the size of these effects is modest. Economist Robert Moffitt, the author of the leading review article on the topic, concluded that most poor single parents would probably be poor even in the absence of public assistance. Furthermore, he wrote, the effects of

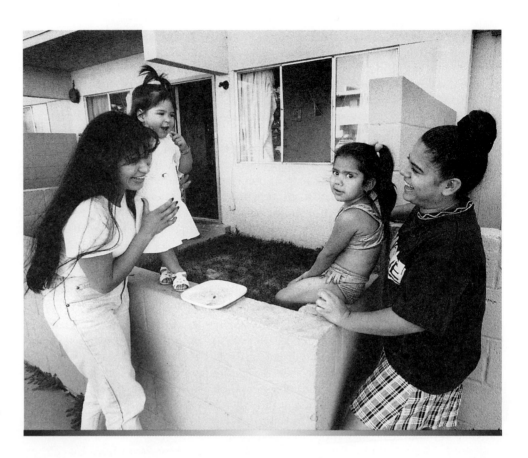

*These teenage
mothers live in a
supported residence
that provides them
with education and
job training.*

public assistance "are not large enough to explain long-run declines in marriage
rates and, in any case, are incapable of explaining recent upward trends in female
headship [single-parent families] because welfare benefits have been declining"
(Moffitt, 1992).

A case can be made, therefore, for increasing, or at the very least, maintaining,
levels of assistance to low-income families with children. It is as follows: (1) children from these families have experienced a considerable decline in well-being;
(2) at least part of the problem is the low incomes of their parents; (3) government programs that provide income assistance have had only modest effects on
the growth of single-parent families and other trends held to be detrimental to
children; and yet (4) these programs substantially raise the standard of living of
poor children. Indeed, some of the advocates of cutbacks acknowledge that in the
absence of adequate public assistance, more children would end up in foster care
or orphanages.

Almost all Western nations provide more financial assistance to parents than the
United States, and this difference, as noted in Chapter 14, is an important reason
why the United States has one of the highest percentages of children who are
poor. Many European countries provide universal child allowances—a fixed annual payment per child that the government pays to all parents, regardless of their
incomes. The closest the United States comes to a universal child benefit is 1997
legislation that provides parents with a $400 tax credit for each child under 17 in
1998 and $500 each thereafter. But this tax credit is not universal because only

families with income tax liabilities receive the credit; if parents don't earn enough money to pay income taxes (which is the case for many low-income families), they don't get the credit.

The argument for assisting poor families through universal benefits rather than means-tested (i.e., available only to parents with incomes below a certain level) benefits, you will recall from Chapter 6, is that universal benefits acquire broad political support among families of all incomes. Some students of public policy have argued that only universal social programs, such as Social Security, gather enough political strength to retain adequate funding over the long run (Skocpol, 1991). The Achilles heel of universal programs, however, is that because of their universal coverage they are very expensive. Programs targeted on the poor are cheaper but command less political support.

One universal program that was nearly established in 1994 was a national health insurance system. The failure of Congress to enact it was particularly unfortunate from the standpoint of family policy because universal health insurance would be a major antipoverty measure for children. The most obvious reason is that so many children, an estimated 10 million in 1995, are not covered (U.S. Bureau of the Census, 1997i). In addition, the lack of health insurance benefits in many part-time and low-wage jobs creates a perverse incentive for parents to apply for, or remain on, the public assistance rolls. This is because parents and children receiving public assistance also receive health insurance through the Medicaid program for the poor. When a parent gives up public assistance to take a job, she may find that she loses all her medical coverage, and she may decide that having protection from large medical bills dictates that she quit her job. The problem has been eased by recent expansions of Medicaid to some children in nonwelfare, low-income families, but the parents of these children are still at high risk of not having health insurance.

In sum, I think efforts to lower the number of teenagers who have babies are important because of the close connection between childbearing outside marriage and persistent poverty. At the same time, one must keep in mind that reducing teenage childbearing won't eliminate persistent poverty. Broader measures to connect young adults from impoverished backgrounds to the world of work are also crucial. Additional programs to provide assistance to single mothers in general, the majority of whom are divorced, are also worth considering. These measures, I have argued, would raise the standard of living of children without significantly affecting the rate of divorce.

SOCIAL CHANGE AND THE PRIVATE FAMILY

During the twentieth century, family relations also changed in ways having to do with intimacy, love, and companionship, a process referred to in Chapter 2 as the rise of the private family. An improved standard of living allowed wives and husbands to focus their attention not only on making ends meet but also on having an emotionally satisfying personal life. The "companionship" marriage became the ideal and remained so through the 1950s. Starting in the 1960s, however, the search for personal fulfillment moved beyond marriage. Sexual intercourse prior to marriage became widespread, cohabitation came to be common and accepted, and the divorce rate doubled. People defined their relations with sexual partners more in terms of their own sense of fulfillment and personal growth than in terms of their social obligation to marry, to have children, or to remain with one partner for life.

People's view of children also changed in the twentieth century. Children came to be seen less as little laborers and more as fragile beings in need of care and nurturing. As the change occurred, the state and the so-called helping professions (social workers, psychiatrists, guidance counselors) began to intervene more directly in the relationship between parent and child. (For instance, recent laws that require physicians and social service workers to report suspected cases of child abuse are consistent with this trend.) Judges increasingly decided court cases according to the "best interests of the child." Courts were more likely to remove children from parents who were unable to care for them or who were viewed as grossly neglectful or abusive. The authorities also passed and enforced compulsory schooling laws, which could be justified by society's collective interest in the adequate rearing of the labor force of the next generation.

To some extent, intervention between parent and child by the state and the helping professions may actually have reduced the privacy of the family. In fact, some European observers of the growth of the welfare state even write of the "deprivatization of the family," the extent to which the private realm has been invaded by the public one (Orfali, 1991; de Singly, 1993). This latter view, however, is only partially correct—at least in the United States. Rather, two contrasting movements have arisen (Glendon, 1989). The first, which has just been discussed, was increasing regulation of parents' relationships with their children. The second was decreasing regulation of adults' intimate relationships with one another.

THE DEREGULATION OF INTIMATE UNIONS

Let us consider the latter development. Prior to the twentieth century, when most families farmed land, marriage was the main way of controlling the flow of wealth across generations. For this reason, landowning parents sought to influence their children's choice of spouses (see Chapter 2). Governments passed laws that reinforced parental control, such as by prohibiting interracial marriages or requiring parental permission. In the twentieth century, as the inheritance of land became less important, legal regulations on marriage weakened considerably. Laws concerning who is allowed to marry, who may marry whom, and who must give permission were overturned by courts or withdrawn by legislatures. For instance, in 1967, the Supreme Court unanimously struck down a Virginia law that prohibited interracial marriage. The judges found the law to be a violation of the equal protection clause of the Fourteenth Amendment to the Constitution. Moreover, the Court wrote,

> The freedom to marry has long been recognized as one of the vital personal rights essential to the orderly pursuit of happiness by free men.

> Marriage is one of the "basic civil rights of man," fundamental to our very existence and survival. . . . Under our Constitution, the freedom to marry, or not marry, a person of another race resides in the individual and cannot be infringed by the State (Loving v. Virginia, 1967).

The sweeping language of this decision suggested that the Court would not look favorably on other state restrictions on marriage. Marriage had become an individual decision, a basic personal right, rather than a socially approved way of transferring property, passing on wealth to descendants, or pooling labor. It had become essentially a private matter—a way of achieving a personally satisfying life. Other court decisions in the latter half of the twentieth century have endorsed a constitutional right to privacy in marriage that would never have been endorsed earlier in the nation's history. Recall from Chapter 7, for instance, that the Supreme Court ruled in 1965 that a state law prohibiting the use of contraceptives by married couples violated marital privacy. By the end of the 1980s, divorce had become an individual decision, as virtually every state enacted some form of "no-fault" divorce law allowing one spouse to obtain a divorce without demonstrating any particular fault or failing on the part of the other spouse, even if the other spouse objected. The law now emphasizes "private ordering," the idea that divorcing parents ought to have broad latitude to negotiate their own financial and custodial agreements (Maccoby & Mnookin, 1992).

An additional facet of the deregulation of marriage is the blurring of the legal and social boundaries between being in a married state and being in an unmarried state. U.S. courts have extended some, though not all, of the rights and protections of married couples to unmarried, cohabiting couples and their children, while maintaining in principle the difference between them. In 1972, you will remember, the Supreme Court extended to unmarried individuals the right of privacy it had found for married persons in 1965 by overturning laws that prevented the sale of contraceptives to unmarried individuals. A series of Supreme Court decisions starting in 1968 have invalidated nearly all laws that discriminate against children born outside marriage. Other Western nations have also ended most forms of discrimination against children born outside marriage and have held parents financially responsible for them. Generally, though, the surge in cohabitation is so new that the law is still in flux.

EXCESSIVE INDIVIDUALISM?

The increasingly private, self-fulfillment emphasis in marriage and cohabitation has been criticized and lamented by some. The issue is whether people's attention to their own personal satisfaction, to the growth and development of their psychological selves, has reached such extreme proportions that their capacity to make commitments to others has atrophied.[3] These "others" include not only family members but also neighborhoods, church groups, and communities—the groupings that give meaning and cohesion to society. In the twentieth-century United States, individualism is what economists call a "normal" good, meaning that the more income people have, the more of it they purchase. The elderly constitute the clearest example: They have used their higher incomes to purchase, or to remain in, separate homes and apartments. Similarly, young adults have used higher living standards to move out of their parents' homes (at least until the recent decline in their labor market prospects). Husbands and wives in unhappy marriages have used their greater economic independence to divorce.

Yet what seems excessive to the observer may seem justified and liberating to the actor. We are fortunate to live in a time and place where the standard of living is sufficiently high that a majority of the population can focus on their personal well-being. This luxury was not nearly as widespread 100, or even 50, years ago. As easy as it is to criticize excesses in others, few of us volunteer to rein in our own pursuit of happiness. Moreover, women's greater independence, some authors argue, has given them more control over their own sexual expression than previous generations had (Ehrenreich, Hess, & Jacobs, 1986). There is a case to be made, in other words, that the emphasis on individualism is an important advance

---

[3]See, for example, Bellah, Madsen, Sullivan, Swidler, & Tipton (1985).

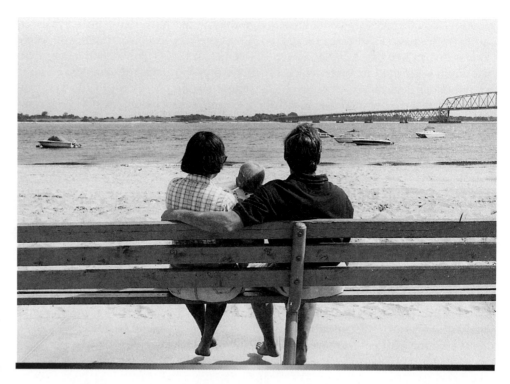

The strengths of the family include the desires of most people to experience lasting bonds of intimacy and to have children.

that has improved societal levels of happiness. And although the case is rarely stated in words, many of us make it with actions in our own lives.

Individualism, it seems to me, can be judged a problem only if it interferes with important social functions. Yet that indeed is the charge, and in the realm of the family the specific charge is that adults have been too preoccupied with their own individual satisfaction to meet their obligations to children. In other words, it is alleged that the rise of the private family, focused on individual emotional satisfaction, has undercut the ability of the public family to carry out its responsibilities to children. There is some truth to this charge. For example, the pursuit of individual fulfillment is one factor in the greater instability of marriages and partnerships, and this instability in living arrangements, in turn, appears to be detrimental to children's well-being. It is a mistake, however, to hold individualism responsible for all of the increase in divorce, single-parent families, and the problems of children: Individualism did not cause the movement of manufacturing jobs from the United States to the Third World and the resulting deterioration in young people's labor market prospects. It did not cause the growth of the service sector of the economy during the twentieth century and the resulting expansion of opportunities in occupations that had been stereotyped as women's work. Culture and commitment have played a role in the case of children, but so has economic change. On the relative importance of each, reasonable people can, and do, disagree.

SHARING THE COST OF STABILITY

Moreover, the greater stability and security of marriage in previous generations were obtained at the cost of restricting women's lives more than men's. The breadwinner-homemaker norm restricted the ability of wives to pursue paid work.

In a society in which money is the main medium of exchange, this restriction left wives dependent on their husbands. It also limited the fulfillment they could receive from achievements outside the home. There are still social conservatives who endorse this arrangement and would favor a return to the dominance of the breadwinner-homemaker family, but they are in the minority.

All others who are concerned about family need to confront the issue of how to enhance the stability and security of intimate unions without making women pay a disproportionate price. Is it possible to develop a new bargain between women and men that can provide both of them with a greater sense of security about their relationship and that can also provide more stability in their children's lives? Valerie Oppenheimer argues that, given their economic difficulties, young men should value having a second earner as a partner more highly than having a stay-at-home wife (Oppenheimer, 1994). But even if they do, one might ask how young women view these unions. In what Arlie Hochschild called a "stalled revolution," women have increased their financial contributions to marriages but men have not increased their household contributions commensurately (Hochschild, 1989). As a result, many wives are faced with a double burden of paid work and home work. Is it any wonder that women, given the option of living independently, find marriage less attractive and that many wives, as Hochschild writes, "cannot afford the luxury of unambivalent love for their husbands"?

If men wish to have the insurance of a second earner, they may need to do more around the house and with the children. There is some evidence that men increased their share of housework moderately between 1975 and 1985 (see Chapter 10). Studies also show that boys in single-parent households do much more household work than boys in two-parent households; it's possible that as the 1970s and 1980s high-divorce-rate cohorts of children reach adulthood and marry, husbands will do a greater share of the domestic work (Goldscheider & Waite, 1991). In addition, it appears that the bargain between cohabiting couples stresses equity in wage earning and housework more than marriage does. If so, some cohabiting couples may carry this more equitable ethic into their marriages (Brines & Joyner, 1993). But there is no good evidence yet as to whether the division of household labor changed further in the 1990s.

Married men are more likely to share the domestic work if they value marital stability, and they are more likely to value marital stability if they also value living with their children every day. In an era of high divorce rates, men are at risk of losing the privilege of living with their children every day because they are rarely awarded (or even ask for) sole custody of children after a divorce. Sadly, from the evidence on divorced men's contact with their children, one might conclude that many men don't care if they see their children every day or even every week. The question is whether their preferences are changing or whether they will begin to change in the years ahead. Articles, books, and movies about the "new" fathers who actively rear their children indicate that our culture is giving men permission to care about raising their children much more than in the 1950s. The spread of joint legal custody also carries the message that fathers should be involved. So far, however, behavioral change appears to have lagged. Perhaps we will have to wait until the men who were divorced in the 1970s and 1980s reach old age and discover how little contact with, and support from, their kin they can muster. Perhaps then younger men will see the long-term costs of underinvesting in their children.

Even if men do change their behavior, divorce rates will probably not fall substantially. When women and men both work for pay, there are simply more alternatives to staying married. The typical ages at marriage are also unlikely to decline very much, especially if the job prospects of less-well-educated young men remain troubled. Cohabitation is likely to remain common and possibly increase. Marriage, particularly lifelong marriage, is unlikely to regain the predominant, indispensable place in family relations that it had in the past.

A SUMMING UP

Through hundreds of articles and books, the debates about the state of the family have bounced between those who argue that it is in deep decline and those who counter that it is in fine shape. Neither assertion is true. The social institution of the family is experiencing a period of great change, handling some of it well and limping through the rest. It is possible that some of the current changes will stretch its adaptability so thin that it will crack, but that judgment is premature. History has shown the family to be a resilient institution, able to alter its form to fit changing circumstances. Yet it is not infinitely adaptable. In examining the state of the family, one must be able to confront its problems without losing sight of its strengths.

One problem is that the family is an institution that was designed for scarcity and is now being asked to perform in an era of greater (although not uniform) prosperity. Throughout most of human history, people have been too preoccupied with subsisting from day to day and season to season to be concerned about personal fulfillment. Marriage and family provided an efficient way to pool the labor of women and men that was necessary to grow food (or earn enough money to buy it), to make or buy clothes and other goods, and to raise future sources of labor, namely children. Today, most people take these basic tasks for granted. Families are now being asked to carry the heavy responsibility of providing not merely sustenance but also emotional satisfaction. It is a relatively new demand, and the institution has not fully adjusted to it.

Another problem is that the family, in most places at most times, has been dominated by men; now it must adapt to a society in which women have substantial (although not yet full) independence. Male dominance was probably enforced first by greater physical strength, but then male dominance became so entrenched in Western law and social norms that the use of physical force usually wasn't necessary. For example, traditional English law held that wives had few legal rights because, upon marriage, the husband and wife became one legal person—effectively, the husband. A contemporary challenge is to modify the institution so that women and men share the benefits and burdens equitably.

The institution was also designed to raise many children in order that some would survive to adulthood; it now is being asked to raise one or two who will almost certainly survive to adulthood. Prior to the twentieth century, most couples did not experience sustained periods without children around because they began to have them soon after they were married and because one or both parents often died before all the children had grown up. Before the twentieth century, then, prolonged childless periods rarely existed by choice. Now an extended period without children in the household is common at the beginning of marriage and almost universal during the latter half. During these times, family relations necessarily focus on the relationship between the spouses. A consensus on what they should offer each other and expect from each other is still emerging.

The strengths of the family include the continuing desires of most adults to experience lasting bonds of intimacy and affection and to have children. Some sociologists think these desires are solely the result of the powerful socialization children receive. But there are theories that suggest they may also have a psychoanalytic component derived from early experiences with parents or an evolutionary component derived from the need to reproduce. Moreover, couples in first marriages can find strong support and guidance in the law and in social norms for the roles of spouse and parent.

In addition, the institution has demonstrated an ability to assume a great diversity of forms in different cultures and different eras. Countless anthropological studies show that non-Western societies have had family systems that are much less centered on the conjugal unit of husband, wife, and children. A final, and probably related, strength, which should humble those who predict its imminent demise, is its ability to outlast its critics. As with Mark Twain, its death has been greatly exaggerated. For instance, a concerned observer wrote in the *Boston Quarterly Review* of 1859: "The family, in its old sense, is disappearing from our land, and not only our free institutions are threatened but the very existence of our society is endangered" (Lantz, Schultz, & O'Hara, 1977, quoted at p. 413). Similar words can still be heard today—along with the words of those who celebrate its supposed disappearance. To be sure, the breadwinner-homemaker family is in decline. But although that type of family is the point of reference for many Americans, in historical perspective it is but a blip on the radar screen. The family is not disappearing, but exactly where it is heading we cannot yet be sure.

SUMMARY

1. Two fundamental changes in the family over the past half century are as follows: (1) The lessened economic dependence of women on men. To some extent, this is a movement back toward the situation of women a century or two ago. (2) The weakening of marriage. Marriage is less dominant as an organizing principle for sexual activity and childbearing. Moreover, the decline of lifelong marriage has led to the emergence of created kinship. In a variety of family settings, people are actively constructing kinship ties outside the boundaries of lifelong marriage. These ties are based more on what people do for one another than on their family-tree relationships. Created kinship ties require continual maintenance or they will lapse; since women do more of the work of maintaining kinship ties, they stand to benefit more from them. Unmarried men, in contrast, may find themselves isolated from kin later in life.

2. The well-being of the elderly has improved: They are living longer and their standard of living is, on average, better. Family members still provide most of the care for the frail elderly. Although minorities and women are not as well off economically as men, changes in the lives of the elderly represent a success story for U.S. social policy. Nevertheless, there are developments on the horizon that are troubling. When the baby boom cohort retires after 2010, there will be more elderly persons and relatively fewer adult children to care for them and to pay Social Security taxes. Because of high divorce rates, many men will not have kept up their ties with their children; therefore, their children may be less willing to provide assistance to them.

3. Divorce is a common experience for nonpoor children (as well as poor ones); we know that divorce raises the risks of some unwanted outcomes. There has also been a large increase in mothers' employment among the nonpoor, but there is no good evidence linking mothers' employment to lowered well-being of children, with the possible exception of children under the age of two. The greatest change for poor children has been the increasing percentage who live in single-parent families. Single-parent families are neither as harmful nor as harmless to poor children as the

extremes of the literature suggest, but they do present some disadvantages to children.

4. One of the major dilemmas in family policy is what mix of policies to adapt that may encourage two-parent families or support single-parent families. Most people agree that teenage childbearing should be discouraged, although there is less agreement on the means of doing so. With regard to divorce, some leaders urge a campaign to discourage it. The author believes such a campaign is unlikely to succeed because it contradicts broad cultural and economic trends. Another strategy is to reduce the income-related difficulties of single-parent families through a child allowance or refundable tax credit scheme that provides benefits to all or most families. These kinds of universal programs can win broad support but are expensive.

5. During the past century, there has been decreasing regulation by the state of adults' intimate relationships with one another. Marriage became fundamentally a private matter, a way of achieving a personally satisfying life. Moreover, court decisions and laws have blurred the boundaries between marital and nonmarital unions. The private, self-fulfilling emphasis in intimate unions has been criticized as excessive, with some justification; yet the emphasis on individualism could also be viewed as an important social advance. The greater security and stability of marriage in previous generations were achieved, in part, by restricting women's lives more than men's. The challenge is to enhance the stability and security of relationships without making women pay the price. A key will be for men to share domestic work more equitably.

FAMILIES ON THE INTERNET

The debates about the state of the family and its future can be monitored on the Internet. On the liberal side, the Council on Contemporary Families (**www.slip.net/~ccf**), newly formed in 1997, defends the diversity of American families and argues that the institution is not in decline. On the center-right is the Institute for American Values (**www.americanvalues.org**), which promotes the idea that the decline of marriage and the increase in single-parent families have harmed children and weakened society. On the right is the Family Research Council (**www.townhall.com/frc**), which supports the "traditional family" in which women stay home to raise children, is strongly pro-life, and opposes gay rights.

GLOSSARY

acquired immune deficiency syndrome (AIDS) A disease, caused by the **human immune deficiency virus (HIV)**, that leaves the body unable to fight against disease.

activities of daily living (ADLs) Personal care activities, including bathing, dressing, getting into and out of bed, walking indoors, and using the toilet.

ADLs See **activities of daily living**.

AFDC See **Aid to Families with Dependent Children**.

affective individualism An outlook on personal relationships that emphasizes the emotional rewards to, and autonomy of, each individual more than that individual's obligations to care for and support others.

Aid to Families with Dependent Children (AFDC) A federal program of financial assistance to low-income families, commonly known as "welfare" until it was replaced by **Temporary Assistance to Needy Families (TANF)** in 1996.

AIDS See **acquired immune deficiency syndrome**.

Alaska natives Native Americans living in Alaska; Eskimos and Aleuts.

alimony Maintenance payments from an ex-husband to an ex-wife.

American Indian The name used for a subset of all Native Americans, namely, those who were living in the territory that later became the 48 contiguous United States.

androgynous behavior Behavior that has the characteristics of both genders.

annulment A ruling that a marriage was never properly formed.

archival research Research that uses printed or written documents stored in libraries or other data archives.

arranged marriage A marriage in which the parents find a spouse for their child by negotiating with other parents.

Asian American A person living in the United States who comes from or is descended from people who came from an Asian country.

assigned kinship Kinship ties that people more or less automatically acquire when they are born or when they marry.

assimilation The process by which immigrant groups merge their culture and behavior with that of the dominant group in the host country.

attachment A bonding to another person that produces feelings of security, comfort, and ease when the other person is nearby.

authoritarian style (of parenting) A parenting style in which parents combine low levels of emotional support with coercive attempts at control of their children.

authoritative style (of parenting) A parenting style in which parents combine high levels of emotional support with inductive control of their children.

authority The acknowledged right of someone to supervise and control others' behavior.

baby boom The large number of people born during the late 1940s and 1950s.

barrio A segregated Mexican-American neighborhood in a U.S. city.

berdache In Native American societies, a man or woman who dressed like, performed the duties of, and behaved like a member of the opposite sex.

bilateral kinship A system in which descent is reckoned through both the mother's and father's lines.

biosocial approach (to gender differences) The theory that gender identification and behavior are based in part on people's innate biological differences.

birth cohort All people born during a given year or period of years.

block grant A fixed amount of money that the federal government gives each state to spend on a set of programs.

blood relatives People who share common ancestors: parents and children, uncles and aunts, nephews and nieces, grandparents and grandchildren.

brideservice A custom in which a prospective bridegroom agrees to work for a time for the bride's family.

bridewealth A custom in which a prospective bridegroom's family makes a gift of money or livestock to the bride's family.

capitalism An economic system in which goods and services are privately produced and sold on a market for profit.

centralizing women Women who specialize in maintaining the links of kinship.

child abuse Serious physical harm (trauma, sexual abuse with injury, or willful malnutrition) of a child by an adult, with intent to injure.

child support assurance system A proposed system under which the state would guarantee that a mother would receive the child support awarded to her up to a certain maximum; the state would then endeavor to collect court-ordered support payments from the father.

cohabitation The sharing of a household by unmarried persons who have a sexual relationship.

cohort replacement model A model of changing public opinion in which each successive birth cohort experiences a different social environment and retains distinctive opinions throughout their adult life.

compadrazgo In Mexico, a godparent relationship in which a wealthy or influential person outside the kinship group is asked to become the *compadre,* or godparent, of a newborn child, particularly at its baptism.

companionate love The affection and partnership felt in a love relationship of long duration.

companionship marriage A marriage in which the emphasis is on affection, friendship, and sexual gratification.

comparable worth A system in which an expert body classifies jobs according to their "worth," as defined by attributes such as skill, effort, responsibility, and working conditions; wages or wage guidelines are then set according to the ranking of jobs.

comparable-worth discrimination A situation in which women and men do different jobs of equivalent value in the same company but the women are paid less.

comparison level for alternatives The level of satisfaction that a person thinks she or he would find in other relationships.

conflict theory A sociological theory that focuses on inequality, power, and social change.

conjugal family A kinship group comprising husband, wife, and children.

consensual union A cohabiting relationship in which a couple consider themselves to be married but have never had a religious or civil marriage ceremony.

contingent workers Workers who are hired temporarily or on a part-time basis and who typically do not receive fringe benefits such as health insurance, retirement pensions, and paid vacations.

coparenting An arrangement whereby divorced parents coordinate their activities and cooperate with each other in raising their children.

courtship A publicly visible process with rules and restrictions through which young men and women find a partner to marry.

courtship stage theories Descriptions of the stages of courtship that young adults must follow if their relationship is to result in marriage.

created kinship Kinship ties that people have to construct actively.

crisis period A period during the first year or two after parents separate when both the custodial parent and the children experience difficulties in dealing with the situation.

distribution of family income The proportion of the total income of all families in the nation that each family receives.

domestic violence Violent acts between family members or between women and men in intimate or dating relationships.

donor insemination A procedure in which semen is inserted into the uterus of an ovulating woman.

Earned Income Tax Credit (EITC) A refundable tax credit to low-income families with a child or children in which at least one parent is employed.

EITC See **Earned Income Tax Credit.**

elder abuse Physical abuse of an elderly person by a nonelderly person.

elderly population The group of people aged 65 years and over.

entitlement A program in which the government is obligated to provide benefits to anyone who qualifies, regardless of the total cost of the program.

era of divorce tolerance The time of a tolerant approach toward divorce, from the middle of the nineteenth century until, in the United States, 1970; the grounds for divorce were widened, and divorce was made more accessible to women.

era of restricted divorce The time of a restrictive approach toward divorce, until about the middle of the nineteenth century; divorces were usually granted only on the grounds of adultery or desertion, and generally only to men.

era of unrestricted divorce The time of a virtually unrestricted access to divorce, from, in the United States, 1970 to the present; divorces are usually granted without restriction to any married person who wants one.

evolutionary psychology The view that human behavior can be explained in terms of evolutionary pressure to behave in ways that maximize the chances of reproduction.

exchange theory A sociological theory that views people as rational beings who decide whether to exchange goods or services by considering the benefits they will receive, the costs they will incur, and the benefits they might receive if they were to choose an alternative course of action.

extended family A kinship group comprising the conjugal family plus any other relatives present in the household, such as a grandparent or uncle.

externalities Benefits or costs that accrue to others when an individual or business produces something.

extramarital sex   Sexual activity by a married person with someone other than his or her spouse.

familial mode of production   A means of production in which the family produces nearly all its own food, makes most of its own clothes, and with the help of others builds its own dwelling.

family wage system   A division of labor in which the husband earns enough money to support his family and the wife remains home to do housework and childcare.

female-centered kinship   A kinship structure in which the strongest bonds of support and caregiving occur among a network of women, most of them relatives, who may live in more than one household.

feminist theory   A sociological theory that focuses on the domination of women by men.

fertility   The number of births in a population.

flextime   A policy that allows employees to choose, within limits, when they will begin and end their working hours.

formal sector   The part of a nation's economy that consists of jobs that meet legal standards for minimum wages, are relatively long-lasting and secure, include fringe benefits such as contributions to Social Security or health insurance, often have possibilities for advancement, and are sometimes unionized.

foster care   The removal of children from their parental home and their placement in another home.

frustration-aggression perspective   The theory that aggressive behavior occurs when a person is blocked from achieving a goal.

functionalist theory   A sociological theory that attempts to determine the functions, or uses, of the main ways in which a society is organized.

gender   The social and cultural characteristics that distinguish women and men in a society.

gender role   The different sets of behaviors that are commonly exhibited by women and men.

generativity   A feeling of concern about, or interest in, guiding and shaping the next generation.

gerontologist   A social/biological scientist who specializes in the study of aging.

Hispanic   A person living in the United States who traces his or her ancestry to Latin America.

HIV   See **human immune deficiency virus.**

human immune deficiency virus (HIV)   The virus that causes **AIDS.**

hunter-gatherers   People who wander through forests or over plains in small bands, hunting animals and gathering edible plants.

hypothesis   A speculative statement about the relationship between two or more factors.

ideal type   A hypothetical model that consists of the most significant characteristics, in extreme form, of a social phenomenon.

immigrant enclave   A large, dense, single-ethnic-group, almost self-sufficient community.

in vitro **fertilization**   A procedure in which eggs are removed from a woman, fertilized in a laboratory dish with sperm from a man, and then inserted into the uterus of either the genetic mother or a surrogate mother.

incest   Sexual relations with one's child, brother, or sister.

independent marriage   A marriage in which the emphasis is on self-development, flexible roles, and communication about problems.

informal sector   The part of a nation's economy that consists of temporary or casual jobs that sometimes offer illegal subminimum wages and that have little security, little possibility for advancement, and no fringe benefits.

initiator (of a divorce)   The person in a marriage who first becomes dissatisfied and begins the process of ending the marriage.

institutional marriage   A marriage in which the emphasis is on male authority, duty, and conformity to social norms.

interactionist approach (to gender differences)   The theory that gender identification and behavior are based on the day-to-day behavior that reinforces gender distinctions.

intergenerational solidarity   The characteristics of family relationships that knit the generations together.

internal economy   The way in which income is allocated to meet the needs of each member of a household, and whose preferences shape how income is spent.

intersexual   A person who is born with ambiguous sexual organs.

intimate outsider   A person, such as a stepparent, who plays a role in a family that is somewhere between that of a parent and that of a trusted friend.

joint legal custody (of children after a divorce)   The retaining by both parents of an equal right to make important decisions concerning their children.

joint physical custody (of children after a divorce)   An arrangement whereby the children of divorced parents spend substantial time in the household of each parent.

Kinsey Report   A 1948 book by zoology professor Alfred Kinsey detailing the results of thousands of interviews with men about their sexual behavior.

labor force All people who are either working outside the home or looking for work.

labor market mode of production A means of production in which people work for pay and thus produce less for their own use at home and buy and sell more on the market.

latent function An unacknowledged, unstated reason behind social actions.

legal custody (of children after a divorce) The right to make important decisions about the children and the obligation to have legal responsibility for them.

lineage A form of kinship group in which descent is traced through either the father's or the mother's line.

longitudinal survey A survey in which interviews are conducted several times at regular intervals.

lower-class families Families whose connection to the economy is so tenuous that they cannot reliably provide for a decent life.

manifest function A publicly stated, acknowledged reason behind social actions.

marital interaction The way in which wives and husbands behave toward each other.

marital rape Sexual assault by a husband accompanied by physical force or the threat of physical force.

marital similarity The general rule that people have a strong tendency to marry others who have similar social characteristics.

marriage market An analogy to the labor market in which single individuals (or their parents) search for others who will marry them (or their children).

matrilineage A kinship group in which descent is through the mother's line.

mediating structures Midlevel social institutions and groupings, such as the church, the neighborhood, the civil organization, and the family.

Medicaid The government program of health insurance for people with incomes below the poverty line.

Medicare The government program of health insurance for all elderly people.

mestizo A person whose ancestors include both Spanish settlers and Native Americans.

middle-class families Families whose connection to the economy provides them with a secure, comfortable income and allows them to live well above a subsistence level.

monogamy A marriage system in which people are allowed only one spouse.

mortality The number of deaths in a population.

nation A people with shared economic and cultural interests.

nation-state A term that combines the governmental and cultural connotations of the two words it comprises.

Native American The name used for the original, indigenous peoples who had settled in America hundreds of years before Columbus arrived.

negative externalities The costs imposed on other individuals or businesses when an individual or business produces something of value to itself.

1965 Immigration Act Act passed by the U.S. Congress which ended restrictions that had blocked most Asian immigration and substituted an annual quota.

no-fault divorce The granting of a divorce simply on the basis of marriage breakdown due to "irreconcilable differences."

nonmarital birth ratio The proportion of all births that occur to unmarried women.

norm A widely accepted rule about how people should behave.

objectivity The ability to draw conclusions about a social situation that are unaffected by one's own beliefs.

observational study (also known as field research) A study in which the researcher spends time directly observing each participant.

oldest-old The group of elderly people 85 years of age and over.

old-old The group of elderly people 75 to 84 years of age.

parallel parenting An arrangement whereby divorced parents gravitate toward a more detached style, going about their parenting business separately.

parental leave Time off from work to care for a child.

passionate love The sexually charged attraction that occurs at the start of many love relationships.

patriarchy A social order based on the domination of women by men, especially in agricultural societies.

patrilineage A kinship group in which descent is through the father's line.

patrilocal A marriage residence rule in which the wife goes to live in her husband's parents' home.

pay equity See **comparable worth.**

peer group A group of people who have roughly the same age and status as one another.

permissive style (of parenting) A parenting style in which parents provide emotional support but exercise little control over their children.

Personal Responsibility and Work Opportunity Reconciliation Act of 1996 (PRWORA) The federal welfare legislation that requires most recipients to work within two years and that limits the amount of time a family can receive welfare.

physical custody (of children after a divorce) The right of a divorced spouse to have one's children live with one.

polyandry A form of polygamy in which a woman is allowed to have more than one husband.

polygamy A marriage system in which men or women (or both) are allowed to have more than one spouse.

polygyny A form of polygamy in which a man is allowed to have more than one wife.

positive externalities Benefits received by others when an individual or business produces something, but for which the producer is not fully compensated.

poverty line A federally defined income limit defined as the cost of an "economy" diet for a family of four, multiplied by three.

power The ability to force a person to do something even against his or her will.

prestige Honor and status in a society.

primary analysis Analysis of survey data by the people who collected the information.

principle of least interest In a dating relationship, the fact that the partner who is less interested in the relationship has more power because he or she could more easily leave it.

private family Two or more individuals who maintain an intimate relationship that they expect will last indefinitely—or in the case of a parent and child, until the child reaches adulthood—and who live in the same household and pool their income and household labor.

privilege A special advantage or benefit enjoyed by some individuals.

procreation The process of having and raising children.

production for exchange value Work for wages outside the home.

production for use value Work that produces goods and services used within the home.

psychoanalytic approach (to gender differences) The theory that gender identification and behavior are based on children's unconscious internalization of the qualities of their same-sex parent.

public family One adult, or two adults who are related by marriage, partnership, or shared parenthood, who is/are taking care of dependents, and the dependents themselves.

public goods Things that may be enjoyed by people who do not themselves produce them.

racial-ethnic group People who share a common identity and whose members think of themselves as distinct from others by virtue of ancestry, culture, and sometimes physical characteristics.

reflexivity A researcher's examination of the nature of the research process that she or he is undertaking.

relationship by blood The sharing of a common ancestor, including cross-generation ties (such as parent and child) and same-generation ties (such as brother and sister).

relationship-specific investment Time spent on activities such as childrearing that are valuable only in a person's current relationship.

remarriage chain A path that links individuals across households through the ties of disrupted unions and new unions.

remittances Cash payments sent by immigrants to family members in their country of origin.

responsive workplace A work setting in which job conditions are designed to allow employees to meet their family responsibilities more easily.

role overload The state of having too many roles with conflicting demands.

scientific method A systematic, organized series of steps that ensures maximum objectivity and consistency in researching a problem.

secondary analysis Analysis of survey data by people other than those who collected it.

selection effect The principle that whenever individuals sort, or "select," themselves into groups nonrandomly, some of the differences among the groups reflect preexisting differences among the individuals.

selection hypothesis The assertion that two groups differ because certain kinds of people select (or are selected into) one group more than the other.

service sector Workers who provide personal services such as education, health care, communication, restaurant meals, legal representation, entertainment, and so forth.

sex The biological characteristics that distinguish men and women.

sex ratio The number of males in a population compared with the number of females.

sex-gender system The transformation of the biological differences between women and men into a social order that supports male domination.

sexual identity A set of sexual practices and attitudes that lead to the formation in a person's mind of an identity as heterosexual, homosexual, or bisexual.

sexual monogamy The state of having just one sex partner.

sexually based primary relationship An erotic, close relationship that is one of strong, frequent, and diverse interdependence that lasts over a considerable period of time.

social capital The economic advantages a person has by virtue of the structure of his or her relations with other people.

social class An ordering of all persons in a society according to their degrees of power, prestige, and privilege.

social exchange perspective The theory that people calculate whether to engage in a particular behavior by considering the rewards and costs of that behavior and the rewards of alternatives to it.

social institution A set of roles and rules that define a social unit of importance to society.

social learning perspective The theory that individuals learn behavior they will later exhibit by observing what others do and seeing the consequences of these actions.

social network A group of people who are linked through interaction with one another.

social role A pattern of behaviors associated with a position in society.

Social Security Act of 1935 The federal act that created, among other provisions, Social Security, unemployment compensation, and aid to mothers with dependent children (later renamed **Aid to Families with Dependent Children**).

socialism An economic system in which the number and types of goods produced, and who they are distributed to, are decided by the government rather than by the actions of a market.

socialization The way in which one learns the ways of a given society or social group so that one can function within it.

socialization approach (to gender differences) The theory that gender identification and behavior are based on children's learning that they will be rewarded for the set of behaviors considered appropriate to their sex but not for those appropriate to the other sex.

specialization model A model of the marriage market in which women specialize in housework and child care and men specialize in paid work outside the home.

spillover The fact that stressful events in one part of a person's daily life often spill over into other parts of her or his life.

state A government that claims the right to rule a given territory and its population and to have a monopoly on force in that territory.

stem family A kinship group comprising parents plus one child who remains at home.

stepfamily A household in which two adults are married or cohabiting and at least one of the adults has a child present from a previous marriage or relationship.

Stonewall riot The 1969 riot to which many writers date the emergence of the gay political movement.

surrogacy A procedure in which a woman agrees to be artificially inseminated with a man's sperm, carry the fetus to term, and then turn the baby over to the man (and typically to his wife) when it is born.

survey A study in which individuals from a geographic area are selected, usually at random, and asked a fixed set of questions.

symbolic interaction theory A sociological theory that focuses on people's interpretations of symbolic behavior.

Temporary Assistance to Needy Families (TANF) A federal program of financial assistance to low-income families that began in 1996, following passage of new welfare legislation. (See **Aid to Families with Dependent Children**.)

total fertility rate (TFR) The average number of children a woman will bear over her lifetime if current birthrates remain the same.

transaction costs The costs of organizing and carrying out exchanges.

'tweeners The group of elderly people who have incomes that place them between the poor, who can qualify for public assistance over and above Social Security, and the middle class, who can supplement their Social Security checks with savings and pensions.

union A stable, intimate relationship between two people who live in the same household but may or may not be married.

union formation The process of beginning to live with a partner either through cohabitation or marriage.

upper-class families Families that have amassed wealth and privilege and that often have substantial prestige as well.

value A goal or principle that is held in high esteem by a society.

welfare state A capitalist government that has enacted numerous measures, such as social security, unemployment compensation, and a minimum wage, to protect workers and their families from the harshness of the capitalist system.

Western nations The countries of Western Europe and the overseas English-speaking countries of the United States, Canada, Australia, and New Zealand.

women-centered kinship A kinship structure in which the strongest bonds of support and caregiving occur among a network of women, most of them relatives, who may live in more than one household.

working-class families Families whose income can reliably provide only for the minimum needs of what other people see as a decent life.

young-old The group of elderly people 65 to 74 years of age.

REFERENCES

Acton, W. (1865). The function and disorders of the reproductive organs in youth, in adult age, and in advanced life: Considered in their physiological, social, and psychological relations. Philadelphia.

Adetunji, J. (1997). Assessing the mortality impact of HIV/AIDS relative to other causes of adult deaths in sub-Saharan Africa. In International Union for the Scientific Study of Population Committee on AIDS (Ed.), *The socio-demographic impact of AIDS in Africa.* Liège, Belgium: International Union for the Scientific Study of Population.

Akerlof, G. A., Yellen, J. L., & Katz, M. L. (1996). An analysis of out-of-wedlock childbearing in the United States. *Quarterly Journal of Economics, 111,* 277–317.

Altman, L. K. (1997, July 15). AIDS deaths drop 19 percent in U.S., continuing a heartening trend. *New York Times,* pp. Al, A4.

Alwin, D. F. (1988). From obedience to autonomy: Changes in traits desired in children, 1924–1978. *Public Opinion Quarterly, 52,* 33–52.

Alwin, D. F. (1990). Historical changes in parental orientations to children. In N. Mandell (Ed.), *Sociological Studies of Child Development* (pp. 65–86). Greenwich, CT: JAI Press.

Alwin, D. F. (1996). Coresidence beliefs in American society—1973 to 1991. *Journal of Marriage and the Family, 58,* 393–403.

Amato, P., & Booth, A. (1997). *A generation at risk: Growing up in an era of family upheaval.* Cambridge, MA: Harvard University Press.

Amato, P. R. (1993). Children's adjustment to divorce: Theories, hypotheses, and empirical support. *Journal of Marriage and the Family, 55,* 23–32.

Amato, P. R. (1994). The implications of research findings on children in stepfamilies. In A. Booth & J. Dunn (Eds.), *Stepfamilies: Who benefits? Who does not?* (pp. 81–87). Hillsdale, NJ: Lawrence Erlbaum.

Amato, P. R. (1998). More than money? Men's contribution to their children's lives. In A. Booth & A. C. Crouter (Eds.), *Men in families: When do they get involved? What difference does it make?* (pp. 241–278). Mahwah, NJ: Lawrence Erlbaum Associates.

Amato, P. R., & Rezac, S. L. (1994). Contact with nonresident parents, interparental conflict, and children's behavior. *Journal of Family Issues, 15,* 191–207.

American Booksellers Association v. *Hudnut.* (1984). 598 F. Supp. 1316 (1984); 771 F. 2nd 323 (1985); 106 S.Ct. 1664 (1986).

American Heritage Dictionary (1982). Second College Edition, New York: Houghton Mifflin.

Ammerman, N. T., & Roof, W. C. (1995). Old patterns, new trends, fragile experiments. In N. T. Ammerman & W. C. Roof (Eds.), *Work, family, and religion in contemporary society* (pp. 1–20). New York: Routledge.

Anderson, E. (1989). Sex codes and family life among poor inner-city youths. *Annals of the American Academy of Political and Social Science, 501,* 59–78.

Anderson, E. (1991). Neighborhood effects on teenage pregnancy. In C. Jencks & P. E. Peterson (Eds.), *The urban underclass* (p. 383). Washington, DC: The Brookings Institution.

Anderson, M. (1971). *Family structure in nineteenth century Lancashire.* Cambridge, England: Cambridge University Press.

Angell, R. (1936). *The family encounters the depression.* New York: Charles Scribner's Sons.

Angier, N. (1993, July 18). Study of sex orientation doesn't neatly fit mold. *The New York Times,* p. 24.

Aquilino, W. S. (1991). Family structure and home-leaving: A further specification of the relationship. *Journal of Marriage and the Family, 53,* 999–1010.

Aquilino, W. S. (1994). Impact of childhood family disruption on young adults' relationships with parents. *Journal of Marriage and the Family, 56,* 295–313.

Arendell, T. (1986). *Mothers and divorce: Legal, economic, and social dilemmas.* Berkeley: University of California Press.

Ariès, P. (1960). *L'Enfant et la vie familiale sous l'ancien regime.* Paris: Librairie Plon.

Ariès, P. (1962). *Centuries of childhood: A social history of family life.* New York: Vintage Books.

Ariès, P. (1985a). Love in married life. In P. Ariès & A. Bejin (Eds.), *Western sexuality* (pp. 130–139). Oxford: Basil Blackwell.

Ariès, P. (1985b). Thoughts on the history of homosexuality. In P. Ariès & A. Bejin (Eds.), *Western sexuality* (pp. 62–75). Oxford: Basil Blackwell.

Astone, N., & McLanahan, S. (1991). Family structure, parental practices, and high school completion. *American Sociological Review, 56,* 309–320.

The average American woman spends 17 years raising children and 18 years helping aging parents. *Newsweek,* (1990, July 16) cover.

Bachrach, C. (1983). Children in families: Characteristics of biological step and adopted children. *Journal of Marriage and the Family, 45,* 171–179.

Baehr v. *Lewin.* (1993). 74 Haw. 530, 74 Haw. 645, 852 P.2d 44.

Bailey, B. L. (1988). *From front porch to back seat: Courtship in twentieth-century America.* Baltimore: Johns Hopkins University Press.

Bailey, M., & Pillard, R. C. (1991). A genetic study of male sexual orientation. *Archives of General Psychiatry, 48,* 1089–1096.

Bailey, M., Pillard, R. C., Neale, M. C., & Agyei, Y. (1993). Heritable factors influence sexual orientation in women. *Archives of General Psychiatry, 50,* 217–223.

Bandura, A. (1973). *Aggression: A social learning analysis.* Englewood Cliffs, NJ: Prentice-Hall.

Bane, M. J. (1986). Household composition and poverty. In S. H. Danziger & D. H. Weinberg (Eds.), *Fighting poverty: What works and what doesn't* (pp. 209–231). Cambridge, MA: Harvard University Press.

Barcus, F. E. (1983). *Images of life on children's television: Sex roles, minorities, and families.* New York: Praeger.

Bartlett, J. (1980). *Familiar quotations* (Ed. E. M. Beck). Boston: Little, Brown.

Baumgarth, W. (1986). The family and the state in modern political theory. In J. Peden & F. Glahe (Eds.), *The American family and the state* (pp. 19–47). San Francisco: Pacific Research Institute for Public Policy.

Baumrind, D. (1971). Current patterns of parental authority. *Developmental Psychology Monographs, 4* (1, Pt. 2).

Baxter, J. (1994). Is husband's class enough? Class location and class identity. *American Sociological Review, 59,* 220–235.

Baydar, N., & Brooks-Gunn, J. (1992). Effects of maternal employment and child-care arrangements on preschoolers' cognitive and behavioral outcomes: Evidence from the children of the national longitudinal survey of youth. *Developmental Psychology, 27,* 932–945.

Bean, F., & Tienda, M. (1987). *The Hispanic population of the United States.* New York: Russell Sage Foundation.

Becker, G. S. (1957). *The economics of discrimination.* Chicago: University of Chicago Press.

Becker, G. S. (1991). *A treatise on the family* (Enlarged ed.). Cambridge, MA: Harvard University Press.

Bellah, R. N., Madsen, R., Sullivan, W. M., Swidler, A., & Tipton, S. M. (1985). *Habits of the heart: Individualism and commitment in American life.* Berkeley: University of California Press.

Belluck, P. (1998, March 20). Black youths' rate of suicide rising sharply. *New York Times,* p. A1.

Belsky, J., & Eggebeen, D. (1991). Early and extensive maternal employment and young children's socioemotional development: Children of the national longitudinal survey of youth. *Journal of Marriage and the Family, 53,* 1083–1098.

Belsky, J., Spanier, G. B., & Rovine, M. (1983). Stability and change in marriage across the transition to adulthood. *Journal of Marriage and the Family, 45,* 567–577.

Bem, S. L. (1981). Gender schema theory: A cognitive account of sex-typing. *Psychological Review, 88,* 354–364.

Bendix, R. (1960). *Max Weber: An intellectual portrait.* New York: Doubleday.

Benería, L., & Roldan, M. (1987). *The crossroads of class and gender: Industrial homework, subcontracting, and household dynamics in Mexico City.* Chicago: University of Chicago Press.

Bengtson, V., Rosenthal, C., & Burton, L. (1990). Families and aging: Diversity and heterogeneity. In R. H. Binstock & L. K. George (Eds.), *Handbook on aging and the social sciences* (3rd ed.) (pp. 263–287). New York: Academic Press.

Bennett, C. (1995, August). *Interracial children: Implications for a multiracial category.* Paper presented at the annual meeting of the American Sociological Association, Washington, DC.

Bennett, N., Bloom, D., & Craig, P. (1989). The divergence of black and white marriage patterns. *American Journal of Sociology, 95,* 692–722.

Berger, B. (1986). On the limits of the welfare state: The case of foster care. In J. R. Peden & F. R. Glahe (Eds.), *The American family and the state* (pp. 365–379). San Francisco: Pacific Research Institute for Public Policy.

Berger, B., & Berger, P. (1983). *The war over the family: Capturing the middle ground.* Garden City, NY: Anchor Books.

Berger, R. J., Searles, P. A., & Cottle, C. E. (1991). *Feminism and pornography.* New York: Praeger.

Bergmann, B. R. (1986). *The economic emergence of women.* New York: Basic Books.

Berk, R. A., Campbell, A., Klap, R., & Western, B. (1992, October). The deterrent effect of arrest in incidents of domestic violence: A bayesian analysis of four field experiments. *American Sociological Review, 57,* 698–708.

Berk, S. F. (1985). *The gender factory: The apportionment of work in American households.* New York: Plenum Press.

Berkner, L. K. (1972). The stem family and the developmental cycle of the peasant household: An eighteenth-century Austrian example. *American Historical Review, 77,* 398–418.

Bernhardt, A., Morris, M., & Handcock, M. S. (1995). Women's gains or men's losses? A closer look at the shrinking gender gap in earnings. *American Journal of Sociology, 101,* 302–328.

Bernstein, A. C. (1988). Unraveling the tangles: Children's understanding of stepfamily kinship. In W. R. Beer (Ed.), *Relative strangers: Studies of stepfamily processes* (pp. 83–111). Totowa, NJ: Rowan and Littlefield.

Berry, M., & Blassingame, J. (1982). *Long memory: The black experience in America.* New York: Oxford University Press.

Besharov, D. J., & Dembosky, J. W. (1996, October 3). Child abuse? Threat or menace? How common is it really? *Slate* [On-line]. Available: www.slate.com (Accessed February 7, 1998).

Besharov, D. J., & Laumann, L. (1994, May). Don't call it child abuse if it's really poverty: Social policies for children. Woodrow Wilson School of Public and International Affairs, Princeton University.

Bettelheim, B. (1976). *The uses of enchantment: The meaning and importance of fairy tales.* New York: Alfred A. Knopf.

Bianchi, S. M. (1995). The changing economic roles of women and men. In R. Farley (Ed.), *State of the Union: America in the 1990s.* Vol. 1 (pp. 107–154).

Bianchi, S. M., & Spain, D. (1986). *American women in transition.* New York, NY: Russell Sage Foundation.

Bianchi, S. M., & Spain, D. (1996). Women, work, and family in America. *Population Bulletin 51,* (3). Washington, DC: Population Reference Bureau.

Billingsley, A. (1992). *Climbing Jacob's ladder: The enduring legacy of African-American families.* New York: Simon and Schuster.

Billy, J. O. G., Tanfer, K., Grady, W. R., & Klepinger, D. H. (1993). The sexual behavior of men in the United States. *Family Planning Perspectives, 25,* 52–60.

Black, A. (1924, August). Is the young person coming back? *Harper's,* p. 340.

Blackwood, E. (1984). Sexuality and gender in certain Native American tribes: The case of cross-gender females. *Signs, 10,* 27–42.

Blake, J. (1989). *Family size and achievement.* Berkeley: University of California Press.

Blank, R. M. (1997). *It takes a nation: A new agenda for fighting poverty.* Princeton: Princeton University Press/Russell Sage Foundation.

Blankenship, K. M., Rushing, B., Onorato, S. A., & White, R. (1993). Reproductive technologies and the U.S. Courts. *Gender & Society, 7,* 8–31.

Bledsoe, C. H. (1980). *Women and marriage in Kpelle society.* Palo Alto, CA: Stanford University Press.

Bledsoe, C. H., & Cohen, B. (Eds.) (1993). *Social dynamics of adolescent fertility in sub-Saharan Africa.* Washington, DC: National Academy Press.

Block, J. H. (1984). *Sex role identity and ego development.* San Francisco: Jossey-Bass.

Blood, R. O., & Wolfe, D. M. (1960). *Husbands and wives: The dynamics of married living.* New York: The Free Press.

Bloom, A. (1994, July 18). The body lies. *The New Yorker,* pp. 38–49.

Blumberg, P., & Paul, P. (1975). Continuities and discontinuities in upper-class marriages. *Journal of Marriage and the Family, 37,* 63–77.

Blumberg, R. L. (1991). Income under female versus male control: Hypotheses from a theory of gender stratification and data from the Third World. In R. L. Blumberg (Ed.), *Gender, family, and economy: The triple overlap* (pp. 97–127). Newbury Park, CA: Sage Publications.

Blumer, H. (1962). Society as symbolic interaction. In A. M. Rose (Ed.), *Human behavior and social processes* (pp. 179–192). Boston: Houghton Mifflin.

Blumstein, P., & Schwartz, P. (1983). *American couples: Money, work, sex.* New York: William Morrow Company.

Blumstein, P., & Schwartz, P. (1991). Money and ideology: Their impact on power and the division of household labor. In R. L. Blumberg (Ed.), *Gender, family, and economy: The triple overlap* (pp. 261–288). Newbury Park, CA: Sage Publications.

Bohannan, P. (1971a). Divorce chains, households of remarriage, and multiple divorcers. In P. Bohannan (Ed.), *Divorce and after* (pp. 128–139). New York: Anchor Books.

Bohannan, P. (1971b). The six stations of divorce. In P. Bohannan (Ed.), *Divorce and after* (pp. 33–62). New York: Anchor Books.

Boocock, S. S. (1991). Childhood and child care in Japan: a comparative analysis. In S. E. Cahill (Ed.), *Sociological studies of child development: Vol. 4* (pp. 51–88). Greenwich, CT: JAI Press.

Booth, A., & Dabbs, James M., Jr. (1993). Testosterone and men's marriages. *Social Forces, 72,* 463–477.

Booth, A., & Edwards, J. N. (1992). Starting over: Why remarriages are unstable. *Journal of Family Issues, 13,* 179–194.

Booth, A., Johnson, D. R., Branaman, A., & Sica, A. (1995). Belief and behavior: Does religion matter in today's marriage? *Journal of Marriage and the Family, 57,* 661–671.

Boserup, E. (1970). *Woman's role in economic development.* London: George Allen and Unwin.

Boswell, J. (1982). Revolutions, universals, and sexual categories. *Salmagundi,* 58–59, 89–113.

Bott, E. (1957). *Family and social network.* London: Tavistock.

Bowers v. *Hardwick,* 106 SCt. 2841 (1986).

Bowles, S., & Gintis, H. (1976). *Schooling in capitalist America: Educational reform and the contradictions of economic life.* New York: Basic Books.

Brand, E., Clingempeel, W. G., & Bowen-Woodward, K. (1988). Family relationships and children's psychological adjustment. In Hetherington & Arasteh (Eds.), *Impact of divorce* (pp. 299–324). Hillsdale, NJ: Lawrence Erlbaum Associates.

Bray, J. H. (1988). Children's development during early remarriage. In Hetherington & Arasteh (Eds.), *Impact of divorce* (pp. 279–298). Hillsdale, NJ: Lawrence Erlbaum Associates.

Brines, J., & Joyner, K. (1993). *Ties that bind: Principles of stability in the modern union.* Paper presented at the Annual Meeting of the Population Association of America, Cincinnati.

Brody, E., Kleban, M., Johnson, P., Hoffman, C., & Schoonover, C. (1987). Work status and parent care: A comparison of four groups of women. *The Gerontologist, 27,* 201–208.

Brody, E. M. (1981). Women in the middle and family help to older people. *The Gerontologist, 21,* 471–480.

Brooks-Gunn, J., Duncan, G. J., Klebanov, P. K., & Sealand, N. (1993). Do neighborhoods influence child and adolescent development? *American Journal of Sociology, 99,* 353–395.

Browning, C. R., & Laumann, E. O. (1997). Sexual contact between children and adults: A life course perspective. *American Sociological Review, 62,* 540–560.

Buchanan, C. M. et al. (1991). Caught between parents: Adolescents' experiences in divorced homes. *Child Development, 62,* 1008–1029.

Bulcroft, R., & Bulcroft, K. (1993). Race differences in attitudinal and motivational factors in the decision to marry. *Journal of Marriage and the Family, 55,* 338–355.

Bumpass, L. L. (1984). Children and marital disruption: A replication and update. *Demography, 21,* 71–82.

Bumpass, L. L., Raley, R. K., & Sweet, J. A. (1995). The changing character of stepfamilies: Implications of cohabitation and nonmarital childbearing. *Demography, 32,* 425–436.

Bumpass, L. L., & Sweet, J. A. (1989). National estimates of cohabitation. *Demography, 26,* 615–625.

Bumpass, L. L., Sweet, J. A., & Cherlin, A. (1991). The role of cohabitation in declining rates of marriage. *Journal of Marriage and the Family, 53,* 913–927.

Bumpass, L. L., Sweet, J., & Martin, T. C. (1990). Changing patterns of remarriage. *Journal of Marriage and the Family, 52,* 747–756.

Burgess, E. W. (1926). The family as a unity of interacting personalities. *The Family, 7,* 3–9.

Burgess, E. W., & Locke, H. J. (1945). *The family: From institution to companionship.* New York: American Book Company.

Burgess, E. W., Locke, H. J., & Thomes, M. M. (1971). *The family: From traditional to companionship* (4th ed.). New York: Van Nostrand Reinhold.

Burkhauser, R. V., & Smeeding, T. M. (1994). *Social security reform: A budget neutral approach to reducing older women's disproportionate risk of poverty,* Policy Brief, No. 2. Syracuse, NY: Center for Policy Research, Syracuse University.

Burt, M., & M. E. Cohen. (1989). Differences among homeless single women, women with children, and single men. *Social Problems, 36,* 508–523.

Burtless, G., & Karoly, L. (1995). Demographic change, rising earnings inequality, and the distribution of personal well-being, 1959–1989. *Demography, 32,* 379–405.

Burton, L. (1990). Teenage childbearing as an alternative life-course strategy in multigenerational black families. *Human Nature, 1,* 123–143.

Buss, D. M. (1985). Human mate selection. *American Scientist, 73,* 47–51.

Buss, D. (1994). *The evolution of desire: Strategies of human mating.* New York: Basic Books.

Butterfield, F. (1997, February 3). '95 data show sharp drop in reported rapes. *New York Times,* p. A1.

Butz, W. P., & Ward, M. P. (1979). The emergence of countercyclical U.S. fertility. *American Economic Review, 69,* 318–328.

Byne, W. (1994, May). The biological evidence challenged. *Scientific American, 270,* 50–55.

Cain, M. (1983). Fertility as an adjustment to risk. *Population and Development Review, 9,* 688–702.

Caldwell, J. C. (1982). *Theory of fertility decline.* New York: Academic Press.

Caldwell, J. C., & Caldwell, P. (1993). The nature and limits of the sub-Saharan African AIDS epidemic: Evidence from geographic and other patterns. *Population and Development Review, 19,* 817–848.

Caldwell, J. C., Caldwell, P., & Orubuloye, I. (1992). The family and sexual networking in sub-Saharan Africa: Historical regional differences and present-day implications. *Population Studies, 46,* 385–410.

Calhoun, A. W. (1919). *A social history of the American family: Vol. 3. From 1865 to 1919.* New York: Barnes and Noble.

Callendar, C., & Kochems, L. (1983). The North American berdache, *Current Anthropology, 24,* 443–470.

Camarillo, A. (1979). *Chicanos in a changing society: From Mexican pueblos to American barrios in Santa Barbara and Southern California, 1848–1940.* Cambridge, MA: Harvard University Press.

Campbell, A. A. (1968). The role of family planning in the reduction of poverty. *Journal of Marriage and the Family, 30,* 236–245, quoted at 238.

Cancian, F. M. (1987). *Love in America: Gender and self-development.* Cambridge, England: Cambridge University Press.

Capaldi, D., & Patterson, G. (1991). Relation of parental transitions to boys' adjustment problems: 1. A linear hypothesis; 2. Mothers at risk for transitions and unskilled parenting. *Developmental Psychology, 27,* 489–504.

Caplow, T., Bahr, H. M., Chadwick, B. A., Hill, R., & Williamson, M. H. (1982). *Middletown families: Fifty years of change and continuity.* Minneapolis: University of Minnesota Press.

Carlson, A. (1986). What happened to the "family wage"? *The Public Interest, 83,* 3–17.

Carp, W. (1991). Family history, family violence: A review essay. *Journal of Policy History, 3,* 203–223.

Carter, H., & Glick, P. C. (1976). *Marriage and divorce: A social and economic study* (Rev. ed.). Cambridge, MA: Harvard University Press.

Castro, Janice. (1993, 29 March). Disposable Workers. *Time,* pp. 42–46.

Cate, R. M., & Lloyd, S. A. (1992). *Courtship.* Newbury Park, CA: Sage Publications.

Cavan, R., & Ranck, K. (1938). *The family and the Depression: A study of 100 Chicago families.* Chicago: University of Chicago Press.

Chafe, W. H. (1972). *The American woman: Her changing social, economic, and political roles, 1920–1970.* New York: Oxford University Press.

Chambers, D. L. (1990). Stepparents, biological parents, and the law's perceptions of family after divorce. In S. D. Sugarman & H. H. Kay (Eds.), *Divorce reform at the crossroads* (pp. 102–129). New Haven, CT: Yale University Press.

Chase-Lansdale, L., Brooks-Gunn, J., & Zamsky, E. (1994). Young multi-generational families in poverty: Quality of mothering and grandmothering. *Child Development, 65,* 373–393.

Chase-Lansdale, L., & Hetherington, E. M. (1990). The impact of divorce on life-span development: short and long term effects. In P. B. Baltes et al. (Ed.), *Life-span development and behavior: Vol. 10* (pp. 105–150). Hillsdale, NJ: Lawrence Erlbaum Associates.

Chase-Lansdale, P. L., Cherlin, A. J., & Kiernan, K. E. (1995). The long-term effects of parental divorce on the mental health of young adults: A developmental perspective. *Child Development, 66,* 1614–1634.

Chase-Lansdale, P. L., & Vanovskis, M. A. (1993). Adolescent pregnancy and child support. In R. Wolons (Ed.), *Children at risk in America* (pp. 202–229). Albany, NY: State University of New York Press.

Cherlin, A. (1977). The effects of children on marital dissolution. *Demography, 14,* 265–272.

Cherlin, A. J. (1978). Remarriage as an incomplete institution. *American Journal of Sociology, 84,* 634–650.

Cherlin, A. J. (1988). *The changing American family and public policy.* Washington, DC: Urban Institute Press.

Cherlin, A. J. (1988, October 27). Child support: Now everyone will be compelled to pay. *The Washington Post,* p. 23.

Cherlin, A. J. (1990). The strange career of the "Harvard-Yale Study." *Public Opinion Quarterly, 54,* 117–124.

Cherlin, A. J. (1992a). Infant care and full-time employment. In A. Booth (Ed.), *Child care in the 1990s* (pp. 209–214). Hillsdale, NJ: Lawrence Erlbaum Associates.

Cherlin, A. J. (1992b). *Marriage, divorce, remarriage* (Rev. and enlarged ed.). Cambridge, MA: Harvard University Press.

Cherlin, A. J. (1993, December 30). Making deadbeats pay at work. *New York Times.* p. A19.

Cherlin, A. J. (1995). Child care for poor children. In P. L. Chase-Lansdale & J. Brooks-Gunn (Eds.), *Escape from poverty: What makes a difference for poor children.* Cambridge, England: Cambridge University Press.

Cherlin, A. J., & Chamratrithirong, A. (1988). Variations in marriage patterns in central Thailand. *Demography, 25,* 337–353.

Cherlin, A. J., Chase-Lansdale, P. L., & McRae, C. (1998). Effects of parental divorce on mental health throughout the life course. *American Sociological review, 63,* 239–249.

Cherlin, A., & Furstenberg, F. F., Jr. (1988). The changing European family: Lessons for the American reader. *Journal of Family Issues, 9,* 291–297.

Cherlin, A., & Furstenberg, F. F., Jr. (1992). *The new American grandparent: A place in the family, a life apart.* Cambridge, MA: Harvard University Press.

Cherlin, A. J., Furstenberg, F. F., Jr., Chase-Lansdale, P. L., Kiernan, K. E., Robins, P. K., Morrison, D. L., & Teitler, J. O. (1991). Longitudinal studies of the effects of divorce on children in Great Britain and the United States. *Science, 252,* 1386–1389.

Cherlin, A. J., Kiernan, K. E., & Chase-Lansdale, P. L. (1995). Parental divorce in childhood and demographic outcomes in young adulthood. *Demography, 32,* 299–318.

Chodorow, N. (1978). *The reproduction of mothering: Psychoanalysis and the sociology of gender.* Berkeley: University of California Press.

Christensen, K. E., & Staines, G. L. (1990). Flextime: A viable solution to work/family conflict? *Journal of Family Issues, 11,* 455–476.

Clark, R. L. (1990). Income maintenance policies in the United States. In R. H. Binstock & L. K. George (Eds.), *Handbook on aging and the social sciences* (pp. 382–397). New York: Academic Press.

Clarkberg, M. (1997). *The price of partnering: The role of economic well-being in young adults' first union experience.* Bronfenbrenner life course center working papers: Vol. 97–11. Ithaca, NY: Cornell University (33 pp.).

Clarkberg, M., Stolzenberg, R. M., & Waite, L. J. (1993). Attitudes, values, and the entrance into cohabitational unions [Discussion Paper 93-4]. Chicago:

Population Research Center, National Opinion Research Center, and the University of Chicago.

Clymer, A. (1992, September 11). Family leave bill sent to president. *New York Times,* p. A26.

Coale, A. J., & Zelnik, M. (1963). *New estimates of fertility and population in the United States.* Princeton: Princeton University Press.

Cohen, R. (1971). Brittle marriage as a stable system: The Kanuri case. In P. Bohannan (Ed.), *Divorce and after* (pp. 205–239). Garden City, NY: Anchor Books.

Cohen, S., & Katzenstein, M. (1988). The war over the family is not over the family. In S. Dornbusch & M. Strober (Eds.), *Feminism, children, and the new families.* New York: The Guilford Press.

Coleman, J. (1988). Social capital in the creation of human capital. *American Journal of Sociology, 94* (Suppl.), S95–S120.

Collier, J., Rosaldo, M., & Yanagisako, S. (1982). Is there a family? New anthropological views. In B. Thorne & M. Yalom (Eds.), *Rethinking the family: Some feminist questions* (pp. 25–39). New York: Longman.

Collins, R. (1971). A conflict theory of sexual stratification. *Social Problems, 19,* 3–21.

Conger, R. D., Elder, J., Glen H., Lorenz, F. O., Conger, K. J., Simons, R. L., Whitbeck, L. B., Huck, S., & Melby, J. N. (1990). Linking economic hardship to marital quality and instability. *Journal of Marriage and the Family, 52,* 643–656.

Cook, K., O'Brien, J., & Kollock, P. (1990). Exchange theory: A blueprint for structure and process. In G. Ritzer (Ed.), *Frontiers of social theory: The new syntheses* (pp. 151–181). New York: Columbia University Press.

Cooney, T. M., & Uhlenberg, P. (1990). The role of divorce in men's relations with their adult children after mid-life. *Journal of Marriage and the Family, 52,* 677–688.

Cott, N. (1977). *The bonds of womanhood: Woman's sphere in New England, 1780–1835.* New Haven, CT: Yale University Press.

Cottrell, L. S., Jr., Hunter, A., & Short, J. F., Jr. (1973). *Ernest W. Burgess: On community, family, and delinquency.* Chicago: University of Chicago Press.

Cowan, C. P., & Cowan, P. A. (1987). Men's involvement in parenthood: Identifying the antecedents and understanding the barriers. In P. W. Berman & F. A. Pederson (Eds.), *Men's transition to parenthood* (pp. 145–173). Hillsdale, NJ: Lawrence Erlbaum Associates.

Cowan, P. A., & Cowan, C. P. (in press). Becoming a family: Research and intervention. In I. Sigel & E. Brody (Eds.), *Family research, vol. 2.* Hillsdale, NJ: Lawrence Erlbaum Associates.

Cowley, G. (1997, May 19). Gender limbo. *Newsweek,* pp. 64–66.

Crenshaw, A. (1994, July 18–24). Paying the price for being married. *Washington Post National Weekly Edition, 21.*

Cretney, S. (1993, December). Step-parentage in English law. Paper presented at the International Colloquium on Stepfamilies Today, Paris.

Crimmons, E. M., Saito, Y., & Ingegneri, D. (1989). Changes in life expectancy and disability-free life expectancy in the United States. *Population and Development Review, 15,* 235–267.

Family Impact Seminar. (1990, January) The crisis in foster care: New directions for the 1990s [Background briefing report]. Family Impact Seminar. Washington, DC.

D'Antonio, W. V. (1985). The American Catholic family: Signs of cohesion and polarization. *Journal of Marriage and the Family, 47,* 395–405.

Danziger, S., & Weinberg, D. (1986). *Fighting poverty: What works and what doesn't.* Cambridge, MA: Harvard University Press.

Darling, C. A., Kallen, D. J., & VanDusen, J. E. (1984). Sex in transition, 1900–1980. *Journal of Youth and Adolescence, 13,* 385–399.

Darwin, C. (1871). *The descent of man and selection in relation to sex.* New York: Appleton.

Das Gupta, M., & Bhat, P. N. M. (1997). Fertility decline and increased manifestation of sex bias in India. *Population Studies, 51,* 307–315.

Davis, J. A., & Smith, T. (1997). General social surveys [On-line]. Available: www.norc.uchicago.edu/gss.htm (Accessed November 7, 1997).

Davis, J. A., & Smith, T. W. (1996). General social surveys, 1972–1996. In *Cumulative Codebook.* Chicago: National Opinion Research Center.

Davis, K. (1937). Reproductive institutions and the pressure for population. *Sociological Review, 29,* 289–306.

Davis, K. (1985). The meaning and significance of marriage in contemporary society. In K. Davis & A. Grossbard-Schechtman (Eds.), *Contemporary marriage: Comparative perspectives on a changing institution* (pp. 1–22). New York: Russell Sage Foundation.

Davis, N., & Robinson, R. (1988). Class identification of men and women in the 1970s and 1980s. *American Sociological Review, 53,* 103–112.

de Singly, F. (1993). *Sociologie de la famille contemporaine.* Paris: Editions Nathan.

Degler, C. N. (1980). *At odds: Women and the family in America from the revolution to the present.* New York: Oxford University Press.

Degler, C. N. (1990). Darwinians confront gender; or, there is more to it than history. In D. L. Rhode (Ed.), *Theoretical perspectives on sexual difference* (pp. 33–48). New Haven, CT: Yale University Press.

D'Emilio, J., & Freedman, E. B. (1988). *Intimate matters: A history of sexuality in America*. New York: Harper and Row.

Demos, J. (1970). *A little commonwealth: Family life in Plymouth Colony*. Oxford: Oxford University Press.

Desai, S., Chase-Lansdale, L., & Michael, R. T. (1989). Mother or market? Effects of maternal employment on the intellectual ability of 4-year old children. *Demography, 26,* 545–561.

di Leonardo, M. (1987). The female world of cards and holidays: Women, families, and the work of kinship. *Signs, 12,* 440–453.

Diamond, M., & Sigmundson, H. K. (1997). Sex reassignment at birth: Long-term review and clinical implications. *Archives of Pediatric and Adolescent Medicine, 151,* 298–304.

Donnelly, A. C. (1994, June). National Committee to Prevent Child Abuse.

Dornbusch, S. M., Carlsmith, J. M., Bushwall, S. J., Ritter, P. L., Leiderman, H., Hastorf, A. H., & Gross, R. T. (1985). Single parents, extended households, and the control of adolescents. *Child Development, 56,* 326–341.

Dornbusch, S. M., & Strober, M. H. (1988). Our perspective. In S. M. Dornbusch & M. H. Strober (Eds.), *Feminism, children, and the new families* (pp. 3–24). New York: The Guilford Press.

Duggan L., Hunter, N., & Vance, C. S. (1985). False promises: Feminist antipornography legislation in the U.S. In V. Burstyn (Ed.), *Women against censorship* (pp. 130–151). Vancouver: Douglas and McIntyre.

Dumon, W. (1992). *National family policies in EC-countries in 1991.* Brussels: Commission of the European Communities, Directorate General for Employment, Industrial Relations and Social Affairs.

Duncan, G. J. (1984). *Years of poverty, years of plenty.* Ann Arbor: Institute for Social Research, University of Michigan.

Duncan, G. J. (1991). The economic environment of childhood. In A. C. Huston (Ed.), *Children in poverty* (pp. 23–50). New York: Cambridge University Press.

Duncan, G. J., & Hoffman, S. D. (1985). Economic consequences of marital instability. In M. David & T. Smeeding (Eds.), *Horizontal equity, uncertainty, and economic well-being* (pp. 427–467). Chicago: University of Chicago Press.

Duncan, G. J., & Hoffman, S. D. (1991). Teenage underclass behavior and subsequent poverty: Have the rules changed? In C. Jencks & P. Peterson (Eds.), *The urban underclass* (pp. 155–174). Washington, DC: The Brookings Institution.

Duncan, G. J., & Rodgers, W. (1991). Has children's poverty become more permanent? *American Sociological Review, 56,* 538–550.

du Plessix Gray, F. (1990, 19 February). Soviet women. *The New Yorker,* p. 55.

Dworkin, A. (1985). Against the male flood: Censorship, pornography, and equality. *Harvard Women's Law Journal, 8,* 1–30.

Easterlin, R. A. (1980). *Birth and fortune.* New York, NY: Basic Books.

Edwards, J. N. (1991). New conceptions: Biosocial innovations and the family. *Journal of Marriage and the Family, 53,* 349–360.

Eggebeen, D. J., & Hogan, D. P. (1990). Giving between generations in American families. *Human Nature, 1,* 211–232.

Eggebeen, D. J., Snyder, A. R., & Manning, W. D. (1996). Children in single-father families in demographic perspective. *Journal of Family Issues, 17,* 441–465.

Ehrenreich, B., Hess, E., & Jacobs, G. (1986). *Remaking love: The feminization of sex.* Garden City, NY: Anchor Books/Doubleday.

Ehrhardt, A. E. (1985). The psychobiology of gender. In A. S. Rossi (Ed.), *Gender and the life course.* New York: Aldine.

Eisenstadt v. *Baird.* (1972). (Vol. 438, p. 405). U.S.

Elder, J., Glen H. (1975). Age differentiation and the life course. *Annual review of Sociology, 1,* 165–190.

Elder, J., Glen H., Conger, R. D., Foster, E. M., & Ardelt, M. (1992). Families under economic pressure. *Journal of Family Issues, 13,* 5–37.

Elkin, F., & Handel, G. (1984). *The child and society: The process of socialization* (5th ed.). New York: Random House.

Ellwood, D. (1988). *Poor support: Poverty and the American family.* New York: Basic books.

Ellwood, D. T., & Summers, L. (1986). Poverty in America: Is welfare the answer? In S. H. Danziger & D. H. Weinberg (Eds.), *Fighting poverty: What works and what doesn't* (pp. 79–105). Cambridge, MA: Harvard University Press.

Emerson, R. M. (1972). Exchange theory, Part II: Exchange relations and network structures. In J. Berger, J. Zelditch, M. & B. Anderson (Eds.), *Sociological theories in progress: Vol. 2.* New York: Houghton Mifflin.

Emery, R. E. (1989). Family violence. *American Psychologist, 44,* 321–328.

Engels, F. (1972). *The origin of family, private property, and the state.* New York: International Publishers.

England, P. (1994). [Review of the Book *Gender play: Girls and boys in school*]. Contemporary Sociology, 23, 282–283.

England, P., & Farkas, G. (1986). *Households, employment, and gender: A social, economic, and demographic view.* New York: Aldine.

Entwisle, D. R. (1985). Becoming a parent. In L. L'Abata (Ed.), *Handbook of family psychology and therapy: Vol. 1* (pp. 557–585). Homewood, IL: Dorsey Press.

Entwisle, D. R., & Doering, S. G. (1981). *The first birth: A family turning point.* Baltimore: Johns Hopkins University Press.

Epstein, C. F. (1988). Toward a family policy: Changes in mothers' lives. In A. J. Cherlin (Ed.), *The changing American family and public policy* (pp. 157–192). Washington, DC: Urban Institute Press.

Erikson, E. H. (1950). *Childhood and society.* New York: W. W. Norton.

Eschbach, K. (1993). Changing identification among American Indians and Alaska natives. *Demography, 30,* 635–652.

Evans, M. D. R. (1986). American fertility patterns: A comparison of white and nonwhite cohorts born 1903–1956. *Population and Development Review, 12,* 267–293.

Fagot, B. I. (1974). Sex differences in toddlers' behavior and parental reaction. *Developmental Psychology, 10,* 554–558.

Fagot, B. I., Leinbach, M. D., & Hagan, R. (1986). Gender labeling and the adoption of sex-typed behaviors. *Developmental Psychology, 22,* 440–443.

Farley, R., & Allen, W. (1987). *The color line and the quality of life in America.* New York: Russell Sage Foundation.

Federal Interagency Forum on Child and Family Statistics. (1997). *America's children: Key national indicators of well-being.* Washington, DC: U.S. Government Printing Office.

Feminists for Free Expression. (1997). Available: www.well.com/user/freedom (Accessed November 8, 1997).

Ferree, M. M. (1990). Beyond separate spheres: Feminism and family research. *Journal of Marriage and the Family, 52,* 866–884.

Fine, G. A. (1987). *With the boys: Little league baseball and preadolescent culture.* Chicago: University of Chicago Press.

Fischer, D. H. (1978). *Growing old in America.* New York: Oxford University Press.

Fitzpatrick, M. A. (1988). *Between husbands and wives: Communication in marriage.* Newbury Park, CA: Sage Publications.

Flandrin, J. L. (1985). Sex in married life in the early Middle Ages: The church's teaching and behavioral reality. In P. Aries & A. Bejin (Eds.), *Western sexuality: Practice and precept in past and present times* (pp. 114–129). Oxford: Basil Blackwell.

Folbre, N. (1994). Children as public goods. *American Economic Review, 84,* 86–90.

Fonow, M. M., & Cook, J. (1991). Back to the future: A look at the second wave of feminist epistemology and methodology. In M. M. Fonow & J. Cook (Eds.), *Beyond methodology: Feminist scholarship as lived research* (pp. 1–15). Bloomington: Indiana University Press.

Forrest, J. D., & Singh, S. (1989). The sexual and reproductive behavior of American women, 1982–1988. *Family Planning Perspectives, 22,* 206–214.

Fortune. (1991, May 20).

Foucault, M. (1980). *The history of sexuality: Vol. 1. An introduction.* New York: Vintage Books.

Fox, R. (1967). *Kinship and marriage.* Harmondsworth, England: Penguin Books.

Fox, R. (1993). Babies for sale. *The Public Interest, 111* (Spring), 14–40.

Frazier, E. F. (1939). *The Negro family in the United States* (Rev. and abridged ed.). Chicago: University of Chicago Press.

Freedman, E. B. (1990). Theoretical perspectives on sexual difference: An overview. In D. L. Rhode (Ed.), *Theoretical perspectives on sexual differences* (pp. 257–261). New Haven, CT: Yale University Press.

Freedman, R., Chang, M., Sun, T., & Weinstein, M. (1994). The fertility transition in Taiwan. In Thornton & Lin (Eds.), *Social change and the family in Taiwan* (pp. 264–304). Chicago: University of Chicago Press.

Friedan, B. (1963). *The feminine mystique.* New York: Dell.

Friedman, D. E., & Galinsky, E. (1991). Work and family trends. In S. Zedeck (Ed.), *Work and family* (pp. 1–18). San Francisco: Jossey-Bass.

Frieze, I. H. (1983). Investigating the causes and consequences of marital rape. *Signs, 8,* 532–553.

Frieze, I. H., & Brown, A. (1989). Violence in marriage. In L. Ohlin & M. Tonry (Eds.), *Family violence* (pp. 163–218). Chicago: University of Chicago Press.

Furstenberg, F. F., Jr. (1976). *Unplanned parenthood: The social consequences of teenage childbearing.* New York: The Free Press.

Furstenberg, F. F., Jr. (1981). Implicating the family: Teenage parenthood and kinship involvement. In T. Ooms (Ed.), *Teenage pregnancy in a family context* (pp. 131–164). Philadelphia: Temple University Press.

Furstenberg, F. F., Jr (1987). The new extended family: The experience of parents and children after remarriage. In K. Pasley & M. Ihinger-Tallman (Eds.), *Remarriage and stepparenting: Current research and theory* (pp. 42–61). New York: The Guilford Press.

Furstenberg, F. F., Jr., Brooks-Gunn, J., & Morgan, S. P. (1987). *Adolescent mothers in later life.* Cambridge, England: Cambridge University Press.

Furstenberg, F. F., Jr., & Cherlin, A. J. (1991). *Divided families: What happens to children when parents part.* Cambridge, MA: Harvard University Press.

Furstenberg, F. F., Jr., & Condran, G. A. (1988). Family change and adolescent well-being: A re-examination of U.S. trends. In A. J. Cherlin (Ed.), *The changing American family and public policy* (pp. 117–155).

Furstenberg, F. F., Jr., & Nord, C. W. (1985). Parenting apart: Patterns of childrearing after divorce. *Journal of Marriage and the Family, 47,* 893–904.

Furstenberg, F. F., Jr., Sherwood, K. E., & Sullivan, M. L. (1992). *Daddies and fathers: Men who do for their children and men who don't.* Parents' Fair Share Demonstration. New York: Manpower Demonstration Research Corporation.

Furstenberg, F. F., Jr., & Spanier, G. B. (1984). *Recycling the family: Remarriage after divorce.* Newbury Park, CA: Sage Publications.

Gagnon, J. H., & Simon, W. (1973). *Sexual conduct: The social sources of human sexuality.* Chicago: Aldine.

Galinsky, E. (1992). *Work and family: 1992 status report and outlook.* New York: Families and Work Institute.

Galinsky, E., Bond, J. T., & Friedman, D. E. (1993). *The changing workforce: Highlights of the national study.* New York: Families and Work Institute.

Galston, W. (1990/1991). A liberal-democratic case for the two-parent family. *The Responsive Community,* 14–26.

Gans, H. (1982). *The urban villagers: Group and class in the lives of Italian-Americans.* New York: The Free Press.

Garfinkel, I. (1992). *Assuring child support: An extension of social security.* New York: Russell Sage Foundation.

Gatz, M., Bengtson, V. L., & Blum, M. J. (1990). Caregiving families. In J. Birren & W. Schaie (Eds.), *Handbook of the psychology of aging* (3rd ed.) (pp. 404–426). Orlando, FL: Academic Press.

Geffner, R., Rosenbaum, A., & Hughes, H. (1988). Research issues concerning family violence. In V. B. Van Hasselt, R. Morrison, A. S. Bellack, & M. Hersen (Eds.), *Handbook of family violence* (pp. 457–481). New York: Plenum Press.

Gelles, R., & Cornell, C. P. (1990). *Intimate violence in families* (2nd ed.). Newbury Park, CA: Sage Publications.

Gelles, R. J. (1987). *Family violence.* Newbury Park, CA: Sage Publications.

Gelles, R. J., & Straus, M. A. (1979). Determinants of violence in the family: Toward a theoretical integration. In W. R. Burr, R. Hill, F. I. Nye, & I. L. Reiss (Eds.), *Contemporary theories about the family: Vol. 1* (pp. 549–581). New York: The Free Press.

Gelman, D. (1992, February 24). Is this child gay? Born or bred: The origins of homosexuality. *Newsweek,* pp. 46–53.

Geronimus, A. T. (1991). Teenage childbearing and social and reproductive disadvantage: The evolution of complex questions and the demise of simple answers. *Family Relations, 40,* 463–471.

Geronimus, A. T., & Korenman, S. (1992). The socioeconomic consequences of teen childbearing recon-

sidered. *Quarterly Journal of Economics, 107,* 1187–1214.

Gerth, H., & Mills, C. W. (1946). *From Max Weber: Essays in sociology.* New York: Oxford University Press.

Gilkes, C. (1995). The storm and the light: Church, family, work, and social crisis in the African-American experience. In N. Ammerman & C. Roof (Eds.), *Work, family and religion in contemporary society* (pp. 177–198). New York: Routledge.

Gill, R. (1991). Day care or parental care? *The Public Interest, 105,* 3–16.

Gillis, J. R. (1985). *For better or worse: British marriages, 1600 to the present.* Oxford: Oxford University Press.

Glass, J. L., & Estes, S. B. (1997). The family responsive workplace. *Annual Review of Sociology, 23,* 289–313.

Glendon, M. (1987). *Abortion and divorce in Western law.* Cambridge, MA: Harvard University Press.

Glendon, M. (1989). *The transformation of family law: State, law, and family in the United States and Western Europe.* Chicago: University of Chicago Press.

Glenn, N. D. (1990). Quantitative research on marital quality in the 1980s: A critical review. *Journal of Marriage and the Family, 52,* 818–831.

Glick, P. C. (1984). Marriage, divorce, and living arrangements: Prospective changes. *Journal of Family Issues, 5,* 7–26.

Gold, S. (1993). Migration and family adjustment: Continuity and change among Vietnamese in the United States. In H. McAdoo (Ed.), *Family ethnicity* (pp. 300–314).

Goldberg, C. (1998, January 16). Public still backs abortion, but wants limits, poll says. *New York Times,* p. A1.

Goldin, C. (1977). Female labor force participation: The origin of black and white differences, 1870 and 1880. *Journal of Economic History, 37,* 87–108.

Goldscheider, C., & Uhlenberg, P. (1969). Minority group status and fertility. *American Journal of Sociology, 74,* 361–372.

Goldscheider, F., & Goldscheider, C. (1994). Leaving and returning home in 20th century America. *Population Bulletin, 48* (4).

Goldscheider, F. K. (1990). The aging of the gender revolution: What do we know and what do we need to know? *Research on aging, 12,* 531–545, quoted at 533.

Goldscheider, F. K. (1997). Recent changes in the U.S. young adult living arrangements in comparative perspective. *Journal of Family Issues, 18,* 708–724.

Goldscheider, F. K., & Goldscheider, C. (1993). *Leaving home before marriage: Ethnicity, familism, and generational relationships.* Madison: University of Wisconsin Press.

Goldscheider, F. K., & Waite, L. J. (1991). *New families, no families? The transformation of the American home.* Berkeley: University of California Press.

Golombok, S., Spencer, A., & Rutter, M. (1983). Children in lesbian and single-parent households: Psychosexual and psychiatric appraisal. *Journal of Child Psychology and psychiatry, 24,* 551–572.

Gonzalez Baker, S. (1996). Homelessness and the Latino paradox. In J. Baumohl (Ed.), *Homelessness in America* (pp. 132–140). Phoenix, AZ: Oryx Press.

Goode, W. J. (1963). *World revolution and family patterns.* New York: The Free Press.

Goode, W. J. (1971). Force and violence in the family. *Journal of Marriage and the Family, 33,* 624–636.

Goode, W. J. (1982). *The family* (2nd ed.). Englewood Cliffs, NJ: Prentice-Hall.

Gordon, L. (1988). *Heroes of their own lives: The politics and history of family violence.* New York: Viking.

Gordon, M. (1964). *Assimilation in American life.* New York: Oxford University Press.

Gottman, J. M. (1979). *Marital interaction: Experimental investigations.* New York: Academic Press.

Gottman, J. M., & Levenson, R. W. (1987). The social physiology of marriage. In P. Noller & M. A. Fitzpatrick (Eds.), *Perspectives on marital interaction* (pp. 182–200). Philadelphia: Multilingual Matters.

Gove, W. R., Style, C. B., & Hughes, M. (1990). The effect of marriage on the well-being of adults. *Journal of Family Issues, 11,* 4–35.

Gray, F. (1990). Soviet women. *The New Yorker,* p. 55.

Greeley, A. M., Michael, R. T., & Smith, T. W. (1990, July/August). Americans and their sexual partners. *Society, 27,* 36–42.

Greenhalgh, S., & Li, J. (1995). Engendering reproductive policy and practice in peasant China: For a feminist demography of reproduction. *Signs: Journal of Women in Culture and Society, 20,* 601–641.

Greeno, C. G. (1989). *Gender differences in children's proximity to adults.* Doctoral dissertation, Stanford University, Palo Alto, California.

Greenstein, T. N. (1990). Marital disruption and the employment of married women. *Journal of Marriage and the Family, 52,* 657–676.

Greenstein, T. N. (1993). Maternal employment and child behavioral outcomes: A household economics analysis. *Journal of Family Issues, 14,* 323–354.

Gregory, R. G., Anstie, R., Daly, A., & Ho, V. (1989). Women's pay in Australia, Great Britain, and the United States. In R. T. Michael, H. I. Hartmann & B. O'Farrell (Eds.), *Pay equity: Empirical inquiries* (pp. 222–242). Washington, DC: National Academy Press.

Greven, P. J. (1970). *Four generations: Population, land, and family in colonial Massachusetts.* Ithaca, NY: Cornell University Press.

Griswold del Castillo, R. (1979). *The Los Angeles barrio, 1850–1890: A social history.* Los Angeles, University of California Press.

Griswold v. *Connecticut.* (1965). 381 U.S. 479.

Groopman, J. (1997, August 11). To be poor and infected with H.I.V. *New York Times,* p. A29.

Gross, J. (1994, April 25). After a ruling, Hawaii weighs gay marriages. *New York Times,* p. A1.

Grossman, F. K., Eichler, L. S., & Winikoff, S. A. (1980). *Pregnancy, birth, and parenthood.* San Francisco: Jossey-Bass.

Grubb, W., & Lazerson, M. (1988). *Broken promises: How Americans fail their children.* Chicago: University of Chicago Press.

Gutman, H. G. (1976). *The black family in slavery and freedom, 1750–1925.* New York: Pantheon Books.

Guyer, J. (1988). Dynamic approaches to domestic budgeting: Cases and methods from Africa. In D. Dwyer & J. Bruce (Eds.), *A home divided: Women and income in the Third World* (pp. 155–172). Palo Alto, CA: Stanford University Press.

Gwartney-Gibbs, P., & Stockard, J. (1989). Courtship aggression in mixed-sex peer groups. In M. A. Pirog-Good & J. E. Stets (Eds.), *Violence in dating relationships* (pp. 185–204). New York: Praeger.

Haas, L. (1992). *Equal parenthood and social policy: A study of parental leave in Sweden.* Albany: State University of New York Press.

Haines, M. R. (1996). Long-term marriage patterns in the United States from colonial times to the present. *The History of the Family, 1,* 15–39.

Hajnal, J. (1982). Two kinds of preindustrial household formation systems. *Population and Development review, 8,* 449–494.

Haldeman, D. C. (1991). Sexual orientation conversion therapy for gay men and lesbians: Scientific examination. In Gonsiorek & Weinrich (Eds.), *Homosexuality: Research implications for public policy* (pp. 149–160). Newbury Park, CA: Sage Publications.

Hall, C. (1990). Strains in the firm of wife, children, and friends? Middle-class women and employment in early nineteenth-century England. In P. Hudson & W. Lee (Eds.), *Women's work and the economy in historical perspective* (pp. 106–131). Manchester, England: Manchester University Press.

Hall, S. (1904). *Adolescence: Its psychology and its relations to anthropology, sociology, sex, crime, religion and education.* 2 vols. New York: Appleton.

Halpern, R. (1993). Poverty and infant development. In C. H. J. Zeanah (Ed.), *Handbook of infant mental health* (pp. 73–86). New York, NY: Guilford Press.

Hamer, D. H., Hu, S., Magnuson, V. L., Hu, N., & Pattatucci, A. M. L. (1993). A linkage between DNA markers on the X chromosome and male sexual orientation. *Science, 261,* 321–327.

Hampton, R. L., & Newberger, E. (1985). Child abuse incidence and reporting by hospitals: Significance of severity, class, and race. *American Journal of public Health, 75,* 56–60.

Handler, J. (1995). *The poverty of welfare reform*. New Haven, CT: Yale University Press.

Hansen, K. V. (1989). Helped put in a quilt: Men's work and male intimacy in nineteenth-century New England. *Gender & Society, 3,* 334–354, quoted at 338.

Hareven, T. K. (1982). *Family time and industrial time*. Cambridge, England: Cambridge University Press.

Harjo, S. (1993). The American Indian experience. In H. McAdoo (Ed.), *Family Ethnicity* (pp. 199–207).

Harrell-Bond, B. E. (1975). *Modern marriage in Sierra Leone*. The Hague: Mouton.

Hartmann, H. I. (1976). Capitalism, patriarchy, and job segregation by sex. *Signs, 1,* 137–169.

Harvey, D. (1993). *Potter Addition: Poverty, family, and kinship in a heartland community*. New York: Aldine de Gruyter.

Haveman, R. (1996). Does the growth in male earnings inequality reflect changing opportunities or changing choices? In AEI Conference Summary [On-line]. Available: American Enterprise Institute for Public Policy Research.

Hawes, J., & Nybakkan, E. (1991). *American families: A research guide and historical handbook*. New York: Greenwood Press.

Hawes, J. M., & Hiner, N. R. (Eds.). (1991). *Children in historical and comparative perspective: An international handbook and research guide*. (pp. 31–70). New York: Greenwood Press.

Hayes, C. D. (1987). *Risking the future: Adolescent sexuality, pregnancy, and childbearing*. Washington, DC: National Academy Press.

Hayes, C. D., Palmer, J. L., & Zaslow, M. L. (1990). *Who cares for America's children? Child care policy for the 1990s*. Washington, DC: National Academy Press.

Heclo, H. (1986). The political foundations of antipoverty policy. In S. Danziger & D. Weinberg (Eds.), *Fighting poverty: What works and what doesn't* (pp. 312–340). Cambridge, MA: Harvard University Press.

Hendrick, S. S., & Hendrick, C. (Eds.). (1992). *Romantic love*. Newbury Park, CA: Sage Publications.

Henrikson v. *Gable*. 412 N.W. 2nd 702. (Mich. app. 1987).

Henry III, W. A. (1993, September 20). Gay parents: Under fire and on the rise. *Time*.

Hernandez, D. J. (1993). *America's children: Resources from family, government, and economy*. New York: Russell Sage Foundation.

Hertz, R. (1986). *More equal than others: Women and men in dual-career marriages*. Berkeley: University of California Press.

Herzog, E., & Sudia, C. E. (1973). Children in fatherless families. In B. Caldwell & N. Ricciuti (Eds.), *Review of child development research: Vol. 3* (pp. 141–232). Chicago: University of Chicago Press.

Hetherington, E. M. (1972). Effects of father absence on personality development in adolescent daughters. *Developmental Psychology, 7,* 313–326.

Hetherington, E. M. (1987). Family relations six years after divorce. In K. Pasley & M. Ihinger-Tallman (Eds.), *Remarriage and stepparenting* (pp. 185–205). New York: The Guilford Press.

Hetherington, E. M., & Clingempeel, W. G. (1992). Coping with marital transitions. *Monographs of the Society for Research in Child development, 57* (Nos. 2–3).

Hetherington, E. M., Cox, R., & Cox, M. (1978). The aftermath of divorce. In J. Stevens & M. Mathews (Eds.), *Mother-child, father-child relations* (pp. 148–176). Washington, DC: National Association for the Education of Young children.

Hetherington, E. M., & Jodl, K. M. (1994). Stepfamilies as settings for child development. In A. Booth & J. Dunn (Eds.), *Stepfamilies: Who benefits? who does not?* (pp. 55–79). Hillsdale, NJ: Lawrence Erlbaum.

Hirosima, K. (1997). Projection of living arrangements of the elderly in Japan: 1990–2010. *Genus, 53,* 79–111.

Hochschild, A. R. (1983). Attending to, codifying and managing feelings: Sex differences in love. In L. Richardson & V. Taylor (Eds.), *Feminist frontiers: Rethinking sex, gender, and society* (pp. 250–262). Reading, MA: Addison-Wesley.

Hochschild, A. R. (1989). *The second shift: Working parents and the revolution at home*. New York: Viking.

Hochschild, A. R. (1997). *The time bind: When work becomes home and home becomes work*. New York: Henry Holt and Company.

Hoeffer, B. (1981). Children's acquisition of sex-role behavior in lesbian-mother families. *American Journal of Orthopsychiatry, 51,* 536–544.

Hoem, B., & Hoem, J. M. (1988). The Swedish family: Aspects of contemporary developments. *Journal of Family Issues, 9,* 397–424.

Hofferth, S. (1984). Kin networks, race, and family structure. *Journal of Marriage and the Family, 46,* 791–806.

Hofferth, S. D. (1992). The demand for and supply of child care in the 1990s. In A. Booth (Ed.), *Child care in the 1990s: Trends and consequences* (pp. 3–25). Hillsdale, NJ: Lawrence Erlbaum.

Hofferth, S. L., Brayfield, A., Deich, S., & Holcomb, P. (1991). *National child care survey, 1990*. Washington, DC: Urban Institute Press.

Hoffman, K. L., Demo, D. H., & Edwards, J. N. (1994). Physical wife abuse in a non-Western society: An integrated theoretical approach. *Journal of Marriage and the Family, 56,* 131–146.

Hoffman, S. D., & Duncan, G. J. (1988). What are the economic costs of divorce? *Demography, 25,* 641–645.

Hoffman, S. D., Foster, M., & Furstenberg, F. F., Jr. (1993). Re-evaluating the costs of teenage childbearing. *Demography, 30,* 1–13.

Hogan, D., Hao, L., & Parish, W. P. (1990). Race, kin networks, and assistance to mother-headed families. *Social Forces, 68,* 797–812.

Holmes, S. (1990). Day care bill marks a turn toward help for the poor. *New York Times,* p. E4.

Hotz, V. J., McElroy, S. W., & Sanders, S. G. (1996). The costs and consequences of teenage childbearing for the mothers and the government. *Chicago Policy Review, 1,* 55–94.

House panel leader jeered by elderly in Chicago. *New York Times* (1989, August 19) p. 8.

Howell, N. (1979). *Demography of the Dobe Kung.* New York: Academic Press.

Hsia, H.-C., & Scanzoni, J. H. (1996). Rethinking the roles of Japanese women. *Journal of Comparative Family Studies, 27,* 309–329.

Huber, J. (1991). A theory of family, economy, and gender. In R. L. Blumberg (Ed.), *Gender, family, and economy* (pp. 35–51). Newbury Park, CA: Sage Publications.

Hurtado, A. (1995). Variation, combinations, and evolutions: Latino families in the United States. In R. Zambrana (Ed.), *Understanding Latino families* (pp. 40–61). Thousand Oaks, CA: Sage.

Ihinger-Tallman, M., & Pasley, K. (1987). *Remarriage.* Newbury Park, CA: Sage Publications.

Ingrassia, M., & McCormick, J. (1994, April 25). Why leave children with bad parents. *Newsweek,* pp. 52–58.

Institute for Social Research. (1998). The Monitoring the Future study [On-line]. Available: www.isr.umich.edu/src/mtf/ (Accessed March 21).

Isaacs, S. L., & Holt, R. J. (1987). Redefining procreation: Facing the issues. *Population Bulletin, 42*(3).

Jacklin, C. N. (1984). Sex-typing behavior and sex-typing pressure in child/parent interaction. *Archives of Sexual Behavior, 13,* 413–425.

Jacobellis v. *Ohio.* (1964). 378 U.S. 184.

Jacobson, C. K., & Heaton, T. B. (1991). *Social Biology, 38,* 79–93.

Jacobson, P. (1959). *American marriage and divorce.* New York: Rinehart.

Jehl, D. (1994, June 15). President offers delayed proposal to redo welfare. *New York Times.* p. A1.

Jencks, C. (1994). *The homeless.* Cambridge, MA: Harvard University Press.

Jencks, C., & Peterson, P. (1991). *The urban underclass.* Washington, DC: The Brookings Institution.

Jeter, J. (1997, August 15). 'Covenant marriages' tie the knot tightly. *The Washington Post,* p. A1.

Johnson, A. M., Wadsworth, J., Wellings, K., Bradshaw, S., & Field, J. (1992). Sexual lifestyles and HIV risk. *Nature, 360,* 410–412.

Johnson, W. R., & Skinner, J. (1986). Labor supply and marital separation. *American Economic Review, 76,* 455–469.

Jones, J. (1985). *Labor of love, labor of sorrow: Black women and the family from slavery to the present.* New York, Basic books.

Juhn, C., Murphy, K., & Pierce, B. (1993). Wage inequality and the rise in returns to skill. *Journal of Political Economy, 101,* 410–442.

Kalish, S. (1995). Multiracial births increase as U.S. ponders racial definitions. *Population Today, 23,* 1–2.

Kalmijn, M. (1991a). Shifting boundaries: Trends in religious and educational homogamy. *American Sociological Review, 56,* 786–800.

Kalmijn, M. (1991b). Status homogamy in the United States. *American Journal of Sociology, 97,* 496–523.

Kalmuss, D. (1984). The intergenerational transmission of marital aggression. *Journal of Marriage and the Family, 46,* 11–19.

Kamerman, S. B., & Kahn, A. J. (1987). *The responsive workplace: Employers and a changing labor force.* New York: Columbia University Press.

Katz, J. (1976) *Gay American history.* New York: Harper and Row.

Katz, M. (1989). *The undeserving poor: From the war on poverty to the war on welfare.* New York: Pantheon Books.

Kaufman, J., & Zigler, E. (1987). Do abused children become abusive parents? *American Journal of Orthopsychiatry, 57,* 186–192.

Kaus, M. (1992). *The end of equality.* New York: Basic Books.

Kellam, S. G., Ensminger, M. E., & Turner, R. (1977). Family structure and the mental health of children. *Archives of General Psychiatry, 34,* 1012–1022.

Keller, S. (1991). The American upper class family: Precarious claims on the future. *Journal of Comparative Family Studies, 22,* 159–182.

Kelley, H., Berscheid, E., Christensen, A., Harvey, J., Huston, T., Levinger, G., McClintock, E., Peplau, L., & Peterson, D. (1983). *Close relationships.* New York: Freeman.

Kelley, H. H. (1979). *Personal relationships.* Hillsdale, NJ: Lawrence Erlbaum Associates.

Kempe, C. H., Silverman, F. N., Steele, B. F., Droegemuller, W., & Silver, H. K. (1962). the battered child syndrome. *Journal of the American Medical Association, 181,* 17–24.

Kertzer, D. I. (1991). Household history and sociological theory. *Annual Review of Sociology, 17,* 155–179.

Keshet, J. K. (1988). The remarried couple: Stresses and successes. In W. R. Beer (Ed.), *Relative strangers: Studies of stepfamily processes* (pp. 29–53). Totowa, NJ: Rowan and Littlefield.

Kessler, R., House, J., & Turner, J. (1987). Unemployment and health in a community sample. *Journal of Health and Social Behavior, 28,* 51–59.

Kiernan, K. E. (1992). The impact of family disruption in childhood on transitions made in young adult life. *Population Studies, 46,* 213–234.

Kilborn, P. (1997, April 29). Priority on safety is keeping more children in foster care. *New York Times,* p. A1.

Kimmel, D. C. (1992). The families of older gay men and lesbians. In L. Burton (Ed.), *Families and aging* (pp. 75–78). Amityville, NY: Baywood.

Kingston, P. W. (1990). Illusion and ignorance about the family-friendly workplace. *Journal of Family Issues, 11,* 438–454.

Kinsey, A. C., Pomeroy, W. B., & Martin, C. E. (1948). *Sexual behavior in the human male.* Philadelphia: W. B. Saunders.

Kirkpatrick, M., Smith, C., & Roy, R. (1981). Lesbian mothers and their children: A comparative study. *American Journal of Orthopsychiatry, 51,* 545–559.

Kitano, H. H. L. (1988). The Japanese American family. In C. H. Mindel & R. W. Habenstein (Eds), *Ethnic families in America: Patterns and variations* (pp. 258–275). New York: Elsevier Science Publishing.

Kitano, H. H. L., & Daniels, R. (1988). *Asian Americans: Emerging minorities.* Englewood Cliffs, NJ: Prentice Hall.

Klein, J. (1997, 16 June). In God they trust. *New Yorker,* pp. 40–48.

Kobrin, F. E. (1976). The fall of household size and the rise of the primary individual in the United States. *Demography, 13,* 127–138.

Koegl, P., Burnam, M., & Baumohl, J. (1996). The causes of homelessness. In J. Baumohl (Ed.), *Homelessness in America* (pp. 24–33). Phoenix, AZ: Oryx Press.

Kohn, M., & Slomczynski, K. (1990). *Social structure and self-direction: A comparative analysis of the United States and Poland.* Oxford: Basil Blackwell.

Kohn, M. L. (1969). *Class and conformity: A study in values.* Homewood, IL: Dorsey Press.

Kohn, M. L., & Schooler, C. (1978). The reciprocal effects of the substantive complexity of work and intellectual flexibility: A longitudinal assessment. *American Journal of Sociology, 84,* 24–52.

Komarovsky, M. (1971). *The unemployed man and his family.* New York: Octagon Books.

Komarovsky, M. (1992). The concept of social role revisited. *Gender & Society, 6,* 301–313.

Komter, A. (1989). Hidden power in marriage. *Gender & Society, 3,* 187–216.

Kornhaber, A., & Woodward, K. L. (1981). *Grandparents/grandchildren: The vital connection.* Garden City, NY: Anchor Press/Doubleday.

Koss, M. P. (1988). Hidden rape: Sexual aggression and victimization in a national sample of students in higher education. In A. W. Burgess (Ed.), *Rape and sexual assault II* (pp. 3–25). New York: Garland.

Kost, K., & Forrest, J. D. (1992). American women's sexual behavior and exposure to risk of sexually transmitted diseases. *Family Planning Perspectives, 24,* 244–254.

Kotlowitz, A. (1991). *There are no children here: The story of two boys growing up in the other America.* New York: Doubleday.

Kristof, N. D. (1996, 11 February). Who needs love! In Japan, many couples don't. *New York Times,* p. A1.

Ku, L. C., Sonenstein, F. L., & Pleck, J. H. (1992). The association of AIDS education and sex education with sexual behavior and condom usage among teenage men. *Family Planning Perspectives, 24,* 100–106.

Landale, N., & Fennelly, K. (1992). Informal unions among mainland Puerto Ricans: Cohabitation or an alternative to legal marriage? *Journal of Marriage and the Family, 54,* 269–280.

Landale, N., & Forste, R. (1991). Patterns of entry into cohabitation and marriage among mainland Puerto Rican women. *Demography, 28,* 587–605.

Lantz, H., Schultz, M., & O'Hara, M. (1977). The changing American family from the preindustrial to the industrial period: A final report. *American Sociological Review, 42,* 406–421.

LaRossa, R., & LaRossa, M. (1981). *Transition to parenthood: How infants change families.* Newbury Park, CA: Sage Publications.

Larsen, A. S., & Olsen, D. H. (1989). Predicting marital success with PREPARE: A replication study. *Journal of Marriage and Family Therapy, 15,* 311–322.

Larson, A. (1989). The social context of HIV transmission in Africa: A review of the historical and cultural bases of East and Central African sexual relations. In Australian National University (Ed.), *Health Transition Centre Working Papers,* no. 1.

Laslett, B. (1973). The family as a public and private institution: An historical perspective. *Journal of the Marriage and the Family, 35,* 480–492.

Laslett, P., & Wall, R. (1972). *Household and family in past time.* Cambridge, England: Cambridge University Press.

Laumann, E. O., Gagnon, J. H., Michael, R. T., & Michaels, S. (1994). *The social organization of sexuality: Sexual practices in the United States.* Chicago: University of Chicago Press.

Lehrer, E. L., & Chiswick, C. U. (1993). Religion as a determinant of marital stability. *Demography, 30,* 385–404.

Leridon, H., & Villeneuve-Gokalp, C. (1989). The new couples: Number, characteristics, and attitudes. *Population 44, English Selection,* no. 1, 203–235.

LeVay, S. (1991). A difference in hypothalmic structure between heterosexual and homosexual men. *Science, 253,* 1034–1037.

LeVay, S., & Hamer, D. H. (1994, May). Evidence for a biological influence in male homosexuality. *Scientific American, 270,* 44–49.

Levenson, R. W., & Gottman, J. M. (1983). Marital interaction: Physiological linkage and affective exchange. *Journal of Personality and Social Psychology, 45,* 587–597.

Levenson, R. W., & Gottman, J. M. (1985). Physiological and affective predictors of change in relationship satisfaction. *Journal of Personality and Social Psychology, 49,* 85–94.

Lever, J. (1976). Sex differences in the games children play. *Social Problems, 23,* 478–487.

Levinson, D. (1988). Family violence in cross-cultural perspective. In V. B. Van Hasselt, R. L. Morrison, A. S. Bellack, & M. Hersen (Eds.), *Handbook of family violence* (pp. 435–455). New York: Plenum Press.

Levinson, D. (1989). *Family violence in cross-cultural perspective.* Newbury Park, CA: Sage Publications.

Levy, F. (1987). *Dollars and dreams: The changing American income distribution.* New York: Russell Sage Foundation.

Levy, F., & Michel, R. (1991). *The economic future of American families: Income and wealth trends.* Washington, DC: Urban Institute Press.

Levy, R. J. (1989). An introduction to divorce-property issues. *Family Law Quarterly, 23,* 147–160.

Lewis, O. (1965). *La vida: A Puerto Rican family in the culture of poverty—San Juan and New York.* New York: Random House.

Lewis, R. (1972). A developmental framework for the analysis of premarital dyadic formation. *Family Process, 11,* 17–48.

Lewontin, R. (1995a, April 20). Sex, lies, and social science: *The New York Review of Books,* pp. 24–29.

Lewontin, R. (1995b, May 25). Sex, lies, and social science: An exchange. *New York Review of Books,* pp. 43–44.

Lichter, D. T., LeClere, F. B., & McLaughlin, D. K. (1991). Local marriage markets and the marital behavior of black and white women. *American Journal of Sociology, 96,* 843–867.

Lichter, D. T., McLaughlin, D. K., Kephart, G., & Landry, D. J. (1992). Race and the retreat from marriage: A shortage of marriageable men? *American Sociological Review, 57,* 781–799.

Liem, J. H., & Liem, G. R. (1990). Understanding the individual and family effects of unemployment. In J. Eckenrode & S. Gore (Eds.), *Stress between work and family* (pp. 175–204). New York: Plenum Press.

Light, I. (1972). *Ethnic enterprise in America: Business and welfare among Chinese, Japanese, and Blacks.* Berkeley: University of California Press.

Liker, J. K., & Elder, G. H., Jr. (1983). Economic hardship and marital relations in the 1930s. *American Sociological Review, 48,* 343–359.

Lin, C., & Liu, W. (1993). Intergenerational relationships among Chinese immigrants from Taiwan. In H. McAdoo (Ed.), *Family ethnicity* (pp. 271–286).

Lipman-Blumen, J. (1984). *Gender roles and power.* Englewood Cliffs, NJ: Prentice-Hall.

Liss, L. (1987). Family and the law. In M. B. Sussman & S. K. Steinmetz (Eds.), *Handbook of marriage and the family* (pp. 767–794). New York: Plenum Press.

Little, K. (1973). *African women in towns.* Cambridge, MA: Cambridge University Press.

Liu, K., Manton, K. G., & Liu, B. M. (1985). Home care expenses for the disabled elderly. *Health Care Financing Review, 7* (2), 51–59.

Lock, J. H. (1984). *Sex role identity and ego development.* San Francisco: Jossey-Bass.

Locke, H. J. (1951). *Predicting adjustment in marriage: A comparison of a divorced and a happily married group.* New York: Henry Holt.

Logan, J. R., & Spitze, G. D. (1996). *Family ties: Enduring relations between parents and their grown children.* Philadelphia: Temple University Press.

Lomintz, L. (1977). *Networks and marginality: Life in a Mexican shantytown.* New York: Academic Press.

Limnitz, L. (1987). *A Mexican elite family, 1820–1980: Kinship, class, and culture.* Princeton, NJ: Princeton University Press.

Lorber, J. et al. (1981). On the reproduction of mothering: A methodological debate. *Signs, 6,* 482–514.

Loving v. *Virginia.* (1967). 388 U.S. 1.

Luker, K. (1984). *Abortion and the politics of motherhood.* Berkeley: University of California Press.

Luker, K. (1996). *Dubious conceptions: The politics of teenage pregnancy.* Cambridge, MA: Harvard University Press.

Lundberg-Love, P., & Geffner, R. (1989). Date rape: Prevalence, risk factors, and a proposed model. In M. A. Pirog-Good & J. E. Stets (Eds.), *Violence in dating relationships: Emerging social issues* (pp. 169–184). New York: Praeger.

Luster, T., & Small, S. A. (1997). Sexual abuse history and number of sex partners among female adolescents. *Family Planning Perspectives, 29,* 204–211.

Lye, D. N., Klepinger, D. H., Hyle, P. D., & Nelson, A. (1992). *Childhood living arrangements and adult children's relations with their parents.* Annual meeting of the Population Association of America, Denver.

Lynd, R. S., & Lynd, H. M. (1929). *Middletown: A study in modern American culture.* New York: Harcourt, Brace, and World.

Maccoby, E. E. (1990). Gender and relationships: A developmental account. *American Psychologist, 45,* 513–520.

Maccoby, E. E. (1992a). Coping with marital transitions. *Monographs of the Society for Research in Child Development 57* (nos. 2–3).

Maccoby, E. E. (1992b). Family structure and children's adjustment: Is quality of parenting the major mediator? In M. Hetherington & W. G. Clingempeel (Eds.), *Coping with marital transitions* (pp. 230–238).

Maccoby, E. E. (1998). *The two sexes: Growing up apart, coming together.* Cambridge MA: Harvard University Press.

Maccoby, E. E., & Jacklin, C. N. (1974). *The psychology of sex differences.* Palo Alto, CA: Stanford University Press.

Maccoby, E. E., & Mnookin, R. H. (1992). *Dividing the child: Social and legal dilemmas of custody.* Cambridge, MA: Harvard University Press.

MacDonald, K., & Parke, R. (1984). Bridging the gap: Parent-child play interaction and peer interactive competence. *Child Development, 55,* 1265–1277.

Macfarlane, A. (1970). *The family life of Ralph Josselin.* Cambridge, England: Cambridge University Press.

Macfarlane, A. (1978). *The origins of English individualism.* Oxford, England: Basil Blackwell.

Manegold, C. S. (1993, April 8). To Crystal, 12, school serves no purpose. *New York Times,* p. A1.

Manegold, C. S. (1994, August 25). Quiet winners in house fight on crime: Women. *New York Times,* p. A19.

Manning, R. C. (1991). Redefining obscenity. In R. M. Baird & S. E. Rosenbaum (Eds.), *Pornography: Private vice or public menace?* Buffalo, NY: Prometheus Books.

Manning, W. D. (1993). Marriage and cohabitation following premarital conception. *Journal of Marriage and the Family, 55,* 839–850.

Manning, W. D., & Smock, P. (1995). Why marry? Race and the transition to marriage among cohabitors. *Demography, 32,* 509–520.

Marcus, S. (1964). *The other Victorians: A study of sexuality and pornography in mid-nineteenth-century England.* New York: Basic Books.

Mare, R., & Winship, C. (1991). Socioeconomic change and the decline in marriage for blacks and whites. In C. Jencks & P. Peterson (Eds.), *The urban underclass* (pp. 175–202). Washington, DC: The Brookings Institution.

Mare, R. D. (1991). Five decades of educational assortative mating. *American Sociological Review, 56,* 15–32.

Markman, H. J., Floyd, F. J., Stanley, S. M., & Storaasli, R. D. (1988). Prevention of marital distress: A longitudinal investigation. *Journal of Consulting and Clinical Psychology, 56,* 210–217.

Markman, H. J., & Kraft, S. A. (1989). Men and women in marriage: Dealing with gender differences in marital therapy. *The Behavior Therapist, 12,* 51–56.

Marsiglio, W. (1992). Stepfathers with minor children living at home: Parenting perceptions and relationship quality. *Journal of Family Issues, 13,* 195–214.

Marsiglio, W. (1993). Adolescent males' orientation toward paternity and contraception. *Family Planning Perspectives, 25,* 22–31.

Martin, J., & Martin, E. (1978). *The helping tradition in the black family and community.* Chicago: University of Chicago Press.

Martin, L. G. (1989). The graying of Japan. *Population Bulletin, 44,* 1–43.

Martin, T. C., & Bumpass, L. L. (1989). Recent trends in marital disruption. *Demography, 26,* 37–51.

Marx, K. (1959). The eighteenth brumaire of Louis Bonaparte. In L. S. Feuer (Ed.), *Marx and Engels: Basic writings and philosophy* (pp. 318–348). Garden City, NY: Anchor Books.

Marx, K. (1977). *Capital:* Vol. 1. New York: Vintage Books.

Masheter, C. (1997). Healthy and unhealthy friendship and hostility between ex-spouses. *Journal of Marriage and the Family, 59,* 463–475.

Mathews, J. (1993, October 11–17). The quiet move toward benefits for gay couples. *The Washington Post National Weekly Edition.*

May, E. T. (1980). *Great expectations: Marriage and divorce in post-Victorian America.* Chicago: University of Chicago Press.

May, E. T. (1988). *Homeward bound: American families in the cold war era.* New York: Basic Books.

Mayer, S. E. (1997). *What money can't buy: Family income and children's life chances.* Cambridge, MA: Harvard University Press.

McAdoo, H. (1988). *Transgenerational patterns of upward mobility in African-American families.* Newbury Park, CA: Sage Publications.

McCurdy, K., & Daro, D. (1994). Current trends in child abuse reporting and fatalities: The results of the 1993 annual fifty state survey [Working Paper no. 808]. National Committee to Prevent Child Abuse. Chicago.

McGue, M., & Lykken, D. T. (1992). Genetic influence on risk of divorce. *Psychological Science, 3,* 368–373.

McLanahan, S., & Sandefur, G. (1994). *Growing up with a single parent: What hurts, what helps.* Cambridge, MA: Harvard University Press.

McLanahan, S. S. (1983). Family structure and stress: A longitudinal comparison of two-parent and female-headed families. *Journal of Marriage and the Family, 45,* 347–357.

McLanahan, S. S. (1994). The consequences of single motherhood. *The American Prospect, 18,* 48–58.

McLaughlin, D. K., & Lichter, D. T. (1997). Poverty and the marital behavior of young women. *Journal of Marriage and the Family, 59,* 582–594.

McLeod, J. D., & Shanahan, M. J. (1993). Poverty, parenting, and children's mental health. *American Sociological Review, 58,* 351–366.

McLoyd, V. C. (1990). The impact of economic hardship on black families and children: Psychological distress, parenting and socioemotional development. *Child Development, 61,* 311–346.

Mead, L. (1992). *The new politics of poverty: The nonworking poor in America.* New York: Basic Books.

Menaghan, E. G. (1989). Role changes and psychological well-being: Variations in effects by gender and role repertoire. *Social Forces, 67,* 693–714.

Merton, R. K. (1968). *Social theory and social structure* (Enlarged ed.) New York: The Free Press.

Meyer, D. R., & Garasky, S. (1993). Custodial fathers: Myths, realities, and child support policy. *Journal of Marriage and the Family, 55,* 73–89.

Meyering, A. (1990). La petite ouvrière surmenée: Family structure, family income, and women's work in nineteenth-century France. In P. Hudson & W. Lee (Eds.), *Women's work and the economy in historical perspective* (pp. 132–156). Manchester, England: Manchester University Press.

Michael, R. T., Hartmann, H. I., & O'Farrell, B. (1989). *Pay equity: Empirical inquiries.* Washington, DC: National Academy Press.

Michael, R. T., Laumann, E. O., & Gagnon, J. H. (1992). The number of sexual partners of adults in the United States. Harris School of Public Policy Studies, University of chicago.

Mills, D. M. (1988). Stepfamilies in context. In W. R. Beer (Ed.), *Relative strangers: Studies of stepfamily processes* (pp. 1–28). Totowa, NJ: Rowan and Littlefield.

Min, P. (1993). Korean immigrants' marital patterns and marital adjustment. In H. McAdoo (Ed.), *Family ethnicity* (pp. 287–299).

Mintz, S., & Kellogg, S. (1988). *Domestic relations: A social history of American family life.* New York: The Free Press.

Mischel, W. (1966). A social-learning view of sex differences in behavior. In E. E. Maccoby (Ed.), *The development of sex differences* (pp. 56–81). Palo Alto, CA: Stanford University Press.

Mitterauer, M., & Sieder, R. (1982). *The European family.* Chicago: University of Chicago.

Modell, J. (1985). Historical reflections on American marriage. In K. Davis & A. Grossbard-Schectman (Eds.), *Contemporary marriage: Comparative perspectives on a changing institution* (pp. 181–196). New York: Russell Sage Foundation.

Modell, J. (1989). *Into one's own: From youth to adulthood in the United States.* Berkeley: University of California Press.

Modell, J., Furstenberg, F. F., Jr., & Strong, D. (1978). The timing of marriage in the transition to adulthood: Continuity and change 1860–1975. *American Journal of Sociology, 84* (Suppl.), S120–S150.

Modell, J., & Hareven, T. K. (1973). Urbanization and the malleable household: An examination of boarding and lodging in American families. *Journal of Marriage and the Family, 35,* 467–479.

Moffitt, R. (1990). The effect of the U.S. welfare system on marital status. *Journal of Public Economics, 41,* 101–124.

Moffitt, R. (1992). Incentive effects of the U.S. welfare system: A review. *Journal of Economic Literature, 30,* 1–61.

Money, J., & Tucker, P. (1975). *Sexual signatures: On being a man or a woman.* Boston: Little, Brown and Company.

Moore, J. W., & Cuéllar, A. B. (1970). *Mexican Americans.* Englewood Cliffs, NJ: Prentice-Hall.

Morgan, S. P. (1988). Sons, daughters, and the risk of marital disruption. *American Journal of Sociology, 94,* 110–129.

Morgan, S. P., McDaniel, A., Miller, A. T., & Preston, S. H. (1993). Racial differences in household and family structure at the turn of the century. *American Journal of Sociology, 98,* 798–828.

Morgan, S. P., & Waite, L. J. (1987). Parenthood and the attitudes of young adults. *American Sociological Review, 52,* 541–547.

Morioka, K. (1996). Generational relations and their changes as they affect the status of older people in Japan. In T. K. Hareven (Ed.), *Aging and generational relations: Life-course and cross-cultural perspectives* (pp. 263–280). New York: Aldine de Gruyter.

Morley, R. (1994). Wife beating and modernization: The case of Papua New Guinea. *Journal of Comparative Family Studies, 25,* 25–52.

Morrison, D. R., & Cherlin, A. J. (1995). The divorce process and young children's well-being: A prospective analysis. *Journal of Marriage and the Family, 57,* 800–812.

Mortimer, J. T., & London, J. (1984). The varying linkages of work and family. In P. Voydanoff (Ed.), *Work and family: Changing roles of men and women* (pp. 20–35). Palo Alto, CA: Mayfield.

Mosley, J., & Thomson, E. (1995). *Fatherhood: Contemporary theory, research, and social policy* (W. Marsiglio, Ed.) (pp. 148–165). Thousand Oaks, CA: Sage.

Moynihan, D. (1973). *The politics of a guaranteed income: The Nixon administration and the family assistance plan.* New York: Random House.

Murray, C. (1984). *Losing ground: American social policy, 1950–1980.* New York: Basic Books.

Murstein, B. I. (1970). Stimulus, value, role: A theory of marital choice. *Journal of Marriage and the Family, 32,* 465–481.

Nakonezny, P. A., Shull, R. D., & Rodgers, J. L. (1995). The effect of no-fault divorce law on the divorce rate across the 50 states and its relation to income, education, and religiosity. *Journal of Marriage and the Family, 57,* 477–488.

Nanda, S. (1990). *Nanda, neither man nor woman: The Hijras of India.* Belmont, CA: Wadsworth.

National Aging Information Center. (1996). *Limitations in activities of daily living among the elderly* [www.aoa.dhhs.gov/naic]. Washington, DC: U.S. Administration on Aging (17 March, 1998).

National Opinion Research Center. (1997). General Social Survey [On-line]. Available: http://www.icpsr.umich.edu/GSS (Accessed August 29, 1997).

Neilson, J. M. (1990). Introduction in J. M. Neilson (Ed.), *Feminist research methods: Exemplary readings in the social sciences* (pp. 1–37). Boulder, CO: Westview Press.

Neuhaus, R. J. (1988). Renting women, buying babies, and class struggles. *Society, 25,* 8–29.

Newman, K. (1988). *Falling from grace: The experience of downward mobility in the American middle class.* New York: The Free Press.

NICHD Early Child Care Research Network. (1997). The effects of infant child care on infant-mother attachment security: Results of the NICHD study of early child care. *Child Development, 68,* 860–879.

Nicholas, D. (1991). Childhood in medieval Europe. In J. M. Hawes & N. R. Hiner (Eds.), *Children in historical and comparative perspective* (pp. 31–52). New York: Greenwood Press.

Nock, S. L. (1998). *Marriage in men's lives.* New York: Oxford University Press.

Norton, M. B. (1984). The evolution of white women's experience in early America. *American Historical Review, 89,* 593–619.

O'Brien, J. E. (1971). Violence in divorce prone families. *Journal of Marriage and the Family, 33,* 692–698.

O'Connell, M., & Bloom, D. E. (1987). Juggling jobs and babies: America's child care challenge. In *Population Trends and Public Policy Reports,* no. 12. Washington, DC: Population Reference Bureau.

O'Connell, M., & Moore, M. (1980). The legitimacy status of first births to U.S. women aged 15–24, 1939–1978. *Family Planning Perspectives, 12,* 16–25.

Oda, T. (1991). Tradition and innovation of the Japanese family in an aging society: Focusing on family support of the elderly. In *Proceedings of the Nihon University International Symposium on Family and the Contemporary Japanese Culture: An International Perspective* (pp. 361–406). Tokyo: University Research Center, Nihon University.

Ogawa, N., & Retherford, R. D. (1993). Care of the elderly in Japan: Changing norms and expectations. *Journal of Marriage and the Family, 55,* 585–597.

O'Hare, W. (1992). America's minorities—the demographics of diversity. *Population Bulletin, 47* (4).

Olasky, M. (1992). *The tragedy of American compassion.* Washington, DC: Regnery.

Olasky, M. (1997). Charitable aid should replace government welfare. In C. P. Cozie & P. A. Winters (Eds.), *Welfare: Opposing viewpoints* (pp. 56–64). San Diego, CA: Greenhaven Press.

Oliver, M., & Shapiro, T. M. (1995). *Black wealth/white wealth: A new perspective on racial inequality.* New York: Routledge.

Olson, J. S. (1979). *The ethnic dimension in American history.* New York: St. Martin's Press.

O'Neill, N., & O'Neill, G. (1972). *Open marriage: A new life style for couples.* New York: Evans.

O'Neill, W. L. (1967). *Divorce in the progressive era.* New Haven, CT: Yale University Press.

Oppenheimer, V. (1970). The female labor force in the United States. *Population Monograph Series, 5.* Berkeley: Institute of International Studies, University of California.

Oppenheimer, V. K. (1988). A theory of marriage timing. *American Journal of Sociology, 94,* 563–591.

Oppenheimer, V. K. (1994). Women's rising employment and the future of the family in industrial societies. *Population and Development Review, 20,* 293–342.

Oppenheimer, V. K., Blossfeld, H.-P., & Wackerow, A. (1995). United States of America. In H.-P. Blossfeld (Ed.), *The new role of women: Family formation in modern societies* (pp. 150–173). Boulder, CO: Westview Press.

Oppenheimer, V. K., Kalmijn, M., & Lim, N. (1997). Men's career development and marriage timing during a period of rising inequality. *Demography, 34,* 311–330.

Oppenheimer, V. K., & Lew, V. (1995). American marriage formation in the 1980s: How important was women's economic independence? In K. O. Mason & A.-M. Jensen (Eds.), *Gender and family change in industrialized countries* (pp. 105–138). Oxford: Clarendon Press.

Orfali, K. (1991). The rise and fall of the Swedish model. In Prost, A., & Vincent, G. (Eds.), *A history of private life: Vol. 5, Riddles of identity in modern times* (pp. 417–449). Cambridge, MA: The Belknap Press of Harvard University Press.

Orloff, A. (1993). Gender and the social rights of citizenship: The comparative analysis of gender relations and welfare states. *American Sociological Review, 58,* 303–328.

Ortiz, V. (1995). The diversity of Latin families. In R. Zambrana (Ed.), *Understanding Latino families* (pp. 18–39). Thousand Oaks, CA: Sage.

Oxford English Dictionary (2nd ed.). (1989). Oxford: Clarendon Press.

Ozment, S. (1983). *When fathers ruled: Family life in reformation Europe.* Cambridge, MA: Harvard University Press.

Padian, N., Shiboski, S., & Jewell, N. (1991). Female-to-male transmission of human immunodeficiency virus. *Journal of the American Medical Association, 266,* 1664–1667.

Pagelow, M. D. (1988). Marital rape. In V. B. Van Hasselt, R. Morrison, A. S. Bellack & M. Hersen (Eds.), *Handbook of family violence* (pp. 207–232). New York: Plenum Press.

Pagnini, D. L., & Morgan, S. P. (1996). Racial differences in marriage and childbearing: Oral history evidence from the South in the early twentieth century. *American Journal of Sociology, 101,* 1694–1718.

Pagnini, D. L., & Rindfuss, R. R. (1993). The divorce of marriage and childbearing: Changing attitudes and behavior in the United States. *Population and Development Review, 19,* 331–347.

Pahl, J. (1989). *Money and marriage.* Hampshire, England: Macmillan.

Palmer, J. L. (1988). Financing health care and retirement for the aged. In I. V. Sawhill (Ed.), *Challenge to leadership: Economic and social Issues for the next decade* (pp. 173–214). Washington, DC: Urban Institute Press.

Palmer, J. L., & Gould, S. G. (1986). The economic consequences of an aging society. *Daedalus, 115* (1), 295–323.

Papanek, H. (1973). Men, women, and work: Reflections on the two-person career. *American Journal of Sociology, 78,* 852–872.

Papernow, P. (1988). Stepparent role development: From outsider to intimate. In W. R. Beer (Ed.), *Relative strangers: Studies of stepfamily processes* (pp. 54–82). Totowa, NJ: Rowan and Littlefield.

Parcell, T. L., & Menaghan, E. G. (1994). Early parental work, family social capital, and early childhood outcomes. *American Journal of Sociology, 99,* 972–1009.

Parish, W. L., Hao, L., & Hogan, D. P. (1991). Family networks, welfare, and the work of young mothers. *Journal of Marriage and the Family, 53,* 203–215.

Parke, R. D. (1996). *Fatherhood.* Cambridge, MA: Harvard University Press.

Parkes, C. M., & Hinde, J. S. (1982). *The place of attachment in human behavior.* New York: Basic Books.

Parsons, T. (1942). Age and sex in the social structure of the United States. *American Sociological Review, 7,* 604–616.

Parsons, T., & Bales, R. F. (1955). *Family, socialization, and the interaction process.* New York: The Free Press.

Pate, A. M., & Hamilton, E. E. (1992). Formal and informal deterrents to domestic violence: The Dade County spouse assault experiment. *American Sociological Review, 57,* 691–697.

Patterson, C. J. (1992). Children of lesbian and gay parents. *Child Development, 63,* 1025–1042.

Patterson, C. J. (1994). Children of the lesbian baby boom: Behavioral adjustment, self-concepts, and sex-role identity. In B. Greene & G. Herek (Eds.), *Contemporary perspectives on gay and lesbian psychology: Theory, research, and applications,* pp. 156–175. Newbury Park, CA: Sage Publications.

Pearlin, L., & Johnson, J. (1977). Marital status, life-strains, and depression. *American Sociological Review, 42,* 704–715.

Pearlin, L. I., & McCall, M. E. (1990). Occupational stress and marital support. In J. Eckenrode & S. Gore (Eds.), *Stress between work and family* (pp. 39–60). New York: Plenum Press.

Pearsall, P. (1987). *Super marital sex: Loving for life.* New York: Doubleday.

Peplau, L. A. (1991). Lesbian and gay relationships. In J. C. Gonsiorek & J. D. Weinrich (Eds.), *Homosexuality: Research implications for public policy.* Newbury Park, CA: Sage Publications.

Peters, E. H. (1986). Marriage and divorce: Informational constraints and private contracting. *American Economic Review, 76,* 437–454.

Peterson, G. W., & Rollins, B. C. (1987). Parent-child socialization. In S. K. Steinmetz (Ed.), *Handbook of marriage and the family* (pp. 471–507). New York: Plenum Press.

Peterson, J. L., & Zill, N. (1986). Marital disruption, parent-child relationships, and behavior problems in children. *Journal of Marriage and the Family, 48,* 295–307.

Phillips, R. (1991). *Untying the knot: A short history of divorce.* Cambridge, England: Cambridge University Press.

Pillemer, K., & Finkelhor, D. (1988). The prevalence of elder abuse: A random sample survey. *The Gerontologist, 28,* 51–57.

Pinker, S. (1997). *How the mind works.* New York: W. W. Norton.

Pleck, E. (1987). *Domestic tyranny: The making of American social policy against family violence from colonial times to the present.* New York: Oxford University Press.

Pleck, J. H. (1977). The work-family role system. *Social Problems, 24,* 417–427.

Pleck, J. H. (1985). *Working wives/working husbands.* Beverly Hills, CA: Sage Publications.

Pleck, J. H., & Ku, L. C. (1990). Sexual activity, condom use, and AIDS awareness among adolescent males. *Family Planning Perspectives, 22,* 206–214.

Podhisita, C. (1984). Marriage in rural northeast Thailand: A household perspective. In A. Chamratrithirong (Ed.), *Perspectives on the Thai marriage,* publication no. 81 (pp. 69–110). Salaya, Thailand: Institute for Population and Social Research, Mahidol University.

Pogrebin, L. (1983). *Family politics: Love and power on the intimate frontier.* New York: McGraw-Hill.

Polachek, S. (1979). Occupational segregation among women: Theory, evidence, and a prognosis. In C. Lloyd (Ed.), *Women in the labor market* (pp. 137–157). New York: Columbia University Press.

Pollock, L. A. (1983). *Forgotten children: Parent-child relations from 1500 to 1900.* Cambridge, England: Cambridge University Press.

Popenoe, D. (1988). *Disturbing the nest: Family change and decline in modern societies.* New York: Aldine de Gruyter.

Popenoe, D. (1991). Family decline in the Swedish welfare state. *The Public Interest, 102,* 65–77.

Popenoe, D. (1994). The evolution of marriage and the problem of stepfamilies: A biosocial perspective. In A. Booth & J. Dunn (Eds.), *Stepfamilies: Who benefits? Who does not?* (pp. 3–27). Hillsdale, NJ: Lawrence Erlbaum.

Popenoe, D. (1996). *Life without father.* New York: Free Press.

Portes, A., & Jensen, L. (1989). The enclave and the entrants: Patterns of ethnic enterprise in Miami before and after Mariel. *American Sociological Review, 54,* 929–949.

Portes, A., & Sensenbrenner, J. (1993). Embeddedness and immigration: Notes on the social determinants of economic action. *American Journal of Sociology, 98,* 1320–1350.

Portes, A., Stepick, A., & Truelove, C. (1986). Three years later: The adaptation process of Cuban and Haitian refugees in South Florida. *Population research and Policy Review, 5,* 83–94.

Presser, H. B. (1989). Can we make time for children? The economy, work schedules, and child care. *Demography, 26,* 523–543.

Presser, H. B. (1994). Employment schedules among dual-earner spouses and the division of household labor by gender. *American Sociological Review, 59,* 348–364.

Preston, S. H., & Kono, S. (1988). Trends in the well-being of children and the elderly in Japan. In J. L. Palmer, T. Smeeding, & B. B. Torrey (Eds.), *The vulnerable* (pp. 277–307). Washington, DC: Urban Institute Press.

Preston, S. H., Lim S., & Morgan, S. P. (1992). African American marriage in 1910: Beneath the surface of census data. *Demography, 29,* 1–15.

Preston, S. H., & McDonald, J. (1979). The incidence of divorce within cohorts of American marriages contracted since the civil war. *Demography, 16,* 1–25.

Purcell, P., & Stewart, L. (1990). Dick and Jane in 1989. *Sex Roles, 22,* 177–185.

Qian, Z. (1997). Breaking the racial barriers: Variations in interracial marriage between 1980 and 1990. *Demography, 34,* 263–276.

Qian, Z., & Preston, S. H. (1993). Changes in American marriage, 1972 to 1987: Availability and forces of attraction by age and education. *American Sociological Review, 58,* 482–493.

Quadagno, J. S. (1994). *The color of welfare: How racism undermined the war on poverty.* New York: Oxford University Press.

Queen, S. S., Habenstein, R. W., & Quadagno, J. S. (1985). *The family in various cultures* (5th Ed.). New York: Harper and Row.

Rainwater, L., & Smeeding, T. M. (1995). Doing poorly: The real income of American children in a comparative perspective. *Luxembourg Income Study, Working Paper 127* [On-line]. Available: www.lissy.ceps.lu/index.htm (Accessed April 17, 1998).

Rainwater, L., & Yancey, W. L. (1967). *The Moynihan report and the politics of controversy.* Cambridge, MA: MIT Press.

Raley, R. (1995). Black-white differences in kin contact and exchange among never married adults. *Journal of Family Issues, 16,* 77–103.

Raley, R. (1996). A shortage of marriageable men? A note on the role of cohabitation in black-white differences in marriage rates. *American Sociological Review, 61,* 973–983.

Rank, M. R., & Cheng, L. (1995, August). Welfare use across generations: How important are the ties that bind? *Journal of Marriage and the Family, 57,* 673–684.

Reiner, W. (1997). To be male or female—that is the question. *Archives of Pediatric and Adolescent Medicine, 151,* 224–225.

Reinharz, S. (1992). *Feminist methods in social research.* New York: Oxford University Press.

Reiss, I. L. (1960). Toward a sociology of the heterosexual love relationship. *Marriage and Family Living, 22,* 139–145.

Reno v. *American Civil Liberties Union.* (1996). 929 F. Supp. 824.

Report cites heavy toll of rape among the young. (1994, June 23). *New York Times,* p. A12.

Reskin, B., & Padavic, I. (1994). *Women and men at work.* Thousand Oaks, CA: Pine Forge Press.

Richardson, L. W. (1977). *The dynamics of sex and gender: A sociological perspective.* Boston: Houghton Mifflin.

Riley, N. (1996). China's missing girls: Prospects and policy. *Population Today, 24,* 4–5.

Riley, N. (1997). Gender, power, and population change. *Population Bulletin, 52* (1).

Riley, N., & Gardner, R. W. (1997). *China's population: A review of the literature.* Liège, Belgium: International Union for the Scientific Study of Population.

Rindfuss, R. R., Morgan, S. P., & Swicegood, G. (1988). *First births in America: Changes in the timing of parenthood*. Berkeley, CA: University of California Press.

Rindfuss, R. R., & VandenHeuvel, A. (1990). Cohabitation: A precursor to marriage or an alternative to being single? *Population and Development Review, 16,* 703–726.

Rivera, R. R. (1991). Sexual orientation and the law. In J. C. Gonsiorek & J. D. Weinrich (Eds.), *Homosexuality* (pp. 81–100). Newbury Park, CA: Sage Publications.

Roberts, R. E. L., Richards, L. N., & Bengtson, V. L. (1991). Intergenerational solidarity in families: Untangling the ties that bind. *Marriage and Family Review, 16,* 11–46.

Robins, P. K. et al. (1980). *A guaranteed annual income: Evidence from a social experiment.* New York: Academic Press.

Robinson, J. P. (1988, December). Who's doing the housework? *American Demographics,* p. 24ff.

Robinson, R. V. (1993). Economic necessity and the life cycle in the family economy of nineteenth-century Indianapolis. *American Journal of Sociology, 99,* 49–74.

Rodgers, J. L., Nakonezny, P. A., & Shull, R. D. (1997). The effect of no-fault divorce legislation on divorce rates: A response to a reconsideration. *Journal of Marriage and the Family, 59,* 1026–1030.

Rodgers, W., & Thornton, A. (1985). Changing patterns of first marriage in the United States. *Demography, 22,* 265–279.

Roe v. *Wade.* (1973). 410 U.S. 113.

Roschelle, A. (1997). *No more kin: Exploring race, class, and gender in family networks.* Thousand Oaks, CA: Sage.

Rosen, E. I. (1987). *Bitter choices: Blue-collar women in and out of work.* Chicago: University of Chicago Press.

Rosenmayr, L., & Kockeis, E. (1965). *Umwelt und familie alter menschen.* Berlin: Luchterland-Verlag.

Ross, C. E., & Mirowsky, J. (1988). Child care and emotional adjustment to wives' employment. *Journal of Health and Social Behavior, 29,* 127–138.

Ross, C. E., Mirowsky, J., & Huber, J. (1983). Dividing work, sharing work, and in-between: Marriage patterns and depression. *American Sociological Review, 48,* 809–823.

Rossi, A. S. (1977). A biosocial perspective on parenting. *Daedalus, 106,* 1–31.

Rossi, A. S. (1984). Gender and parenthood. *American Sociological Review, 49,* 1–19.

Rossi, A., & Rossi, P. (1990). *Of human bonding: Parent-child relations across the life course.* New York: Aldine de Gruyter.

Rossi, P. (1994). Troubling families: Family homelessness in America. *American Behavioral Scientist, 37,* 342–395.

Rothman, E. K. (1984). *Hands and hearts: A history of courtship in America.* Cambridge, MA: Harvard University Press.

Roussel, D. (1988). *La famille incertaine.* Paris: Éditions Odile Jacob.

Rubin G. (1975). The traffic in women. In R. R. Reiter (Ed.), *Toward an anthropology of women* (pp. 157–211). New York: Monthly Review Press.

Rubin, J. Z., Provenzano, F. J., & Luria, Z. (1974). The eye of the beholder: Parents' views on sex of newborns. *American Journal of Orthopsychiatry, 44,* 512–519.

Rubin, L. B. (1976). *Worlds of pain: Life in the working-class community.* New York: Basic Books.

Rubin, L. B. (1983). *Intimate strangers: Men and women together.* New York: Harper and Row.

Rubin, L. B. (1992). *Worlds of pain: Life in the working-class family* (Rev. ed.). New York: Basic Books.

Rubin, L. B. (1994). *Families on the fault line.* New York: HarperCollins.

Ruggles, S. (1987). *Prolonged connections: The rise of the extended family in nineteenth century England and America.* Madison, WI: University of Wisconsin Press.

Ruggles, S. (1994). The transformation of American family structure. *American Historical Review, 99,* 103–128.

Ruggles, S. (1997a). The effects of AFDC on American family structure. *Journal of Family History, 22,* 307–325.

Ruggles, S. (1997b). Reply to Oppenheimer and Preston. *Demography, 34,* 475–479.

Ruggles, S. (1997c). The rise of divorce and separation in the United States, 1880–1990. *Demography, 34,* 455–466.

Russell, D. E. H. (1982). *Rape in marriage.* New York: Macmillan.

Ryan, M. P. (1981). *Cradle of the middle class: The family in Oneida County, New York, 1790–1865.* Cambridge: Cambridge University Press.

Ryder, N. B. (1980). Components of temporal variations in American fertility. In R. W. Hiorns (Ed.), *Demographic patterns in developed societies* (pp. 15–54). London: Taylor and Francis.

Sandefur, G., & Tienda, M. (1988). *Divided opportunities: Poverty, minorities, and social policy.* New York: Plenum Press.

Sandefur, G. D., & Liebler, C. A. (1997). The demography of American Indian families. *Population Research and Policy Review, 16,* 95–114.

Sapiro, V. (1990). The gender basis of American social policy. In L. Gordon (Ed.), *Women, the state and welfare* (pp. 36–54). Madison: University of Wisconsin Press.

Scanzoni, J. (1972). *Sexual bargaining: Power politics in American marriage.* Englewood Cliffs, NJ: Prentice-Hall.

Scanzoni, J., Polonko, K., Teachman, J., & Thompson, L. (1989). *The sexual bond: Rethinking families and close relationships.* Newbury Park, CA: Sage Publications.

Schaefer, R. T., & Lamm, R. P. (1998). *Sociology* (4th ed.). New York: McGraw-Hill.

Schlafly, P. (1978). *The power of the positive woman.* New York: Jove Publications.

Schneider, D. (1980). *American kinship: A cultural account* (2nd ed.). Chicago: University of Chicago Press.

Schneider, D., & Smith, R. (1973). *Class differences and sex roles in American kinship and family structure.* Englewood Cliffs, NJ: Prentice-Hall.

Schoen, R., Greenblatt, H. N., & Mielke, R. B. (1975). California's experience with non-adversary divorce. *Demography, 12,* 223–244.

Schoen, R., Urton, W., Woodrow, K., & Baj, J. (1985). Marriage and divorce in twentieth century American cohorts. *Demography, 22,* 101–114.

Schoen, R., & Weinick, R. M. (1993). Partner choice in marriages and cohabitations. *Journal of Marriage and the Family, 55,* 408–414.

Schor, J. B. (1992). *The overworked American: The unexpected decline of leisure.* New York: Basic Books.

Schwartz, P. (1994). *Peer marriage.* New York: Free Press.

Schwartz, P., & Rutter, V. (1998). *The gender of sexuality.* Thousand Oaks, CA: Pine Forge Press.

Scott, J. (1986). Gender: A useful category for historical analysis. *American Historical Review, 91,* 1053–1075.

Scott, J. F. (1965). The American college sorority: Its role in class and ethnic endogamy. *American Sociological Review, 30,* 514–527.

Sedlak, A. J. (1991). *National incidence and prevalence of child abuse and neglect: 1988. Revised report.* Rockville, MD: Westat, Inc.

Sedlak, A. J., & Broadhurst, D. D. (1996). *Executive summary of the third national incidence study of child abuse and neglect.* Washington, DC: National Center on Child Abuse and Neglect, Administration for Children and Families, U.S. Department of Health and Human Services.

Seidman, S. (1991). *Romantic longings: Love in America.* New York: Routledge.

Seltzer, J. A. (1991). Relationships between fathers and children who live apart: The father's role after separation. *Journal of Marriage and the Family, 53,* 79–101.

Serbin, L. A. (1984). The early development of sex differentiated patterns of social influence. *Canadian Journal of Social Science, 14,* 350–363.

Serbin, L. A., Sprafkin, C., Elman, M., & Doyle, A. (1984). The early development of sex-differentiated patterns of social influence. *Canadian Journal of Social Science, 14,* 350–363.

Sexton, J. (1996, May 12). As reports of child abuse rise, officials split up more families. *New York Times,* p. A1.

Shanas, E. (1980). Older people and their families: The new pioneers. *Journal of Marriage and the Family, 42,* 9–15.

Sharp, R. (1993, September 14). In latest recession, only Blacks suffered net employment loss. *Wall Street Journal,* p. 1.

Sheehan, S. (1995, December 11). Ain't no middle class. *New Yorker,* pp. 82–93.

Shelton, B. A., & Agger, B. (1993). Shotgun wedding, unhappy marriage, no-fault divorce? Rethinking the feminism-Marxism relationship. In P. England (Ed.), *Theory on gender/feminism on theory* (pp. 25–41). New York: Aldine de Gruyter.

Shelton, B. A., & John, D. (1993). Does marital status make a difference? Housework among married and cohabiting women. *Journal of Family Issues, 14,* 401–420.

Sherman, L., & Berk, R. (1984). *The Minneapolis domestic violence experiment.* Washington DC: The Police Foundation.

Sherman, L. W., & Smith, D. A. (1992, October). Crime, punishment, and stake in conformity: Legal and informal control of domestic violence. *American Sociological Review, 57,* 680–690.

Shilts, R. (1988). *And the band played on: Politics, people, and the AIDS epidemic.* New York: Penguin Books.

Shinn, M., & Weitzman, B. (1996). Homeless families are different. In J. Baumohl (Ed.), *Homelessness in America* (pp. 109–122). Phoenix, AZ: Oryx Press.

Shoemaker, N. (1991). Native American families. In J. Hawes & E. Nybakkan (Eds.), *American families: A research guide and historical handbook* (pp. 291–317). New York: Greenwood Press.

Silverstein, C. (1991). Psychological and medical treatments of homosexuality. In Gonsiorek & Weinrich (Eds.), *Homosexuality* (pp. 101–114).

Silverstein, M., & Bengtson, V. L. (1997). Intergenerational solidarity and the structure of adult child-parent relationships in American families. *American Journal of Sociology, 103,* 429–460.

Silverstein, M., & Waite, L. (1993). Are blacks more likely than whites to receive and provide social support in middle and old age? Yes, no, and maybe so. *Journals of Gerontology, 18,* S212–S222.

Skocpol, T. (1991). Targeting within universalism: Politically viable strategies to combat poverty in the United States. In C. Jencks & P. E. Peterson (Eds.), *The urban underclass* (pp. 411–436). Washington, DC: The Brookings Institution.

Skocpol, T. (1992). *Protecting mothers and soldiers: The political origins of social policy in the United States.* Cambridge, MA: The Belknap Press of Harvard University Press.

Smeeding, T. M. (1990). Economic status of the elderly. In R. L. Binstock & L. K. George (Eds.), *Handbook on aging and the social services* (pp. 362–381). New York: Academic Press.

Smeeding, T., Torrey, B. B., & Rein, M. (1988). Patterns of income and poverty: The economic status of children and the elderly in eight countries. In J. L. Palmer, T. Smeeding & B. B. Torrey (Eds.), *The vulnerable* (pp. 89–119). Washington, DC: Urban Institute Press.

Smith, A. (1776). *The wealth of nations.*

Smith, D. B. (1980). *Inside the great house: Planter family life in eighteenth-century Chesapeake society.* Ithaca: Cornell University Press.

Smith, D. S. (1973). Parental power and marriage patterns: An analysis of historical trends in Hingham, Massachusetts. *Journal of Marriage and Family, 35,* 419–428.

Smith, D. S. (1979). Life course, norms, and the family system of older Americans in 1900. *Journal of Family History, 4,* 285–298.

Smith, D. S., & Hindus, M. (1975). Premarital pregnancy in America, 1640–1971: An overview and interpretation. *Journal of Interdisciplinary History, 5,* 537–570.

Smith, J. P. (1994). Marriage, assets, and savings [Working paper]. RAND Corporation, Santa Monica, CA.

Smith, J. P., & Ward, M. P. (1985). Time-series growth in the female labor force. *Journal of Labor Economics, 3* (Suppl.), S59–S90.

Smith, P. K., & Daglish, L. (1977). Sex differences in parent and infant behavior in the home. *Child Development, 48,* 1250–1254.

Smith, S., Blank, S., & Bond, J. (1990). *One program, two generations: A report of the forum on children and the Family Support Act.* New York: Foundation for Child Development.

Smith-Rosenberg, C. (1975). The female world of love and ritual: Relations between women in nineteenth-century America. *Signs, 1,* 1–29.

Smolensky, E., Danziger, S., & Gottschalk, P. (1988). The declining significance of age in the United States: Trends in the well-being of children and the elderly since 1939. In J. L. Palmer, T. Smeeding & B. B. Torrey (Eds.), *The Vulnerable* (pp. 29–54). Washington, DC: The Urban Institute Press.

Snarey, J. (1993). *How fathers care for the next generation.* Cambridge, MA: Harvard University Press.

Snipp, C. M. (1989). *American Indians: The first of this land.* New York: Russell Sage Foundation.

Soldo, B. J., & Agree, E. M. (1988). America's elderly. *Population Bulletin, 43* (3).

Soldo, B. J., & Hill, M. S. (1993). Intergenerational transfers: Economic, demographic, and social perspectives. *Annual Review of Gerontology and Geriatrics, 13,* 187–216.

Sommers-Flanagan, R., Sommers-Flanagan, J., & Davis, B. (1993). What's happening on music television: A gender-role content analysis. *Sex Roles, 28,* 745–753.

Sonenstein, F. L., Ku, L., Lindberg, L. D., Turner, C. F., & Pleck, J. H. (1997). New data on sexual behaviors of teenage males [On-line]. Available: www.urban.org/family/teenmale.htm (Accessed December 1, 1997).

Sonenstein, F. L., Pleck, J. H., & Ku, L. C. (1989). Sexual activity, condom use, and AIDS awareness among adolescent males. *Family Planning Perspectives, 21,* 152–158.

Sonenstein, F. L., Pleck, J. H., & Ku, L. C. (1991). Levels of sexual activity among adolescent males in the United States. *Family Planning Perspectives, 23,* 162–167.

South, S., & Lloyd, K. (1992). Marriage opportunities and family formation: Further implications of imbalanced sex ratios. *Journal of Marriage and the Family, 54,* 440–451.

South, S. J. (1991). Sociodemographic differentials in mate selection processes. *Journal of Marriage and the Family, 53,* 928–940.

Spain, D., & Bianchi, S. M. (1996). *Balancing act: Motherhood, marriage, and employment among American women.* New York: Russell Sage Foundation.

Spanier, G. B., & Furstenberg, F. F., Jr. (1987). Remarriage and reconstituted families. In M. B. Sussman & S. K. Steinmetz (Eds.), *Handbook of marriage and the family* (pp. 419–434). New York: Plenum Press.

Spira, A., et al. (1992, December 3). AIDS and sexual behavior in France. *Nature, 360,* 407–409.

Spitze, G., & Logan, J. (1990a). More evidence on women (and men) in the middle. *Research on Aging, 12,* 182–198.

Spitze, G., & Logan, J. (1990b). Sons, daughters, and intergenerational social support. *Journal of Marriage and the Family, 52,* 420–430.

Stacey, J. (1983). *Patriarchy and socialist revolution in China.* Berkeley: University of California.

Stack, C. (1974). *All our kin: Strategies for survival in a black community.* New York: Harper and Row.

Stanley, S. M., Markman, H. J., St. Peters, M., & Leber, B. D. (1995). Strengthening marriages and preventing divorce: New directions in prevention research. *Family Relations, 44,* 392–401.

Stark, E., & Flitcraft, A. (1988). Violence among intimates. In V. B. Van Hasselt, R. Morrison, A. S. Bellack & M. Hersen (Eds.), *Handbook of family violence* (pp. 457–481). New York: Plenum Press.

Starr, J., Raymond H. (1988). Physical abuse of children. In V. B. Van Hasselt, R. Morrison, A. S. Bellack & M. Hersen (Eds.), *Handbook of family violence* (pp. 119–155). New York: Plenum Press.

Starving a child to death. [Editorial]. (1996, September 5). *New York Times,* p. A22.

Steiner, G. (1981). *The futility of family policy.* Washington, DC: The Brookings Institution.

Steinhauer, J. (1994, August 20). Increasingly, employers offer benefits to all partners. *New York Times,* p. A1.

Steinmetz, S. K. (1987). Family violence: Past, present, and future. In M. B. Sussman & S. K. Steinmetz (Eds.), *Handbook of marriage and the family* (pp. 725–765). New York: Plenum Press.

Stern, M. (1987). *Society and family strategy: Erie County, New York* (pp. 1850–1920). Albany: State University of New York Press.

Stets, J. E. (1992). Interactive processes in dating aggression: A national study. *Journal of Marriage and the Family, 54,* 165–177.

Stets, J. E., & Straus, M. A. (1989). The marriage license as a hitting license: A comparison of assault in dating, cohabiting, and married couples. In M. A. Pirog-Good & J. E. Stets (Eds.), *Violence in dating relationships* (pp. 33–52). New York: Praeger.

Stiglitz, J. E. (1988). *Economics of the public sector* (2nd ed.). New York: W. W. Norton.

Stoller, E. P., & Pugliesi, K. L. (1989). Other roles of caregivers: Competing responsibilities or supporting resources? *Journal of Gerontology, 44* (Suppl.), S231–S238.

Stone, L. (1977). *The family, sex, and marriage in England 1500–1800.* New York: Harper and Row.

Straus, M. A., Gelles, R., & Steinmetz, S. K. (1980). *Behind closed doors: Violence in the American family.* Garden City, NY: Anchor Press/Doubleday.

Straus, M. A., & Gelles, R. J. (1986). Societal change and change in family violence from 1975 to 1985 as revealed by two national surveys, *Journal of Marriage and the Family, 48,* 465–479.

Studer, M. (1991). Quality of center care and preschool cognitive outcomes: Differences by family income. *Sociological Studies of Child Development, 5,* 49–72.

Suarez, Z. (1993). Cuban exiles: From golden exiles to social undesirables. In H. McAdoo (Ed.), *Family ethnicity: Strength in diversity* (pp. 164–176). Newbury Park, CA: Sage Publications.

Swartz, M. J. (1958). Sexuality and aggression on Romonum Truk. *American Anthropologist, 60,* 467–486.

Sweeney, M. M. (1997, March). *Women, men, and changing families: The shifting economic foundations of marriage.* Paper presented at the annual meetings of the Population Association of America, Washington, DC.

Sweet, J. A., & Bumpass, L. L. (1987). *American families and households.* New York: Russell Sage Foundation.

Swidler, A. (1980). Love and adulthood in American culture. In N. J. Smelser & E. H. Erikson (Eds.), *Themes of work and love in adulthood* (pp. 120–147). Cambridge, MA: Harvard University Press.

Symons, D. (1979). *The evolution of human sexuality.* New York: Oxford University Press.

Tanfer, K., Grady, W. R., Klepinger, D. H., & Billy, J. O. (1993). Condom use among U.S. men, 1991. *Family Planning Perspectives, 25,* 61–66.

Tanner, M., Moore, S., & Hartman, D. (1995, September 19). The work versus welfare trade-off: An analysis of the total level of welfare benefits by state. *Policy Analysis* [On-line] No. 240. Available: www.cato.org/pubs/pas/pa-240.html (Accessed February 7, 1998).

Tanner, N., & Zihlman, A. (1976, Part 1). Women in evolution. *Signs, 1*(3), 585–608.

Tasker, F., & Golombok, S. (1995). Adults raised as children in lesbian families. *American Journal of Orthopsychiatry, 65,* 203–215.

Tatara, T. (1993). U.S. child substitute care flow data for fiscal year 1992 and current trends in the state child substitute care populations [Voluntary Cooperative information System Research Notes, no. 9]. Washington, DC: American Public Welfare Association.

Thibaut, J., & Kelley, H. H. (1959). *The social psychology of groups.* New York: John Wiley.

Thoits, P. A. (1986). Multiple identities: Examining gender and marital status differences in distress. *American Sociological Review, 51,* 259–272.

Thoits, P. A. (1992). Identity structures and psychological well-being: Gender and marital status comparisons. *Social Psychology Quarterly, 55,* 236–256.

Thomas, D. (1990). Intra-household resource allocation: An inferential approach. *Journal of Human Resources, 25,* 635–664.

Thorne, B. (1982). Feminist rethinking of the family: An overview. In B. Thorne & M. Yalom (Eds.), *Rethinking the family: Some feminist questions* (pp. 1–24). New York: Longman.

Thorne, B. (1992). Feminism and the family: Two decades of thought. In B. Thorne & M. Yalom (Eds.), *Rethinking the family: Some feminist questions* (Rev. ed.) (pp. 3–30). Boston: Northeastern University Press.

Thorne, B. (1993). *Gender play: Girls and boys in school.* New Brunswick, NJ: Rutgers University Press.

Thornton, A. (1985). Reciprocal influences of family and religion in a changing world. *Journal of Marriage and the Family, 47,* 381–394.

Thornton, A., Axinn, W. G., & Hill, D. H. 91992). reciprocal effects of religiosity, cohabitation, and marriage. *American Journal of Sociology, 98,* 628–651.

Thornton, A., Axinn, W. G., & Teachman, J. D. (1994, May). *The influence of educational experiences on cohabitation and marriage in early adulthood.* Paper presented at the annual meeting of the Population Association of America, Miami.

Thornton, A., Chan, M.-C., & Sun, T.-H. (1984). Social and economic change, intergenerational relationships, and family formation in Taiwan. *Demography, 21,* 475–499.

Thornton, A., Chang, J., & Lin, H.-S. (1994). From arranged marriage toward love match. In A. Thornton & H.-S. Lin (Eds.), *Social change and the family in Taiwan* (pp. 148–177). Chicago: University of Chicago Press.

Thornton, A., & Fricke, T. E. (1989). Social change and the family: Comparative perspectives from the West, China, and South Asia. In J. M. Stycos (Ed.), *Demography as an Interdiscipline* (pp. 128–161). New Brunswick, NJ: Transaction Publishers.

Tienda, M. (1989). Puerto Ricans and the underclass debate. *Annals of the American Academy of Political and Social Science, 501,* 105–119.

Tilly, L. A., & Scott, J. W. (1978). *Women, work, and the family.* New York: Holt, Rinehart, and Winston.

Toshio. T. (1993). *U.S. child substitute care flow data for FY 92 and current trends in the state child substitute care populations.* VCIS research notes, vol. 9. Washington, DC: American Public Welfare Association.

Trafford, A. (1982). *Crazy time: Surviving divorce.* New York: Harper and Row.

Treas, J. (1993). Money in the bank: Transaction costs and the economic organization of marriage. *American Sociological Review, 58,* 723–734.

Treas, J., & Bengtson, V. L. (1987). The family in later years. In M. B. Sussman & S. K. Steinmetz (Eds.), *Handbook of marriage and the family* (pp. 625–648). New York: Plenum Press.

Tribe, L. (1990). *Abortion: The clash of absolutes.* New York: W. W. Norton.

Trussell, J. (1988). Teenage pregnancy in the United States. *Family Planning Perspectives, 20,* 262–272.

Tsuye, N. O. (1992, August). *Work and family life in Japan: Changes and continuities.* Annual meetings of the Population Association of America. Pittsburgh.

Turner, J. (1986). *The structure of sociological theory* (4th ed.) Chicago: Dorsey Press.

Tzeng, J. M., & Mare, R. D. (1995). Labor market and socioeconomic effects of marital stability. *Social Science Research, 24,* 329–351.

U.S. Administration on Children and Families. (1996, September). Fact sheet: Personal Responsibility and Work Opportunity Reconciliation Act of 1996. [On-line.] Available: www.acf.dhhs.gov/programs/opa/facts/prwora96.htm (Accessed March 6, 1998).

U.S. Bureau of Justice Statistics. (1994a). *Violence against women: A national crime victimization survey report.* Washington, DC: U.S. Government Printing Office.

U.S. Bureau of Justice Statistics. (1994b). *Violence between Intimates* [NCJ-149259]. Selected findings. Washington, DC: U.S. Government Printing Office.

U.S. Bureau of Labor Statistics. (1988). *Labor force statistics derived from the Current Population Survey, 1948-1987.* Washington, DC: U.S. Government Printing Office.

U.S. Bureau of Labor Statistics. (1991). *Employment and earnings, 38,* (1). Washington, DC: U.S. Government Printing Office.

U.S. Bureau of Labor Statistics. (1993). *Work and family: Changes in wages and benefits among young adults.* Washington, DC: U.S. Government Printing Office.

U.S. Bureau of Labor Statistics. (1997). Labor force statistics from the current population survey. Series LFS21000030. Washington, DC: U.S. Bureau of Labor Statistics.

U.S. Bureau of the Census. (1975). *Historical statistics of the United States, Colonial Times to 1970.* Washington, DC: U.S. Government Printing Office.

U.S. Bureau of the Census. (1983). *America in transition: An aging society.* Current Population Reports, series P23-128. Washington, DC: U.S. Government Printing Office.

U.S. Bureau of the Census. (1991a). *Family disruption and economic hardship: The short-run picture for children.* Current Population Reports, Series P60-23. Washington, DC: U.S. Government Printing Office.

U.S. Bureau of the Census. (1991b). *Fertility of American women: June 1990.* Current population Reports, Series P20-454. Washington, DC: U.S. government Printing Office.

U.S. Bureau of the Census. (1991c). *Household and family characteristics. March 1990 and March 1989.* Current Population Reports, Series P20-447. Washington, DC: U.S. Government Printing office.

U.S. Bureau of the Census. (1991d). *Marital Status and Living Arrangements: March 1990.* Current Population Reports, Series P20-450. Washington, DC: U.S. Government Printing office.

U.S. Bureau of the Census. (1991e). *Statistical abstract of the United States, 1991.* Washington, DC: U.S. Government Printing Office.

U.S. Bureau of the Census. (1992a). *The Asian and Pacific Islander population in the United States: March 1991 and 1990.* Washington, DC: U.S. Government Printing Office.

U.S. Bureau of the Census. (1992b). *Marital status and living arrangements: March 1992.* Washington, DC: U.S. Government Printing Office.

U.S. Bureau of the Census. (1992c). *Marriage, divorce, and remarriage in the 1990s.* Washington, DC: Government Printing Office.

U.S. Bureau of the Census. (1992d). *Statistical abstract of the United States, 1992.* Washington, DC: U.S. Government Printing office.

U.S. Bureau of the Census. (1993a). *Hispanic Americans today.* Washington, DC: U.S. Government Printing Office.

U.S. Bureau of the Census. (1993b). *The Hispanic population of the United States: March 1992.* Washington, DC: U.S. Government Printing Office.

U.S. Bureau of the Census. (1993c). *Household and family characteristics: March 1992.* Current Population Reports, Series P20-467. Washington, DC: U.S. Government Printing Office.

U.S. Bureau of the Census. (1993d). *Marital status and living arrangements: March 1993.* Current Population Reports, Series P20-468. Washington, DC: Government Printing Office.

U.S. Bureau of the Census. (1993e). *Money income of households, families, and persons in the United States: 1992.* Current Population Reports, Series P60-184. Washington, DC: U.S. Government Printing Office.

U.S. Bureau of the Census. (1993f). *Poverty in the United States: 1992.* Current Population Reports, Series P60-185. Washington, DC: U.S. Government Printing Office.

U.S. Bureau of the Census. (1993g). *Statistical abstract of the United States, 1993.* Washington, DC: U.S. Government Printing Office.

U.S. Bureau of the Census. (1993h). *We the Americans: Asians.* Washington, DC: U.S. Government Printing Office.

U.S. Bureau of the Census. (1994a). *Marital status and living arrangements, March 1993.* Current Population Reports, Series P20-478. Washington, DC: U.S. Government Printing Office.

U.S. Bureau of the Census. (1994b). *Statistical Brief SB/94-3RV, The Earnings Ladder: Who's at the bottom, Who's at the top?* Washington, DC: U.S. Government Printing Office.

U.S. Bureau of the Census. (1994c). *Who's minding the kids? Child care arrangements: Fall 1991* [Current Population Reports, Series P70-36]. Washington, DC: U.S. Government Printing Office.

U.S. Bureau of the Census. (1995). *Child support for custodial mothers and fathers: 1991.* Current Population Reports, Series P60-187. Washington: U.S. Government Printing Office.

U.S. Bureau of the Census. (1996a). Interracial married couples: 1960 to present. *Living Arrangements* [Online]. Available: www.census.gov (Accessed: March 1, 1998).

U.S. Bureau of the Census. (1996b). *Marital status and living arrangements, March 1994.* Current Population Reports, Series P20-484. Washington, DC: U.S. Government Printing Office.

U.S. Bureau of the Census. (1996c). *Marital status and living arrangements, March 1995 (Update).* Current Population Reports, Series P20-491. Washington, DC: U.S. Government Printing Office.

U.S. Bureau of the Census. (1996d). *Poverty in the United States: 1995.* Current Population Reports, Series P60-194. Washington, DC: U.S. Government Printing Office.

U.S. Bureau of the Census. (1996e). *Statistical abstract of the United States: 1996.* Washington, DC: U.S. Government Printing Office.

U.S. Bureau of the Census. (1997a). *The Asian and Pacific Islander population of the United States.* Washington, DC: U.S. Government Printing Office.

U.S. Bureau of the Census. (1997b). *Family characteristics: March 1996* (update). Current Population Reports Series P20-495. Washington, DC: U.S. Government Printing Office.

U.S. Bureau of the Census. (1997c). *Health insurance coverage: 1996.* Consumer Income, Series P60-199. Washington, DC: U.S. Government Printing Office.

U.S. Bureau of the Census. (1997d). *Hispanic population from the March 1994 current population survey.* Washington, DC: U.S. Government Printing Office.

U.S. Bureau of the Census. (1997e). *Household and family characteristics: March 1996 (Update).* Current Population Reports, Series P20-495. Washington, DC: U.S. Government Printing Office.

U.S. Bureau of the Census. (1997f). *Money income in the United States, 1996* [Series P20-197]. Current Population Reports. Washington, DC: U.S. Government Printing Office.

U.S. Bureau of the Census. (1997g). *Poverty in the United States: 1996.* Current Population Reports, Series P60-198. Washington, DC: U.S. Government Printing Office.

U.S. Bureau of the Census. (1997h). *Results of the 1996 race and ethnic targeted test.* Washington, DC: U.S. Government Printing Office.

U.S. Bureau of the Census. (1997i). *Statistical abstract of the United States, 1997.* Washington, DC: U.S. Government Printing Office.

U.S. Centers for Disease Control. (1988). *Understanding AIDS: A message from the Surgeon General.* Washington, DC: U.S. Government Printing Office.

U.S. Centers for Disease Control and Prevention. (1994). *HIV/AIDS surveillance report.* Washington, DC: U.S. Government Printing Office.

U.S. Centers for Disease Control and Prevention. (1997). *HIV/AIDS surveillance report.* Washington, DC: U.S. Government Printing Office.

U.S. Department of Health and Human Services. (1997). *Trends in the well-being of America's children and youth: 1997* [Office of the Assistant Secretary for Planning and Evaluation]. Washington, DC: U.S. Government Printing Office.

U.S. House of Representatives. (1993). *1993 Green Book: Overview of entitlement programs.* Washington, DC: U.S. Government Printing Office.

U.S. House of Representatives, Committee on Post Office and Civil Service. (1992). Hearings, "America's

Changing Profile." Serial no. 102–64. Washington, DC: U.S. Government Printing Office.

U.S. House of Representatives, Committee on Post Office and Civil Service. (1994). Hearings, "Review of Federal measurements of race and ethnicity." Serial no. 103-7. Washington, DC: U.S. Government Printing Office.

U.S. House of Representatives, Committee on Ways and Means. (1996). *1996 Green Book.* Washington, DC: U.S. Government Printing Office.

U.S. National Center for Health Statistics. (1979). *The national nursing home survey: 1977 summary for the United States.* Vital and Health Statistics, Series 13, no. 43. Washington, DC: U.S. Government Printing Office.

U.S. National Center for Health Statistics. (1986). *Aging in the eighties: Age 65 years and over and living alone, contacts with family friends, and neighbors.* Advance Data from Vital and Health Statistics, no. 116. Washington, DC: U.S. Government Printing Office.

U.S. National Center for Health Statistics. (1987). *Aging in the eighties: Functional limitations of individuals 65 and over.* Advance Data from Vital and Health Statistics, vol. 133. Washington, DC: U.S. Government Printing Office.

U.S. National Center for Health Statistics. (1991a). Advance report of final natality statistics, 1989. *Monthly Vital Statistics Report, 40* (8, Supplement). Washington, DC: U.S. Government Printing Office.

U.S. National Center for Health Statistics. (1991b). Advance report of final natality statistics, 1991. *Monthly vital Statistics Report, 42* (3, Supplement). Washington, DC: U.S. Government Printing Office.

U.S. National Center for Health Statistics. (1991c). Advance report of final marriage statistics, 1988. Monthly Vital Statistics Report 40 (4, Supplement). Washington, DC: U.S. Government Printing Office.

U.S. National Center for Health Statistics. (1993a). Advance report of final natality statistics. *Monthly Vital Statistics Report, 41* (9 Supplement). Washington, DC: U.S. Government Printing Office.

U.S. National Center for Health Statistics. (1993b). Annual summary of births, marriages, divorces and deaths: United States, 1992. *Monthly Vital Statistics Report, 41,* (13). Washington, DC: U.S. Government Printing Office.

U.S. National Center for Health Statistics. (1993c). Births, marriages, divorces, and deaths for 1992. *Monthly Vital Statistics Report, 41,* (12). Washington, DC: U.S. Government Printing Office.

U.S. National Center for Health Statistics. (1993d). Firearm mortality among children, youth, and young adults 1–34 years of age, trends and current status: United States, 1985–90. *Advance Data from Vital and Health Statistics, no. 231.* Washington, DC: U.S. Government Printing Office.

U.S. National Center for Health Statistics. (1993e). *Morbidity and Mortality Weekly Report, 42* (20). Washington, DC: U.S. Government Printing Office.

U.S. National Center for Health Statistics. (1994). Advance report of final natality statistics, 1992. *Monthly Vital Statistics Report, 43* (5, Supplement). Washington, DC: U.S. Government Printing Office.

U.S. National Center for Health Statistics. (1995). Annual summary of births, marriages, divorces, and deaths: United States, 1994. *Monthly Vital Statistics Report, 43,* (13). Washington, DC: U.S. Government Printing Office.

U.S. National Center for Health Statistics. (1996). Advance report of final natality statistics, 1994. *Monthly Vital Statistics Report 44* (11). Washington, DC: U.S. Government Printing Office.

U.S. National Center for Health Statistics. (1997a). Advance report of final natality statistics, 1995. *Monthly Vital Statistics Report, 45,* (11, supplement). [Online]. Available: www.cdc.gov/nchswww/nchshome.htm (Accessed December 24, 1997).

U.S. National Center for Health Statistics. (1997b). Annual summary of births, marriages, divorces, and deaths: United States, 1996 [July 17]. *Monthly Vital Statistics Report, 45,* (12). Washington, DC: U.S. Government Printing Office.

U.S. National Center for Health Statistics. (1997c). Characteristics of elderly nursing home residents: Data from the 1995 national nursing home survey. *Advance Data from Vital and Health Statistics, 289.* Washington, DC: U.S. Government Printing Office.

U.S. National Center for Health Statistics. (1997d). Fertility, family planning, and women's health: New data from the 1995 National Survey of Family Growth. *Vital and Health Statistics,* Series 23, no. 19. Washington, DC: U.S. Government Printing Office.

U.S. National Center for Health Statistics. (1997e). Report of final natality statistics, 1995. *Monthly Vital Statistics Report, 45,* (11, supplement). Washington, DC: U.S. Government Printing Office.

U.S. National Research Council Panel on Adolescent Pregnancy and Childbearing. (1987). *Risking the Future: Adolescent Sexuality, Pregnancy, and Childbearing.* Washington, DC: National Academy Press.

U.S. Office of Management and Budget. (1978). Race and ethnic standards for federal agencies and administrative reporting. *Federal Register 43, Statistical Policy Directive 15,* 19269–19270.

U.S. Senate, Special Committee on Aging. (1988). *Aging in America: Trends and projections.* Washington, DC: U.S. Government Printing Office.

Udry, J. R. (1994). The nature of gender. *Demography, 31,* 561–573.

Udry, J. R. (1997). Limits of gender socialization in girls. University of North Carolina at Chapel Hill: Carolina Population Center.

Udry, J. R., Morris, N. M., & Kovenock, J. (1995). Androgen effects on women's gendered behavior. *Journal of Biosocial Science, 27,* 359–368.

Uhlenberg, P. (1979). Demographic change and the problems of the aged. In M. W. Riley (Ed.), *Aging from birth to death* (pp. 153–166). Boulder, CO: Westview Press.

Uhlenberg, P. (1980). Death and the family. *Journal of Family History, 5,* 313–320.

Uhlenberg, P. (1993). Demographic change and kin relationships in later life. *Annual Review of Gerontology and Geriatrics, 13,* 219–238.

Umberson, D. (1987). Family status and health behaviors: Social control as a dimension of social integration. *Journal of Health and Social Behavior, 28,* 306–319.

United Nations. (1995). *World population prospect: The 1994 revision.* NY: United Nations.

United Nations Centre for Social Development and Humanitarian Affairs. (1989). *Violence against women in the family.* New York: United Nations.

van Poppel, F., & de Beer, J. (1993). Measuring the effect of changing legislation on the frequency of divorce: The Netherlands. *Demography, 30,* 425–441.

Vaughan, D. (1990). *Uncoupling: Turning points in intimate relationships.* New York: Vintage Books.

Verhovek, S. H. (1994, May 9). Texas capital ends benefits for partners. *New York Times,* p. A1.

Veroff, J., Douvan, E., & Kulka, R. A. (1981). *The inner American: A self-portrait from 1957 to 1976.* New York: Basic Books.

Waite, L. J. (1995). Does marriage matter? *Demography, 32,* 483–507.

Waite, L. J., & Lillard, L. (1995). Til death do us part: Marital disruption and mortality. *American Journal of Sociology, 100,* 1131–1156.

Waller, W. (1937). The rating and dating complex. *American Sociological Review,* pp. 727–734.

Waller, W. (1938). *The family: A dynamic interpretation.* New York: Dryden.

Wallerstein, J. S., & Blakeslee, S. (1989). *Second chances: Men, women, and children a decade after divorce.* New York: Ticknor and Fields.

Wallerstein, J. S., & Kelly, J. B. (1980). *Surviving the breakup: How children and parents cope with divorce.* New York: Basic Books.

Watkins, S. S., Menken, J. A., & Bongaarts, J. (1987). Demographic foundations of family change. *American Sociological Review, 52,* 346–358.

Weber, M. (1949). *The methodology of the social sciences.* New York: Free Press.

Webster v. *Reproductive Health Services.* (1989). 109 S. Ct. 3040.

Webster, P. S. Orbuch, T. L., & House, J. S. (1995). Effects of childhood family background on adult marital quality and perceived stability. *American Journal of Sociology, 101,* 404–432.

Webster's Third New International Dictionary of the English language, unabridged (P. B. Gove, Ed.). (1976). Springfield, MA: Merriam.

Weinraub, M., Clemens, L. P., Sockloff, A., Ethridge, T., Gracely, E., & Myers, B. (1984). The development of sex role stereotypes in the third year. *Child Development, 55,* 1493–1503.

Weinrich, J. D., & Williams, W. L. (1991). Strange customs, familiar lives: Homosexualities in other cultures. In J. C. Gonsiorek & J. D. Weinrich (Eds.), *Homosexuality: Research implications for public policy* (pp. 44–59). Newbury Park, CA: Sage Publications.

Weisner, T. S. (1987). Socialization for parenthood in sibling caretaking societies. In J. B. Lancaster (Ed.), *Parenting across the life span: Biosocial dimensions* (pp. 237–270). New York: Aldine de Gruyter.

Weiss, R. S. (1975). *Marital separation.* New York: Basic Books.

Weiss, R. S. (1990). Bringing work stress home. In J. Eckenrode & S. Gore (Eds.), *Stress between work and family* (pp. 17–37). New York: Plenum Press.

Weitzman, L. J. (1979). *Sex role socialization.* Palo Alto, CA: Mayfield.

Weitzman, L. J. (1985). *The divorce revolution: The unexpected social and economic consequences for women and their children in America.* New York: The Free Press.

Welter, B. (1966, Summer). The cult of true womanhood. *American Quarterly,* pp. 151–174.

West, C., & Zimmerman, D. H. (1987). Doing gender. *Gender and Society, 2,* 125–151.

Westat Incorporated. (1981). *The national study of the incidence and severity of child abuse and neglect.* Washington, DC: National Center on Child Abuse and Neglect.

Weston, K. (1991). *Families we choose: Lesbians, gays, kinship.* New York: Columbia University Press.

White, L. (1994). Stepfamilies over the life course: Social support. In A. Booth & J. Dunn (Eds.), *Stepfamilies: Who benefits? Who does not?* (pp. 109–137). Hillsdale, NJ: Erlbaum Associates.

White, L. K. (1990). Determinants of divorce: A review of research in the eighties. *Journal of Marriage and the Family, 52,* 904–912.

White, L. K., & Booth, A. (1985). The quality and stability of remarriages: The role of stepchildren. *American Sociological Review, 50,* 689–698.

Whyte, M., & Parish, W. (1984). *Urban life in contemporary China*. Chicago: University of Chicago Press.

Whyte, M. K. (1990). *Dating, mating, and marriage.* New York: Aldine de Gruyter.

Williams, W. L. (1986). *The spirit and the flesh: Sexual diversity in American Indian culture*. Boston, MA: Beacon Press.

Williamson, O. (1981). The economics of organization: The transaction cost approach. *American Journal of Sociology, 87,* 548–577.

Wilson, K., & Portes, A. (1980). Immigrant enclaves: An analysis of the labor market experiences of Cubans in Miami. *American Journal of Sociology, 86,* 295–319.

Wilson, W. J. (1987). *The truly disadvantaged: The inner city, the underclass, and public policy.* Chicago: University of Chicago Press.

Wilson, W. J. (1996). *When work disappears.* New York: Knopf.

Wines, M. (1992, September 24). Vote is set today on veto by Bush. *New York Times,* p. A20.

Winship, C., & Mare, R. D. (1992). Models for sample selection bias. *Annual Review of Sociology 18,* 327–350.

Witke, R. (1967). Mao Tse-tung, women, and suicide in the May fourth era. *China Quarterly, 31,* 128–147.

Wolf, M. (1972). *Women and the family in rural Taiwan.* Palo Alto, CA: Stanford University Press.

Wong, M. G. (1988). The Chinese American family. In C. H. Mindel, R. W. Habenstein, & J. Wright (Eds.), *Ethnic families in America: Patterns and variations* (pp. 230–257). New York: Elsevier Science Publishing.

Wright, E. (1976). Class boundaries in advanced capitalist societies. *New Left Review, 98* (3), 41.

Wright, E. O., Shire, K., Hwang, S.-L., Dolan, M., & Baxter, J. (1992). The non-effects of class on the gender division of labor in the home: A comparative study of Sweden and the United States. *Gender & Society, 6,* 252–282.

Wright, G. C., & Stetson, D. M. (1978). The impact of no-fault divorce law reform on divorce in the American states. *Journal of Marriage and the Family, 40,* 575–580.

Wright, Lawrence. (1994, July 25). One drop of blood. *The New Yorker,* pp. 46–55.

Wu, L. L., & Martinson, B. C. (1993). Family structure and the risk of a premarital birth. *American Sociological Review, 59,* 210–232.

Wulczyn, F. H., & Goerge, R. M. (1992). Foster care in New York and Illinois: The challenge of rapid change. *Social Service Review, 66,* 278–294.

Yamamoto, C., & Kojima, K. (1996). Nuptiality and divorce in Japan: 1994 [In Japanese]. *Journal of Population Problems, 52,* 36-51.

Yanagisako, S. (1985). *Transforming the past: Tradition and kinship among Japanese Americans.* Stanford, CA: Stanford University Press.

Yanagisako, S. J., & Collier, J. F. (1987). Toward a unified analysis of gender and kinship. In J. F. Collier & S. J. Yanagisako (Eds.), *Gender and kinship: Essays toward a unified analysis* (pp. 14–50). Palo Alto, CA: Stanford University Press.

Yasuba, Y. (1962). *Birth rates of the white population in the U.S., 1800–1860.* Baltimore: Johns Hopkins University Press.

Young, I. M. (1994). Making single motherhood normal. *Dissent, Winter,* 89–93.

Young, M., & Willmott, P. (1986). *Family and kinship in east London.* London: Routledge and Kegan Paul.

Zaretsky, E. (1986). *Capitalism, the family, and personal life* (Rev. and expanded ed.). New York: Harper and Row.

Zelizer, V. (1985). *Pricing the priceless child: The changing social value of children.* New York: Basic Books.

Zeng, Y., Ping, T., Baochang, G., Yi, X., Onhua, L., & Yongping, L. (1993). Causes and implications of the recent increase in the reported sex ratio at birth in China. *Population and Development Review, 19,* 283–302.

Zill, N. (1988). Behavior, achievement, and health problems among children in stepfamilies: Findings from a National Survey of Child Health. In E. M. Hetherington & J. D. Arasteh (Eds.), *Impact of divorce, single parenting, and stepparenting on children* (pp. 325–368). Hillsdale, NJ: Lawrence Erlbaum Associates.

Zill, N. (1992, August 26–28). *The changing realities of family life and the condition of children in the United States.* Meeting on Children and Families, Aspen Institute Domestic Strategy Group, Aspen CO.

Zill, N., & Rogers, C. C. (1988). Recent trends in the well-being of children in the United States and their implications for public policy. In A. J. Cherlin (Ed.), *The changing American family and public policy* (pp. 31–115). Washington, DC: Urban Institute Press.

PHOTO CREDITS

Chapter 1
Opener, p. 2 Harry Cutting/Monkmeyer; p. 7 Joel Gordon; p. 14: *above right and below right,* Erika Stone; *left:* Alan Carey/The Image Works; p. 21 David Wells/The Image Works; p. 23 Gerard Fritz/Monkmeyer; p. 35 Ursula Markus/Photo Researchers.

Chapter 2
Opener, p. 38 Culver Pictures; p. 40 National Gallery, London/Art Resource, NY; p. 43 Burns Archive; p. 44 Culver Pictures; pp. 47 and 50 North Wind Picture Archives; p. 54 Culver Pictures; p. 57 The Library of Congress; p. 66 Corbis/UPI-Bettmann.

Chapter 3
Opener, p. 74 Nita Winter/The Image Works; Fig. 3-1 p. 76 National Museum of American Art, Smithsonian Institution/Art Resource, NY; p. 81 Elizabeth Crews/The Image Works; p. 83 Elizabeth Crews/Stock Boston; p. 95 Spencer Grant/Photo Researchers; p. 101 Raphael Gaillarde/Gamma-Liaison.

Chapter 4
Opener, p. 106 Gale Zucker/Stock Boston; p. 113 George Cohen/Impact Visuals; p. 120 Elizabeth Crews/Stock Boston; p. 129 Beryl Goldberg.

Chapter 5
Opener, p. 134 Joel Gordon; p. 141 Margaret Miller/Photo Researchers; p. 149 Spencer Grant/Monkmeyer; p. 155 Erika Stone; p. 160 Alan Carey/The Image Works; p. 161 Randy Matusow/Monkmeyer; p. 164 Lionel Delevingne/Stock Boston.

Chapter 6
Opener, p.168 Angel Franco/NYT Pictures; p. 171 Elizabeth Crews/Stock Boston; p. 175 Sang Fu-pao/New China Pictures/Eastfoto; p. 177 NYT Pictures; p. 179 Jim Whitmer/Stock Boston.

Chapter 7
Opener, p. 196 North Wind Picture Archives; p. 202 Corbis-Bettmann; p. 208 Joel Gordon; p. 209 Corbis-Reuters; p. 214 Alice Austen/Courtesy of the Staten Island Historical Society, Historic Richmond Town, Staten Island, NY 10306; p. 224 Betty Press/Monkmeyer; p. 227 Porter Gifford/Gamma Liaison.

Chapter 8
Opener, p. 232 Carolyn Hine/The Picture Cube; p. 239 Mimi Forsyth/Monkmeyer; p. 241 North Wind Picture Archives; p. 244 Superstock; p. 255 Joel Gordon; p. 256 Harriet Gans/The Image Works; p. 263 Ursula Markus/Photo Researchers.

Chapter 9
Opener, p. 272 Susan Lapides/Design Conceptions; p. 275 AP/Wide World Photos; p. 282 Nita Winter/The Image Works; p. 287 Atsushi Akusada/AP/Wide World Photos; p. 289 Mike Kagan/Monkmeyer; p. 291 Bill Bachman/Photo Researchers; p. 293 Peter Menzel/Stock Boston; p. 295 Norman Y. Lono/NYT Pictures; p. 297 M.B. Duda/Photo Researchers.

Chapter 10
Opener, p. 302 Judy Gelles/Stock Boston; p. 307 Rajesh Vora/The Image Works; p. 308 Sean Sprague/Impact Visuals; p. 317 Gale Zucker/Stock Boston; p. 319 Harry Cutting/Monkmeyer; p. 329 Mike Mazzaschi/Stock Boston.

Chapter 11
Opener, p. 334 Marilyn Humphries/Impact Visuals; p. 338 Corbis-Bettmann; p. 353 David Strickler/Monkmeyer; pp. 359 and 361: © 1994 Donna Ferrato/DOMESTIC ABUSE AWARENESS PROJECT, NYC from the book *Living With the Enemy* (Aperture).

Chapter 12
Opener, p. 364 Charles Gatewood/The Image Works; p. 367 Corbis; p. 382 Judy Gelles/Stock Boston; p. 388 Erika Stone/Photo Researchers; p. 390 Arlene Collins/Monkmeyer.

Chapter 13
Opener, p. 396 Spencer Grant/Monkmeyer; p. 404 Peter Byron/Monkmeyer; p. 408 Howard Dratch/The Image Works; p. 413 Corbis-Bettmann; p. 415 April Saul.

Chapter 14
Opener, p. 424 Bob Kramer/The Picture Cube; **p. 426** Suzanne DeChillo/NYT Pictures; **p. 428** Kindra Clineff/The Picture Cube; **p. 435** Steven Weinrebe/The Picture Cube; **p. 437** Nubar Alexanian/Stock Boston; **p. 439** Harry Cutting/Monkmeyer; **p. 443** Joel Gordon; **p. 445** Mimi Forsyth/Monkmeyer.

Chapter 15
Opener, p. 464 Jean-Claude Lejeune/Stock Boston; **p. 471** Peter Menzel/Stock Boston; **p. 473** Tom Cruze/Chicago Sun-Times; **pp. 476, 479** Alexander Lowry/Photo Researchers; **p. 482** Nita Winter/The Image Works.

Chapter 16
Opener: p. 494 Barbara Rios/Photo Researchers; **p. 499** Thomas Craig/The Picture Cube; **p. 501** Corbis-Reuters/Bettmann; **p. 503** Jim Goodwin/Photo Researchers; **p. 505** James Carroll/Stock Boston; **p. 512** Courtesy of the Children's Defense Fund; **p. 514** Jonathan Meyers/Monkmeyer; **p. 518** Erika Stone.

ACKNOWLEDGMENTS

Chapter 1

Page 10, Table 1.1: Mark Mellman, Edward Lazarus, and Allan Rivlin. 1990. "Family Times, Family Values," in David Blankenhorn, Steven Bayme, and Jean Bethke Elshtain, eds., *Rebuilding the Nest: A New Commitment to the American Family.* Reprinted by permission of Family Service America, Families International, Inc., Publishers.

Page 34: Alice S. Rossi. 1984. "Gender and Parenthood," *American Sociological Review* 49: 1–19, 15. Reprinted by permission of University of Chicago Press and the author.

Chapter 2

Page 69, Fig. 2.2: Donald J. Hernandez. "Percentage of Children Aged 0–17 Living in Each of Four Types of Families, 1790–1989," *America's Children: Resources from Family, Government, and the Economy.* Reprinted by permission of Russell Sage Foundation.

Chapter 3

Page 88: *The American Heritage College Dictionary,* Third Edition. Copyright © 1997 by Houghton Mifflin Company. Reprinted by permission.

Page 97: Alice S. Rossi. 1984. "Gender and Parenthood," *American Sociological Review* 49: 1–19. Reprinted by permission of University of Chicago Press and the author.

Chapter 4

Page 108: Susan Sheehan. 1995. "Ain't No Middle Class," *The New Yorker* (December 11). Copyright © 1995 by Susan Sheehan. Originally appeared in *The New Yorker.* Reprinted by permission of Lescher and Lescher, Ltd.

Page 123, Fig. 4.4: James A. Davis and Tom W. Smith. 1996. *General Social Surveys,* 1972–1996: Cumulative Codebook. Reprinted by permission of National Opinion Research Center.

Page 125, Fig. 4.5 and Page 126: Alice S. Rossi and Peter H. Rossi. 1990. *Of Human Bonding: Parent-Child Relations Across the Life Course.* Copyright © 1990 by Walter de Gruyter, Inc., New York. Reprinted by permission of Walter de Gruyter and the authors.

Chapter 5

Page 139, Fig. 5.1: William P. O'Hare. 1992. "America's Minorities—The Demographics of Diversity," *Population Bulletin* 47, 4: Table 5. Reprinted by permission of Population Reference Bureau, Inc.

Page 145, Fig 5.2 and Page 146, Fig. 5.3: Reynolds Farley and Walter R. Allen. 1989. *The Color Line and the Quality of Life in America,* Table 6.1. Reprinted by permission of Russell Sage Foundation.

Page 146: Andrew J. Cherlin and Frank F. Furstenberg Jr. 1992. *The New American Grandparent: A Place in the Family, A Life Apart,* p. 15. Published by Harvard University Press. Reprinted by permission of the authors.

Pages 148-149: Andrew J. Cherlin. 1992. *Marriage, Divorce, Remarriage,* revised and enlarged edition. Copyright © 1981, 1982 by the President and Fellows of Harvard College. Reprinted by permission of Harvard University Press.

Page 156: Nancy S. Landale and Katherine Fennelly. 1992. "Informal Unions Among Mainland Puerto Ricans: Co-habitation or an Alternative to Legal Marriage?" *Journal of Marriage and the Family* 54: 2, p. 272. Copyright ©1992 by the National Council on Family Relations, 3989 Central Avenue, N.E., Suite 550, Minneapolis, MN 55421. Reprinted by permission.

Page 158: Alejandro Portes and Julia Sensenbrenner. 1993. "Embeddedness and Immigration: Notes on the Social Determinants of Economic Action," *American Journal of Sociology* 98: 1320–50, University of Chicago Press.

Page 159, Fig. 5, Box 1: William P. O'Hare. 1992. "America's Minorities—The Demographics of Diversity," *Population Bulletin* 47, 4: Table 10. Reprinted by permission of Population Reference Bureau, Inc.

Chapter 6

Page 181, Fig. 6.1: National Opinion Research Center. 1997. *General Social Survey.* Reprinted with permission.

Chapter 7

Page 206, Fig. 7.1: Robert T. Michael, Edward O. Laumann, and John H. Gagnon. 1992. "The Number of Sexual Partners of Adults in the United States," unpublished paper, Harris School of Public Policy Studies, University of Chicago, 1992. Reprinted by permission of Robert T. Michael.

Page 207, Fig. 7.2: Jacqueline Darroch Forrest and Susheela Singh. 1990. "The Sexual and Reproductive Behavior of American Women, 1982–1988," *Family Planning Perspectives* 22: 206–214. Reprinted with permission from *Risking the Future: Adolescent Sexuality, Pregnancy and Childbearing.* Copyright © 1987 by the National

Academy of Sciences. Courtesy of National Academic Press, Washington, DC, and Allan Guttmacher Institute.

Page 213: John Boswell. 1982. "Revolutions, Universals and Sexual Categories," *Salmagundi,* 58–59: 89–113. Reprinted by permission of Salmagundi.

Page 215, Fig. 7.3: Edward O. Laumann, John H. Gagnon, Robert T. Michael, and Stuart Michaels. 1994. *The Social Organization of Sexuality.* Copyright 1994 Edward O. Laumann, Robert T. Michael, CSG Enterprises, Inc., and Stuart Michaels. Reprinted with permission of University of Chicago Press.

Pages 216, 217: Richard Lewontin. 1995. "Sex, Lies and Social Science," *The New York Review of Books* (1995a 20/4) pp. 29, 44. Copyright © NYREV Inc.

Chapter 8

Page 236, Fig. 8.2: Larry L. Bumpass and James A. Sweet. 1989. "National Estimates of Cohabitation," *Demography* 26: 615–625. Reprinted by permission of Demography and the authors.

Page 253, Fig. in box: Newsweek. 1986. "The Marriage Crunch," *Newsweek* (June 2). © 1986, Newsweek, Inc. All rights reserved. Reprinted by permission. Photo © 1986 Mark Kozlowski/STOCKLINE.

Page 254, Fig. 8.3: Scott J. South. 1991. "Sociodemographic Differentials in Mate Selection Processes," *Journal of Marriage and the Family* 53: 4, p. 932. Copyright © 1991 by the National Council on Family Relations, 3989 Central Ave., N.E. Suite 550, Minneapolis, MN 55421. Reprinted by permission.

Page 259, Fig. 8.4: Larry L. Bumpass, James A. Sweet, and Andrew Cherlin. 1991. "The Role of Cohabitation in Declining Rates of Marriage." *Journal of Marriage and the Family* 53: 4, pp. 913–927. Copyright © 1991 by the National Council on Family Relations, 3989 Central Ave., N.E. Suite 550, Minneapolis, MN 55421. Reprinted by permission.

Page 259: Larry L. Bumpass, James A. Sweet, and Andrew Cherlin. 1991. "The Role of Cohabitation in Declining Rates of Marriage," *Journal of Marriage and the Family* 53: 4, pp. 913–927. Copyright © 1991 by the National Council on Family Relations, 3989 Central Ave., N.E. Suite 550, Minneapolis, MN 55421. Reprinted by permission.

Page 267: Arthur A. Campbell. 1968. "The Role of Family Planning in the Reduction of Poverty," *Journal of Marriage and the Family* 30: 2, p. 238. Copyright © 1968 by the National Council on Family Relations, 3989 Central Ave., N.E. Suite 550, Minneapolis, MN 55421. Reprinted by permission.

Chapter 9

Page 277, Fig. 9.1: Francesca M. Cancian. 1987. *Love in America: Gender and Self-Development.* Reprinted by permission of Cambridge University Press and the author.

Page 279: Deanna L. Pagnini and S. P. Morgan. 1996. "Racial differences in marriage and childbearing: Oral history evidence from the South in the early twentieth century," *American Journal of Sociology* 101: 1694–1718. Reprinted with permission of University of Chicago Press.

Chapter 10

Page 321, Fig. 10.3: John P. Robinson. 1988. America's Use of Time Project: University of Maryland, Data for 1965 and 1975, and America's Use of Time Project: University of Michigan, Data for 1985, in *American Demographics,* Dec. 1988, pp. 24ff. Reprinted by permission of American Demographics Inc., America's Use of Time Project, University of Maryland, and John P. Robinson.

Page 323, Fig. 10.4: Catherine E. Ross and John Mirowsky. 1988. "Child Care and Emotional Adjustment to Wives' Employment," *Journal of Health and Social Behavior* 29: 127–138. Reprinted by permission of American Sociological Association.

Page 324: Leonard I. Pearlin and Mary E. McCall. 1990. "Occupational Stress and Marital Support," *Stress Between Work and Family,* pp. 39–60. Copyright © 1990 Plenum Press. Reprinted by permission of Plenum Press and Leonard I. Pearlin.

Page 324: Robert S. Weiss. 1990. "Bringing Work Stress Home," in John Eckenrode and Susan Gore, eds., *Stress Between Work and Family,* pp. 17–37. Copyright © 1990 Plenum Press. Reprinted with permission of Plenum Press and Robert S. Weiss.

Chapter 11

Page 341, Fig. 11.1: Murray A. Straus and Richard Gelles. 1986. "Societal Change and Domestic Violence from 1975 to 1985 as Revealed by Two National Surveys," *Journal of Marriage and the Family* 48: 3, p. 471. Copyright © 1986 by the National Council on Family Relations, 3989 Central Avenue, N.E. Suite 550, Minneapolis, MN 55421. Reprinted by permission.

Page 345, Fig. 11.2: Edward O. Laumann, John H. Gagnon, Robert T. Michael, and Stuart Michaels. 1994. *The Social Organization of Sexuality.* Copyright 1994 Edward O. Laumann, Robert T. Michael, CSG Enterprises, Inc., and Stuart Michaels. Reprinted by permission of University of Chicago Press.

Page 347, Fig. 11.3: Karen McCurdy and Deborah Daro. 1993. "Current Trends in Child Abuse Reporting and Fatalities: The Results of the 1993 Annual Fifty State Survey," Working Paper no. 808, National Committee for Prevention of Child Abuse, 1994. Reprinted by permission.

Page 356: Marc. J. Swartz. 1958. "Sexuality and Aggression on Remonum, Truk," *American Anthropologist,* 60–3 (June): 467–486. Reprinted by permission of American Anthropological Association.

Page 356, Fig. 11.4: Mary P. Koss. 1988. "Hidden Rape: Sexual Aggression and Victimization in a National Sample of Students in Higher Education," in Ann Wolbert Burgess, ed., *Rape and Sexual Assault II,* pp. 3–25. Copyright © Garland Publishing. Reprinted by permission.

Page 358: Jan E. Stets, 1992. "Interactive Processes in Dating Aggression: A National Study". *Journal of Marriage and the Family* 54: 1, pp. 165–177. Copyright © 1992 by the National Council on Family Relations, 3989 Central Avenue, N.E. Suite 550, Minneapolis, MN 55421. Reprinted by permission.

Chapter 12

Page 370, Fig. 12.1: Andrew J. Cherlin. 1992. *Marriage, Divorce, Remarriage,* revised and enlarged edition. Copyright © 1981, 1992 by the President and Fellows of Harvard College. Reprinted by permission of Harvard University Press.

Page 378, Fig. 12.2: Larry L. Bumpass and James A. Sweet. 1987. Figure from *American Families and Households.* Reprinted by permission of Russell Sage Foundation.

Page 384, Fig. 12.3: Judith A. Seltzer. 1991. "Relationships between Fathers and Children Who Live Apart: The Father's Role after Separation," *Journal of Marriage and the Family* 53: 1, p. 86. Copyright © 1991 by the National Council on Family Relations. 3989 Central Avenue, N.E., Suite 550, Minneapolis, MN 55421. Reprinted by permission.

Chapter 13

Page 403, Fig. 13.1: Larry L. Bumpass, James A. Sweet, and Andrew Cherlin. 1991. "The Role of Cohabitation in Declining Rates of Marriage," *Journal of Marriage and the Family* 53: 4, pp. 913–927. Copyright © 1991 by the National Council on Family Relations. 3989 Central Avenue, N.E., Suite 550, Minneapolis, MN 55421. Reprinted by permission.

Pages 405 and 406, Fig. 13.2: Anne C. Bernstein. 1988. "Unraveling the Tangles: Children's Understanding of Stepfamily Kinship," in William R. Beer, ed. *Relative Strangers: Studies of Stepfamily Processes,* pp. 83–111. Reprinted by permission Rowman & Littlefield Publishers, Inc.

Page 407: Jamie K. Keshet. 1988. "The Remarried Couple: Stresses and Successes," in William R. Beer, ed. *Relative Strangers: Studies of Stepfamily Processes,* pp. 45–46. Reprinted by permission Rowman & Littlefield Publishers, Inc.

Page 409: Andrew J. Cherlin and Frank F. Furstenberg Jr. 1992. *The New American Grandparent: A Place in the Family, A Life Apart,* p. 158. Reprinted with permission of the authors.

Page 414: Patricia Papernow. 1988. "Stepparent Role Development: From Outsider to Intimate," in William R. Beer, ed. *Relative Strangers: Studies of Stepfamily*

Processes, p. 81. Reprinted by permission Rowman & Littlefield Publishers, Inc.

Chapter 14

Page 425: Catherine S. Manegold. 1993. "To Crystal, 12, School Serves No Purpose," *The New York Times* (April 8). Copyright © 1993 by The New York Times Company. Reprinted with permission.

Page 431, Fig. 14.1: Duane F. Alwin. 1990. "Percentage selecting characteristics as one of the three most important emphases in childrearing, by class," in Nancy Madell, ed., *Sociological Studies of Child Development,* vol. 3, pp. 65–86. Copyright © 1990 by JAI Press. Reprinted by permission.

Page 442, Fig. 14.2: Sandra L. Hofferth, April Brayfield, Sharon Deich, and Pamela Holcomb. 1991. *National Child Care Survey,* 1990. Copyright © 1991 by Urban Institute Press, Washington, DC. Reprinted by permission.

Page 450, Fig. 14.3: Eugene Smolensky, Sheldon Danziger, and Peter Gottschalk. 1988. "The Declining Significance of Age in the United States: Trends in the Well-Being of Children and the Elderly since 1939," in John L. Palmer, Timothy Smeeding, and Barbara Boyle Torrey, eds, *The Vulnerable,* p. 33. Copyright © 1988 by Urban Institute Press, Washington, D.C. Reprinted by permission.

Page 452, Fig. 14.4: Donald J. Hernandez. 1993. *America's Children: Resources from Family, Government, and Economy.* Reprinted by permission of Russell Sage Foundation.

Page 454, Fig. 14.5: Greg J. Duncan. 1991. "The Economic Environment of Childhood," in Aletha C. Huston, ed., *Children in Poverty.* Reprinted by permission of Cambridge University Press.

Page 459, Fig. 14, Box 1: Timothy Smeeding, Barbara Boyle Torrey, and Martin Rein. 1988. "Patterns of Income and Poverty: The Economic Status of Children and the Elderly in the Eight Countries," in John L. Palmer, Timothy Smeeding, and Barbara Boyle Torrey, eds., *The Vulnerable,* p. 89, Table 5.2. Copyright © 1988 by Urban Institute Press, Washington, D.C. Reprinted by permission.

Chapter 15

Page 465: Andrew J. Cherlin and Frank F. Furstenberg Jr. 1986. *The New American Grandparent: A Place in the Family, A Life Apart.* Published by Harvard University Press. Reprinted with permission of the authors.

Page 469, Fig. 15.2: James A. Sweet and Larry L. Bumpass. 1987. *American Families and Households.* Reprinted by permission of the Russell Sage Foundation.

Page 470: Alice S. Rossi and Peter H. Rossi. 1990. *Of Human Bonding: Parent-Child Relationships Across the*

Life Course, p. 142. Copyright © 1990 by Walter de Gruyter, Inc., New York. Reprinted with permission of Walter de Gruyter and the authors.

Page 476: *Webster's Third New International ® Dictionary,* p. 2169. Unabridged © 1993 by Merriam Webster Inc.

Page 489, Fig. in Box: Naohiro Ogawa and Robert D. Retherford. 1993. "Care of the Elderly in Japan: Changing Norms and Expectations," *Journal of Marriage and the Family,* 55: 3, p. 589. Copyright © 1993 by The National Council on Family Relations, 3989 Central Avenue, N.E. Suite 550, Minneapolis, MN 55421. Reprinted by permission.

NAME INDEX

SUBJECT INDEX